COMPROMISED:

Clinton, Bush and the CIA

Terry Reed
John Cummings

S.p.i.
BOOKS

A Division Of Shapolsky Publishers

Compromised: Clinton, Bush And The CIA

S.P.I. BOOKS
A division of Shapolsky Publishers, Inc.

Copyright © 1994 by Terry Reed and John Cummings

All rights reserved under International and Pan American Copyright Conventions. Published in the U.S.A. by Shapolsky Publishers, Inc. No parts of this book may be used or reproduced in any matter whatsoever without written permission of Shapolsky Publishers, Inc., except in the case of brief quotations embodied in critical articles or reviews.

ISBN 1-56171-249-3

For any additional information, contact:

S.P.I. BOOKS/Shapolsky Publishers, Inc.
136 West 22nd Street
New York, NY 10011
212/633-2022 / FAX 212/633-2123

Manufactured in Canada

10 9 8 7 6 5 4

Dedicated to those intelligence assets denied.

For Marilyn Trubey and Joe Dunlap, without whose devotion to the defense of others this book would, at best, have been written from a prison cell.

T.R.

For Bruce and Sebastian, the 6th.

J.C.

This book deals with the Central Intelligence Agency co-opting the Presidency and how Black Operations, like a cancer, have metastasized the organs of government to the point where the malignancy cannot be removed without destroying the government it was designed to initially preserve.

Harry S. Truman, the man who created the CIA in 1947, alluded to this as far back as the 1960s when, in the twilight of his life, he stated his concern in a letter to a magazine editor about what the agency was becoming, only a little more than a decade after its creation.

The former president, never a man to mince words, voiced the fear that the CIA was out of control and that what it was doing was not what he had intended, nor what a democracy needed.

HARRY S TRUMAN
INDEPENDENCE, MISSOURI

June 10, 1964

Dear Mr. Arthur:

Thank you for the copy of LOOK with the article on the Central Intelligence Agency. It is, I regret to say, not true to the facts in many respects.

The CIA was set up by me for the sole purpose of getting all the available information to the President. It was not intended to operate as an international agency engaged in strange activites.

Sincerely yours,

Harry Truman

Dear Mr. William B Arthur
LOOK Magazine
488 Madison Avenue
New York, New York 10022

CONTENTS

CAST OF CHARACTERS

Diana Aguilar —Real estate agent in Mexico and friend of the Reeds.

Tommy Baker —Little Rock private detective involved in "finding" Terry Reed's stolen airplane.

Wayne Barlow —Terry Reed's FBI "handler" in Oklahoma City.

Cecilia Barlow —Barlow's wife.

Richard Behar —*Time* magazine reporter.

Jerry Bohnen —Investigative reporter in Oklahoma City.

Jozsef Bona —KGB agent.

Emile Camp —A pilot involved in Contra pilot training operation in Mena, Arkansas.

Lazaro Cardenas —Governor of the Mexican State of Michoacan.

John Cathey (Oliver North) —Terry Reed's CIA handler and the man who put Reed into play with Barry Seal.

Steve Clark —Former Arkansas Attorney General and original attorney for Terry Reed's civil lawsuit in Arkansas.

Bill Clinton —President of the United States and former governor of Arkansas.

Hillary Clinton —Clinton's wife and former member of one of Little Rock Arkansas' top law firm.

Roger Clinton —Bill Clinton's brother who was convicted on a narcotics charge and who then implicated major figures in Arkansas.

William Cooper —Former Air America pilot who worked in Contra supply operation and was shot down over Nicaragua.

Linda Crow —Little Rock secretary.

John Desko —Former United States Air Force Intelligence specialist and best friend of Terry Reed.

William Duncan —Former Internal Revenue Service agent whose investigation in Arkansas was compromised by CIA.

Joe Dunlap —Investigator for Federal Public Defender's Office in Wichita, Kansas, who handled Reed's case.

Edwin Enright —Former head of FBI office in Oklahoma City and man who introduced Terry Reed to Oliver North.

Joe Evans —Barry Seal's mechanic who worked for Contra in Arkansas.

George Fenue —Hungarian businessman and intelligence operative.

Vincent Foster —Former law partner of Hillary Clinton who served as White House counsel and allegedly committed suicide.

Raul Fierro —"Commandante" of Guadalajara Airport.

Robin Fowler —Federal prosecutor in Wichita, Kansas.

Max Gomez (Felix Rodriguez) —CIA man who ran operations in Mexico for "Operation Screw Worm." A man close to George Bush.

Lawrence Graves —Chief of Staff for Arkansas Attorney General Winston Bryant.

John Wesley Hall —Little Rock attorney who was first involved with the Reeds' civil right lawsuit.

Cherryl Hall —A social and business friend of Janis Reed's in Little Rock.

Wally Hall —Sports editor of the Arkansas Democrat, and Cheryl's husband.

Fred Hampton Jr. —CIA asset and owner of Rich Mountain located in Mena, Arkansas.

Webster (Webb) Hubbell —Little Rock attorney and close political associate of Bill and Hillary Clinton. Now an Associate United States Attorney General.

Mark Jessie —FBI agent in Little Rock, Arkansas.

Robert Johnson —Purported attorney for Southern Air Transport and the man in charge of the CIA's *Operation Screw Worm*.

Patrick Juin —Mexican citizen and friend of the Reeds who witnessed key events while Reed was in Mexico.

Patricia Juin —Wife of Patrick.

Dan Laster —Little Rock bond dealer implicated in federal drug investigation and ex-employer of Roger Clinton.

Mitchell Marr —Terry Reed's CIA handler in Mexico.

Mark McAfee —Little Rock businessman who entrapped CIA man in Arkansas.

Ramon Medina (Luis Posada Carriles) —Cuban exile assassin who was in charge of Contra ground training for CIA *Operation Jade Bridge* in Nella, Arkansas.

Bob Nash —Bill Clinton's top industrial development aide during his governorship and liaison between Clinton Administration and the CIA.

Larry Nichols —Arkansas State employee who "framed" Steve Clark and who later exposed Clinton's philandering.

Steve Robison —Janis Reed's defense attorney in Wichita.

Tom Ross —FBI agent in Hot Springs, Arkansas.

Akihide Sawahata —Resident CIA Agent in Little Rock.

Adler Berriman (Barry) Seal —Key CIA contractor during Arkansas based Contra flight training (*Operation Jade Bridge*) and clandestine weapons delivery (*Operation Centaur Rose*) programs.

Finis Shellnut —Seth Ward's son-in-law man and the man who coordinated Barry Seal's airborne cash deliveries.

Frank Theis —Federal Judge in Wichita, Kansas who acquitted Reed of mail fraud charges.

Richard Tingen —Canadian businessman and owner of Chapala Realty in Mexico.

Leroy Tracta —CIA Agent in Latin America and handler of Barry Seal.

Marilyn Trubey —Terry Reed's defense attorney in Wichita.

Seth Ward Jr. —Father in law of Webb Hubbell, Arkansas industrialist and political power broker.

Seth (Skeeter) Ward III —Seth Ward's son.

Emery West —Hungarian emigré, Terry Reed's former employer and mentor in Oklahoma City.

Pat Weber (Amiram Nir) —Israeli intelligence operative who alerted Reed of "coup" within the American Government and the man who briefed then Vice President George Bush on the Iran Contra Affair.

Russell Welch —Arkansas State Police investigator in Mena.

Raymond (Buddy) Young —Former Chief of Security for Bill Clinton and the key man in the false criminal case brought against the Reeds.

AUTHOR'S NOTE

By TERRY KENT REED

When I finished this book and pondered in search of a title, I reflected on its contents. My mind executed a sort of instant replay, cover to cover.

I saw myself and the people described within moving in fast-forward, jerky, almost comical motion. At times, my mental video data bank stopped, rewound and "froze" the action so I could more closely study the scene and analyze motives and behavior.

Then, from deep within my mental thesaurus, the word that accurately describes the common thread that holds together their, and my, motivations, came to mind.

COMPROMISE.

I leafed through the weathered pages of my Webster's New Universal and found the word so aptly applied.

com·pro·mise: kom'pramíz'
1. a mutual promise, or agreement.
2. to surrender or give up one's principles.
3. to lay open to danger, suspicion, or disrepute; to endanger the interests of.

Because I *compromised* my values and principles while working for the Central Intelligence Agency, I found myself saying "YES," when I should have been saying "NO".

When Bill Clinton, as a young governor, agreed to a *compromise* with the CIA, he not only surrendered his principles for the benefit of a mutual agreement, he opened the State of Arkansas, and this Nation, to danger, suspicion and disrepute.

Most certainly, in retrospect, the actions of Clinton, Oliver North, myself and others were well intentioned, but, did indeed endanger the interests of the United States. As is so adeptly said: I found myself doing all the right things for all the wrong reasons.

However, when I finally found the courage to say "No", when I could no longer *compromise* my beliefs between right and wrong, a chain of events unfolded forcing my family and myself to flee and go into hiding, traveling more than 30,000 miles over a period of months. My wife and I and our three small sons serpentined as fugitives, evading the FBI and, more frighteningly, the CIA that I had worked for.

How had we become fugitives? Why had the FBI falsely labeled us "armed and dangerous"? Why was Bill Clinton's Chief of Security manipulating government computers to falsely label me a drug trafficker? Why were my wife and I indicted and the criminal justice system used in an attempt to discredit and silence me? Why did people in the Reagan/Bush government want me killed?

KNOWLEDGE. I have knowledge of deep, dark, dirty government secrets that *compromised* individuals in positions of power, people who do not want my information *compromised*.

Knowledge, my teachers taught me, was power. They failed to point out that knowledge can also be deadly.

THIS BOOK IS ABOUT THAT KNOWLEDGE.

John Cummings, my co-author, is the person responsible for my divulging this knowledge; to use pen and paper to chronicle the events that led up to my conversion from being an asset of the CIA to that of a liability. John came to me in 1991 and attempted to convince me that only within the pages of a book could I be assured that the truth of what happened would not be stifled or altered.

He suggested I reveal *everything*, not only to safely record the events as they occurred, but to relieve my mind of the burden I was carrying. I was reluctant. I did not want to *compromise* other intelligence assets and possibly ongoing covert operations. I foolishly felt a courtroom was the only proper forum to bring a culmination to this ordeal.

However, as John had sermonized and predicted, justice is often just an illusion.

At least it is when a sitting and former President can be *compromised*, in a federal courtroom, from the clandestine activities in which I was involved. John was right. The government, he said, would make certain that no mahagony-paneled courtroom ever heard this volatile story.

And so, I'm going instead to the court of public opinion and you can be the judge and jury.

As I take my oath for you, the reader, I make one promise: I will not *compromise* the truth. I want to set the record straight for my children's sake so that they will know from reading this book what really happened and how, hopefully, they and others can avoid the pain my wife and I are still suffering.

To my surprise and amazement, writing *Compromised* has proved emancipating and therapeutic. It has evolved into an intense, yet wonderful journey of self-discovery. Capturing this story on paper has enabled me to better understand my actions; to redefine myself; and emerge from this nightmare with my soul and my family intact.

It nearly destroyed me to be ejected form the secret cabal to which Oliver North and others had granted me membership; to be discarded, discredited, abandoned and labeled a threat.

It devastated my wife and me when TIME magazine, in April of 1992, ran a full page article which branded me a liar.

It hurt to find that in our time of need no one was willing to come forward to help us prove the truth and clear my name.

We grieved to discover that organizations and individuals who claim to search constantly for the truth simply turn their backs if the truth doesn't fit their version of reality.

This book became the vehicle to set the record straight and redeem my self-esteem. I'm not a public figure like some of the people who populate this book. In fact, it was only recently that I peeled back their code names and discovered who some of the people I was dealing with actually are, what their secret agenda was, and what the real consequences of my involvement with them meant.

I had operated under many mistaken assumptions, in part due to my own headstrong faith, and strict training. And yet, ironically, the same unyielding constitution that got me into this, got me out.

My intention in life was to combine my love of family and flying with business success and sense of purpose. Like those I admire...people such as Thomas Alva Edison, Henry Ford, the Wright Brothers, Zora Arkus-Duntov, Chuck Yeager, Joe Ida, Harry Truman—I wanted to put back into society more than I took out.

The type of person I just described would never have envisioned being sought out by the Central Intelligence Agency, being recruited as an asset, being *compromised* and then labeled a liability. Never would I have imagined that the low-profile operatives I was put into play with at the beginning of this odyssey would eventually become a modern American folk hero, an Attorney General...and even the President of the United States.

Bizarre things happened to me in Arkansas as I and others made our way carefully through the crack in the Congressional *compromise* strategically built into the Boland Amendments for the purpose of allowing secret aid for the Contras. During this CIA "black operation" in support of what later became known as Iran-Contra, I unknowingly became a witness to power...and the abuse of it. Because of my knowledge, I became a liability not only to my government handlers, but to some very powerful people as well.

As I sat in a dimly-lit World War II ammunition storage bunker outside Little Rock, Arkansas, I observed the CIA *compromise both major political parties*. I attested to something that I, like others, had often wondered about: does the CIA sponsor candidates to the office of U.S. President?

The answer is yes.

I witnessed the creation of a counterfeit president.

Taken out of context, this is difficult to believe. But when one steps back from the explosiveness of the question and simply considers the mechanics of going from being a poor boy in Arkansas to the highest, most powerful office in the land, one begins to wonder... How is this possible?

One answer is ambition, lots of hard work, and blind luck. But I know, from first-hand experience, that is not always the case.

Another answer is CIA conspiracy to elevate the "proper candidates" to this supreme seat of puissance.

By now you may be thinking I'm a "conspiracist." That is not the case. I am a realist from Missouri, a place synonymous with stubbornness. Our founding principle is: SHOW ME.

I've been shown. And, through my experiences as chronicled in this book, I will attempt to show you.

But why should you give me credence? There have been others who didn't— initially. The federal judge who sat in my appraisal didn't believe me at first. But at the end of my criminal trial and ordeal, after discovering governmental misconduct, that he had been misled, and that I had been wrongfully charged, he acquitted me.

Having been found innocent in the courtroom, I was then "convicted" in the media. This disinformation effort to discredit me in order to minimize the damage to Bill Clinton's Presidential campaign culminated in a TIME magazine article on April 20, 1992.

What an irony! Seeing my face atop a full-page article calling me a liar, a cheat and a charlatan. By TIME making me famous, for all the wrong reasons, reminded me of what Lily Tomlin had said: "I always wanted to be somebody, but I should have been more specific."

Why me? What had I done? Why was my credibility called into question? These are some of the questions answered in this Byzantine story.

I was not only a witness to power and its abuse, I saw with my own eyes the hypocrisy of our "war on drugs". I learned first-hand, while working on an intelligence operation, that our government's stated drug policy had been *compromised* by the CIA, which just couldn't say "no" to the unbridled power derived from illicit drug profits.

When I discovered a government that couldn't say "no," I said "no." I'm still paying the price for that decision.Since all of this occurred, a lot has changed for me and my family, who were also victimized and shared my pain. Most of what has happened was negative. But a positive aspect is I rediscovered myself in this crucible.

This experience provided me with a rare opportunity. I was forced to go back and reassemble the pieces of myself that I had lost along the way, to recapture the values I cherished as a young man—values that made me an intelligence asset, but ultimately turned me into a liability.

As you read *Compromised,* I hope you will see me come full circle from the starry-eyed, patriotic over-achiever with Midwestern values to a man who hits moral bottom while working for the CIA. You will travel with a man who suddenly realized he must resurrect his morality, find himself once again and fight back against overwhelming odds.

THIS BOOK IS ALSO ABOUT REDEMPTION. But when I set out to redeem my values and drew my line in the sand, I was not allowed to return to a normal and productive life. Instead I became a disposable asset to the CIA. I had done nothing wrong, yet I was indicted, simply because I knew too much and had to be silenced. Neither the CIA, George Bush nor Bill Clinton could afford to leave me with what I cherished most: my credibility.

For more than two-and-a-half years, the Reagan-Bush Justice Department acquiesced in the plot to silence me and strip me of my credibility by framing me and converting me into a felon. They failed.

And though I was tried in Federal Court and found not guilty, I've learned that in this country, being innocent is not enough. The stigma remains and, at best, I have been elevated to the status of "an acquitted felon."

How did I get from "there to here?" I am a true baby-boomer, born in 1948, and a product of the Cold War.

Vivid recollections of my childhood in a small town, besides being smothered with love, include being molded by parents, school and church to accept the responsibilities of being an American male...duty, honor, country. These were not the words of some military academy's doctrine, etched in stone to be learned later in life...they were instilled in me from birth.

The world's most powerful man at the close of World War II, and a fellow Missourian who helped shape my life, Harry S. Truman, embraced and espoused the principles of freedom I accepted as religion.

The Cold War period was one of such international paranoia, political unrest and global instability that it fathered such terms as ICBM, super-power, nuclear holocaust, radiation shelter and The Domino Theory.

Truman, the only man who knew the weight that had to be borne for making the decision to use "THE BOMB", openly feared World War III. As he traveled in retirement, delivered speeches and spoke of the necessity to counter communist aggression around the world, I listened.

On January 20th, 1966 I was a high school senior wrestling with teenage temptations to rebel and reject my training. On that same day, a speech written by Truman was read in Jerusalem where the Harry S. Truman Center for Advancement of Peace was being inaugurated.

When I read his words they became the potion that my youthful soul needed to distance myself from those of my generation who were finding it unfashionable to have feelings of patriotism.

"We meet at a time in history, in a world beset with troubles and hostilities in many places. It is a world of evolution and revolution. An unimagineable catastrophe of a Third World War hangs like a dark cloud over all mankind. What so many in places of leadership do not seem to realize, that if petty bickerings and squabbles are not peacefully resolved, the situation could get out of hand—as it has so many times in the past. But the next time, it will not be a Third World conflict—it could well be the last folly of man—and likely the last of man on this earth.

"There will be no Noah's Ark to save and repopulate the species—the waters will be deadly as well—for any life to survive....

"[Wars] are made either by power-hungry adventurers, fanatical zealots, empire builders, false prophets, crusading conquerors, or too often depraved madmen.

"They incite, arouse and provoke their subjects to acts of war. In each case there is first an act of war by an aggressor. Whenever there is an aggressor—there inevitably has to be a choice for the offended nation—that of either surrender or defensive action. Then, the fat is in the fire—and the flames usually spread."

Truman's logic on U.S. involvement in Southeast Asia flowed parallel to his views that America could not ignore its United Nations obligation, and that President Johnson was unfairly critized for his commitment to the conflict.

"But the President is badly served in his task, as is the nation, by those irresponsible critics, or side-line hecklers who neither have all the facts—nor the answers.

"For my part I have reason to believe that our presence in South Viet Nam, as is our presence in other places on the globe, has but one purpose, and that is to help keep the peace, and to keep ambitious aggressors from helping themselves to the easy prey of certain newly formed independent nations.

"If we abandon these, to the new marauders and the 'Little Caesars' - we are again headed for deep trouble.

"If we should commit the grave folly of abandoning the United Nations, or allowing the defaulters to curb its effectiveness, we will be setting the stage for a third world war...

"Our purpose is honorable. We covet no territory. We look for no special privileges.

"The new Imperialists, however, who pose in the guise of liberators continue to spread misunderstanding and distortion of our intentions, to obscure their own designs.

"By now, it should be clear to all, that attempts at exploitation or subjugation of other peoples by any power is a threat to the peace and security of all...

"For us, in the words of Woodrow Wilson, 'there is but one choice, and we have made it.'"

With those words, I made my decision. I would do as my elders requested and serve my country. To me, this was reality. Compared to the rest of the world, my world *was* worth fighting for. The young males with whom I grew up had a sense of duty, and an obligation to defend not only our country but our way of life. They sought to fulfill the mandate bestowed on the United States as a result of World War II; where a victorious, great nation that led the world in democratic reform, had inherited the responsibility to prevent World War III.

This sense of debt and obligation formed the values I embraced and cherished and they set me apart from those who were always looking for the free or easy ride. I was trained to do things the hard way; there was no easy way. Life seemed simple. Things were black and white, right and wrong, worth fighting for or not. Your elders made decisions that you followed and it was not your place to question their judgement until you became an adult.

How quickly we forget that the future of the USSR could not be predicted in the '60s. Nikita Khrushchev, pounding his shoe on the podium at the U.N., and shouting, "We will bury you", was the topic of social studies discussions when I was a student in junior high school. Russia was no wounded giant or decaying super-power in 1967 when I made the decision to serve my country and help create what Truman referred to as "conditions of freedom and justice in the whole world."

Truman was the man who personified my core beliefs. The same man whom Republican President George Bush, Democratic contender Bill Clinton, and independent candidate H. Ross Perot tried so hard to emulate and identity with during the 1992 Presidential elections.

In 1967, I entered the United States Air Force. My duty and my path were crystal clear. The world appeared to be on the brink of nuclear meltdown unless we all did our fair share to prevent it. I would pay my dues to the nation and society would repay me by allowing me to live my life in freedom, and in a safer world. I simply planned to follow the yellow brick road. The lines that separated the highway from the ditches were defined by reflective tape that not only glowed in the dark, but seemed to electrocute those who veered off course.

This seemingly simplistic view of life and youth did not mean I was simple-minded. My friends and I simply saw no real alternative. This was the necessary initiation into adulthood and maturity.

I felt then, as I do now, that this is still the right way to be reared. Youths in their teens and early twenties are not programmed sufficiently to question their elders. And if a nation cannot rely upon its youth to obey, to pay the price of freedom, what does it really have? I was taught that if you feel the values you are asked to defend are not worth the risk, then you should renounce your citizenship and leave. Simply go elsewhere, some place that does not levy demands on its citizens.

In many ways, I feel the course of what happened to me is the course of what has happened to our country.

I, like many Americans, feel the nation has slowly slid from the acme of freedom and self-government to the complex, fragmented form of governmental gridlock and *compromise* we have today. A government that operates long on money and short on ideals. A government comprised of spin doctors, handlers, lobbyists and talking heads, instead of the frankness and honesty radiated by Truman.

When I hit bottom while working for the CIA, I compared myself to an alcoholic, realizing that he either had to quit or die. If I continued on the course set me for me by others, I would *compromise* my entire code of ethics and I might as well be dead.

I was learning quickly that life and people dilute your value system, and it was all so easy to turn your back and give in a little bit at a time. I suddenly realized it was past time to make a major heading change or course correction in my life. Somehow I had ended up in the ditch with nearly everyone else. I needed to get my values and my life back on the yellow brick road. I'm still paying for that difficult decision. Weak people, those in the ditch, I have discovered, don't like the strong, the ones who crawl back to the highway.

Back on the road, I looked around and wondered how I had made this ill-conceived journey. How had I deviated so far off course and missed my original destination? One degree of heading change at a time, I realized. Then, the words of my grandfather came to me, saying: "If ya didn't plan on takin' the trip, why did ya pack your bags?"

Thus began the process of self-analysis that led to this book.

Oddly, the very same qualities for which the world of Military Intelligence sought me out, would lead to my divorce from civilian intelligence operations. I apparently had more patriotism than the CIA had bargained for. My love of my country had evolved into contempt for the government and I refused to be *compromised*, as Bill Clinton and others I was dealing with had been.

As Oliver North and I worked on our "black" project for the CIA, we analyzed America's ills and debated the medication necessary to recoup the nation. By reviewing the principles this country was founded upon and comparing its present condition to those principles, it's obvious that democracy has failed to insure that the founding principles are maintained. We came to the conclusion "that democracy doesn't work."

North and I felt the most paramount threats to our system of liberties had not come from the communists he and I had been programmed to hunt down and kill. The enemy came from within our own ranks. The decay of the voice of the people is what threatened us most. WE THE PEOPLE were being bypassed and our representation undermined through a breakdown in our built-in-system of checks and balances. The budget DEFICIT was to blame. The breakdown was occurring by not making each and every one of us pay as we go. Credit was an easy, evil siren by which to be lured, and one that eventually would bring an end to our way of life. Economic collapse was not all we feared. By not forcing the American public to pay for its way of life, to simply allow the public to "charge it," they were being lulled into a state of governmental non-participation that would eventually put the power of the government into the hands of only a few of the "ruling class". Karl Marx always said democracy doesn't work. We were afraid he was right.

Voter rebellion was what was needed and that revolution was being contained by not forcing the American people to be held individually fiscally accountable. There was no "feedback" to those who ruled us. Congress, we felt, was to blame for allowing the DEFICIT to exist. This had to be changed. Our first priority would have been to return this country to its original capitalistic foundation of "pay as you go."

Financial sacrifice was only one method of personal compensation to our governing system. There was another method and like the deficit, it too was a "D" word...DRAFT. It represented personal sacrifice, or better stated: repayment to America for the privilege of living here...a responsibility that should be accepted by all...men and women alike.

Again, the check and balance, the "feedback" to the political leaders could only be effective in times of national crisis if the entire spectrum of citizenry was represented. The Vietnam debacle, whether avoidable or winnable, would have had a quicker outcome if all the socioeconomic groups were equally represented and had equally paid the price of enforcing our national foreign policies.

That's how simply Oliver North and I saw things back then. And I still believe they are valid solutions to our nation's ills.

North and I did not conspire to overthrow our form of government, but simply to return it to the basic principles on which it was founded. The crisis of leadership and the sorry state of affairs that produced the Vietnam War, a war that touched and changed us both, showed us it was impossible to solve the nation's problems within its present, corrupted system.

Just as a trim tab on an airplane wing can slowly correct a plane's heading, my involvement with the secret cabal, designed to operate outside of the main body of government, attempted to correct the heading of the country. Ours was not a plot to replace democracy, just fine tune it and return it to the state of *true* democracy our founding fathers had intended.

To me, the Cold War can be compared to a game of Monopoly. Simply put, the ideology was to control or own all the property on the game board. In the Cold War, as in the game, if your opponent goes bankrupt his assets are liquidated and you win. Thus is the case of the USSR. The Kremlin is out of the game...for now at least.

How do I feel, as a Cold Warrior, about its defeat? I feel both honored and saddened. I completed my mission, the one for which I was trained. I destroyed my enemy. But yet the victory is hollow, and I, like others, see the present danger of our ways. Now that it's gone, I miss my old enemy, the USSR. I can now see its qualities. The USSR was, in fact, a stabilizing force for the world. What has replaced it is more unpredictable than it ever was.

Those now leading this country must deal with this instability and power vacuum in the world. But these are the same people who denigrate the principles I learned as a youth. They are the ones who rationalized their way out of serving their country and now seemingly claim that holding political office somehow repays that debt they welched on. They are the elite cadre of pseudo-intellectuals who not only evaded the draft, but seem to have disdain for those who served. They view veterans as less cerebral and lacking the intellectual capacity to understand the subtleties of world affairs.

Having worked in intelligence most of my adult life, I'm acutely knowledgeable of the rules that control classified material. I was, therefore, torn in writing this book for fear I might *compromise* classified data and methodology. One element I felt compelled to expose is the fact that there is no real government war on drugs. I feel this, the American people have a definite right and need to know. Other operations this book deals with, I felt initially, needed to be protected.

But, my co-author, John Cummings, convinced me otherwise. The public, he insisted, also has the right to know about the CIA sponsoring candidates for the U.S. Presidency and, thereby, *compromising* themselves and their values. We wrote this book because, otherwise, there would be no assurance that the truth would ever be told. I have decided to take the risk and, hopefully, I am not exposing any on-going classified projects or methodology.

Despite what I know about Bill Clinton's involvement with the CIA, I still voted for him. I, like many Americans, voted for change. This country had to get rid of George Bush and the outdated, misguided attitudes demonstrated by his wing of the Republican Party. Hopefully, our congressional leaders will take note and realize the American people will no longer stand by idly while witnessing the hawking and wholesaling of this once great land.

But right now, I have a more immediate problem—larger and more complex than any with which I've ever attempted to deal—that of raising three young sons, three young men who may be asked someday to serve their country, to pay *their* dues.

What kind of values do I instill in them to ensure this country survives? At the same time, how can I moderate the code of conduct I seek to instill, to unselfishly serve for the security of all, and yet alert them they may be exploited by this virtue?

Do I teach them to obey the establishment and work for change only within the defined framework of government? Or do I teach them there is a proper time to rebel and do as the American Declaration of Independence instructs, to take up arms and change what is wrong?

I fought the Vietnam War, I fought the Justice Department and now I am fighting TIME magazine. On April 16, 1993, I filed a lawsuit against TIME in a New York federal court under the federal libel statutes.* I am determined to prevail.

Terry Kent Reed
Somewhere in the U.S.

---

*   Terry K. Reed vs Time Warner, Inc., Time Inc. Magazine Company, and Richard Behar; United States District Court, Southern District of New York , case # 93 Civ. 2249. Exhibit A, TIME article "Anatomy of a Smear". (See document section at the end of chapter 36)

A word about the quotes in this book. I was a paid intelligence professional. I was recruited, selected, trained and compensated in great part for my ability to organize facts, events, analyze motives and mentally retain them.

Some quotes in this book are not verbatim.

In some instances, scenes in this book were reconstructed from notes and memories of the events, meetings and conversations shortly after they took place. *All* quotes are expressed in the spirit, intent, tone and inflection of the person or the participants in the included conversation.

Ethnic slurs and profanity are in no way intended to insult anyone or any particular ethnic group. They are factual and included to recreate authenticity in the dialogue between persons quoted in this book.

CHAPTER 1

PATRIOTIC TIME BOMBS

As a nation,
You should never test
Your very best,
While at home
You leave the rest.
                    —Terry Kent Reed, 1971

"Fucking Nixon and Kissinger! They're the real war criminals here," Oliver North lamented. North and his companion were talking heatedly about the blame—and guilt—cast upon the military in the wake of the Vietnam debacle.

Terry Reed replied, "Yeah. If those two bastards were put on public display in POW cages, maybe history wouldn't repeat itself."

At their first meeting on February 24, 1982, in Oklahoma City, Oliver North and Reed had discovered they were cut from the same cloth. They had lived parallel lives, served their country in parallel ways and had been the victim of parallel lies from the nation's leaders who had sent men to die and then sat back to debate its morality. Both men were seeking the same elusive thing: A chance to redeem the military institutions and the men they loved.

Although neither realized it at the time, they were patriotic time bombs produced in the same Cold War Factory.

"Us good soldiers seem to be disposable," North said over and over as he sat under the penetrating view of J. Edgar Hoover, whose portrait hung in all FBI offices like this one in Oklahoma City. North then professed to be working for the Central Intelligence Agency and used a cover name. His code name for this project was "John Cathey."

As the CIA man continued to sermonize, Terry Reed was astonished to find someone who was articulating the same frustration and anger he felt about the fate of those who had served their country, put their lives on the line and were then abandoned. In too many cases men like them had even paid the supreme price for freedom....death. And for what, the man he knew as "John Cathey" asked?

The words stirred images and thoughts of the forces in Terry's life that had influenced his decision to serve his country.

* * *

A lump was forming in the young cadet's throat and his eyes were beginning to well-up as he listened to Harry S. Truman on that spring day in 1966. The former president, then nearly 82 and, his voice wavering, exhibited the spark and determination of the man who had made a decision that affected the world forever.

The man from Missouri had taken care of *his* soldiers in 1945. He had nuked the enemy, gotten the war over with and brought 'em home...victorious.

The speech delivered that day in Carthage, only 20 miles from Lamar, the Missouri town where Truman had been born, was having a profound effect on 18-year-old ROTC cadet, Lieutenant Colonel Terry Kent Reed, "A" Company commander, Detachment No. 19, Fifth U.S Army Instructor Group.

Terry and the other cadets of his elite unit were frozen at rigid attention on the Carthage Senior High School parade field, preparing to pass in review to convey respect for Truman, the man responsible for their unit's creation. The community's leaders were respectfully assembled to pass on to their youth the principles they embraced, the core of our freedom: duty, honor, country.

The scene resembled a Norman Rockwell painting. Here was a small southwestern Missouri town of 10,000 founded in 1842 and steeped in Civil War history. Named after the ancient North African city, Carthage was the site of the world's largest active marble quarry, with many capitol buildings in the North being built of the coveted white marble. Its vast resources of agriculture and lead and zinc mining made it a major asset to the Union's war-making capability causing the North to sacrifice many soldiers in attempts to keep the minerals out of Confederate hands.

Carthage, the county seat of Jasper County, was the site of the first land battle of the War Between the States, the location of some of the most savage guerrilla fighting, and where the North and South first tested their full scale battle resources and abilities. Jasper County was the location of the war's first extended campaign for the entire length of the war (1861-1865), which heightened guerrilla warfare tactics as opposing armies attempted to control this vital Mississippi River transportation artery.

The Battle of Carthage on July 5th, 1861, became the focal point of Missouri's struggle over whether or not to withdraw from the Union. For three years, both sides took turns occupying the town. On September 22nd, 1864, Confederate guerillas finally burned Carthage to the ground.[1]

The bloodshed certainly had an effect on the local citizenry. The census of 1860 noted the county population as 6,883. By war's end only 30 full-time residents were left.

Having to live under ongoing occupation by warring armies made the citizens of Carthage survivors, and wary of all government authorities. Reed's great-grandfather was a mule-trader and political organizer who prided himself on being able to buy mules, stolen from both armies, and then sell them to whichever army was occupying Carthage at the time. He, like the others left alive, had only survived by clinging to their wits and making the best of a bad situation. Perhaps this spit-in-the-eye-of-authority attitude was best manifested in Reed's grandfather who refused throughout his life to buy a fishing license, saying, "God put the fish there, not the State of Missouri." For his anti-government stance, he ended up paying fines levied by the game wardens far and above the cost of the license.

This independent, stubborn and enterprising attitude captured by the local newspaper of 1861, *The Southwest News*. Its motto was, "Independent in all things, neutral in nothing", creating an environment that turned this region for a time into a sanctuary for misfits, malcontents and miscreants who became America's folk heroes, and often, its "most wanted."

The list includes Belle Starr, the Dalton, Younger and James gangs, Quantrill's Raiders and even, in this century, Bonnie and Clyde. And, of course, Harry S. Truman.

By the end of the 19th Century, Carthage prided itself at having more millionaires per capita than any other town in America, having completely rebuilt itself and grown beyond its agrarian heritage by establishing a thriving, diverse industrial and manufacturing base centered around the mining industry. The town boasted sidewalks paved in marble and granite, which defined grids studded with Victorian mansions built by the wealthy and rivaling anything Eastern cities offered.

This centerpiece of American values, with its marble-constructed town square court house, complete with castle-like turrets and a clock that struck with a frequency that rivaled Big Ben, was where Terry Reed was raised—twenty miles from the birth place of Harry S. Truman.

Truman, besides being a statesman and farmer, was a personal hero of Terry's, an example by virtue of his common sense attitude toward life and society. In Truman's mind things were either right or wrong. Terry shared that headstrong faith, based on values instilled by his strongly independent and religious-minded parents. It was part of a value system the young Reed knew was worth defending and, if necessary, dying for.

Consequently, there was no doubt in his mind of his purpose in life as he stood on the drill field in 1966 at Carthage High School. That day, he set out on the same path as Oliver North. That day, the field in Carthage and the parade grounds at North's Annapolis were one and the same. It was the day the Carthage ROTC unit received the highest award that could be given. They had been rated the best in the nation and the man who had fought for the unit's origination and accreditation, Harry Truman, had been invited to present the award. The cadets had presented the former President with an engraved Wilkinson saber as a token of appreciation to the man who immortalized the words, "The buck stops here".

This scene of patriotism and duty did not reflect the entire nation's sentiment, however. Much of the country was in turmoil. As the former President extolled patriotism and honor, Lyndon Johnson was grappling with the problems of the Vietnam war. More than 400,000 U.S. "advisors" were on the ground in Vietnam. Riots were tearing American campuses and cities apart. Thousands carried banners saying "Make Love, Not War," and draft cards were being torn and burned. America's ally, Canada, was becoming the fashionable place for many draft-age youth to sit out the war.

Truman would have none of this, though, as he looked out across the field to the assembled cadets and crowd, and told them about duty, honor and country.

"In 1792 George Washington, President of the United States, asked Congress to start a military training program for the safety of this country. He was not successful in obtaining it.

"President after President has made the same request. We have made progress but we still have not integrated universal training programs.

"Our Government is founded on the principle of the consent of the governed. We believe that government is the servant of the individual and not his master. Jefferson like Washington and Hamilton was well aware that a strong military establishment was vital to the preservation of our liberty. All these early patriot leaders knew that effective military forces are not possible without proper training and able leadership. They all remembered Washington's struggle for men and leaders to win the revolution...

"The spirit of our people has never been war-like. Our ancestors came to this country to find peace and freedom. That is what we have always wanted. That is what we want now.

"But there is a great difference between being peaceful and being passive. It's impossible to have world peace unless we are able and willing to stand up for our rights and the rights of the free world...

"The welfare of the nation and the world is in the hands of its young men. They must attain the knowledge and ability to carry on....

"Institutions such as this great school give young men lessons and leadership training and the fundamentals of a good education....

"Never before in the history of the world has a great nation followed the path which we followed after the German and Japanese surrenders in 1945. We helped to rehabilitate the defeated countries just as we did our allies.

"Never in the history of the world had that happened before. It comes very nearly being the Golden Rule on a world basis.

"Young men and women study your history, study the great leaders in history and try to live by the Ten Commandments and the Sermon on the Mount.

"You will be happy, you will make others happy and the country will be safe for the future."

Cadet Lieutenant Colonel Reed, Alpha Company commander with his Sam Brown Belt glistening in the sun and his saber drawn, had to fight back the tears. The discipline and challenges of ROTC had been Terry Reed's right of passage, forcing him to shed his shyness, build his self-esteem, and grow mentally and physically to levels he had never dared to dream possible. In Carthage, this haven of Middle American values, being an ROTC officer and leader carried the same status as varsity "jock." And here he was, standing at attention before his company, the group of cadets that he had lead and molded through out his year as their Co. These twenty students were a product of his undivided effort and most assuredly reflected the pride instilled in them by himself and the man who had made the monumental decision to end World War II.

Having risen to be one of only six company commanders, Terry saw himself as among the elite. Moreover, his company was the best of the six. And he was going to do what Harry Truman told him, serve his country. The draft dodgers and protestors be damned! "The nation can count on us", the young Reed and many others in his battalion pledged.

If anyone was as proud as Terry that day, it was his father. In battles across Africa and Europe, Harry Reed had helped defeat the Nazis and now he was passing the torch to his son, the eldest of six children. For 18 years, the young Reed had been taught by his father to honor his family, community and country.

Terry was the quintessential product of Middle America. Sown like patriotic seed on the plains, his destiny was to be harvested for the nation's use. He spent laborious nights shining shoes and polishing brass for open ranks inspections, and finding it sometimes necessary to study into the early morning hours to make the required straight A-grade average. It had been no easy task, but it had been worthwhile, culminating in that proud moment, one that had a profound and lasting impact on the young Missourian. He had proved capable not only to his parents and teachers, but more importantly, to himself as well.

This new "crop" of dedicated young men, for the most part born of veterans of World War II, was reaped by the government and sent on the fruitless and unsupported mission to halt the advance of communism in Southeast Asia.

By the Fall of 1967, Terry was in college but facing the draft, and was torn between duty and education. As the male enrollment in the school he was attending began dwindling due to increased draft quotas, he felt pangs of guilt. Hadn't he, after all, suffered and excelled during those years in ROTC to prepare himself for military service?

Although intellectually curious and eager to learn, his country needed him now. Knowing he had no other moral choice, he shopped all the military services and decided to join the Air Force, which he hoped would enable him to acquire valuable skills while fulfilling his military obligation.

Time of war terrifies most mothers and Terry's mother, Martha Reed, was somewhat relieved to see that her son was more interested in after-burners and jet fuel than bayonets and gunpowder. She knew the price that one can be asked by our country to pay, having lost a younger brother in World War II. Terry felt that from all the services the Air Force offered the best continuing college education program available while serving on active duty. After a battery of tests at the recruiting station in Joplin, Missouri, he was excited to find that due to high test scores, he was qualified for "any job the Air Force has."

Further testing at the Armed Forces Induction Center in Kansas City, and later at Amarillo, Texas, during basic training, indicated to the Air Force they were dealing with "intelligence material". Terry and one other airman from their flight of 120 were summoned one day to the base psychiatrist who told them "the Air Force is considering you for a highly-placed, sensitive job...intelligence."

After attending basic military intelligence school at Lowry Air Force Base in Denver, Reed honed his insidious skills at the 2nd Reconnaissance Technical Squadron at Barksdale AFB in Louisiana. By the late summer, 1969, he was informed that he had been selected for Defense Secretary Robert S. McNamara's top-secret project, code named Igloo White. The hard work and long hours of studying had again paid off. He had rivaled the Air Force's best.

So, at the age of 21, armed with Midwestern and religious values, a near-photographic memory and a top-secret security clearance given him by the Defense Intelligence Agency (DIA), he set out on what he saw as a patriotic course built upon his earlier years in ROTC.

With very little fanfare and an overloaded B-4 bag, Air Force Sergeant Terry K. Reed, AF16962257, departed Travis Air Force Base, California on October 9, 1969. He and the plane's load of human replacements for the war headed West, to where the action was....and where a Marine by the name of Oliver North had just been promoted to First Lieutenant and was winding down his tour of duty in I Corp near the Demilitarized Zone in the northern area of South Vietnam.[2]

Then came the reality of Southeast Asia.

YEAR: 1969
PLACE: NAKHON PHANOM, RTAFB THAILAND
SUBJECT: TASK FORCE ALPHA
CLASSIFICATION: TOP SECRET, NO FOREIGN DISSEMINATION
CODE NAME: "IGLOO WHITE"

This shadowy, wing-level unit had a brigadier general as its commander and reported directly to 7th Air Force headquarters in Hawaii, bypassing the usual intelligence reporting channels in southeast Asia. From there, the intelligence information Task Force Alpha (TFA) collected went straight to the Pentagon where select briefers kept the Joint Chiefs and the Secretary of Defense informed on the success of the unit's secret mission.

This was the heart of McNamara's pet project, the so-called "electronic fence" that was to manage the interdiction and destruction of North Vietnamese resupply traffic flowing south along the primitive road complex known as the Ho Chi Minh trail. It extended over 400 miles from North Vietnam, through Laos and Cambodia, into South Vietnam.

The complex task was in the hands of trained military and civilian technicians operating IBM's latest secret creation—the world's largest computer, code named 360E, the "E" designating experimental. Working with the Department of Defense, IBM had pushed computer technology beyond the envelope as it was then defined. This project was the center-piece of the efforts of the Johnson administration to contain the war to Vietnam. It's primary mission was to cut off the supply routes afforded the enemy in the dense, triple-layer jungle canopy of Laos, and prevent stockpiling of supplies needed for another Tet offensive.

Located on the southern shores of the Mekong River in primitive northeastern Thailand, this remote Royal Thai Air Force base housed the DOD's supercomputer system. Protected by earthen-filled steel revetments, the futuristic, single-story facility extended below ground, protected by a camouflaged steel roof designed to take three direct hits by mortar fire without penetration. The technology contained within its walls was considered so advanced for its day that extreme measures had been taken during the construction phase to prevent it from falling into communist hands. The entire facility was wired with explosives to be detonated in the event the base was ever over-run.

The computers' pulse was monitored by teams of Air Force and civilian technicians in the command center known as the plot room or "floor". This futuristic battle station was dimly-lit and sunken into a hemispherical arrangement resembling a small amphitheater. The back-lit, Plexiglass targeting boards that glowed in the room's eerie darkness gave the appearance of a high-technology bull ring, comparable to the science fiction flight deck of the Starship Enterprise in the *Star Trek* series.

The continuous twinkling of the sensor-activation lights mounted on Plexiglass screens combined with the latest technological breakthrough, LED (light-emitting diodes) clocks calibrated to read hundredths of a second, gave the visitor an advanced warning of the technology housed within Task Force Alpha's facility.

In a nutshell, and if all worked well, an appropriately cleared visitor to TFA would learn the following: As the "gooks", as the enemy was called, moved their supplies under the cover of darkness, foliage and clouds along the road segments in Laos, code-named "Steel Tiger", they were unaware of the airborne command post, an EC-121R, high above them at 35,000 feet.[3] This predecessor of the present-day AWAC system was armed with the latest classified electronic wizardry whose primary task was "monitoring" the electronic signals from a "string of sensors" that specially-equipped aircraft had previously dropped adjacent to the road segments below. Upon impact with the ground, the camouflaged sensors buried themselves up to their plastic antenna, which were designed to blend into the jungle foliage making them nearly impossible for the enemy to detect or locate.

When enemy truck traffic passed along these "seeded" road segments they unknowingly "activated" the sensors through seismic or sometimes audio vibration. This sent an electric signal skyward to the AWAC-style plane, via which the data was relayed to the "floor," or command center, of the plot room at TFA. There, the 360E began a series of calculations that would guide a specially-equipped and armed F-4 aircraft to an airborne point in space to coincide with the moving target. If all went well, a bomb would fall, seemingly out of nowhere, onto an unsuspecting enemy.

This advanced concept, in theory, would give the Air Force the ability to "kill" all trucks, day or night and in any weather conditions. It was exciting for Reed to be participating in an operation with such advanced technology that even the budget for it was classified. The price tag for TFA's internal operations, not counting aircraft and ordinance, was over $1 million a day. By early 1971, shortly after Terry left, the official and classified ordinance reports showed that over 2.2 million tons of bombs had been dropped on Laos. This secret air war was costing $10 billion a year and the Air Force was claiming that up to 12,000 Soviet-built Zil-57 cargo trucks had been "killed" per year.

The Royal Thai Air Force base, from which TFA operated, was also the home of another offshoot of the super-computer. Its code name was "Teaball," Seventh Air Force's special controlling facility that directed air strikes from EC-121s early-warning radar planes code named "Disco".[4] Its purpose was to coordinate air strikes and provide U.S. pilots operating over North Vietnam with advance warning of enemy fighter intercepts. TFA's computer was so advanced it could identify Soviet MIG aircraft by model number, track their fuel burn and even warn American pilots as to the skill of the individual enemy pilot. This was achieved by intercepting airborne radio voice communications in TFA's plot room. There they could compare stored enemy pilots' voice prints to the one in the plane, determine his name, relay to the American combatant his opponents proficiency in flying, and most frightening of all—relay the number, if any, of American aircraft shot down in aerial dog-fight engagements.

Reed's job as a target selector and photo analyst was to focus primarily on a 50-by-15 square mile road segment known as the Route 23 complex, winding out of the mountainous and rugged MuGhia Pass from North Vietnam into Southern Laos. The route flowed around, over and through the volcanic karst formations which were riddled with caves, affording the North Vietnamese Army (NVA) subterranean protection for the never-ending B-52 strikes, code named Arc Light. This key segment of Laotian real estate was vital to the NVA resupply effort for its troops in South Vietnam. Without tons of munitions, food, and fuel moving south on a regular basis, the enemy stockpiles in Cambodia and elsewhere would quickly exhaust themselves leaving NVA regulars ill-equipped to continue their offensive efforts in South Vietnam. Terry and his team would use the tell-tale records of the sensor activations to determine where the enemy had hidden truck parks and storage areas along the jungle-shrouded route. By melding these electronic "tips" on where the enemy was hiding, combined with other intelligence provided by photo-reconnaissance and pilot reports, Reed's team was responsible for selecting the impact point of tons of high explosives delivered by aircraft.

The lives of many American flyers were relying upon the thoroughness in which Reed and his team did their job. The NVA was shooting back with some of the most sophisticated and concentrated aerial defenses Russia had ever built. "Flak traps," as they were known were placed throughout MuGhia Pass, and portions of Southeast Asia were actually being more heavily defended than Moscow. As a group supervisor, Terry briefed Air Force forward air controllers (FAC's) and F-4 jet pilots on not only the suspected location of North Vietnamese supply convoys, but these anti-aircraft artillery (AAA) positions as well. Six hours after a typical briefing, Terry and the returning pilots would study the bomb damage assessment (BDA) photos of the previous air strikes. Those retaliatory briefings, given also to the CIA, were Terry's introduction as to how legitimate covert operations are misused to disguise black, or illegal, operations. The CIA was "on the ground" in Laos despite Richard Nixon's public denial. He conveniently misled the public by making statements shrouded in deceit such as, "There are no American troops in Laos", the operative word being "troops."

But those weren't the only briefings Reed gave. There were those "special requests" that put him into contact with the civilian "spooks" who were doing secret work for "the customer," the Central Intelligence Agency. These were men under contract by the CIA, which was fighting its own secret war in Laos and it depended upon Task Force Alpha (TFA) and men like Reed to provide them with "fresh" intelligence so that they could carry out their own deadly agenda. The Air Force officially denied any linkage to the CIA.

But Terry knew the truth. So at the age of 21, he had come to accept as routine the heavy responsibility of making life and death decisions. He had also come to accept the fact that the government and the military had to deceive the American public to accomplish its national security objectives.

The rationale for this deception: the American public would not tolerate knowing that the war had spread beyond North and South Korea. Though supposedly a "neutral country," a half-million combat sorties had been flown and over a million tons of bombs had been dropped on the small nation prior to Terry's arrival.

But those massive and relentless air attacks only interrupted the enemy traffic. The secondary explosions Reed's team was rewarded for producing on the ground in Laos, were reverberating all the way to Washington. All of this ordinance was being dropped secretly and illegally on a country with whom we were not at war. Senator Stuart Symington (D-Mo.) would announce in public hearings, "we have been at war in Laos for years, and it's time the American people knew more of the facts."[5]

This disclosure was made in October, 1969, the month Terry arrived in Thailand, and it wasn't until five months later that President Nixon acknowledged for the first time U.S. "involvement" in Laos.

From the CIA's station headquarters in the capital of Vientiane, Reed knew the CIA was more than just a little involved. It was pulling the strings and bribing the ruling right-wing Laotian officials living off the misery of their own people. For each bombing raid, a "fee" was paid to Laotian Prince Souvanna Phouma for the "bombing rights." Terry began to think cynically of the U.S.

government when learning that it was literally renting Laos for its secret and non-existent war.

And who was coordinating the "non-existent" effort in Laos for the CIA?—Air America, the obscure, "humanitarian" airline that secretly shuttled lethal and humanitarian supplies along with personnel throughout the region with "civilian" pilots. The reconnaissance photos these pilots needed in order to locate their remote jungle airfields and targets came from TFA. With the assistance of Air America pilots for "target tips," Terry and his unit applied their deadly skills. From the portable trailer in which he worked, equipped with the technology to analyze airborne and satellite reconnaissance, Terry dug in for the duration of his 12-month stay. Words such as "Heavy Hook," "56 SOW," "Spookie," "Raven," "Nail," "Bug," "FRAG," "HABU," "Black Crow," "Paveway," "Wild Weasel," "KS-72," and "Mark 86" proliferated his vocabulary, and became the dialogue of his trade.

But though Terry Reed worked in a 21st-Century space-age environment, where he lived was something else. The air-conditioning necessary to keep the computers cooled and operational didn't exist in the airmen's living quarters. Their "hooches," as they were called, were overcrowded, infested with mosquitos and built on stilts to keep the cobras out during the sun-baked dry season and the torrents of water out during the monsoon season. This stark contrast between living and working quarters, combined with the sweltering heat and the relentless noise from day and night takeoffs and landings was draining.

The air was pounded 24 hours a day by the rotor blades of patrolling helicopters trying to prevent North Vietnamese Army (NVA) saboteurs from penetrating the perimeter of the remote base. Because of its strategic northern location, 100 miles due west of the Demilitarized Zone separating North and South Vietnam, the base housed special search and rescue units whose job was to rescue downed airmen. Nakhon Phanom (NKP) was a perpetual beehive of activity requiring Reed and most of the other men to work twelve hour shifts, often seven days a week.

The reality of the human carnage brought on by the war was visibly displayed to Terry when giant C-130 transport planes landed full of body bags that were piled along the runway enroute to the mortuary in Saigon. Observing Thai soldiers nonchalantly sorting the corpses by nationality triggered the realization of the fragility of life. While contemplating his own mortality and sitting in the sizzling heat awaiting personnel replacements from "the world," Terry would first meet a man with whom he would later bond for life.

It was December 1969 and the man from Erie, Pennsylvania, nicknamed Roger Ramjet by his intelligence school classmates, would walk down a C-130 loading ramp and into Terry's life.

Terry was surveying the group of "jeeps" (new arrivals) from the States who appeared to be simultaneously suffering from heat shock, culture shock, homesickness, fear and jet lag, when he first noticed Ramjet. He behaved differently than the remainder of the new arrivals wandering across the sweltering flight line.

The other "sheep" were aimlessly following some imaginary leader. But not Ramjet. He appeared to be alone, in charge, and more interested in inspecting the steel and sand-bagged revetments protecting the F-4 Phantom aircraft. He had a way about him...an aura that radiated an instinct to survive, and an innate curiosity for these sophisticated instruments of war.

Ramjet had spotted the TFA sign Reed was holding, threw his gear into Reed's truck, and said in his soft-spoken, monotonal voice, "My name's John Desko. I'm from Erie, PA. I came here to blow shit up, win this war, and get outta here."

On the trip to the barracks, the conversation shifted from war to the hidden benefits of serving abroad.

"Is it true that B-52 pilots can smuggle in Jap bikes by hiding them in the bomb bay? If that's the case, then I'm lookin' for a Kawasaki triple."

Being a motorcycle fanatic himself, Reed and Ramjet hit it off immediately as they dug in for their one-year tour of duty in this outpost from hell. They became friends for life and both would later say that their main task during this time was keeping each other sane. This bond for life was not forged on some safe and secure college campus. It was deeper and more serious. Their Alma Mater would be Task Force Alpha. It was here they would lose their virginity and naïveté about truth, deceit and the way the world of "intel" *really* operates, not the way they had been taught in Denver. They would soon discover that their unit was actually the "secret supermarket of intelligence material" to not only the Air Force but other "customers" they couldn't mention, particularly the CIA.

The CIA relied extensively upon Air America for logistics support to conduct their unstated objectives in Southeast Asia. Air America was described to the outside world as a humanitarian airline with bases in Vientiane, Laos, and Udorn, Thailand. With the majority of its aircraft painted white and bearing no military markings, Air America and its pilots shuttled some extremely "sensitive and lethal cargo" along with the rice and medical supplies it air dropped to friendly forces in the Plain of Jars in Northern Laos. That sensitive cargo included bootlegged intelligence material, secretly provided to the CIA by Task Force Alpha through this "shuttle service." Through this operation, Reed met some strange, rogue pilots who wore solid gold chains and flight suits with no insignia. The gold was for emergency bartering in case of a shootdown and their sanitized flight suits were supposed to give them the appearance of civilian pilots.

These pilots knew that if shot down and captured, their country would deny any knowledge of their mission or existence. By volunteering for this hazardous and secret duty they received compensation for their "black" services far above the going rate for "legal flights." If they survived, they could go home wealthy. If they didn't, their next of kin would probably never know the truth surrounding their death.

One of these pilots was a man by the name of William Cooper. He was then in his mid-40's and shuttling C-123's and DC-3's between TFA and Vientiane laden with, among other things, illegally provided aerial photography, photography that had been "sanitized" to be used for special CIA bombing missions to places openly banned by the President and Congress. Cooper was a nobody in 1970, but would become famous, or perhaps infamous, when he crashed and died in 1986 in Nicaragua at the controls of a C-123K filled with guns and gringos. That crash would usher in the era known as Iran-Contra.

TFA, or the "project" as it was known, would also house another of the dirty secrets of the Vietnam War—the fact that U.S. servicemen were being sacrificed to accomplish bombing objectives in Laos.

In a diplomatic chess game, Air Force decision-making had been "neutered."

Instead of a "flying armada" that could have destroyed North Vietnam's industrial capability, it had been turned into an instrument to achieve Nixon and Kissinger's political agenda that included "détente" with the Chinese.

Instead of raining fire non-stop on North Vietnam until the enemy quit, Air Force fire power became the diplomatic "stick" in Kissinger's "carrot and stick" policy.

The "carrot" was the curtailment of bombing in the North in exchange for an "honorable peace," which meant a pre-arranged American withdrawal before the political and military collapse of South Vietnam. The "stick" was the punishment side of the equation that Nixon would use to force the Vietnamese to negotiate like gentlemen at the bargaining table in Paris, showing the American's back home that he couldn't be bullied by the likes of Le Duc To and Ho Chi Minh.

Caught in the middle of this political chess game were men like Reed. His job at TFA was to select the impact point for the bombs the Air Force was "allowed" to drop. In compliance with the Geneva Accords and the rules of engagement, Terry had to insure that the bombs did not fall on humanitarian targets, such as hospitals—and POW camps built by the North Vietnamese along the trail network of Steel Tiger.

Hanoi, in a cold-blooded attempt to keep the road network open, had placed clusters of POWs in concentration camps at key junctions in the road network. Intelligence reports indicated that many of these POWs, who were being used as "human shields," had been transferred from camps in the Hanoi-Haiphong region to augment the captured American flyers shot down over Laos. By this time nearly 400 airmen had been downed while flying over this neutral nation.

By the spring of 1970, this human shield tactic was effectively preventing the Air Force from bombing those critical road junctions, allowing the North Vietnamese to build stockpiles in the south in preparation for a another Tet Offensive.

Hanoi was insidiously exploiting America's compliance with the humanitarian constraints placed on its Air Force. Largely due to the effectiveness of TFA's interdiction efforts, the NVA could not stockpile sufficient fuel to launch a mechanized or tank offensive in the South. They had become so daring in Laos, however, as a result of the success of their "American Human Shield Program" that they initiated a daring program to construct a POL (petroleum) pipeline, which would supply fuel to the Soviet-built Zil-57 supply trucks, thereby allowing them to haul containerized fuel to depots in the south. Reed's team and the Air Force sat helplessly watching the construction of pumping stations down Steel Tiger, normally protected in karst caves and in close proximity to these POW camps.

Major decisions affecting the war were in many cases influenced by political events in the United States. One such event was the killing of four Kent State students by National Guardsmen in the spring of 1970. Kent State had erupted on May 4, 1970 in response to the U.S. invasion of Cambodia, a sign that the war was spreading. The political backlash and the public outcry from the Cambodian invasion forced the cancellation of a planned military ground invasion of Laos to destroy the petroleum pipeline under construction there, and to free the POWs.

The bullets that killed the students in Ohio had symbolically ricocheted all the way to Terry's trailer in Thailand. On a fateful day in mid-May, an Air

Force captain walked into Terry's targeting shop and ordered that computerized "fail safes" that prevented inadvertent bombing of the POW camps be removed.

"Pull the map tacks," the captain commanded. Terry and the other enlisted men were shocked and appalled when the officer told them a policy change had been made and that the POW camps would no longer be protected from bombing operations.

A small mutiny ensued and ended shortly thereafter, with the stunned airmen standing at rigid attention while a full colonel read them the Uniform Code of Military Justice, specifically the section about the consequences of refusing to obey a direct order. They were guaranteed immediate lodging in the federal penitentiary at Fort Leavenworth, Kansas, if the orders were not obeyed immediately, and told that replacements from Hawaii would be there within 24 hours. The replacements *would* follow the lawful orders being given. It was going to happen, with or without their cooperation.

Hadn't the American prisoners taken an oath, after all, and signed a service agreement to pay "the supreme price" if necessary? This was the logic the colonel applied. And who were the men paying the supreme price? Young men like Terry Reed and Oliver North were seeing the nation's very best slain needlessly to avoid upsetting geopolitical goals that only Richard Nixon and a select few could secretly articulate.

The red tacks came down and so did the bombs.

In retrospect, Terry came to understand how the military had appealed to his logic, of sacrificing the few to save the many. But, in the process, they had also exploited his sense of duty. The result was that he went home missing a part of himself, much like those who returned missing limbs. Except no one could see what he had lost.

No one except Oliver North, who 10 years later would return with that missing part, honor, and offer to graft it back on.

This heinous decision to bomb the POW camps, which Terry could not and would not talk about for years for fear of violating his secrecy oath that could send him to prison, haunted him. He would learn first hand that day that "national security" could be successfully used to mask the crimes committed by his own government.

Terry tried to rationalize what he had been forced to do since his brother, Gary, was an enlisted man still in harm's way and serving with the U.S. Army at a fire base near the uninhabitable and dangerous Demilitarized Zone. Maybe the action had prevented another Tet and had likewise saved his brother's and other soldiers' lives. It was time to block the incident from his mind and go back to "the world," the name GIs gave to America. Terry returned home on leave to no parades or welcoming bands at the bus station. "Where was Harry Truman now," he thought?

Dressed in his Air Force blues and wearing his Accommodation Medal, National Defense and Vietnam campaign ribbons, Terry suppressed his anger out of respect for his father. It had been four years now since that day on the parade field; the cheers had faded and the flags now were wrapped around the KIAs' (killed in action) caskets. Reed had grown to suspect that his Midwestern values had been exploited by the government. But worse yet, he felt that his elders had let him down. Why were the youth being forced to rebel and bring attention to the injustices brought on by our own government? Why were the adults not in the streets instead of the youth, protesting the inequities of the draft and the lack of a stated foreign policy? Why were the young paying the price both abroad and in the streets of America? It saddened him deeply.

It was like a scene from *All Quiet on the Western Front* when the young, battle-scarred German soldier returned home realizing that the flag-waving, the martial music and the heroic speeches did not prepare him for the realities of comrades dying in agony.

As Terry looked around he came to the unthinkable realization that possibly those who had stayed at home were the smart ones. They, at least, were intact, and not finding it necessary to defend the actions of their country abroad. How easy it was for them to rationalize their opposition and non-action.

At that time, news was focusing on all the negatives spilling out of the bloody conflict. An Army lieutenant named William Calley had become the measure of military morality. His actions in a village called My Lai later became known as the My Lai Massacre. Just coming home was turning into a battle of its own.

"Why can't those hippie soldiers kick their asses like we did the Nazis?" the elder Reed asked as they sat in the front porch swing that spring day in 1971. "I think this proves our society lacks any real values. And it's all my generation's fault. We gave you too much and you don't appreciate what you have. You're all soft. This must be how Rome decayed. You guys have been over there too long. Besides, the papers say you're winning. I don't understand."

"Not true," Terry replied. "The papers are lying; the government is lying. You can't know how bad we're losing. If it were up to the Air Force, we'd nuke 'em and be home by the Fourth of July."

The young Reed knew that body counts of enemy dead and bomb damage estimates were being "cooked" to keep the American public from knowing the truth of how badly the war was going. General William Westmoreland, the military's supreme commander, would later pay a price for perpetuating these battlefield myths.

Terry, now a staff sergeant in Air Force intelligence, had grown up believing in what Superman had called "truth, justice and the American way." Those beliefs had been shattered. There was no truth in this war. Where was the justice in it all? Was this the American way? He couldn't tolerate the thought of being considered a warmonger for his efforts to serve his country. He did not blame the military for what was happening, it was the political leaders who were at fault. The elders, they were the ones who were wrong and should be held accountable.

"It's a different war, Dad. The people aren't behind us. Our government won't let the military win. To tell the truth, Dad, I've grown to admire the determination of the people we're fighting. They're dedicated survivalists and in this thing for the long haul. They aren't going home until they're victorious or dead."

Terry's disillusionment only grew after being re-assigned to stateside duty. He found a country gripped in a generational war with students rioting on the campuses and the older generation wrapped in an Orwellian orgy of denial and self-deception.

He had not told his father, who had returned from World War II to cheering crowds and congratulations from his neighbors, that military authorities had warned the young airman not to wear his uniform in the Los Angeles airport because of the harassment he would encounter. His father had never had to wipe spit off his uniform.

His aging father had been sired by a different America and still believed that America always fought on the side of right. "You're so lucky to have been born an American," his father repeatedly said during Terry's youth. "This is the greatest country in the world."

Believing that, how could the older man now believe that the country they had both loved and now served had become mired in a minefield of lies and deception? The answer, he decided, was impossible to convey to those of his father's generation. He wouldn't attempt to destroy his father's illusions. Some myths should be sacred.

He simply told an unbelieving father that he shouldn't always believe the newspapers, what he saw on TV... or his government. Victory in Southeast Asia, the young man knew, was not only not at hand, it was not even on the horizon.

As the two Reeds sat on the porch and tried to span the generation gap, many of the troubling revelations of America's secret agenda were yet to surface. And the young sergeant was forbidden to talk about the terrible secrets he was carrying inside him. Laos, he knew, was the place his fellow soldiers were being discarded wholesale.

The reality of men being put needlessly in harm's way and a war being fought without public support while Congress debated its morality was a stark contrast to what his father had known and what the son had come to expect. It changed Terry's life forever.

It was a bitter and disillusioned man who left the Air Force five years later and went about his life. He considered the whole experience as something perverse, a kind of "national masturbation" where the best seeds are needlessly ejaculated. Gone forever, they will never bear fruit.

But Terry thought as he embarked on civilian life that at least he had put government duplicity behind him. He would find, however, that one never really gets out of intelligence. He had attained the knowledge and self-discipline that made him an asset, literally. His Air Force file highlighting his patriotic efforts and honorable discharge now went to the Central Intelligence Agency, to be held for future use.

> *If you can't call it a war,*
> *Then don't call me.*

—Terry Kent Reed, 1976

1. Ward L. Schrantz, *Jasper County, Missouri, in the Civil War*, Carthage, Missouri, 1923.
2. Ben Bradlee, Jr., *Guts and Glory, The Rise and Fall of Oliver North*, Donald I. Fine and Co., New York, 1988, p-86-87.
3. John Morrocco, *Rain of Fire, the Air War 1969-1973*, (Boston Publishing Co. 1985), p. 38.
4. Ibid, p. 145
5. Ibid, p. 194

REQUEST AND AUTHORIZATION FOR PERMANENT CHANGE OF STATION - MILITARY
(If more space is required, continue on reverse)

The following individual will proceed on Permanent Change of Station:

ASSIGNMENT DATA

1. GRADE, LAST NAME, FIRST, MIDDLE INITIAL, AFSN/SSAN	2. SHIPPING AFSC/CAFSC	3. ☐ OVER 4 YRS. SERVICE (Sgt only)
A1C REED, TERRY K 491-52-8196	20650	

TDY

4. PURPOSE OF TDY	5. TDY ENROUTE ADDRESS
attend crs 3OZR8045-5 Intelligence Area Studies(SEA) Class starts 10 Sep 69 grad 7 Oct 69	In/out processing Section, Bldg 345 Lowry AFB, CO 80230

6. NO. OF DAYS	7. TDY REPORTING DATE	8. SECURITY CLEARANCE
29	between 0800 and 1200 hours, 8 Sep 69	TOP SECRET

9. UNIT, MAJOR COMMAND, AND ADDRESS OF UNIT TO WHICH ASSIGNED	10. UNIT, MAJOR COMMAND, AND ADDRESS OF UNIT FROM WHICH RELIEVED
ALPHA TASK FORCE(BACAF) APO San Francisco 96310	2 Recon Tech Sq(SAC) Barksdale AFB, LA 71110

11. TED	[X] PCS WITH PCA (EDCSA) 15 Oct 69	☐ PCS WITHOUT PCA
12. REPORT TO COMDR, NEW ASSIGNMENT NLT	13. DALVP Yes	14. LEAVE ADDRESS 328 N Garrison Carthage, MO 64836

TRAVEL DATA

15. INDIVIDUAL ELECTED TO SERVE	☐ ACCOMPANIED	☐ UNACCOMPANIED TOUR	☐ DEPENDENTS PROHIBITED WITHIN OVERSEA AREA

16. TRAVEL OF DEPENDENT(S) IS AUTHORIZED ☐ CONCURRENT ☐ TO A DESIGNATED POINT WITHIN CONUS	17. AUTHORITY FOR CONCURRENT TRAVEL	18. TPC WITH __8__ DAYS TRAVEL TIME PERMITTED

19. MODES OF TRANSPORTATION AUTHORIZED FOR OVERSEA TRAVEL [X] MIL ACFT ☐ MIL VESSEL ☐ COML ACFT OR VESSEL	20. REPORT TO MAC PASSENGER SERVICE COUNTER AT NET _____ (Hour and Date) NLT _____ (Hour and Date)

21. AIR MOVEMENT DESIGNATOR	22. FLIGHT NO. OR NAME OF VESSEL	23. EXCESS BAGGAGE AUTHORIZED 34 POUNDS 2 PIECES	24. DISLOCATION ALLOWANCE CATEGORY

25. DEPENDENTS *(List names of dependents and DOB of children)*

FISCAL

26. PCS EXPENSE CHARGEABLE TO
5703500 320 P577.02 410 440 S503725

Esther M. Marks, Cert Agt

27. TDY EXPENSE CHARGEABLE TO
5703400 300 0448.03 408 409 463 S525002

28. CIC	29. AUTHORITY AND PCS CODE
4 5 048 5776 503725	AFM 39-11 PCS CODE J 10N40077

30. REMARKS OJT STATUS R. SERVICING CBPO: 56 Cmbt Spt Gp, APO San Francisco 96310. Orders will be indorsed to include reporting instructions to PAE. Introduction and/or purchase of privately owned firearms into SEA is prohibited. Amn will receive M-16 tng before reporting to PAE. SUB PROJ CODE: 0448.03

31. DATE	32. TYPED NAME AND GRADE OF CBPO OFFICIAL	33. SIGNATURE
30 Jul 69	C E GUTHRIE SMSGT, USAF	

34. DESIGNATION AND LOCATION OF HEADQUARTERS DEPARTMENT OF THE AIR FORCE HQ 2AF (SAC) BARKSDALE AFB, LA 71110	35. SPECIAL ORDER NO. A-508	36. DATE 30 Jul 69
	37. TDN FOR THE COMMANDER	

38. DISTRIBUTION	39. SIGNATURE ELEMENT OF ORDERS AUTHENTICATING OFFICIAL
50 - Indiv, 28 - CBPO (ADM), this stn 4 - BCRF, this stn, 1 - DXI, BCASMP, SVSH 46 COMSOT-1, 3 - 2RTSq, 1 Pstl Off New Unit, 6 - CBPO, 56 Cmbt Spt Gp, APO San Francisco 96310, 6 - DASPO, this HQ Rcvd: 30 Jul 69 PM	*(seal: HEADQUARTERS OFFICIAL SECOND AIR FORCE)* A. L. TSCHEPL, COL, USAF Dir of Admin

AF FORM 899 MAR 68   PREVIOUS EDITIONS OF THIS FORM ARE OBSOLETE.

1-1. Above, Air Force orders assigning Terry Reed, with his Top Secret clearance, to Task Force Alpha, code name "Igloo White," in Thailand. This operation, known unofficially as "McNamara's Project", after the Secretary of Defense at the time, was one of the nation's most secret units.

CITATION TO ACCOMPANY THE AWARD OF

THE AIR FORCE COMMENDATION MEDAL
(FIRST OAK LEAF CLUSTER)

TO

TERRY K. REED

Staff Sergeant Terry K. Reed distinguished himself by meritorious service as Imagery Interpretation Specialist, Day Shift, Targets Section, Exploitation Branch, 432 Reconnaissance Technical Squadron, Udorn Royal Thai Air Force Base, Thailand, from 4 February 1974 to 23 January 1975. During this period Sergeant Reed displayed outstanding initiative, professionalism, and technical ability which contributed immeasurably to the completion of assigned reconnaissance projects and intelligence collection efforts. His work in the development of Target Intelligence Kits, prepared in support of United States Support Activiti Group contingency planning, contributed significantly to the accomplishment of the mission of the 432 Reconnaissance Technical Squadron and the mission of the United States Air Force in Southeast Asia. The distinctive accomplishments of Sergeant Reed reflect credit upon himself and the United States Air Force.

1-2 The citation, above, was given to Reed at Udorn, Thailand, Headquarters for Air America.

SGT, SSGT AND SGT PERFORMANCE REPORT

I. IDENTIFICATION DATA

1. LAST NAME · FIRST NAME · MI	2. AFSN:	3. GRADE
REED, TERRY K.	SSAN: FR491-52-8196	Sergeant

4. ORGANIZATION, LOCATION, AND COMMAND	5. RESERVE WARRANT OR COMMISSION GRADE AND AFSN	6. REASON FOR REPORT
Task Force Alpha Nakhon Phanom RTAFB, Thailand (PACAF)	None	☐ NO REPORT 1 YEAR ☐ CHANGE OF REPORTING OFFICIAL ☒ NO REPORT 6 MONTHS ☐ DIRECTED BY _____

7. PERIOD OF REPORT & SUPERVISION

FROM	THRU	NR DAYS
18 Sep 69	17 Mar 70	158

II. DUTIES:

PAFSC 20650 DAFSC 20650 CAFSC 20650 Current Duty: Shift NCOIC, Photo Exploitation Branch for Task Force Alpha (Named USAF Unit, Wing Level). Supervises daily interpretation by designated shift personnel of photography essential to unit mission and preparation of resulting intelligence reports. Additionally responding to requests for targeting actions and aiding in the preparation of briefing aids and special intelligence products as required.

III. PERSONAL QUALITIES

		N/O	0	1	2	3	4	5	6	7	8	9
1. PERFORMANCE OF DUTY: Consider the quantity, quality, and timeliness of his work in the duties described in Section II.	REPORTING OFFICIAL											X
	INDORSING OFFICIAL											X
2. WORKING RELATIONS: Consider how well he used his ability to communicate (oral and written) and to get along with others to improve his overall performance.	REPORTING OFFICIAL											X
	INDORSING OFFICIAL											X
3. TRAINING: Consider how well he discharges his responsibilities as an OJT supervisor, trainer, or trainee and in other efforts to improve his technical knowledge and educational level.	REPORTING OFFICIAL											X
	INDORSING OFFICIAL											X
4. SUPERVISION: Consider how well he supervises, leads, uses available resources, and maintains good order and discipline.	REPORTING OFFICIAL											X
	INDORSING OFFICIAL											X
5. ACCEPTANCE OF NCO RESPONSIBILITY: Consider his acceptance of responsibility for his actions and those of his subordinates.	REPORTING OFFICIAL											X
	INDORSING OFFICIAL											X

		BR	BH	N/O	0	1	2	3	4	5	6	7	8	9
6. BEARING AND BEHAVIOR: Consider the degree to which his bearing and behavior on and off duty improve the image of Air Force NCOs.	REPORTING OFFICIAL	X	X											X
	INDORSING OFFICIAL	X	X											

IV. OVERALL EVALUATION

		N/O	0	1	2	3	4	5	6	7	8	9
How does he compare with others of his grade and Air Force specialty? Promotion potential is an essential consideration in this rating.	REPORTING OFFICIAL											X
	INDORSING OFFICIAL											X
	1ST ADDITIONAL INDORSING OFFICIAL	X											

1-3. One of Terry Reed's military proficiency reports written while serving at Task Force Alpha.

V. COMMENTS OF REPORTING OFFICIAL *(Be factual and specific. Add any comments which increase the objectivity of the rating.)*

FACTS AND SPECIFIC ACHIEVEMENTS: During this rating period, Sgt Reed has performed his duties in an outstanding manner. As a shift supervisor, he eagerly assumed numerous responsibilities and directed the work of his photo interpreters with great efficiency. As a photo interpreter himself, Sgt Reed performed in a truly outstanding manner. His high quality work resulted in the production of many lucrative targets which were subsequently struck by aircraft yielding impressive bomb damage statistics and disrupting major sections of an opposing forces' logistical complex. Outstanding as a supervisor and as a photo interpreter, Sgt Reed also excelled as an organizer. When his branch was tasked with scanning a large quantity of special aerial photography, he set up the operating procedures and then undertook a major portion of the scan himself. His efforts were largely responsible for the location of major new sections and the update of many older sections of hostile lines of communication. Because of his versatility, Sgt Reed was often given a variety of special projects. His production of graphics for presentation to high ranking civilian and military officials won him frequent praise and recognition. STRENGTHS: Uncommon intelligence and efficiency combined with excellent leadership ability make Sgt Reed an outstanding NCO. OTHER COMMENTS: I recommend that Sgt Reed be promoted to Staff Sergeant at the earliest opportunity. This duty performed in Southeast Asia.

VI.	REPORTING OFFICIAL		
NAME, GRADE AND ORGANIZATION	DUTY TITLE	SIGNATURE	
LAURENCE J. ZIMMERMAN, Capt, Task Force Alpha (PACAF)	OIC, Photo Exploitation Branch	*Laurence J. Zimmerman*	
		DATE 25 Mar 1970	

VII.	INITIAL INDORSING OFFICIAL		

Based upon frequent observation of his work, I concur with the above raters. Sgt Reed has continually proven himself to be an outstanding NCO. Reliance upon his abilities, and personal knowledge have been rewarded repeatedly with the production of intelligence outstanding in quality and quantity. His graphics are some of the finest and most professional materials I have ever seen. Each one presents the information clearly and simply, insuring that the information is conveyed to the viewer. I highly recommend him for promotion to Staff Sergeant.

NAME, GRADE AND ORGANIZATION	DUTY TITLE	SIGNATURE	
JAMES D. TURINETTI, Capt, Task Force Alpha (PACAF)	Chief, Photo Interpretation Division	*James D. Turinetti*	
		DATE 25 Mar 1970	

VIII.	ADDITIONAL INDORSEMENT		

I agree with the rating official. I have observed Sgt Reed often, and he is clearly an outstanding NCO. Difficult tasks could always be assigned to him with the assurance that they would be completed successfully. His in-depth knowledge and versatility earned him the respect of every man he worked with. I highly concur with the recommendation that Sgt Reed be promoted at the earliest opportunity.

NAME, GRADE AND ORGANIZATION	DUTY TITLE	SIGNATURE	
HAROLD A. BELLES, Col, Task Force Alpha (PACAF)	Director of Intelligence	*Harold A. Belles*	
		DATE 25 Mar 1970	

IX.	ADDITIONAL INDORSEMENT		
NAME, GRADE AND ORGANIZATION	DUTY TITLE	SIGNATURE	
		DATE	

GPO : 1969—O—348—16—BCB13-1 336-817

1-4. An unclassified description of Reed's activities at Task Force Alpha. The majority of this work was performed in support of the CIA and Air America.

CHAPTER 2

THE SOONER CONNECTION

J. Edgar Hoover continued to glare from his ominous portrait in the Oklahoma City FBI office.

"Fucking Nixon and Kissinger!" Oliver North said once again.

"Yeah," Terry Reed replied.

The first meeting between the two Vietnam-era veterans had been arranged by Edwin Enright, the SAC (Special Agent in Charge) of the Oklahoma City FBI regional headquarters. But this was no ordinary meeting, and no ordinary FBI office.

The leased federal office complex was located in the building housing Sooner Federal Savings and Loan, whose logo, a giant neon pig, sat astride the roof above them. The FBI offices, consisting of the entire two floors situated atop the high-rise structure, had leaded walls to interdict electronic eavesdropping. The restricted basement floors below were a giant swat-team arsenal and a secret motor pool.

Terry did not know the man he was dealing with was Oliver North. He had used the cover name "John Cathey." When they had been introduced, "Cathey" had flashed government "creds"—Central Intelligence Agency credentials—with, as Terry recalled later, "the photo, the eagle and the whole nine yards."

This was not a chance meeting, of course. Terry and North had been brought together by Enright for a reason. The Oklahoma City office had a reputation of being run by men sympathetic to White House policy and their SACs were willing to intervene on its behalf. Prior to Enright's tenure, this office was headed by Oliver (Buck) Revell, who became the FBI's Executive Assistant Director and that agency's liaison with Oliver North, who would later solicit Revell's help in limiting the Iran-Contra investigation.[1]

Enright had arranged for both men to have lunch earlier at Cappuchina's, an up-scale hangout favored by the agents, because "Cathey" and Enright believed that Terry could be useful to both agencies.

Enright was pleased that both men appeared to have hit it off. And with good reason, for they discovered that day that they both had carried back from Southeast Asia the same emotional scars.

The lean, neatly dressed man in the business suit with the boyish grin and the gap between his teeth reminded Terry in some ways of *Mad* magazine's Alfred E. Newman. Cathey told Terry that he was reporting directly to the National Security Council on matters dealing with defense-related espionage.

Terry felt honored that he was being put into play with someone who reported to the level of the White House. He had dealt extensively with the CIA through Air America during his Air Force intelligence days in Southeast Asia, but now he was being put into a new and more significant loop involving the dark side of civilian intelligence gathering.

Terry caught himself reminiscing about the events and turns in his life that had led to this eventful meeting. As he looked back at the six years since his discharge from the Air Force, he could barely believe the rapid and successful transition he had made to civilian life. The time from his January 1976 separation until now seemed a blur.

The first entry on his checklist of "must do" items after discharge had been to enroll in civilian flight training. The Air Force had reneged on its promise to send Terry to flight school. They had told him if he would re-enlist and finish his college degree, he would be guaranteed a slot in pilot training. But, due to congressionally- imposed manpower reductions as a result of the termination of the Vietnam War, the Air Force had an over-abundance of pilots.

But flying had become his obsession. For this reason, his first objective had been to exhaust his entire entitlement from the GI Bill in a civilian pilot training curriculum. After shopping around to find just the right flight school, he discovered Mizzou Aviation in Joplin, Missouri. What drew Terry like a magnet to Mizzou wasn't necessarily that the school offered an FAA approved training curriculum that was licensed to strict government standards, but rather the fact that Mizzou's manager and chief pilot examiner, John P. Brown, had a reputation that preceded himself. Brown was known as the hardest, toughest, strictest, most demanding, professional, son-of-a-bitchin' flight examiner in the entire mid-west—causing most student pilots to flee to schools beyond his authority and reach to schools that adhered to less demanding standards.

Being a person who enjoyed doing things the hard way, and getting his money's worth, Terry zeroed in on and Mizzou and Brown. After all, if he was going to go to all this effort and expense to learn to fly, he wanted to be good.

Terry was successful in attaining his flying goal and spent his last dollar of entitlement on JP-4 (jet fuel) in pursuit of his advanced jet rating. He had made it at last. He had his wings. He had his commercial/instrument pilot's license which included his "torch" (jet) rating and all instructor certificates to boot.

Terry worked full time during the two years he attended flight school. Besides providing him with necessary cash to attend school and support himself, the job did something else equally as important. It introduced him to the world of American business. His job as a manager of an industrial equipment rental firm put him into contact with building contractors, finance people, and heavy equipment manufacturers and suppliers.

This awakened his entrepreneurial spirit.

Terry was seeing first-hand the invasion of Japanese and other foreign tools and implements into the American work place. Companies like Makita, Kubota, Mikasa, Bosch and Stihl were looking for a toe-hold in the American economy from which to launch major competitive assaults against American manufacturers. This both excited and saddened him. He identified what he thought to be tremendous opportunity in the marketing segment of the foreign onslaught, but what interested him the most was the comparison of this activity to warfare.

Surely, he thought, the American manufacturers would have to fight back.

If not, they would obviously be over-run and destroyed. Surely this great nation wouldn't allow that to take place. He could easily see that Japanese products were far superior to America's. After all, his company in Joplin, Missouri, utilized many different makes and models daily in the worst possible battle grounds—the rental market. Without a doubt, tested side by side, the foreign tools were vastly superior. They performed more reliably and most importantly, needed less maintenance. Surely, he thought, American firms would have to re-tool their factories, redesign their products, and fight back!

"Factory automation," he thought back in 1979, would be the coming thing. American firms would be forced to automate and up-grade their facilities in a major way—for the first time since World War II. That would be it. He would combine his newly documented flying skills with the world of manufacturing. He set out to find an aggressive young company that would offer him the opportunity for which he felt he was so justly qualified.

First, he hired on as a flying salesman for an aluminum extrusion company in Kansas. The company president Joe Ida, himself a pilot and one of America's originators of the technology of "squirting" heated aluminum through a die, immediately took note of Terry's industrious, disciplined work ethics. Ida took Terry under his wing and introduced him to his thriving and growing customer base.

This brought Terry into contact with all the major aircraft builders, many of their sub-contractors, and their machinery builders. This world of metal, computer technology and industrialists, he discovered, was exactly what he had been searching for. He instantly took root and began to mature and grow in this new-found environment. With the skills and freedom to pilot himself between sales accounts, Terry normally had the jump on the competition, which was still wondering "How does a person actually get to Hays, Kansas?" after finally locating it on a road map. He simply flew there, got the order, and flew on to other "strategic targets." It seemed so simple.

And he was noticing something else: the lack of discipline of his "enemy," the competition. For the most part, he was discovering civilians were lacking in skills that the Air Force had not only instilled in him, but had demanded.

He was normally more organized, better prepared, and, in most cases, better trained than his foes. Simply, they seemed to be "inferiorly equipped," as they used to say in Air Force intelligence.

It reminded him of debriefing USAF F-4 Phantom crews who were making air raids in North Vietnam. Those who engaged the enemy in MIG dog fights toward the end of Linebacker II (the last authorized bombing of the North), normally reported "no contest—they're inferiorly equipped." Reed was beginning to enjoy the world of business when he met Emery West, president of Northwest Industries in Oklahoma City, in November of 1979. West had been shopping for a corporate pilot to fly the company's aircraft. The firm expanded it's computer controlled machine tool sales activity beyond Oklahoma and into Texas, Louisiana, Kansas, Missouri and Arkansas.

What had made Terry's résumé stand out among the other 600 applicants for the flying job was "Air Force Intelligence" and his nearly three years living in Asia. West figured Terry's familiarity with Asian customs would be advantageous in negotiating with the Asian machine tool suppliers he was courting. And his intelligence background made him instant "mentor material" since

West himself had spent most of his adult life interfacing with the CIA, FBI, and KGB.

Emery West was an escapee of the 1956 Hungarian revolution, who then emigrated to the West and later received asylum in the U.S. He was still drawn to the world of intrigue masked within intelligence operations. Reed's hiring offered him a chance to interact with someone from the shadow world once again.

Terry's assets combined with his understanding of manufacturing technology, love of flying and ferocious business acumen made him an instant success at Northwest Industries (NWI) and within the machine tool industry. He had proven himself time and time again to West until ultimately he was made the company's executive vice-president and became West's protégé.

Together they embarked on building a high-technology manufacturing/marketing firm with offices in five cities and dealers in four more. They were involved in the expansion of this endeavor when Terry flew Emery to the Chicago machine tool show in the new company plane in September of 1980. There they discovered that Hungary had a machinery display and was soliciting Western trading partners.

As West and Reed chatted with the Hungarians that day, the groundwork was laid for Northwest Industries to become a communist bloc trading partner, and Terry's life had suddenly veered back into the world of intelligence gathering. West had "offered Reed up" to the FBI as point man to monitor the KGB moles "planted" within the Hungarian trading company and operating in the U.S. This relationship with Reed had proved so successful for the FBI that they stayed in touch with him even after he left Northwest Industries in 1981 to start his own machine tool and automation consulting firm. As fate would have it, Terry's first order of business in January, 1982, had been to become a dealer for Toshiba Machine Tool, Inc., headquartered in Chicago. He was not aware that Toshiba was under investigation by the FBI and CIA for suspicion of selling American defense technology to the Russians. But he was about to find out. Someone at the CIA had retrieved his Air Force file, and he was now being interviewed by a representative of the Agency.

* * *

"I've reviewed your military record," Cathey continued intently, "and considering your technical knowledge you'll have the perfect cover for helping us nail this dirty Jap company you are brokering for."

The world of high-tech spying was nothing new to Terry. He was already an FBI asset and had just spent the last 16 months spying (he preferred to call it "monitoring") on a KGB-infested Hungarian machine tool company for his FBI handlers.

"Barlow tells me you're good at this," Cathey said to him. "Barlow" was a reference to one of Enright's counter-intelligence agents, Wayne (Buzz) Barlow, who had been Terry's prime handler in the Hungarian project. Their relationship had grown into something more personal as Barlow and his wife, Cecelia, had become intimate friends with Terry and his wife, Janis.

"With your military background, you won't need a security briefing," Cathey continued, "and considering your technical knowledge you'll have the perfect cover for moving freely within the Toshiba organization."

It was clear that Cathey had already familiarized himself with Terry's military service record, something not available to everyone. Cathey had also been impressed with Terry's background in aviation, high-technology manufacturing and international trading.

Prior to continuing his conversation, Cathey turned his attention to Enright. This bulldog-jowled J. Edgar Hoover clone, both physically and mentally, sat staring at them from the far end of the conference table through his puffy, bloodshot eyes. He gave the appearance of a man near burn-out.

"We're getting into a sensitive area here, Ed," Cathey said to Enright. "I'm sure Terry is aware of the problem of a CIA agent operating within the CONUS (referring to the Continental U.S. where laws bar the CIA from operating). Let's not create any needless problems. I'm sure you'll agree you should excuse yourself before I continue."

After Enright grudgingly left the room, Cathey's briefing centered on information developed from foreign agents who had uncovered something highly disturbing to the U.S. Government. From the evidence available, it was obvious that Toshiba Machine Tool, a division of the giant Japanese electronics conglomerate, was illegally exporting restricted technology to the Soviet Union. But beyond that, Cathey said, the company had also stolen secret defense information and apparently provided it to the Soviets along with the equipment to use it.*

"We about shit when Barlow informed us you had become a Toshiba dealer," Cathey continued, in a much more relaxed tone. "Talk about luck! We've been watching Toshiba for quite some time but have been unable to nail them in the act. And Barlow tells me we're getting two agents for the price of one. It's not very often we find an asset who has a cooperating wife. She really gets into this, huh? That's great."

Based on Cathey's comments, Barlow must have thoroughly briefed Cathey prior to the meeting. Barlow, in essence, had "sponsored" Terry into the intelligence club, a prerequisite for membership.

Wives can be a problem for assets. Some spouses can never adjust to a world of deceit where things are never quite what they seem. Barlow had passed on to Cathey Terry's wife's excitement over being part of the cloak and dagger world that the Reeds had become drawn into.

As Terry and Cathey reminisced and traded war stories, Terry told him about how his relationship with Barlow had started and realized that Buzz had become more than a handler. They were now friends, or so Terry thought. The bond between them had flourished initially because of their common interest in flying. Although Barlow had been a carrier pilot in the Vietnam years, his first bonding with Terry came in the cockpit of a 1980 twin Cessna 414, N2693F, in October, 1980, high above the plains of Oklahoma.

---

* Five years later, the U.S. Government would reveal that Toshiba Machine Tool had provided the Soviets with technology to produce silent submarine propellers that could elude sonar detection. The KGB orchestrated, between 1982 and 1984, the purchase by the USSR of four machine tools and associated computer programs directly from Toshiba. The scandal resulted in the indictment of Toshiba executives in Japan. Toshiba's president did the "honorable thing" and committed suicide. Sales of Toshiba Machine Tool products were banned in the U.S. for five years. Secretary of Defense Casper Weinberger said the illegal exports "caused significant damage to the security of Japan and the United States."

* * *

Even though the temperature outside at 10,000 feet was below freezing, per-spiration was beading on Barlow's balding head. Barlow, in the left seat, was, in pilot's jargon, clearly "behind the airplane" as he attempted to deal with the "emergency" Terry had created.

"Goddam it, I don't know what you did, but *please* give me back the left engine! I'm rusty at this! It's not fair to do this on our first training flight!"

Terry was evaluating Barlow's flying performance and, in flight instructor's jargon, was conditioning him to become "receptive to learning". In order to test Barlow's responses to an in-flight emergency, he secretly had shut off the fuel valve to the left engine and was now watching this ex-hot dog carrier pilot lose his cool over Duncan, Oklahoma. Reed was amazed that this Annapolis grad was not demonstrating "the right stuff" pilots always admired.

Barlow's "cover" at Terry's firm was to be that of a company co-pilot, and Terry, the man in the right seat and a certified flight instructor, was trying to get Barlow's pilot proficiency up to speed. It would be necessary for "Buzz" to demonstrate competency to be added to the aviation insurance policy covering NWI's plane. It had been a long time since Barlow had flown and Terry seized the chance to gently wring out his FBI student.

"You gotta tell me the procedure from your checklist for a restart or I'll die right along with you. Keep your mind working. Come on, engage your brain!"

Slowly, Barlow began to research his data bank of flying knowledge to find the computer disk in his mind labeled "pilot." He awkwardly but methodically began prioritizing his cockpit workload and groping with the procedures to deal with the simulated emergency Terry had created as a "real-time" test.

"Hey, this thing performs pretty good on one engine," Barlow said after suc-cessfully "caging" the left engine.

"Don't get cocky," Terry smiled, "or I'll shut down your right one, too."

After restoring power to the engine, and promising no more simulated emer-gencies, Terry set the auto pilot so they could ease the tension and get on to the other business at hand, namely spy work.

The KGB had gone on a buying spree. They had learned that Lenin's words were quite true: "A capitalist's only religion is money." The Soviets didn't have to steal the technology they desperately needed and couldn't produce. They simply had to come to America and buy it. The Japanese were more than will-ing to do business, even if they didn't really own what they were selling. And what the Japanese couldn't provide them, the KGB was apparently going to "procure" through legitimate business ties they were establishing in North America.

"Barcorp in Canada is loaded with KGB," Barlow said, referring to a ma-chine tool trading company that was importing communist bloc equipment for sale to the West. "You need to keep me informed of all the players you come in contact with from Technoimpex, and especially be wary of a guy by the name of Jozsef Bona. He's a card-carrying KGB agent."

Mention of Bona's name caused Terry to give Barlow his undivided atten-tion. He had already met Bona the month before at the International Machine Tool Show in Chicago. Terry remembered him as an aging version of James Bond, a man in his mid-50s who could drink all day and all night without it ever seeming to affect him. His suave, European demeanor was highlighted by his thick, bushy mustache and deep set eyes. Bona was smooth, witty, intelligent, and articulate. Terry irritated Barlow later when he told him that he thought Bona was much smarter than the FBI agents he'd met.

Referring to Bona, Barlow said, "He's been in India, Pakistan and Africa that we know of. He speaks seven languages and is a lovable, cunning son of a bitch. He's suspected in at least three deaths of foreign agents. I want to hang his fuckin' head on my wall! Will you help me?"

"What do you have in mind? Just because I'm a pilot doesn't mean I invite danger."

Reed was a little apprehensive. From his intelligence school training he had been told that, in many areas, the KGB out-gunned even the CIA. He didn't know if the Oklahoma City FBI office could be a match for the Kremlin's finest.

"I'll back you up and be your shadow in anything I ask you to do," Barlow said. "I need your help because I'm technically weak in manufacturing."

Reed agreed to help nail Bona which would apparently be a big scalp for Barlow to have hanging from his belt.

The Technoimpex that Barlow had referred to was the Hungarian government-run trading company and Barcorp, in Toronto, was its Canadian trading partner. Bona had told Terry facetiously, "Technoimpex is not the East Bloc venereal disease it sounds like."

And from what Barlow had said, the KGB's North American operations were based in Toronto. Cathey would later tell Terry that his CIA oversight of this espionage operation was also based there.

The prematurely-balding Barlow was a linguist fluent in Russian and Magyar. His remaining hair was thick and graying, his face unlined except for the laugh wrinkles around his eyes. Small in stature, he was unpretentious and professional and did not have the usual "cop" demeanor found in many agents.

The job of a counter-intelligence agent is to look for people who work for hostile intelligence services or people who have access to plans and activities of those services. The objective is to learn the plans of these intelligence services, neutralize their operations, induce defections and undermine the credibility of their agents.

Barlow had worked in counter-intelligence the majority of his FBI career. He was placed under cover in Terry's firm when it became one of the first American companies licensed to market computer-controlled machine tools and equipment produced in Hungary, then a Soviet Bloc country.

The FBI knew that this experiment in East-West détente would serve as a possible conduit for the theft of American technology, especially computer technology. Such technology was a specialty of Terry's Oklahoma-based firm, Northwest Industries, Inc., in Oklahoma City. Northwest's founder and president, Emery [Veda] West was no stranger to the world of East-West intrigue. As a political prisoner, he had escaped from his native Hungary during the 1956 uprising and was given asylum in the U.S., but was never completely trusted. The FBI saw every émigré as a possible KGB "plant," or "mole". Enright had been West's handler for years and conveyed privately to Reed his concerns about West's true allegiance.

Terry's job for the FBI was to discuss technical aspects of machine tools and to be aware of the technology the Hungarians wanted. Terry was also the person designated to travel to Hungary when possible and report on Soviet manufacturing capabilities.

Barlow's job was to identify KGB agents and eavesdrop on their conversations in their native language. His undercover placement at Northwest Industries and the company's mandatory "cooperation" were U.S. government prerequisites for obtaining the necessary State Department licenses allowing trade with Hungary. To do his job, Barlow had to pose as the company's pilot. But he hadn't flown since his Navy days and Terry was assigned the task of reintroducing Barlow to the cockpit.

The friendship flourished over many emptied bottles of Chivas Regal in the latter months of 1980. But Terry at that time was still a third wheel in Barlow's social circle because of Terry's bachelorhood. The two men's "gray" friendship expanded to a social one when Terry began dating his future wife, who would later be accepted into the world of "spook" (the slang term for intelligence operative, or spy) marriages by Barlow and his wife.

For a man who had professed to need only an airplane, a credit card and a condom to have a good time, a strange thing had begun to happen to Terry in late February, 1981. He had been a bachelor with a vengeance, making up for the fact that he had been in Southeast Asia during the sexual revolution. His activities had gone far beyond just selling machine tools in the oil patch.

Terry had not been looking for love in his countless rendezvous when he reluctantly agreed to a blind date with Janis Kerr. She was an aggressive, attractive and liberated woman with a keen eye for business whose real estate career was flourishing during the oil boom in Oklahoma.

As he pulled into the driveway to pick her up for their first date, a peculiar sensation came over him. From the visual clues he was noting, he began to get his hopes up that this woman might be "different." Here was a perfectly manicured brick home, 1930's vintage, with an old fashioned wooden porch swing on the large screened-in front porch. There was also a Mercedes 300D in the drive. He liked her taste in cars, and decided to forgive her for buying a diesel.

"Ummh," he thought. "Here's an independent woman who must be successful in her own right. Maybe this female is different."

As soon as he stepped into her living room that cold February night, he *knew* she was different. Not the typical glass and chrome furniture with Herculon love seat he was so accustomed to seeing in the apartments of his other dates. Two wing back chairs sat in front of the fireplace where gas logs cast a warm glow in the cozy parlor. The vaulted ceilings, hardwood floors, antiques, and Impressionist paintings displayed her distinctive tastes. As he sipped his scotch and water from the Waterford glass she had just purchased in Ireland, he surveyed her book case—Somerset Maugham, Robert Frost, Carlos Casteneda, the writings of Dag Hammarskjold, Dickens, Michener, and *Everything You Ever Wanted to Know About Sex but Were Afraid to Ask*. The gamut.

"I've got to get to know this woman," he thought.

"So how did you end up in Oklahoma?" Terry asked as they dined at Sullivan's Restaurant later that evening.

"That's a good question," she said, becoming noticeably distant and appearing to be reflecting back to distant memories.

"How did I?" she asked of herself in a confused tone. "Time, certainly has a way of erasing one's motivations."

But Terry's earlier dinner conversation discussing the Vietnam War and the sixties had triggered nearly-forgotten images...images she would later share with him...images of a key event...a turning point in her life.

The light green 1966 GTO sat parked on the overlook of the industrial town of North Kansas City, Missouri, as the smoke stacks along the Missouri River belched out their nightly doses of pollution. The location known as Water Works Park was a popular parking place for local teenagers and the site of many back seat conquests. The year 1968 had come to a bloody close for Americans torn between country, causes, communism and social revolution.

The windows of the vehicle that John Z. DeLorean created during his stint at Pontiac Motor Division were foggy as a result of the heavy breathing inside.

Much to her date's frustration, Janis Kerr, the 17-year-old passenger in the car that night in January, 1969, was not going to surrender her virginity for many reasons; not the least of those being the physical barrier known as the four-speed console that separated their naugahyde bucket seats.

But she had a lot more than sex on her mind, much to the dismay of the "jock" in the left seat hell-bent upon a course of adding another notch to his gun. The screaming sirens of morality, religion, and the conflict of just being a teenager in the late 60's were definitely interfering with her date's plans that January night.

The Tet offensive in Vietnam had turned the war around a year earlier. Some of her older male school mates had already been drafted or had volunteered in order to fight enemies that she only read about in newspapers, which the United States Government coldly referred to as "body counts." But the war for her, as well as most of the citizens of the industrial community north of the Missouri River where she had been raised, was little more than a nightly abstraction beamed electronically into a secure living room.

But now that she was on the threshold of womanhood and experiencing the biological instincts of motherhood, she began to question, even rebel, at the thought of needless death on both sides—classmates had already returned from Southeast Asia in body bags.

"So what's wrong? You're so distant, Janis. Why can't you just let go and have fun with this? Everybody else is! These are the 60's! We're the love and peace generation, right?"

She straightened her rumpled clothing. "We're supposed to be, I guess. But right now our love and peace generation is either hiding out in the education system to avoid the draft, or plain old hiding in Canada. Most are either burning buildings and protesting or being shot at in Vietnam. I want to get involved....you know....organize, protest. This war is wrong. Look at this Tet offensive. It's obvious our government is lying to us. We're not winning over there. We need to bring our soldiers home."

"You can't protest! Your parents won't let you," he said mockingly. "They're so strict they would throw a fit if I didn't have you home by 10 o'clock. Christ, you don't have the guts to even tell them about me. Some protester!"

This angered the girl raised in the affluent Baptist church in Northtown. Just being with him, she believed, was a sign of protest. Her parents didn't even know about Dan. He was older, 23 years old in fact, and from her parents' viewpoint would have represented the Devil himself. She could only imagine what they would have thought had they known what he was trying to accomplish that winter's night.

Janis' mother, a strict Baptist and fifth grade school teacher, would never have allowed her oldest daughter to date an "older man." This occasional clandestine date with Dan was probably the most rebellious thing this straight-A, straight-laced student had ever done.

"You'd better take me home. I wouldn't want you to get in trouble for taking someone out that's under age," she snapped.

While the car containing the two silent occupants headed to her best friend's house to drop her off, she was still smarting from his comments. She had to admit to herself that he was right. She had to get out from under her parents' thumbs to mature and find herself. A plan was formulating in her mind. She would escape! She would leave home! She would no longer be smothered by her restrictive parents and the church she was forced to attend three times a week. Janis would later laugh about how she never got to see more than just the beginning of "The Wizard of Oz," which aired on a Sunday night each year. She had to leave for church just as Dorothy's house crashed on top of the wicked witch and the movie turned to Technicolor. She grew up believing the entire movie was in black and white!

But built within this religious system to control the minds of their youth was a basic flaw. And this flaw, lying right under the noses of the deacons of the Baptist church, was a product of their own doing and support: Oklahoma Baptist University.

OBU, 375 miles southwest of Kansas City, was a place she had learned about from the church's "underground youth network." It was a place that the products of this strict Baptist rearing could "flee" to with the consent of their parents, who believed that their young adults were receiving the very best education, conducted in a rigid religious environment.

If they only knew! As most males living near a parochial college can attest, the annual shipment of freshman female arrivals into these institutions are a bundle of hormonal time bombs, just ticking away waiting for someone or something to activate the detonator. The influx of teenagers that were convinced they had been suppressed their entire lives made for a formidable student body, determined to make up for lost time now that they were out from under the daily monitoring of parental guidance.

"Dan, I won't be seeing you after tonight," she said as the car pulled up in front of the her friend's home. "I think you should date someone else. I've made a decision to get out of here and go to college in Oklahoma. I'm going to get involved with the movement against the war and try to make a difference. You're right, I just can't let go and have fun, at least not in this town. Maybe Kansas City is a good place for you, but not for me."

As the 389-cubic-inch engine caused the rear tires to spin, leaving dual black marks, the driver "went through the gears," breaking the silence of the quiet residential neighborhood. Janis Kerr felt more at peace.

She was going to do things HER way! 1969 was the eve of America's second revolution and she wanted in on it—head bands, granny glasses, bell bottoms, birth control pills. The sex, drugs, and rock 'n roll generation was upon her.

She was realistic enough to know, however, that she needed a sound education to effectively compete heads up in a male dominated society, and she was determined to attain one. She was already beginning to feel like a second class citizen, noticing how society was placing demands on only the male population. Why wasn't the government demanding she register for the draft? Women may have come a long way, but they still had a long journey ahead of them. She wasn't going to handicap herself by staying here and limiting her goals and ambitions.

After retreating to her friend Merrillyn's bedroom that night, she outlined her

life strategy and how she would explore the world before settling down and having
children with Mr. Right.

"What kind of person do you think you'll marry?" Merrillyn asked.

"Well, if I do ever get married, all I know is, he'll have to be exciting!" she said.
Little did she know.

As she arrived home the following Sunday morning to dress for church, her mother
opened the door, giving her the once-over to see if there was any external evidence
of wrong-doing.

"Mom, Dad, I've made a decision," Janis said. "I'm going to go to OBU with
Merrillyn and get a degree in Education." She knew her mother would approve,
considering her own profession.

"Oh, Janis, we're so glad. We knew our prayers would be answered," her mother
said as she hugged her.

The plan had worked! Her life was finally just beginning!

"Sorry if my question disturbed you," Terry said somewhat confused by Janis'
long silence. "I was just curious how you chose Oklahoma City. I thought maybe
we shared some acquaintances since I have old friends that moved here to
attend Bethany Nazarene College."

Their first few encounters after this pleasant but uneventful blind date centered around conversations on a variety of subjects. Janis had just finished
Margaret Truman's book about her father, Harry S., and told Terry how much
she admired the man from Missouri.

"You know, he was so unpretentious and pragmatic. I feel a real affinity for
this man," she said. "Maybe it's because I grew up with an aura about Truman.
You know, having been raised in Kansas City, all of the school kids went on a
yearly field trip to the Truman Library. Oftentimes ole Harry himself was there
and would play the piano for us. He was just so down to earth and amiable.
Plus, he was so much more intelligent than most people gave him credit. Did
you know he loved to read the classics? I mean the *real* classics like the writings
of Sophocles and Plato. And Chopin was his favorite composer. He's not the
hick from Missouri all those arrogant, blue-blooded politicians tried to portray
him as."

As Janis continued her book review and analysis of Truman's political stance
as well as his marriage, Terry was becoming more and more intrigued. Here
was an intelligent female he could really talk to.

She wasn't desperately searching for a husband. It seemed like so many of
the women he went out with were seeking a step-father for their kids from their
"previous commitments," as much as a husband.

By late February, they both decided to take their relationship beyond the
conversation stage and into the Ramada Inn, next door to the Crash and Burn
Club in New Orleans, famous for its aviation architecture and whose building
was constructed to partially engulf a giant old Lockheed Constellation 4-en-
gine passenger plane. He invited her to spend Mardi Gras week with him in
New Orleans, where he was attending a machine-tool show. Terry had carefully
selected a room overlooking the club, which had the plane's left wing and the
three-ruddered tail jutting from the building. He was big on symbolism.

But more than electricity was generated between them, and strange things
began to happen inside his head that weekend. Caught up in the energy of
Bourbon Street and the madness of the Mardi Gras crowd, something struck

him. For the first time in years, he was totally oblivious to the hordes of attractive women around him. "But why?" he asked himself.

And Janis, that independent woman who was determined to stay that way, was having the same, frightening revelations. Here was a handsome, successful man, a pilot with airplanes and sports cars at his fingertips who seemed oblivious to all these trappings. He was so unlike the "oilies" she had dated in the past with their gold chains and Rolexes—men so impressed with themselves. She had found them generally to be insecure, shallow, and hedonistic. Here was a man with a *mind*. That's it. That's what she was falling in love with. The first time she had ever called him at home she was surprised to find him there. When she had asked him what he was doing he had said, "Actually, I'm reading Pythagorus. I need to brush up on the Pythagorean theorem so I can apply it to the project I'm involved in." What a change from the jocks she had been seeing, whose only knowledge of theories involved the "Split T" or the "Quarterback Shuffle."

And that first Saturday morning she spent with him in New Orleans she felt a childish delight and warmth as they lay in bed and laughed at Wylie Coyote and Roadrunner cartoons. This man was so unpretentious. And as they talked about their goals she realized that they both had the same basic, intrinsic values.

By the time Sunday night rolled around, as Janis was asleep in the right seat beside him in the twin-engine Piper Seminole heading back to Oklahoma City, Terry's mind returned to what the Air Force had taught him about developing a battle plan for any contingency. His "target" he decided, was sleeping right beside him.

"Goddam!" he thought to himself, "I'm falling in love!"

As their relationship developed, Terry found his mind filled with strange and new thoughts. Up until the point he had met her, he could bond mentally only with other males in a true team environment where words were not always necessary; a world where ideas and attitudes are shared without the usual excuses required between men and women. It was all no-fault. No facades or veneer existed. He had never met a female he could relate to and still not feel constantly accountable.

When he was with Janis, he sensed that somehow together they were greater than the sum of their two identities, that together they became a critical mass, explosive and lethal when joined together. He saw the potential power within the relationship and knew that it could be harnessed in a positive way, or become destructive. This both fascinated and frightened him.

Together, he believed, they were capable of anything—both good and bad. The negative in this type of relationship, he realized, was that there was no brake. He believed that the combination of their personalities could prove fruitful or fatal, since she was not only with him, but ahead of him, in some respects. They both yearned to walk on the wild side, something mandatory for a life in intelligence, but a quality not especially practical when it comes to evaluating risk. Two and a half months later, on May 16th, after a whirlwind courtship, they were standing at the altar in Golden, Colorado. They knew they were making a decision based not on lust, but on logic and love. Each had gone though a previous marriage and both had been part of the lonely singles scene for years. With tears in their eyes, they were hoping that *this* commitment was forever and, this time, for all the right reasons.

As the sun streamed through the skylight in the chapel ceiling, and, after exchanging the traditional vows, he put the ring on her finger, kissed her softly and made one personal vow. He made her a promise: "It'll never be boring." The words proved to be prophetic. In the years ahead, as she lay awake crying, fearful for her safety and that of her children, she often wished for boredom. Much to her chagrin, he had kept his vow.

But, from the moment they were married, she became a willing participant in the world of international intrigue, never dreaming then that the government would in the future define this to mean "accomplice." They enjoyed a brief weekend honeymoon at the Brown Palace in Denver, knowing that they were going to have a truly one-of-a-kind June honeymoon—behind the Iron Curtain.

After they were married, Cecelia and Wayne Barlow threw a party for the newlyweds at their home in Edmond, Oklahoma. Cecelia embraced Janis and, in a reference to the incestuous spook world, whispered, "We're so glad to have you in the family." It became a spy-wife's support group where women like Cecelia could share their feelings openly without violating security. Cecelia and Janis were both petite, vivacious, intelligent women—always ready for a good time—and stimulated by the lives their husbands led.

A great deal of trust is required of couples in such situations. Some questions have to go unanswered. They are different in many respects and often gravitate to a world of their own. They cannot easily mix with "non-spook" couples since they must always be guarded.

Cecelia Barlow had identified in Janis the qualities she would need to maintain her marriage, namely the ability to totally trust your mate, ask few questions and still find the dark side of the intelligence world intriguing.

And now, Janis had become the wife of a spook, a secret title that excited her. This new circle of friends her new husband was exposing her to were definitely different. The Barlows, she thought, seemed normal enough on the surface, but underneath was something else that fascinated her.

Janis immediately liked "Buzz," his nickname from his Navy days. She saw a soft side in him and liked the influence he had on her husband. He was always sharing his latest literary discoveries with Terry, who tended to be content reading technical manuals, *Aviation Weekly* or *Car and Driver magazine*. She would often find them in intense discussions about Buzz's most recent book, from *Sidhartha, Kahlil Gibran,* and *Illusions.* His choices were all indicative of a man who had advanced beyond the world of covert activities and who, in reality, was torn between the life he had chosen and that of a simple, intellectual, non-violent existence. His privately stated goal, in fact, was to move back to Portland, Oregon, and open a candle shop, hardly the contentious quest one might expect of an undercover agent.

On the horizon was an important espionage trip to Hungary. Terry's ostensible purpose as vice president of Northwest Industries was to sign a corporate trade agreement with a Hungarian machine-tool manufacturer.

But Enright and Barlow had seized on this chance for some spying, simply because Terry could travel there and they couldn't. He would be exploring the bowels of the East Bloc manufacturing companies from which the USSR was buying its most advanced manufacturing equipment. It was a unique chance to evaluate the USSR's technical capabilities in both hardware and electronics, and especially computer technology. Now they wanted Terry to

do what they were trying to prevent the Hungarians from doing in this country—spy!

* * *

The Reeds spent the 4th of July in 1981 on the "Pest" side of the Danube.
Terry would meet men he would later be put into play with, and under far
different circumstances. Two of these men, George Fenue and Mike Szilagyi,
were people that the Reeds came to enjoy and like immensely. They entertained the Reeds royally during their visit to Hungary and Janis was made to
feel like a visiting dignitary when they arrived in Budapest. She found herself
being greeted at the airport with bouquets of roses, and she and Terry were
immediately whisked away to their hotel in a chauffeur driven car.

Although she had traveled extensively throughout Europe, this was her first
visit to a communist Bloc country and she was intrigued by the bleakness and
lack of color. Everything appeared gray and oppressive, except the spirit of the
people whom she found to be delightfully charming with their satirical sense
of humor honed to a razor's edge. She was also impressed with their intellect
and knowledge of American history that rivaled what she herself knew of her
country.

As she lay awake one night in Budapest, she realized her fantasies were
being brought to life. She and Terry were both well aware they were being
followed wherever they went. By whom, they were not sure. A cold chill had
sent shivers through her body when, on the day of their arrival in Budapest, a
voice out of nowhere "suggested" she put her camera away. And now, she found
herself being both apprehensive and tantalized by the thought of re-consum-
mating their marriage in the Hotel Olympia, while secret cameras and micro-
phones were most likely recording them. Oh well, they both decided, if that
were the case they would at least give the KGB voyeurs something to look at. No
paranoia was going to spoil this honeymoon. She thought then that she had
married James Bond. She was unbelievably happy. Kansas City now seemed
like someplace on another planet.

But behind this facade was deadly serious business. The FBI had an agenda
for Terry. They wanted to know, most of all, the level of the Soviets' manufacturing capability and the type of computer-memory technology being developed.

This memory, known as a "bubble memory," was the world's most advanced
state of the art for that time. Computer-controlled machine tools shared this
memory technology with advanced weapons systems. By Terry's analyzing a
machine tool capability, it would be possible to evaluate the level attained by
the Russians in advanced memory design for weaponry. The FBI believed that
this cruise missile technology had not been perfected at this time by the Soviets. Or had it?

Terry's "investigation" discovered that the Soviet Bloc did, indeed, possess a
rudimentary design, but it was still experimental and far too large for weapons
applications. The Soviets definitely lagged far behind the West in this weap-
ons-critical technology. But the Soviets could make rapid advancements if they
pirated the technology from the right trading partner in America. This was
what concerned the FBI.

* * *

Back home in Oklahoma, Cecelia Barlow didn't want to know about Hungarian technology. She wanted to know about the Danube, the shops, the food, the
clothes and the people Janis had met.

"So tell me about the men," she said. "What are they like? Are they all just
obnoxiously macho? Did you really meet Joe Bona? A real KGB agent? I've
heard so much about him!"

As the women drank their Hungarian wine and discussed the trip off in the
corner of the Barlow's den, Janis told Cecelia, "You would not believe the road
crews there. I about died when I saw them. The men wore only their bikini bathing trunks. That's it! That and their combat boots. And these guys are not petite.
Most of them look like professional wrestlers! But my, do they have good tans!"

Oblivious to the giggles in the corner, Barlow debriefed Terry about the technical aspects of the trip. It had been highly-productive for the FBI to have someone moving freely within Soviet manufacturing circles. Barlow felt he might
soon get his long-awaited opportunity to nail Bona.

By October of 1981, Barlow still didn't have Bona's head, but Terry's attention was off of communism and onto capitalism. While working on a manufacturing project, Terry had come to know some Japanese executives of the American division of Toshiba Machine Tool. One of them, Takashi Osato, who was
based in Houston, was impressed with Terry's marketing capability and offered what Terry saw as a once in a lifetime opportunity—a Toshiba dealership
for Oklahoma and Northern Texas if Terry would leave his job at Northwest
Industries and start his own company.

"Buzz, I've got good news and bad news," said Terry over lunch at
Cappuchino's in early November. "The good news is I've been offered a chance
to start my own company, and I'm going to. The bad news is I won't be your
eyes and ears on the Hungarian project any longer. I'm resigning from Northwest Industries."

Barlow was visibly upset. The departure meant he would be losing his key
asset, but Terry had spent many hours making his decision and Barlow was not
going to stand in his way, no matter how much he protested. Within the ensuing weeks, however, KGB super-spy Bona let Terry know that he wanted to
retain their relationship, regardless of Terry's employment status with NWI.
For this reason, and others that would later become clear, Barlow wanted to
stay in Terry's shadow. He wanted to be kept informed of all requests and
movements of his KGB adversary.

By December, Barlow had undergone a complete turnabout. He was ecstatic
about Terry's career decision to link up with Toshiba. The reason didn't become clear until February, 1982, when Enright called Terry and said, "I've got
somebody in my office who you need to meet. Why don't we all have lunch at
the usual place."

Oliver North, using his alias John Cathey, came into Terry's life during lunch
that day over cups of cappuchino and talk of their mutual enemy. "Fucking
Congress," Cathey kept saying. And Terry shook his head in agreement.

As the day wore on through the meeting with Enright and the briefing taking
place under the neon pig, Terry sensed something hauntingly familiar about
the well-groomed man from the CIA who looked out of place in a business suit.
He had a GI knot in his tie.

They had met before, Terry was sure. But where? And when?

Suddenly it came to him as the day was winding down. He turned to "Cathey" and nearly shouted, "NKP! That's where I saw you. You were a Marine, right? And your name isn't Cathey, right?"

NKP was Nakhom Phanom Royal Thai Air Force Base where Terry had worked with Task Force Alpha, the elite and Top Secret unit. It had hosted many visitors from other services, the CIA and Air America. The Marines had, in fact, been the major force behind the sensor development program.

Chagrined but smiling the CIA man nodded and said, "Damn, you do have a good memory. But I'd just as soon you forget about that for the time being."

He was glad to forget it. Thinking of Task Force Alpha was not his favorite thing. Too much scar tissue. His service there became the timer ticking away, the catalyst that armed the patriotic time bomb inside him.

"How about it?" Cathey asked. "Can I factor you in on this? Help me hit a home run on this Toshiba thing and there may be a big promotion in it for you down the road."

* * *

Terry could still hear himself saying "yes" to the man from the CIA as he drove home that evening to tell his wife about his abnormal day.

Not just anyone could be handed off to the CIA on such an important project as this. He began to recap the major events in his life that had led to the point where he had become the right man in the right place with the right credentials. Maybe his pain and dedication had not been in vain after all.

1. *Report of the Congressional Committees Investigating the Iran-Contra Affair*, (U.S. Government Printing Office, 1988), P. 287.

Memorandum

To : SAC, OKLAHOMA CITY (190-OC-49753) (P)   Date 7/17/90

From : MDE ▓▓▓▓▓▓▓▓▓▓▓▓ b7C

Subject : REQUEST OF JERRY BOHNEN,
KTOK-AM 10 Radio, for
information regarding
Northwest Industries, Inc.;
FREEDOM OF INFORMATION ACT REQUEST;
OO: OKLAHOMA CITY

        Pursuant to a Freedom of Information Act request,
the following files and/or serials should not be destroyed
prior to 7/96:

(s) b1

DO NOT SERIALIZE

MAINTAIN AS TOP SERIAL

336528
Cashlyd by 9103▓▓▓▓▓ b7C
Sarily on: OADR
12/1/92

ALL INFORMATION CONTAINED
HEREIN IS UNCLASSIFIED
EXCEPT WHERE SHOWN
OTHERWISE

2-1. FBI memorandum cover sheet from Freedom of Information Act request [FOIA] initiated by Oklahoma City investigative reporter Jerry Bohnen in an attempt to gain data on
Terry Reed's company Northwest Industries. Redaction begins!

FD-36 (Rev. 5-22-78)

FBI

TRANSMIT VIA:
☐ Teletype
☐ Facsimile
XX AIRTEL

PRECEDENCE:
☐ Immediate
☐ Priority
☐ Routine

CLASSIFICATION:
☐ TOP SECRET
☐ SECRET
☐ CONFIDENTIAL
☐ UNCLAS E F T O
☐ UNCLAS

CONFIDENTIAL

Date _____ 2/27/81

TO: SAC, CHICAGO

FROM: SAC, OKLAHOMA CITY ▉▉▉▉ (P)

▉▉▉▉▉▉▉▉▉▉

OO: Oklahoma City

▉▉▉▉▉▉▉▉▉▉▉▉▉▉
▉▉▉▉▉▉▉▉▉▉▉▉▉▉▉▉▉▉▉▉
▉▉▉▉▉▉▉▉▉▉▉▉▉▉▉▉▉▉▉▉

      NWI is currently negotiating with Technoimpex to
modify General Numeric computers to operate with Technoimpex machine
tool centers and thereafter market the centers in the United
States.

LEAD: INFORMATION CONTAINED
           IS UNCLASSIFIED   9803 ▉▉▉
           WHERE SHOWN
CHICAGO   11/20/92
▉▉▉▉▉▉▉▉▉▉▉▉▉▉▉▉▉▉▉▉▉▉

                        CONFIDENTIAL   174
                                                        168
                        Classified and Extended by
  2 - Chicago   Reason for Extension FCIM, II, 1-2.4.2 (2) (3) 2-27-01
  2 - Oklahoma City   Date of Review for Declassification _____
  (4)

                                                   Searched _____
                                                   Serialized _____
Approved: _____   Transmitted _____ (Number) (Time)   Per _____

2-2. Heavily redacted FOIA document which clearly shows FBI interest in the business
relationship between Reed's company, NWI, and the Hungarian firm, Technoimpex.

CG  (S) b1

(2) (S) b1

(2) (S) b1

(2) (S) b1

(S) b1

LEADS

OKLAHOMA CITY

AT BETHANY, OKLAHOMA. Will determine the following:

1.  (2)(S) b1

2. Furnish Chicago the name of the owner of Northwest Industries for search through Chicago indices. (S)(U)

3. (S) b1

4. (2)(S) b1

CONFIDENTIAL

-2*-

2-3. Heavy redaction of the above secret FOIA document provided to Bohnen proves by default that NWI was heavily involved in counter intelligence activities.

FBI

TRANSMIT VIA:

☐ Teletype
☐ Facsimile
☐ _____

PRECEDENCE:

☐ Immediate
☐ Priority
☐ Routine

CLASSIFICATION:

☐ TOP SECRET
☐ SECRET
☐ CONFIDENTIAL
☐ UNCLAS E F T O
☐ UNCLAS

Date _____

(s) b1

PAGE TWO OC ████ SECRET

FOR INFORMATION OF BUREAU AND CHICAGO NWI'S CIVIL SUIT AGAINST
TECHNOIMPEX, JOZSEF BONA AND OTHER TECHNOIMPEX OFFICIALS SETTLED IN
U. S. DISTRICT COURT, WESTERN DISTRICT OF OKLAHOMA ON JANUARY 12,
1983. AS PART OF THE SETTLEMENT NWI WAS ORDERED TO TURN OVER TO
THE ATTORNEY FOR TECHNOIMPEX, IDENTIFIED AS THE LAW FIRM OF BAKER
AND MC KENZIE OF CHICAGO, FIVE COMPUTER BOARDS GIVING THE THREE
HUNGARIAN MACHINING CENTERS SIMULTANEOUS 3 AXIS OPERATION AND
ALSO CONTAINING PROGRAMMABLE CHIPS. THE ATTORNEY FOR TECHNOIMPEX
IS TO HOLD THE BOARDS AS AN OFFICER OF THE COURT UNTIL TECHNOIMPEX
CAN MAKE APPLICATION TO HAVE THE BOARDS EXPORTED TO HUNGARY. THE
ATTORNEY HAS BEEN ORDERED BY THE COURT TO DENY ACCESS TO THE
BOARDS TO TECHNOIMPEX UNTIL APPROVAL HAS BEEN RECEIVED FOR EXPORT.
IF APPROVAL TO EXPORT IS NOT OBTAINED FROM THE DEPARTMENT OF
COMMERCE, THE BOARDS WILL BE RETURNED TO NWI.

(s) b

SECRET

2-4. Note line 3 of above FOIA document. Jozsef Bona is the KGB agent whom Special
Agent Barlow was shadowing. The discussion of the computer boards shows FBI concern
that U.S. Defense technology contained within the memory circuits of the boards may fall
into Soviet hands.

June 16, 1981

To Whom It May Concern:

I Terry K. Reed, SS# 491-52-8196, was honorably dis-
charged from the U.S. Air Force on January 5, 1976,
from Griffiss Air Force Base, Rome, New York. Prior
to my discharge, I worked within the USAF intelligence
community and possessed a top secret security clearance.
Upon discharge, I was given a travel restriction which
limited the foreign countries that I could visit for a
period of two years from date of discharge. I realize
that that restriction has expired but I feel it is in
the best interest of everyone concerned to inform you
of the following:

I am presently the vice president of Northwest Industries,
Inc., 6900 N.W. 63rd, Bethany, Oklahoma. My corporate
duties are taking me and my wife, Janis, on a business
trip to Hungary beginning late June to early July of this
year. Besides Budapest, my business will take me to
several other cities within Hungary for the purpose of
evaluating the manufacturing capacity of several foreign
plants. I am traveling with the full knowledge and
approval of Mr. Edwin Enwright, the acting chief of the
Oklahoma City FBI office.

Sincerely,

Terry K. Reed
Vice President
Northwest Industries

cc: Emery West

TULSA, OK
CONROE, TX

ARLINGTON, TX
ODESSA, TX

NWI

NORTHWEST INDUSTRIES, INC.
CNC MACHINE TOOL SPECIALISTS
ENGINEERING, SALES, SERVICE

6900 N.W. 63rd
BETHANY OKLAHOMA 73008
405/721-1460
405/721-5266

TERRY REED
VICE PRESIDENT

TULSA OFFICE
. 79th East Avenue
OK 74145
2-0460 664-8666

DALLAS OFFICE
360 Place, 1201 N. Watson Rd.
Arlington, TX 76010
817/640-1738
Odessa, TX 915-333-1591

HOUSTON OFFICE
410 S. Trade Center, PKY Suite A-1
Conroe, TX 77302
713-273-1523

2-5. Terry Reed's business card at Northwest Industries (NWI)—the technology trading com-
pany he worked for when he began his civilian intelligence activities along with the letter
Reed wrote to NWI President Emery West, who secretly forwarded it to Edwin Enright,
FBI's top man in Oklahoma, in case anything untoward happened to Reed during a trip to
Hungary.

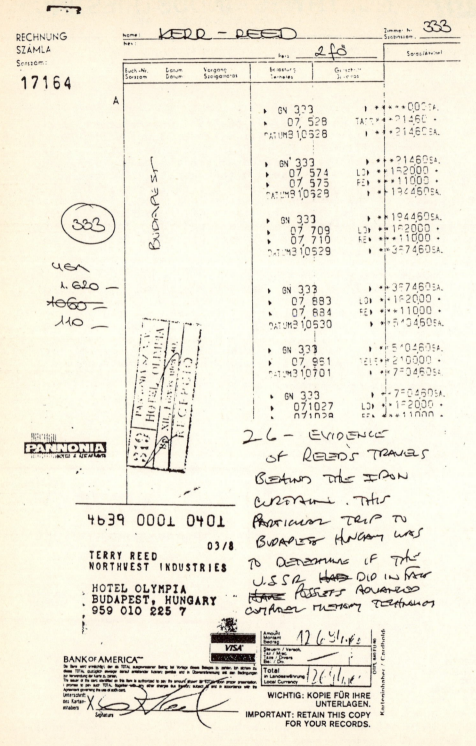

2-6. Evidence of Reed's travels behind the Iron Curtain. This particular trip to Budapest, Hungary was to determine if the USSR did in fact possess advanced computer memory technology.

M. I. SZILAGYI
M. Sc. Eng. & Ec.
CNC Machine Tools Export Dept.

"TECHNOIMPEX..
HUNGARIAN MACHINE INDUSTRIES FOREIGN TRADE COMPANY
BUDAPEST V., Dorottya u. 6.   Tel.: 184-055 — Telex: 22-4171
Address: H-1390 BUDAPEST P.O.B. 183

CLARA MOLDOVÁNYI

"TECHNOIMPEX..
HUNGARIAN MACHINE INDUSTRIES FOREIGN TRADE COMPANY
BUDAPEST V., Dorottya u. 6.   Tel.: 184-055 — Telex: 22-4171
Address: H-1390 Budapest, P.O.B. 183

LÁSZLÓ S. BÁRDOS
Head of NC Dept.

"TECHNOIMPEX..
HUNGARIAN MACHINE INDUSTRIES FOREIGN TRADE COMPANY
BUDAPEST V., Dorottya u. 6.   Tel.: 184-055 — Telex: 22-4171
Address: H-1390 BUDAPEST P.O.B. 183

DÉNES TIHANYI M. E.
SALES ENGINEER
NL-DIVISION

SZERSZÁMGÉPIPARI MÜVEK   572-066
(MACHINE TOOL WORKS)   TEL.: 571-881
BUDAPEST, IX., SOROKSÁRI ÚT 160. TELEX: 22-5733

JENÖ HAZAI
DIRECTOR

MACHINE TOOL WORKS
MILLING MACHINE FACTORY
2501 ESZTERGOM
SÁGVÁRI ENDRE U. 28.   TELEX: 22-5634
H U N G A R Y   TELEFON: 281.

Dipl. Ing. MÁTYÁS TÁLAS
Konstrukteur

WERZEUGMASCHINENWERKE   SZIM ESZTERGOMI
FRÄSMASCHINENFABRIK   MAROGEPGYAR
E s z t e r g o m   E s z t e r g o m
Telefon: 158 — Telex: 22-5634 Ságvári Endre u. 28.
                               UNGARN

R. GÁBOR HORACEK M. E.
COMMERCIAL DIRECTOR
MEMBER OF THE BOARD OF DIRECTORS

SZERSZÁMGÉPIPARI MÜVEK
(MEACHINE TOOL WORKS)
1102 BP. X., LIGET U. 22.   TELEFON: 572-066
                               TELEX: 22-5364

2-7. Hungarian business cards Reed collected on his trip. Reed was told by the FBI that the director, Matyas, was a KGB chief.

TOSHIBA MACHINE CO. AMERICA

9219 KATY FREEWAY, SUITE 206
HOUSTON, TEXAS 77024
TELEPHONE:
AREA 713 932-8850

Home Office
7328 Niles Center Road
Skokie, Illinois 60076
Telephone
Area 312 676-4372
Telex 724439

August 31, 1982

Reed, Kerr & Associates
1117 Northwest 63rd Street
Oklahoma City, OK 73116

Attention of Mr. Terry Reed

Dear Mr. Reed,

I am deeply grieved to learn of the death of your father,
and I wish to express to you my heartfelt condolences. I
share your sorrow in this sad event.

Sincerely yours,

Takashi Osato

2-8. Letter of condolence from Takashi Osato of Toshiba Machine Tool Company to Reed
at time of his father's death. Shows closeness of relationship between Reed and Toshiba as
Reed spied upon the firm at the request of his FBI and CIA handlers.

CHAPTER 3

PROJECT DONATION

"This is a hell of an opportunity. Finally, we have a President that understands we gotta fuck Congress and take care of our obligations around the world. We've got goddam communists taking over countries in our hemisphere. We're gonna kick their ass, this time."

As John Cathey spoke, he and Terry Reed were in a world of their own, oblivious to the yuppie crowd of Oklahoma City's elite, sipping their drinks under the shade of Cappuccino's forest green awnings.

The empty demitasse cups on their table had been pushed aside as the two men studied a napkin that Cathey had turned into makeshift diagram material. Even someone watching from afar would have realized, from the men's body language and posture, that they were having an intense and intimate conversation.

It was March 11th, 1983 and a typical Oklahoma City spring day, sunny with gusts of wind from across the prairie. It was only mid-morning but the early lunch crowd was already starting to gather.

Cathey's voice, though low key, radiated excitement and enthusiasm. Cathey had just been promoted to head what he told Terry was "Project Donation." This would prove to have dire consequences later for Terry, who, at the time, realized that Reagan was digging in for a major battle with Congress over supplying the Contras and was preparing to find the aid he needed from *any* source necessary.

For Terry and Cathey, it was *déjà vu.* Their old festering wounds were starting to bleed again. Congressional on-again, off-again whimsy, so reminiscent of Vietnam, angered both of them. This they would not and could not tolerate, This, they agreed, given a chance and the right leader. Once again, people were being put in harm's way without the backing they needed.

Cathey had informed Terry that highly-placed people in Washington had decided to pull him out of the high-technology espionage operation that had brought them together originally. Although Cathey considered the work important for national security, like most people not fully versed in the world of technology, Cathey personally found it boring and somewhat intimidating. Technology transfer, he confided, was not his true calling.

He had been a Marine combat officer in Vietnam and, with this new assignment, Cathey considered himself back "in the action" he longed for. Over the course of the past year, while tracking illegal Toshiba exports, the two men had exchanged many war stories. But Reed still only knew his CIA handler by his alias, "John Cathey."

North's activities during this period, from 1982 to the spring of 1984, have been highly-classified and kept totally under wraps to this day. Researchers have had little success uncovering his activities during that period. They have been told through leaks that North worked on some "bizarre," highly-classified projects for FEMA, the Federal Emergency Manpower Agency.[1] No witnesses have come forward to reveal what North really did under this cloak of secrecy.

Whatever he might have been doing for FEMA, North was busy running agency errands and using the FBI as a conduit. During that time, Terry's method of contacting North was through the FBI. North had told him, if he needed to talk, to call collect to an FBI office in Buffalo, N.Y., ask for a "Mr. Carlucci," another North code name, and leave a telephone number where Terry could be contacted. North would then call him back after the message was relayed to him.

Terry had assumed that the reason for Buffalo was its geographic proximity to Toronto, where North had said he was based because of KGB activity there. Lake Ontario would provide the deniable link between Agency and FBI collaboration. It also meant that Terry could have no record of telephone communication with North. It was built-in deniability and Terry understood how that worked. No paper, no trail, was the rule pounded into his head in intelligence school.

The Cathey-Reed meeting in Oklahoma City that March day came at a critical time for the Reagan administration. Six months earlier, Congress had passed the first Boland Amendment barring the use of funds "for the purpose of overthrowing the government of Nicaragua." And as Cathey and Terry spoke, 37 congressmen were drafting a letter to the President, warning him that CIA activities in Central America could be violating the law.[2] A month later, reporters visiting Contra training camps in Central America wrote that the U.S. "secret war against Nicaragua's leftist Sandinista regime has spilled out of the shadows."[3]

Because of the setback in Congress for his Nicaraguan policy, Reagan was going over the lawmakers' heads directly to the people. He was planning a dramatic appearance the following month at the Orange Bowl in Miami on the anniversary of the Bay of Pigs invasion as a major public relations gambit to rally support for his Nicaragua initiative. North and others had hoped to use this appearance for massive fund-raising, lobbying and propaganda purposes. Their targets were wealthy benefactors who hopefully would supplement the Contra's secret foreign assistance and establish an underground supply network.

The formation of this underground supply network was what North had referred to at the beginning of this meeting as his "opportunity."

With his Alfred E. Newman grin from ear to ear, exposing the gap in his front teeth, Cathey looked up from the napkin sketches.

"Ain't this great? Nobody loses. I found a secret source of not only money, but hardware, too. Wouldn't you know it, it'd be available through fucking insurance companies. Only in America!" Cathey exclaimed.

On the napkin before them was a blueprint for the "money pump" Cathey had discovered. If Congress wouldn't appropriate tax money for the Contras, then the CIA would have to become "creative," think like businessmen and provide a way for the Contras' backers to write off their "contributions" as a business expense.

Money was always welcome, but there were problems with the cash donations North was seeking. Most people he had approached for monetary donations were only interested in contributing if they could take a tax deduction. But "questionable" tax deductions are not only highly traceable, the preferred cash contributors were in short supply and the money still had to be converted into hard assets. There was another angle to solving the problem: go directly after the hardware needed for the Contra support. The side of this equation that most fascinated Terry was the insurance angle that North briefed him on.

Through the insurance scheme, a donor could make a contribution of a hard asset, such as an airplane, helicopter or a yacht, and the "loss" incurred by a conspiring or "participating" insurance company could be offset or underwritten through something Cathey described as "loss brokering."* Cathey told Terry an amendment to the federal tax laws allowing this practice had actually been signed into law years earlier, but had recently been strengthened.

Cathey was not totally clear on the mechanics of the brokering, but told Terry it would allow the participating, or in this case CIA-controlled, insurance company to go shopping for the hardware items the Contras needed. Once the item and donor were located and it was determined which insurance company held the policy on it, the CIA's company could then buy the "liability" portion of the policy from the unsuspecting insurance company holding it.

Up to this point, it was all done on paper since no loss has actually occurred. The CIA knew that no one outside the insurance industry would ever understand this as it only pertained to federal liquidity ratios levied upon the insurance industry.

Then, when the "donated" item disappeared, the loss, or now real liability, would automatically flow through to the insurance company working secretly with the CIA. This company would then pay for the loss and take a tax deduction. The taxpayer, or the federal deficit in this case, picked up the bill.

The complexity of the system required a napkin for explanation.

"Ain't capitalism grand!" Cathey said of the idea as Terry began to comprehend the scheme. "It's based on Ben Franklin's principle of a penny saved is a penny earned."

By reducing tax liability, and therefore reducing the amount of taxes owed the government, money is saved, and, therefore, earned.

"Yeah. But is all this legal?" Terry asked. "Doesn't the guy donating the hardware have to go along with all this? Or do your people just go out requisitioning things?" Terry was comparing this to the form of "borrowing" that is commonly done in the military. Servicemen don't view requisitioning as stealing, simply a redistribution of supplies, seeing as how "it all belongs to Uncle Sam."

Cathey assured him there was definitely no need for stealing. Economic downturns in the Texas-Oklahoma oil patch had been a blessing for the program.

---

*   Net income for the "losing" insurance company would continue to increase because of
      tax breaks that were allowed from underwriting losses. Loss-reserve selling allows one
      insurance company to sell future claims to another company, giving the first company
      immediate income from the purchase, and from the unused claim money. The buying,
      or second, company is provided with instant tax write-offs through mandatory, tax-
      exempt cash "set aside" requirements.⁺

"Believe you me, since the oil boom busted, we probably have plenty of people right here in Oklahoma, and especially Texas and Louisiana, that want to donate all kinds of things they now don't need, and can't sell," Cathey speculated. "I'm sure there'll be lots of 'oilies' just lined up trying to give us Lear jets, helicopters, yachts, all kinds of crap. No, we won't have to steal. The mother lode is right here in the *Sooner State*. To be a donor and to profit, all you have to do is have insurance on your donation, look the other way, and don't come looking for it."

"That's interesting. But why are you telling me all this?" Terry asked.

"I know the circles you travel in," Cathey said. "You rub elbows with lots of fat cats in the oil patch. I was thinking maybe you could steer me to possible donors. And you could tell them there's no danger in all this. We 'own' the insurance company, so no flat-foot investigators are going to come around asking questions. We've already thought of that."

Through the Toshiba affair Cathey had become aware of the affluent manufacturing circles Terry moved in. He realized that Reed was on a first-name basis with many of the wealthy, right-wing businessmen who were owners of the manufacturing companies. He had sold many of them expensive computer-controlled manufacturing equipment, transactions valued in the millions of dollars. A lot of them, risk-takers by nature and profession, were now caught in a cash crunch because of the collapse of their local economies and the banking industry that had underwritten their oil-drilling operations. They needed cash from any source. Why not get it from their own insurance company by "trading off" a high-value luxury item they could easily get along without?

Cathey did not know these men and he needed someone who could approach them on a personal basis. He hoped Terry would be a channel to them and act as a kind of "fund-raiser" for the donor program. This was obviously an early effort by Oliver North to find big-money people, an effort that went full-blown in ensuing years and resulted in the private contributions of such fat cats as Adolph Coors, the brewing magnate and Helen Garwood, a wealthy Texas widow who ended up donating more than $2.5 million in cash and stock. These contributions and others were made available through the private fund-raising efforts of men like Carl (Spitz) Channell and Richard Miller.[5] North sought out these and other conservative minded business men to form the nucleus of a "private donation" network to solicit tax exempt contributions for the Contra causes. One such organization controlled by Channell, the National Endowment for the Preservation of Liberty (NEPL), raised more than $10 million from private contributors.[6] (See chapter end.) It was a true capitalistic operation, with the blessing of the CIA, to thwart the wishes of Congress.

Terry told Cathey he was fascinated by the whole operation, approved of the concept and wished him well. But it was not a good time for him to get involved, he already had too many irons in the fire. He and Janis had a six-month-old son, Duncan, their first child. In addition to the other demands on his time, he was trying to keep Janis happy by completing the construction of their new nursery. Being anxious, first-time parents, they had shared their bedroom with Duncan until now, but the baby needed a nest of his own so that his weary parents could get a full night's rest. He would definitely have no time for fund raising, and he had to admit to himself that he doubted its legality, no matter what financial manipulations the CIA had devised.

"And in addition to all the other irons I have in the fire," Terry added, "we're going to Florida tomorrow to an Ultra-light fly-in. I've decided to do a little market analysis, and if things go well, I may be buying part of a Ultra-Light manufacturing plant located near Kansas City."

As of late, Reed had become very involved with a manufacturing firm in Olathe, Kansas, that was building one-man sport planes, the latest craze in aviation. Ultra-lights did not require a pilot's license to operate and were quickly becoming a new industry within aviation. A flying event held annually in Lakeland, Florida, called Sun 'N Fun, was being billed that year as a major Ultra-Light marketing event.

Terry informed Cathey that he would be flying his private four-seater Piper Turbo Arrow, N2982M, to Florida the next day and would be taking with him, along with Janis, an old attorney friend and his wife from Joplin, Missouri.

Cathey expressed a desire to go along, since he had always wanted to see a major Ultra-light event, and he thought Ultra-Lights had a definite military application. But five adults can't fly in a plane designed for four people, so that was out of the question.

But Cathey wasn't yet finished with the sales pitch for the donor program. "Hey, maybe you want to get in on this. You have an airplane. Perhaps you want to donate it?" he asked Terry.

Terry was perplexed. Yes, he had an airplane. But for a donor to profit under Cathey's formula, he would have to have a large equity in it. Otherwise, the donor would simply be losing something that he needed. This made no sense in his case.

"Hey, my plane is financed at the bank. I don't think I have any equity in it at all. For your plan to be attractive to a donor, doesn't he need equity in the asset? Besides, I need my plane. I use it continually in business," Terry said.

Cathey was confused. His grin was gone as he pondered Terry's words. Apparently his plan was flawed. It wasn't for everyone. He picked up his pen and wrote "equity" on the napkin.

"I hadn't thought of that," he confessed. "I see why you're a businessman and I work for the CIA."

Throughout the Toshiba affair, Cathey had appeared to be impressed with Terry's business acumen. He was seeing an aggressive business style that mirrored military warfare. Terry's "take no prisoners" attitude had come from his military training, which he was realizing had a definite business application. All those hard days and nights in Southeast Asia had not been for naught. Not only did his military days give him the discipline and attitude necessary to succeed, but more importantly his "wild oats" were already sown. While most of his competition, or "enemies," cruised the singles bars and nursed hangovers the next day, he was home working late into the night getting ready for tomorrow's battles.

The talk then turned to social things. Cathey said he was going to stay over and suggested Terry and his wife join him for dinner. "I'm sorry, John," Terry said. "This thing about having a baby is putting a cramp in my social life. Janis and I have added a new term to our vocabulary... babysitter."

"Yeah, the last time I saw your wife...when was it...in October, right?," Cathey asked, then adding without waiting for an answer. "She was all wore out. Hope she liked the roses I brought her. Too bad she couldn't have held off a little longer so that your son could have shared my birth date...oh well, at least we're both Libras."

Cathey was referring to his visit to Oklahoma City on Oct. 5, 1982, the day after the Reeds' son, Duncan, was born in Mercy Hospital. That day he accompanied an ecstatic new father to Janis' hospital room where she lay recovering from 12 hours of natural childbirth. Terry had learned over the course of "interfacing" with Cathey that his birthday was October 7th, 1943. Oliver's and his son's birthdays would be celebrated three days apart.

The primary purpose of Cathey's visit that October day was to see what he could do to repair the disintegrating relationship between Terry's firm and Toshiba Machine Tool since Reed's information was apparently more valuable than Terry had realized. Terry had been "monitoring" Toshiba for 10 months and, as common practice, the "handler," i.e. Cathey, did not inform the "asset," i.e. Reed, the true value of the vital information Terry was passing on. This is done for security reasons and to keep the asset calm and in character so that the significance of his role remains unknown to him.

Toshiba had proved it not only had the ability to screw up the balance of power in the world, it had also been screwing its dealer network and had reneged on its contract with Terry's new firm. This had put Terry in a position of having to file a state lawsuit against Toshiba to force it to honor its contract.

Working with the Japanese had been quite an education for Terry. He had learned they were exploiting the American legal system by trying to apply Japanese custom to American business practices. Their insistence on keeping written contracts to a minimum and, focusing instead on the Japanese custom of handshakes to seal agreements, was becoming a major area of litigation in American courts.

"We no need paper, only word," they customarily said. This had forced him to defend his position as a dealer with Toshiba when they attempted to violate his oral contract with them.

Terry's duties as a Toshiba dealer gave him free access to the company's bonded warehouse in Houston, a place where neither U.S. Customs or any other federal agency could go. Armed with the FBI and CIA's "shopping list" of questions, he would visit Houston twice a month for sales training and, most importantly, inspect the conditions and specifications of equipment shipped from Japan, still crated and awaiting release to the American market.

Cathey had told Terry that agents in Japan were tracking the crating and shipping of certain "key" models of machine tools that possessed the capability to manufacture highly-classified defense-related parts. The KGB had expressed great interest in one particular model of machine and was trying to purchase it anywhere, and anyway, they could. What bothered the CIA was that at least two of these $1 million machines had been built and shipped from Japan to bonded warehouses within the U.S. and then had "disappeared." They had been tracked going into warehouses, but they had never come out.

Considering the value of this equipment, logic dictated that they would not be warehoused for long periods of time and had probably been somehow "pirated" out of these facilities.

What the Agency needed Terry to do was actually quite simple. The old formula of "who, what, when, where and how" had to be applied and solved. Terry's eyes and ears were critical to relaying inside information about how these machine tools were "vanishing" and if possible, to where were they being shipped.

Terry's lawsuit initiated against Toshiba due to the unexpected business rift had, in effect, brought his involvement with Toshiba to an end, and with it, his work for the FBI.

At this meeting, Cathey was forced to disclose to Terry the importance of the information he had been passing on. Without him, Cathey said, they were "blind and deaf" and the States-side portion of the operation was in jeopardy. It suddenly became apparent to Terry just how important an asset he had been. Cathey was grasping at straws and began looking for a way, any way, to repair the business rift.

Cathey had surprised Terry at the earlier October meeting by displaying his seeming lack of business acumen. The CIA handler sought to mend the break by offering to pay Terry for the damages Toshiba had inflicted. This had made no sense whatsoever, forcing Terry to point out: "Hey, money doesn't solve these kinds of problems. Business relationships are based on contracts and trust. They've fucked me and your money can't change that. This is about honor. You should understand that."

From Terry's viewpoint, John Cathey's Project Donation had started and ended with that March meeting. And he had been of no real value to the Agency since the prior October, due to the Toshiba rift. Terry felt he was simply out of the spook business, for now, and was in no position to contribute further.

Instead, Terry spent the balance of the time that afternoon sharing with Cathey his new-found high. The exhilaration of a Vietnam comrade finally doing what he wanted: Getting another shot at the commies, and Congress. At that time, Terry was not interested in getting directly involved with Cathey's new war. He had a living to make and all the past spook work had been voluntary, with no real compensation for his time and effort.

But times and circumstances change.

* * *

"What do you mean my plane's not there?" Terry questioned. "Is this some kind of a joke?"

Terry was in the Olathe County Courthouse in Kansas, a short distance southwest of Kansas City, researching some incorporation files. It was 11 AM on March 24th, 1983. At the other end of the telephone was the receptionist at Mizzou Aviation in Joplin, Missouri.

"No it's not here. It wasn't here this morning when we came to work and we figured you had picked it up."

"Well, I didn't, so, if you're sure it's missing, call the police." He was upset.

Twelve days previously, Janis and Terry had begun their planned trip from Oklahoma City to Florida by way of Joplin to pick up his friends. That was the day Janis had learned her husband was in fact made of "the right stuff" when he calmly and skillfully handled an in-flight emergency. Their single-engine plane suddenly decided to deposit six quarts of oil on the windshield, the result of three broken pistons.

Terry had been able to nurse the ailing plane to Joplin, "change underwear" and pick up his waiting friends. He rented an aircraft for the remainder of the trip and turned his plane over to Mizzou Aviation, the fixed base operator at the Joplin Airport, to be repaired. Mizzou was where Terry had gone to flight school, and had later worked as a flight instructor. The plane had remained in

Mizzou's custody until the morning of the 24th when he called to see if the airplane was repaired and ready to be picked up.

As he hung up the pay phone in Kansas, the haunting recollection of the "donation" sales pitch from Cathey, a few days earlier on March 11th, came to mind. But he had certainly not agreed to any donation—or had he? There had been a subsequent conversation with Cathey after their initial talk. A week and a half later, on March 21st, Cathey had telephoned Terry at his office in Oklahoma City for what had seemed to be a purely social conversation.

Cathey asked about the Ultra-light show and Terry casually chatted with him about the near catastrophic plane incident and the fact that his plane was at the Joplin Airport being repaired.

"Are you sure, you don't want to donate it?" Cathey had asked in a joking manner after considering the sizeable repair bill that would be forthcoming. Terry shrugged it off as a bit of friendly banter.

After leaving the Kansas courthouse, he drove to Joplin in a borrowed car to find out what had happened to his plane. What he learned there proved to be very unsettling. On the afternoon of March 23rd, the aircraft had been repaired and then tied down beside the airport beacon tower. For some unexplained reason, the mechanic in charge of the repair put the engine and airframe log books in the pilot's seat but did not bother to lock it.

This perplexed Terry since even student pilots are trained early on never to carry those log books in the airplane. The reason? Doing so is an added invitation to theft since it's almost impossible to sell an aircraft without its log books. It would tip off a buyer that the plane is probably stolen. It's like trying to sell a car without the title.

When questioned later why he had been so careless, the mechanic answered that he had no excuse and that it was simply inadvertent. But Terry was more upset over the way the theft was being handled, since no one could assure him that anyone in law enforcement was actively searching for the plane.

Terry decided to take matters into his own hands and called his FBI handler, Buzz Barlow, at his home in Edmond, Oklahoma, to ensure that the theft was entered in the FBI's National Crime Information Center in Washington. Barlow assured Terry that he would confirm the entry of the theft, and Terry returned home by commercial airliner from Kansas City, upset and suspicious.

This plane was more than utilitarian to Terry. In addition to its being impeccably maintained, Terry knew its complete service history since its delivery from the factory. He had flown it during his training as a commercial and instrument student, and felt that he had lost an old friend, one he would probably never see again.

To add to his mounting problems and inconveniences from the theft, his irreplaceable, original pilot log books also were gone. He had left them in the plane when he turned it over to Mizzou for repairs. These books reflect a pilot's credentials, and without them it is difficult, if not impossible, to prove flight time and ratings history. Terry set about the difficult and time-consuming task of trying to reconstruct his flying history.

He eventually sent his insurance claim to his carrier in Wichita, Kansas, and, after much foot-dragging, finally was awarded $32,950 on June 13th, 1983, for his loss. The insurance company's bank draft was made out to both Terry and Lakeshore Bank of Oklahoma City, which held a $27,000 lien on the plane. After deducting the amount of the lien, the accrued interest, the monthly payments he made after the plane was stolen, and rental bills for other aircraft used while awaiting payment from the insurance company, he netted approximately $1,500 in "revenue." He had been fortunate, but he was still without his log books.

Three days after receiving and signing over the check to Lakeshore, Terry got another unexpected social call from Cathey. In that conversation peppered with humor, Cathey theorized the plane was probably "south of the border and being put to good use by now."

Cathey expressed a desire to stay in closer contact with Terry because his new project, he said, was getting exciting and "taking on new dimensions." Terry, he thought, might be i-n-t-e-r-e-s-t-e-d. Cathey said he would keep his friend posted.

By August of 1983, Terry had decided to acquire partial ownership of the Ultra-Light company in Kansas and, along with two other partners, move it to Little Rock, Arkansas. His old boss, mentor and friend from Kansas, Joe Ida, had propositioned Terry with an offer that was hard to refuse. Ida and an old friend, Seth Ward, from Little Rock were interested in bidding on the now defunct company in Kansas and moving it to Arkansas, where Ward lived. He said Terry could have equity in the company if Terry would forgive the $35,000 debt owed him by the now-bankrupt Kansas firm and be willing to manage the new company being formed from the deal.

Terry not only saw this as a fair deal and an opportunity, but also a way to relocate his machine-tool company, Reed, Kerr and Associates Inc., to Arkansas, where a more diverse manufacturing economy was developing. And it was less centered around the oil industry.

Much to his wife's initial dismay, Terry felt it was in their best interest to uproot the family and sell their restored Victorian home in Oklahoma City, which had been their labor of love.

Throughout this *"Sooner connection"* phase of intelligence "handoffs" in Oklahoma, Terry believed that he had made only one true friend, Buzz Barlow. By now, their relationship was a close, personal one and Barlow and his wife voiced regret repeatedly that the Reeds were planning to leave Oklahoma.

By late August, they finally sold their house and the Barlows hosted a going-away party. On August 23rd, Cathey unexpectedly called Terry at home.

"I hear through Enright that Buzz says you guys are moving to Arkansas," he noted. "I really can't talk about it on an unsecure line, but we've got an exciting project in the works down there and I think there may be a slot for you. One that'll maybe even pay you this time."

Terry was interested. The money would certainly be nice, especially since Janis would not be working for a while after their move to Arkansas. She was hoping to be a full-time mother to their son.

"Hey, if you're interested, it's best I just put you into play with the guy that's going to be running the operation for me. I'll make the introduction and have him look you up. I'll tell him you're a good guy."

"How do I know who he is and where to find him?" Terry asked.

"He'll find you...and his name is Barry Seal."

Terry had just been handed off to a man whose name would come to haunt those who worked with him.

It was another step closer to the abyss.

50   TERRY REED AND JOHN CUMMINGS

1. Ben Bradlee Jr., *Guts and Glory, The Rise and Fall of Oliver North*, Donald I. Fine Inc., 1988, pp. 132-4.
2. Public Law 97-377, Defense Appropriations Act for Fiscal Year 1983, Sec. 793
3. *Newsweek*, April 11, 1983, P. 46.
4. *Wall Street Journal, Bill Targets Tax Breaks for Self-Insured Reserves*, October 12, 1981.   Dun & Bradstreet Reports, *Insurance Crisis, Who's To Blame for High Insurance Rates*, March/April, 1986 pp. 40-43; Wall Street Journal, *Oil Company Captives See New Tax Liabilities*, November 8, 1982; Wall Street Journal, *Risk Managers Increase Investment Savvy*, October 11, 1982; Internal Revenue Code, Title 61, Paragraph 601, subdivision .276.
5. Bradlee, *Guts and Glory*, PP.226-28.
6. *Report of the Congressional Committes Investigating the Iran-Contra Affair*, (U.S. Government Printing Office, 1988), p. 85.

The Channell-Miller Contra Assistance Network

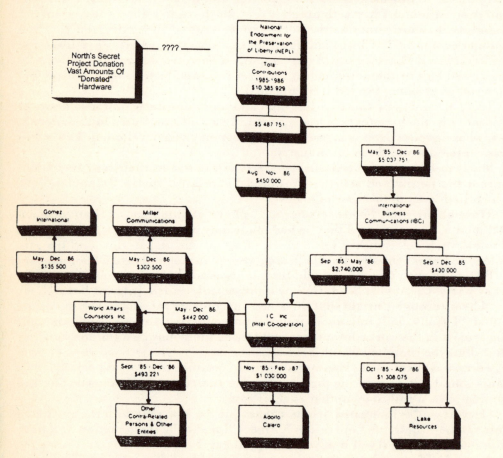

This chart represents the money flow of the Channell-Miller Contra Assistance Network.

Source: Senate Select Committee on Secret Military Assistance to Iran and the Nicaraguan Opposition and House Select Committee to Investigation Covert Arms Transactions with Iran.

3-1. Chart showing the complexity of the corporate relationships set up to raise funds for the Contras. The chart also suggests a probable connection between the corporate entities and "Project Donation."

CHAPTER 4

INTO THE LOOP

As the Lear 23's jet engines spooled to take-off RPM and the turbine-temperature needles rose to the red-limit markers, Barry Seal assumed the flight instructor's posture in the right seat.

With his arm around the back of the pilot's seat occupied by Terry that late December day in 1983 at Mena, Arkansas, Seal told Terry "now release the fucking brakes and let's have some fun." Terry appeared tense.

"Relax, you're gonna like this," Seal assured him. "A Lear jet behaves similar to the Citation that you're rated for, except things happen faster."

Terry had always wanted to fly what pilots call "the businessman's fighter plane." And now he was getting his chance as he and Seal started their return trip to Little Rock, and continued to fine-hone their friendship newly found in the cockpit of N13SN.

Terry had been in Arkansas less than three months and the man Cathey had said would find Terry had done just that.

The white jet accelerated abruptly to V-1 and Seal reminded his "student" that it was "time to fly." Terry gingerly pulled back the pilot's yoke and much to his amazement, the plane leaped skyward. He had flown a lot, but this was truly fucking fun, with twin capital "F's."

Seal knew flying. But he was also a renaissance man, multi-talented and faceted, something that had enabled him to survive the many other troubles then besetting him. By the winter of 1983, as they headed back to Little Rock, Seal had begun to recognize that Terry shared some of those multi-talented traits. And, more importantly, besides flying, he knew manufacturing as well.

And Terry also begun to realize something. He was beginning to sort out from among Seal's talents his intriguing ability to handle the government handlers who thought they were handling him.

It was clear that Seal was not impressed with these men who worked for the government, people Seal looked down on as having limited ambition. "Fucking GS suits (slang for General Salary Schedule)," he had called them. "No balls, and very little brains."

In six words, Seal had articulated what Terry had come to realize since his days in Oklahoma when he began to realize that he had foolishly allowed the government to use his talents over and over, monopolizing his time and knowledge, with no compensation and no apparent appreciation of a businessman's necessity to generate cash flow.

As the jet assumed a heading of 077 degrees and was soaring through 15,000 feet, Terry turned to Seal and said: "Maybe we can trade off services. I'll teach you about manufacturing if you'll train me to handle these GS bean-counters so I can have a plane like this."

Seal smiled. "It's a deal," he replied.

In short, Seal knew his business and Terry saw him as a mentor in dealing with "the suits." But what did Seal really see in Terry? Clearly, Seal had many ventures going and was shopping for reliable "subcontractors." But, until this trip to Mena, Seal had not appreciated Terry's in-depth knowledge of manufacturing techniques, or simply how things are made.

From childhood Terry, the oldest of six children, had been the "weird kid" who always wondered how things were made. As his friends swung baseball bats in his Little League days, Terry was pondering machines. He was more curious about the type of machinery required to manufacture bats than he was in learning the art of using one.

Terry's curiosity as a young man was a gift from his father who, in addition to being a schooled jeweler, worked on top-secret research and development projects for rocket engines at the Rocketdyne Division of North American Rockwell in Neosho, Missouri. Dinner conversation in the Reed house in Carthage, Missouri, was often about thrust requirements needed to orbit payloads in outer space and the machinery needed to manufacture rocket engines.

In fact, instead of sports, what had "tripped his trigger" as far back as grade school, was the wail of an internal combustion engine at red-line RPM. Young Terry's fascination with all things mechanical would accelerate him on a course of building backyard and garage motorized inventions that would astound adults.

Friends recalled him winning a debate with his seventh-grade science teacher concerning the inner workings of a car starter. His love of speed, engines and aluminum was what directed his attention to airplanes.

And now here he was, at the throttle of "Bill Lear's orgasm," a Lear-23! As Seal demonstrated a series of aileron rolls while still maintaining a heading, it wasn't taking Terry long to become addicted to the smell of kerosene that was powering Seal's jet instead of the high octane fuel Terry was used to using.

After the Air Force had reneged on its promise to send him to flight school, he had eventually attained his type-rating in Cessna Citation jets at Flight Safety International in Dallas, a very expensive education, and had amassed more than 2,000 hours flight time.

All the money Terry had put into his aviation studies now seemed worthwhile as Seal cancelled the IFR flight plan, handed over the controls of the craft streaking through the Arkansas skies and said: "It's your airplane. Wring this bitch out and show me what you're made of."

Terry met the challenge and with a "shit-eatin' grin," snapped the airplane into a left banked wing-over maneuver, fighter pilot-style. He brought the plane's heading to north and rolled, wings level while diving toward his "target," the airport setting atop Winthrop Rockefeller's Petit Jean Mountain. The airspeed indicator was now at VMO...306 knots indicated. He held the Lear approximately 100 feet off the ground as they buzzed the runway and then slowly began pitching the nose skyward beyond 45 degrees of pitch-up attitude.

Reed nursed the stick rearward forcing the craft and its occupants to pull an estimated four G's in order to catapult the plane into the complicated chandelle maneuver he was attempting.

Seal cautioned, "Watch out for the compressor stall! Push it over the top and recover this thing. I'm overweight and these G's are gettin' to me."

After Terry recovered from the maneuver and leveled off at 17,500 feet, Seal turned and said: "Guess I'm too old for this shit. OK, hot dog, let's take it back to base. You got the right stuff."

By the time Seal and Terry landed at Little Rock's Adams Field, a bond between the two men was developing so strong that Seal violated a cardinal rule of intelligence. He would now tell Terry something he didn't "need to know."

They went directly to the coffee shop inside the building housing Central Flying Service. There, Seal began by telling Terry the real reason why they had just made the trip to Mena in the rural mountainous area of Western Arkansas and to the firm called Brodix Manufacturing. Seal had told Terry he held an interest in the Brodix firm that was, as far as anyone knew, an aluminum foundry and machining company that was slated to "expand" into something new, and *SECRET*.

"It's time I let you know the truth about what we want to do at Brodix," Seal said. "Let's have some coffee and you can tell me all you know about the investment casting process."

Terry was puzzled. "Investment casting is normally for close-tolerance precision steel parts," he replied. "I just came from an aluminum foundry. What's your interest in application for steel?"

"Guns, what else?" Seal replied as he peered over his coffee cup.

Without either man saying it, Seal and Terry had just crossed the Rubicon. The lives of both men were then changed forever. That day a chain of events was set in motion that would lead Terry to learn eventually what was really going on in Arkansas: the state was going to be the secret *source* of weapons for the Contras, as well as a major training base and trans-shipment hub for weapons. Seal, because of the mutual trust that was being developed, had divulged to Terry information that he had not been cleared to reveal.

"I'll have to talk to our *friend* on this (a coded reference to John Cathey), but I need you in on this project. It's more difficult to make weapons parts than they led me to believe."

Seal explained that a New Jersey gun-manufacturing company had been purchased—lock, stock and barrel—and was being moved to Arkansas to quietly and discreetly produce weapons components for the Contras.

This was clearly another facet of what was later described in the Congressional hearings on the Iran-Contra Affair as CIA Director William Casey's plan to have CIA-owned proprietaries, or front businesses, become the bypass conduit around a whimsical Congress. The Director saw these flip-flopping Congressional attitudes as obstacles to the Reagan Administration's controversial and unpopular foreign policy initiatives.

Continuous on-and-off Congressional bans on American military aid to the Contras was creating a shortage in the arms supply for the Nicaraguan operation. This "drought" was depleting the level of arms in the reservoir to a critically low level. Firms that normally supplied the Defense Department had been barred by Congress from supplying the Contras because of those Congressional bans. Casey wanted to establish a continuity to the supply effort, hopeful that the White House objective of overthrowing the Sandinistas could be attained through eventual armed internal rebellion.

Terry, having seen unnecessary loss of life in Southeast Asia, put himself in the shoes of the Contra soldiers. How could they, he thought, have even a chance of survival without at least a minimum stock of weapons? In Vietnam, he had been put in harm's way while Congress debated the morality of the "conflict." Now, it was happening again, only this time to a group of "freedom fighters", as President Reagan called them, in a country so close to his own. The Congressional jockeying continued to rage on.

The recent moving of a New Jersey arms-manufacturing company to Arkansas was not merely, as the state would claim, the result of vigorous recruitment by the Clinton administration. It was instead, Seal said, the result of behind-the-scenes CIA decisions to make Arkansas the equivalent of a "proprietary." But, nonetheless, it would help Bill Clinton deliver on his campaign promises to provide "jobs for Arkansans."

Iver Johnson's Arms Inc., the firm brought to Arkansas from New Jersey, was one steeped in American history. Originally established in Massachusetts during the American Revolution, it had helped arm the colonial soldiers to fight the British. It already had ongoing military and civilian arms contracts that would allow it to operate openly under the usual scrutiny of the Treasury Department's Bureau of Alcohol, Tobacco and Firearms.

Under federal law, arms companies must create a paper trail for tracking and control of all weapons, especially for components that go into fully-automatic weapons. The M16, the weapon used by American military services, is a weapon requiring this documentation and control. All international sales require an End-User certificate, which traces the weapon from origin to destination. The Boland Amendments, which banned sales to the Contras, effectively forced the CIA to find a source of weapons without such certificates.

This secrecy required to produce the non-traceable parts posed an immediate problem for Iver Johnson's. Iver Johnson's was working on a classified contract with the United States Navy to produce a .50-caliber sniper rifle. This required government inspectors' scrutiny of the company's operations in its new location in Jacksonville, Arkansas.

To circumvent this scrutiny, the decision had been made to cast critical, and untraceable, parts at a location other than Jacksonville. Seal explained, as they sat in the coffee shop, that Brodix would contain that casting operation. The trip to Mena was now beginning to make sense to Terry.

Because Iver Johnson's was an established firm, it provided instant cover for the clandestine work that was slated to be done in Mena.

On paper, Philip Lynn Lloyd, a wealthy Arkansas businessman with close ties to the Arkansas bond industry, was listed as a principal in the company and the man responsible for its relocation to Arkansas.* Terry was learning that Lloyd was probably just a "cover" for the project.

"So now that you know what we're up to, what will it take in the way of machinery to cast and machine the lower receiver housing of the M16?" Seal asked.

"I'll need blue prints and I'll need to know quantities," Terry replied.

The lower receiver housing is the major part that differentiates the M16, fully automatic, military assault weapon from the AR-15, the semi-automatic version that is sold to the public in sporting goods stores.

---

* Lloyd was convicted in Federal Court in Little Rock in December, 1990, of nine counts of bankruptcy fraud and conspiracy stemming from the concealment of more than $500,000 worth of assets when his personal financial empire collapsed.[1]

Federal law requires that during production each receiver housing be stamped with a serial number and documentation be created that will track it from cradle to grave. Obviously, the CIA did not want serial numbers on weapons going to the Contras during a period when Congress had banned the sales.

Seal and Terry ended their first arms discussion pleased with themselves. Seal had found a local confidant who understood machine tools and Terry felt honored that he was being entrusted with such important secret knowledge. He felt that the window of opportunity was opening and he decided to leap through it. He had been in Arkansas less than three months and the man Cathey had said would find him had done just that.

Things were going well for the Reeds in Arkansas. They had temporarily moved into an upscale apartment on the west side of Little Rock, the "in" place to be. Terry's new Ultra-light company named Command Aire was getting a lot of good press representing, as it did, the efforts of the state to attract new industry.

The Reeds found that being part of this effort was the key to membership in Little Rock society. In just a few months, they had an overview of the social and political pecking order there. Because one of the principals in Terry's company, Seth Ward, was a socialite and a Little Rock industrialist, Terry already was traveling in high social and political circles. This newly-found status led to an introduction to Hillary Clinton, the wife of the governor, who worked at the prestigious Rose Law Firm*, THE Arkansas law firm, where Webb Hubbell, Ward's son-in-law and former Little Rock mayor, was a partner. This firm, which was handling Terry's company's product liability work, was the unofficial pipeline to the governor.

While establishing his new ultralight business, Terry visited the Rose Law Firm often. These lawyers were most definitely "in the loop" as the Arkansas oligarchy was dragged kicking and screaming into the twentieth century.

This was not your typical law firm whose strict charter kept them primarily aligned with the pursuit of civil justice... Deal brokering was the firm's specialty. All that was missing was Monty Hall screaming, "Let's make a deal!"

The icons of Little Rock's business community flowed through the firm's front door. Terry realized Seth Ward had taken him directly into the heart of the beehive where things were really made to happen in Arkansas.

The Who's Who in Arkansas congregated a short distance down the hall from Webb Hubbell's office. There Hillary Clinton, the Queen Bee, anointed

---

* From the time of Clinton's successful presidential bid in late 1992 and the publication date of this book, the Rose Law Firm has surfaced repeatedly in the news as having been the "bull pen" for up-and-coming Washington influence peddlers and people who used their prior relationships, professional and personal, with Bill and Hillary Clinton as a conduit to positions of power in Washington. The list, so far, includes:

1. Vincent Foster—the now-deceased, former law partner of Hillary Clinton who moved to Washington to serve as White House council and then suspiciously, allegedly committed suicide after not properly handling some rather minor scandals which erupted at the onset of the Clinton Administration.

2. Webster Hubbell—now serving as Number Two man in the Justice Department and rumored to be the man running interference for the Clintons as the brewing Whitewater[2] scandal develops. He is rumored to be the man actually *running* Justice.

her subjects and gave her blessing to meticulously prepared contracts outlining proposed business ventures.

"Webb's office is right next door to the Governor's", Seth Ward joked about Hubbel's proximity to Hillary Clinton's office. "*She* wears the pants in the family," Ward continued, "And she's a stone-cold son-of-a-bitch. Kicking ass in a man's world. I wish I had a daughter like that... Hell, for that matter, I wish I had a son like that," Ward mumbled in reference to his only male offspring, Skeeter, a somewhat passive and foolhardy yuppie type who had already left a string of business failures in his wake.

Terry was finding that in 1984 Arkansas' young governor, Bill Clinton, was no hero to a lot of these people. Ward and others often spoke contemptuously of Clinton behind his back, calling him a wimp and referring to him as their "token politician." They made it clear they had no respect for any man whose wife was the major bread winner and often referred to him as the "boy governor." It was clear from the back stabbing comments made by Ward and his cronies that Clinton was viewed as a political light weight who was long on promises and short on delivery. They said he lacked true political finesse, was too damned wishy-washy, and never cut a deal with anyone that he wasn't forced to *compromise* on later.

Terry figured their distaste for Clinton had more to do with his "progressive attitudes" and his quest to attract out-of-state businesses which were a major threat to the established power base. Clinton just didn't fit their mold of what a consummate politician should be. Their political hero was still Wilbur Mills, once a powerful Congressmen who grabbed the nation's attention when he drove drunk into the Potomac tidal basin with his mistress, a former stripper named Fannie Fox.

But Mills' wife had never worked. Instead, she had spent her time attending meetings of the Daughters of the Confederacy. These elite and pretentious southern belles of Little Rock, who retrieved their fur coats from storage at the first sign of a frost, viewed Hillary Clinton as a social outcast because of her "uppity, liberated, northern attitudes", the fact that she had a career and her audacity, when first marrying Bill, to not take her husband's last name. After his only political defeat, she apparently realized this was something to be reckoned with and promptly became Hillary Clinton rather than Hillary Rodham. Now she's both.

To Janis Reed it seemed as though she had driven accidentally through a time warp on her trip to Little Rock. Although the distance from Oklahoma City to Little Rock along I-40 was only 270 miles due *east*, she found it was like going back 100 years in time. She discovered that the average male in Arkansas believed that—next to Appomatox—Arkansas' blackest date in history was the day women won the right to vote. Not only were women's rights barely acknowledged, but civil rights in general barely existed. Janis was astounded by the racial prejudice she encountered.

"You won't believe the discussion I had today," she remarked to her husband one night during dinner. "Some people at my real estate seminar asked me which school Duncan was going to attend. I told them I had him in Montessori school part time and I was happy with it. Oh, they said, that's not what they meant. They meant when he goes to kindergarten. I said he's only a year and a half old! Then they proceeded to tell me that I'd better get him on the waiting list for certain private schools. 'So what's wrong with the neighborhood school?', I said. They said 'oh honey, you don't want your child going to school with colored children.' Terry, some of the women are my age and younger. It's not like they're old ladies who remember the Civil War. I asked them why they were so prejudiced. And you know what? Everyone responded with a look of disbelief.

"'Honey, what do you mean prejudice? Why I even let my maid's husband wait for her in the parlor in my house last week. I thought at that time my dead mama would be rolling over in her grave. We're not prejudiced. We just think it's best for all of us not to have our children co-mingling. And we know a lot of Negroes who feel the same way.'"

Education was the issue that continuously dominated the newspaper headlines while the Reeds lived in Arkansas. The need to improve their education system—which ranked nearly dead last in comparison to other states—came down to a supposed lack of qualified teachers. Clinton took a political lead on the issue, pressed hard and finally got the Legislature to pass mandatory teacher testing, despite the outcries of the teachers. The Reeds were infuriated, however, when, the day before the test was to be administered, the previously sealed and secret test was "leaked" to the media and printed in its entirety in the local newspaper. Despite outcries that the entire test had been "*compromised*," it was administered anyway and, needless to say, the vast majority of the teachers passed.

Arkansas' movers and shakers, the sons of the Old South, hated "carpetbaggers and Yankees" like Clinton's wife. (Hillary claimed Chicago as home.) For them, the Civil War still was being fought. This pervasive reactionary attitude precluded any real economic advancement for the state, unless, of course, there was something in it for the good ole boys. True status was reserved usually only for people whose grandfathers had traded slaves and cotton at the Peabody Hotel in Memphis 150 years before.

Despite these obstacles, Terry was moving up. He had even shared the men's room with Governor Clinton at the segregated Little Rock Country Club. Anybody who was anybody urinated there—provided, of course, he was white.

And it was often in the men's room where many of the back door deals were struck while a black man held the cologne and soap and towel for the Arkansas' "Bond Daddies" who did their insider trading and got the advance word on what would be the most lucrative "politically-wise" investments.

Old South protectionist attitudes had put in place usury laws that capped interest rates in Arkansas. To get around this cap, and make their money perform, the municipal bond industry was developed as a vehicle to give the Arkansas' elite a way to invest their money outside the state, where higher rates were legal. As a result, a small "Wall Street" had sprung up in Little Rock and the people who operated it were called "Bond Daddies."

One of them was Dan Lasater, a man very close to Bill Clinton and whose firm, Lasater & Co., was handling more than $300 million annually in preferred state bond activity. The state was using the Rose Law Firm as its bond counsel for much of this activity. It was one big happy family.

Terry reminisced about the first time he had met Lasater, a man in his mid-30s who delighted in flaunting his wealth. Lasater hadn't been traveling alone that day. He had been the person who introduced Terry formally to Barry Seal.

Lasater was also displaying a "trophy" that eventful November day in 1983 when he walked into Command Aire's Ultra-Light factory unannounced. The "trophy" was Roger Clinton, the governor's trouble-prone, half-brother.

"I'm Dan Lasater and this is my driver, Roger Clinton. He's the governor's brother," Lasater said referring to the hyperactive young man next to him. As Lasater started to swagger into the factory area as if he owned it, Terry's eye shifted to a rather large man standing in the doorway. Unlike Lasater, this man was behaving like a guest and demonstrating some manners.

"Oh yeah," Lasater continued. "I guess I should introduce a client of mine. This is Mr. Barry Seal."

Terry shook hands with the neatly-dressed man who appeared robust, but overweight. As the entourage walked into the factory, Lasater and Clinton ran off to look at the colorful Ultra-Light on static display. As they walked slowly together, Seal turned to Terry and spoke in a slow and cordial southern drawl, "We have a common *friend* who says you have some talent I need."

"Does this common *friend* have a name?"

"John Cathey."

Terry had just been handed off, again, into a new loop.

In using Adler Berriman Seal, Cathey and the CIA were turning in desperation to a "hidden" asset with automatic deniability...a man with a *handle*. Seal was a man with a past, a man with a criminal record and a man the CIA could do business with when they needed performance.

Nicknamed "Thunder Thighs" because of his size, Seal was the type of man about whom movies are made. In fact, a movie about Seal, named *Double Crossed*, was made in 1991 though it minimalized the extent of Seal's true connections to the intelligence community, portraying him as a drug-trafficker-turned-informant who was assassinated after the White House blew his cover. True as far as it went. But Terry would learn there was much more to Seal than just that.

Seal was considered by those in his inner circle as the consummate pilot. At the age of 26, he had been the youngest 747 pilot in the nation. But his commercial aviation career with TWA was brought to an early and abrupt end in 1972 when he was arrested in New Orleans for alleged violations of the Mutual Security Act of 1954, which bars the export of explosives without approval of the State Department. A DC-4 owned by Seal and loaded with 13,000 pounds of C-4 explosives, primercord and blasting caps was seized in Shreveport, Louisiana. The government contended these were explosives earmarked for anti-Castro groups operating in Mexico. But the charges were never fully tried and the case was later dropped without any real explanation. During Seal's trial, two key government witnesses failed to appear. A mistrial was declared and the charges were later dismissed by an appeals court. A CIA source revealed to co-author John Cummings that the Agency, in fact, aborted the case because it feared that CIA assets' names might be revealed in court.

At this first meeting with Reed, Seal described himself this way: "I'm a contractor. I specialize in transportation. Whatever there is to transport, I transport. I have certain connections within the government, and I presently have a contract that you may have interest in. I'll talk to you later, privately."

Terry knew to press no further and accepted Seal for what he appeared to be: a wealthy businessman with high intelligence connections. After all, look who had brought them together, Oliver North, aka "John Cathey."

Seal would later refer to himself as a "calculated risk taker" who "needed excitement" in his life. The CIA apparently knew he also had the talent, organization and the *cojones* to get the job done. But a lot more was going on in Seal's life at the time that Terry was unaware of.

Seal was one of those hidden assets who had been kept on the shelf for years, a kind of black reserve force. But Seal was already isolated, beyond the normal arms-length relationship for built-in deniability. This would become a problem. The lack of professional intelligence leadership within this cut-out would result ultimately in critical mistakes being made.

As Lasater tested the suspension of the Ultra-Light in the showroom by bouncing up and down in it in his $1,000, three-piece business suit and high-priced Gucci shoes, Terry and Seal agreed to meet again later, when they could talk privately, without the presence of company that was demonstrating such boorish behavior.

"So Barry tells me you don't need to be a pilot to fly one of these things," Lasater said, referring to the Ultra-Light.

"That's not what I said, Dan," Seal said shaking his head in disgust. "You have to be a pilot, you just don't need a license. There's a big difference between the two. Hey, I think this is a sure-fire way for you to kill yourself. Let's get out of here. I need an investment banker that's alive."

Roger Clinton ran in a state of high excitement to open Lasater's limousine door and the uninvited entourage departed.

* * *

Later that same month Seal returned to Little Rock for "banking purposes" and took the opportunity to invite Terry to dine with him. At that dinner meeting, which was much like a job interview, Seal thoroughly debriefed Terry about his Air Force intelligence background and other special qualifications he had.

As Terry was talking about his second tour in Southeast Asia and his unit's support of air drops in Cambodia, Seal interrupted, "Stop right there! What exactly did you do? Were you involved in that? I mean in a hands-on capacity?"

Terry told him that selecting drop zones for supplies delivered by air was part of his job as a photo-intelligence analyst in Thailand, which was only one facet of his highly specialized training at Air Force Intelligence School at Lowry Air Force Base in Denver. At Udorn, Thailand, he said, his team had been in charge of many aspects of C-130 aerial delivery, including crew training and ground support. Also of great interest to Seal in this conversation was the revelation that Terry's Air Force unit, Task Force Alpha, supported Air America, the CIA's airline.

"So, besides being a flight instructor, you speak Spanish and you know how to coordinate with aircrews in order to put the shit on target?"

Terry nodded.

"You're hired. But I got a more pressing problem right now. When can you go with me to Mena?" Mena was not only the site in which Seal had moved his aircraft operations from Louisiana, but he now co-owned a manufacturing facility there as well.

The "more pressing problem" for Seal at that moment was not finding someone who was a flight instructor with knowledge of aerial delivery, rather he needed immediate manufacturing advice, which Seal knew was Terry's profession. Seal needed to set in place several things in Arkansas, one of which was an underground arms manufacturing network.

Throughout the month of December, the two men became better acquainted through repeated telephone conversations, and by personal visits whenever Seal showed up in Little Rock to make his numerous "deposits" at Lasater's firm.

At that time Terry was wearing two hats, one as a principal in Command Aire and the other as president of Reed, Kerr & Associates, an automation consulting and marketing firm. In Oklahoma, he had been instrumental in starting an Ultra-Light air park, which the Federal Aviation Administration viewed as an airport requiring licensing under Part 157 of Federal Aviation Rules (FARs). Seal was drawing upon both the manufacturing *and* aviation talents Terry possessed.

By January, 1984, a month after visiting Brodix Manufacturing in Mena with Terry, Seal needed to get something else underway. He had to find a site in a remote area around Mena that would serve as a secret base to train Contra pilots in air-delivery techniques.

At this time, a restaurant named SOBs (Shrimp, Oysters, Beer) situated on the north bank of the Arkansas River in Little Rock and close to Terry's factory, had become their hangout. Seal, who lived in Baton Rouge, Louisiana, liked the Cajun atmosphere and the restaurant's resident ragtime band.

"Christ, Cathey didn't tell me we gotta teach these fuckers to fly, too!" Seal said referring to the Contras. "It was my initial understanding these guys would all be skilled pilots and all we had to do was teach them how to hit the fuckin' target, with a palletized load of supplies. I guess the truth of the matter is the fuckin' Nicaraguans don't have any pilots. Some fuckin' freedom fighters!"

Seal had unforeseen problems because the Agency had suddenly discovered that, like it or not, the CIA would have to create a "Contra Air Force" with people who had motivation but little else. And Cathey, a former infantry officer, either hadn't recognized this or he had kept the fact from Seal. These crews were needed desperately to reduce the CIA's exposure in case one of the supply planes was shot down. If that happened, Seal had warned, the crew "had better be beaners," so the world would not discover the Boland Amendment was being violated.

Seal desperately needed someone who knew FAA requirements for setting up an airport.

"Tell me about this airport you started in Oklahoma City," Seal said as he built his salad from the ice-filled bathtub that served as SOB's salad bar. "Especially the part about FAA licensing if you're near a vector airway."

From his conversations with Terry, Seal was now aware of Reed's prior involvement with a group of Oklahoma businessmen who had sought an FAA permit to build a private airstrip north of Oklahoma City. Seal had become concerned about FAA notification requirements and didn't want to be in violation of any FAA rules as this would bring immediate and unwanted attention to the training site.

"Better yet, why don't I just put you on board officially as an aviation consultant while I figure out exactly how you fit in to all this," Seal suggested.

"Sounds good to me. What do I need to do?" Terry replied as he loaded his plate with radishes.

1. *Arkansas Business,* December 17, 1990.
2. *Newsweek,* January 24, 1994.

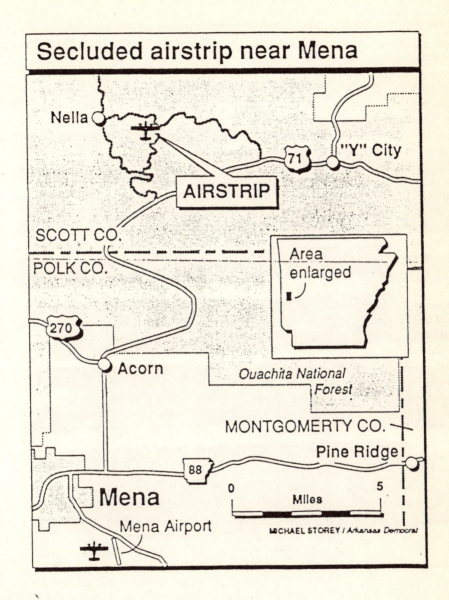

Secluded airstrip near Mena

Nella

"Y" City

71

AIRSTRIP

SCOTT CO.

POLK CO.

Area enlarged

270

Acorn

Ouachita National Forest

MONTGOMERY CO.

Pine Ridge

88

Mena

0   Miles   5

Mena Airport

MICHAEL STOREY / *Arkansas Democrat*

4-1. Map; above showing location of secret air training strip set up for CIA operations "Jade Bridge" and "Centaur Rose" by Reed and Barry Seal at Nella, in Western Arkansas. (Credit *Arkansas Democrat*).

ADMINISTRATIVE:

    The following investigation was conducted by
SA THOMAS W. ROSS at Polk County, Arkansas, on January 20,
1984:

4-2. Censored FBI report obtained by Terry Reed and his attorney Robert Meloni through
court discovery. The date of January 20, 1984 is significant in that Reed and Seal were
selecting the Nella site at precisely that time. Whatever the FBI's function was as the strip
went into operation remains hidden behind government black ink.

CHAPTER 5

GETTING OFF THE GROUND

"Bank tighter to the left. More! More! There it is, offa my left wing. What do ya think?" Barry Seal asked from the right seat of his Lear jet, N83JA.

It was a clear, cold January day in 1984 as Terry Reed and Seal circled a remote area of Western Arkansas at an altitude of 5,000 feet MSL (mean sea level). Terry, still somewhat uncomfortable piloting the high-performance jet, was concerned about the plane's stall speed as they exceeded 45 degrees of bank in order to bring the field Seal was referring to into view.

"OK, I got it now. It's definitely remote and I like the surrounding terrain. But does the topography look similar to Nicaragua?" Terry asked.

"Yeah. They'll love it. They'll think they're home," Seal answered, "Now, if we can just teach 'em to stuff an airplane into 2,500 feet without killing themselves, maybe uncle sugar will give us a big r-e-w-a-r-d! Let's go land at Mena and drive back up here to see how it looks from the ground."

Maps of the area below refer to it as the town of Nella. But only Rand-McNally—and God—know where it is for sure. (See chapter end.) It is not now, and never was, a town. In it's best days it was only a wide spot in the road, a road house, a stagecoach stopover point, a watering hole before entering the Oklahoma territory. The area reminded Reed and Seal of the movie *Deliverance*, where Burt Reynolds and a group of city slickers discover the beauty and danger of backwoods rural living while on an all male canoeing and camping trip.

The nearest town, about 12 miles to the south, is Mena, population 5,000. In describing Mena, a local law enforcement officer told one of the authors "If ya wanna pick up girls here, you gotta go to your family reunion." Seal had earlier selected this heavily-wooded location, along with two others, to be the possible site of the Agency's clandestine bivouacking and training area.

Terry had officially been on board the operation only two weeks. He and Seal were flying to Mena that day in order to have an engineering discussion with J.D. Brotherton, the president of Brodix Manufacturing and, on the way, Seal had wanted to show Terry the primary site he was considering. After the meeting at Brodix, which was to outline the computer-controlled machine tools necessary to produce the needed weapons parts, Terry and Seal attempted without success to drive to the Nella site. One thing they discovered: Security would not be a major problem if they chose the Nella site. It was almost impossible to find it on the ground, even with a map and compass.

But the two did eventually survey the area and conclude it would be a perfect training base, serviced only by primitive dirt roads maintained by the

United States Forest Service for fighting forest fires within the Ouachita National Forest and accessible safely only by four-wheel drive vehicles. They immediately identified that the mountainous terrain within the region would not only add realism to the flight training, but add danger as well.

Terry was instructed to return later to do a more thorough survey of all three sites, not only evaluating ground conditions, but—more importantly to Seal—to consider the strict FAA rules governing the airspace above the land. If the site was not selected properly, commercial aviation could be adversely affected and bring about unwanted FAA licensing requirements. Of concern to Terry was the ability to use ground based navigation aids already in place in Western Arkansas as a way to locate the field in inclement weather and at night. Seal initially had not paid enough attention to this.

It was now clear that the problems to be dealt with were increasing. On the flight back to Little Rock, Terry noted, "As I survey these sights, I should take into consideration the proficiency level of the pilots that'll be using the field. That surrounding terrain could be pretty dangerous, especially in bad weather. They still peel about a half a dozen flatlander pilots off of Rich Mountain every year."

Chuckling, Seal replied, "I got some good news and some bad news. The good news is Cathey says the beaners know how to fly single engine airplanes. The bad news? Barely."

This was becoming more and more like Richard Nixon's "Vietnamization" program, Terry thought. His mind drifted back to Thailand where, in 1973, the U.S. Air Force was tasked with trying to teach Vietnamese pilots not only to fly Mach 2, but to use such advanced western technology as the toilet. All within one life span. It was simply impossible to do, Terry had discovered first hand.

Seal's headquarters in Arkansas was based at Rich Mountain Aviation, situated in a brand new building at the southwest end of the Inter-Mountain Regional Airport in Mena. From there, Seal said he had based his aircraft refurbishing and retrofitting activities, another facet of his business activities.

Terry, familiar with the aviation world as he was, was impressed not only by the building, but the quality of the major airframe repair and modifications going on there. This was no backwoods operation, even though it was located in the backwoods.

Terry completed the surveys over the ensuing month during which time he met Seal's Mena "network" consisting primarily of Fred Hampton, Joe Evans and Emile Camp. Hampton, he was informed, was a second-generation fixed base operator who lived in the area and had operated Rich Mountain Aviation prior to Seal's arrival. But Terry could tell by Hampton's demeanor, that though he was the purported owner, he was not the man calling the shots. Seal called the new facility "my new building" when he toured it with Terry.

Evans, Seal had said, was an Air Force-trained, "cracker jack" aviation mechanic and the only man Seal truly trusted to work on his personal airplanes. It was clear that they went back together many years.

Camp was a pilot and a business associate of Seal's. Camp said he was involved with Seal in the purchase and sale of airplanes in Baton Rouge. Later Terry would learn that Seal and Camp had met originally in a Honduran jail, where they had both been incarcerated for drug trafficking. Both were from Louisiana. Neither seemed at the time to be anything other than prosperous businessmen. Terry and Camp were about the same age and immediately took a liking to each other.

By the following month, February, 1984, the first Boland Amendment was in effect and the Contras in the field in Central America were beginning to feel its impact. The little money Congress had appropriated for them was running out. National Security Advisor Robert (Bud) McFarlane would assign to Oliver North the job of "holding them (the Contras) together in body and in soul."[1] The CIA was obviously under tremendous pressure by the Reagan administration to get things going in Nella.

This was evidenced by Seal's demeanor at SOBs when he and Terry met that month. As the ragtime band played its last few bars of "Dixie" and the roar of the patrons died down, the two men at the corner table finished their dinner. Seal wolfed down the last of the three-dozen oysters, washed them down with a gulp of soda, belched, lifted himself slightly from his chair and passed gas.

Now for business. He pushed the plates aside and grabbed a paper napkin to use as stationary. He turned to Terry and said, "Okay, you're the high-powered aviation consultant, where in the hell are we gonna build this goddam airstrip? It's time for a decision. Our *friend* (the way Seal always referred to "Cathey") says we gotta come on line sooner than planned. So what's your decision? Adjacent to the federal land to the west or under the Hog-2 MOA?"

Reed and Seal had spent several laborious hours scanning the aviation charts, taking into account all the aeronautical considerations for site selection. The protected airspace above the Nella location, known in pilots circles as an MOA, made this site ideal. Combining that with the ability to pin point the area's location from inside the plane's cockpit by use of a LORAN (long range navigation) receiver, made the Nella location the best of the three potential candidates for the clandestine airfield.

Terry was prepared for Seal's question. After hours of research and field work, he had made his selection. "Our main considerations," he said, "should be security, a 'real-time' training environment and the logistics of bivouac. I vote for Nella."

Barry agreed that more rural than Nella, you couldn't get. He took the napkin and drew a diagram of general runway alignment and said, "You work up the LORAN (map) coordinates and I'll relay the info to Cathey."

With the decision on site location now made, the *black* operation "Jade Bridge" could begin. Prefabricated chicken houses would be erected in order to blend in with the countryside and to serve as makeshift barracks for the Contra trainees who would be brought in. Headquarters would be located in an old farmhouse already existing on the north end of the property. Construction would begin to greatly improve a grass landing strip which already existed and would ideally serve as a landing field and practice DGZ, or drop zone.

Terry knew that this would meet basic Air Force standards designated as the Bare Base Concept. He had, in fact, been attached to the 4th Tactical Fighter Wing in North Carolina that perfected the concept of operating a fighter wing unassisted in an extremely remote location.

The heavily-forested site at Nella provided shelter, water and enough level ground for aircraft operations. Seal was pleased with Terry's work and he said he was passing the good word up to Cathey about his new-found friend and asset.

During this period, Oliver North, who was still known only to Reed as John Cathey, was living up to his reputation for being "action oriented" and "bypassing red tape." CIA Director William Casey was, by now, his "teacher or philosophical mentor" to whom North looked regularly for help and advice. However, Clair George, then the CIA deputy director for operations, saw North as a man whose ideas often were extreme, "crazy" or "hare-brained."[2]

By viewing it through his personal prism, North was continuously interpreting President Reagan's September, 1983 finding (a Presidential decision), which outlined United States policy in Central America.

The finding sought to use military action only as a means to force a diplomatic settlement, not, as North viewed it, a de facto declaration of war against Nicaragua. In a memorandum to National Security Advisor Robert (Bud) McFarlane a month after the Nella start-up decision, North proposed significant military actions against the Sandinistas, the details of which are still classified under the guise of national security. The operations being implemented by Seal in 1984 were clearly part of North's scheme to win the conflict militarily.[3]

Several of these hare-brained schemes of North's may have been what Seal was getting Reed involved with in Arkansas. Seal would later confide to Reed that there were going to be two separate, compartmentalized operations based out of the Mena area. The one Terry was becoming sucked into, involving flight training and aerial delivery techniques, was code-named *"Jade Bridge"*. It's aircraft call sign was designated *"Boomerang"*. The second was the ferrying of large quantities of arms and munitions from Arkansas to staging areas in Central America. This tributary to the Agency cut-out was code named *"Centaur Rose"*, and its aircraft call sign was *"Dodger"*.

* * *

During March, Terry was working night and day. He had a business to run, but his heart was in the spook world. He worked late into many nights preparing a training outline similar to the one used in the Vietnamization program and based upon the anticipated skill level of the pilots that were to be trained. Often Janis would wake up in the middle of the night to find her husband at work at his desk. She marveled at his ability to exist on three or four hours of sleep a night and his ceaseless high-energy level.

Seal knew that there were at least two other pilot training sites in place in the continental United States. His knowledge led him to inform Terry that the students the Nella facility was to receive would be recent graduates from the other two sites. They would have basic piloting skills that would allow them to fly single-engine aircraft in soft instrument conditions (marginally bad weather). Once in operation, Nella would upgrade the students to multi-engine status and teach them air-drop techniques.

But all was not rosy for Terry. There were problems developing in the Ultra-Light industry. Another company producing these sport airplanes had just been hit with a major liability judgment running into millions of dollars. As a result, the insurance companies underwriting the liability for this industry were getting skittish. Terry's backers, like Ward, were becoming nervous. It was their deep pockets that plaintiffs could reach into if their firm suffered a similar misfortune.

Until April 1, 1984, Command Aire had taken all the necessary legal steps to prepare itself for customer-related aviation accidents, but not for what happened that day. April Fool's day took on a new meaning for Terry as he lay in the dirt and rubble next to his totally-destroyed Ultra-Light. The accident had taken place southwest of Little Rock on Seth Ward's Triple-S Ranch. As an ambulance raced across the field toward him, Terry, fully conscious, frantically tried to dislodge himself from the wreckage, fearful of a fire from the spilled fuel.

While testing a customer's plane the brand new engine had "seized" in flight and Terry had been unable to glide back to the open field. He crashed in the woods among 60-foot high pine trees. His right foot was crushed on impact. He was taken to St. Vincent's Hospital in Little Rock where he underwent emergency surgery lasting more than eight hours.

After the surgery, doctors informed Terry that if circulation did not properly return, the foot might have to be amputated. Due to his stubbornness and overly-cautious attitude toward addictive drugs, he refused to take any painkillers and lay awake suffering miserably in a cold sweat, reliving all the dangers he had faced in his life. He brought up memories of his childhood, when he built and raced go-carts, had grown into motorcycles, and his two years in Southeast Asia without a scratch during more than 2,000 hours of flight time. He had, he thought, been a lucky man. But now he had almost "bought the farm" from a freak accident while doing something unimportant. As he writhed in agony, his life took on a new meaning and he began to philosophize about life and death and about the Contras who were willing to lay down their lives for a cause.

Janis stepped softly into his room and found her husband semi-delirious from the pain. "You know you made all the local news shows," she whispered. "I guess when they called the ambulance, someone said there had been a plane crash. The news dispatcher envisioned a 747 rather than a single engine plane. The place was swarming with camera crews."

He grimaced even more. The last thing a good pilot wants is to "plane crash" in the headlines.

"How's Duncan? He saw me crash?"

"I think he's a little too upset. He's telling everyone his daddy's foot has a boo-boo. He's got his doll, Archie, in a cast. Actually, poor Archie is in a body cast and he looks a lot worse than you do. When I called my parents to tell them about the crash, my mother about fainted, she was so upset. But when I called your mother, do you know what she said? She said 'well, he's been too lucky too long.' Of course, she caught the next bus out of town and is on her way down to take care of you. Can you believe the difference in mothers? Mine raised two daughters and yours raised six kids.....listen to me," she said abruptly as her voice broke, "I'm just rambling. Dammit I'm so mad at you. I was so scared."

Janis started sobbing as she laid her head on his chest. "Do you know you almost got killed? You could be dead right now. Duncan almost lost his father. I had to sit in that waiting room all night, not knowing how you were, or if they were going to cut your leg off."

Terry interrupted. "Janis, listen to me. Calm down. I have to talk to you."

He told her he had made a decision, that he wanted her to be part of it and to understand—to try and understand—what he was trying to deal with. He finally realized that he was mortal. And he wanted to use his life for something significant, something more than money. The most significant thing he could think of was getting deeply involved in the Contra cause. If he had to die, he wanted to die for a cause.

The military cadet from Carthage had been resurrected.

Two days later, Terry looked up from his bed and saw Seal standing beside him. "Hey partner, you almost bought the fuckin' farm, huh? Janis tells me your heart's bruised and almost dislodged. Did ya go down makin' decisions, or did you freeze?" This is what pilots always want to know, wondering what they will do when the time comes."

"I got an opportunity to sorta prove myself...to myself, Barry. Yeah, I was thinkin' all the way down all right. But, most important to me was I flyin' all the way to the ground instead of freezin'...or prayin' to God. I was analyzing my options and acting on them all the fucking way to impact. I think my old instructor, John Brown, would be proud, if he knew. Don't laugh, but I'd like to think I performed as if I had 'the right stuff'."

Seal had sat down next to the bed and the two talked seemingly for hours about life and death, causes and the rest. They even discovered something more they had in common and had not realized. They both had the same birthday, July 16th.

"Barry, I've come to a decision. I want in. Full time. This may sound stupid, but, if I die, I want to die for something important and I think the Contra cause is important."

"You're hired...again."

Terry had made his pact and he was at peace with himself.

Over the course of the next three months, Terry underwent two more operations, rehabilitation and he even designed and built his own cast support from Ultra-Light parts.

"What's that noise," Janis wondered as she walked in the door from work one afternoon. In the kitchen she found Duncan sliding around in his Big Bird house shoes amidst a cloud of white dust, "Snow mommy, it's snowing in the kitchen, watch me skate in the snow!", he shrieked.

She was flabbergasted by the sight of her husband with his foot propped up on a chair and his saber saw in his hands. He was cutting his cast off.

"You're supposed to leave it on six more weeks. What's Dr. Blankenship going to say?"

"Hey I know how things work," Terry barked. "Our bodies are like machines, and I know machines. The way I have it figured, if I saw the top part of this cast off and put this rubber tip on my heel I can exert my full body weight on my heel, and, by constructing the foot support properly, I will exercise my damaged foot muscles each time I walk. I'm getting rid of my crutches and building this brace. It makes perfect engineering sense."

"All right Dr. Reed, it's *your* foot," she answered. "But you'd better not bitch about pain or come to me for sympathy. I'm tired of hearing you moan in your sleep. I think you're a terrible patient. I'm going to start taking your pain pills if you don't, just to make living with you more tolerable."

"Come on, it's not so bad," he joked. "At least we get to park in handicap parking, don't we? The orthopedic surgeon told me I'm his first survivor of a foot injury of this magnitude. He wants to send my X-rays on a nationwide tour to all the medical schools. Maybe we'll get royalties."

"You are the eternal optimist," she said unable to hold back a smile.

The crash had temporarily removed him from his Ultra-Light business, but

Terry had spent most of his recuperation time working on the Contra flight training outline. He had made his decision to divest himself of the Ultra-Light company, something that did not make Seth Ward and his other partners happy. But the spook world again had his interest and the accident would be the perfect excuse to extricate himself from the business.

June 11th was Janis' birthday and Terry's gift to her was making it has last day in the Ultra-Light business. She was happy about this because she didn't like her husband working with Ward.

She had grown to dislike the man intensely due to his overbearing ways and his tendency to siphon off the desperately-needed company cash flow to satisfy his insatiable greed. He was a millionaire, but, inside his head, he was still the poor boy from "Dogtown," or North Little Rock, who needed to reinforce his ability to get the best of people in business deals. This was the way some Little Rock businessmen said Ward had made his fortune, by screwing his business partners. Janis considered him the ultimate bigot and sexist.

He had been a Marine fighter pilot in World War II and said he had flown with the famous "Pappy" Boyington and his "Black Sheep" squadron in the South Pacific. His favorite saying was: "Pappy was a pussy."

Ward was tall, 6'4', and gruff. But he could ooze charm when he wanted something from you. He would admit privately to Terry that he made his fortune by suing out-of-state companies for violating Arkansas' usury law, or its cap on interest. He had a reputation for using the legal system to his advantage. He was disliked by his neighbors and had only one true friend that Terry knew of. And Seth wasn't above trying to take advantage of him, financially. And the one running legal interference for him was none other than his son-in-law, Webb Hubbell, a former Chicago Bear tackle, a member of the Rose Law Firm and now a high-ranking official of the Justice Department. Terry and Ward split with bad blood between them.

On June 12th, Seal picked Terry up in Little Rock and flew him to Mena. Ground work on the field at Nella was about to start and drainage was a prime concern. Seal borrowed a pickup truck from Hampton, drove to Nella and both men "walked the field" to make one last inspection before the bulldozers started. Terry, actually, "limped the field."

While photographing the field from a knoll east of it, Seal turned to Terry and asked: "You want to be an instructor? I've hired a guy from Tulsa and another's coming down from Nebraska. Between them and Camp, that'll make four if you're on board. But I shit you not, this is gonna be dangerous. You told me that you love to fly at night, and I could easily work you in to the night schedule if you're interested. You want it?"

"Does the Pope shit in the woods? Is a bear Catholic?"

Terry had now entered another loop. He was no longer just a consultant, he was now embarked on a course he had set in his hospital bed. He had committed himself and there would be no turning back.

As they flew back that day, it was briefing time again. Seal began by saying the job came with some perks. "We'll find you an airplane and part of our deal is you can keep it over in Little Rock. Consider it a company car. Evans will perform all your maintenance at Rich Mountain and he will have a secret source of bulk fuel for you to use, so that you won't be running up traceable fuel bills. The guy from Tulsa will be in charge of scheduling. He has created a perfect cover, which all the instructors are to use. If anyone asks you who you're training, just tell them you're a contract instructor with Ross Aviation and working in their foreign student department."

Ross Aviation was a real company in Tulsa, Oklahoma, about 100 miles west of Mena. In addition to being a contract cargo firm, it operated a major flight training program and had a large foreign student enrollment. Its foreign student pilots, and those of another Tulsa aviation school, Spartan, literally filled the skies in this region during training, primarily in Cessna 150s. Many of their students were from the Middle East and Mexico. This would be a perfect cover for the Nella instructors since many of the Ross instructors were hired on a contract basis. Air traffic controllers would think nothing of hearing a panicky student screaming in a foreign tongue during a moment of stress.

"Have I left anything out?" Seal asked.

"What about communications? Surely, I don't use my home phone for scheduling, do I?"

"Oh I forgot. As soon as we land I'll take you by OSI and I'll introduce you to Aki."

"Aki? That sounds Japanese."

The fat man grinned. "It is. He's a slope."

Back in Little Rock, both men got into Terry's car and headed for 1217 Rebsamen Park Road, near the Arkansas River and within view of the State Capitol Building. The building was a nondescript, single-story building with rough wood siding situated next door to a pizza parlor. Aki Sawahata and his company, Overseas International (OSI), occupied the south half of the building.

Sawahata, neatly-dressed in a business suit, quickly closed a door at the end of the building as Seal and Terry walked in. Not knowing Terry, Sawahata clearly did not want the stranger to see whatever was in the room.

Terry was surprised and amused when Sawahata handed him a business card with his firm's acronym OSI, which to intelligence people meant Office of Special Investigations, the military equivalent of the CIA.

"*Ohio, guizmas?*" Terry was mustering up his best Japanese.

"You speak Japanese?" Sawahata asked amazed.

"Just enough to keep foreign nationals guessing," Terry grinned.

"In that case, I'll correct your Japanese. It's afternoon, so it's *konichiwa*."

"Well, in Southeast Asia, I always lived for *kumbawa* (night). That's when you go to town and play with the girls," Seal chimed in.

Sawahata was smiling. He seemed to be taking an immediate liking to Terry.

Seal, who made the formal introductions, suggested going to a local oriental restaurant where they could talk without being overheard by Sawahata's two employees. Terry was learning how modern intelligence works. Real companies, doing real business, are used for cover—just like the Mafia.

The firm had filed its incorporation papers with the Arkansas Secretary of State's office only three months earlier, on February 29, 1984. The papers listed as its officers Sawahata and a man identified as James Robinson of Clinton, Arkansas. Its ostensible business was developing trade for American companies wishing to conduct business with Japan.

Sawahata told Terry that the firm was set up primarily to export bulky commodities, preferably raw materials, back to Japan. In his words, the ships from Japan come over full and often return empty. His job was to fill the returning ships with cargo Japan needed. Arkansas had some of the resources his company was shipping: pulpwood, bauxite, and rice.

Terry later learned that wasn't all Overseas International was shipping. The tea-break that afternoon at Fu Lin's, the Chinese restaurant at 320 S. Victory, near the State Capitol Building, centered on communications.

"Now this is a little sensitive since CIA agents aren't supposed to be operating in the U.S.," Seal uttered in a guarded tone. "But Aki here is the Agency's resident guy. All three of us have a common *friend*. From your point of view, Terry, Aki's your secure communications link. He has all the radio gear at his office. We'll all communicate through him. That way, since he's local, you won't have any long distance phone charges on your phone over ta Mena."

While Terry was still absorbing all this newly passed information, Seal added. "While we're talkin' about phones, do not ever, ever, ever use any of the pay phones in Mena. They're all bugged."

"How do you know?", Terry asked.

"I had Aki have em' bugged, for security reasons... let's just say we're huntin' for a mole. Get it?"

Terry knew to ask no further about the "mole". He knew what the term meant and assumed Seal and Sawahata were concerned about having a double agent in their midst. He cleared his mind of that eerie thought and got back to what was said earlier about secure communications.

Terry could see the beauty of the setup. He could contact Sawahata by local phone, and then would have no need to call anyone else. The Agency had taken care of communications security, it appeared, but he was curious if they used telephone lines or air waves.

"What kind of communications capability do you have? Just so I'll know," Terry asked Sawahata. "I mean, is it secure? And can you talk on aircraft frequencies?"

"Aki can communicate with God and the devil can't even jam him," Seal answered. That was all Terry needed to know.

"So, Terry-san, Barry tells me you know quite a bit about manufacturing. I find that very interesting," Sawahata said. "It is something I do not know very much about. And Company has tasked me with some oversight in this area. Maybe you could assist me if I get it cleared from higher up."

"Aki, I already took Terry to Brodix," Seal said. "And I told him about Iver Johnson's." Sawahata appeared uneasy. This had been a major breach of security. Seal had revealed the formation of the arms manufacturing network, without getting approval from Cathey. And Sawahata, the local man in charge, now was learning for the first time that Terry had been brought into a loop for which he had not been cleared.

Terry was already realizing that things were being run on the sloppy side, not the way things were done in Air Force Intelligence. There, no one was ever brought into a loop for which he was not specifically cleared. And the person had to have an absolute need to know.

"From operational point of view, Terry, I will be your primary contact from this point on," Sawahata said. "Mr. Seal is out of state a lot, so from now on just consider me your boss. I'm glad to have you with us. You come highly recommended by Mr. Cathey."

What Terry didn't know then—and what Sawahata didn't say, was that Seal had something else to do for the Agency, something that had become more urgent and immediate—priority *numero uno*. Seal, who knew how to always tell "the suits" what they wanted to hear, had done just that.

Seal had passed on to them that the Sandinistas were dirty, and providing the Medellin Cartel with safe haven and a trans-shipment point for mega-loads of cocaine heading north to America. Just what the White House needed to convince a recalcitrant Congress to approve military aid for the Contras. As Seal spoke that day in Little Rock with Terry and Sawahata, the CIA was getting ready to equip his C-123K military cargo plane called "The Fat Lady" for a sting to ensnare the Sandinistas.

On the way back to Sawahata's office, Terry saw a problem that had not been discussed. "Barry, when I get my new airplane, where am I suppose to base it? I bring this up because there is no private hangar space available here in Little Rock."

"For the time being, I've made a deal with Little Rock Air Center. I've got an old friend over there I can lean on for you. They only have tie down space available for now, though. And we will need better facilities, once this thing is fully operational."

Sawahata injected: "I went out to North Little Rock Airport recently and saw some private hangars under construction. Maybe you can get one of those."

"Yeah, that would be great. I still need a place to store my Ultra-Light, too," Terry said.

Seal winced. "Wasn't one brush with death in one of those crazy things good enough for ya?"

"Hey, you know us pilots. Calculated risk takers, isn't that what you say?"

After dropping off Sawahata, and on the way to the airport, Seal took the opportunity to give Terry some cautionary advice. "Hey, I know you're all gung-ho on this. But if I were you, I would go slow," Seal said. "There's no guarantee here on how long this may last. For all we know, Cathey could get his way and the fuckin' Marines could invade Nicaragua tomorrow. This whole Mena thing could come to an end before it even gets started. In other words, I wouldn't consider this a fulltime job. I wouldn't want to see you and Janis hurt economically."

Terry understood that assets had no GS rating, nor did he want one. He had cashed his last government paycheck when he left the Air Force and vowed then never to collect one again.

With that in mind, he told Sawahata he wanted to "volunteer" for the night shift at Mena and do his training under cover of darkness, always his favorite time to fly. The other instructors had no problem with that, since that was the most dangerous time to fly in mountainous terrain.

This would also give him the daytime hours to stay active as a machine-tool consultant. A good cover, he thought.

1.   Testimony of Oliver North, *Hearings*, 100-7, Part I, 7/7/87, p. 54
2.   *Ibid*, 7/13/87, p. 40
3.   Memo by North/Constantine Menges, 10/19/83, subject "Special Operations: Nicaragua."

CHAPTER 6

AMERICA'S BANANA REPUBLIC

The black C-130 military cargo plane banked into a perilous 60-degree descending turn as the pilot maneuvered to align the giant transport for the final approach to Mena.

The craft went full flaps as the pilot pushed full left rudder, putting the plane into a right forward slip, descending rapidly toward it's target, the threshold of the 5,000-foot runway 17.

It was an unorthodox maneuver for a plane of that size and as Terry Reed kept his vision locked on the approaching craft, he remarked to Joe Evans who was standing nearby, "This damn July temperature is just like Southeast Asia. The hotdog pilot in the 130 better watch the density altitude at this elevation. He's flying like he was trained by Air America!"

Though Terry didn't know it at the time, that was precisely the case. He did not recognize the elderly pilot initially. It had been 14 years since their farewells in Thailand. He was about to be reunited with Bill Cooper.

When the cargo ramp descended and the shrill whine of the turbines spooled down, neither Terry nor the other three waiting instructors were quite prepared for the 20 ragtag Nicaraguan "Freedom Fighters" who walked down to the tarmac. By this time in the afternoon on July 8, 1984, the ramp had been heated to frying-pan temperatures by the sun over Arkansas.

Evans turned to Terry. "Yeah," the mechanic with the weather-beaten face said. "Barry tells me most of these pilots they're gonna use down there in Central America are ex-Air America cowboys. I guess your job is to lasso these young mavericks and teach them how to fly heavy iron. I sure don't envy you guys. Just look at 'em."

Terry was shocked. Somehow, he had expected to see soldiers with bloused pant legs, combat boots and berets. Instead what straggled off the C-130 were men in blue jeans, mismatched colors and Adidas and Nike sneakers. They looked like they had just left a blue-light special at K-Mart.

The only commonality in their "uniform" appeared to be their Levi jeans, some stonewashed, some not, and their Sporty's Pilot Shop private pilot flight kits. Rayban sun glasses adorned their faces, as if they were hoping to emulate the look of the stereotypical super-macho Latino pilot. It triggered in Terry's "stress syndrome" a flashback to Vietnamization where Laotian men stood wearing Raybans and brand new flight suits while picking their noses up to the second knuckle.

"Fuck," exclaimed Evans. "*I* don't even have Raybans!"

The arriving students were quickly moved out of the Sunday afternoon's heat and into the Rich Mountain hangar while the plane's other occupants sat about their assigned tasks. Although Terry would not learn Richard Brenneke's name—or the purpose of his trip—until later, he appeared to be a member of the crew and the person responsible for the skid-mounted cargo that was off-loaded into another Rich Mountain hanger. What the crates contained was not discussed, but seemed to be important nevertheless.*

Why had they all come to Arkansas?

Because of the Boland Amendment—or to be precise, the three Boland Amendments passed in varying form. The legal force of these amendments, attached to Congressional-approved appropriation bills that Reagan was forced to sign into law, is still being debated by scholars. They were intended to bar direct military aid to the Contras training *in Central America* by U.S. government personnel. But by dissecting the fine print, North and Agency attorneys apparently decided that having the military *loan* the equipment to this operation—run by contract employees *in the United States*—was not a violation.

Why North and the CIA undertook this operation in Arkansas to circumvent the Boland Amendment was clearly because they were barred by law from doing it themselves. But before they could establish *when and where* they wanted to set up the operation, they first had to define *what* they wanted to do there. They then had to decide *who* would be their proxy. And implementing the *"how"* would depend on their skewed legal interpretation that use of non-government personnel, or contract employes, would not be a Boland violation.

The CIA knew *what* had to be done. The Nicaraguans desperately needed skilled flight crews that could resupply ground troops engaged in a highly-mobile guerrilla war where resupply can be accomplished only with air drops. This was being done with American contract crews who were at great risk of being exposed if they were shot down and captured.

In deciding *where* to locate the training base, a map of the United States is needed. Initially, all perimeter states, or border and coastal states, must be eliminated because of the concentration of federal law enforcement and coastal defense agencies such as the Coast Guard, the Air Force, the Navy, the FBI, the Drug Enforcement Administration and U.S. Customs.

From what is left, a state must be chosen. It has to be rural, under-populated and have terrain similar to Nicaragua's. It should also be a state with a political mind set similar to the banana republics that the CIA operates so successfully in. It must possess the right political environment and political power base that would view the Agency as a "welcomed industry" and a way to enrich itself while picking up a "political marker" from Washington for a future favor. In short, an accomplice.

Arkansas was the only state that qualified perfectly in each category. And the icing on the cake was the fact that Arkansas already had become the dumping ground for federal facilities no other state wanted, such as the U.S. Army

---

* Brenneke would later testify that most of the crates contained weapons and other gear to be used in the training program. He would also say that he found cocaine in some of the crates and while on the ground at Mena, called Donald Gregg, then Vice President George Bush's chief of staff, and complained about the drugs. He quoted Gregg later as saying that was none of his business. Brenneke later claimed his role in this affair was that of a money-launderer for the Agency, that he worked out of Panama where the flight had originated and that he had just thumbed a ride on the flight.[1]

chemical weapons plant in Pine Bluff and the nuclear storage area in Pea Ridge.

So here they were, finally, in Mena. As the students dragged their B-4 bags into the sweltering hangar, the whole scene was reminiscent of in-processing procedures at Don Muang International Airport in Bangkok, Thailand, where all GIs first arrived for their in-country tour of duty in Southeast Asia. The only thing missing was a bevy of oriental hookers waving through the fences at this latest load of "raw meat" arriving from "the world."

The arriving "Freedom Fighters" dropped their gear and were drawn immediately to the white Cessna 404 up on jacks, with its cowlings and inspection plates removed. They were peering with awe and curiosity into the plane's crevices, realizing that, if they "made the grade", this would be the type of plane they'd be flying.

The sleek, twin-engine craft was exposing its internal engineering marvels inherited from the factory in Wichita, Kansas. The plane was considered a "cabin class" aircraft since it had an "air-stair" or clam-shell door on the left rear side that allowed passengers to board by climbing the self-contained staircase. The seating arrangement in this particular plane had six seats in the rear and a "cabin" up front for the pilot and co-pilot. With the large internal cargo area and "potty" in the aft area, this plane appeared gargantuan compared to the light single-engine aircraft in which the students had been trained. It must have made them feel unsure of ever having the ability to master such a large craft.

The instrument panel, which contained a full set of gauges for both pilot and co-pilot, housed twin air speed indicators showing the plane capable of speeds of up to 237 knots. The fuel-injected and turbo-charged Continental engines could propel the plane to altitudes above 25,000 feet. To them this was the ultimate challenge.

Terry entered the hangar along with Emile Camp and the other two flight instructors, pseudonymed "Nebraska" and "Oklahoma."

The man who appeared to be in charge called the wandering group together for in-processing. It was not unlike that first day in Bangkok, filling out forms listing next-of-kin and being briefed on the essentials such as mail deliveries from Central America.

The majority of the briefing was conducted by an Hispanic dressed in fatigues and known only to the flight instructors as "Diego," the "temporary field commander" on loan from Panama who had the bearing and attitude of an experienced military drill instructor and professed to be an ex-helicopter pilot.

"Take those fuckin' sunglasses off, soldiers!" he shouted at the motley crew of trainees, who appeared to be worn out from their flight. He informed them that the four men standing behind him were the "contract instructors" who would teach them advanced flying techniques, and, in particular, aerial resupply procedures they would use in combat—if they measured up and didn't wash out.

Diego then joined the students as the instructors were asked to introduce themselves and recap briefly their individual aviation backgrounds. The students were then given copies of the Cessna 414 information manual, which, for the purpose of their classroom work, would become their "bible." They were told to memorize it from cover to cover and be prepared at any time to answer questions based on its content.

A brief outline of the aviation curriculum was discussed and they were told that it would be the instructors' job to upgrade them to multi-engine aircraft, giving them the ability to fly safely in the more advanced 400 series-style aircraft.

Once that was accomplished, they would be taught aerial delivery procedures and how to apply these techniques in a hostile environment, meaning when someone was shooting at them from either the ground or air with a combination of both small arms fire or missiles or, even worse, from interceptor aircraft.

The four instructors, who by now knew each other fairly well, were working from lesson plans they had developed which capitalized on their particular expertise and strengths.

A key lesson learned from Vietnam was the need for an expert ground controller at the infantry-company level, whose job was to coordinate the delivery safely from the ground. In other words, he became "air traffic control" in the field and in many cases the success of a mission depended on him.

In this first class of 20, four men were there to become these ground controllers. The U.S. Army had developed this joint training technique where controllers train with flight crews to learn what a pilot has to contend with during these maneuvers.

By now, the skid-mounted cargo containing the field equipment and weapons had been brought into the hangar and each man was given his issue and told to board the white, one-ton Chevy grain truck presently backing into the hangar. The six-foot high sideboards of the truck would shield the occupants from view as they headed for nearby Nella. The only thing that might have seemed odd to the local residents that day occurred when Ramon Vanardos, the truck driver and the man assigned to be the local "supply sergeant," stopped later at a local fast-food joint and ordered 60 cheeseburgers and 60 orders of fries—"to go."

Terry and the other instructors followed in his S-10 Chevy Blazer as the truck turned off U.S. Highway 71 nine miles north of Mena and west of what is called "Y" City. The truck could barely negotiate portions of the narrow dirt road maintained for the U.S. Forest Service to fight fires in that area of the Ouachita National Forest.

The students were being tossed about the truck bed as the vehicle forded Clear Fork, one of the creek beds running off the Belle Fourche River. "Oklahoma," one of the flight instructors in Terry's blazer, noted, "God, I wish we could take pictures of all this. No one's ever gonna believe this happened after it's all over. Surely the government's gonna invade Nicaragua before we get these guys trained, don't ya think?"

Terry answered, "Yeah, I'm sure you're right. Based on what I've seen we have to work with, we're only gonna need five years to get these guys up to speed." Everyone laughed. The worst was yet to come.

What is called Nella is nothing more than a wider place in the dirt road, an intersection in the woods six miles from the highway. About a mile and a half east from the intersection, after passing the Shiloh Country Church, was the 109-acre property to be used for the practice drop zone and training base.

Local property records show that the land had been purchased in October, 1982, at about the time Barry Seal first arrived in Mena and set up his operational headquarters at Rich Mountain Aviation. Though Seal put up most if not all the money for the land, about $50,000, Fred Hampton and his wife were listed as the nominal purchasers. Hampton, the fixed base operator at Rich Mountain, suddenly began to deposit large amounts of cash in his bank during this period, after being on the verge of bankruptcy only a few years earlier.

The land was an ideal training site. It bordered huge reserves of heavily-forested federal land to the southeast and northwest. Just about anyone could operate with impunity. Forest rangers were told by their superiors to stay out of this area except in extreme emergencies and to ignore activities that were military related. Terry was told by Seal that U.S. Army Special Forces personnel stationed 30 miles to the north at Fort Chaffee, who were on continuous maneuvers in the area, provided security by "shadowing" the site. The soldiers, unofficially, would "co-mingle" with the students during maneuvers and war games and be bivouacking near enough to fend off any wandering campers or peering eyes. What Seal had neglected to tell Terry, but he would later learn, was the "shadows" had shadows—in the form of the FBI.

The only thing that would have seemed strange to anyone wandering into the area was the new and expansive barbed wire fencing, anchored to steel posts, strung around the site. The poverty-stricken farmers in the area used only homemade wooden fence posts that they cut themselves from the surrounding forest.

There was other "security," too—in many ways the best that money could buy. Seal confided to Terry that the people who lived in the area had been "purchased," and would be getting "government subsidies" that didn't originate from the Agriculture Department. In other words, they were paid to see, hear and speak no evil of the Agency's operation.

As Varnados' truck made a right turn and headed south into the property, it passed the dilapidated old farm house that had been converted to mask a training headquarters and command post. This was Varnados' home. He told anyone who might ask that he was living there as a caretaker. Behind the house was a satellite dish and a steel mast supporting an antenna similar to what a ham radio operator would use. Via satellite, Akihide Sawahata in Little Rock could talk to this facility on a secure frequency, as could the training aircraft.

"This is neat. Who would guess this old farmhouse is packed with state-of-the-art communications gear?" said Nebraska, a former Special Forces officer, as Terry's Blazer slowly went by and angled down a hill behind the house toward three brand new Butler-style, pre-fabricated chicken houses.

These weren't your normal gabled roof, sheet metal chicken houses, a common site in Arkansas, home of Tyson's chicken. However, the scene captured the image that prompted H. Ross Perot to call it "the Chicken State" when he was running for the Presidency. These were actually high-tech portable barracks. Camouflaged to look like chicken houses, two were living quarters and one was used for a classroom. One of the two used for quarters also housed the latrine and mess hall. All consumables, such as food, were government issue and supplied from Fort Chaffee.

In addition to having plumbing and electricity, they were fully insulated and built on temporary wooden foundations, not the usual concrete. They were heated and cooled by portable military climate control units, which were mounted externally. An equipment shed behind the farmhouse sheltered the portable military generators and lighting equipment that would be used to guide the aircraft toward the field for simulated night airdrops. Also housed there was the Ford Cub tractor that towed the military trailer containing a 400-gallon tank where fuel for the generators was stored.

Within view of the complex, farther down the hill, one could see that what had been a pasture was now a usable landing strip. The 2,300-foot north-south runway area had been sodded and additional drainage provided to carry off the water resulting from the expected summer torrential rains. Varandos had recently mowed the strip with a belly-mower attached to the tractor's under-carriage and the hay that had been planted along the edges of the strip was ready to be harvested. On the west side of the field was a camouflage netted area suitable for aircraft parking.

Truly, the CIA had thought of everything. The Agency had at its disposal all the modern, air-transportable equipment similar to the type that the American public would discover years later as it watched "Operation Desert Storm" un-fold on television. Nothing had been left to chance. They were bivouacked!

The students had been told to dig in for a four-month intense training pro-gram. It would not only include flight training, which they looked forward to with excitement, but a continuation of basic ground combat training to trans-form the trainees into spit-and-polish soldiers. This they hated.

"Diego" was the drill instructor. His job was to continue basic military train-ing and discipline. After deboarding from the truck's cab, and in typical mili-tary fashion, he ordered the men out of the truck and into their "barracks". They were instructed to "return looking like soldiers" for a briefing in the "class-room."

The four instructors waiting in the classroom were now somewhat taken aback as the students were transformed by having shed their slovenly civilian attire and replaced it with military-looking, sanitized GI jungle fatigues.

The students, they had been told, were the children of the Central American elite, people who had seen their property and businesses seized by the Sandinistas. To them, the Sandinistas were simply communists taking orders from Moscow and Havana.

"*Boland es un Communista,*" the students would chant while double-timing in formation, a phrase to be taught to them by their permanent drill instructor who had not yet arrived from El Salvador.

It was apparent to Terry that whatever else the U.S. government and others might have been doing, they had certainly taken the trainees' blind hatred of communism to a new level. They had gotten their "minds right" on the issue of motivation. Having studied the psychology of learning in the Air Force's Lead-ership Academy and again during FAA Flight Instructor training, Reed consid-ered them over-hyped and, therefore, overconfident and dangerous, consider-ing the training they were facing.

The *first* thing he would have to do was, just as the flight instructors manual said, "*gain their confidence.*" He realized in order to accomplish that objective he would initially be forced to show them what they *didn't* know about flying. He had to convert them from their "*overly confident state*" and return them to one of "*being receptive to the learning process.*" In other words, the instructors decided, they would scare the hell out of the students once they were in the air.

The trainees seated themselves at the metal tables placed in rows in front of the four instructors.

What ensued was a classified, detailed briefing of the training program and what was expected of the students to successfully complete the course. Each instructor, in turn, told the students what aspect of the aviation program he was responsible for and why he had been recruited for this covert program.

They were made aware of the fact that "Oklahoma" was actively involved with an international flight training school licensed by the Federal Aviation Administration and would train them from the same FAR 141 curriculum. The students appeared elated and honored that they would have to meet stringent American "airman-check" procedures and would be learning something that they could use the rest of their lives—if they lived through the dangerous multi-engine training.

"Oklahoma" addressed them: "I don't speak Spanish. And I hope that's not a problem. But my first task will be to test all of you on basic single-engine and FAA regulation knowledge in order to determine your level of proficiency before advancing to the multi-engine course. In other words, view me as your hurdle to flying the twin-engine plane you saw in the hangar today. I will be your check pilot as you advance throughout your training."

It was clear Oklahoma was by-the-book and brought to the program the necessary FAA "attitude." The students, recently graduated from their single-engine instrument curriculum conducted elsewhere in the U.S., knew what a check-pilot was. They immediately identified Oklahoma as "Mr. Chicken Shit." He would allow no deviation from the rules.

Nebraska was next. He produced the training materials prepared for Phase I of their flight training. A realization of the written work that would be involved brought a collective groan . As he distributed the stacks of booklets, he briefed them in a very military, monotone voice.

"I taught helicopter flying for the U.S. Army during Vietnam. My style is to pretty much follow the Army's method of instruction. If you don't stay up with your ground school work, you're fucking grounded. Diego will administer all ground material to you and I fully expect all assignments to be completed on schedule or you simply don't fly. If you do not maintain the required 70 percentile passing grade for each phase, you are permanently grounded and you will be sent home. Any questions?"

From his military bearing and emotionless style of his delivery he was readily identifiable. He was Chicken Shit No.2 in both the air and on the ground.

Emile Camp was next. His Louisiana drawl wowed them.

"I just want y'all to be good pilots and the kind of students that I'm proud to sign off as havin' schooled under me. I'm sure ya'll will work hard so we can getcha flyin' that twin-engine Cessna on one engine in bad weather and full of bullet holes, with proficiency. My job, besides flyin' with ya and gettin' ya up ta multi-motor speed, is ta keep ya in good airplanes. And as ya know, we've selected the 400 series Cessna to be the airplane ya'll be 'type-rated' in for the purpose of graduation. After that, you'll be upgraded to the Beech 18 if we have one available, and if ya can handle a tail-dragger."

By his laid back style, it was obvious that Camp was a likeable guy, a noticeable dichotomy between him and the previous two men they had heard.

Then came Terry. He initially spoke in Spanish, which they clearly enjoyed.

"La solamente cosa que yo amor a mas de avuelta es una muchacha bonita sin ropas y con pequenas nalgas." (The only thing I love more than flying is a beautiful, young, naked woman with a small ass). This evoked cheers and catcalls.

"Do you guys think you have the 'right stuff'?" Terry asked, once the macho commotion settled down. "Well I'm your primary night instructor, and I'm going to teach you all about the 'fright stuff.'" Some of those who hadn't yet mastered the subtleties of the English language required a moment of interpretation from fellow students. Then, again there was laughter. Terry continued.

"But, in all seriousness, I like flying at night, which is how I trained for the majority of my ratings. Therefore, I have volunteered to be your nighttime instructor. That does not mean I am *loco*. Multi-engine flying is demanding, but it should also be fun. This course will be very dangerous, especially the night training, and I will demand nothing short of excellence from all of you. But, it is my style to let you fly the airplane from hour one. You will learn nothing by me flying the plane for you. I already *know* how to fly it. My job is to *teach* you. I admire your motivation for volunteering and I will do my best to help you liberate your country. Any questions?"

The student nearest the front of the class, who had been focusing on the "prosthesis" Terry had built to keep from using crutches, asked, "What happened to your foot?"

"I crashed an airplane on April Fool's Day and almost killed myself. I'll try to prevent you from doing the same." They thought he was joking at the time, but they would learn the truth later. But he had lied about being crazy, he *was* a little *loco*.

It was dusk outside and time for taps. The students had taken note of the difference in the men who would teach them. A flight schedule was passed out covering the next two weeks of scheduled activities. From the looks on their faces, the trainees were aware of the complex task ahead. As the four instructors left the room, Diego announced.

"Reveille is at 0430 hours, fall out in full flight gear behind the barn after breakfast at 0530."

You could hear the moans in the darkness outside over the sounds of the crickets and the lowing of animals.

After returning the other instructors to Mena that night, and while driving back to Little Rock on the darkened Highway 270, Terry used the time to meditate upon what seemed like the strange, dual... yes, surrealistic, life he was leading.

How many other "Nellas" are there out there? And how many other guys out there are living a dual existence? A few? Many? Is this what America has become, having to go underground to do what its leadership thinks is right? Is this the government I'm dealing with? Am I working for the government? Or is there more than one government? If so, how many? Should I feel honored or ashamed to be singled out for this? Am I a traitor or a patriot?

Has democracy broken down, as Lenin said it would? Is it dead? Or is this its rebirth? Or has it always been like this and I was just never involved? Is the CIA right? Is Congress right and really reflecting the people's will this time? Is there such a thing as the "people's will?" Is this how we got into the Vietnam war, or how we got out?"

The haunting questions raced through his mind.

Then, he thought about the hospital, lying there and talking with Barry Seal. He had almost died that day, needlessly. He felt he had been given a second chance...a chance to die right. How you die, he then realized, is something a person does have a degree of control over.

Had the American Colonists sneaked off to covert camps where foreigners would teach them how to fight the British? Had the countries who trained the Colonists debated the morality of it all? He began to feel like a dog chasing his tail. There's no place to go for these answers, he decided. You just have to live it out, he decided, and see if you die right. Who is John Cathey, really? How did Barry Seal fit into all of this? Who is Seal— really?

Terry became so engrossed in his thoughts he hadn't realized he had driven the entire distance back to Maumelle until his headlights lit up the front of his house at No. 8, Ten Tee Circle near the 10th tee of the private golf course. He turned off the ignition and just sat until his wife approached the car and said: "You look like you could use a beer. I'll trade you one for your thoughts."

A sudden surge of pain emanating from his injured foot brought him around. "Yeah, I'll take the beer, but you don't want to know what I was thinking."

1.   Oral deposition given to the Arkansas Attorney General's office, June 19, 1991, page 16.

CHAPTER 7

TAIL-NUMBERS GAME

"Terry-san, I will come by your house and pick you up," Akihide Sawahata said on the telephone. "We need to meet Barry at the airport. We will both fly to Mena with him and then you can fly us back in your new 'Company' airplane."

Hot damn, Terry Reed thought. Maybe he wouldn't have to answer all those questions that nearly burned out his brain while driving back from Mena the previous night. The world looked different after a good night's sleep. The reality was he wouldn't be driving back from Mena anymore, he'd be flying. July 9th, the calendar said. It was 7 AM.

He hurriedly finished his coffee and playfully slapped Janis' backside while she was showering and said, "Aki's coming by to get me. We're going to Mena to pick up my airplane. Don't forget, communication security is in effect. Don't *ever* call me over there. Only call OSI in the event of an emergency. If anyone is curious, just tell them I'm working on an engineering project at Brodix Manufacturing."

Janis came out of the shower and gave him one of those 'I know, I'm not stupid' looks, and then began assisting him in wrapping his cast in plastic so that he could bathe.

While doing so she lectured, "Terry, you act like I was new at this game. All that time in Oklahoma with Buzz and then Cathey...did I ever embarrass you, even one time? I may not have gone to intelligence school...but I've had a great teacher."

Terry reasoned his instructional attitude must have made her defensive. He hadn't meant to upset her, he just wanted to be certain there were no spook related screw-ups originating from the Reed household. He recalled the conversation with Seal and Sawahata about tapped phones in Mena and could only conclude that his phone was being "monitored" as well. One breech of communication security at this early stage of Agency employment would probably mean instant termination. A lot was riding on this program and he assumed it was being shadowed by Washington.

After coaxing Janis to repeat one more time that she would never violate Agency security procedures by calling him at Rich Mountain Aviation in Mena, and that she would only use Overseas International's local number, and only then if it were a matter of life or death, he crawled into the shower.

Once inside and with her out of reach, he could hear her mimic, "I know, this is different, this a big opportunity for both of us".

Sawahata was soon parked in Terry's driveway where both men drove off toward the Little Rock Airport by way of the Maumelle Highway, as it was called. On the way, Terry asked Aki to stop at Arkansas Machine Tools, a company owned by Mark McAfee, one of Terry's business associates in the machine tool industry.

"I need to drop off a quotation on a particular machine on the way to the airport," Terry informed him. Little did he and Sawahata realize then that this would be a BIG mistake—for both of them.

Terry had met McAfee in his first days in Arkansas when Seth Ward had brought him in to Command Aire's facility to appraise their equipment for insurance. From that first meeting, it was obvious that McAfee had a problem. He wasn't just hyper. *He was really hyper*! Terry initially didn't know why, but would later learn of his addiction to diet pills. And they obviously weren't working for what they were intended.

McAfee, a short man in his early 40s, was a person who needed to accept the reality that designer blue jeans could no longer encompass his rapidly-expanding girth. He needed to get out of The Gap-style clothing stores, where teenage salesgirls titillated him as they measured his in-seam, and over to Sear's Big Men's department.

He had big problems in all three categories of life. Categories Terry called the three M's—money, morals and marriage. Under Terry's theory, if you simultaneously have trouble with any two of the M's, you had big problems. And McAfee had major problems in all three.

First, McAfee had big money problems. Like a lot of machine tool dealers, he had been unable to understand that the oil boom was only a "spike" on the EKG chart of machinery sales. This was a very common problem among equipment suppliers throughout the Midwest who were becoming insolvent. McAfee had overextended himself financially and was refusing to properly deal with the fact that he was already in Chapter 11 bankruptcy and court-ordered reorganization. Worst of all, he still deluded himself, believing he was an astute businessman and financial guru.

Reed observed that McAfee was refusing to deal with the financial problems he was having. He had opened up secret bank accounts that he had hidden from his creditors...and the Bankruptcy Court. One secret expenditure was to finance the $12,000 purchase of a 1982 mist-green Corvette. He had been foolish enough to take Reed into his confidence and tell him he was diverting large amounts of cash from his bankrupt firm to a new machine tool company he had secretly formed and named ARMCO. In addition, he had gone into a totally unrelated and losing venture to manufacture rowing-machines that was also sucking capital from his bankrupt firm. He was forced to hide assets and used equipment from trade-ins and moved them across the state line to Memphis in preparation for the time when creditors would seize everything.

McAfee had also purchased a $125,000 airplane, a single-engine blue Beech Bonanza that was hidden from creditors at the North Little Rock Airport. A twin-engine Beech Baron he previously owned had already been seized. His idea of "reorganization" seemed to be to downsize to an airplane he didn't really need.

McAfee had sought out Terry and made him an attractive offer. His business failure had begun to destroy his relationship with his equipment suppliers, forcing him to get really creative.

Recalling Seal's earlier admonition that Mena was not necessarily a permanent job, Terry had kept his business options open. After leaving the Ultra-

Light company, he had established a limited business relationship with McAfee that would be beneficial to them both and allow Terry to keep his hand in the machine tool industry.

They agreed that Terry would use his company, Reed, Kerr & Associates, to take over the distribution of machine tool lines that McAfee was losing. In turn, McAfee would share his customer base, which Terry would solicit, thereby attempting to introduce them to product lines that he had represented before moving to Arkansas. This agreement benefited both men, enabling them to profit from each other's efforts and, when they agreed, to share in revenues from business that they otherwise wouldn't have. Terry viewed this as a relationship of convenience, where his company simply operated under the same roof as McAfee's. Terry would receive clerical support and would not have to invest in the overhead associated with starting a new company in Arkansas.

This arrangement put Terry in contact with the woman who was both McAfee's secretary, and mistress, a shapely blonde named Linda Crow. McAfee was immediately protective of her and without reason appeared jealous of Terry. McAfee used her as a punching bag and, at the same time, a life preserver. He was someone who was barely keeping his head above water. He wanted her to rescue him emotionally from his failing marriage so that he could later shed her when he reached the safety of shore, in someone else's arms, no doubt.

Upon being introduced to Sawahata that morning, and learning of OSI's international trading connections, McAfee became increasingly hyper. McAfee urgently needed $350,000 in order to get creditors off his back and forestall his foreclosure. It was obvious to Terry that McAfee somehow saw Sawahata as his financial savior. McAfee was having his usual morning "high" from his pills and it was nearly impossible for Terry to pry Sawahata away from him. Within 15 minutes, McAfee had in desperation scatter-gunned 10 different business ideas at Sawahata, hoping he would go for one of them.

Back in the car, Sawahata turned to Terry and remarked: "Holy Buddha! What is that guy all about?"

Terry laughed. "You just did too good of a sales job, Aki. I guess your exporting cover just has a way with people, especially people that are desperate and going broke."

On the way to the airport, he cautioned Sawahata about McAfee's financial and emotional condition and told him to stay away from him. But the damage had been done. Sawahata unfortunately had given McAfee his business card.

Sawahata took the journey to the airport as an opportunity to outline to Terry the scope of his duties. "Terry-san, I talked to Mr. Cathey and he spoke very highly of you. It appears you are perhaps the only trained intelligence person involved in the Nella operation. Therefore, I am going to rely on you completely to keep me informed as to exactly what going on there, as well as in Mena."

"What do you mean by 'exactly'?" Terry asked. "Are you referring to all aspects of the flight training, or what?"

"It is just that we have brought in some very non-professional people for deniability and they must be continually monitored to insure professionalism in overall operation. So, please, tell me everything you hear or see or even suspect is going on," Sawahata answered.

"Is there someone you don't trust?" Terry asked. "Tell me now, if this is the case. My life may be depending on these people."

"It is my nature not to trust. And that has been reinstilled by my training. But I need to trust you, completely. You will be Agency eyes and ears for this project and, considering you understand Japanese culture, hopefully we can become special friends, too. I like your family."

"Do you trust Barry? Is he the problem?" Terry asked.

"All assets who have freedom of movement, especially internationally, are difficult to control. Barry is probably in that category of asset."

"So you want me to spy on Barry, too?" Terry was beginning to feel uneasy.

"I do not like that word 'spy'. Just observe and report."

"How shall I report, in writing? Or some other method?"

"No, we have perfect cover already," Sawahata answered. "You are businessman and so am I. We will get together at least once a week, maybe for lunch. That way, government can pay. We call benefit of job." They laughed as they sat waiting in the parking lot adjacent to the Little Rock Air Center and near a distinctive gold Mercedes 450 SEL with Arkansas plates on the rear, and a razorback hog plate on the front.

Seal had already landed his Lear jet, which was being refueled, and approached the waiting car. "Terry, why are you hanging out with a slope, didn't you get enuffa that in Southeast Asia.

"Fruck you, fat man," Sawahata said laughing. "Just for that, I will not give you keys to Mercedes I have for you."

"Oh, well, in that case,...whose the fuckin' Chink you're with, Terry? I think I fucked his sister in Southeast Asia, or maybe it was his mother, or grandma..."

Seal's banter would not have been as light-hearted had he known what was going on in Washington.

The previous day had been interesting for Terry, but it was becoming a nightmare for Seal. He was now caught in the jaws of the Iran-Contra nutcracker. Although Terry didn't know it, Seal had been working as an informant for the Drug Enforcement Administration long before they met. But his DEA handlers were losing control.

Seal had learned that the Sandinista government was allowing the Medellin cartel to use Nicaragua as a trans-shipping point for cocaine. To catch the Sandinistas "in the act," the CIA had planted a camera in Seal's C-123K * military cargo plane to record the loading in Nicaragua. But a tug of war had developed between the White House, the CIA and the DEA over this juicy piece of information that Ronald Reagan just could not sit on. The propaganda value was so hot that everyone wanted a piece of the credit.

When Seal returned from his successful surveillance mission the night before, his DEA handlers had received the disturbing news that the conservative *Washington Times* newspaper knew all about his mission and was about to break the story.

It was clear that the White House, and Oliver North in particular, had leaked the story after seeing an opportunity to tell President Reagan what he wanted to hear, embarrass the Sandinistas and, at the same time, win some Congressional support for the Contras.

---

*   The Fairchild C-123 Provider troop and cargo transport is powered by 2 Pratt and Whitney 2300 horsepower R-2800-99W radial engines. Two additional turbo jet engines can be mounted to increase take-off performance. Length=76 feet, Wing span=110 feet. Maximum take-off weight=60,000 lbs. Maximum level speed=228 mph. Maximum range=1035 miles.

The exposure of Seal's mission posed great peril to "the fat man." If it were made public, the Cartel would know that Seal was the informant who had set them up. Like the Mafia, they were ruthless and didn't tolerate stool pigeons.

While Terry had contemplated the meaning of life as he drove home from Mena the previous night, Seal's life was hanging by a thread.

But if Seal was worried he gave no indication of it that day in Little Rock. He gave his new car a "walk around," nodded with approval and joked, "Thanks Aki. Now I'll blend in with the bond daddies here in Arkansas. But let's get goin', I'm in a hurry! I've got to get down to Florida on business and we need to get Terry into his new airplane so he can go impale himself on the side of Rich Mountain with a load of beaners."

* * *

The white Lear jet, three spooks full, flew to Mena where Seal had a brief discussion with his chief mechanic, Joe Evans, that centered around problems with his C123, "The Fat Lady," the plane Barry had so affectionately named and the one he had flown to Nicaragua for the drug sting. Seal then abruptly departed for Florida.

Terry's new airplane, parked in the Rich Mountain hangar, was a 1977 Cessna 404, a twin-engine craft bearing the tail number N36998. After a thorough inspection, Terry sought out Evans, who was responsible for maintenance on all planes used for training. It was Terry's practice to talk directly to the man who had signed off the maintenance log.

"So, is she ready to go? I was hopin' to see something a little better looking," Terry inquired skeptically. "Is this all you have?"

Evans handed him the necessary documentation on the plane and, in his West Virginia hillbilly drawl, said, "She may look a little rough around the edges, but, mechanically, I'd bet my life on her. I've been over her with a fine tooth comb."

"Good. That's what you're gonna do. Let's go fly it." Terry always believed that, to assure tip-top maintenance, the mechanic who had deemed the plane airworthy should ride in it. This practice had kept him alive so far.

"What's the matter? Don't you trust me? Hell, Barry does," Evans challenged.

"Look at my foot. I got this by trusting another mechanic, and it still hurts. No offense, but get in the airplane. Come on Aki, go with us."

Evans, a FAA certified and licensed aircraft mechanic and 10-year Air Force veteran, held the highest rating, A&I, which meant aircraft inspector and was Seal's personal mechanic and longtime friend. Evans was clearly unhappy. But as Terry had just learned back on April Fool's Day, it's the little things that'll sneak up and kill you. Terry would later come to share Seal's respect for Evans, but this was the first plane he'd flown that Evans had certified as airworthy.

Once airborne, and with Sawahata in the back seat, Evans took the controls while Terry read the maintenance logs. "Shit! This thing has new engines and propellers on it, they're near zero-time. Where did this thing come from?"

"Emile (Camp) delivered it. He said it was one of the fleet he and Barry were brokering through their business," Evans replied. "He told me to tell you that mechanically she's in great shape, and they're gonna get a guy down here from Ohio to put new radios in it for ya. You'll probably fly this one for six months or so and then, in the spring, we'll put her in Junior's shop for paint and interior. Then, you'll get a new one. But she'll do for now. She's a fine airplane."

While Evans was distracted, Terry was performing his favorite check-out proceedure, reaching down to the floor between the two pilot seats and switching off the fuel valve to the right engine. As expensive as flying is, Terry lived by the Air Force motto that all flying should a continuation of training. And besides, since he and the other instructors and students would be putting their lives in Joe's skilled hands, he wanted to see if Evans would question his own mechanicing ability during a simulated emergency in a plane he had recently deemed airworthy.

Moments later, the Continental engine burbled, backfired and the propeller went automatically to full increase.

"Crap, what happened?" Evans yelled.

"I don't know, didn't you just sign it off? You did the maintenance."

Terry responded. Evans began to grope with the controls, but still had not identified the problem as fuel starvation. Evans frantically instructed Reed to switch on the auxiliary fuel boost pumps and became overly engrossed in scanning the engine instruments for a clue to the powerplant's demise. Terry was rating Evan's performance as that which would lead to a fatal flat-spin condition if he didn't adjust the plane's attitude and regain heading control. Joe had failed to input proper rudder pressure and manage his airspeed when the Cessna entered into an abrupt right-bank descending turn as a result of the decaying airspeed and asymmetrical thrust.

"Can I have the plane?" Terry asked.

Evans gladly surrendered the controls.

Terry input the left rudder, pitched the nose forward in order to gain speed and get the air speed needle away from the VMC red line. Rolling wings level he switched the fuel valve to the on position and restored power to the right engine.

Sawahata, who had just come along for the ride and was not a pilot, was kneeling on the floor praying to Buddha and probably wondering at the same time if he should convert to Christianity. After realizing that this had only been a simulated "emergency," Aki exhaled, "You *are* fruckin' crazy. Seal told me that about you."

"Oh, relax, Aki," Terry reassured him, "We're just calculated risk-takers. Didn't Barry tell you?"

Evans did not appreciate the humor, but he came to have an understanding of the guy in the left seat of the Cessna. He learned that Terry understood maintenance procedures, knew how planes worked and wasn't afraid to fly them on the ragged edge.

Reed was happy with the plane's performance. Someone had been taking pretty good care of it before Camp and Evans got it. But who that was would not be known to Terry until much later. He would find that this aircraft, and all the others he ended up using in Mena, were apparently stolen, and very likely part of "Project Donation," which "John Cathey" had sketched out for Terry on the napkin in Oklahoma City more than a year earlier.

* * *

Six years later, investigative reporter Jerry Bohnen of radio station KTOK-AM in Oklahoma City, an expert in aircraft registration, found something very interesting and unsettling about the planes Rich Mountain maintained for the training program, code named Boomerang.

By accessing two different and unconnected computerized databases, Bohnen discovered a highly sophisticated stolen aircraft laundering system housed within the government that could only have been put in place by someone with access to government-controlled computers and records. The cleverly-devised system had been created by use of a loophole that stonewalls aircraft tracking and enables "someone" in possession of a stolen aircraft to "launder" it and give it a new identity, or "N number" that will make it appear that it is not stolen.*

The scheme retrieves from the government's computers the tail number of a clean airplane of the same make and model as the stolen aircraft. Only personnel having in-depth knowledge, and access, to government databases could retrieve the needed make and model to match the stolen plane. Of key importance is finding a clean plane based in a geographic region far from the planned operation area of the stolen one. Otherwise, two identical planes of the same make and model and bearing the same N-number could possibly, and disastrously, appear at the same airport.

The objective is to assure that the stolen airplane appears legitimate since its N-number would not appear on any law enforcement "hot sheets." The scheme's complexity, like that of Project Donation, was matched only by its deviousness.

For example, the tail number of the plane Terry had just flown was N36998. According to what Bohnen found by checking its true serial number, it was stolen March 1, 1983 from Falcon Field near Atlanta, just three weeks before Terry's plane had been stolen at Joplin. At the time of the theft, the plane's registration number was N3241B. The Falcon Field case is still unsolved.

Based on new information that Bohnen has developed, it appears possible the federal government has for years been "borrowing" aircraft both stolen and unstolen, with and without the owners' cooperation, for use in "sting" operations. Terry learned later from subpoenaed discovery in his civil rights lawsuit, that Rich Mountain Aviation in Mena, Arkansas had access to N numbers that had not even been issued by the FAA. Inside information like this could only have come from government sources.

Bohnen found the FAA has no apparent desire to be informed about "hot" airplanes and had no system to flag them as stolen even if they are informed of a theft. Since the government controls both the FAA registration records system and the FBI's National Crime Information Center (NCIC), it would be a simple matter to mask something like "Project Donation" and any other related government misconduct. Maybe "John Cathey" hadn't invented this program after all, and was only using an existing system to benefit for the Contra cause.

---

*   An N number is the aircraft equivalent of an automobile license plate except that it is painted on the plane, not bolted on as with cars. Terry was given seven different airplanes to use for the Nella training operation. (See chapter end.)

Changing tail numbers is nothing new. It's like changing license plates on stolen cars. Seal required altered numbers while working for the government because it enabled him to move more freely, making it more difficult for him to be traced or followed. A deputy sheriff in Mena revealed he had seen tail, or N, numbers of planes inside the Rich Mountain hangar being taped over to alter the N numbers, and in some instances, two planes receiving the same number.

The Mena airport, known officially as the Inter-Mountain Regional Airport, had by this time become well-known in aviation circles as one of the few places in the entire country where an aircraft owner or pilot could get "anything" done, legally or otherwise.

Available there, or nearby, were complete overhaul and retrofit facilities that included major airframe modifications, engine overhaul, along with paint and interior work—very unusual when you consider this remote area and the fact that Dallas, the headquarters of American Airlines and a city built on aviation, is only 150 miles southwest.

A pilot coming to Mena had a reason. And lower repair rates—"eggs are cheaper in the country"— were only part of the reason. First, there are stringent documentation and reporting regulations requiring mechanics to file with the FAA a Form 337 detailing alterations made to any aircraft after a plane is built and sold. Failure to file this form exposes the mechanic to prosecution, suspension of his license and a possible prison term. The original intent of this reporting was to insure that no modifications were made that were not approved by the original manufacturer. This, simply, was to insure safety.

But the DEA stepped in when the airplane became the transporter of choice for drug traffickers. Form 337, the DEA found, was the perfect vehicle to monitor modifications that are normally performed to aircraft used in nefarious activities. Any modification that extends the range of the plane or alters the number or size of the cargo doors automatically flags that aircraft, and its owner, as a possible drug smuggler.

Smart pilots involved in nefarious activities know this and look for repair facilities and mechanics who will break the law and not file the 337. Mena was such a place. For a price, anything was possible.

Intelligence agencies share with drug traffickers a need not to leave a paper trail. That's why the CIA sent Seal to Mena in 1982 and set up its "fixed base operation" there. The government secretly paid to modify several of Seal's "sting" aircraft there since the DEA didn't want a paper trail either.*

However, in 1984, all Terry knew was that Rich Mountain was used as the maintenance facility for the Nella flight training operation, and that Seal relied on that company as the source of his retrofitting and maintenance for his airplane brokering firm in Baton Rouge, Louisiana. Everything he needed, Seal told him, was there, including Goodner Bros. paint shop across the field, which had a spray booth large enough to hold a massive C-130 transport plane. Terry was impressed.

Terry and Sawahata departed Mena that day only after he repeatedly promised his passenger that there would be no more simulated emergencies. He decided to fly north and try out his new, $12,000, top-of-line, ITT McKay high-frequency radio. While orbiting the Nella strip he handed the radio to Sawahata

---

* This was revealed to one of the authors by a DEA source.

and said: "Barry says you can talk to God, let's see if you can talk to the Devil. Try to raise Varandos and see what's going on down there."

Once Sawahata had established radio contact, Vanardos informed Terry that "Nebraska" was at the "pick-up" site getting some new "chickens." This meant he was at Waldron, Arkansas, approximately 10 miles north of Nella, the airport that the students would be trucked to and from via fire roads for their daily training. It provided a 4,000-foot runway in a less mountainous area and was ideally situated for primary multi-engine training.

While circling above, Reed could see Nebraska's high-wing, aerobatic Citabria aircraft parked under the camouflage netting at the Nella field. This two-place, tandem, STOL (short take-off and landing) plane was Nebraska's personal aircraft and, with weather permitting, he used it for commuting to and from the field.

"OK, I guess he's got his hands full, and my passenger and I have to get back to base, so I'll see you guys tomorrow night at the pickup site at 1900 hours," Terry said.

On the way back, Sawahata informed Terry that he had arranged for his plane to be hangared temporarily at the Benton Airport 20 miles southwest of Little Rock. This was the best he could do, he said, until more suitable storage could be found nearer Maumelle.

"Shit, you mean with all the assets of the Agency, they can't build us a fucking hangar?" Terry asked.

Sawahata smiled and said: "We're working on that."

* * *

The first 30 days of the training program were dedicated to Phase I operations, attempting to upgrade the students to a level of proficiency for multi-engine operations with all aircraft systems functional. It had been an intense month for all four instructors and, fortunately, no one had been killed, yet.

The Latinos were doing fairly well in the air, but, on the ground it was a different story. Nebraska was upset. He was beginning to realize that it wasn't the U.S. Army with which he was working; he simply couldn't ground everyone.

Diego wasn't measuring up either, and appeared to be losing control of the ground school. Terry was putting in long hours at night, on weekends and even, occasionally, during the day. But it was paying off. Everyone was getting used to one another and the "bugs" were being ironed out.

The lesson plan called for a method of training that had been proved effective in Vietnam, putting more than one student at a time in the airplane. Homer (Red) Hall, Seal's avionics technician from Ohio, had by now installed a completely new stack of Collins Pro-Line digital avionics in Terry's plane. He had also wired the plane for multiple head-sets, so that the students riding in back could monitor all cockpit conversations between the instructor and the student pilot in the left seat. The four-month course called for 40 hours of dual instruction for each student. Since the students were being trained in groups of four, this would give each trainee 120 hours of observation, or "osmosis" training time, and 40 hours of hands-on time for a total of 160 hours.

A typical training sortie included these four students, one instructor and approximately four hours of tense, sweaty, low-altitude work.

It was "July hot" in Arkansas. From the sound of the massive insects impacting on the windshield at low altitude, they could easily be mistaken for birds. Students and instructors alike were taking GI-issue salt pills and malaria tablets. To Terry, it was like being back in Southeast Asia. But the students felt right at home in this near-tropical climate and joked that if they lost the war in Nicaragua they would come back here and become wealthy landowners.

By now, most landing training was being conducted out of 12 airports of various sizes in Western Arkansas. The majority of the air work, or dangerous flight operations, were kept within the confines of what is defined on aviation charts as MOAs (military operations areas). An MOA is an area of select air space set aside by the FAA and labeled as a high risk area for pilot operations. A key reason for selection of the Nella site was due to its location, "under the floor" of the Hog-2 MOA, whose airspace encompassed a range of 100 to 4,000 feet AGL (above ground level). A combination of the Hog-2 and Hog-3 airspace gave the instructors an area of about 1,500 square miles of protected air space in which to train. Terry and Seal selected this training site because of the MOAs' location within a triangular navigation area defined by the Ft. Smith, Hot Springs and Rich Mountain VORs (ground-based radio navigation aids). It offered not only protected airspace, but a mixture of all types of instrument and visual approaches.

These MOAs were used primarily for training flights from Fort Chaffee and Little Rock Air Force Base, as well as simulated F-4 Phantom dog fight exercises from jets of the Air National Guard unit stationed at Fort Smith. Use of this airspace for commercial or private use was very limited due to the dangerous training environment existing within it. This made it ideally suited for the Nella operation, since their operations were also dangerous, and it reduced the risk of being detected.

The instructors had mutually decided, in the interest of safety and privacy, that the practice air drops would take place only in the confines of the Nella field. The field, besides providing a clear drop zone of sufficient size to make an emergency landing if needed, would surely be remote enough to prevent any unwanted FAA investigations, since it is illegal to throw objects from airplanes.

The good flying time was early morning, late evening and into the night due to reduced temperatures, improved visibilities and because the skies were less bumpy from thermal activity. After 9 AM on a typical day, flying below the haze layer, normally 5,000 feet MSL, was like riding a bucking bronco, which added to the stress and strain, especially considering the aircraft were not air conditioned.

All in all, Oklahoma, "Mr. FAA," had found the Hispanic students competent, considering their mission. The instructors didn't view them as Kamikaze trainees, but took into consideration that Nicaragua would not require the same navigation and communications discipline as the TCA (terminal control area) at a huge commercial airport like Chicago's O'Hare.

At a flight instructor meeting held earlier, Terry voiced concern that Oklahoma and Nebraska were too much "by the book." By the time the trainees performed to their standards, he said, the Sandinistas would be building runways on the banks of the Rio Grande, in preparation for their invasion of Texas.

The students seemed to really like Terry, sensing that he was giving them realistic and practical training that they needed to survive.

His best student at the time, Juan No. 1 as Terry called him, was at that stage where students become dangerous, not through inability, but rather though overconfidence. It was Sunday afternoon, August 5th, as the twin Cessna sat on the south end of the 6,000-foot runway at Petit Jean Airport, FAA designator MPJ.

With Juan in the left seat, and three others in the back, they prepared for takeoff. The training plan for the day, as far as Juan knew, was to practice "touch-and-go" landings on several hard-surface runways in Western Arkansas.

Terry had just decided to modify the lesson plan without Juan's knowledge. Juan was, without a doubt, the best in the group and reminded him of the old comic strip character Steve Canyon, a natural flyer. He had the potential to be a very good flyer if he could bring that cocky attitude under control and survive this phase of training. Terry's old instructor had used humiliation to keep him in line, so, he decided to force Juan to "lose it" in front of the group. This would be a lesson for everyone.

After conversing with the students sitting in the back via the Dave Clark intra-cockpit communication system, he had them compute short-field takeoff distance for the plane, taking into account their weight and the field conditions. When they came up with their answers, he then turned to Juan and said: "Tell me the numbers and the procedure for short-field takeoff." He knew them all and rattled them off with precision.

Juan, by this time had logged 15 hours of training with both engines running. Terry decided it was time to show him the dangerous side of multi-engine flying. He could recall his FAA examiner asking him during his oral examination for his multi-engine instructor's rating, "Why does a twin-engine airplane have two engines?" The answer was, the examiner later explained: "Because it won't fly on one." Juan was about to find that out.

With the brakes locked and Juan bringing the engines up to red-line manifold pressure, 41 inches, and tachometers to the red-line RPM of 2,700, Terry called "brakes release."

After acceleration to flying speed, Juan deftly rotated at exactly the right "numbers" and skillfully held back the air speed as the plane climbed steeply to clear the simulated 50-foot obstacle. With Juan's attention fully on the mountain in front of him, Terry grabbed the red engine mixture knob for the right engine and pulled it all the way to the rear. The engine quit.

They were now in the realm of flight known as "behind the power curve." And the young pilot discovered that strange phenomenon the FAA calls "swimming in glue."

"Heading. Air speed. Air speed! Pick up on the heading, pick up on the heading! Goddam it, pick on the fucking heading!" Terry shouted.

As the air speed needle descended below the red line on the air-speed indicator, Terry realized it was time to quit talking and do the thing all instructors hate to do, take over the airplane. It is a sign of instructor failure, he had been taught.

But Juan wasn't letting go. Steve Canyon, the throttle jockey, was now frozen to the controls and Terry had only one avenue left as the plane began to buffet, stall and roll abruptly to the right. He had to kill the left engine, too.

Scrambling for the left mixture knob, Terry shut down the left power plant, elbowed Juan sharply in the rib cage and shoved the control yoke forward in order to wrench it from Juan's grasp. He finally let go.

They were now in a 6,500-pound glider heading toward the Arkansas River Valley, which luckily was 700 feet below the elevation of the field they had just departed. With the plane now in a shallow, wings level, stabilized dive, Terry held his breath as he pushed both mixture knobs forward after retarding both throttles to idle. While executing the recovery, he could hear his No.1 student mumbling "madre de Dios." The windmilling power plants burbled and returned to life.

Juan later said Jesus had been responsible for the restart of both engines that day. That really irritated Terry. God and religion had nothing to do with it, he told them. "Pilots fly airplanes," he said. "God only talks to dead pilots."

Under the column "engine out procedures," Terry, back in Little Rock later that night, graded Juan with a 5... "below acceptable standards." Somehow that seemed an understatement, since he too had scored badly that day. He was the instructor and the person responsible for the safety of the flight. But it had been near disaster, partially due to the same trait he was trying to correct in Juan. Over-confidence! It angered him in his silence at his desk in Maumelle.

This time, he thought, they could all have died. Would this have been a nobler way to die than the Ultra-Light accident?

One thing for sure, this had been a lesson for everyone. Terry learned not to drop his guard for an instant. Flying, he was reminded once again, just had a way of keeping a person humble.

The loud ringing of the phone brought him out of his meditation. It was Seal and he was in Little Rock. "Come on out to the airport, I've got a present for you. Something to make your life a little less exciting."

At the airport, Seal produced two Honeywell night vision systems. "Where did you get these?" Terry asked.

"I got a friend in GSA (General Services Administration) supply. I can get anything. Have Red (Hall) wire your plane for these. That way you won't kill yourself on the side of some mountain and bring this whole operation to an end. Oh, by the way, I hear we'll be gettin' a new camp commander real soon and from what I hear about this guy, your students will definitely get caught up on their ground work. He's supposed to be a real motherfucker!"

August 31, 1990

John Cummings
19 Wedgewood Avenue
East Northport, N.Y.

Dear John,

I apologize for my tardiness on this informantion. It's an election year for us and other duties are calling.

Anyway, let's start the rundown on the 7 airplanes Terry Reed says he flew while training pilots at Mena. As I indicated in some of our telephone conversations, he kept logs on the planes. Sometimes he had registration or N numbers as well as the serial numbers. It's kind of unusual for a pilot to keep serial numbers. But Reed says he learned the practice from the pilot who taught him at Springfield, Missouri. And in actuality, it's a good practice. Because it's easy to change N numbers, but not serial numbers.

These are the planes he says he flew, their registration numbers as he recorded them, their serial numbers as he recorded them and the kind of airplane they were:

1) N36998 sn 404-0090 1977 Cessna 404
2) N5425G sn 404-0045 1977 Cessna 404
3) N69889 sn 421B-0529 1974 Cessna 421 B
4) N5774C sn 402C-0042 1979 Cessna 421 B
5) N9490Y sn BA-540 1963 G18S Beech
6) N8275T sn 348170016 1981 Deneca
7) N4677W sn 13-273 1978 Rockwell Commander

What's most interesting and peculiar is how each of the planes as Terry Reed knew and flew them and recorded them in his log books was a stolen airplane 'at the time.' By checking the registration numbers 'at the time' anyone would have learned they were real and legitimate airplanes and not stolen, or so it would seem. For instance, plane number one, N36998 in the time frame fitting Reed's use was a 1977 Cessna 404 belonging to the Cessna Aircraft company in Belgium. But it had a different serial number. Plane number two, N5425G was recorded with the Faa as Sale reported, out of Winter Haven, Florida. It too had a different serial number. Plane number three, N69889 belonged to the Coca Cola Bottling Company of Elizabethtown, Kentucky. Plane four, N9490Y was owned by Rainbow Islands Cargo Inc of Honolulu, Hawaii. Plane number six, N8275T had a registered owner of Ranger Aviation Enterprises Inc of San Angelo, Texas. And airplane number seven, N4677W was owned by Kent B. Sands of Bellevue, Washington.

Stay with me. It sounds complicated but it's not! Okay so far the registration numbers on the airplanes flown by Reed belong to other planes of the same make, but located in other parts of the country. And those registration numbers are not listed as stolen. So Reed's planes are carrying 'false' registration numbers. So his planes 'appear' legitimate.

Now checking the serial numbers of the planes flown by Reed, we learn they're stolen!

Plane number one again, N36998 or serial #404-0090 turns out to be a Cessna 404 stolen March 1, 1983 from a Falcon Field near Atlanta, Georgia. It was flown at the same time under N3241B. Its disappearance, which has never been solved, was questionable. I've talked to the Insurance people. Three guys, including an air line pilot, out of Georgia owned the plane. The insurance company questioned the theft and there was civil litigation in the Georgia courts over the settlement. An insurance company officer told me the air line pilot later was arrested for carrying dope on board one of his airliners in Florida. There was a stink over it but the pilot was later released and either cleared or charges dropped. It was insured by Fireman's Fund Insurance and Associated Aviation Underwriters.

Plane Number two, flown by Reed as N5425G, was also a 1977 Cessna 404 Titan. But its real Registration was N5425G. It was stolen in November of 1984 from an airfield at Addison, Texas which is part of Dallas. It was owned by Holmes Leasing company of Dallas. Insurance was carried by Aviation Office of America in Dallas, Texas. Again the theft involved drugs! The President of Holmes Leasing was a John Holmes. His attorney tells me Holmes' partner was dealing dope. The plane was apparently missing on a dope flight when two guys cracked it up loaded with Pot or some such stuff just across the border in Mexico. Turns out there were several people indicted in the drug operation. Holmes was not one of them. He and his attorney, understandably were extremely nervous in discussing the theft etc.

Plane number three, N69889 turned out to be N5SF, also a 1974 Cessna 421. It was stolen in January of 1985 from Orlando, Florida. Marshall Boone owned the plane at the time. I interviewed him. He indicated it was stolen after he had just installed a new radar system and other avionics as well as a new right engine. About 3 weeks later or perhaps a month, he couldn't recall exactly, the plane turned up crashed just off shore of Rutter Cut Key in the Bahamas.

7-1. Letter from investigative reporter Jerry Bohnen to co-author John Cummings spelling out results of Bohnen's research into aircraft used for pilot training in Arkansas. It shows that the planes were stolen but bore the "N" numbers of "clean" planes. (two pages.)

The tail was still visible and a friend of Boone's took pictures, which indicated the registration number had been changed with tape to resume 5S8 or 5SB. Maps were found in the plane indicating it had been flown in Colombia and Venezuela. He said he first learned of the crash when a federal law agency called him.

Plane number four, N5774C, turned out to be N5779C, again a 1979 Cessna 402C. It was stolen September 2, 1983 from Palm Beach International Airport at West Palm Beach, Florida. It was owned by Planeholder Inc, a Florida corporation out of Miami. I've never been able to talk to anyone about this theft. But notes in the aircraft file indicate the plane was stolen early in the morning, refueled at Boca Ratan. The passenger seats were removed and the occupants were believed to be a female and a Jamaican male. The plane's never been found. CAse remains unsolved.

Plane number five, N9490Y was really N9412, again a 1963 Beech 18. It was owned by Perkiomen Airways Ltd of Reading, Pennsylvania and was stolen July 1, 1983. In Puerto Rico, where Perkiomen had some sort of a mail route contract. The insurer was Aviation Office of America. I could never locate the owner. But a former employee told me the company filed bankruptcy in the Spring of '83' and he wouldn't put it past the principal owner to let the plane disappear. Regardless, the plane has never been found. The case remains unsolved.

Plane numer six, N8275T, was really N8280D, a 1981 Piper Seneca. Yes, there was a Seneca flown by Reed. I recall you mentioning Seale's fondness of Senecas. Anyway, this airplane was stolen January 1, 1985 from Tampa, Florida where it was owned at the time by Topp of Tampa Airport Inc which is now Airofly Tampa Inc. Jamie Jordan of Topp of Tampa owned the plane about 5 to 6 months before it disappeared from the Tampa airport. It was insured by U-S AIG or U-S Aviation Underwriters. The plane was never recovered.

Plane number seven, N4677W was really N4697W, a 1978 Rockwell Commander. It was reported stolen in a very bizarre case in September 1983 from Washington State. No insurance on the plane. This was the only plane of the 7 which was recovered after being stolen. However after its theft in 1983 in an admitted theft by the owner who was in a legal dispute with the bank, the plane reappeared in January or February 1990. The owner didn't know where the plane was all these years, or so he claims. And by all circumstances it might be the case. He had 2 friends steal the plane and arranged for them to know where it was to be located but not tell him. The pilot died several months later and reportedly didn't tell the owner where the plane was hidden. Very strange tale.

Summarizing these 7 planes, the registration numbers belonged to unstolen planes located elsewhere around the country. But the serial numbers, which aren't routinely checked or observed easily, proved the planes were stolen.
The FAA no longer maintains files reflecting if airplanes are stolen.
But a check with the International Aviation Theft Bureau, phone 301-694-5444 proved the planes were listed as stolen.
A Bob Collins handles the bureau and ran the checks for me.

Now if you take Reed's own airplane, it makes 8 planes which were stolen and flown under Registration numbers belonging to legitimate and unstolen airplanes elsewhere around the country. Further, the planes of the legitimate registration numbers were the same model and year of the ones actually being flown by Reed in Arkansas. Think about that one! It'd take a little research to find matching planes. I could do it. But what kind of drug operation, if this is what Reed was doing, or as far as that goes a Contra training operation, would take the time to research the airplane background? Perhaps one with government connections? Think about it. ANyone who steals an airplane for a few days of drug-hopping missions just tapes over the N number to make it appear to be something else. They then usually ditch the plane inthe ocean or abandon it, right? But not Seale and his boys. No, they needed the planes for a little longer. Now either Seale and his people were extremely sophisticated, or they had the assistance of some very well heeled backers.
They couldn't afford to be snatched or tripped up by the usual tape method of registration alterations. They had to employ a far more sophisticated method. That's why it seems almost out of character for the way Reed's plane was found and observed with taped numbers. Remember the private detective who says he 'stumbled' onto the airplane when the wind blew open the door described the supposed sloppy job of taping over the registration numbers? It's totally out of character! It doesn't fit Seale's operational methods. Somebody obviously set up Reed, trying to make it appear he was sloppy and a stupid crook! I don't buy it.
By the way, in case you've never known. Reed's airplane had a registration number belonging to an identical Piper airplane hangared in Columbus, Ohio. The plane was sold to a West German and exported. Interesting point. It is near Columbus, Ohio where supposedly there might have been some kind of Contra training operation. And it is near Columbus where an avionics firm, with defense contacts, is located. Seale's old buddy, Homer 'Red' Hall worked for the avionics firm, and supposedly received 750-thousand from Seale to do avionics work on his airplanes. It proved so profitable for Hall, he left Ohio and moved to Mena for a while.
    Well, enough. If you need more, call or write.
Sincerely,

Jerry Bohnen

CHAPTER 8

THE BOMBER

The training schedule posted on Aki Sawahata's wall in OSI's secret communications room showed it was a "no fly day" for Terry Reed. Sawahata had informed Terry that there would be *certain* days, and nights, that he should "stay away" from the Mena area. He wasn't told why, but he knew better than to ask. After all, he didn't have a need to know.

But Terry could not help but notice there was a definite pattern to these "no-fly" days. They normally coincided with Seal's frequent Little Rock visits to see investment banker Dan Lasater.

Terry used his "stand down days," days not involved in training, to concentrate on his machine-tool sales activities throughout Arkansas. The deal he had struck with Mark McAfee allowed him to use McAfee's office and secretary to prepare the lengthy and complex quotations that were required to bid on projects. He was at McAfee's office when Sawahata telephoned him. Unfortunately, McAfee overheard Linda Crow say, "Terry, the call's for you. It's your Japanese friend, Aki."

It was a bad move on Sawahata's part. McAfee had taken his pills and was so hyper he could make an inanimate object nervous. Before Terry could pick up the call, McAfee grabbed the phone and began rattling off 10 new "get rich quick" schemes with which he hoped Sawahata would want to get involved.

"I've been layin' awake all night, just thinkin' about you!!!!!! Forklifts! Forklifts! That's it! Forklifts! That's what Japan needs. Let's export rebuilt forklifts to Japan. I know a company that rebuilds forklifts. We can buy 'em cheap. You got the ships to ship 'em in. We can make a killing. What do you think?"

By this time, and since the call was for him anyway, Terry was listening in.

"I do not think so," Sawahata answered. "You ever hear of Toyota of Japan. They biggest forklift manufacturer in world. Why they want to buy used forklifts from you?"

"How about weedeaters? That's another idea I have! Hell, they're made right here in Arkansas. I know where the factory is. We can buy 'em cheap and ship thousands over there. What do you think?"

"Mr. McAfee, you sound too excited. We Japanese go slow in business. Maybe I come by someday and we can talk in detail. But, right now, I need to speak with Mr. Reed."

"Yeah, Mark." Terry spoke into the phone. "This call's for me. And, besides, you've been to Japan. How many lawns did you see in Tokyo that would need a weedeater."

McAfee slammed down the phone, breaking the receiver in half. A stream of obscenities followed. "I got a sense of urgency here!" he screamed. "Nobody realizes there's a sense of urgency here! Linda, get your ass in here and close the door!"

With McAfee off the phone, Sawahata proceeded: "Terry-san, Can you leave that place and call me ASAP? We have emergency."

The "emergency" was the mechanical breakdown of a plane with Nebraska and four students aboard in Hot Springs, a resort city west of Little Rock. They had to be extricated and returned to Waldron before a lot of questions were asked. Hot Springs is a very public place and the gambling hub of Arkansas. It was the height of the horse racing season. How could you explain a Cessna 404 filled with Latino "freedom fighters" just sitting in the sweltering sun outside the terminal?

Sawahata wanted Terry to fly a "round robin" to Hot Springs, pick up the five men, fly them back to Waldron where their vehicle was parked, then pick up Joe Evans and repair parts at Rich Mountain and then fly him back to Hot Springs for the repairs.

Terry successfully rescued the "downed" Contras before the *enemy* found them and began unwanted interrogation. He returned the group safely to Waldron and then launched immediately for Mena. It had been a successful SAR mission (search and rescue), lacking only to return Evans to Hot Springs.

When Terry landed at Mena, he noticed that Seal's C-123 was there, along with a camouflaged U.S. Army truck parked outside. He had not known Seal was in town. Terry walked into the hangar and past the security guard, who seemed to recognize him. The Rich Mountain clerical employees were nowhere to be seen. Normally, at least one could be found wandering around the hangar carrying a clipboard. Terry was looking for anyone who knew Evans' whereabouts. One of these workers told federal investigators years later, there were certain days, usually when Seal was there, when they were not allowed into the hangar area. This was one of those days.

The unexpected event that day, the breakdown of Nebraska's plane, had drawn Terry accidentally into yet another loop...guns! He wasn't prepared for what he saw. All the overhead lights had been turned on because blankets covered the windows. Laid out on tables in the corner of the hangar were weapons parts. Several gun crates, bearing U.S. Army markings, were open on the floor. Terry could see the military nomenclature stenciled on one of the crates.

"Stock, M16, 24 each."

At one table three Army personnel wearing fatigues were busy assembling rifles and putting the now-completed weapons in a new crate. But, even more curious, these crates were made of white pine that bore no markings at all. As he casually approached and looked inside one of the unmarked crates, he saw layered rows of M16 parts known as lower receiver housings.

Movement from a different direction caught his eye. Terry saw Seal and Evans getting out of a twin-ruddered, twin-engine Howard airplane parked in the hangar.

"You musta been running that plane of yours at red line," Seal said. "We weren't expecting you quite yet. The slope had called and said he had a problem. Joe's got the parts boxed up. You better get him on over there pretty quick."

Seal's demeanor was casual, apparently figuring that what Terry had seen, he had seen. And he could be trusted. As Terry and Evans started to leave the hangar, Seal stopped him and suggested, "Hey, I'm spending the night in Little

Rock, let's do SOBs. I'd invite Evans to go with us, but he'd try to make us take him to Snug Harbor. I got that shit out of my system in Vietnam."

Seal was laughing as he crawled back into the Howard. Snug Harbor Tavern and Grill was a North Little Rock dive and strip joint on the Arkansas River. A prerequisite for the strippers, Terry decided after one visit there, was to have varicose veins and "low beams". Nipples that pointed straight down. The girls performed their nude dance acts on sheets of plywood supported by saw horses. Real class. This is where the true rednecks and GIs from the nearby Camp Robinson hung out. It was the stop of last resort on payday when all the other women had turned them down. Considering all the brawls there, the rumor was that the bouncers searched you at the door to make sure you DID have a weapon. It was definitely Evans' kind of place.

Flying enroute to Hot Springs, Evans was extremely quiet. Finally he spoke: "I guess you got an eyeful back there in the hangar." He paused. "Aw well, sooner or later you'd found out anyway."

"What's going on?" Terry asked, sure now that Evans would fill him in.

"Shit, you can't fight a war without guns, you know that," Evans said referring back to his military experience. He chuckled. "We're just sorta makin' some. You know how it is, you were in the Air Force. We just sorta 'requisitioned' some parts that were layin' around."

Terry let it go at that. He hadn't expected to hear even that much. As their plane was being handed off to the Hot Springs tower, Evans asked: "Have you met the Tasmanian devil, yet?"

"Who?" Terry asked bemused at the thought of the Warner Brothers cartoon character who devours everything in sight.

"The guy Barry flew in. The new camp commander. Boy, he's somethin'. I feel sorry for your students with that son of a bitch up there. He looks fuckin' mean."

Evans was referring to an infamous Cuban exile mercenary, Ramon Medina. Unknown to them at the time, his real name was Luis Posada Cariles, a known terrorist with CIA connections dating back to the Bay of Pigs.

Posada, or Medina, at that time was supposedly serving time in a Venezuelan prison for planting a bomb aboard a Cuban airliner on October 6, 1976, that exploded and killed everyone aboard as it took off from Jamaica.

But obviously, he wasn't in Venezuela, at least not in the summer of 1984, when he suddenly appeared in Nella. According to reliable accounts, the CIA helped Posada escape. Felix Rodriguez, a veteran CIA agent and key player in the Iran-Contra scandal, would later say that elements of the Enterprise had aided in the escape and Medina was brought into the Contra resupply project. By the following year, September, 1985, Medina would be based in El Salvador managing the day-to-day operations.[1]

Leaving Evans in Hot Springs to repair the crippled plane, Terry completed the "round robin" and flew back to Benton.

That night, Seal showed up late in Little Rock for dinner with Terry. At this meeting, Seal seemed uneasy and preoccupied. He had planned to get there in time to stop by Dan Lasater's firm, Lasater & Co., before it closed. It was 8PM.

"My plans have changed," he said. "I won't be spendin' the night here, and I need you to do me a favor in the mornin'. I've got a briefcase out in the car that's got some money in it to give to Dan. It's for a sure-fire investment deal he's turned me on to."

This was the first time Seal, or anyone, had asked Terry to handle money. Again, without seeking it, Terry was crossing over into another facet of the operation—the money loop.

The ragtime band was playing and they were at their usual corner table. "I'm gonna need someone I can really trust *and I mean really trust.* I know the slope is havin' me watched. Hell, he's even asked Evans to spy on me. Ain't this a great business? Everybody's fuckin' watchin' everybody while Daniel Ortega's gettin' ready to shove a big dick up Uncle Sam's ass, or should I say the vice president's ass."

He paused and stared intently at Terry. "At some point, Terry, you're gonna havta decide who ya really trust, too. So it's time to decide. Me or the slope. Who ya gonna go with?"

Terry's Air Force training had not prepared him for this "allegiance tug of war"—of having to choose between people he had thought were on the same side. It was obvious that Sawahata was playing everyone off against the other. But Seal seemed way ahead of him.

"Look" Seal continued, "you told me a long time ago, you wanted to learn how to handle the suits, well I'm ready to teach ya, but I gotta know you're on my side. Play things Sawahata's way and he'll be using you forever while he gets promoted from one GS fucking level to the next."

Terry thought for a moment and then said, "OK, but what's this shit about the vice president?"

"Oh that's somethin' I probably shouldn'ta said. Let's just say I came into possession of certain sensitive information about the Bush family on my last trip to Central America."

"OK, but if this is a relationship built on trust, first, what have you been doing in Central America?" Terry asked.

"Lotsa things. Some of which I can't tell you about. You really don't need to know, and I guarantee you don't *want* to know, so you don't become a liability, too. But the part I want to talk to you about tonight, if you're in, is guns and money. You sure you're in?"

"Barry, I'm not *totally* stupid," Terry replied with some emotion. "I've pretty much pieced together on my own that you're flyin' weapons down south. And I would assume that you're doing that with the blessing of the CIA and the White House...this operation is too large and too well equipped to otherwise exist undetected. I would also assume that you are motivated for reasons other than patriotism. Barry...I fought a war in which I was paid nothing. It'd certainly be nice to fight and win one, not only to heal a bunch of old wounds, but serve my country and get paid as well. Yeah, if that's what you're talking about...count me in."

Seal then divulged to Terry that he had, in deed, been flying weapons, like the ones he had seen earlier that day, from Mena to storage facilities in El Salvador and elsewhere. He had recently obtained the C-123, he said, because the size of the shipments were exceeding the size of his supply aircraft.

The part that fascinated Terry, and which Seal called the "decoy operation," involved Seal's ownership or "use" as he put it, of "two of everything." He said there were two C-123s that had the same tail number and, from all outward appearances, were identical.

"Where in the hell do you get C-123s?" Terry asked.

"Where do you think?—the Agency, of course. They got shit hid all over the

place. Planes left over from Southeast Asia, mostly old Air America stuff." Seal
added that he had two Navajos and two Senecas airplanes, two wives and two
girl friends. From his experience, a spare was always necessary in case something, or someone, broke down. And, more importantly, in this case, it was for
a diversion of attention to distract and send pursuers in the wrong direction or
have the ability to appear to be in two places at the same time.

But despite the humor, Seal was clearly worried. And now his dinner companion was worried, too. He was worried about allegiance. Were Sawahata
and Seal really just setting him up to test his loyalty. Should he tell Aki about
this meeting? Was the table bugged? Was this a test of his allegiance to the
CIA?

For the time being, Terry decided to play along. You can't make an intelligent decision without good intelligence, he had been taught.

"OK," Terry said. "So you're flying guns down, big deal! I suspected something was going on concerning weapons, ever since our discussions back in
December about casting M16 parts. What's secret about that?"

"What you walked in on today was the U.S. Army's and National Guard's
'donation' of parts to make it all happen," Seal answered. "This is extremely
sensitive. And if Sawahata finds out that you know about it, he'll get upset.
You know these government shits, they don't trust anybody. So anyway, keep
that quiet, will ya? But more importantly, let's get down to the money. I have
need of a shadow, a decoy."

As both men talked, Terry moved closer to Seal. He didn't want to miss the
slightest detail. The band was beginning to drown out the conversation. It was
getting really interesting.

"There's a lot goin' on here besides patriotism," Seal said in his usual monotone. "There's big money bein' made offa all this weapons stuff. I'm flyin' lots
of cash back in here to Arkansas, money that a guy would be hard-pressed to
explain how he came by, if the FAA ramp checked him. So, if you're interested,
I got the need for a good pilot that can tuck it tight at night and not get squeamish when wake turbulence hits ya. I've flown with ya and I know ya don't get
squeamish. Ya wanna do it?"

"Sure, tell me more."

It was napkin time again. Seal sketched out a diagram of how two aircraft
could "join" in flight, temporarily appear as one radar return, or blip, on an
air traffic controller's screen, and then have the *primary* aircraft "disappear"
and be replaced by the *rendezvous* aircraft. To the controller, it would appear
as if nothing had happened. He still would be tracking only one airplane. What
the controller would not realize was the aircraft he was "handling" had been
switched with another. Seal even had a humorous term for this procedure. He
called it "piggybacking", appropriately, for someone operating in Arkansas,
where the state symbol is a razorback hog.

Seal said this technique had been taught him by the CIA as a way to penetrate foreign airspace with two aircraft that would appear as one on the ground
controller's screen. The second aircraft has the ability to "drop off" the screen
and fly to a secret destination. This was devised by the CIA as a means of
penetrating and exiting foreign airspace while on intelligence missions.

"So that's real interesting, but what's the application here in Arkansas?"

"The Agency's having me move in large quantities of cash from foreign sources
for 'investments' here," Seal replied. "Lasater's part of that operation. When

we sell the weapons I'm flying down there, the profits in cash are flown back here for depositin'. Trouble is, the Agency doesn't want anyone to know about the profits. So, if I'm being followed out of Central America, and, if someone knows I'm carrying the cash, I need a way to throw them off my tail." That's where Terry and piggybacking would come in.

"OK, so what do I do?"

"I have two Seneca II's that are identical. November 8658 echo and November 8049 zulu," Seal said. "I'll leave one here in Little Rock, at Little Rock Air Center for you to use as the rendezvous aircraft. We'll work up an exact time and altitude to rendezvous above Texarkana. You'll join in behind me on my tail—and I mean on my fucking tail! I want you to be able to count the rivets that mount the tail hook. Use your night vision system. Then after 'you' become 'me' you just proceed on up to Mena and land. It's that simple."

"Let's go out and practice this somewhere in the daytime," Terry suggested.

"Sounds good to me. I'll bring Camp, he's in on this, too. And you know what's great? He and you look a lot alike. At a distance, with you sitting in the airplane, I've confused you for him."

"Let's go back to the gun deal," Terry suggested. "Is there anything else you can tell me. I'm just curious. I saw what appeared to be Army personnel in there assembling them."

"Remember those fuckin' M16A1's...you know the ones that were first used in Vietnam, the ones that jammed when exposed to sand? The Army's got a bunch of that model and wants to get rid of them. What better place than Nicaragua? And the cool part is we get to sell them to the Contras and the Agency pockets the profits. A little secret source of revenues Congress don't know about."

"Is this your brainchild?" Terry asked.

"No. I'd like to take credit for it, but this is Mr. Cathey's doing, or at least he's takin' credit for it. Only problem he didn't think of is we can't sneak the whole fuckin' weapon outa Uncle's inventory, only the main components. There's paper tracking on the full-auto stuff. So we build these guns up from parts inventory primarily and then add some 'home brew,' you know, the parts Brodix are casting. The beauty of this is: no paper, no trail."

Back in the parking lot, Seal went to his Mercedes, opened the trunk and handed Terry a locked briefcase. "Do me a favor. Take this by Dan's place first thing in the morning and don't leave it layin' around unguarded. It's a sizeable deposit, courtesy of Uncle Sam."

"Can I ask where you're goin'? I thought you were gonna spend the night?" Terry asked.

"So did I. Me and the Fat Lady have an appointment down south. See ya later, piggyback."

Seal *needed* a new friend. By now, Seal's "sting" involving the Nicaraguans had become public even though his name, as of yet, had not surfaced in the media. The story, leaked by North and the White House, had first appeared in the *Washington Times* and the Cartel was now certain that Seal was a U.S. government informant. A subsequent headline in *The New York Times* read: "U.S. Accuses Managua of Role in Cocaine Traffic."

Seal's name was not in the story, but it didn't have to be. The Cartel knew who had flown "The Fat Lady." Now, Seal's cover had been blown and, to the DEA's dismay, his usefulness as an asset was coming to an end. Beltway politics had done him in. His value as a DEA undercover agent and his personal safety were traded off in exchange for convenient headlines that suited the Reagan Administration's agenda to make the Sandinistas look bad...at any expense. Seal had become expendable. His problems were compounded by a turf war not only between federal agencies, but within the individual agencies themselves. A federal investigation of Seal had been started in Baton Rouge and Seal's friends were being hauled before a grand jury.

If the "suits" were turning on him, then Seal could play that game, too. Seal had, as his earlier cryptic remark about the Bush family indicated, acquired some "dirt" of his own that he had kept to himself. And now, he was secretly preparing ways to go on the offensive himself.

As Seal started up the Mercedes, Terry recalled he had one last pressing issue. "Barry, you got any pull with the Chink? He's workin' me to death and I need a weekend off for something special."

"Sure. You know I know how to handle orientals, I could always negotiate the hookers in Asia down. Two for the price of one, normally. What do ya need that's so special?" Barry asked.

"A weekend off to go try to make a baby," Terry replied. "In fact, not just any weekend. Janis and I have plotted her optimum 'window of pregnancy' and I need a couple of days around the first of the month."

"Consider it done, " Seal replied. "I'll take care of the Chink. Surely the CIA understands an agent has to have time to produce more agents."

Terry's crash and the fears it had engendered focused his mind not only on the fragility of life for himself, but his two-year-old son's as well. As he looked back, he believed that his marriage to Janis at that time had reached a new plateau and that they needed now to reinforce their family with a new life. He and Janis had talked, quite clinically, about another child, the need for a "backup." Earlier they had thought that one child would be enough. Like many "Yuppie" couples the "in" thing was to have a trophy that they could show off.

That "trophy," the product of their generation's need to *plan* everything, was their first son, Duncan. They saw him as the perfect child. But, they wondered, what would happen to them and their marriage if an incident like Terry's crash suddenly snuffed out the results of their life's investment in an only child? They didn't want to wait. They were both in their 30s and the biological clock was ticking away.

As a result of Seal's "handling" Sawahata for Terry, and scheduling him deserved time off, Aki had pencilled in September 1 and 2 as "undercover days." Sawahata felt he had outdone himself with the humor of it.

The Reeds put their spook lives on hold for two days and escaped to Eureka Springs, Arkansas, known as "The Little Switzerland of the Ozarks." Terry had to bribe his way into the Crescent Hotel, which was jammed for the Labor Day weekend. The luxury hotel, built by the railroad in 1886, was designed originally for wealthy Yankees who wanted to soak in the mineral waters from the underground springs. It seemed like the fitting place to make a baby.

Suffering the pain of labor nine months later while giving birth naturally to their second son, Elliott, Janis thought about her son being conceived on Labor Day. How fitting!

* * *

The phone rang just as Terry was stepping out the door to head for Lasater's. Seal had told him his contact there for the deposit transaction would be Dan Mangum, the vice president.

"Terry-san," Sawahata said. "I need to see you immediately. We have a problem over there. Can you pick me up at my place?"

"Sure, but I have to make a stop on the way."

After dropping off the briefcase, he pulled into Sawahata's parking lot at OSI. On the way over, his stomach had been in a knot. What, if anything, should he tell Aki?

Had it been a test?

The flight training had been going on for six weeks and Terry had been meeting weekly with Sawahata for lunch at a Chinese restaurant near the State Capitol to brief him on the students' progress. The instructors were concerned. The students' performance in the air was acceptable, but they were scoring substandard on their written work.

It appeared that Diego was losing control. He just didn't seem up to the task of whipping them into shape scholastically. As Terry and the other instructors knew, lack of aviation knowledge can be just as lethal as lack of flying skills. The training schedule was in peril because they could not advance safely to Phase II, or airdrop procedures, until they had mastered all Phase I material. Sawahata was being pressured by Cathey to accelerate the program and drastic measures were being taken.

Sawahata wanted to go to Mena, immediately. He said the new field commander had called a meeting and everyone had to be there. No excuses!

On the flight over to Mena, Terry's instincts were gnawing at him and he decided to tell the credential-carrying CIA man about the previous night's meeting with Seal. He made the right decision.

As the expressionless Japanese sat in the right seat and absorbed the information Terry passed on, he seemed stoic. "In Japan, we have saying we call putting 'dye in water.' It is way of tracking information which you generate in order to observe how it comes back to you. From this you learn many things. No. 1. You learn conduit of information back to you. No. 2. You see if information comes back to you distorted. No. 3, and most important, you see if information comes back at all. You just passed critical test. You are now most definitely trusted one. Terry-san, you make me so happy, and I hope you are not angry at Mr. Seal and me. But we needed to know of your trust for sure." Terry, however, had held back two important things from Sawahata. He did not tell him about Seal's veiled reference to the Bush family and didn't let on that Seal had asked him to keep information secret from Aki, the CIA boss.

What the fulltime spooks had not realized was that Terry had dyed the water, too, and learned a lot. Namely, the Agency was involved in everything Seal was doing and Seal was doing everything with the Agency's blessing.

"Aki, do me a favor," Terry said with a touch of pleading in his voice. "The next time you doubt my trust, please just read my military file. The Air Force entrusted me with great secrets that I passed on to no one unless they had an absolute, operational need to know. Can we please cut through the bullshit and this continuous moral tug of war of pitting people against each other. I have to trust you guys, too."

"OK, this is last test," Sawahata said. "But what kind of sensitive informa-tion did Air Force entrust in you if I may ask?"

"Information about our plans to bomb Japan... again! Only this time, we use *super-boy*." Sawahata did not respond.

They landed and drove to Nella where Medina was shaking everyone's tree. When they drove into the camp, now guarded by sentries, all 20 students were standing at rigid attention as if facing a firing squad.

There had been a sea change since Terry had last seen the camp.

Medina, a man in his 40s and dressed in bloused jungle fatigues with a maroon beret and wearing a sidearm, was storming up and down, swearing in Spanish and acting very Hispanic and macho. The other three instructors were sitting tensely at a picnic table with Varnados taking it all in. A major shape-up was underway. Diego, who clearly had been demoted, had become Medina's adjutant. There was no doubt who was in charge now.

"You pigs are not even worthy of dying for your cause,"

Medina yelled at the students in obvious disgust. "People like you come from soft families! You are soft people from elite families! If you want to stay in this program, you must become hard like me! The Sandinistas are hard! They train hard. They have Russian instructors. They are getting Russian helicopters. They will shoot you down and eat you for lunch!. And I will laugh! If you survive the crash and escape, I will kill you! This is serious business and I will personally shoot the next man who scores below 70 percentile on any written test. I take that back, 80 percentile!"

As he watched, Terry felt certain that Medina was a man who had killed before. The emotions that Medina evoked in Terry were mixed. He had respect for his dedication, but, on the other hand, he felt ill at ease that Medina would threaten his trainees with death in order to motivate them.

Medina had spent the previous day being briefed by Oklahoma about the slow pace of the ground work, low test scores and the general lack of military discipline at the camp. To Terry it reminded him of his first night of basic training at Amarillo, Texas. After landing at the airport, he and the other Air Force recruits stood at rigid attention in the snow while the civilian air travel-ers watched the Training Instructors yell obscenities.

When Medina finished barking at the trainees, he abruptly turned and fo-cused on Nebraska. "So tell me, what would the U.S. Army do to Special Forces commanders in Vietnam who *compromised* classified information? Stand up and tell me!" he shouted.

Medina had discovered from Evans that Nebraska had left classified charts and flight information inside the plane that had been forced to land previ-ously at Hot Springs. Waving them in the air, Medina shouted, "There are lines on these maps that will direct anyone who reads them straight to this facility. These maps coupled with our secret VHF frequencies could be the end to this program."

Nebraska had no response.

"I am immediately appointing my adjutant, Diego, as security officer," Medina declared. "This will not occur again! This operation will not be com-promised while I am in charge. If any of you have anything in your possession, notes, diagrams, anything that is a jeopardy to this operation, turn it over to Diego immediately for destruction."

He told Sawahata to prepare a report about the security breach and "file it with Washington." Medina had made it clear there would be consequences for sloppiness.

To Medina, they all—students and instructors—were soft and needed to be shaped up militarily.

He ended his speech, sat down, and, as military protocol dictated, let his adjutant, Diego, take over. Diego marched to center position and read the new school camp standards. They included new and tightened security procedures along with schedules for stepped-up overnight field maneuvers involving hand-to-hand combat with the Fort Chaffee soldiers. Survival techniques would be stressed such as Air Force escape and evasion training for downed pilots along with search and rescue (SAR) techniques behind enemy lines. He had also arranged for the trainees to fire live ammunition at the Fort Chaffee range for M16s and .45-cal. weapons.

As the briefing wound down, Diego read from his clipboard. "When I call the following names, please step forward. Martinez. Ortega. Lopez. Gutierrez."

Fear was clearly visible in their eyes as they stepped forward. Had they failed? Were they really going to be shot? Nobody had a clue. Until Diego spoke: "Pack your gear. You four men are going to Georgia to flight training school for the Maule aircraft. Your previous instructor in single-engine training has recommended you all for this job. Fall out."

The Maule aircraft was manufactured in Georgia and later became Oliver North's primary STOL, or Short-Field Takeoff and Landing, aircraft for in-field resupply and medical evacuation missions. A high-performance, high-wing single engine airplane, it is renowned worldwide for its ability to take off and land on unimproved air strips.* North would write the following year to CIA Agent Felix Rodriguez, a Bay of Pigs Veteran and a man later recruited by the Enterprise, to expect a shipment of "a number of new Maule aircraft" which would be flown by "Nicaraguan pilots or other Latin Americans—not U.S. citizens." The Enterprise's records would show that they purchased three Maule aircraft and support packages for a total of $183,238.[2]

The decision now reduced the class of 20 to 16 and the four instructors initially concluded this would reduce their workload. Emile Camp was the first to speak as the students dispersed.

"Well that's good. Now that we're down to 16 students, maybe we won't have to work such long hours and can slow down the pace a little bit. That'll mean fewer students per flight or fewer flights, right?"

Medina snapped before the words were barely out of Camp's mouth. "You see! This soft attitude is coming from you civilian instructors. This is what's wrong here. I need military instructors to get these men in shape. No, that does not mean fewer flights! You will fly more hours and do whatever it takes to get them prepared for combat. Their country needs them now. Do you understand?"

"Hey Medina, stick it up your ass sideways, you beaner motherfucker!" Camp shouted back. "I ain't your goddam nigger. So lets' just get it on right fuckin' now!"

Sawahata had to step between the two enraged men. "Gentlemen! Gentlemen! Calm down! The Agency needs to get its money's worth. We have hired

---

*   North interceded with Assistant Customs Commissioner William Rosenblatt to stone-
     wall, or at least, limit a Customs investigation into the shipments of Maule aircraft to
     Central America. [3]

good people. Surely, we can all work together peacefully for our common cause."

The two antagonists glared at the small Japanese man standing between them. They apparently decided that to crawl over their CIA boss in order to take swings at each other would be counter-productive.

They would bide their time. There would future opportunities to settle the vendetta that was building between them. Camp would die six months later in a crash that would leave behind a lot of unanswered questions.

1.   Felix Rodriguez and John Wiseman, *Shadow Warrior.* Simon & Schuster, 1989, pp 290-291.
2.   *Report of the Congressional Committees Investigation of Iran-Contra Affair, Summary of Enterprise Expenditures p. 337*
3.   Ben Bradlee, Jr., *Guts and Glory, the Rise and Fall of Oliver North (Donald I. Fine, Inc. New York, 1988) p. 447*

CHAPTER 9

GOLD MEDAL FLIGHT SCHOOL

Ramon Medina was, indeed, a son of a bitch.

On the ground, it became a non-stop boot camp. Medina posted the scores of daily written tests and each week raised the percentile required for passing, with ninety per cent being the ultimate target. The price of failure, he implied, was a body bag.

He worked them, night and day. Every moment not studying their ground-school texts was spent in guerrilla warfare tactics, as they were divided into teams for simulated combat and ambush training. This meant sloshing through streams and forced marches through the heavily wooded terrain that surrounded them. The dense underbrush, laden with briars, ticks and the insatiably carnivorous chiggers, made even walking difficult in the areas where they concealed their positions while hiding on maneuvers.

Though Terry disliked Medina personally, he admired him professionally. He was quickly turning the students into lean fighting men from the harsh regimen that "The Bomber," as he was called, was putting them through. This made Terry's and the other instructors' jobs easier.

As they jogged at double time until they nearly dropped from heat exhaustion, Medina forced the students to shout cadence and chant "*Boland es un Communista.*" This part of their mental conditioning again reminded Terry of his own basic training experiences.

Medina's 24-hour-a-day regimen was due to the need to quickly get this class trained and into the field. Congress was preparing to pass what became known as the "full Boland" Amendment that prohibited either the CIA, or the Defense Department, "or any other agency or entity of the United States involved in intelligence activities" from providing, directly or indirectly, any military assistance to the Contras.

Their only visitors from the outside world were medical personnel from Ft. Chaffee who came to treat the normal maladies. Their only respite came on Sunday nights when Ramon Varnados brought in *cervezas* to complement the occasional weekend barbecue. From the occasional aroma he smelled, Terry figured the trainees had discovered the illegal relaxant that grew wild in the mountainous region and for which Arkansas was quickly becoming famous.

Pot smoking befitted the Arkansas State slogan at the time, which was: "ARKANSAS, A NATURAL HIGH." It made the Nicaraguans joke that they were fighting not just to drive the communists from their homeland, but to win the war and get back to what they considered to be the home of the "best weed in the world."

Medina had "frozen" the flying curriculum until the trainees ground work improved. There would be no air drop training until the test scores rose to the ninety percentile. Terry and the other instructors used this time in the air to review with the students what they had learned already, namely that a twin-engine airplane "can really be a handful" compared to the single-engine types they had originally trained in.

The flight work review now became an escape from the hostile camp environment created by Medina. The students looked forward to putting on civilian clothes and being trucked to nearby Waldron for the start of each flight training session. Civvies were part of the cover since the students were supposed to be flight trainees from Ross Aviation in Tulsa, and wearing camouflage uniforms would have immediately attracted suspicion.

The flight sessions were becoming longer which required instructors to work in shifts during a specified scheduled flight training class. Instructors would rendezvous at pre-planned airports throughout western and central Arkansas to relieve each other, thereby reducing the amount of takeoffs and departures at Malvern. This would also reduce the chance of being observed and bringing unnecessary attention to the Malvern/Nella area. Security was at the top of everyone's list. Especially Medina's.

The Agency had Oklahoma obtain the tail numbers of the multi-engine airplanes being utilized by the Spartan School of Aeronautics in Tulsa and for use as the false call signs in radio transmissions to air traffic control in the area. That way, if local air controllers on the ground decided to check the "N" numbers of the aircraft they were handling, they would trace them to Spartan, which had a large number of foreign students. All would appear routine.

Terry began to notice that when he was conducting "Boomerang" flight training sorties within the MOAs (military operations areas) and monitoring ATC (air traffic control) communications, he could hear the controllers intentionally divert other air traffic away from the area. He knew that ATC was fully aware of his presence in the area since the transponder lights in the training aircraft gave indications they were being "painted" or observed. Red Hall, Seal's Agency avionics expert, made sure their collision avoidance equipment was fully operational and it showed continuous "interrogation" activity by ATC when flying above 4,000 feet MSL within the MOAs. It seemed obvious that the FAA was providing cover for "Jade Bridge" by attempting to keep unwanted aircraft out of the area.

When he asked Seal about this, Seal said: "Yeah, ain't Uncle great? This is better than operating in any fuckin' banana republic. Here the government can use all its 'resources' for cover."

While flying, Terry was observing increased troop movements on the ground in the Nella area and additional security at the training complex. The camp's "security forces" were fully-armed Anglos wearing sanitized jungle fatigues and who walked around with a defined aura of professionalism and authority. Using late model Army-issue communication equipment, these shadowy security personnel were in constant contact with Medina and his adjutant, Diego.

The increased patrols were a precursor for the new training phase, the phase involving actual air drops that would have to be confined to the Nella strip and adjacent areas. This would mean increased and concentrated air traffic occurring in the area at the height of the tourist and camping season. Even though, as Seal had told Terry, a lot of local people had been given "government subsidies" not to report anything strange they might see, there were some sightings reported nonetheless. For example, Arkansas State Police Investigator Russell Welch said that civilians in the area had sighted a platoon-sized group of camouflaged men crossing the Ouachita River east of Nella "as if they were on a mission."

One local game warden revealed to one of the authors that he had been told to "just keep going" when confronted in the area by two heavily-armed men with a "military bearing." Another was warned away by someone who claimed to be an FBI agent and who exhibited federal credentials.

Another such witness was Bill Duncan, a former Internal Revenue Service Agent who had been sent to Mena to investigate the massive amounts of cash the Agency was inadvertently transfusing into the area's banks. His target had become Rich Mountain Aviation, which he did not know had become a CIA proprietary. During his stay in Mena there, residents told him and other investigators of "numerous reports of automatic weapons fire" in the Nella area, and locals seeing "people in camouflage in the middle of the night, low intensity landing lights around the Nella airport, twin-engine airplane traffic in and about the Nella airport..." Duncan said these reports came from "a variety of law enforcement sources."

And there was increased activity within the hangars of Rich Mountain Aviation at the Mena Airport as well. A secretary at Rich Mountain, Cathy Corrigan, told Duncan that employees were often "forced to stay inside their offices because airplanes would land and strange faces would be around. Folks of Spanish origin would be around that they had not seen before.

In a previously sealed and "classified" transcript of sworn testimony given by Duncan for the purpose of getting Independent Prosecutor Lawrence Walsh's office to investigate the Agency's activities at Mena, Duncan described "great secrecy surrounding the entire operation at Rich Mountain Aviation" in Mena. Duncan testified in his June, 1991, deposition given to the Arkansas Attorney General that there were "airplanes landing in the middle of the night, hangar doors opening, the airplanes going in, then leaving out before daylight... numerous, dozens and dozens of accounts like that."

As the training at Nella droned on, the student body was whittled down. By late September, the head count was down to 16 possible pilots and 4 ground controllers. Terry and the others had already identified about six of the pilots who were marginal at best. But four of these six potential wash-outs spent a lot of time alone with Medina, appearing to be his favorites or "pets." This confused the instructors since these four mediocre aviators were escaping Medina's ferocious wrath, yet they needed it the most. Soon the Gringos would find out why the four were being privately "tutored" and receiving special treatment.

Keeping good on his promise to show the Contras what they'd be flying in Nicaragua, Barry Seal had delivered a camouflaged Fairchild C-123 to the Mena airport. Before landing, and in grand style, Seal buzzed the Nella field, putting the students into a state of euphoria when they saw the massive hulk of the "heavy iron" streaking across the field, barely above the treetops. As an incentive and a reward, the top two students of each week were taken to Mena to sit in and inspect the plane. "Hangar flying", it's called. As they sat in the cockpit staring at the massive array of gauges and daydreaming, it was easy to imagine their thoughts of delivering the "tools of freedom" to their comrades in the field and being celebrated as national heroes. Lying about the barracks, dog-eared and mutilated, were C-123 operations manuals. It wasn't difficult to see that they all considered the Cessna as only a necessary stepping stone to the "baby C-130" they hoped to master.

But new problems were looming both for Seal and for the program. Seal was learning first hand the truth concerning the joke about the four biggest lies, one of which is: "I'm with the government and I'm here to help you." Seal had now learned, as he put it, "Uncle Sam doesn't shoot straight," and that a promise from one part of the government can be completely meaningless to another.

Though Seal had been working closely and effectively with the Drug Enforcement Administration in Florida, the same agency was actually preparing to indict him in Louisiana. John Cathey had tapped Seal because of his aviation skills and his aircraft maintenance facility in Mena. But the DEA and the federal agencies in Louisiana, who had "no need to know" and weren't cleared for knowledge about Nella, were coming after Seal with a vengeance. All they saw in Seal was his Agency-manufactured drug-trafficker profile and cover. They did not realize that his highly sensitive missions were being directed by Oliver North and the Executive branch of government. The multitude of agencies of the Justice Department were simply busy fighting among themselves to see who would be the first to "put another notch in their gun" by bringing him down.

Seal's problem was that Oliver North and the National Security Council could not intervene in his behalf without risking "Centaur Rose" and "Jade Bridge" being *compromised*. If this occurred, an immediate Congressional Investigation centering around Boland Amendment violations would be launched, the results of which could spell disaster for the Reagan Administration. The problem that now tied everyone's hands in the White House was Congress and the stringent language of the newly-enacted Boland II, as it was called. Cathey had alerted Seal to pull out all the stops with training, so that at least some Nicaraguan pilots would graduate and be sent into combat as soon as possible. CIA attorneys were busy studying the small print of the amendment, trying to soften it with their own interpretation, not only as it applied to the government but also to "subcontract" cut-out operations like the one at Nella.

* * *

When Seal returned that day to Mena in late September, 1984, he had dropped off Aki Sawahata at Rich Mountain Aviation and drove to Nella to deliver a new instructor code-named "Idaho."He was a former Air America loadmaster for C-123 aircraft in Thailand. In addition he was a seasoned aerial combat crew member whose main flight function had been to jettison airborne cargo at precisely the correct second in order to hit the DZ (drop zone). For this reason, his job speciality was normally referred to as "the kicker". His experience was ideal, since the C-123 was the plane the students would be using once they relieved the CIA pilots who were conducting the ongoing airdrop operations in Nicaragua.

It was a Sunday afternoon and the instructors and Medina were having their weekly management seminar or "group grope" as Reed preferred to call it. They had been expecting Seal. When the group heard him arrive, they came out of the command post to greet him.

These meetings were supposed to be a time of problem solving and open exchange among the faculty, without the students being present. The pressure from Washington was to accelerate the training schedule, thereby adding to the friction already generated by personality conflicts. For the most part, these meetings were now degenerating into finger-pointing sessions—with Medina being the one doing the pointing. Camp didn't "cotton" to the Latino's arrogant approach which was more often than not causing more "open exchange" than solving problems.

"John Cathey is giving you guys a present," Seal said as he introduced the new instructor. "He's an ex-Air America cargo rigger and 'kicker' from Thailand. You and he should hit it right off, Terry. You guys probably worked on the same railroad in Thailand...layin' Thais."

Barry had a knack of somehow working a sexual reference into most discussions. He seemed especially pleased with himself over this comment—he grinned and slapped Terry on the back.

Seal then turned to Medina and told him that Washington was getting impatient and felt that they were perhaps spending too much time on spit and polish.

"They want to immediately implement the aerial delivery phase of the training, regardless of these guys' military bearing," Seal said. "They're anxious to see some product come out of this school. That's why they're sending in 'Idaho' here. They also told me to tell you it's very important for you to complete your 'extra-curricular' activities."

"Extra-curricular activities" appeared to be code talk that only Seal and Medina seemed to understand.

Medina, Seal and Diego then left for a private meeting while Idaho was introduced to the others. A cargo specialist or loadmaster, like "Idaho" was badly needed and he filled a major void in the "faculty" line-up. He had brought all the necessary ballistics tables used to compute trajectory of palletized cargo based upon weight and frontal area of drag. He said other essential training equipment, such as cargo nets, a pallet and parachutes, would also arrive soon. This signaled to Reed that he was probably a true professional with extensive knowledge and not some "by the seat of his pants" cargo jockey. This was welcome news.

Terry later learned Idaho had worked in the aerial resupply of Angkhor Wat during the siege of the ancient Cambodian city by the Khmer Rouge. This USAF airlift operation had coincided with Terry's last tour in Southeast Asia. "Idaho" had, in fact, been stationed at Udorn in Thailand and based out of the old facilities built by the Japanese during World War II.

After an extensive exchange of experiences and war stories between Terry and the cargo man, they agreed Seal was probably correct in his earlier assumption. It was highly probable that they HAD indeed laid some of the same Thais.

After Seal, Diego and Medina finished their private meeting, Seal approached Terry and, referring to Sawahata said, "Our main chink is back at Rich Mountain, you need to fly him back to Little Rock. I don't have time to fuck with him right now. I got pressin' problems back in Washington." He left alone.

Terry noticed that Seal was not entirely himself. Although jovial, he seemed somewhat preoccupied and distant. Unknown to Terry, he had good reason. Seal had decided that he had to go public in order to protect himself against an impending Louisiana indictment. Seal had been at the center of a major turf war not just between different agencies, but *within* the agencies themselves.

He was alone and discarded by the federal drug agents in Florida, with whom he had worked closely. They appeared to have abandoned him when he most needed them to vouch for him and call off the law enforcement dogs of several agencies in Louisiana. This fear of being discarded and tossed to the dogs had forced Seal to begin taking protective measures of his own. Though the Feds did not know it, Seal had begun secretly recording all his conversations with them.*

The secret tapes are highly embarrassing to the government, particularly the DEA. At one point, DEA agent Ernest Jacobson is asked by Seal what his office wants from him. Jacobson replies: "I don't know what my office wants. My office doesn't know what my office wants." This kind of admission demonstrated that the agencies involved were confused and operating with conflicting agendas.

Seal was in a highly unusual, and *compromising*, position with the government. Informants and assets like Seal rarely work for more than one government agency at a time. Through no design of his own, Seal was working with the DEA, Customs, the FBI, the CIA, the Medellin Cartel and possibly others. None of the government "handlers" appeared to know entirely about the other. By the fall of 1984, Seal probably knew more about the GS "suits" he was dealing with than they knew about him.

In addition to making the tapes, Seal had devised a plan to make his own television documentary, something that would be his insurance policy. He used John Camp, a reporter for Baton Rouge television station WBRZ-TV, to film the piece which was later titled "Uncle Sam Wants You." After it was broadcast on November 20, 1984, Seal told his DEA handlers in Florida that he had cooperated in the TV documentary because he feared the DEA, and the government in general, was preparing to double-cross him—which it ultimately did. The film basically showed Seal being "handled" by his "handlers", complete with him receiving $10,000 in cash as an installment for services rendered. With the agents "entrapped" on the secretly taped video, Seal figured there was no way they could deny his existence or his role in their ongoing investigations.

Shortly after Seal left Nella that day, a late afternoon line of weather began sweeping in from Oklahoma toward Arkansas. It was the type of fast-moving cold front that spawns severe thunderstorms and, worse yet, tornadoes. For this reason, the "group grope" was ended prematurely and the instructors were transported back to Mena in the back of the one-ton gas truck. The bed of the truck was becoming less useful to haul cargo since the tank had been enlarged to allow for the ever-increasing amount of fuel being used by the training aircraft. Joe Evans was finding it necessary to buy fuel throughout the area, which he trucked in to mask the large amounts being used. Terry and the others could only speculate on the magnitude of the program's fuel bill.

Back at Rich Mountain, Sawahata was talking to Evans about modification requirements to two new aircraft the operation had procured. One, a Cessna 402 bearing registration number N 5774C, had already arrived. Terry was told this Cessna would become their primary training plane for the practice air

---

* These are tapes made available to one of the authors by police sources who believed the federal agents would destroy them. Much of their content has never been revealed.

deliveries. Hampton and Evans were in the new hangar having an in-depth engineering discussion about adding a door in the tail that would allow cargo to be ejected from the rear rather than the side, giving it the configuration and appearance of a miniature C-123. This would be essential for the practice air drops of bags of flour instead of real cargo.

The group of aviators decided not to test their luck against the line of towering cumulus clouds that were now looming over Rich Mountain. It was definitely time for some "hangar flying" rather than weather flying.

Evans briefed the group that he hoped he would soon be receiving a World War II vintage Beech 18 tail dragger that would be modified as well. This large, radial engined twin, which had been the primary trainer for most American World War II bomber pilots, would be used as a final upgrade aircraft, giving the students some "round motor" experience just prior to their graduation. The radial engine used in the Beech 18 utilizes the same principles of operation as the Pratt and Whitney engines in the C-123, which would be essential for smooth transition training in Central America.

Sawahata assured Evans the Agency was "looking" for a Beech 18 suitable for modification and wanted to know how long he needed to modify it for their mission.* Evans joked that if he had one in his possession soon, he could have it ready long before the students would be.

As the talk went on, the storm hit Mena assuring that no one could leave for several hours. Sawahata, like Seal, began to seem nervous and distracted. He kept reminding Reed he needed to get back to Little Rock in order to use his secure telephone line for an important call. Terry informed him that no flying could be done safely until the cold front had passed. He reminded Aki of his once-crushed foot that now ached severely due to the change in weather. Sawahata decided it would be prudent to wait.

"Terry-san, all this bad weather makes me think about your company airplane being tied down in Benton," Aki recalled. "Have you found hangar for company plane, yet?"

Terry told Aki that he had discovered there was no available hangar space to be found at any price in Central Arkansas.

"You need to check with builder of new hangars at North Little Rock Airport, again. I do not like to see your plane sitting around so visible. It could invite problems."

Terry agreed to check again with Bill Canino, the developer of the hangar project at North Little Rock.

It was after dark by the time the storm had passed, and everyone began to leave.

Oklahoma, Idaho and Nebraska all flew off in their "Company" planes headed for unknown destinations. Terry and Sawahata filed an IFR (instru-

---

* Apparently it was already "on order." Jerry Bohnen, the Oklahoma investigative journalist, later found that the Beech 18 used there was a 1963 Beech G18S stolen in Puerto Rico on July 1, 1983. Then, its registration number was N 9412, but when flown in the training program bore the tail No. N9490Y. The 1979 Cessna 402C, already in the hangar that day, had been stolen from Palm Beach, Fla. on Sept. 2, 1983 and it was actually N5779C. Evans claimed to author John Cummings that he has no records of any aircraft he ever worked on at Rich Mountain. Strange, since aircraft mechanics customarily retain records of all planes they have worked on, for liability purposes.

ment flight rules) flight plan for the trip back to Little Rock in anticipation of perhaps catching up with the weather that was moving east.

As they took off, Sawahata immediately got on the ITT McKay radio and began talking to the Nella command post about whether the "shipment" had arrived. A new loop was about to open for Terry.

Medina informed Sawahata that the "shipment," whatever it was, had not arrived. Just as Terry was intercepting his flight planned course, Sawahata turned to him and said: "Terry-san, I am sorry to make you do this, but I must ask you to cancel your flight plan and fly me to river at Ft. Smith. I want you to stay at very low altitude and follow Highway 71 on way there."

After canceling his IFR flight plan, Terry changed headings adding, "Hey, no problem, Aki-san. It's your plane and your gas. Where we goin'?"

"We need to look close for U-Haul truck going south on 71. I am worried about its safe passage to Nella. We had near miss recently and truckload of munitions was almost discovered by local police. I am just very worried. Shipment is overdue. It was supposed to arrive by noon today."

Terry slowed the aircraft to minimum controllable airspeed and descended to 1,000 feet above the highway. It was dark and the headlights from highway traffic were needed in order to locate and track the road...but no U-Haul could be seen. On the outskirts of Ft. Smith, Sawahata asked Terry if he knew where "Rock 13" was on the Arkansas River's Kerr-McClellan navigation way near Barling, Arkansas.

After consulting a road map, Terry was able to locate No. 13 Lock and Dam, which Highway 59 utilizes as a bridge to cross the river. He flew over the area and circled in a steep right banked turn, so that Sawahata could look out the right window.

"Aki, what the hell are we lookin' for? If you'll tell me it'll make it a lot easier," Terry asked.

"I need to locate a special barge that should be parked near the dam. It has our shipment," Sawahata replied.

Terry banked the plane in the other direction, to the left, giving himself the vantage angle for viewing the ground. He orbited long enough to ascertain there was no barge, but a U-Haul was parked nearby. Sawahata nervously got on the radio and began talking to the driver, who said his last radio communication with the barge indicated it was heading west just past Ozark, Arkansas. It had been forced to drop anchor and wait out the storm.

Sawahata was relieved. He asked Terry to remain in view of the river and fly toward Ozark. Twenty miles up the river, they spotted a lone barge heading west toward Ft. Smith. It was difficult to notice since it was powering upstream without navigation lights. Aki again got on the radio and began talking with the barge captain to get their estimated time of arrival at Lock 13. Sawahata and Terry loitered in the area until the barge and truck safely linked up.

"What was that all about, Aki?" Terry asked as they headed finally for Little Rock.

"Terry-san, you know rule. You do not have a need to know."

"Well, it seems the pulpwood you say OSI ships to Japan is heading the wrong way, it's going west toward *Okrahoma*. It should be going east toward the Gulf of Mexico, don't you think?" He could not help being facetious, remembering that OSI's cover was to purchase raw materials such as those offered by the timber industry of Arkansas and then export them to Japan.

Terry, again, through no desire of his own, had been exposed to yet another CIA secret, a transportation system that was obviously hauling weapons. From where the barge had originated its journey, he did not know...then. But he was beginning to get a pretty good idea of the transportation route the weapons were traveling.

With what he had witnessed that night, combined with the information relayed to him by Seal about the Army and National Guard's "donation" of weapons parts, Terry had a pretty complete picture of a secret weapons pipeline and its "outflow valve" in Arkansas. As of that night, he also knew weapons were being stored, at least temporarily, at the Nella complex awaiting "Dodger" flights to points south. Did the Boland Amendment have a flaw that purposely allowed this, he wondered?

Months later, after he was put into play with people on the next rung of the good ole boy ladder, he would learn that "special barge traffic" carrying *critical cargo* for operation "Centaur Rose" had its safe transit assured by the U.S. Army Corps of Engineers, which controls the whole Arkansas River. Good idea, Terry thought, no weigh stations, no speed traps, no prying eyes from local sheriffs. It made him wonder: How long had the Agency been using the rivers, largely abandoned by American commerce that favored Interstate Highways? Just like Southeast Asia, he mused. Everything moves by water.

* * *

It was mid-October 1984 and the students were in awe, viewing as they were the first turning of leaves they had seen. The Ouachitas were ablaze with color and the cockpit temperatures were now considerably lower. Ramon Varnados, the major domo of the complex, had to figure out how to operate the sophisticated portable heater units in preparation for cold weather. Army manuals are designed for fifth-grade reading level, which was about Ramon's limit.

Though lacking perhaps in formal schooling, Ramon was nonetheless street smart when it came to making a buck. He had quickly become known as the source of anything that was either hard to find or officially off limits to the students. He had established a major black market in copies of *Penthouse* and *Playboy*, centerfolds of which were prominently displayed on the barracks' walls. This was one of the few "luxuries" allowed by Medina.

The heavy humid air of summer was finally gone and the increased in-flight visibility, coupled with the smoother ride, made flying less tedious and much safer. It was a welcome relief for Terry and the others as they jumped full speed ahead into phase II—airdrops.

"Sixty seconds to mark," said the ground controller's voice to the perspiring Hispanic pilot in the left seat of the Cessna 402.

"Roger, give me a hack at 30 seconds," Ignacio, the captain of the sortie replied, requesting a signal to begin his timing.

Terry was sitting in the right seat traveling at 150 MPH and 500 feet above the treetops approaching the drop zone from the valley to the north of the field. He and his trainee were wearing their Honeywell night vision systems as he spoke to his three students on the intercom system. The two in the back were craning their necks to keep up with the cockpit action.

"You got a visual on the DZ (Drop Zone)?...I didn't hear you confirm with the kicker that the door is open. You're getting behind it, you're gettin' behind it. Read back your departure clearance before we dump this load and things really get busy."

It was obvious that the Hispanic pilot was, in aviation jargon, "getting behind the airplane." Hell, Terry was even being nice to him. So far he allowed him to have all on-board systems operational.

Wonder what he'd do if I gave him a hydraulic system failure, Terry thought to himself. Probably just shit his pants, give up and die, he guessed. For this reason he decided not to induce a simulated in-flight emergency and instead help the floundering student.

"Did you pick up on the hack, Ignacio?" Terry asked. "I've already started my clock, 15 seconds to delivery. I see muzzle flashes in our 1 o'clock. Ramon's up to his usual shit. Call five seconds to Arturo (the kicker in the back). When he calls 'pallets away' break hard left...you got the air speed for it. Remember, you'll be lighter then...and watch out for the mountain. Once we're clear, then dive for the river valley. Take cover below the treetops. I'm sure Ramon's laid a trap for us."

In a squeaky voice, five octaves above normal, the pilot switched his communications selector to the rear position in order to talk to the kicker, and called out *"dies segundos."* It was obvious to Terry that the pilot was under extreme pressure, reverting as he did to his native language. Terry had learned this was an ideal way to assess the stress level of his students who at times were under *severe* pressure in the cockpit.

The two other students, by now standing in the cabin doorway behind, and observing, weren't laughing. They knew they were next. Their job was to take note of the errors made by the man in the hot seat. And it was hot.

The white pop flare at the 12 o'clock position signaled that the aircraft was directly over the drop zone. Terry called "pallets away." The man in the back, the kicker, relayed to the flight crew immediately *"Si..er..I mean yes, pallets away Capitan Terry."*

But it was too late. Before they could break left, they saw the red flashes coming from their 2 o'clock position. This was the coded light signal for a ground-to-air missile launch. Considering the plane's proximity to the light beam, they had not time nor altitude for evasive maneuvers. They were "dead."

Over the radio came Ramon's sinister Latino voice. "You better hope you die in the crash, Ignacio. 'Cause if you survive, I'll hunt you down and capture your young ass. Then I'll torture you to death and enjoy it! And, Ignacio, the Sandinistas will do even worse!"

As the plane continued on its departure route, the pilot was receiving his cockpit critique. "Fuckin' missiles, Ignacio. Ramon got us again. I told you I saw small arms fire in my 1 o'clock" Terry reprimanded. "That was the giveaway. Always listen to your co-pilot. He has eyes, too. You should have aborted. The procedure is to abort. I know you Latinos think retreating is unmanly, but it's how you stay alive in combat."

"Gold Medal Flight School" was in full operation. As per John Cathey's mandate, the curriculum had advanced to the air delivery stage. Terry's role in visual "bombing" training was limited to weekends, when five pound bags of Gold Medal flour were dropped from the tail of the modified Cessna 402. The students scores would be based on whose bags came closest to the target, a big limed "X" in the middle of the Nella strip. The best were given the cut-out gold seals from the Gold Medal bags, which Terry mounted on cardboard.

Terry gave out these mock medals weekly at the "group grope," and the first "award ceremony" marked the only time he had ever seen Medina laugh. Somehow these homemade medals captured the true essence of the entire program for Reed. It reminded him of Southeast Asia when Ho Chi Minh's young soldiers had fought successfully against the vehement fire power of the United States. Yes, he hoped his students, wearing cardboard decorations, could fight back against all odds, just as his respected enemy had done in Laos.

The students had been divided into teams, one of which was "good guys" and the other the "bad guys". The exercise was to simulate a guerilla-style war in which the good guys would conduct hit-and-run attacks on the bad guys. In the real conflict, this would mean having highly-mobile infantry units isolated in the field and requiring resupply from the air. In Vietnam, the U.S. operated with total air superiority. This could not be assured in Nicaragua where the Sandinistas already had Soviet Hind helicopters and MIG jets. It had been decided that this operation needed more emphasis on air-to-ground communications procedures, since the shorter the time the delivery aircraft was exposed to the hostile environment, the greater the chances of survival. And given the geographic boundaries of Nicaragua, with friendly countries north and south and oceans on both sides, the aircraft could penetrate and escape quickly *if* they didn't linger over their drop zones.

The role of the ground controller attached to the good guys was to insure a quick entry and exit of the supplying aircraft. The bad guys' job was to foul up the air delivery by breaking into the ground controller's radio frequency and luring the plane into a "flak trap," as had been the experience in Vietnam during allied search and rescue missions.

The close proximity of opposing forces in a guerrilla-style war, combined with lack of clearly defined battle lines, makes this type of aerial delivery extremely dangerous with accuracy being mandatory. For this reason, the Nicaraguans were being heavily trained in light signals procedures that would allow delivery to take place silently at night with minimum voice exchange. U.S. Army-supplied generators and vertical flood lighting systems provided on-the-ground signaling devices for night deliveries. During the day, flares were used as necessary with more emphasis on voice communication.

As equally important to *uncompromised* communications, the problem of aerial delivery is to safely maneuver the aircraft with respect to the wind to allow for drift of the palletized cargo. This is not only to insure it landing in the right place, but also in the right hands. Good guys on the ground fire flares to enable the pilot and crew to analyze wind speed and direction as well as to signal "pallet away" time when the plane is directly over the drop zone. Coupled with assigning and assessing these aircraft maneuvering tasks, the instructors continuously simulated in-flight emergencies, thus compounding the work load of the crew and honing their skills. It was truly a team effort in the air and on the ground.

With Medina on the ground as "bad guys" commander, aircraft "losses" were high. He was even known to occasionally fire live tracer bullets at night to add realism. The training was intense and, considering the importance of the mission assigned to aerial delivery, it was going to take a lot longer than had been estimated.

Terry often had to shake off his misgivings concerning this backwoods training program. In the regular Army, it would have taken two years to train even the most competent soldiers for these combat aviation tasks. The instructors at Nella had been allotted four months, but were insisting on more time. This fact was not music to John Cathey's ears, but he had no choice other than to go along with the instructors' demands.

The proposed graduation date was extended to November, 1984, if even then. Already, the new Boland prohibition was in effect having passed both houses on October 11th. This one really had some tooth in it. Terry thought of consulting his attorney Mark Stodola, in Little Rock, for a legal opinion to see if he was violating any laws, but he shrugged it off, thinking that would be a violation of security. And anyway, he knew he was working for credentialled CIA Agents like John Cathey and Akihide Sawahata. Surely, he thought, if there was any legal exposure as a result of the wording in Boland, the Agency would be able to deal with it back in Washington. His worries were insignificant compared to the plight of his Contra trainees.

Terry often despaired of them. But he believed they would someday prevail. They were, he believed, like his prior Vietnamese enemies. Though lacking organization, discipline and fighting skills, they compensated with Ho Chi Minh-style dedication and perseverance. He hoped that, if things were reversed and he had to liberate his country, there would be someone to do this sort of training for him.

Night flying was Terry's specialty and, in order to give the students a real time training environment, additional nighttime flight requirements were added to the curriculum. The entire month of October became a blur of images enhanced by night vision systems, with four eight-hour night sessions a week and full weekends, when weather permitted.

Although self-imposed, the instructors began to feel the pressure of the oncoming winter. They established December 1st as the mandatory graduation date since they knew that the severity of winter weather would play a major factor in the flying schedule. Ice storms were severe and common in Arkansas during the winter and the foliage would be gone, further increasing the threat of detection.

* * *

The first day of November, 1984, was an unlucky one for Akihide Sawahata. Regardless of its power, even the CIA cannot plan for the X-factor. And that was Mark McAfee in the case of operations "Jade Bridge" and "Centaur Rose".

McAfee had become a parasite in search of a host to maintain his own existence. He had pried his way into Sawahata's life and now wanted to suck Aki into his own dying organism or, in this case, his business. While wallowing in his decaying financial dilemma, which by now was deep into Chapter 11 bankruptcy, McAfee had, by chance, bought a copy of the *Wall Street Journal*. He had read an article in which an American businessman had been paid a handsome reward by U.S. Customs for preventing the illegal transfer of sensitive technology to a foreign country.

Armed with this information and enough diet pills to open a clinic, he had concocted a plan to create a crime and then solve it. And like the man he had read about in the *Journal*, he would get a handsome reward, and live happily ever after. Or so he thought.

Knowing that Sawahata was in the export business, McAfee leveled his sights on setting up OSI, Sawahata's CIA front firm. After researching to find an item on the prohibited export list, he had selected a product manufactured by Hewlett-Packard known as an integrated circuit cell tester. All he had to do next was lure Aki into a scheme to export such an item through OSI and he could report the crime...and collect his reward.

Unknown to Terry, this plan had been in the works for several weeks and, through McAfee's insistence, Aki had visited Arkansas Machine Tool's facilities where McAfee propositioned him to export the tester to Japan.

Sawahata, not realizing what the item even was, and simply to humor McAfee, had left with a brochure about the tester that McAfee had provided him. That day, Special FBI Agent Mark A. Jessie received a phone call from McAfee asking him to investigate OSI and Sawahata.

Linda Crow, McAfee's secretary and mistress, had accidentally intercepted a return call from Jessie, which she noted on her daily planner.

Sawahata, Terry and the rest of the local CIA group in Arkansas in operations "Centaur Rose" and "Jade Bridge" were unaware of McAfee's machinations. But an investigation of Sawahata would pose problems not only for the Agency's clandestine operations, but for everyone involved as well.

This problem could *compromise* the entire operation!

Date of transcription __2/6/86__

Pursuant to Administrative Subpoena issued January 16, 1986, PAT FUNK, Staff Assistant, Security, SOUTHWESTERN BELL TELEPHONE COMPANY, 1111 West Capitol Avenue, Little Rock, Arkansas, furnished credit information and toll records for Arkansas telephone numbers (501) 394-9907, (501) 394-9910, (501) 394-9914, and (501) 394-9927, which include the period from January 1, 1982, through March 24, 1984.

Investigation on __1/30/86__ at __Little Rock, Arkansas__ File # __LR 12D-283-105__

by __IA LINDA E. DALEY/jhk__ Date dictated __1/31/86__

This document contains neither recommendations nor conclusions of the FBI. It is the property of the FBI and is loaned to your agency; it and its contents are not to be distributed outside your agency.

On 01/25/83, Navajo N-62856, was fueled at Mena, Arkansas.

On 02/01/83, H & L EXPLORATION purchased 300 gallons of 100 LL jet fuel at Poteau under the name of SUPREME HELICOPTER (N2656E)

On 02/18/83, H & L EXPLORATION truck purchased 563 gallons of 100 LL jet fuel under the name of SUPREME HELICOPTER (N2656E). H & L fuel truck was purchased on 10/29/82 by Barry SEAL. The truck was never registered in Louisiana. On 04/20/83, the title from California was surrendered in Arkansas and the vehicle was registered in the name of H & L EXPLORATION. The Certificate of Title was signed by Bill and Barbara ADAMS. Handwriting examples of Bill ADAMS' signature and samples of Joe EVANS' handwriting are one and the same handwriting. The document was signed in Mena, Arkansas. The 1983 Mena Telephone Book has H & L EXPLORATION listed at the Mena Airport, telephone number 501-394-5375. The telephone number was installed in the old RICH MOUNTAIN hangar. Arkansas State Police (ASP) Investigators have photos of the fuel truck at RICH MOUNTAIN AVIATION and the vehicle has been observed at Joe EVANS' house in Mena.

In March or April 1983, Terry CAPEHART noted that aircrafts N-80492, N-80462, and N-7409L has been observed at Joe EVANS' hangar in Mena.

9-1. Above, portions of FBI phone records request and select surveillance reports shows interest in communications in Mena area during "Jade Bridge" and "Centaur Rose" timeframes. Note interest in quantities of aviation fuel being used by Seal's operation.

FM LITTLE ROCK (12D-283) (245D-7)

TO DIRECTOR ROUTINE

NEW ORLEANS (245D-7) ROUTINE

MIAMI ROUTINE

ATTENTION SUPVR. JIM MC NALLY

FRED L. HAMPTON, DBA RICH MOUNTAIN AVIATION; ET AL;

NARCOTICS; OO: LITTLE ROCK (LR 12D-283).

COINROLL; OO: NEW ORLEANS (NO 245D-7) (LR 245D-7).

FBIHQ AND MIAMI DIVISION HAVE ADVISED LITTLE ROCK THAT

DEA DOES, IN FACT, HAVE AN INTEREST IN THE C-123 AIRCRAFT

PRESENTLY AT THE MENA, ARKANSAS, HANGAR FACILITIES OF HAMPTON.

DEA HAS SEVERAL THOUSAND DOLLARS IN ELECTRONIC EQUIPMENT ABOARD

THE C-123.

SUPVR. RON KELLY, LITTLE ROCK, HAS PERSONALLY ADVISED

SHERIFF A. L. HADAWAY OF THE DEA INTEREST IN THE AIRCRAFT,

AND HE HAS AGREED NOT TO SEIZE THE AIRCRAFT.

MIAMI SUPVR. TIM MC NALLY IS REQUESTED TO ADVISE DEA,

1 - 12D-283
1 - 245D-7
RWK/bng
(2)

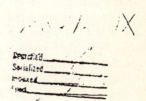

9-2. FBI message showing the DEA's equity in Barry Seal's C-123K, "The Fat Lady" that later crashed in Nicaragua.

CHAPTER 10

CHRISTMAS PAST

Terry Reed just wanted to be a "daddy" for an entire day, but the phone call on Saturday morning of November 3rd, 1984, changed all that. It was one of those points in time when a life's course is totally, and invisibly, changed forever.

Before the call, his agenda for the day had been to put aside his onerous workload. What with the training at Nella and his machine tool business burgeoning, he realized he was totally neglecting his son, Duncan, who had just celebrated his second birthday the previous month.

Terry saw his life accelerate to fast forward and some precious time he and Duncan needed to share was slipping away. He could already imagine the little boy graduating from the Air Force Academy. So for today at least, communism and Nicaragua be damned!

After feeding his son breakfast at home on Bowman Road in Little Rock, Terry's mind returned to his conversation with Barry Seal in July. As they stood on the rise overlooking the Nella strip, Terry had discussed with Seal his hope that flight training at Nella would be only a temporary thing. He hoped that Seal was still scouting around among the spooks for something better suited to Terry's talents—and ambitions.

In good ole boy jargon, Seal had said he would "keep his ear to the ground" for the right opportunity. In late July, Seal returned from a trip outside the country and relayed to Terry something he had heard from "a reliable source."

He said a program was being put together through a cutout in Florida, but it was only then in what he called "the incubation stage." Seal claimed he was not personally involved with the program, but he knew recruitment for it was underway and candidates were being selected through newspapers ads in the west, and southwest. That area of the United States, Seal said, had become a sanctuary for Agency contract pilots and soldier of fortune aviators who preferred states that were more tolerant of survivalist attitudes.

The prospect of working on the program piqued Terry's interest, and he became fascinated with the idea of the CIA using classified ads for recruitment. Right out of the movies, he thought. Who would believe that this was really one of the ways the Agency "reached out to touch someone". Together, he and Seal sat down and wrote out a classified ad with all the right ingredients.

"You need to write up something that outlines what you would like to do and what you consider your strengths, but make it sound just like an ad out of *Soldier of Fortune* magazine," Seal had told him. "I've been told this project is out of the country, so be sure to stipulate you're '*willing to relocate worldwide*.'"

"And, after the ad, then what?" Reed queried.

"The way this works is, if they want to talk to you, they'll get in touch. You may think this sounds hocus-pocus, but you just don't walk into Langley and apply for real spook work."

Terry concluded this must be how the "good ole boy" network was forced to communicate for security reasons. Without his knowing the recipient of the ad, it would be impossible for him to *compromise* the start-up program.

"Pretty slick," he thought.

On July 29th, 1984, an ad appeared in the classified section of the *Denver Post* stressing that T. Kent Reed of Little Rock was seeking a position with an "aggressive *company* that is wishing to develop rapidly." It outlined his qualifications, which included being a commercial pilot with a jet rating and someone who was a "team player, but also a free-thinker seeking a challenging position....willing to relocate worldwide."

By November, Terry had nearly forgotten about the ad. Flight training and his other activities had totally consumed his attention. He had even confided to Seal his feeling that nothing would ever come of it, and that it had probably been a waste of effort and money.

The phone was on its fifth ring as Terry finished wiping the oatmeal from Duncan's face. The remnants of the two-year-old's "feeding" were still splattered on the kitchen floor. Being a father for the first time at age 34 was a lot rougher in some ways than operating in a cloak-and-dagger environment.

"Is this the T. Kent Reed who ran an ad in the Denver Post back in July?" the caller asked. It caught him off guard, but there was a faint recognition of the man behind the voice. After acknowledging the ad, Terry replied, "Yeah, but who's this?"

"This is the voice of Christmas Past. Would you like to talk about the future? I'm now passing through your area conducting job interviews. Do you know a quiet place we can talk?" Terry was especially curious about the word, *future*. The thought of having no future had consumed him since the day his life was nearly snuffed out by the Ultra-Light accident. He quickly agreed to meet the caller, deciding not to question him over the phone about the comment of Christmas past. After all, he figured, this was, hopefully, an Agency interview and everything he said or did was probably part of the pre-employment test.

Suddenly, with the receiver still in his hand, Reed's thoughts turned to the more mundane: Who was going to take care of Duncan? His wife, now more than two months pregnant with their second child, was busy with her real estate business. Fortunately, it took only a few minutes to find a babysitter.

An hour and a half later, Terry turned into the parking lot on the west side of the City Terminal at the North Little Rock Airport where the "voice of Christmas past" he hoped would arrive. The mysterious caller said he could be in Little Rock in two hours.

What caught Terry's eye as he got out of his car was a brand new Maule airplane. Still in lime-green zinc oxide primer with a temporarily applied, taped-on tail number, it was parked near the terminal. Thinking he had a half hour to kill, Terry decided to have a closer look at the Maule, an aircraft he had never had an opportunity to inspect up close. He had seen one of these powerful, single-engine STOL aircraft impressively perform short field takeoffs and landings in a recent air show in Kansas.

As he walked past a pay phone on his way to the ramp where the Maule was parked, the man on the phone lowered the receiver and said, "Hey, Terry Reed? I'm Bill Cooper. You here for a job interview? You put on a little weight since Thailand."

Terry noticed something familiar in the man's eyes. It had been more than 14 years since he had looked into them, but the voice was definitely recognizable. Gradually, he scanned his data bank of mental images and recalled seeing this man wearing a baseball cap and military-style head phones. He was the pilot who had delivered the students to Mena in the C-130 back in July.

As Terry reacquainted himself with Cooper, he noticed in the Maule another pilot, who from photographs he is now sure was William (Buzz) Sawyer from Magnolia, Arkansas. Both men went down in flames in Nicaragua nearly two years later aboard a C-123 carrying guns and gringos, an international incident that revealed what the U.S. government had been denying, that it was supplying the Contras.

"I didn't recognize you that day back in Mena," Cooper said. "If I had, maybe we coulda' had a beer. You used to be a little skinny fucker over there during the war."

"Yeah, and you used to have hair," Terry jibed.

It was a typical vets' reunion. They had not really known each other well during those days back in Nakhon Phanom at Task Force Alpha. Their liaison then was secret, and illegal, since the Air Force was not allowed to "inter-face" officially with the CIA, which is not part of the Defense Department. Terry's unit during the war was in fact giving high-grade intelligence to Air America's "customer," the CIA. Air America was the cut-out.

Cooper then had been flying in DC-3s, or "gooney birds," and C-123s shuttling classified material to Vientiane, Laos, for Air America. Vientiane was the site of CIA headquarters for the illegal air war being conducted in Cambodia and Laos.

Both were younger men in those days. Now in his late 50s, Cooper's upper lip sported more hair growth than the top of his head. He was balding, the sides were turning gray and he had a thick waistline that was probably expanding. But he still had that twinkle in his eye. The look of a weathered Chuck Yeager. A man who had lived on the wild side in his younger days, and who wasn't afraid to still taste excitement when he found it.

As they chatted, the pay phone rang. Cooper answered it and had a short, heated discussion about an aircraft engine. He angrily said goodbye and hung up. He clearly was upset with the person on the other end. He had a major problem to deal with and he expressed the hope Reed could help him with it.

"I'm with the guy in the Maule," he said nodding toward the man sitting in the plane. "I've got another plane parked around the corner on the transit ramp that's got engine trouble. I was lucky to even make it here. And that fucking Joe Evans back there in Mena...well, well the FAA oughta' pull his license if he signs off work like that as being airworthy."

Terry was quickly learning that there was some type of connection between Cooper and Seal's mechanic Joe Evans and an airplane maintenance problem.

Both Terry and Cooper began walking toward the transit ramp. A late-model single-engine Piper Arrow, N30489, was sitting and dripping oil on the tarmac. Cooper said that he picked up this plane at Mena earlier that day, and that he and the other pilot had planned on flying both planes to Florida. The pilot in the Maule was from Arkansas, he said, but did not identify him other than saying he had also been in Southeast Asia.

"Shit, I bet we dropped a valve in that fuckin' Lycoming the way she's blowin' oil," Cooper said, shaking his head and referring to the manufacturer of the aircraft's engine. "I know it's only hittin' on three, based upon how rough she's runnin'. I can't work on it today. We're in a hurry to get this Maule and its cargo on down to Central America. I couldn't locate Evans by phone back in Mena, so I need you to help me find a place to store this bird until I can come back and fix it properly."

"So," Terry said quizzing Cooper, "You been over to Mena and met every-one, even Seal's hillbilly mechanic?"

"Yea, I'm afraid so," Cooper acknowledged. "Evans told me you were flyin' a company plane. I was thinkin' maybe you could hangar this thing for me."

"Didn't they tell you, I don't have a hangar yet. I got my Company plane tied down up in Searcy, about 30 miles north of here. There's no hangar space here at all, Bill," Terry informed.

"We can't leave it tied down in the open, and loaded," Cooper said. "I don't know how I would explain 500 pounds of *Charlie cuatro*. The local cops might not understand."

Terry, of course, knew what *Charlie quatro* was, GI code talk from Southeast Asia for C-4 plastic explosives.

"Goddam, Bill. You got 500 pounds of C-4 in this Arrow?"

"Yeah, and 500 pounds more over there in the Maule. I can't haul it all outta here today," Cooper said. "I gotta get my butt down to Florida by to-night. I gotta attend an important meetin' there. So I guess you'll just have to store it for me 'til I can get back up here."

Is this a job interview, Reed wondered, or some kind of test?

How many criminal statutes apply to knowingly storing C-4 explosives? This had to be a triple-finger no-no, Terry thought. Just being in possession of it was probably against the law. It's like having a body in the trunk of your car! How do you explain that to the police? But what choice did he have? This was an Agency emergency and maybe there were Brownie points involved. Or maybe this was another test of faithfulness and commitment. Seal had often com-plained that working with spooks involved continual "tests" of loyalty. There are no work rules as such for assets other than productivity. "Dying the water," as Sawahata had discussed, was just one of many way of doing this.

"Bill, like I said, there's no hangar space available here. I'm on a waiting list right now. Best I could do is try to arrange for a tie-down spot and stash the C-4 and safeguard it somewhere," Terry offered.

"Well, if you'd do that, I'd be grateful. I can't stay and help you, though. The Charlie cuatro will need someplace secure," Cooper replied. "We gotta get the Maule and its contents down to where the action is. Here's $300. That oughta cover temporary storage for the Arrow and I'll try to get back next month. I really appreciate this."

Both men manually towed the Arrow to a temporary tie-down slot rented under Terry's name. Looking in the plane's side window and seeing a U-Haul blanket covering the explosives, Terry couldn't help but wonder how large a crater 500 pounds of C-4 would make, but he knew that Charlie cuatro was extremely stable.

Afterwards, since it was too chilly and windy to remain outside, they took shelter in the terminal for the interview. The pilot in the Maule stayed in his plane, obviously guarding his cargo.

"Were your ears burnin' last night?" Cooper asked, "Cause I was learnin' all about ya'. I spent the night in Mena, they even took me up to the camp. That's quite a little operation you guys got goin' over there. They speak real high of ya'. Ain't Barry Seal somethin'? And what about this Medina character? I wouldn't turn my back on him for a New York minute. But do you think you'll ever convert those beaners to real pilots? Shit, this reminds me of fuckin' Nixon's Vietnamization program." He laughed at the analogy.

Terry was anxious to find out about the method of communication used by the good ole boy network.

"I'm curious about the ad. Is that how you found me?"

"Yeah, believe it or not, that's how they ran across ya. It makes the "classifieds" take on a whole new meanin', don't it?" Cooper joked. "But I didn't realize that the guy in the ad was the same guy instructin' over at Nella until last night."

Cooper went on to say that he had been recently recruited the same way, after placing a similar ad. Cooper said he was living in Reno, Nevada. Terry concluded that this was part of the "west, southwest" connection Seal had told him about. Seal, unknown to Reed, was spending a lot of time in that area, preparing to testify for the government in several major cases.

Cooper wanted to know what Seal had passed on to Reed about the new operation. Terry told him about what Seal had said, that a whole new program was being created to operate outside the United States. Seal was sure it was an Agency-let contract of some sort, and that flying was involved. If this was the case, Reed wanted to know if he could somehow fit into what was being considered.

Cooper outlined to him the possibility of this cut-out growing into a major offshore operation that would need not only "fearless flyers" but maybe even some savvy businessmen who understood international marketing, something he heard Terry was now involved in. He said that the new crew of Agency oversite operatives were, for the most part, college educated, "business types" that had law degrees and spent most of their time "flying desks instead of airplanes."

"These aren't my kind of people," Cooper admitted. "But times are changin' and so is the way the Agency manages these projects.

"Right now, I don't think anybody really knows what the fuck they're doin'," Cooper added. "All I been told is to scout around for C-123 crews for aerial delivery operations because of all this Boland shit. It appears to me we're startin' up a small Air America-style operation in order to get the Agency further removed, but I think it's hooked to a much larger cut-out somehow. All I know right now is the 'customer' wants lotsa munitions moved.

"Sounds to me like you've acquired a bunch of new talents since you told Uncle Sam to kiss off. You weren't a pilot then. So, for right now, why don't you send me sort of like a résumé and I'll pass it around to see how you could fit in. I'll give you priority handlin'."

"How would I contact you? Surely not through the classifieds again," Terry joked.

"For right now, send me your résumé to the address on this card." It read: Southern Air Transport, 6400 N.W. 36th, Miami, Florida, 33166. "I get mail there. Now there's no big hurry on this. They won't be able to do anything until after the first of the year."

Southern Air Transport (SAT) was an airline Terry had heard about while attending a flight instructor refresher clinic in Denver. He had sat next to a pilot named Doug Perkins who said he had flown for Air America in Thailand, had worked for SAT and was then working for Southern Cross, a worldwide aircraft delivery service. After Reed told the man he had been in Air Force intelligence, the pilot referred to SAT and Southern Cross as "spook outfits," proprietaries of the CIA. It was becoming clear to Terry that SAT somehow had a role in the formation of the cut-out to which Cooper had referred.

At this time, with the stringent Boland Amendment in effect, CIA Director William Casey was sorting his options. Also taking form was clearly what Oliver North later referred to as Casey's dream of an "off-the-self, totally self-sustaining, stand-alone entity that could perform certain activities on behalf of the United States." This idea actually took form later in what became known as "Operation Screw Worm," something that was to have a profound effect on Terry's life.

* * *

The STOL Maule used less than 500 feet of runway as it departed to the southeast with its two spook occupants and its lethal cargo. Terry realized that Duncan would have to wait for his father's attention and his wife would have to dine alone once again.

That night he returned to the airport, driving his brand new Chevy van and downloaded the lethal contents of the disabled Arrow. After having given more thought about the size of the crater that could be caused by an accidental explosion, he knew he couldn't take the C-4 home. Instead, he had selected a location that was remote, hidden, safe and, importantly, where he had easy access: directly behind Mark McAfee's warehouse on the Maumelle Highway.

He carefully avoided potholes on the way. Under the cover of darkness Terry dug a large hole in the side of an earthen embankment that would direct any explosive force away from the building and toward the nearby Arkansas River. He felt like a grave robber. And what would he say if a cop suddenly shone a light on him?

Returning home, tired and covered with dirt, Terry invoked his "spook agreement" with his wife. Each month, he had the right of refusal in answering any three questions...if they were based on "national security" and if Janis didn't have a "need to know." Not the least of the questions that night was, "Where have you been all day, why didn't you baby-sit Duncan, and why didn't we go to dinner?"

He had used up the entire month's allocation and it was only November 3rd.

On Nov. 7th, four days after Cooper left, there was another phone call, this time from a very familiar voice, but one he had not heard since moving to Arkansas.

"Your phone is not secure, so just listen," John Cathey's voice said. "I'm getting glowing reports on you through our guy there, you know, the one who talks funny...he says you're doin' a great job.

"Our fat friend says they couldn't do it without you. But we really need some product out of there ASAP. So I'd like you to devote all of your energy to that end and not get distracted about our other developments going on in Florida."

Terry assumed that the reference to Florida meant Southern Air Transport and Bill Cooper.

"Does this have anything to do with the guy that was here last Saturday...the guy I used to work with in Thailand?" Terry asked.

"Yeah. That's who I'm talking about. He may, in fact, offer you a position. And if you want to get factored in on the new program down there, maybe I can pull some strings on this end and get you in. But for right now, I need your help there."

To Terry, this meant he was getting an "excellent to outstanding" proficiency report from a CIA man at one of the highest levels. From the man who had told him back in Oklahoma that he reported directly to the National Security Council and a man who would later become famous and infamous using his true name— Lieutenant Colonel Oliver North.

"Do you have a way to get in touch with the guy from Florida?" Terry asked. "'Cause if you do, I've got something in storage for him I'd like him to pick up ASAP. But tell him it's in safe keeping for now and not to worry."

"Yeah, he told me about that. I'll pass your message along. Keep up the good work, we need more like you. Let's all dance on Ortega's grave."

It was significant that North, by indirection, had put Terry in orbit with Cooper, Sawahata, Seal and SAT...all in one conversation. By now, Oliver North had been put in charge of keeping the Contras together "in body and soul" as Ronald Reagan had wanted. He was to be the cut-out between the White House and the CIA now that the Boland Amendment had passed.[1] He was the one designated to keep the Administration's obsession with aiding the Contras from bumping head-on into the Boland legalisms. "The U.S. contact with the Nicaraguan Resistance was me, and I turned to 'others' to help carry out this activity," he later testified. The "others" mentioned were a reference to those doing the hands-on, behind-the-scenes work like Reed and men like him.

Over the next two months, the explosives were constantly on Terry's mind. Evans seemed unconcerned about the disabled Piper Arrow tied down in the open at North Little Rock, only complaining, "I got too much fuckin' work to do. Cooper blew up the engine, he can fix it. I got a fuckin' Beech 18 to put a door in. The chink tells me that's my No.1 priority. I only got one boss. If Cooper doesn't show up soon, I'll send Mike over to take a look at it, when he gets back from Ohio."

"Mike" was a black mechanic who worked for Seal periodically at Mena who seemed knowledgeable about both the mechanical *and* electronic aspects of aviation. Mike was unlike Homer (Red) Hall, Seal's main avionics man, who did not appear to have any mechanical background or experience. Evans identified "Mike" to one of the authors as a CIA avionics expert who felt uncomfortable being in Mena since there were virtually no other Blacks in the area.

But "Mike" wasn't in Arkansas at the time in order to assist Evans, so Terry had to put his worry about the plane and the C-4 out of his mind and get on with the business of flight training.

By now, the first group of students were nearing graduation, and it was important for Evans to get the Beech 18 modified and operational so that the students could get their "round-motor" time before graduation.

The Contra pilot "class of '84' was shaking out to be ten pilots and four ground controllers. They were also shaking from the weather. It was a typical late fall in Arkansas, wet and bone-chilling cold. The high humidity always made it feel 30 degrees colder than it actually was. Someone reared in the tropics did not handle that well.

Aki Sawahata had relayed the decision to shut down the school for the winter months once the present students were graduated and the pressure for "product" was satisfied.

"We'll moth-ball the camp until March if we can get just four or five crews graduated and shipped on down there," Sawahata said. This would be a welcome relief for the instructors because winter weather was now impacting the flying schedule.

Seal was showing up more often in Little Rock, in a much better frame of mind and seemingly much more relaxed than before. The lunches at SOBs with Terry were resumed, sometimes including Sawahata who normally preferred his favorite Chinese restaurant one block from the State Capitol.

Seal was probably more relaxed due to his newly negotiated legal status. By this time, Seal had worked out a plea bargain with the government on his Baton Rouge indictment for conspiracy to possess cocaine with intent to distribute and causing a financial institution not to file Currency Transaction Reports (CTRs). On November 19th, 1984, Seal agreed to plead guilty to one reduced count on each charge. But the bottom line for Barry was the happy news that he would be given no prison sentence time.

Even without the CIA's direct intervention in his behalf, Seal had again manipulated the Feds, proving once again how he could "handle his handlers." Sawahata, whose hands were obviously tied since helping Seal in Baton Rouge could have exposed Seal's role in the black operations in Arkansas, made no mention of any of this to Reed. Outwardly, Seal seemed to believe that his problems were behind him, but they were really only beginning.

This, of course, was not part of the agenda discussed while Seal, Sawahata and Terry were having lunch in Little Rock just prior to the graduation set for early December.

"If Joe Evans doesn't get that Beech 18 modified in time, Aki, I'll give 'em all a ride in 'The Fat Lady'," Seal offered, in an extremely jovial mood. "That ought to get their rocks off for 'em. We can have 'em kick a pallet of cash outa the cargo door and see if they can hit the fuckin' lawn at the State Capitol."

Seal started laughing, but Sawahata saw no humor in this comment and appeared nervous. Money had only been discussed once in Reed's presence, and that was during "the test" when Seal had revealed in August that he was flying into Arkansas with money he said was made from weapons sales. Terry had passed this discussion along to Sawahata, who appeared to know about the money all along. He knew that Seal was depositing heavy dollars at Lasater's firm, and, from this statement about the Capitol, Reed had deduced that the state government was somehow intertwined with "Centaur Rose." He knew better than to ask questions, but, by piecing together Seal's comments, especially those about the "donations" of weapons parts by the Arkansas National Guard, he was beginning to get the big picture. The state must be in on it.

This all made sense. How long could an operation like this go on undetected by those at the top? Maybe he wouldn't get into any legal trouble if the C-4 were discovered. The thought of the state, and most certainly the Arkansas State Police, being involved in the Agency's operations gave him comfort.

"Will six graduates be enough, Aki?" Terry asked. "Because, realistically, we need to wash out six guys."

Aki seemed confused with the number. It seemed too small from what he could remember. How had 20 students turned into 6 graduates?. It was napkin time.

On the napkin, Reed wrote:

    20 = original trainees
    -4 = Maule designees
    -4 = ground controllers
    -6 = washout
    -14 students .... 20 - 14 = 6

"So what are names of six you want to wash out?"

Terry listed the six names that he felt were unsafe and incapable of upgrade training in Central America.

Sawahata took out his pen and circled four of the six and said: "OK, you wash out other two, but these four guys must be graduated, they are part of 'special team' Mr. Medina is in charge of." These were the "pets" that were getting special attention and "tutoring" from Medina and Diego. There also had been unexplained absences for these four and the excuse had always been "they're ill." The instructors knew this was a ruse, but assumed they "didn't have a need to know," and were being misled.

"Are you asking me or telling me to graduate these four guys, Aki?" Terry asked. "Because, in my professional opinion as a flight instructor, they're dangerous and will probably get someone killed..."

"That's the whole idea, Terry," Seal broke in, "to get someone killed! Tell him, Aki. He does have a need to know. Aviation is serious business, and I sympathize with him not wanting these four guys running around the skies of Central America bein' incompetent in an airplane. If you don't tell him, I'm goin' to."

Sawahata did not like what Seal was doing, and saying. Sawahata was obviously holding back on something very touchy, and sensitive. Without saying a word, he opened his brief case and pushed across the table a booklet entitled "Assassination Manual." The existence of this manual, which had been written specifically for the Contras in 1983, had ignited a fire-storm in Congress when it had been made public earlier in September.

"Terry-san, you were in a war," the CIA man said." Many lives can be saved if right people die. It is very important for Agency to 'place' some pilots in a position to be able to shorten conflict. These four guys have been selected for very special mission to eliminate key Sandinista leaders. It is important they graduate with proper credentials so that they may penetrate Nicaraguan aviation community and get near their targets."

Terry was speechless. He really didn't want to know any more than he had just been told. He would find out later about Medina's background as an assassin and a saboteur of civilian aircraft. The Agency, in selecting Medina had clearly tapped a man with the right credentials to train paid killers.

Terry stared at Seal. Nobody said a word. Finally, to break the silence, Terry spoke, "I understand. Thanks for telling me. They'll be signed off. Tell Washington there will be 10 'graduating' pilots, 4 ground controllers, 4 transfers and 2 washouts. That'll be the graduating class of 1984."

When lunch was over, Seal got Terry aside and told him to hold the evening open for dinner. He was going to Lasater's to make another "deposit," but Barry had "some important shit I gotta talk to you about."

That night, at SOBs, Terry was waiting for both Seal and Janis. They were both late as the band was warming up. It was 7 PM and at that hour the bar turns into bedlam.

After Barry arrived and they realized it was so late it was unlikely that Janis would show, Seal tipped the waiter for their favorite table in the corner. The conversation centered, of course, on aviation.

"So what are you flyin' right now? I've sorta lost track. Are you in a Cessna?" Seal asked.

"Yeah, I just switched out. I turned in N36998, a 404 and Evans gave me a newer Titan, N5425G. It's a nicer plane. While we're on the subject, do I keep the Company airplane this winter while the school is in mothballs?"

"Sure. All of this is on Uncle. Rule No. 1. Soak him for all you can get. But I do want you to trade out around the first of the year to a Seneca. I've got a special project of my own goin' on and you'll need to be in a Seneca for security purposes."

"What's the special project?"

"Right now, Emile and I are piggybacking the cash I told you about as it comes in from down south," Seal told him. "We're using two Senecas that are identical to each other, and I figure a third one would really confuse any overly curious Air Traffic Controller if the going gets tough."

The Seneca given Terry by Evans right after New Year's 1985 was a 1981 Piper Seneca believed to have been stolen only a few days before in Tampa, Florida. The Cessna Titan Reed traded out in order to get the Seneca, it was later learned, had been stolen from Addison Field near Dallas, in November, 1984, only weeks before Evans gave it to Reed.

"Sure that's fine. Do I talk to you or Emile about detailed instructions?" Terry asked.

"Talk to Emile and he'll give you the Seneca right around the first of the year."

"What's significant about the first of the year?"

"The tithing is gonna really go on the increase, come January 1."

"Tithing?"

"Yeah, the dime that the state's workin' on for lettin' the Agency's operation go on here," Seal answered. "You didn't think somethin' this big could be goin' on without havin' to pay for it. Shit, you were in Southeast Asia. Didn't you tell me we had to pay some fuckin' prince in Laos every time the Air Force dropped a bomb there? You see it's all the same, just one fuckin' banana republic after another."

The "dime" Seal referred to was the 10 percent being charged the CIA by high Arkansas state officials for allowing the Agency to operate in Arkansas. The word tithing Terry had learned back in his Sunday school days in the Nazarene Church. The term meant 10 per cent of your money would be given the church and, in return, as the Bible proclaimed, you would get it back 10 fold. And this was undoubtedly true for the CIA.

Arkansas was providing cover for the Agency's illegal airplane modifications, Contra training operations, arms shipments and, from what Seal revealed, ways to invest the black money that was being made from its gun-running to Central America. So that's why the singer Glen Campbell called Arkansas the "land of opportunity".

* * *

Graduation day was Sunday, December 16th, 1984. Miraculously, no one had been killed during the training program. But four months had stretched into five and a half. Everyone was happy that it was finally over and everyone was graduating. Only the 14 grads were present at the ceremony in Rich Mountain's hanger where it had all started on that hot day back in July.

Medina said, without elaboration, that he had "eliminated" the two wash-outs once the instructors advised him they weren't cut out for combat aviation.

Evans had, in fact, modified the Beech 18 that gave the students three weeks of "round motor exposure." And Seal had taken them all for a ride in "The Fat Lady." With Christmas approaching, visions of *fiesta* and a break from the ordeal of training danced in their heads. Sawahata, without explanation, did not show up for the ceremony. Only the instructors, Medina and Diego attended and Reed gave each of the graduates "gold medals" and authentic pilots' log books showing their training. The only omission in the log book entries was the classified location in which the training had taken place.

All expressed the hope that when Operation Jade Bridge could finally be acknowledged publicly that the students would be allowed to count this training toward obtaining American pilot certificates. Right now they had no real gringo licenses, only their "capability" and their log books.

What was unspoken was the instructors instinctively knew that the young Latins were not ready for what was facing them. They needed at least six months more training. The faculty agreed that if the students received the proper up-grade training for the C-123 aircraft and had ideal conditions, they could prob-ably perform. That meant, however, having the entire flight crew alive and functioning in a plane that had all its systems fully operational. But these are optimum conditions that rarely exist in combat. And Terry knew that. He felt that he and the others were simply filling a square for the CIA. If a supply plane went down and someone was going to die, as Barry had put it, "it'd better be beaners at the controls."

Yet, the motley crew that arrived in jeans and Rayban glasses had now turned into men with military bearing.They were no longer a mockery to the Raybans they were wearing. To them, this was as important as a cadet or midshipman leaving the service academies. There were even some tears. Reed could only think about how he felt when leaving for Southeast Asia.

War is a hand-me-down deal, he thought. His father had handed him off to the government and he had returned safely, bearing only psychological scars no one could see. Now, he was participating in the ancient process, replenish-ing the supply of warriors. Only the weapons had changed.

This had been a tough year for Terry. He had survived a crash, had set new goals for himself, and entered the dark world of being a spook. And suddenly here it was, at year's end.

No one knew for sure if there would even be another class. If the Nicaraguan conflict elevated into a major shooting war in Central America, civilian subcontractors certainly would not be needed. The edge of uncertainty robbed the occasion of its festive atmosphere for all.

Ramon Varnados would be the only one left behind. He had moth balled the camp. The Army had repossessed their equipment "on loan" and ATC controllers were certain to see an abrupt decrease in traffic handled from "Ross and Spartan Aviation Schools."

The only perks for the instructors were the fact that they could continue to use their "Company airplanes" until the next class, if there was one. This had been a year of learning for everyone. Everything was in place. Aircraft had been "procured", modified and were now being stored in Louisiana. The instructors all knew they could do a better job quicker with the next class of "freedom fighters," if there was a next class.

As the black C-130 taxied into position outside the hangar, the roar of the turbo-prop engines going through beta, causing the plane to back-up, became deafening. With the C-130 crew shutting down only the two engines on the port side, it was a sign it would be a quick turn-around. There wouldn't be a lot of time for emotional goodbyes as the instructors helped load the gear aboard the giant plane.

As Medina boarded with Diego, Reed could see Medina staring right through Emile Camp, who was helping with the cargo. It was obvious that the tension between them had not abated since that first confrontation. Camp, sensing the stare, turned to Medina and said: "Ramon, hope there's no hard feelings. I'll see you in the spring."

Medina stared back with no expression and said coldly: "I doubt that."

Camp shrugged off the comment, thinking Medina wasn't coming back to Nella. He was wrong.

It gave Reed cold chills to see the four designated assassins boarding the plane. He was, he felt, releasing a deadly infection into the world.

When the plane taxied out, Emile Camp approached Terry and began talking. "Barry tells me he talked to ya' about gettin' a Seneca. I'll have it for ya' right after the first of the year. We can then talk 'bout the cover operation I need ya' to help us with. But, for right now, I'm shuttin' down for Christmas. Don't know about you, but I need some time off with my family. Hey, does the resident chink pay Christmas bonuses?" He laughed.

By now, the increased Agency aircraft activity centered at Rich Mountain Aviation was generating unwanted attention from other aircraft shops located at the Mena Airport who were seeking new business. The high profile image of the larger aircraft such as the Cessnas and Navajos and the Lear was beginning to require the use of less conspicuous planes, if the operation was to remain discreet.

Because of the impending and increased "cash flow" into Arkansas, the Agency had decided to use light twin-engine Piper Senecas for this activity. As Terry Capeheart, the Polk County Arkansas Deputy Sheriff at the time later testified during Federal Investigations into Seal's activities at Mena: "The Senecas just didn't stand out" and he overlooked their significance. Capeheart, who now operates an FAA-approved aircraft engine overhaul facility, described the Seneca as "a real common airplane and favors a couple of other airplanes from a distance unless you're quite familiar with them..." Seal and the Agency knew what they were doing. They always seemed far ahead of their main competitors, namely other federal agencies.

Reed was now being invited into the money loop, in a big way. The downsizing side of the Agency's operation by converting to lower profile, twin engine Piper Seneca II aircraft was in preparation for an increase or up-sizing in the amount of *green flights* (sorties carrying cash) that would be traversing through Arkansas' skies.

Both Terry and Camp breathed a sigh of relief as the black C-130 carrying the graduates lumbered down the runway, took off, retracted its landing gear and cleared the tree line at the south end of the Mena airport. It banked southeast, headed for Homestead Air Force Base in Florida where, before returning to Central America, the graduates would be turned loose for a week of debauchery—paid for by Uncle Sam.

Lord help the hookers there, Terry thought.

1.   North testimony, *Hearings*, 100-7, Part I, 7/9/87.

CHAPTER 11

'WETA OKAMI'

Terry began 1985 with a traditional kiss under the mistletoe and a series of resolutions vowing, in no particular order, to become a millionaire by the time he was 40, to lose 20 pounds, to spend more time with his now-expanding family and reduce the number of keys he carried to three (house, car and airplane).

He had observed that the fewer keys you carried, the more status and freedom you possessed. He also felt that the fewer keys the less complicated your life. This may have been his goal as 1985 began, but the Boland Amendment and William Casey's dark plans to circumvent it would produce the opposite result for him.

Things were going well financially, and his second child was on the way. Sawahata had been impressed with Reed's "performance." Labor Day had taken on a double meeting because there was now scribbled on the calendar another "labor" day in May, Janis' estimated due date.

The Reeds were becoming a regular part of the Little Rock social scene. They had grown beyond the "cotton mouths" (Southern elitist snobs) Seth Ward had put them in touch with and Terry was now making friends with people such as Mark Stodola, an attorney who had just run unsuccessfully for County Prosecutor but was still considered an up and coming political threat.

Terry and Janis had been there 15 months, had settled in and were looking for a larger home as a "nest", in anticipation of the new baby. Terry was elated. He was sure, at long last, he was finally on his way up the good ole boy ladder. "John Cathey" had assured him he was on the fast-track, and he waited with enthusiasm for the success he was sure would come. The crash, rekindling within him an awareness of his mortality, had triggered a metamorphosis. He now knew where he was going and how he was going to get there.

When Aki Sawahata called him in mid-January, the headlines talked of little else but Nicaragua. Reed was sure the United States was about to invade. He was certain there would be no more classes at Nella, particularly in light of Barry Seal having told him that he shouldn't view the Nella operation as anything permanent. He had hoped Aki had news from Cathey telling him he was about to move up.

Sawahata asked Reed to meet him for lunch at their usual place near the Capitol. At Fu Lin's, over won-ton soup, Reed turned the conversation to business. "I now have a hangar at the North Little Rock Airport. I was able to get one last week, but it's not housing the Company airplane. I put Bill Cooper's plane in there...the one with the bad engine. And I sure wish you would lean on someone in order to get rid of it and the *Charlie cuatro*."

"Oh, it is good you have hangar. We will need it for increase of special flight activity here," Sawahata replied. "I will reimburse you monthly for its cost. You are going to need it to hangar your new Company airplane, if you accept my offer. I need you to be in courier pilot flying operation with Mr. Seal and Mr. Camp. If you are interested we can fly to Mena tomorrow so you can trade airplane and have one just like theirs."

Terry was disappointed to hear Sawahata talking only of local flying. He was hoping that Cooper had cleared things with Cathey and he'd be offered a long-term position in the "new operation."

"But Aki, it was my understanding when I last spoke with Mr. Cathey that he was considering me for a position in the new operation in Florida," Terry said. "Has there been any change in the plan down there? I would really like to grow beyond all of this 'spooky' flight activity."

"Terry-san, I need you right here. I need a pilot to move me around and to help supervise operations here in Arkansas. And you know a lot more about manufacturing than I do. In fact, I have big problems in manufacturing right now. You are in a good place for now. All of these things take time, and it is best for now you show Agency that you will do what they think is most important."

It looked like Reed was being offered a "promotion" within Sawahata's loop in Arkansas, but not an exciting and mysterious "off shore" Agency job. At least not for now. Sawahata then expressed his doubts about the Nella Operation, "Jade Bridge," continuing and was concerned about whether Seal could devote any more time to "Operation Centaur Rose." Since this was his only option at the time, Reed suppressed his disappointment and agreed.

"OK, Aki. You've got yourself a flying, manufacturing engineer, for now at least. But I still want to send my résumé on to Florida as Bill Cooper suggested. You got any problems with that? I still don't want to do this forever."

"OK, if you insist. But I am afraid they will steal you away from me," Sawahata added. "Good guys are hard to find. I like your aggressiveness in everything you do. In fact you remind me of Japanese expression...*weta okami.*"

"What the fuck is a *weta okami*?"

Sawahata laughed as he slurped his noddles into his mouth and grinned. "We say...hungry wolf. That is good name for you. From now on I call you *weta okami.*"

Was this good or bad, Terry thought. His first Agency code name, and it was in Japanese.

The next day *"Weta Okami"* and Sawahata flew to Mena to trade airplanes. Reed turned in his twin Cessna and picked up a 1981 twin engine Piper Seneca N8275T that had just been freshly painted in order to match Seal's Seneca, N8049Z, and Camp's, N8658E. From all outward appearances, they were identical.

That day, the three pilots had an operational discussion in Rich Mountain's new hangar while Sawahata listened. Chief among the topics was "piggy-backing," to avoid detection. This diversionary tactic was already working flawlessly and had gone undetected with Seal and Camp, so far.

Seal had told Reed that he had been flying in large quantities of cash packed in duffel bags containing sophisticated electronic transmitters to serve as homing devices to locate the airborne jettisoned "green backs". This was the CIA's "money loop" in Arkansas. Now, they were adding a third plane flown by Reed that would serve solely as a decoy. He was going to be part of an elaborate airborne deception that masked these deliveries. In the course of these activities, he would eventually learn who was getting these airborne cash deposits; something that already had him very curious.

Seal outlined a plan that Reed considered ingenious as it unfolded. No high-ranking Air Force war planners could come up with anything better suited to evade the enemy. "The Agency has devised a way to make this almost idiot-proof," Seal began in a military-style briefing tone. "I'll cover how we safely jettison and relocate the cargo from the "green flights" and Emile will talk about piggy-back flight procedures."

Terry was reminded of his Air Force days as an Intelligence Briefer where Intelligence Analysis normally remain highly specialized and give only that portion of the stand-up briefing in which they were considered an expert.

"Most smugglers are dumb shits, and their own people can't be trusted," Seal lectured, while producing a yellow legal pad and pencil. "All it takes to bring down the whole operation is to have an internal leak and a tip-off about the location of a drop zone. With *our* method of operation there is no way the drop zone location can be compromised."

"How's that possible?" Reed asked.

"'Cause I don't even know where the fuck it is until I jettison the load and note my location on the LORAN (Long Range Navigation equipment). The plane that is piggy-backing sees the load go, denotes the same coordinates as a backup and never relays the coordinates by radio in the air."

"So how do you find the cash?" Reed wondered aloud.

"We have a homing beacon located with the cargo. Once we're sure the jettison was executed unobserved, there are several things we can do. Let me list them for ya.

"Option number 1: We can go back and get it since we know the geographic coordinates to within a few meters of the kickout point.

"Option number 2: We can verbally relay the coordinates to a pickup crew on a secure and scrambled frequency. Then they fly a helicopter into the drop area. Or

"Option number 3: We simply use the LORAN to navigate to a predetermined spot and jettison it near some "friendly forces", who just happen to have a receiver that'll track the frequency of the transmitters in the bag.

"Combine that with the fact that the piggy-back split gives anyone watchin' us two targets to follow—neither one of which is carryin' anything at that point—and ya got a pretty damn fool-proof system. Courtesy of Uncle Sam."

Referring to the duffel bags, Reed asked, "You just said transmitters. Is that plural?"

"You're a flyer. You know a pilot needs at least two of everything just to be sure one works. You wouldn't want to lose $3 million in cash, would you, just because some fuckin' $2,000 radio didn't work?"

As he listened and absorbed what Seal had said, Terry looked at Sawahata, who was smiling, and added, "You did not think it was only Federal Express that could always deliver, did you?"

Terry realized this entire scheme could not have been possible a few years earlier. Prior to that time, only the military used bulky and costly LORAN navigation equipment (long range navigation), which automatically triangulates airborne position through the use of a minimum of three ground-based, low-frequency transmitters and gives the pilot a cockpit readout of his latitude and longitude, continuously, down to the nearest second of a minute.

Major breakthroughs in LORAN technology in the late 70's and early 80's had drastically shrunk the size of the equipment and lowered the price to a few thousand dollars.

The ability to know precisely where he was with respect to the surface gave Seal's planes the ability to jettison cargo, in this case money, and to know within meters the aircraft's location when it did so. That means Seal didn't need a pre-arranged drop zone and could drop his "cargo," whenever and wherever he chose.

Camp now borrowed Seal's tablet and began sketching a diagram of radio fixes in Western Arkansas. Apparently it was time for his portion of the briefing.

"I'll draw ya a map of a typical mission. This won't be exact, but the concept's there," Camp drawled in his friendly Southern tone.

Whereupon Camp drew a line of flight that showed two airplanes that already were in tightly packed piggy-back formation and enroute to the Texarkana VOR flying at exactly the same airspeed, tracking the same course and within a few feet of the same altitude. These two planes would be flying nearly stacked on top of each other with the one at the bottom position being only slightly more than one airplane's length behind the one above.

He then drew a line to represent Reed's plane rendezvousing and joining with them from below and climbing ever so cautiously until Reed's craft became the bottom plane, flying likewise slightly more than one airplane's length behind the plane above him. That would create a tightly packed three plane formation spaced approximately twenty feet below each other and slightly staggered, front to rear. The planes would then be in such close proximity that, to a ground based FAA Air Traffic Controller, they would appear as only one plane. He would be seeing only one "blip", or radar return, on his screen, not three, due to inherent errors in radar systems.

It would be the job of Camp's plane, the one flying in the top position, to be the "primary diversion plane" for Seal's plane, the "green plane" or the one carrying the cash. Reed's plane, or the "secondary diversion plane" would be flying "shadow position" and escort Seal's plane all the way to the "target" or DZ (drop zone).

Upon crossing the VOR, Camp showed how his airplane would continue into Mena on the original flight plan *filed* by Seal. Reed's, or the shadow aircraft, would change headings with Seal's plane and divert to the *nonfiled* destination, Little Rock, while staying in close formation with the "green plane."

Once near Little Rock, Camp said, it would be Reed's job to begin communication with air traffic control there and to "radar-mask" the fact there were two aircraft instead of only one. During this electronic masking procedure, Seal's plane would abruptly dive down to tree-top level, placing it below radar detection altitude, and jettison his cargo over a pre-selected drop zone west of Little Rock.

Reed's plane, which would purposely remain under radar surveillance by ATC, would then continue on and land at Little Rock, while Seal would depart the area undetected by radar and head south. If all went as before, Camp said, he would be on the ground in Mena without ATC or anyone else being the wiser. ATC would think they had handled only one airplane, which had originated at a hypothetical Point A, and landed at Point B, Mena.

The purpose of Reed's plane would be to further confuse ATC in the remote chance they had detected more than one aircraft as they separated over the Texarkana VOR. With Reed's plane continuing on and landing at Point C, Little Rock, the chances of anyone discovering there were three planes were remote at best. Even if someone wanted to ramp-check Reed's plane once on the ground at Little Rock, Camp noted, he would be carrying nothing. It was an airborne shell-game with the "pea" no longer under any of the three shells. By the time it was over, Camp said, the "pea" would be gone.

What Camp just traced out was what Seal had described earlier as "No. 3" on the list of options for dropping and recovering a payload of CIA cash.

"You only left one thing out Emile," Seal interrupted. "Terry, when you rendezvous with us, before you come down ta join us, take a real close look to see if Camp and I are bein' tailed. Those U.S. Customs Citations are painted black and are real hard to spot, so use your night vision goggles and look real close. If ya see anything, come up on our frequency and sing out."

"What happens if that's the case?" Reed queried

"You abort and just head on back ta Little Rock," Camp replied. "Barry and I will know we're bein' followed, so we got several options. We would probably just split up, givin' him two targets ta chase, most likely. But you don't worry 'bout that...that's our problem."

Reed had some concerns. This question he directed to Sawahata. "Aki, is this all legal? Sounds like we're going to great lengths to avoid detection by other Feds. Who do we consider our enemy here?"

"Terry-san, we are CIA! We are not law enforcement. We are not Justice Department. We are not Treasury Department. We are CIA! We answer to Director who answers to President. You are dealing with very top level. These other agencies are not in loop. They not cleared for major foreign policy decisions. CIA has to work this way all over world. We are not breaking law. We are above law." The CIA man had spoken.

With the speech by Sawahata out of the way, Reed had another question and a suggestion. "I assume this will take some pretty good flying and coordination? I would like all three of us to go out in the MOA and practice a little close formation work before we attempt this, especially at night. One thing that could blow our plan is to have three identical Senecas crash within a mile of each other."

"We'll do better than that," Seal said. "Tomorrow, weather permitting, we'll just go out and fly this whole mission in daylight, only difference bein' I won't be carryin' any cash."

"Barry, of the three ways to do this, it appears to me that No. 3 bears the greatest risk of discovery. Who's safeguarding the location of the drop zone you have set up in Little Rock?" Terry asked.

Sawahata interjected with the answer. "I am... Agency is. The drop is a 'safe' field we have selected because people that own land there are under our control. So do not worry about that. Your job is just be shadow for Barry."

Sawahata wanted the three to begin their practice flights right way. "There is major pressure for increase in Agency deposits in Arkansas," he said.

"Barry, maybe I'm just being nosey, but can't you just continue making deposits at Lasater's like you've been doing all along," Terry remarked.

"That was only tithin' money," Seal answered. "We're talkin' about much more than that now. It seems this has worked so well, Mr. Sawahata's people have decided to make a major investment here."

Sawahata was upset. "Barry-san, you should not talk so freely about Agency investments. They are confidential."

"Aw fuck, Aki," Seal said. "He's gonna figure all this shit out anyway, now that he's part of it. Terry didn't fall off no turnip truck yesterday. And besides, I trust him a lot more than I trust those Little Rock fucks you're runnin' around with. They're just a bunch of goddam politicians with their hands stickin' out."

Reed was somewhat surprised by what he had just heard. He probably didn't need to know everything he was hearing and Sawahata was right to be concerned. Reed figured that the loose lips were probably the result of too many "contractors" being involved.

What he was witnessing, without totally realizing it, was the inherent friction that comes with any intelligence operation. The tension between the administrators, or GS bean-counters like Sawahata, who live by a rule book designed to regulate a glacial bureaucracy, and the assets like Seal who are totally action-oriented and results driven and bristle at rules and accountability, was constantly apparent. Caught in the middle of this operational tug-of-war was Terry. He felt strangely comfortable in this situation though. It was reminiscent of the military where troops in the field held contempt for the "fat cats" with safe jobs back at headquarters.

The next morning at 0830 hours, the weather did permit. Reed was orbiting high above the Texarkana VOR (ground based navigation transmitter) at 10,500 feet in a right-hand holding pattern on the 156-degree radial of the fix. At exactly the prescribed rendezvous time, he spotted Seal and Camp's identical Senecas flying in picture-perfect, piggy-back formation heading northerly, tracking the 336-degree radial of the Shreveport VOR at 4,500 feet MSL.

He had been monitoring their air-to-air conversation on the discreet frequency of 122.97, which ground control did not monitor. He knew by Seal and Camp's position reports they were nearing DUBOW intersection, a navigational fix 17 miles south of Texarkana on vector 13 (FAA designated air highway).

Seal's voice came on the radio first. "You got a visual on us yet, Terry? It'll be easier to spot us at night 'cause (only) Emile will have his navigation lights on."

"Roger, I've got a visual on you. You're in my 12 o'clock low except you're tucked in so tight all I can see form here is one airplane," Terry replied.

"That's the way it's supposed to be," Seal answered. "Get on down here with us. Convert your altitude to air speed and try to tuck in under me before we get to the VOR."

Terry dove his Seneca down to join Seal and Camp at their 4,500-foot altitude, reversing course and coming in up under Seal, who was below Camp. He inched into position under Seal's plane until he could "count the rivets" that attached the tailhook to the bottom of Seal's.

At this point, they were layered like slices of bread in a club sandwich. The three aircraft flying in formation like this made Terry flash back to the thought of three B-52s flying in a "cell" formation while on an "Arc Light" bombing mission over Laos. Reed could tell by the way Seal and Camp were flying in unison that they had done this many times before. He wasn't quite ready yet to get as close to Seal as Seal was to Camp.

Seal, since he could not see Reed, needed the radio to instruct him.

"Now, I'm gonna have to jibber-jabber a lot since you're in my six (meaning out of sight in the back and below)," Seal said to Reed in a relaxed, Cajun drawl. "When we do this for real, we'll keep radio communications to a minimum. But, for right now, I'll just talk ya though it.

"I'm showin' about 10 DME (distance-measuring equipment) from Texarkana and I'm squawkin' nuthin' as you should be also, Terry," Seal instructed.

By squawking, Seal was referring to their airborne radios called transponders, whose purpose is to amplify radar signals bounced off aircraft by ground-based radar. By his reference to "squawkin' nuthin'," Seal meant his transponder was turned off at this point as was Reed's. Only Camp's would be operational and ATC ground would be tracking only him.

At this point, Seal added, "Emile is on center frequency and squawkin' [their assigned code]. Just prior to the fix, Emile's gonna ask for ident. When he does, I'm gonna bank right in a standard rate turn in order to pick up vector 573 to Hot Springs. Now, be careful there, 'cause you gotta turn with me at the same angle and everything, or you'll get in my wake turbulence and it can get pretty hairy. So, when Emile says 'roger ident,'... ident will be the word we both execute the turn on, and be sure to use standard rate. Any questions?"

The three aircraft in a tri-level piggyback formation continued tracking toward the Texarkana VOR as Camp simulated radio conversation with enroute traffic control (ATC) in Memphis. Just as Seal had warned Reed, the moment Camp responded with the word "ident" Seal banked his plane right in order to intercept the 030-degree radial of the Texarkana VOR outbound in a northeasterly direction.

It was all Terry could do to keep tucked in tight and follow Seal's plane through the dangerous maneuver, while wondering what this would this be like at night. Camp's plane continued outbound on the 322-degree radial headed toward the Rich Mountain VOR, while Reed wrestled with his aircraft that was, in fact, experiencing turbulence from Seal's wake.

"Remember what they taught you in flight school, Terry. My wake flows outward and downward. Try to stay exactly in my six and you'll have a smoother ride."

On the real flight, Camp would have continued on and landed at Mena, but, for this practice mission, he rejoined the other two planes, and was busy taking photographs of Reed and Seal's planes flying in perfect unison and now stabilized on the course taking them to Hot Springs.

"From here you two look like you're either re-fuelin' in mid-air or tryin' ta fuck each other," Camp joked over the radio.

Next, it was necessary for them to make a controlled descent together down to the proper altitude for aircraft flying eastbound. This was no easy task. It took an immense amount of concentration. Terry thought about the problems of doing this maneuver at night. He had often watched in awe the way the Air Force Thunderbirds, the precision flying team, maneuvered their aircraft within feet of each other while streaking through the sky. But could they do it at night, without lights? He wondered.

"Terry, at the Hot Springs VOR, you turn your transponder on to twelve hundred and start talking to Little Rock approach. That'll make us about 45 miles out of Adams Field. When they assign you a squawk code, and the instant you say, 'Roger ident,' I'm gonna dive directly in front of you in order to get down to the deck while your (radar) return is still blossoming on their scope," Seal radioed.

What Seal was describing to Reed was a clever way of masking any secondary radar "returns" bouncing off his aircraft by utilizing an inherent error within the ATC's radar system. When a controller assigns a special squawk code to an aircraft he is "handling," he asks the pilot to press a button on his transponder, thus differentiating it from other aircraft on his scope. When the pilot does this, his "return" on the controller's scope blossoms, or enlarges, considerably. Seal was taking advantage of this procedure in order to better evade radar detection.

Just like clockwork, Reed began communicating with Little Rock ATC while over the Hot Springs VOR.

"Little Rock approach, this is Seneca, eight-two-seven-five Tango, level three thousand five hundred, tracking the zero-seven-one degree radial of Hot Springs VOR, squawking twelve hundred, inbound Adams."

"Roger Seneca seven-five Tango, squawk two-seven-four-three and ident."

"Roger, Little Rock, Seneca seven-five Tango is going to two-seven-four-three and squawking ident."

The moment the word "ident" left Terry's lips, Seal's aircraft abruptly dove from its position directly in front of and slightly above Terry and went straight over his nose, catching him unprepared for the severe wake turbulence or disturbed air generated by Seal's maneuver.

After recovering control of his aircraft and scrambling to locate the pilot's clip board that had fallen from its mount as a result of the severe jolt, Terry could hear Seal laughing on their discreet frequency, the one ATC couldn't hear.

"Oh, I forgot to tell ya, Terry. When I split, it can get real rough back there. Ask Emile. He damned near wiped out the first time, too."

Terry knew he had been set up since he could hear Camp laughing, too. Just as the area directly behind a boat provides a water-skier with a smooth surface, flying slightly above or below and directly in line with another plane is not turbulent. But exiting that smooth air space and crossing the wake can produce a very rough ride.

Meanwhile, with his aircraft now again stabilized, Terry took time to notice Seal skimming along at tree-top level tracking inbound toward I-430 looking for the drop zone. This run was for practice, so, approximately 10 miles southwest of Adams, Reed canceled his destination flight plan and all three pilots turned west and flew back to Mena.

After a thorough debriefing on the ground of the practice run, they decided to try it again one more time for safety's sake. After a second dry run, all three felt confident with the maneuvers and coordination involved. All that was left was the real thing...at night.

As the three aircraft split up near Little Rock in order to go their separate ways later that afternoon, Seal came on their discreet frequency and said to Terry, "Go to the Chink's office, he'll give you your rendezvous instructions for the real run."

* * *

Two nights later, just before midnight, Reed was holding at his assigned altitude. It was a cold January night, but crystal clear and ideally suited for the business at hand.

If all went well, and Reed was able to locate his incoming target from the south, he would be home in less than two hours.

Right on cue, Terry could hear Camp's voice talking to the Memphis Air Traffic Control Center about an intermittent "transponder problem." He was eavesdropping on center frequency to determine the location of Seal and Camp's piggy-backing Senecas, which were then departing the Shreveport VOR enroute for Texarkana.

Reed's adrenalin was flowing as he strained to establish visual contact with the other two, who should be lower and, based on their last position report, 30 miles out. He was anxious to make visual contact and depart the holding pattern. Waiting, he was discovering, was the worst part. It only gave him time to think about all that could go wrong. Once things began to happen, he knew, his mind would be occupied with the mechanics of it all, and the tension would subside.

Camp's distant red and green navigation lights were a welcome sight. Seeing Emile's red position light on the right, reminded him of a saying that he had learned during training: "Red on right returning". It meant the target was coming toward you.

Seal and Camp could not see Terry however, because his navigation lights were off. To let them know he was there, and to make sure he identified the right target, he came up on the discreet frequency 122.97.

"Dodger" one and two this is "Dodger" three. I've got a visual on you. Request identification."

Just as they had worked out, Camp silently flashed his strobe lights momentarily, allowing Reed to make certain he had found the right target. As they had practiced, Terry's job was to now gain enough air speed in his descent down to their altitude to enable him to reverse course and tuck up under Seal's plane without over-running them or lagging behind. While doing this, he would take the opportunity to scour the area for the U.S. Customs "flat black Citation jets" he had been warned might be on Seal's and Camp's tail. All was clear.

By the time they all reached DUBOW intersection he was in position and waiting for Camp to give the coded signal "ident" as they approached the Texarkana VOR. His eyes strained to maintain visual contact on Seal's plane. He focused solely and completely on Seal's tail-hook allowing for the most minute adjustments in spacing.

"Roger, ident," he heard Camp's voice saying just as his DME read "1 nautical mile." This meant they were in fact, directly over the VOR, since their altitude put them one mile above the ground.

This time he was more prepared to stay with Seal as they made the turn toward the Hot Springs VOR.

In the distance to his left, he could see Camps' aircraft continuing on to its destination at Mena. With his and Seal's transponders in the "off" position, and Camp's "on", Air Traffic Control had unlikely noticed his and Seal's separation from the *bright* radar blip they were observing that night bouncing off of Camp's plane, amplified by his transponder.

"You still with me Dodger 3?" Seal asked as the lights of Hope, Arkansas came abeam off their right wing.

"Roger, Dodger 2," Reed acknowledged. "On my mark begin 500 FPM [foot per minute rate of] descent to three thousand five hundred. Five, four, three, two, one, mark."

This time their communication was abbreviated and their parallel descent went flawlessly with both aircraft leveling out as one at 3,500 feet MSL, still separated vertically by only a few feet. As they approached the Hot Springs VOR, Reed could hear Camp communicating with Memphis center and getting permission for a visual approach into Mena. He would soon be on the ground.

As rehearsed, Terry now activated his transponder, after dialing in 1200, and turned on his navigation lights. He then called Little Rock approach while over Hot Springs and requested radar services in anticipation of his landing at Adams Field. They responded by assigning him a squawk code of 3477 and asking him to ident. The dangerous part was not over, yet. He knew full well the severity of Seal's wake turbulence that he would encounter as Barry prepared to dive his plane through Reed's line of flight.

"Roger, Little Rock approach, this is Seneca eight-two-seven-five Tango showing thirty DME out of Little Rock, level three thousand five hundred, squawking three-four-seven-seven, identing."

Seal dove, but this time Reed had made sure he was directly behind him and encountered only one severe jolt as he flew through Seal's "dirty air." As he continued communicating with Little Rock, he watched Seal's plane from his left window as it skimmed along I-30 approaching the clover leaf intersection with I-430. Seal, who had gained air speed in the descent, was now ahead of him. Terry was wondering what the motorists were thinking if they sited the "UFO" Seal was piloting, as it streaked along, lightless, toward Little Rock.

Seal picked up on the well-lit highway intersection, his "IP," a bomber pilot's jargon for his "initial point" on a bombing run, and headed north. Terry still didn't have a need to know about the location of the drop zone, but he couldn't help but notice Seal orbiting in a steep left-hand turn over a field containing a horse boarding stable off Terry's left wing.

In the dark void below Seal's plane, Terry could see what appeared to be the headlights of two motorcycles serpentining in the field below. This had to be the secret "drop zone," because he observed Seal's plane bank abruptly to the right in order to open the passenger side door enabling the cargo to tumble earthward.

It was a beautiful execution of a right-hand, 90-degree bank wing over, he thought, as he marveled over Seal's flying ability. The two headlights on the ground converged on the same spot and became motionless. Reed assumed they had found the cargo.

Then it hit him. SHIT!!!!!! "That's the Triple-S ranch," Reed said out loud.

But he had to put this out of his mind quickly and comply with his landing instructions. He observed Seal's plane departing silently southward as planned.

Once on the ground at Adams Field, he proceeded to a transit tie down slot at Little Rock air center. There, he would wait long enough to answer any questions, if approached, and then proceed home.

What Reed had observed, again without wanting to, was that the CIA's "night depository" was owned by someone he knew, namely, Seth Ward, his ex-partner in the Ultra-Light business. The duffel bag containing the money had landed right in the middle of Ward's horse ranch, the same ranch near which Reed had crashed the previous April.

Moreover, Terry knew who lived there and kept motorcycles stored in the barn. It was Ward's son-in-law, Finis Shellnut, whom Reed remembered as a man exiled to the ranch to dig post holes as punishment for marrying Ward's youngest daughter, Sally, and taking her off to Dallas and away from Ward's Godfather-like control.

Shellnut worked for Dan Lasater, Bill Clinton's personal friend and the man who employed Clinton's brother, Roger, as his chauffeur. Lasater & Co., Lasater's firm, was where Seal had been doing his "tithing." Reed was sure there was a connection between the tithing money Seal was depositing personally and the money being dropped into the night.

Ain't Arkansas a nice, cozy, small world, Reed thought.

* * *

The next morning Sawahata called Reed at home, requesting him to come to OSI.

"You did excellent job on first mission. You, Mr. Seal and Camp make very good aerobatic team. Agency money is safely 'on deposit' now. Thank you...very very much. But, Terry-san, I have major pressing problem I need to discuss with you. Lot more to this manufacturing world than I was briefed on prior to starting all this parts business. I need your help with technical details concerning quality control of these parts."

Spread on Sawahata's desk were gun parts with yellow tags marked "rejects."

"I get feedback from John Cathey that some guns jam, guns which use parts built here in Arkansas. Jesus Christ, all these specifications and little numbers on blueprint are enough to drive me crazy. This is your field, Terry-san, so please help."

What Sawahata was realizing was what originally had seemed an easy way to circumvent the law requiring that weapons suppliers document their production and sales through end-user certificates, had some hidden pitfalls. It was a flawed plan if the parts didn't work. Sawahata was learning that precision manufacturing is an applied science requiring lots of expertise that can only be acquired over many years of experience.

Sawahata's CIA training hadn't prepared him to deal with mechanical problems. So, he was now forced to take Terry into his confidence, even though Reed wasn't fully cleared for it. But he needed help, and fast, because Cathey was on his back.

"Where can we go to find the necessary instrumentation for thorough quality-control analysis of this part?" Terry asked as he inspected the lower receiver housing of an M16 that he held in his hand.

"We go Iver Johnson's," Aki said. "They have all necessary equipment, I think."

Both men got into Sawahata's car and drove to nearby Jacksonville, Arkansas, northeast of Little Rock, where the Iver Johnson's Arms, Inc. was located. There, Sawahata introduced Reed to J.A. Matejko, a manufacturing engineer, who was very much in the CIA's loop regarding the building of these weapons parts.

After a tour of the facility, Terry and Sawahata settled into a discussion with Matejko centering around his firm's inability to consistently hold critical tolerances on the weapons parts he was manufacturing. Sawahata had been told the weapons were jamming from heat buildup when operated on full automatic mode.

"The problem is we can machine the parts dead nuts (accurately) on our new Hitachi machining centers," Matejko said. "And Brodix (in Mena) is doing an excellent job of investment casting these parts. But our stack-up tolerances just go all to hell as a result of the sloppy work from our metal plater."

"Oh," Reed asked, "you don't have in-house metal plating capabilities?"

"No, we can't get licensed by the fucking EPA (Environmental Protection Agency). You'd think the CIA could lean on someone and get us a license if this work is so damn important," Matejko said.

Here again, due to the constraints of a covert operation, the X-factor, came into play and big problems had been created for the Agency. To make perfect weapons parts with the necessary close tolerances, Iver Johnson's needed to have a metal-plating capability in its own plant. This, in turn, required EPA licenses to dispose of the residual wastes containing dangerous heavy metals. These licenses are difficult and time-consuming to obtain and the Iver Johnson's had been unable to get the EPA bureaucracy to respond.

Reed learned Razorback Metal Processors, a firm located on the west side of the Little Rock Airport, was doing the plating for Iver Johnson's.

"So does the metal plater know what these parts are, and the tolerances that are required? Or is he just in the dark about all this?" Terry asked.

"Oh, no," Sawahata said. "We pay them special price in order insure secrecy surrounding these pieces. I made special trip there when this project first got started. Problem is not money. They being paid handsomely for 'special services.' They know who customer is. Problem is I think they are...how do you say...dumb-ass rednecks."

Since no one in the group was from Arkansas, they all had a good laugh.

Reed and Matejko knew what was wrong and it was not controlling tolerances while machining the part. Rather, it was the amount of material being added during the chrome-plating process, to the bore area where the bolt slid back and forth during firing.If this process was not controlled properly, too much metal could be added, thereby reducing the clearance between the sliding parts. This, combined with the slight swelling of the bolt due to heat build-up from the explosion of the cartridge in the rifle's chamber, was causing the bolt to jam.

The solution was simple, yet difficult. If Iver Johnson's couldn't be licensed by the EPA, a quality plater who truly understood weapons manufacture would have to be found. But this was a risky step, because it would involve taking another company into the arms loop. That would be a security problem for Sawahata.

Using the *Arkansas Directory of Manufacturers for 1984*, Reed began his search for a company with the expertise to do the job. He used the Standard Industrial Classification Code, or SIC, code 3471, used for electroplating, to identify relevant companies in the state. There were a total of 14 in Arkansas at that time. Most of these turned out to be too large to approach, or the types of companies that run continuous in-house production for high volume work. He needed a special company, preferably one that understood the exacting requirements of gun production.

Terry flew Sawahata around the state to visit the small firms, but they turned out to be ill-equipped and too "back-woodsy" to handle the task. In frustration, Reed turned to an old friend named Jack Kreps who was co-owner of Aerofab, a company in Batesville, Arkansas. Kreps, who had been in manufacturing for years in Arkansas, recommended a company Reed had previously heard of, Choate Machine and Tool in Bald Knob, about 50 miles northeast of Little Rock. Reed located the nondescript and low-profile firm on page 290 of the Arkansas directory.

The owner, Garth Choate, had just constructed a new building and was expanding his general-purpose machining business into a products line that included survivalist gear and gun accessories. When Sawahata and Reed met Choate, they knew they had found the right guy. He recognized the opportunity to get high-profit work, which was not being competitively bid on by other companies. On the surface he appeared to be an all-around good guy who hated "communists" and, most importantly, he knew how to keep a secret.

Choate was an individualist with a vengeance. Guns were his thing. He and Sawahata developed an instant rapport based on their mutual needs. Terry began to think that a new SIC code would have to be created just for Arkansas. One entitled "Agency-Friendly Companies." He joked with Sawahata that the code should be 0007. Aki liked that and said he'd pass the suggestion on to Cathey.

Choate Manufacturing was not only able to solve the immediate crisis, but later expanded into areas of plastic-injection molding in order to produce critical parts and components being depleted from the National Guard inventory such as folding weapons stocks.

Terry, over the course of the next two and a half months, acted as Sawahata's "air taxi-pilot" and manufacturing advisor-expert. Performing in that unique capacity, he was beginning to see Arkansas from a new perspective—through the eyes of the CIA. Sawahata was getting a new perspective, too. On his business calls around the state with Terry, he was learning about manufacturing, something the Agency needed to know more about. He was an avalanche of questions, constantly picking Reed's brain, taking notes and filing reports.

With Reed as the pilot, and Sawahata paying the fuel bills, the two melded into *a black ops manufacturing team*. From Sawahata's constant line of questioning, it was obvious to Reed that the Agency viewed Arkansas as its very own banana republic and its new-found manufacturing base, as something to be exploited and developed, when the right companies were identified.

But, most of all, the CIA found what it truly needed: a convenient operations headquarters where questions weren't asked, where the moonshine mentality saw "the law" as "revenuers," those who wanted to deprive them of a living, and, most importantly, as noted on page 10 of the Arkansas Directory of Manufacturers, the state kept "government red tape" to a minimum.

This whole period with Sawahata was turning into one big "audition" without Terry realizing it. Sawahata was getting inside his head and was becoming comfortable with the world of machine tools to which Reed had introduced him. Without his knowing it at the time, Sawahata was filing the equivalent of military proficiency reports on Reed. Sawahata had named Reed well.

He <u>was</u> a "hungry wolf" who was ruthless when it came to business. "Terry-san," he had said. "You very aggressive guy when it comes to business."

"I ought to be Aki, I learned the hard way from my Japanese suppliers. Their motto hasn't changed from the days of World War II."

"Oh...what motto you refer to."

"Take No Prisoners."

It was a strange alliance. Each had become the other's protégé. Sawahata was learning about technologies hidden within manufacturing processes and Reed was learning the fine art of running an intelligence operation and keeping his lips sealed.

Terry was learning there were definite hidden benefits to working with the Agency, namely there was a secret good ole boy network. New business could just fall in your lap, out of nowhere, it seemed.

While flying one day, Sawahata gave Reed an important sales lead. "You need make visit to Piggot, Arkansas. You know where is?"

"Yeah, it's not too far from Blytheville, where I was stationed in the Air Force. What's going on there?"

"Oh, let us just say I have inside tip from Washington. A new company called MRL has moved in. I think they will need some manufacturing expertise and new equipment based upon Agency contract they will be getting soon."

Reed loved it. Flying the Agency had its fringe benefits, all right. In this case, he was getting an inside tip on a potential customer before the firm even arrived in Arkansas. After checking out the lead, he discovered from the Chamber of Commerce at Piggot, a small town in the northeast corner of Arkansas, that, in fact, a St. Louis-based company, Missouri Research Labs Inc. (MRL) was starting a printed circuit board manufacturing operation.

As Reed developed the MRL account, he met Sawahata's secret contact, Gary Brandon. Brandon had come down from the St. Louis operation and, through him, Reed learned that MRL had secret military contracts through its Electronic Manufacturing Services Group in Albuquerque, New Mexico. That group, however, couldn't produce any weapons parts for the Agency in New Mexico because of documentation requirements and government inspectors at that plant. It had become necessary to start up this facility in Arkansas and disguise it as a general purpose printed circuit board operation to get away from prying eyes.

Seal told Terry later that the facility produced untraceable circuit boards and critical electronic components used in stinger missile guidance systems being made for the Agency. The stinger is a hand-held, ground-to-air missile that can be fired like a bazooka by an individual to disable aircraft. Seal could only speculate why they needed "no trail" stingers. Probably to arm some banana republic and then blame it on some unsuspecting government or private weapons exporter.

Terry sold Brandon some computer-controlled metal fabrication equipment whose purpose was to make electronics enclosures or black boxes to encase sophisticated electronics gear.

Sawahata snickered when he first told Reed about MRL and revealed to him that the Arkansas Development and Finance Authority (ADFA) had "the inside track" on this new operation because the state was making "preferential loans" to the company to capitalize its operation. Reed didn't ask any prying questions about this state-backed lending agency. He would learn later that the state had given MRL a $1.5 million loan in late 1984.

It seemed curious to Reed that Sawahata was getting inside information about ADFA's activities, however.

ADFA was receiving an increasing amount of media exposure. By now it was mid-February, 1985, and the local newspapers were filled with reports about Bill Clinton's formation of ADFA, set up to act as a bonding firm to finance industrial expansion in the state. Its mandate was to lend money at preferred rates either to local companies needing money to expand or as a source of low-cost recruitment capital needed to lure out-of-state manufacturing firms to Arkansas.

Reed knew about the Arkansas Industrial Development Commission (AIDC), whose board was appointed by the governor and served as a task force to attract new industry. This commission, however, had no money of its own. It simply took its clients, businesses wishing to relocate there, to existing financial institutions such as the Little Rock "bond daddies," already operating in Arkansas. Lasater & Co. was a firm that had been receiving on an average of $300 million annually in this state bonding activity. Clinton, through the formation of ADFA, was, in effect, replacing the private bonding firms with ADFA and putting the state itself into the bond business.

The source of the state's capitalization, however, had been a point of curiosity for Reed. It had never been fully explained where ADFA's money would come from. He had even gone so far as to ask his attorney, Mark Stodola, a political insider in Little Rock, about the source. Reed and Stodola both thought ADFA was a good idea, but Reed found it odd that no other state seemed to be doing this. Stodola didn't know the source of the capital, and only assumed tax revenues would be used. This didn't seem to make sense, since the state budget had no funds earmarked for ADFA and the State Constitution barred deficit financing.

"Sure is a great idea," Reed said in Stodola's office. "But my expertise is in manufacturing, and I know what kind of money you're talking about to build modern factories that have state-of-the-art automation. You're talking about the need for a hell of a lotta money, millions. Where are they going to get it?"

"Beats me," Stodola said shrugging his shoulders. "That's Bill Clinton's problem. It's his idea."

* * *

But Clinton had a secret source—one nobody would have guessed. Reed would soon learn who the source was and who was in charge of the state's "money machine."

It was mid-February and Reed was at Rich Mountain having his Seneca undergo a "100-hour inspection." Camp was there for the same reason and the two men were assisting Joe Evans by removing inspection plates on their near-identical aircraft.

Word was filtering back through the spook pipeline that another flight-training class was being formed. Reed and Camp were speculating that somewhere in the United States, probably Ohio from the hints their previous class had dropped, another single-engine class was nearing graduation.

Sawahata had already put out the word that, unless they heard differently, to anticipate a March arrival of "more beaner freedom fighters wearing Raybans."

"Shit," Camp said. "Just what I need. Another fuckin' summer with Ramon. I was really beginning to enjoy this night-flyin' activity with Barry. It's a hell of a lot easier, more safe and it pays better than risking your life daily with these commie killers from down south."

"Yeah, I was wondering how often they have you flying," Terry said. He had only flown that one mission for the drop at the Triple S. Since then Sawahata's other activities had kept him occupied, but he knew Seal and Camp had been burning the midnight oil, literally.

"Three time a week on the average. And Barry says if the duffel bags get any bigger, he'll need to enlarge the door on his Seneca just to be able to jettison the cash," Camp jokingly answered.

"Considerin' the size of Barry, and he fits through the door, you must be talkin' some big duffel bags," Terry added, referring to Seal's physique which was taking on record dimensions as of late.

"Yeah, he tells me we're movin' normally $3 million per sortie. I wish I was workin' on 10 per cent like the state. I'd be retirin' soon."

By Reed's calculations that was about $9,000,000 a week falling out of the sky and into the hands of Governor Bill Clintons' friends. By his calculations that was nearly $40,000,000 a month arriving by Federal Express' secret competitor, *The CIA's Green Flight Express.* If the state was getting 10%, as Seal had said, plus the temporary use of the entire amount, that could explain why lots of money was being thrown around to attract out-of-state industry.

Reed wished he could confide in his lawyer Stodola about what he knew. Stodola would never have suspected the CIA was Arkansas' secret source of capital. That would sure finance a lot of "new industry" for Clinton, Reed thought.

And the best part was, it wouldn't cost the Arkansas tax payer anything.

CHAPTER 12

STRANGE ALLIANCE

In black operations, Terry Reed was finding, danger was never further away than the telephone.

He could hear it ringing as he entered his new residence on the 10th Tee of the Maumelle Golf Course. It was late Wednesday afternoon of February 20, 1985, and he had just finished a hectic day overseeing some Agency manufacturing problems.

All that was on his mind now was enjoying a Scotch and water at his new wet bar, which had a picturesque view of the golf course and a tributary of the Arkansas River. His hard work was beginning to pay off, but trouble was at the other end of the phone he was about to answer.

Sawahata was on the line with some really bad news. "Emile Camp's airplane is missing," he said. "It is past due on a flight from Baton Rouge to Mena. I am telling you this because there is search activity going on, and I am sure it will be on news tonight. I do not want you over there drawing attention to yourself."

"How overdue is he?"

"Only several hours, but Barry and I fear worst."

The crash report would say that Camp died when his white Seneca with black, gray and red trim, registration No.N8658E, crashed into the north face of Fourche Mountain, eight and a half miles north of the Mena airport, as he was heading southeast. The National Transportation Safety Board (NTSB) crash examiner later reported that there was no fuel found in the engine fuel lines, and both fuel quantity gauges read "zero" at time of impact. There was no post-crash fire. Camp had simply run out of gas, Terry and Seal later concluded.

But how??

Camp had been on very simple flight that day. He was to fly from Baton Rouge to Mena and the flight plan he filed with New Orleans Flight Service estimated his time in route as two hours. Block No. 12 of his flight plan estimated he had three hours of fuel on board. He was flying an airplane he knew intimately and had operated and maintained for more than two years. Combined with the fact that he was current in all his FAA ratings, and would be executing an approach into an airport he was familiar with, it should have been, in pilot's jargon, "a walk in the park." Or as Barry Seal would say, "as easy as finding your dick in the dark."

But that's not what happened!!

He departed Baton Rouge at 11:12 AM CST. At 12:55 PM, Camp was cleared for an approach at Mena Inter-Mountain Regional Airport. He then radioed Fred Hampton at Rich Mountain at 12:55 PM, saying he would be landing in "10 or 15 minutes" making his intended flight within the two hours he had estimated. But he never landed at Mena and was declared missing at 2:12 PM, the time when his fuel would have been exhausted, the crash report said.[1]

This was simple math. That meant that Camp should have had at least an hour's fuel on board when he went down. But there was no fire. The wreckage was found two days later in a small area 200 feet below the mountains' crest. The NTSB listed the cause as pilot error. But Seal and Terry didn't buy that and wondered what the aircraft was doing so far off course.

The prescribed instrument approach procedure would have taken Camp to the south and east of Mena, far away from Fourche Mountain, one of the high points in the mountainous area. The aircraft was equipped with the latest array of communication and navigation equipment, including state of the art LORAN-C. And, strangely, there was no record of any further communication with anyone after Camp's last call to Rich Mountain Aviation. Why not? If he had been in trouble, surely he would have radioed Rich Mountain or ATC, or both.

Camp was an experienced pilot. Any student pilot will tell you what you do in a situation like this. If you find yourself confused and off-course, you never descend. Instead you implement the three "C's"—climb, confess and comply.

Camp's last communication with ATC placed him at 4,000 feet MSL. The instrument approach procedure called for the pilot to maintain a minimum altitude of 3,400 feet MSL until established inbound on the approach course. Once established inbound, Camp was then authorized to depart his mandated 3,400 foot altitude and descended for the landing at Mena. Even then, procedures dictated he would not be authorized to descend below 2,580 feet prior to establishing visual contact with the airport runway. *So why did the aircraft impact the mountain at 2,200 feet, and over 8 miles from the airport?* There was no way Camp could have had the field in sight from that distance.

But even more disturbing was Seal's disclosure to Terry after he had inspected the wreckage. He revealed that certain engine controls and switches were set in positions at time of impact that would indicate Camp was trying to get a restart on his right engine. Where, Seal wondered, did the fuel go? The NTSB made no mention of the missing fuel or anything else.

Arkansas State Police Investigator Russell Welch, the resident state police investigator in Mena, noted in his investigative report of the incident that Fred Hampton, the "on paper owner" of Rich Mountain Aviation, the Agency's aviation front company, told him he believed the plane had been "sabotaged" to prevent Camp's testifying about Seal's "sting" operation in Nicaragua for the CIA and DEA. He also told Welch that Camp was carrying documents on board dealing with the C-123 that Seal had used in the sting. No documents were found in Camps' wreckage. This C-123, "The Fat Lady," would be the 'very same plane' the world would see protruding from the Nicaraguan jungle more than 18 months later after crashing during a CIA mission with a load of Contra arms aboard.

Polk County Sheriff A.L. Hadaway, himself a pilot, became alarmed when he heard of the circumstances surrounding the crash. Considering Camp's flying experience he thought it all didn't add up and said, "He [Camp] could find this airport at night and land without lights; I've seen him do it."

But Rudy Furr, the airport manager at Mena, told reporters of rumors he heard coming out of Rich Mountain Aviation that were even more alarming, "I've heard murder, that Camp had a bomb on board, that he had 500 pounds of cocaine and that he had $3 million in cash."

When Reed heard the suspicious circumstances surrounding the crash and the rumors about the $3 million dollars, he privately concluded that perhaps Camp had been on a "green flight" and for some unexplained reason had deviated from his destination of Mena. It just didn't make sense though, since Seal wasn't piggy-backing with him. It was possible Emile was trying to loose a "tail", or maybe he was being followed by a U.S. Customs plane and was attempting to evade it. The element of the whole affair that was injecting paranoia into Reed was the rumor of sabotage. No matter how good a pilot a person is, if someone tampers with a plane and covers his trail properly, the plane will most certainly fall out of the sky.

Terry had lost a friend that day. It wouldn't be the last. Sawahata put all of his pilots on red alert while all aspects of the crash were investigated. He told Terry to be particularly cautious while pre-flighting his Company plane. Seal cautioned Terry to be especially critical of the type and quantity of fuel being taken on when refueling. They didn't know how it had been done to Camp, but all indications pointed to a saboteur in their midst.

Another unsettling aspect to Terry was that Camp had earlier that very month exchanged planes with him for maintenance purposes. Terry had flown Camp's now destroyed Seneca N8658E to North Little Rock after the trade and he and Sawahata had flown it for several days while Red Hall performed avionics maintenance on Terry's. Afterwards, Camp had continued to fly Terry's until they finally rendezvoused to re-trade. That meant that, if someone was out to get Camp, they may have also tampered with Reed's plane. Even after an absolutely thorough personal inspection of his Seneca, Terry still felt uneasy operating the craft for the next few days.

With Camp gone, Seal's importance to the government as a witness only increased. He and Camp had been the only gringos who could testify with direct knowledge about the Cartel bosses. Now, Seal was the only one who could testify about the link between the Contra operations and drug trafficking. And unbeknownst to anyone in Arkansas at that moment, was the resurrection of some key CIA assets in Miami, fanatic exile Cubans who had helped the Agency carry out its black and dirty operations around the world. They had become the Agency's willing assassins and saboteurs.

Camp had already had a run in with one of them, Ramon Medina. But soon there was to be another, even more deadly one named Felix Rodriguez, who used the code name "Max Gomez." He was already being brought into the loop by Donald Gregg, Vice President George Bush's National Security Advisor. Terry would meet "Max" very soon.

Sawahata had a more immediate problem, however. He needed a replacement instructor to take Camp's place for the "Class of '85."

Oklahoma was tasked with finding a replacement since he already had a list of known spook pilots as a result of his father's service with the Agency. It didn't take him long to locate a suitable replacement right there in Oklahoma. The only problem this second Oklahoman presented is what would be his call sign. He would have to be called "Tulsa."

The replacement was a pilot with considerable aviation talent. In addition to having flown both fixed wing and fling-wing (helicopter) aircraft for Air America, he was an FAA certified aircraft mechanic working in Tulsa at a commercial airliner overhaul facility. What most impressed everyone was the fact that he had been a test pilot for a firm in Coffeeville, Kansas which had been responsible for the development of an STOL aircraft called the "Helio Stallion."

With his short stature, receding hairline and cherubic face, Tulsa bore a resemblance to the rock 'n roll singer Elton John. But his quiet and bashful demeanor was deceiving. He was something else when he got into an airplane. He lived on pure 100-proof adrenalin and was unaccustomed to taking orders. Everyone was wondering how he and Ramon would interface.

"Tulsa" was happy to be "recalled." He, Terry and Idaho got along because of their mutual "railroad" experience overseas. They spent a few days together updating their lesson plans and exchanging war stories.

Contrary to the Contra class of '84, this time the instructors and Sawahata seemed ready for the arrival of the students at Nella. As they waited at Rich Mountain for the arrival of the Class of '85, Ramon Varnados was taking the camp out of mothballs and there were early indications of spring. Varnados had been busy using a landscaping box-blade behind the tractor to repair the erosion that winter weather had inflicted on the sod airstrip.

When the truck with the students arrived, Medina and Diego were already with them barking orders. It was apparent that things would go smoother, since these arrivals already seemed to be in a higher state of discipline than the previous class was when it started.

It appeared that this batch of Freedom Fighters was already accustomed to Medina's "lack of punishment is reward enough for a job well done" management philosophy. Terry could certainly relate to that dictatorial leadership style and sympathize with the trainees. It was the same one honed and embraced by the Strategic Air Command (SAC), in which he had served.

Medina informed the instructors that there had been a higher washout rate in the single-engine training due to the application of higher standards. The quality of this new class would therefore be higher, he predicted. It was definitely smaller, only 14 this time. This made everyone happier.

Medina took the opportunity, with everyone present, to give a motivational briefing. He said he had been in Central America and that a CIA ground-based invasion by the Contras was in the offing. Key Sandinista leaders would soon "disappear," he said confidently, but he did not elaborate on this. Terry got the chills hearing that, remembering as he did the "assassins" Medina and the others had trained at Nella. He could only assume that the assassin students would have something to do with the "disappearance" to which Medina referred.

What became known as the Iran-Contra operation was finally in full swing. The White House by now had turned up the heat. President Reagan was implying that the Sandinistas were receiving training and supplies from our declared enemies in Iran, stating that "most of the prominent terrorists groups" in the world were giving "advice and training" to Nicaragua.[2] He neglected to mention Americans arms were being secretly sent to Iran to help free our hostages. Nor did he mention the CIA was secretly arming the Contras. With Medina back in Nella, Felix Rodriguez was on his way to El Salvador to aid in the training of counter-insurgents.

1985 was quickly becoming "the Year of the Contra". From what Terry was learning about Seal's "airdrops", it seemed a great deal more money, more than the previous $40 million a month, was coming into Arkansas. He could only assume that, once this money was "invested" through the maze built within the Arkansas bond business, the Contra effort was benefiting from these gargantuan "night time deposits". These tremendous sums over shadowed the healthy "donations" from wealthy right-wingers that were being solicited by Lieutenant Colonel Oliver North's non-profit network operating out of Washington. These donations, by comparison, were a drop in the bucket and were probably just being used to mask the existence of the real cash that Seal was flying in. Theirs' was probably only "seed money" being used to cover the CIA's banking trail, Terry and Seal theorized.

After the Medina briefing, and prior to the instructors leaving for the day, Sawahata introduced Medina and Diego to "Tulsa" and explained he was the replacement instructor for Camp.

"I certainly hope you don't show the side of insubordination Mr. Camp displayed while teaching here," Medina said to Tulsa. "It was not good for the morale of my troops to see such open disregard for a person of my stature."

Tulsa, with a wad of mint Skol in his mouth, spit on the ground, splattering tobacco juice on Medina's spit-shined jungle boots.

"I don't cotton too much to all this military shit, that's why I got out of the Air Force and was sheep-dipped* in order to work for the Agency," he said. "My job is to turn these guys into good pilots. And I'll die tryin' to do that. You and I'll get along just fine as long you keep out of my way and let me do that."

Medina had picked on the wrong guy again. He had underestimated Tulsa probably because of his demeanor. Reed could tell by the twinkle in Tulsa's eyes that he was ready and confident of the outcome. So did Medina who did nothing but give Tulsa a piercing Hispanic stare. Sawahata bristled and was getting ready to intervene. But there was no need, Medina only cursed in Spanish and walked away. The group was off to a great start again, Terry thought.

On the way back to Little Rock, Sawahata confided to Terry that he was afraid there was a connection between Camp's death and Medina, and that the bad blood between them had just seemed to fester without end. He wanted Terry to keep his eye on Medina's actions toward Tulsa and report immediately if Terry felt that Medina was going to do more than give Tulsa his macho evil eye.

"I don't see what Agency sees in these fucking Cubans," Sawahata said. "They seem crazy to me. They are like trained police dogs, except one is never quite sure who master is."

"Yeah, I wish we would go ahead and invade down there in order to cut out all these non-professionals," Terry responded. "I don't mind telling you Aki, I don't like to be associating with people like Medina. I sure hope you put in a good word for me when this is all over so I can get beyond this type of work. My wife doesn't want me to end up like Emile, especially with two sons to raise."

---

*   By "sheep-dipped" he was referring to a procedure used by the CIA from 1959 to 1975 to set up a secret army in Southeast Asia. Select volunteer pilots were flown to aircraft carriers, which are American soil, mustered out of the military and, in exchange for time still owed Uncle Sam, given contracts of employment with Air America—meaning the CIA. That made it all legal.

"Why you say son? You no have new baby yet?" Aki asked.

"Technology, Aki. Haven't you heard of ultra-sound? Janis had one last week. It's definitely a boy, or it has two umbilical cords."

Terry and Sawahata were becoming close friends. By spending countless hours with Aki over the past several months, Terry thought he knew almost as much about the CIA's activities in Arkansas as Sawahata did. His combination of flying and his expertise in manufacturing, as well as loose security, had exposed him to the many operational loops. But even extensive inside knowledge didn't prepare Terry for what happened March 13th, 1985....

The phone call that morning was from Linda Crow, Mark McAfee's secretary/mistress. She was frantic, Mark was off on another diet-pill binge and even more incoherent that normal. In fact, he had taken time out that morning to punch her around a little just to show how much he loved her.

She was approaching her limit and could no longer contain her belief that he was becoming mentally ill. "Terry, you gotta come by the office real fast, Mark's not here right now and I have to talk to you about something real important," she said sobbing.

Terry could tell by the tone of her voice that she desperately needed a friend. She had confided in Janis that Mark was becoming more violent with her and she didn't know how much longer she could tolerate his punishment. Terry's new home in Maumelle was only four miles away, so he got in his car and drove over.

When he arrived, Linda was pacing in the parking lot and chain-smoking. She clearly was a nervous wreck. "Terry, I gotta talk to you before Mark gets back. And you shouldn't be here when he returns. I think he's actually going crazy. It's those damn diet pills. He's gonna hurt someone, Terry. He's even carrying a gun now, everywhere he goes. He thinks everyone's out to get him. And I know this sounds stupid, but I love him. You just gotta help me handle him."

How could he help?, Terry wondered. Another classic example of a nice woman getting involved with a married man whose life was out of control and he wouldn't take action to repair it. McAfee, at this point, reminded Terry of an aircraft in a terminal dive. Its air speed had grown so high that in order to pull it out, you'd have to pull so many "G's" it'd tear the plane's wings off.

He had basically written off McAfee. And he told her so.

"You've got to get away," he said to her. "Just quit, pack your things and leave this town. Janis and I will help you with money if you need some. It just pains us, Linda, to see you let him treat you like this."

"Terry, it's not only me. He's gonna hurt other people, too. "

"Like who?"

"Your friend, Aki. I don't know how to tell you this, Terry, it sounds too bizarre. But Mark is trying to get Aki in trouble with the FBI. Some damn harebrained plan of his to get rich quick and make a lot of money as a reward from the government."

This really got Terry's attention.

"Linda, slow down and tell me all you know about what you just said."

She confessed that, as far back as November, McAfee had been communicating with the FBI office in Little Rock concerning what he said was "a devious plan by a Japanese firm to steal and export prohibited American technology."

As Linda paced, and smoked, the significance of what she had said began to sink in. This could be a major disaster, not only for the Agency, but the entire Contra training effort, since Terry did not know who, beyond the CIA, was in on the Arkansas operation.

"Linda, do you know who he's been talking to at the FBI?"

"Oh it's a real funny name, I've heard him call up here several times and talk to 'Mark.' He always goes in his office and closes the door when he's talking to him, but I think I wrote it down once on my daily planner."

After retrieving her planner, and searching the previous months, she finally found where she had scrawled the name "Mark Jessie, FBI."

Armed with the information just given him, Terry headed for Sawahata's office. The compact man from the CIA turned visibly white when he heard what Terry told him. He frantically searched his file cabinet until he found the folder labeled "Mark McAfee." Within it was a brochure of a Hewlett-Packard integrated circuit cell tester.

"Terry-san. This guy must be crazy! I did not even know what it was when he showed it to me. I still do not know what it is. We have major security problem. This is emergency. I need a drink!"

By now, it was approaching lunchtime. Both men decided to get away from OSI and go to their usual haunt in order to think and formulate a plan.

Two perfect Rob Roys on the rocks still didn't seem to calm Sawahata's nerves. His paranoia began to run rampant. He began to reconstruct conversations McAfee had lured him into over the phone, now believing he had been secretly taped and McAfee had given the tapes to the FBI.

"Problem is, Terry-san, we do not know how far investigation had progressed. They have had many months to be spying on me." The word "spying" struck Reed as pure irony.

"If I had known about this earlier, I could have had Washington implement damage control, but, with investigation so many months old, perhaps many people within FBI, who were not in proper loop, now know about my activities," Sawahata said. "Is major problem for me! I LOSE FACE! All my Agency training did not prepare me for crazy rednecks like McAfee! Another drink for me, please."

Sawahata was most concerned about the political embarrassment this could cause the CIA. What if this information was leaked to Reagan's opponents on Capitol Hill? Aki's career would surely be over. But he had been reared in Japan, where personal disgrace was overshadowed by something else. Aki feared he had blackened the image of the Agency and disgraced it. And for this he could not be forgiven.

He even feared he would be "terminated" from his job, which takes on a more ominous meaning in intelligence parlance. It means you're dead.

"I must take vacation immediately," the distraught Sawahata confided. "Worse thing can happen right now is for FBI to interview me. We are at critical stage of program, all phases are operational now. Jade Bridge and Centaur Rose are successful, thanks in part to your help. I think program is self-running at this point. With Bruce's help maybe you can cover for me for awhile. I need to think things out in Washington. Come with me, I must introduce you to someone."

"Bruce" was one of Sawahata's employees. All Terry knew, up to this moment was that Bruce functioned as an office manager. He handled the day-to-day details of the export business that masked the real activities of OSI. When he had met him months earlier, Terry had been told by Sawahata that Bruce was from northwest Arkansas and spoke five languages. The emergency had forced Sawahata to reveal Bruce's true role.

And that wasn't the only intelligence rule broken that day. To guarantee security, operatives *never* come in contact with anyone in their chain of command other than the person directly above and below them. The "one up, one down rule" is what keeps the program secure and the identity of its people from being discovered in the event any single individual is compromised. Prior to this emergency, Terry was unaware of and had "no need to know" about the man Sawahata interfaced with and the *state's link* to the operation.

But now Sawahata was forced to take Terry to the "someone" he had just mentioned—and that someone had his office in the south wing of the Arkansas State Capitol.

He could tell Sawahata was accustomed to frequenting the place as he parked his nondescript four-door Oldsmobile Cutlass in a "no parking" zone in front of the Capitol, an area normally reserved for dignitaries.

It was close to noon and Sawahata was concerned about catching this "someone" before he left for lunch. He walked briskly into the building with Terry close behind. As they turned down a hall heading through the south wing they entered a door that read "Arkansas Industrial Development Commission." Inside was a stately room decorated with period furniture.

The receptionist was on the phone, but recognized Sawahata and motioned him to a seat. After she hung up, she asked Sawahata if he had an appointment.

He said no, but told her it "very important to see Mr. Nash immediately." He could not wait until after lunch, he said. Nash emerged from the office a few minutes later, clearly ill-prepared for what he was about to hear.

Sawahata moved close to the other man and, in a panicky low-tone voice, said: "We have emergency. I have to leave town immediately. Let us go inside for private meeting. This gentleman with me is Mr. Reed. You know who he is."

The man who ushered both men into his office was Bob Nash, whose official title then was Senior Assistant to the Governor For Economic Development. Terry was taken back by his appearance, he was a perfect double for Bill Cosby, back in the days when the actor starred in "I Spy," a television series about a businessman in Europe who was in reality an American intelligence agent.

After closing the door to his office, Nash expressed anger that Sawahata was speaking so freely in front of Terry. "Aki, are you sure you want Mr. Reed in on this meeting. This is very awkward. What's this all about? I have lunch scheduled with you for tomorrow. Can't this wait?"

"No," Sawahata answered. "And Mr. Reed is cleared for everything I am going to say. We have difficult situation that becomes major embarrassment for all of us. A local businessman has reported me to FBI here in town and we are not certain how far investigation into OSI's activities may have progressed."

Nash was clearly distraught. He motioned both men to a small, round antique table near the west wall of the stately office. As they sat down in the Chippendale-style chairs, Terry noticed the fireplace on the south wall and Nash's giant, dark, antique mahogany desk. Everything in the room was neatly arranged, giving it the appearance that not a lot of work was done there.

Nash sat back in his chair, leaving Sawahata nervously hunched over the table. As Sawahata chattered on, Nash kept looking at Terry as if to gauge his reaction to Sawahata's narrative about "the emergency."

Nash listened intently, shifting his focus back and forth between the two men across from him. He was making Terry uneasy with his intense stares.

When Sawahata had finished, Nash said in a slow calculated tone that bore no discernible accent of any kind: "I want you to understand, Mr. Sawahata, I'm not necessarily agreeing with the way this is being handled. It appears to me that *you*, Aki, have contributed to this problem. And now you've set in place a plan to take care of these problems that is obviously going to affect me and this office. I suppose all we can do now is take a wait-and-see attitude after you go to Washington and inform your people about our problem here. Of course, I'll have to have a meeting with my people and make them aware of all this. Maybe we can exert some control at our level over the local FBI."

After a long silence, Nash turned to Terry and said: "What do you think, Mr. Reed? You know this McAfee character better than we. How far will he pursue this scheme of his?...I mean, if he doesn't see a response out of the FBI?"

"From what I understand from his secretary, he's totally unpredictable at this point", Terry said. "The good news, from your point of view, is he's not politically connected as far as I'm aware. I think if someone in the FBI were to humor him and convince him there was an on-going investigation, he would probably cause no further problems in this area, for now at least. But he is a loose cannon, and he's desperate."

"I like the way you think. Maybe this office can unofficially intervene with the FBI," Nash suggested. "That would buy us the time we need for Mr. Sawahata to get Washington on top of this. Maybe the problem isn't as large as we think."

Nash and Terry had dissected the problem clinically like surgeons and divided it into two categories: areas that could be dealt with and areas that could not. Sawahata, on the other hand, saw it only one way. In his mind, he was the source of the problem. He was the professional in charge. Terry was afraid Aki was about to fall on his sword over this.

"So, gentlemen," Nash said. "I have a busy schedule this afternoon. Mr. Reed, I would like to have a private conversation with Mr. Sawahata. But, considering the turn of events today, I think you should plan on meeting me for lunch tomorrow in Aki's stead. He will be busy in Washington, I'm sure."

Terry left and waited outside by Sawahata's car. As he looked up at the Capitol Dome, a replica of the dome in Washington, his mind was reeling with thoughts that disturbed him.

The significance of the meeting was beginning to impact on him. He had now been drawn, through no design of his own, to the pivotal point of the intelligence loops that were orbiting around Arkansas. What he had just learned wasn't taught in political science classes.

Here he was at the core. Like Dorothy, he had looked behind the curtain and seen the true "Wizard."

Here was what seemed a strange alliance. A state run by Democrats in bed with a Republican administration in Washington, and both conspiring to evade Congress' prohibition against aiding or abetting the Contras. It was so steeped with hypocrisy.

Was the CIA the invisible force that had the power to *compromise* these political pillars of the nation?

Were these same invisible forces orbiting only in Arkansas or throughout the nation? He wondered. But why limit it to the nation? Perhaps the world functioned under one control. Could that control be the CIA? Was there a secret alliance of agents worldwide who operate as they please?

Religion, he had come to realize, was a form of social control. Was politics as well? Was it just a game like professional sports, simply to divert public attention from what was really happening? Was it all just a placebo?

While driving back to OSI, Terry was strangely quiet and withdrawn. He was feeling manipulated by the social order he had been raised to obey and now he had doubts about his previous motivations in life.

"You're awfully quiet, Terry-san," Sawahata said after a few minutes.

"Aki I've got to ask you a question. It's funny I've never asked, considering all the time we've spent together. Are you a Republican or a Democrat."

"I am a political atheist. I work for the CIA."

"What does that mean?"

"That means Agency is politics. Agency is the government. Everything else is just puppets, a big game, Terry-san. You did not know that?"

If Terry Reed was not a liability before, he certainly was now. Those who see behind the curtain are always a threat. It was like someone telling the Pope in the 1300s that the world was really round and that it did, indeed, revolve around the sun, rather than the other way around.

But those who feared him would not pull the trigger themselves. They would not resort to such "dirty", "mob-style", methods. They would use a much more clean, convenient and safe way to "terminate" him. Simply manufacture a criminal profile, construct a crime, and let the "system" do the rest. Reed would find that when irritated, the United States Government could simply use its internal resources to "eliminate" an asset.

* * *

Terry had a restless night as he lay half-awake analyzing what was occurring and his feelings about it. He could now recall Sawahata's comments after he came down the Capitol steps.

"Terry-san. Thank you very, very much," he had said.

"This is major embarrassment for me. I called Washington from Mr. Nash's office. I need to go get on secure line and explain problem in detail. But it looks like they can help. Too early to know for sure, but I must leave for Washington tonight. I am so glad you are my backup. I know I can count on you. Mr. Nash likes you."

Just as it is performed in combat, Terry had been given a field promotion, one bestowed on the spot during battle by a field commander when the officer above you in rank has been put out of action. Akihide Sawahata's injuries were not physical though. He had been *compromised!*

But he lay awake thinking that maybe his "field promotion" was the result of Sawahata's deserting his post. He wondered if Nash was aware of Sawahata leaving Little Rock that night when he had earlier in the evening showed up at Terry's house with his wife, two children and what appeared to be all their worldly goods in suitcases and boxes with string wrapped around them and their names on the labels.

Sawahata has been evasive about his plan to return, if ever, when he drove up unexpectedly and talked to Terry in his driveway that night. He hadn't even remained long enough to say goodbye to Janis, who was out showing homes to prospective buyers. His Japanese wife was typically obedient and acted as though she didn't even know why they were leaving.

"I talk to Washington," Sawahata said. "They want me out of here for awhile. They need time to analyze problem. You should alert everyone in Mena and Nella, especially Mr. Seal. Just tell him we have big security problem. He will understand. You go to lunch with Bob Nash tomorrow. Everything will be OK. I do not know when I return, it is up to Agency." With that brief *sayonara*, he was gone.

The next day, March 14th, the conversation began casually as the two men gazed at each other across their egg drop soup at Fu Lin's. The banter was light, with each taking measure of the other, not unlike a blind date. Circumstance had thrust them together.

Nash had taken the intervening time to brief himself on Terry since he seemed to know a lot about his background as they talked. Reed knew little about Nash, but assumed the Black man hadn't attained this post by being stupid. He could only assume that there were faceless people behind Nash based on his comment yesterday that he had to discuss the matter with "my people."Terry felt that would be a good starting point to switch from the social talk to business.

"I'm at a disadvantage here, since I really don't know what my role is now," Terry told Nash. "Aki explained to me yesterday that I would be a liaison to your office. I presume you've had time to talk to the people you referred to yesterday. Are they in agreement with me performing as this liaison?"

"I don't mind telling you we're all walking on eggs right now. My people have been thoroughly briefed, and we all see the necessity of someone filling Mr. Sawahata's shoes during his untimely absence. To answer your question, yes, we feel you're suited to perform as liaison, considering your background and knowledge of the program here in Arkansas. I don't have to tell you how sensitive this situation is."

"What are my duties and who do I report to?"

"You sure do get right down to it, don't you, Mr. Reed? I like directness, it's something I don't come in contact with often, working, as I do, in the Capitol."

Nash outlined to Terry that he was expected to be Nash's "eyes and ears" in operations Jade Bridge and Centaur Rose, whose code names were known to him.

What worried him most, he said, was political fallout. He went on to say that he understood why the CIA was resorting to subcontractors, "characters" he called them, who by design had been recruited because of their "seedy background." These people bothered him the most and they needed "adult supervision." Terry saw Nash as the equivalent of the liaison, and "accountant," to the Laotian prince who had rented his country to the CIA years ago.

All Nash really wanted to know, it was clear, was if all was going well. To alert him of any potential problems before they developed and, most importantly, about all "the deliveries" at the ranch outside town, especially if they were on time...and with correct tallies.

"We will need to have lunch at least once a week, maybe more often if the situation demands," Nash told him. "Obviously, I'm not wanting written reports on this. You just keep track of who, what, where, when, why and, mostly importantly, how much, and we'll get along great. I'm sure Mr. Sawahata will return soon, but in the meantime, I'd like to say it's refreshing to work with an Anglo."

Terry now understood Laotian Prince Souvanna Phouma's motivation. It was money, pure and simple. There were no politics in Laos...or in Arkansas. There was only power, and offerings had to be made. He lay awake wondering—if there was truly a "wizard" in the Land of Oz, he was probably for sale too.

After stopping by to see Bruce, Terry discovered through OSI's secure communications that Seal was in Mena. He got into his plane and headed west, thinking about Sawahata's admonition to alert Seal of the new developments. This he wanted to do in person.

After listening to Reed recite the details of the "emergency" that led to Sawahata's fleeing the state, Seal, in his usual relaxed way, said: "So the Chink just discovered we was bein' investigated, huh? Hell, I've known about that ever since that dumb ass McAfee shit called the FBI back in November."

"You've known about this, all along? And you didn't tell Aki?" Terry asked somewhat startled.

"Naw, I figured he needed some excitement in his life. That desk job of his will be his death yet." He couldn't stop laughing.

"You didn't answer my question. How did you know about the investigation?" Terry asked.

"I'm gettin' the best intelligence money can buy. I call it payin' commissions, Terry, you know how the world works. You were in Southeast Asia. Everybody over there was on the fuckin' take. You had to bribe...pay somebody a fuckin' commission ta get anything done, didn't ya? Ain't no different here. It just costs a little more."

"Are you telling me you're buying inside information from the FBI? Are they in on this operation, too?" Terry asked, reflecting back to the comments Nash had made about contacting someone at the FBI.

"Well, you might say the Agency has a couple of moles in the FBI that are supposed to be runnin' cover for us over here. You know, CI (Counter Intelligence) types. That's the kind J. Edgar could never quite trust or control." The Fat Man was vibrating with laughter. It was the first time Terry had seen him laugh since Camp had been killed.

"That's the kind of Fed you never want to turn your back on. These crossover types," Seal said between breaks in laughter. Terry had experience with this kind of agent back in Oklahoma while working with Wayne Barlow. Barlow was a "bridge agent" whose salary was paid by the FBI, but he was closer to the CIA in heart and mind than his FBI bosses would have liked.

"But I'm glad you brought me this information, Terry. And I'm sorry to see Aki takin' everything so serious and leavin' town and all. But, hey...that means ya got promoted, huh? I always like to see my friends movin' up in the world. Ya never know when that can come in handy. Wanna go with me to slop the hogs?"

Terry was confused by the terminology. But he decided to ride along anyway to have dinner at a local diner with Barry. They had all been too busy recently and Camp's death had left them in a somber mood. The "hook-it and ride" attitude was gone now that they believed a murdering saboteur was in their midst. Seal even had another mechanic brought down from Ohio, a person he said he really trusted. He privately told Terry that "Mike," the Black man from

Puerto Rico, was sent in by the Agency to insure the aircraft were not tampered with. Mike was in charge of avionics inspections to insure none of the other Company planes were sabotaged as they suspected Camp's had been.

Driving north out of the airport complex in a one-ton Chevy truck, Seal stopped at the intersection of the airport road and the east-west highway at the north end of the field. While waiting to turn, Barry noticed a nondescript four-door sedan heading east toward them. As Seal pulled on to the highway, he began flashing his headlights at the oncoming car and pulled off the road into a service station parking lot on the north side of the road.

"Yep, it's time to slop the hogs," he said. "Reach under your seat and see if you find a paper bag."

Terry found a brown paper sandwich bag, the type used for lunches. It was neatly wrapped around its contents and sealed with masking tape. Its contents were approximately a half-inch thick and felt like money. As the car Seal had signaled pulled off the road and approached the truck on the driver's side, Seal chuckled, "Terry, meet my *very own* FBI Special Agent, and I do mean *own*. In fact, everybody should own one, they can come in handy. He's one of my inside guys and it's time to make my monthly installment payment for intelligence. Hand me the sack please."

As the car pulled within inspection distance, Terry noticed it had all the markings of an "undercover" FBI car; black wall tires, little hub caps and small antennas. It appeared that the man in the approaching vehicle was uneasy, probably due to Terry's presence in the car with Seal.

"You earned it this time," Seal said as tossed the bag into the window of the other car. Terry could not see the man's face at this point, but he could hear the other man say, "Who's that with you?"

"It's the guy out of Little Rock that flies around with the Chink. Speakin' of which he just ran off to Washington yesterday with his butt on fire due to an 'in-ves-ti-ga-tion' he got wind of out of the Little Rock FBI office." Seal couldn't hold back the laughter and began shaking as he added: "Ain't that a hoot? Shit, you told me about that back in November."

The FBI man obviously didn't want to have this conversation in daylight, nor hang around and socialize. He made his excuses and abruptly departed. As the agent drove out of earshot, Seal added, "Ain't money great, Terry? With it, you can buy damn near anything." He then gave the Arkansas Razorback yell while spinning the truck tires in the dirt: "SOOOOOOEEE pig."

Terry realized Seal had just bribed the FBI!

After dinner that night, and while driving back to the airport, Terry turned the conversation to his future once again. He had gotten a promotion, he thought, but he was still in Arkansas training Contras. Not his idea of a career.

"Barry, what have you heard about Cooper's operation down in Miami?" Is it gonna be up and running soon? Or was that just a false start?" Terry questioned. "I sent my résumé down there, but haven't heard anything back."

"Oh yeah, I forgot ta tell ya," Seal said. "Yeah, I been down south, and I can tell ya this isn't somethin' you wanna get involved in. You know, I know Janis and I think she envisions some kind of life of luxury livin' abroad with you playin' spook and that's not what's goin' on down there. These are all cowboys...old cowboys I might add. And the livin's hard and the pay ain't great. You better write that one off. I don't wanna be responsible for gettin' your wife mad at ya."

Although Seal did not spell it out, he was obviously warning Terry away from the shoddy operation being organized by Southern Air Transport in Miami. This was the "small Air America" Cooper had referred to in his conversation with Terry back in November. The pilots were based in Honduras and living in primitive quarters. While Richard Secord was billing the Enterprise an average of $10,000 a month for each pilot, he was paying them no more than $4,500 to fly combat missions with shoddy aircraft and antiquated equipment.

As Seal dropped Terry off at his plane, he gave him one of those looks and said, "So what's Bobby Nash got you doin', besides spyin' on me? I hear he refers to me as one of those 'seedy characters' over in Mena." He started laughing. Terry wondered if Seal had Nash's office bugged when he heard the term "seedy character"—Nash's exact words.

"Don't let him turn ya into Bill Clinton's bookkeeper like he did the Chink," Seal said, as he again spun his tires and drove off leaving a trail of dust.

1. National Transportation Safety Board Accident report, May 5, 1985.
2. Compilation of Presidential Documents, Vol. 21, #5, at 91-92.

CHAPTER 13

FEEDING FRENZY

"Goddam! I don't know what all you been doin' up there in Arkansas for the Agency, but you sure got some people's attention down here in Florida. If I didn't know you better, I'd accuse you of brown-nosin'. I attended a meeting yesterday in which you were the major topic of discussion.

"John Cathey was down here for an operational discussion and I was elected to give you a call in order to bounce an idea off of you. You got a minute to listen?"

The call had caught Terry by surprise. It was March 16, 1985. He was scheduled to fly that night at Nella and was hoping to sleep late, but it was Saturday morning and Duncan had bounced into his bed at the crack of dawn for the Saturday morning cartoon ritual. Bill Cooper's call had caught him right in the middle of a children's cartoon show, "The Roadrunner Hour", that he and Duncan were watching in bed. It was their favorite show. They especially liked Wile E. Coyote because he never gave up and was ceaselessly innovative. Sooner or later, he would catch that critter.

After changing phones to leave Duncan undisturbed, Terry heard Cooper outline a concept he said had been "kicked around" during the recent Miami meeting. Southern Air Transport (SAT), he noted, was in charge of transportation for an operation he couldn't discuss over the phone. Based upon Agency reports that were falling into the hands of "Cathey," the "customer", as he put it, was considering a start-up operation perhaps based in Mexico that could use talent Terry possessed.

They wanted Terry to do a feasibility study for a machine-tool company that would operate as a front in Mexico. Cooper went on to say that SAT was not set up to handle this type of operation, although they would be in a position to contribute heavily to the transportation side of the plan. They could provide air transport for "heavy things" that would look a lot like large machine tools. If the study indicated that the plan could work, it would require living abroad, something he knew would excite Janis.

"Sure, I'm interested, but I'm awful busy right here in Arkansas. I guess I could talk to these people about this and maybe they can find a replacement for me up here."

Cooper was quick to react to that. "Don't tell them about this, right now. That could be a real touchy subject. Don't want to tip the apple cart. As I understand it things are goin' real smooth up there, except for the problem with the Chink. We don't want to upset the state officials with our plans. Do you get the drift?"

It was clear from what Cooper was saying that the Agency didn't want any-one connected with the State of Arkansas to know what they were contemplat-ing. "Why" was not discussed.

"By the way, yesterday I saw a Fat Man we both know," Cooper said crypti-cally. "He said you weren't interested in crewin' for me down there. And if that's the case, I'll take your name off the list. It sounds like your plate's pretty full right now. This same Fat Man will have more details on this Mexican subject when he returns to Arkansas. In the meantime, drop me a line and give me your thoughts."

Terry was intrigued. Two days later, on March 18, he wrote and mailed Cooper a letter addressed to him in care of SAT. Terry had not seen Seal, but he wanted to get his interest in the operation on record fast. As a "PS," he addressed an issue he had not wanted to raise with Cooper on the phone. The *Charlie Cautro*. At the end of the letter, Terry wrote: "Your storage item is fine, but PLEASE expedite its pickup."

Terry's meeting with Bob Nash for lunch that day had been called to discuss "damage control", or how to contain the FBI's investigation of Aki Sawahata.

"We were able to extract some very interesting information from the local FBI office," Nash told him. "It sounds almost too good to be true, but, appar-ently, Mr. McAfee's 'crime' was handed off to an FBI agent who's under the control of the Agency, S.A. Mark Jessie. He was given the case since it involved an investigation into international espionage, his area of expertise."

"When I talked to Linda Crow, she felt McAfee had been talking to other people at the FBI office before he was put into touch with Special Agent Jessie. What about those people? Is your source sure there's not some kind of parallel investigation going on into OSI's activities?" Reed asked.

"Well, we are dealing with the *federal government* and anything is possible. For that reason, the state has requested that Mr. Sawahata not return until we're assured this near-calamity has blown over. In the meantime, you just keep reporting to me."

"I have a rather sensitive question to ask you, Bob," Terry interjected. "And don't answer if it offends you or violates my need to know. Did you have any advance warning of this 'near-calamity,' as you put it, prior to Sawahata tell-ing you last week? And did you have to buy that information from the FBI? Or did they volunteer it freely?" Reed was "fishing" to find out if Nash was buying his intelligence, just as Seal was.

"I had no advance warning," Nash answered. "I'm sure you could see it came as a shock to me. I don't wish to answer the other question. But why did you ask about buying information?"

"I just figured that if you had a relationship with the FBI, your office would have been forewarned about any investigation of OSI's activities. I've been directly involved in this program since last July and I'm curious if someone might not be 'looking' at me. Can you ask your contact at the FBI if I'm under any sort of investigation?" Nash stared at Reed, appearing to analyze his moti-vation for the earlier question. Reed added, "I was just curious about security. Advance warning of incoming ICBMs is something I dealt with in the Air Force."

"I'll have my sources with the bureau check everyone involved in 'Bridge' and 'Rose' to be assured this doesn't happen again. That should have been Mr. Sawahata's job. He's the Fed in charge of this program, or...so we thought."

Based upon Nash's statement that the state had not been forewarned by the

Feds, it appeared to Terry that Barry Seal was getting much better "intelligence" with his "commission system" than the Clinton administration was through official channels. Seal confessed he had known about the investigation into Sawahata since last November.

As Terry sat eating his egg roll, he realized he hadn't asked Seal the most important question: Why hadn't Seal alerted anyone? Or, if he had, who did he alert and why was no action taken? Terry wanted to keep to himself the knowledge Seal had given him the previous week at Mena about paying commissions. For all he knew, Nash might be on Barry's payroll, too. He wanted the answers to come directly from Seal's mouth, as he seemed to have better intelligence.

Terry was beginning to sense a definite, divisional rift between the state and federal governments. Nash and the state appeared to not be in the "federal loop." But Terry wondered. Was the CIA playing with these guys from the state and setting them up for some kind of "fall?" The Clinton administration was certainly amassing lots of potentially damaging political exposure, he thought.

Terry left Nash and flew to Dallas, the site of the nearest Mexican consulate, to familiarize himself on the legalities of setting up a foreign corporation in Mexico. He had taken to heart what his grandfather had told him years ago while fishing...strike while the iron is hot, and he wasn't going to let this opportunity pass him by, even in light of the field promotion.

What he had already learned was that the Mexicans refused to conduct serious business either over the phone or by mail. The man he had spoken with there after repeated calls, Consul-General Raul Gonzalez Certosimo, said Americans had reduced business to the impersonal. He insisted on a face to face meeting with any serious investors that were interested in developing Mexico. At first Terry thought this was a cultural thing, a formality and a carry-over from Spain and Cortez. But the truth, he would find later, is Mexican officials know it's impossible to hand someone a sack of cash over the phone. He found government representatives were extremely cautious when it came time to collect "special processing fees" and usually conducted this type of business only on a one-on-one level.

Terry was burning up with anticipation about the thought of an Agency backed Company. He and Seal had had a lengthy classroom discussion about CIA "cut-out" operations and "proprietaries." This had been the foundation of their early-on agreement to exchange Terry's manufacturing knowledge for Seal's knowledge of how to handle "handlers." Seal knew a world where intelligence manuals didn't exist, where the unthinkable isn't written down. In all of Terry's years in Air Force intelligence, he had never seen a textbook on how to manage a proprietary. Seal was a proprietary all by himself.

Terry was hearing a lot about Southern Air Transport in Miami, a long-standing Agency front, and decided it would be a good model to study. At one point, SAT was listed as the CIA's largest proprietary, with assets of more than $50 million and employing more than 8,000 people. The CIA, overall, is estimated to have several hundred fronts operating in the United States and overseas.[1]

Seal informed Terry that SAT was serving as a holding company for the CIA and secretly owned other black companies. *Weta Okami* smelled opportunity with this new knowledge. He was particularly intrigued by the concept of proprietary companies controlling other cut-outs.

Seal had become Terry's sponsor in the black world and his instructor in this undocumented training environment. The CIA at one level operated without controls and was truly a paperless company without auditable ledgers and shaded from the eyes of Congress' General Accounting Office. This was the level on which Seal operated and Terry, realizing the benefits, wanted to join him.

To further tantalize Reed, Seal said he saw burgeoning opportunities for anyone with "business smarts" and a good idea. He said the Agency was seriously lacking in ideas and needed innovative and creative people who could perform a service. In other words, they needed good subcontractors.

This fit right in with William Casey's belief that intelligence could only be gathered accurately and efficiently by people outside government who were legitimately connected to the international business community. Casey believed you recruit from the field whomever you need and *then* send them to "spy school." Casey once told one of the authors that during World War II he had learned a lot from the British method of melding the business and intelligence communities. "They're one and the same," he had said.*

CIA Director Stansfield Turner's approach to CIA management was just the opposite. Turner, Casey's predecessor, believed that you turned CIA-trained professional spies into businessmen to penetrate the areas where intelligence was needed. Terry had already been to spy school and was now involved in international trade. Seal saw him as a "shoo-in."

"Terry, the opportunity is right now if ya want it," Seal had told him. "You don't apply for the kinda job I have. You gotta be aggressive and make your own slot. These guys claim ta hate it, but they admire a level of aggressiveness that borders on insubordination, understand? Between the CIA and their Nicaraguan operation, and the DEA and their objectives, there are GS bean counters standin' on street corners with sacks of cash and no ideas.

"You've obviously got some talent they need or they wouldn't be talkin' to ya. I'd pursue it if I was you. For the most part, I'm just a pilot to them. I transport what they want transported and keep my mouth shut. You, on the other hand, you've developed expertise that they badly need. If they're talkin' an offshore operation controlled by SAT, or some other big proprietary, you better jump at the opportunity. And keep me posted on what it is they got in mind for ya. I'd be real curious if there's some way I could work into that, too, if it's offshore."

Seal had become a kind of coach, calling the plays and scouting the opposition. His comments about working himself into this offshore operation were a surprise to Terry. Seal had seemed totally "self-contained." He had his own businesses, his own airplanes, what appeared to be lots of money, prestige and an ability to handle the handlers. Why, Terry wondered, would he be interested in getting involved in yet another operation? Wasn't he ever satisfied?

---

*   Casey said this to co-author John Cummings during an impromptu conversation at a political dinner in New York in 1979. Cummings brought up the topic of intelligence because he was interested in Casey's view on the mass firing of CIA employees by then-CIA Director Stansfield Turner. Casey was an old intelligence hand, having been part of the fledgling U.S. intelligence agency, the OSS (Office of Strategic Services), during World War II and the man responsible for running agents in Germany. Casey was a major figure on Wall Street and served as head of the Securities and Exchange Commission under Richard Nixon and was also a key behind-scenes player in the Republican Party.

But Terry did not know about the problems Seal was having with his handlers, nor did he know of the Agency's plan to bring the Arkansas operation to an abrupt halt as soon as the current class at Nella was graduated.

"So why would you be interested in an offshore operation?" Terry asked. "Aren't you pretty well set up in Louisiana? Wouldn't it be difficult for you to get involved in another fulltime operation?"

"It's like my daddy said, ya don't catch fish unless ya got a baited hook in the water. And I'm always trollin' for somethin'. Besides," Seal added, "with the problems the Chink brought on, I'm sure they'll shut "Bridge" down right after graduation."

And it looked like graduation, projected for August, would be coming along on schedule. Things were going much smoother with the "Contra Training Class of '85," which had been broken down to 10 pilot trainees and four ground controllers. To everyone's surprise Medina entered into a truce with Tulsa, who was a real "soldier of fortune" type, spoke fluent "border" Spanish and often bunked at the complex several days at a time. Tulsa appeared to be taking over the official position of being the unofficial linkage to U.S. Army Special Forces from Fort Chafee, who began co-mingling with the trainees immediately.

The best test of teaching is observing the student applying his newly acquired knowledge. With the feedback from the field in Central America about the performance of the class of '84, the instructors had a model from which to fine tune the curriculum. In short, most of the mistakes made during the previous year's training were being eliminated.

Due to his workload, and because the possible opportunity in Mexico was what he truly wanted a shot at, Terry worked out an arrangement with Tulsa to take over some of the night-time flight training, reducing his role and his workload.

His "interface" time with Bruce at OSI and his weekly lunches with Nash in Little Rock to report the number of "green flights," or cash deliveries, as well as his developing machine-tool business, were consuming a lot of Terry's time. This forced him to reduce flight instruction at Nella to an average of two nights a week and weekends.

The source of the "green" was still a mystery to Terry. But, by his own accounting, an average of $40 million a month was being air-dropped by Seal over the Triple-S Ranch. The image of the dollars pouring from the skies reminded him of psychological warfare flights in Southeast Asia where millions of leaflets were dropped in order to win the allegiance of the civilian population during the war. He wondered if the "greenbacks" were having the same effect here in Arkansas.

He was curious, though. Was it taking this many portraits of dead American presidents to "win over" the Arkansas power structure? Or was something else going on? He was amused at the Congressional skirmishes over funding. Only a few weeks later, on April 24, he would read Congress had refused to appropriate $14 million in Contra aid, an amount that wouldn't keep the Contras going for a week. Terry knew how much money it takes to fight a war. Task Force Alpha, his old unit in Thailand, used up $1 million a day just on internal operational and administrative costs, and that was 15 years earlier. He and Seal had theorized that these miniscule amounts of funding, debated for weeks on the Senate floor, were merely a test of political wills.

By early April, a more personal problem was beginning to bother Terry. He had a hangar, but he couldn't park his airplane in it. He brought this up while dining with a "shady character" from Mena at SOBs.

"I can't get Evans off his butt to fix the Arrow I have stored in my hangar. He's always too busy and I have no way to contact Cooper about it. You got any ideas? I'd love to get my plane into town and Cooper's out."

"Yeah. Borrow Mike for a day," Seal replied as he downed his soft drink. "He's a good mechanic and I'll tell him you need his services."

Shortly thereafter Terry flew to Mena, picked up Mike and flew him back to the North Little Rock Airport. By using an instrument known as a bore-scope, Mike was able to inspect the internal condition of the engines' cylinders and pistons and confirmed Cooper's original diagnosis. It would require a complete new cylinder, piston and associated parts that Mike had to order from the factory.

This didn't get the plane out of the hangar, but the first step had been taken. When he later again brought up the subject of the *Charlie Cuatro* during a discussion with Barry, his only reply was, "Maybe they'll forget you got it and you can keep it. A person never know when he's gonna need 500 pounds of C-4. At least that's what my grandpappy used to say." He loved Seal's humor.

The Arrow and the Charlie Cuatro would have to wait. Terry had his hands full trying to fill Sawahata's shoes. His goal had become to do the best he could and hopefully "bootstrap" his existing knowledge into the foreign operation, if it ever became a reality.

By now it was mid-April and the goals Terry had set for the new year were not being met. He had lost no weight, had added new keys to his key chain and hadn't spent additional time at home. He was, of course, working diligently on the fourth resolution, to become a millionaire in four more years.

By now, things were also going smoothly within the secret arms manufacturing loop. Contractors and subcontractors were brought on line, some knew who the "customer" was, while others did not.

Through Bruce, Terry learned that there was bi-monthly barge traffic receiving "special handling" by the Army Corps of Engineers as it trans-shipped caches of weapons silently upstream to Lock 13 at Fort Smith, where ground transportation took over for the short drive to Mena. Seal's "Dodger" flights took over from there, transporting the badly needed weapons to staging areas in Central America.

Reed was beginning to feel he was smack in the middle of a strange quagmire. He was learning, often by accident and osmosis, about everything, but was in charge of nothing.

But if Terry felt he had no authority, Seth Ward thought just the opposite. From what Ward had learned from his private intelligence network at the Rose Law Firm, he had decided that Terry was in charge, at least of the CIA's weapons business. As Reed taxied his plane onto his aircraft tie-down spot at the North Little Rock Airport, after a return trip from Piggot, Ward was waiting in his 450 SL silver Mercedes. The convertible's Navy blue top was up due to the windy conditions that day.

Ward approached him as he was tying down the aircraft and asked in his usual overbearing manner, "Been out flyin', huh? Where ya been?" Terry did not want to answer specifically.

"Went to visit a customer. Why?"

"Where, up in Piggot? Or over in Mena?"

It was obvious Ward was on to something. He was letting Terry know that he was aware of some locations where the CIA manufacturing was going on. Terry used evasive tactics, to no avail. Ward told him to get into his car because he wanted to talk. Once inside, Ward got right in his face.

"OK. Have it your way. Play games," he snickered. "Better tell your people I know what's goin' on at Iver Johnson's. Hey, I own a company and I want some of that work. Go tell whoever's in charge that Skeeter (his son) wants in on this." Terry said nothing, got out of the car and started to walk away.

This lack of response apparently infuriated Ward, who crawled out of the sports car and yelled, "Now ya done made me mad, Terry." He kept walking until he caught up to Reed, grabbed his arm, spun him around and stuck his face into Terry's—Marine drill instructor style.

"I'm the one who sponsored you into Arkansas, and you better show me some respect! You owe me! Now I'm not askin'...I'm tellin' ya...POM and Skeeter better have a slot made for 'em at the government trough...or else some real bad publicity might start leakin' its way into the papers. Not to mention that Web [Hubble] is a close personal friend of the County Prosecutor's. So don't provoke me, Terry. Go tell whoever you answer to that the Wards are comin' in. We got the horsepower and this is our backyard. Get it?" With that he walked away.

Terry felt he was suddenly auditioning for a remake of the film *The Godfather*. There were many similarities, he was realizing, between what he had heard about the behavior of organized crime bosses and this self-labeled "Little Rock Industrialist" who was obviously comfortable in the role of "enforcer." The only difference so far was Reed could not recall an instance in any of the Mob movies he had seen where one warring faction was threatening to go to the police for help. Ward's threat to seek revenge through the friend of his son-in-law, Web Hubbell, was a reference to Pulaski County Prosecutor Chris Piazza, a very powerful man in Little Rock. Terry could only theorize what sort of problems Piazza could create for the Agency's operations. But, as Terry analyzed the Seth Ward debacle, the short term solution to this power play seemed simple, but would come with a lot of long term risk. Ward must be let in.

The company Ward had referred as the one demanding a slot at the feeding trough was one with which Terry was familiar. It had been the source of some Ultra-Light parts during the period the two men had been business partners. It was called POM Inc., which stood for Park on Meter. It was a major manufacturer of parking meters and its factory in Russellville, Arkansas, was owned and operated originally by Rockwell International. In the 1984 edition of the Arkansas Directory of Industry, on page 155, their expertise was defined as "parking meters, screw machine parts and power press parts." It was obvious that Ward had taken into account the capabilities of his equipment, which could in fact, just as easily build gun parts as it could parking meter parts. An outside observer would probably never have been able to tell the difference in the company's behavior if they got into the "gun loop."

Ward had purchased the company for the specific purpose of buying his son, Seth Ward II, or Skeeter as he was called, a job and a title. But Skeeter was president in name only. The younger Ward had had a string of business ventures that had turned into failures and the elder Ward once confided to Terry: "I decided to buy a company so big that Skeeter couldn't fuck it up.

"I really want my son to be an entrepreneur like you," he privately told Terry, whom he liked. "But I'm afraid he takes after his mother's side of the family." Ward was six feet, four inches tall, but his only son was five foot, six inches, taking after his short, Scandinavian mother who had been a professional opera singer in her youth.

The elder Ward, then in his late sixties, was the embodiment of the World War II Marine fighter pilot he had once been. A cross between Seths' two personal heroes, John Wayne and Robert E. Lee.

Reed both admired and hated the man at the same time. His aggressive, fighter-pilot business style was something Terry wanted to emulate. Ward had a sixth sense when it came to refining a problem to its core and then solving it. Terry couldn't help but admire a person who could build a sizeable financial empire within his own lifetime.

At a "Business School 101" banking luncheon, Terry had marveled at how Ward could manipulate the starch-collar banking community who always managed to say "no" to the poor people. It was fun to watch him hypnotize the banker to the point where he took all the risks and Ward would get most of the profits, if the venture was successful.

At this luncheon, Terry observed Ward lure an unsuspecting banker into a shaky business deal by convincing him that he was going to invest a large quantity of his own capital into the venture and that the bank needed to match or exceed his investment in order "to stay in the game." In fact, Terry knew Ward was putting in nothing, since he had inflated the books on the acquisition they were discussing. That's where he first heard Ward say to a young, eager banker: "There's a big difference between horsepower and horse shit. Are you in, or are you out? It's time to belly up to the bar, son."

What Terry didn't like was Ward's predator attitude, his view that all other humans were simply cannon fodder to be used and discarded at his convenience. This attitude was probably what got him through World War II and contributed to his "us" vs. "them" fighter-pilot mentality. He boasted to Reed he had "slaughtered" many Japanese during the Pacific campaign, and it was apparent he had carried this "slaughtering" mentality into civilian life and the business world. He was used to getting his way in whatever he did and he was now not *asking*, but *demanding*, a piece of the Agency's arms business.

Terry knew problems were in the offing. The sharks were gathering with the scent of blood in the water. It was Agency blood and Agency money Ward was after. If Ward knew about it, certainly others like him did, too. It was a breach of security plain and simple.

Before he was able to talk to Nash, Seal arrived in town for some "personal bankin'" at Dan Lasater's investment banking firm where Terry had earlier made the cash deposit.

At the usual dinner spot on the river, Terry brought up the problem. "I know this guy. This is blackmail, plain and simple. He wants in on the parts business or he's going to blow the lid on this, or so he says. But what bothers me is we have a leak. How'd he find out?"

Seal, who prided himself on knowing everything, was truly surprised. There was something, after all, that he didn't know and that involved a connection between the Triple-S Ranch and Ward.

"Now who is this old fart, exactly?" Seal asked. "I know he was involved with you in the Ultra-Light business, but how does he make the connection to us (the CIA) and the parts business? That's what interests me the most," Seal said, giving his undivided attention.

"Probably the most direct connection right now, and I can think of others, is the Triple-S Ranch where you're depositing 'the green.' He owns it and his son-in-law, Finis Shellnut, is the go-fer that lives out there."

"I thought that was Dan's place all this time! And I know this guy, Finis. He works for Dan as a bondsman. Now ain't that interestin'. But how could he have found out about the parts? Finis has nuthin' to do with that. I don't talk about anything except money when I'm at Dan's. Finis doesn't know who's flyin' the planes. And even if he did, how would he make the connection?"

What was bothering Seal was that there was a peripheral relationship, which he had not been aware of, between people he had been banking with and the people who controlled his drop zone for "the green" . He was discovering that the man who said he owned the property was not the true owner at all. Why had he been misled? he wondered.

Also, a man Seal knew only as a bond salesman and employee of Lasater's was in reality the man living at the Triple-S Ranch and the one retrieving the cash. But the connection between Shellnut and Ward intrigued him the most.

"Well maybe that explains some of the shortfall I've been accused of lately concerning my nightly deposits," Seal theorized.

When asked what he meant, Seal said: "The books don't match. When I pick up the cash down south, it's all accounted for, supposedly. And I've been accused lately of havin' my hand in the till. Maybe this guy Finis is pocketin' a little for the Ward family. Think I'll go talk to Dan about that. But you were sayin' there's another connection to Ward as well."

"Yeah. He's got a pipeline right into the governor's office."

"OOOWHEEE. Teeeell me about that!" Seal exclaimed, sliding closer to Terry.

"Ward's oldest daughter, Suzy, is married to Little Rock's ex-Mayor, Webb Hubbell. Besides being a close personal friend of Bill Clinton's, Webb is a big wheel at the Rose Law Firm here in Little Rock. And guess whose office is right next to Webb's?"

"With all this incestuous shit goin' on, I hate ta take a guess. What are ya gonna say, Bill Casey?"

"Naw, better than that," Reed laughed, "How about Hillary Clinton, the Governor's wife."

"Bingo! There's your fuckin' leak. Somebody in state government had to inform the Ward family about the parts business through Webb Hubbell and I'll betcha that somebody is Bill Clinton himself, if he's as close a friend to Hubbell as you say. You gotta expect these kinda problems in this business. This is not blackmail, Terry, it's nepotism. This is how it works in a banana republic."

Seal sat quietly digesting what he had heard, along with his oysters. When the band quieted enough to continue the conversation, Seal said: "So Ward has basically threatened us, huh? Let him in or what? Let's call his bluff. It could get real interestin'. This whole thing is turnin' out to be somethin' very unprofessional. Let's bring it to a head right now! Tell him The Fat Man from the Agency said to go fuck himself."

Terry was confused about Seal's confrontational stance. Ward was the kind of person that would react to a response of this type with a like response and he could see the FBI getting yet another "tip." Reed could imagine the front page of the Arkansas Democrat: "FBI DISCOVERS SECRET CIA-BACKED GUN RING HERE." The lead in to the story would say: "Terry Reed, a local businessman was arrested by FBI agents yesterday and charged with more than one hundred counts of Federal and State arms violations..." He didn't want to think about it.

"I really don't see what's to be gained from that approach, Barry," Terry countered.

"Hey, you're the one who said you wanted to live abroad and work for the Agency. Run a front company, you said. If ya want to get out of here real fast, one way is to expose it, forcing the Agency to shut it down. That means they would have a sooner need of your Mexican operation. You and I could run it together. That's all I was thinkin'."

As the two men parted that night, Terry could tell Seal was abuzz with what he had learned about the almost incestuous relationships of some very important Arkansans. To Reed, the term *razorback conspiracy* was becoming a very befitting title for the power-based marriage of convenience between banking, manufacturing, politics, the CIA and greed. Seal confided that this new-found knowledge would be valuable to him, especially the connection between the governor's mansion and the drop zone. In effect, on a napkin in SOBs that night, he traced a path from the Triple-S Ranch, to Lasater's firm, through the Ward family, into the Rose Law Firm and, finally, in the back door of the governor's mansion. Seal said he wasn't quite sure how he was going to use this information. His only warning to Terry was the same expression heard at the rodeo as the cowboy in the shoot spurs the Brahma Bull, " get ready to 'hook it and ride'."

All this made Terry uneasy and more determined than ever to get the Mexican business plan off the ground. If, in fact, there was something to pursue, Terry wanted to get going with it. Things were beginning to come apart in Arkansas, he felt. Sawahata had fled and Nash was concerned solely with political damage control. Ward was trying to muscle in on the "action." Seal seemingly wanted to do as the cavalry is instructed when abandoning their fortifications and "burn the fort", then it appeared he wanted to retreat to Mexico. Barry had said only one thing that night Terry agreed with completely— it was all turning into something "very unprofessional." It was becoming one big Chinese fire drill.

Seal's kamikaze stance and what seemed to Terry an unfounded sense of urgency were unquestionably related to the full plate of problems facing him in various parts of the country. Seal was about to go into the Witness Protection Program since he now had a $500,000 price placed on his head by the Medellin Cartel—and he and his government handlers knew it.

As a result of the White House leaks concerning the Sandinistas' involvement in narcotics trafficking, Seal's undercover identity as drug pilot Ellis McKenzie had been *compromised*. The Medellin Cartel now knew that Seal was the one who had penetrated their organization, was working for the Feds and had masterminded the CIA and DEA's photographing of the Nicaraguan "sting". The photos not only purported to document Daniel Ortega's people assisting in the transhipping of cocaine, but had ensnared some high ranking Cartel bosses as well. Jorge Ochoa, one of the leaders of the Cartel, wanted to repay McKenzie/Seal for his excellent undercover work by killing him. And Ochoa had the network and the money to get the job done.

Perhaps this was why Seal was demonstrating such a reckless attitude, a side of him Terry had never seen in the past. Based on Seal's behavior, Terry felt it was time to talk to Nash about Ward/POM's demand to be let in. Surely he would see it as another security risk for the state and could perhaps exert some degree of control over the Ward family. Terry assumed Nash was briefing Governor Clinton, and Clinton could maybe "lean on Ward" by rationalizing with Webb Hubbell, through his wife Hillary, through the Rose Law firm. The lines of communication were becoming so complicated, Terry nearly needed a diagram.

These meetings by now were reminding him of what the military called "stand-up briefings." Nash appeared only wanting to be entertained with the "numbers of it all", such as how many "green missions" had been flown, how many barges went up the river, etc. But this rendezvous at the restaurant would be a special one for Terry. Nash's reaction to the Ward development would have a major bearing on what Terry would do next.

Prior to the meeting, Terry met with Bruce to see if there was some way Sawahata could be contacted. He told Bruce things had "escalated" beyond control. It was now April. Whatever risks would be involved with Sawahata's return were far less than his staying away, Terry figured.

Bruce promised to try, saying he had a way to contact people "back east" in case of an emergency. Terry said to consider it an emergency and then left for the restaurant.

Before Terry could bring up the subject of the "new development," Nash informed him of something that showed who was really in charge, at least at the state level.

Nash let him know that a decision had been made to bring a new firm into the weapons loop. It was called POM and was located at Russellville.

"I'm sure with all your talent, you'll be able to get these guys up to speed quickly on their contract," Nash said, in a rather demeaning tone. "I understand you know the owners and you should all be able to work well together."

Terry objected immediately. He told Nash about the confrontational meeting with Ward at the airport and said he believed this amounted to blackmail. "How can somebody like this be trusted?" Terry asked. "He'll sell us all out to the highest bidder. I know what motivates this man and it's power. Give him 30 days and Seth'll be running the whole show and eventually compromise the entire program."

"I'm sorry you feel that way. You must be listening too much to the 'big man in charge'", Nash responded. This was the way Nash always referred to Seal, never using his name. He continued, "But my card reads Arkansas Industrial Development Commission. Money is flowing here as a result of our state's backing our country's national foreign policy. We need to take advantage of this opportunity, and companies native to Arkansas should be the first to benefit. POM is a native Arkansas company and I don't need to remind you that the Ward family is highly-connected politically. I suggest we just leave it at that and go on about our business."

Terry digested Nash's attitude and decided to feign acceptance in order to end this meeting. He needed time to assess what his next move would be in light of such reckless, selfish and irresponsible behavior. Right then, he was contemplating the option of getting out of the "land of opportunity" before disaster struck.

Nash was apparently filling the power vacuum left as a result of Sawahata's departure, and, from the way he talked, he also didn't have much love for Seal. It sounded like power-play time, and Reed wanted no part of it.

Before he could return home that day, a call was made to his house by J.A. Matejko from Iver Johnson's Arms, Inc. When Terry returned the call, he was told by an upset Matejko, "Terry, I don't know what's goin' on, but you need to get over here real quickly. I got a problem."

At Jacksonville, an hour later, Terry and Matejko huddled in his office. Matejko began, "All I know is, some big old crazy fart named Seth Ward and claiming to be connected to the governor's office barged in here today demanding blue prints for what he said was secret CIA work he knew was going on here. After I told him I didn't know what he was talking about, he got all upset, pushed me aside, came in here and used my phone without permission. I could hear him askin' the operator for the phone number for the governor's mansion. Then he sat there and wouldn't leave. I tried to ignore him, but the old asshole just sat there. It finally came lunch time and I left.

"But then later I get this call on an unsecure phone from a guy named Skeeter Ward who says he's in Russellville. He proceeds to tell me that he's bid on and won a government contract to build gun bolts. He wants me to mail him the blueprints tomorrow so he can order the steel in order to run the job. What in hell's goin' on here?"

The feeding frenzy had already started.The maggots were starting to swarm over the cadaver. Unprofessional was an understatement now. This was serious.

Terry had to act fast. He had always found Skeeter Ward, despite his flaws, to be somewhat reasonable...when he wasn't around his father and trying to impress him with his business savvy. Terry told Matejko he would look into the mess. He then flew to Russellville to control the meltdown he saw coming.

"What's it gonna take, Skeeter, to get your dad under control and out of Iver Johnson's. Hell, he's camped out over there, blabbing about 'CIA-made gun parts' in front of people who don't even know what's going on," Terry asked, already predicting the answer.

"Well, it's pretty simple. Just give me some work so that he thinks he's got you all over a barrel, and I think he'll go away. You know dad. He's not happy unless he's stabbin' someone and twistin' the knife," Skeeter replied with a grin.

Terry realized there was no reasonable method to prevent the "muscling in" of the Ward family, at least not in the short term. He returned with blueprints to an M16 bolt and carrier assembly. Iver Johnson's discretely subcontracted to POM the task of secretly producing 500 units a month. Like cells maturing and dividing, the loop had expanded, on its own.

This was not a new problem for the Agency. As in any banana republic, it dealt with, once the puppet government is up and running, it gets greedy, arrogant—and even begins to think it's really running things.

Arkansas was no different. What Terry was seeing was the seamy, dirty, internal power struggle common to the evolution of any Third-World government. Bill Clinton had made big promises to the electorate. Most people weren't questioning the new-found prosperity from new industry moving into the state. Nor were they questioning the state-backed financing that made it possible. But growth has a way of becoming addictive and Governor Clinton's ballot casters were wanting more frequent fixes.

The insiders, like Ward, knew it was feeding time for the *hogs* and they were lining up at the secret government trough. This was growing beyond what the Agency had envisioned. Its plan did not include the good ole boy nepotism that was beginning to take over. Aside from being a feeding frenzy, it was also a power struggle, plain and simple.

Millions in cash were pouring in as a result of the Boland Amendment's prohibiting military aid or support to the Contras. What the Agency had thought was a haven for laundering black funds and ill-gotten gains had fueled a raging fire now requiring constant replenishment. Nash and the Clinton Administration seized upon this to go one step further. They could utilize the cash *float* to their advantage and the Agency couldn't complain.

The Clinton Adminstration took advantage of the Agency's *compromised* position and began loaning out these secret funds to select industries. The state's financial problems evaporated, just as Oliver North's had when, on April 1st, 1985 he began cashing Contra traveler's checks for his personal expenses.

Governor Clinton was as least as smart and he knew an opportunity when he saw it. And opportunities like this don't come along every day. Was that why Arkansas Development and Finance Authority (ADFA) was formed?*

Seth Ward and businessmen like him were the first to reap the benefits. ADFA records reflect that Ward was one of the first to "belly up to the bar," as he put it. POM, according to these records, received a $2.75 million loan on December 31, 1985 that was used to build an addition to its Russellville plant and to purchase equipment necessary to fulfill its obligations to its new-found "customer," the same one Air America had served. And who processed the extensive paper work for the POM loan? None other than Webster Hubbell, the attorney for the firm, the son-in-law of Seth Ward, the Rose Law Firm partner of Hillary Clinton, the personal friend of Bill Clinton, and now, in 1993, the Associate Attorney General of the United States.

* * *

The month of May was frantic. Terry now considered his *number one* priority in his spare time was to concentrate on his Mexican business plan. He decided to best himself by developing a *"black prospectus"* that was so attractive the CIA couldn't resist implementing it. He would take the plan to a level of maturity that would force a decision to be made, one way or another.

The parts loop now had one new member, POM, which was finding out it was more difficult to build MIL-SPEC parts for guns that it was parking meter components. It was determined that POM's antiquated manual equipment was incapable of consistently holding the tight tolerances that Ivers Johnson's was

*   ADFA was created in 1985 under State Legislative Act 1062 as successor to the Arkansas Housing Development Agency to finance qualified agricultural business enterprises, capital improvement facilities, health-care facilities, housing developments and *industrial enterprises* (italics ours). Its 10 public board members are chosen by the Governor. It raises its money through bond issues, but was given initial capitalization of $6 million from the State Treasurer. Neither state tax funds nor the state's credit is pledged directly to guarantee the ADFA bonds. But, under a separate law enacted the same year, should ADFA defaults exhaust the $6 million, the "authority is authorized to...draw funds for principal and interest from the State Treasurer."[2]

capable of doing on their state of the art Computer Numerically Controlled (CNC) equipment. This was forcing the younger Ward to begin searching for new equipment of the (CNC) variety to upgrade his capabilities.

"There's more to this government shit than dad and I thought there was," Skeeter complained. He even asked Terry to recommend brands of computer-controlled lathes to manufacture the bolt in question. Terry found this amusing since he and Matejko had purposely selected one of the most difficult parts to be made. In Air Force jargon, Reed had tossed them a bone and they were busy chewing on it. This bought everyone some time to deal with POM.

Terry learned from Bruce that Sawahata, who had been "cooling off" in Japan, would be returning the latter part of May. None too soon, Reed thought.

The Nella training was in full swing. No one had crashed, although new security was added because the local sheriff's office had begun investigating what it thought was a major drug operation being conducted at the Mena Airport.

Police in Louisiana, frustrated by the protection Seal was receiving from the DEA in Florida, felt they were being stonewalled by the Feds and that "some kind of invisible evil force" was keeping them at bay.*

They had alerted the local authorities in Mena and asked them to surveil Seal's planes. The sheriff's office was now photographing everyone arriving in any of Seal's known aircraft. This led to Terry being photographed in front of Rich Mountain Aviation on one occasion as he alighted at Mena for aircraft repairs. The then-sheriff, A.L. Hadaway, said later that he believed Terry to be "military or CIA," adding: "I didn't take him for any drug trafficker."

A return on the Agency's investment in Arkansas had been realized, in spite of the risks involved. Oliver North, knowing of the success of Operations "Centaur Rose" and "Jade Bridge" in Arkansas, wrote a memo to National Security Advisor Robert McFarlane dated May 31st, 1985, that spoke cryptically of the trained Nicaraguans coming into play along with Seal's delivery of arms. Entitled "The Nicaraguan Resistance: Near-Term Outlook," it talked of "plans to transition from *current arrangements* (Anglo air crews supplied by SAT) to a consultative (sic) capacity by the CIA for all political matters and intelligence" once Congress lifts restrictions. "The only portion of current activity which will be sustained as it has since last June (1984), will be the *delivery* (by Seal) of lethal supplies."

The resupply operation, "Centaur Rose", out of Mena, was also in full swing. Arms that had been stockpiled over the winter months at Nella were finding their way through "holes in the American defense network" and into the waiting hands of the Contra soldiers. Feedback from the front told of the Class of '84 performing heroically, but still unable to fly C-123s without the aid of Anglo pilots.

Terry was relieved when Cooper finally arrived in Little Rock to repair the Arrow N 30489 and deliver it to Central America along with the C-4. At least that was the plan when he arrived in mid-May.

Terry provided Cooper with tools and picked up the spare parts from Joe Evans in order to replace cylinder No. 1 on the 200-HP, fuel-injected Lycoming

---

*   Local police in Louisiana along with Federal agents there felt that Seal was being
     protected from their investigation through Seal's manipulation of federal agencies
     elsewhere.

engine. Terry "assisted" during the successful "surgery." But other problems were found. Cylinders Nos. 2,3 and 4 were burnt and scored and needed replacement as well. The engine damage was the result of "the fuckin' hillbilly mechanic over in Mena" not adjusting the fuel mixture properly, Cooper said. The aircraft was not in condition to make the long flight to Central America, so it was decided to risk the short flight back to Mena so that Evans could "fix his own fucking mistakes."

The C-4 would have to stay where it was, for now. Terry was happy just to get his hangar back and to be able to use it for its intended purpose...to store his own Company provided airplane.

Flying his own Seneca II, Terry escorted Cooper, who ferried the unairworthy Arrow back to Mena, where he turned it over to Rich Mountain maintenance for a major overhaul. Cooper had come to Arkansas for more than one reason though. He had identified areas of deficiencies in the previous class. Since he was involved in the field upgrade training for C-123s, he decided to help update the lesson plans for the instructors at Nella.

Tulsa had just received a 1974 Cessna 421, N69889, which he was using as his primary training aircraft. While there, Cooper elected to ride along as a check pilot on that afternoon's training sortie. The Cessna used by Tulsa had been stolen from Orlando, Florida, the previous January and was actually tail number N 5SF, according to Jerry Bohnen's research.(See Bohnen's Letter, Chap. 7.)

After returning from Tulsa's flight, it was Terry's turn at bat. That night near sundown he, four students and Cooper as "check airman" departed Waldron, Arkansas for a workout.

After several hours of air work within the Military Operations Area (MOA) over Western Arkansas, Cooper volunteered to assume right seat (instructor) duties in order to give Terry a respite. While sitting in the back and observing this aging aviator, Terry could see first-hand what a really good pilot he was. Cooper was performing engine-out procedures for the students in the dark over mountainous terrain in an airplane loaded near gross weight. Here was a man whose mind performed as Terry hoped his own did. It became a contest for the student to attempt to "load Cooper up" with a combination of in-flight emergencies until the safety of the flight would be jeopardized.

Terry marveled at Cooper's ability to prioritize his workload regardless of the degree of difficulty of the assigned task and his ability to control his fear. Here was a 60-year-old man with a mind like a bear trap causing Terry to realize he had found a role model for himself when he reached his 60s.

What a way to go, Terry thought as Fort Smith Approach vectored the twin Cessna to a heading that would intercept the localizer of the ILS (Instrument Landing System) and cleared them for a practice approach to runway 25.

If you have to die at the age of 60, as Terry's father had of cancer, now this definitely was a better way to go, he thought. Being splattered all over the Boston Mountains while doing something you love and are good at, had to be better than writhing in agony as his dad had done in his final weeks.

This pudgy, bald-headed guy, at his age, should be home bouncing grandchildren on his knee. But here he was; his left engine feathered, adjusting his approach for a simulated hydraulic failure, dealing with a simulated in-flight fire checklist, repeating his memorized missed-approach procedures to his student and still with time to chat with ATC about the thunderstorm that was brewing to the west. All of this while manually flying the airplane, wearing an instrument hood to block his outside view, and all done from the right seat.

If only there were more time to get to know this man better, Terry thought. What made this guy tick? Is stress the secret of youth? He had never met Chuck Yeager, but he couldn't imagine any man cooler in the cockpit than Cooper.

After successfully executing the missed approach at Fort Smith, it was Terry's turn again in the instructor seat. This time, Cooper wanted Terry to go through some simulated emergencies with his students, an area of weakness of the earlier class. The storm was now upon them. Torrential rain was pummeling the plane as it impacted the water droplets at 160 MPH.

With a young Nicaraguan, Leonel, at the controls, they were setting up an approach for a simulated delivery at the Nella field. The flustered trainee was concentrating solely on the mountainous terrain and preoccupied with the aerial delivery. He was needlessly exposing his aircraft to simulated hostile ground fire by blindly following the panic filled instructions from the ground below. By not using all available sensory data and selecting the most logical approach course to the DZ, he was being lured by the enemy into an aerial ambush...a deadly small caliber flak-trap. Cooper knew instinctively from his combat experience with Air America that Leonel was "fucking-up by the numbers." This was exactly how slow-flying cargo pilots get killed and lose their crew, the bird and its contents.

The rain drops were like millions of little missiles hitting the fuselage, deafening the trainee as he attempted to maneuver the aircraft, respond to the ground controller and control his fear all at the same time. As he initiated a left turn in the darkness, Cooper leaned forward and whispered to Terry "shut down the left engine, let's see what this fuckin' beaner's made of."

The blackened cockpit was illuminated only by the glow from the twinkling avionics on the instrument panel. Leonel didn't see the hand reach toward the engine control quadrant. Terry deftly pulled back the red knob on the left engine mixture control causing the three-bladed Hartzell propeller mounted on the gear-driven 375 HP, fuel-injected and turbo-charged Continental engine to immediately go to low RPM, high-drag windmill mode. The aircraft yawed abruptly to the left. Terry didn't speak until the plane rolled beyond 60 degrees of bank angle, hoping Leonel would identify the problem and respond accordingly.

"Rudder...rudder...right rudder! Now, attitude, bank angle, airspeed! Leonel...what the fuck are you doing? Why am I seeing trees in my windshield?" The young pilot, lacking visual reference to the horizon, seemed to freeze on the control yoke, disbelieving the data being presented to him on the aircraft's artificial horizon.

"I'm gonna die with you. Did you go to Mass today? I didn't, I'm not ready to die. If I can't talk you though this recovery, we're all gonna go down together. Now, believe your instruments! Push hard right rudder! Roll wings level, and lower the nose." Slowly, Leonel regained attitude control of the aircraft while wrestling to control the vertigo that was earlier consuming him.

"Now, watch your airspeed; don't let it get away from you. Now, nail that blue line. Look at the altimeter... remember where the ground is! Atta-boy, now let's shut down the bad one...dead foot, dead engine...remember? We need to climb...soon!"

Leonel feathered the left engine's windmilling propeller, sufficiently eliminating enough drag to allow the Cessna to begin a shallow climb out of the pitch black, mountainous Nella valley. Once the aircraft was stabilized, trimmed and climbing back to altitude, Terry looked back to see Cooper, his bald head shimmering in the done light, shaking his head.

"If this is the best you got, I suppose they'll have to do. There's a big rush down there to get these guys in the air in order ta replace the contract crews. The commies are gettin' the best combat hardware Moscow has ta offer. Hind choppers and all the fuckin' SAMs ya can name and number. The Agency is afraid we'll lose a crew and expose the whole program."

A prophetic remark!

On the run back to Little Rock from Mena, Terry turned the conversation to what most interested him, namely Mexico. Cooper professed that he was not really in the decision-making loop for that.

Cooper said he had become a "slave" to a hot sweaty airfield in Central America that was reminiscent of Thailand. He talked of unairworthy, "antique" aircraft fitted with inferior avionics. After detailing the Agency's airlift operation he was involved in, he joked: "Yeah, I guess I've become an antique, too. But it is nice to get your adrenalin goin' again. I been reunited with a bunch of my old Air America flyin' buddies. Livin' there's a bitch... but, hell, it gets us away from our bitches. And it sure beats playin' golf with all the old farts."

This group was what the media later referred to as the "over the hill gang," old flyers who just couldn't let go. They had been reactivated secretly by the Enterprise and they saw it as one last hurrah before their juices gave out.

"It's great to get back in 123s, even if it is just upgrading your beaners to heavy metal category," Cooper added.

But Terry wanted to know about Mexico.

"I was at SAT (Southern Air Transport in Miami) and set in on that one big meeting," Coop told him. "I think these guys are pretty hot on this idea of a cut-out down there. This guy from Washington, John Cathey, is a fan of yours."

Terry then brought Cooper up to date on the ongoing "catastrophes" in Arkansas. The "feeding frenzy" taking place by Arkansas manufacturing companies, the loose security and the turf war Seal had warned him about that was developing between competing law enforcement agencies who were convinced there was major illegal goings on at Mena and wanted to get a piece of the action.

Cooper laughed. "I guess Southeast Asia had its advantage over Mena. It was a lot farther away and they didn't have any fuckin' Feds snoopin' around there. If they had, we'd all ended up in jail."

Terry assumed this was a reference to the rumors that circulated wildly during the Vietnam war that Air America crews were allegedly involved in nefarious activities. Namely heroin smuggling out of the Golden Triangle defined by the geographical intersections of Burma, Laos and Thailand.

Terry went on expressing his concerns about the Mena operation. "It's getting so bad over there, you had better not plan on any graduating classes after this one. Tell whoever's in charge down there that we'll be lucky to complete this one. We got Feds falling over Feds and local cops investigating them."

The FBI in Louisiana, feeling that they were being stonewalled and kept in the dark by their own and other federal agencies, decided to conduct what appeared to be a "sting." (See chapter end.) An undercover FBI agent, Special Agent Oscar T. Eubank, using the alias of Sonny Eggleston, flew into Mena in a stolen Cessna T-210, N5468A, and asked Rich Mountain, the CIA's fixed base operator, to make illegal modifications on the plane. If the FBI had been successful in getting this work done on a "hot" plane, the ironic effect would have been a Fed entrapping a Fed.

Seal thought this was hilarious. As the Agency's chief asset there, he even secretly funded a federal lawsuit charging the FBI and the local police with, in effect, doing damage to the Agency's business. The suit was later mysteriously dismissed, but Terry saw all this as totally unprofessional behavior and a risk to security.

Cooper thought this was hilarious, too.

As Terry dropped him off at Little Rock to catch a commercial flight back to Miami, Cooper said after being entertained by the stories, "Sounds like you need a SAR (search and rescue) flight to extricate you from this mess up here. When I get back to Miami, I'll do some snoopin' around and see if there's sincere interest on this Mexican thing for ya. In the meantime, give these beaners hell for me, 'cause, if you don't, I will when I get 'em down south."

On Sunday May 19th, Terry gave in to his wife's demand that they mingle socially with what Janis called "more normal people." They decided to have a picnic at a campground on the Arkansas River with one of her real estate co-workers Cherryl Hall, who was a close friend and confidant and her husband Wally, the sports editor of the *Arkansas Democrat*.

Terry, like any other husband, had to give way to spousal pressure. A picnic was the last thing on his mind since he had been told Sawahata was on his way back. But Janis demanded that her husband spend some time with *her* that afternoon. The new baby was active and kicking and Janis was now fully nested having decorated the new nursery.

After a day-long picnic, watching their children play together and listening to Wally talk about jocks, they all returned to the Reeds' house on the golf course and decided to have a barbecue.

Janis and mother nature had other plans. While in the middle of the barbecue on their deck overlooking the river, Janis walked out from the kitchen and said, "My water just broke." With her husband as her coach, and after an agonizing 19 hours of labor, she gave birth to their second son, Elliott, who weighed eight pounds, 10 ounces. Now there was a little *Weta Okami* and a backup for Duncan.

Sawahata finally returned from his long absence, without his family, on June 1st and was quick to congratulate Terry on his new son and on how well he held the operation together. After all, hadn't Aki played a part in it by giving him the time off to go to Eureka Springs? Terry had even wanted to make "Eureka" Elliott's middle name. Janis saw no humor in that. They settled on "Kent Kerr."

Reed spent the better part of a day bringing Sawahata up to date. He had spent the bulk of this time in Japan, he said, and his family was still there.

"Agency send me out of country," he told Terry. "I lose considerable face. But, they give me opportunity to return and repair things here. I understand you have big problems with state officials. You can relax now, I am in charge. I will not fail again."

It sounded like the Agency was perhaps exploiting Aki and using his Japanese culture against him. By taking him back and giving him another chance, they probably reasoned he would work twice as hard as he had before leaving, since, in Japan, failure is taken as a personal disgrace and Aki had earlier failed...at least in his own mind. It's like in the Mob, he "owed them one."

All emphasis was on flight training going into the month of June. Sawahata knew he was working on borrowed time and all efforts were being marshalled for damage control. Most of this effort, from what Sawahata said, was attempting to control the law enforcement agencies that were trying to close in on the Agency's operation.

Aki said, "The jig is up, as they say in the South. Do not know how much longer we will be able to keep nosy sheriff, DEA, FBI, IRS, and Customs out. Things are so bad FBI has every fucking pay phone in Mena bugged. Please, Terry-san, tell other instructors to speed up training so we can close operation."

Terry heard of sandwich bags of cash being distributed throughout the Mena area for added "security" and allegiance.

But the "X-factor" had to be dealt with again. In mid-June, Terry was on a night training sortie when a secure distress call was relayed to him from the command post. Seal had blown an engine while returning on a "Dodger" flight and had been forced to make a precautionary landing at Texarkana.

"Arkansas aircraft Boomerang 1, return to Waldron immediately," Medina's voice said over the aircraft's ultra-high frequency ITT McKay radio. "We have an emergency."

Terry was sure someone had crashed. He flew directly to Waldron as instructed and taxied up to the white one-ton truck parked at the end of the field.

"Who's dead?" he asked Ramon Varnados while the students got into the truck.

"Nobody yet. But ya need ta get immediately over ta the Texarkana airport. Barry blew an engine and was able ta put her down over there. But he's carryin' some sensitive cargo and wants ya ta come pick it up ASAP."

Terry flew to Texarkana. He found Seal sitting in a Rockwell Commander, N4677W. The left engine cowling was lying on the ground and light was reflecting from the oil smeared on the left wing. Reed had no knowledge of it, but this was another stolen and recycled plane. This one had disappeared nearly two years earlier in Washington State. It was a 1978 Rockwell Commander whose actual registration number had been N 4697W. This plane had been an easy changeover, only one number had to be altered. In January, 1990, it suddenly and mysteriously reappeared at the same airport from where it had earlier disappeared. This was the only one of the seven aircraft used by Seal that was ever seen again.

"I already checked her out," Seal said in his usual laid-back tone. "She's dead on arrival and I need to get outta here. I got a duffel bag inside. You need to drop me off at Mena and then high-tail over to Russellville to deliver this."

In addition to the duffel bag, Terry noticed Seal had two pilot map cases sitting between the pilot and co-pilot's seat. Barry entered the craft and Reed could view him disconnecting wires from the aircraft's main electrical buss that led to the two map cases. Once disconnected, he carefully packed the excess wiring and cables into the boxes and handed them to Terry, saying, "don't drop these babies, they're fragile." Terry loaded them in his plane along with the duffel bag.

"What are these?" Terry asked.

"Some real valuable electronics on loan from the Agency. I can't leave these lyin' around, they're not just for anyone's use You might call these the '*key to the secret door*.'" Terry let it go at that, concentrating on the task of flying the short hop to Mena.

During the flight, Seal commented, "Wouldn't ya know it. Damn-near crashed on my last mission. That's the way it always happened in Vietnam too, didn't it Reed?"

The two men then engaged in a conversation about pilots they had known who had "bought the farm" in freak accidents, when Seal suddenly changed the subject.

"As soon as we get ta Mena, I'm gonna split. You gotta get this duffel bag over to Russellville and into the greedy little hands of Skeeter Ward. He should be waiting at the airport in his plane."

"Skeeter? I presumed this would be dropped at the Triple-S Ranch as usual."

"Naw, there's $300,000 in here, earmarked for a special project." He started laughing.

"Wanna let me in on the humor?"

"Naw, Terry. No offense, but, you don't have a need to know. But since you know the Wards, you're gonna love the punch line to this joke." He had no time to question Seal further, they were now on final approach to Mena.

After dropping Seal at Mena, Terry flew off to Russellville with the duffel bag full of cash. Several months would pass before he would see Seal again. In less than two weeks, Seal would be entering the Witness Protection Program beginning an extended period of courtroom appearances as a key government witness.

Upon landing at Russellville Municipal Airport, Terry spotted a late-model Beechcraft Bonanza parked at the west end of the field. Its landing lights began flashing when Terry's plane approached. On the ground control frequency of 122.7 which he was monitoring, he heard Skeeter's voice say "Barry, can you see my lights, is that you? You're late."

When Terry responded "No, but Barry sent me with something for you," Ward didn't respond.

Terry taxied up to Ward's plane, shut down his engines and got out with the duffel bag. Skeeter was not comfortable with seeing Terry. He remained in his plane and opened his door.

"Where's Barry?" Skeeter asked nervously.

"Back in Mena. He says there's $300,000 here for you."

"He told you that!?"

Ward seemed shocked that Terry knew what was in the bag.

"Yeah, is there a problem?"

"No, just give it to me, I need to get outta here. But I think Seal's playin' games with all of us."

Ward taxied off immediately and performed no engine run-up, no magneto check or any flight prelim.

Skeeter continued violating every rule in the book as he skidded his plane onto the runway and took off with a tail wind, something a pilot is trained never to do unless in an emergency.

Terry guessed this must have been an emergency. As he watched the Bonanza rotate at mid-field, staying close to the ground to build airspeed and then departing while flying low over the Arkansas River with no navigation lights, Terry thought: Shit! Skeeter's flying like someone carrying contraband!

1. CIA BASE, a computer data base on the CIA compiled by former intelligence officer Ralph McGehee, Herndon, Virginia,1992.
2. ADFA annual report, 1988, p. 6.

SAC (12D-283) (P)   7/19/84
Attn: SUPERVISOR RONALD WAYNE KELLY

SA THOMAS W. ROSS

FRED L. HAMPTON, dba
RICH MOUNTAIN AVIATION;
ET AL.
NARCOTICS
OO: LITTLE ROCK

ADMINISTRATIVE:

          This memo is not to be disseminated outside this agency.

          On July 16, 1984, SA CLIFFORD H. DYAR III advised that
a single engine aircraft had been recovered through undercover
buy in LR 87C-18534. He advised that to protect the ongoing
undercover operation, the aircraft should be recovered by local
authorities and returned to owner. SAs DYAR and OSCAR T. EUBANK
are aware of the efforts to have an undercover agent contact
captioned subjects at the MENA AIRPORT and both are in agreement
that the recovered aircraft could be utilized for this purpose.

          It is requested that SA EUBANK, in an undercover capacity,
fly recovered aircraft to subject's hangar at the MENA AIRPORT for
repairs and/or modifications. Tentative arrangements have been made
to have the aircraft recovered by the Polk County Sheriff's Office
after a three or four-day period.

          It is felt that SA EUBANK and appropriate undercover
personnel can recontact subjects concerning the airplane, with
the object of establishing themselves as narcotics traffickers,
in accordance with the initial objectives on which this
investigation was instituted.

2 - LR 12D-283
2 - LR 87C-18534
1 - SA CLIFFORD H. DYAR III
1 - SA OSCAR T. EUBANK
1 - SA EUGENE L. CROUCH
TWR:jn
(7)

13-1. Evidence of an FBI "sting" against CIA assets operating out of Mena, proving that
crimes are invented to trap people. (two pages.)

On November 6, 1984, Special Agent OSCAR T. EUBANK flew a Cessna 210, tail number 5468A, from North Little Rock, Arkansas, to Mena, Arkansas.

Upon landing at Mena, Arkansas, the plane was taxied to RICH MOUNTAIN AVIATION where it was parked.

At RICH MOUNTAIN AVIATION, CECIL RICE was contacted and SA EUBANK, using the nom de plume of SONNY EGGLESTON, asked Mr. RICE to place a dark tint on the aircraft windows and to install bladder tanks.

Mr. RICE agreed that this could be done and it was agreed that a later telephone contact be made so that price could be discussed.

SA EUBANK then departed after tying down the aircraft in front of a hangar with faded paint which indicated it was owned by RICH MOUNTAIN AVIATION.

Investigation on 11/6/84   at Mena, Arkansas   File # LR 87C-18534

by   SA OSCAR T. EUBANK/kf   Date dictated 11/13/84

SEARCHED ___ INDEXED ___
SERIALIZED ___ FILED ___
NOV 27 1984

               x Airtel   2/8/84

TO: SAC, NEW ORLEANS (245D-7)

FROM: SAC, LITTLE ROCK (245D-7) (P)

SUBJECT: COINROLL;
           OO: NEW ORLEANS

Re Little Rock teletype to New Orleans

ADMINISTRATIVE:

On January 26, 1984, SA LARRY CARVER, DEA, Little Rock, Arkansas, advised that he has made arrangements for their aircraft to be piloted by DEA Agent, which will be utilized in an undercover operation in which HAMPTON and EVANS will be periodically contacted at RICH MOUNTAIN AVIATION in Mena. SA CARVER advised that the operation is tentatively scheduled for mid-February, 1984.

DEA undercover Agent will be accompanied by Little Rock Division pilot, SA OSCAR T. EUBANK.

CHAPTER 14

COMPANY-PAID VACATION

It was June 1985 and the White House was pulling out all the stops. Donations for the Contras were being extorted from third-country cut-outs, from the King of Saudi Arabia and the Sultan of Brunei, and from right-wing fat cats in America.[1]

Operations "Centaur Rose" and "Jade Bridge" had been a huge success. Pilots had been trained and no one had been caught in the act, yet. In fact, few people were even aware of what was going on. The Agency had resorted to civilian "contractors" in its time of crisis and the Arkansas operations were likely becoming a model to be studied at CIA Headquarters in Langley, Virginia. Despite the congressional debates, the Reagan Administration had found the "thin line"—that dark area, between legal and illegal. Unknown to people like Terry Reed, the decision was being made to duplicate this entire program "offshore," where top to bottom control and security can be bought for less in a more cost effective banana republic.

Aki Sawahata had now become Terry's primary, and one-way communications pipeline to Oliver North, aka John Cathey, and into Southern Air Transport in Miami. But, while Terry was feeding information into this pipeline, he was getting nothing back.

So, he was excited when Bill Cooper telephoned him on June 22nd and said, "I did some pokin' around for ya, like ya asked and have been asked to relay this message. They got some guy comin' in this who hasn't been identified yet. I'm bein' told he's another SAT Agency guy, and my inside contact on this tells me they'll be wantin' ya to take a trip to Mexico soon in order ta firm up your plan. I guess you mentioned havin' some kind of ex-business partner down there already and that's got 'em goin' full rich on your deal. Their after-burner isn't kicked in yet, but the ITT gauge is readin' high enough it could ignite at any time. By the way, how's my class comin'?"

Hidden in this collection of flight jargon was the clear indication that Terry's business plan for Mexico was beginning to bear fruit. From what Reed was hearing the Agency seemed especially interested in the aspect of the plan that could possibly include some old business acquaintances of Reed's who were already operating in Mexico...the Hungarian firm Technoimpex.

Cooper went on to ask for a specific date when Terry could undertake a "fact-finding mission" to Mexico. He added he was returning to Central America and needed to pass on Terry's prospective itinerary for the trip to some "new player" who was down there and who was real interested in heading this operation.

Although Cooper pressed Reed for a trip timetable he could relay to the unspecified "head shed", Terry could not give him one. Cooper's call had caught him ill-prepared and Terry's schedule was a full one. Cooper said he was under pressure to do a "quick turn-around" in Miami and told Terry to forward his answer to him at SAT.

On June 24th, the following Monday, Terry wrote Cooper. He'd been thinking about the call all weekend. It wasn't only the CIA who had to buy into his business plan for a machinery firm that could serve as an intelligence front, Terry had to sell his wife on it, as well. It had been two years since he or his wife had had a real vacation. This would be a perfect chance to kill two birds with one stone, develop his plan and take his wife away for a while.

There was no way Janis would agree to him leaving her behind while he toured Mexico. He still had to sell her on the idea of hectic schedule juggling of her real estate activities. And like many a *gringa*, she thought of Mexico as someplace dirty where you can't drink the water and street urchins accost you on every corner.

Janis was fully aware of Terry's flirtation with Mexico and the Agency's business plan he was creating. Because of this she had ordered and already received the State Department travel advisory calling the neighbor to the south a "third world...dangerous country" full of *banditos* and with highways so unsafe you can't drive at night. "Bring your own car parts," it recommended. Terry, who had lived in and traveled by motorcycle throughout Thailand, another "dangerous" Third World country, saw this simply as arrogant State Department propaganda. He knew that traveling in the United States could be far more dangerous.

In the written plan he had submitted, Terry had included the possibility of bringing in outside investors with international ties beyond the U.S. He had speculated that a Hungarian firm operating in Mexico City might be interested in a joint venture of some type. He felt this would help camouflage the new venture, just as Iver Johnson's had done in Arkansas. It had been an established firm brought in with local investors supplying some of the startup capital.

By "penetrating" an existing machine-tool operation, through a stock purchase or merger, he had written, would be one way to avert less official scrutiny. And this probably would be necessary anyway, due to a Mexican law in effect then requiring 51 per cent ownership by a Mexican national. Terry recalled that George Fenue, one of his ex-business partners in the Northwest Industries/Hungarian machine tool venture, had told him their trading company, Technoimpex, planned to expand to Mexico. He wondered if this had been the case.

He had gone through his old rolodex and located the name of an old KGB "ally," Jozsef Bona, the kingpin of the Technoimpex joint venture with his firm Northwest Industries, back in Oklahoma City. After a couple of well-placed calls, he discovered Bona's head was still not on a pole outside FBI Special Agent Wayne Barlow's house in Edmond, Oklahoma. He was, in fact, alive and well and functioning as director-general of an industrial machinery firm called Cortec, S.A. headquartered, as luck would have it, outside of Mexico City.

When Reed reported earlier about bringing in a company with East Bloc ties, his unseen handlers began panting. As Seal had told him, "I don't know what ya said to them, but whatever it was, say it again. They're really hot on this now."

International "camouflage" had been Reed's central theme. The concept was to put a high-technology trading company in a Third World country—in this case Mexico—and develop the proper supply conduit that could deliver "things," in addition to machine tools, the company's cover business. The timing was perfect. Reed's report quoted the Mexican consul Terry had spoken with in Dallas, who had said: "Presidente de la Madrid (Mexico's president) is looking very favorably on granting exclusions to current law and allowing 100 per cent ownership status to companies that offer Mexico an opportunity to develop an export economy. Machine tools are essential to Mexico's manufacturing plan and I will help you."

In mid-1985, Mexico's major source of hard currency, oil exportation through the government-owned and operated industry known as Pemex, was in dire straits. With the price of oil in a free fall, Mexico was focused almost totally on attracting tourists with pockets full of green backs or any other stable foreign currency. They were apparently getting very serious about supplementing their tourism dollars with those from export manufacturing.

With the assistance of the *Instituto Mexicano de Comercio Exterior* in Dallas, Reed thoroughly researched the pertinent international and Mexican laws governing the exportation and importation of high-technology equipment into Mexico. The only obstacles Terry could foresee were the human ones and the X-factor. Mexico, he had learned, was totally centralized with all decisions being *personal ones* and made only at the federal level in Mexico City. For this reason, Reed had said it was essential to visit Mexico City and personally tour the ports capable of handling heavy cargo.

He found a big disparity between what he was being told by Mexico's commerce experts and the printed data supplied to foreign businessmen by the Mexican Government concerning port facilities, warehousing, cartage services and overland trucking companies. Since it appeared the written data was incorrect and obsolete, he decided it was necessary to see first hand what physical barriers and limitations the "proprietary" might encounter. He wanted to make absolutely certain that what he proposed in his plan to the Agency would actually work.

But Sawahata said "no frucking way" when Terry approached him about the need for a couple of weeks off to make an Agency-related trip to Mexico.

"Terry-san, Washington and Mr. Cathey put major pressure on me to graduate current students. Decision has been made. This will be last class due to difficulties controlling politicians here in Arkansas. I need your undivided attention to duties at hand. I need to keep very low profile and desperately need your assistance. If you help now, I will do everything in my power to assist in getting you to Mexico later, if that is what you want."

Terry agreed reluctantly. He would bide his time and build his base of support within the Agency. He had been told Cathey was on his side already and now, with Sawahata, he figured that would be two Agency people pulling for him. That combined with Seal's support and Cooper's helped to make it a lock. That's what he hoped, anyway.

For that reason he would have to delay the Mexico trip until graduation time, scheduled for August. Janis, who loved Europe but decided she already hated Mexico, reluctantly penciled in the last week of August and the first week of September as tentative dates of a "working" vacation. Summer became a blur.

Terry's days were devoted to machine tool sales and Agency weapons parts activity. Nights and weekends were for training sorties. Elliott was two months old and crying for dinner that only mommy could provide when Cathey called that Friday night on July 19th.

"I was just going through my birthday list for special people," Cathey announced. "Sorry I overlooked your birthday on the 16th. I just noticed you and the Fat Man have the same birthday. It makes me think you *calculated risktakers* were all born under the same sign. There must be something to that astrology crap. But, Happy Birthday! Hell, you're still young, you're only 37. I hear nuthin' but good things about you from Sawahata. I guess you really helped out during his little emergency down there. I know about your other interest and I've been talkin' to a guy who you need to meet. I understand you'll be taking a little Company-paid vacation in late August and I'll try to get you guys together while you're on that trip. He's fluent in Spanish and has special interests in getting involved with you on this, if the Company pursues it. By the way, have you made contact with that Red guy in Mexico City?"

Terry was impressed that Cathey knew when his birthday was. He responded that he was ready for a change of scene. "Gosh, it's been so long since I've had any R&R, I feel like I've been on a remote tour in Southeast Asia and they lost my rotation papers."

Cathey laughed. "Take the wife and kids and don't eat the worm in the tequila bottle."

Cathey's cryptic reference to "the Red guy" was to Bona, a top-ranking KGB agent who they both knew from the prior "*monitoring activities*" Reed had performed for the FBI. Cathey did not identify the person he wanted Reed to meet in Mexico and he wondered if it were the same guy Cooper had referred to earlier.

* * *

The second and last graduation ceremony conducted as a result of operation Jade Bridge took place on August 25th, 1985, at the Nella camp. Terry had flown Sawahata over for the non-marked event with Janis back in Maumelle frantically packing for the trip to Mexico. The ceremony was short but the otherwise festive event was dampened by the fact that the complex was now closing down. Within a matter of days, nothing would be left, except the ground scars where the portable buildings once stood. Medina and Diego would leave with the class of 12 (two had been "eliminated") for Central America. Only those connected with the operation would know for certain that it ever existed.

Sawahata was being secretive about his future, but had apparently re-gained enough face to continue his Agency duties as an Oriental spook. He had let it slip that he would soon be attending a language school specializing in middle-eastern cultures. Hopefully, Aki had learned an important lesson in Arkansas and would not now become entrapped by some Arabic equivalent of McAfee.

All were breathing a sigh of relief that Rich Mountain Aviation was still standing despite the fact that police and federal agents were closing in on what they thought was drug money laundering, or so Sawahata said. As far as anyone knew, the weapons manufacturing would continue indefinitely. Since "Cen-

taur Rose" was not being terminated, but only relocated, Sawahata had told
Reed the parts would probably be shipped to the alternative assembly and
staging site, MRL in Piggot, after Mena and Nella were shut down. Why hadn't
he thought of that he wondered? Piggot was near the Mississippi River, and
that would definitely be the cleanest way the Agency could transport the weapons. Shit...waterways again.

At the graduation ceremony, Sawahata discreetly said to Reed, "Terry-san, I
will keep my promise. I talked to Mr. Cathey yesterday, and he said he talked
to you. He is considering you for big promotion. I will help any way I can.
Contact me through Bruce when you get back from Mexico."

Based on Aki's private briefing, Terry was beginning to feel he was also graduating. Maybe he was finally getting his chance to get out of the minors and into
the big league. He certainly hoped so. Now would be an excellent time to be
promoted out of Arkansas. The arms business that the Agency was leaving behind, he felt, was riddled with eminent disaster as long as sub-contractors like
the Ward family were involved.

The other instructors were going their own ways, somewhat saddened by the
uncertainty of events which may result from their hurried curriculum and the
dangers that lay ahead for their "*Latino Freedom Flyers*" in Central America.

But Terry was sure their unified unselfish effort had been worth it. The
countless hours of sacrifice, danger, intrigue, and confrontation with seemingly insurmountable problems were now somehow put into focus. Terry was
glad he had taken a personal stand, had become involved and had contributed
to a cause in which he fervorently believed.

He hadn't demonstrated on campus back in the sixties, so up until now he
had not experienced the feeling of exhilaration as a result of taking matters
into your own hands, and to rebel. But he now knew. He, John Cathey, Barry
Seal and the others had rebelled. They had not silently sat by while people
seeking freedom screamed out from the pain of oppression. Instead they had
acted. "Fuck Congress!", Cathey and Seal had both said. And Reed wholeheart-
edly endorsed their most articulate view.

What a terrific movie this whole adventure would make, he thought, but
who would ever believe it? And, little did he know, it was only time for inter-
mission.

Cathey had called Terry several days earlier to give him his travel itinerary
for Mexico. "I understand you're driving to get the flavor of it all, so if possible
you need to be in Vera Cruz on the 31st. I've got the name of a hotel there that
comes highly recommended by your contact. It's name is Hotel M-O-C-A-M-B-
O. It's supposed to be a five-star place or so Max says."

"Who's Max?"

"Oh yeah, I almost forgot. A guy by the name of Max Gomez will find you
there. Be sure to register under your own name."

Gomez was the codename for Felix Rodriguez, who had been involved with
the Enterprise since January when brought in by Donald Gregg, then-Vice President George Bush's National Security Advisor. Less than a month later, North
wrote Rodriguez asking him to use his influence with the El Salvadoran military to provide aircraft maintenance facilities for planes resupplying the
Contras. Rodriguez was a man who prided himself on having friends in high
places. One of these was George Bush, with whom he had been photographed
on more than one occasion.

* * *

Janis waited until the last minute to transfer her real estate workload to Cherryl
Hall, not really knowing for sure that her workaholic husband would actually
take a trip. In any case, she was hoping he wouldn't go because she wanted to
go somewhere else. All she could recall of Mexico was torrential rains and the
misery of Montezuma's revenge in otherwise beautiful Cancun. The thought of
taking the children on a 3,500-mile driving vacation in a Chevy conversion
van to a Third World country didn't quite fit her image of a foot-loose, yuppie
couple sipping piña coladas by the pool under a *palapa*.

Late in the evening of August 25th, they left loaded down with— what else—
bottled water, pampers, passports and immunization records for everyone.

After crossing the border and sitting and breathing diesel smoke emanating
from the long line of trucks waiting for Mexican customs, the border urchins
were upon them trying to sell local Mexican tabloid newspapers with photos of
maimed bodies. To calm his wife, he told her the usual line: "Hey, this is an
adventure. Cheer up. What's the worst that can happen?"

After departing Matamoros where they bought their Mexican car insurance,
he was glad he was driving and not flying. As their van dodged the craters on
Highway 180 he couldn't help think about the fragility of the machine tools
that would have to be shipped into Mexico. He turned to Janis, who, between
taking care of the children and reading the map, was also doubling as a traveling secretary.

"Take note of the condition of this highway. Based upon the road surface,
any machine tool shipment to Mexico City could not originate at Brownsville,
Texas. They would have to be flown in. That ought to make SAT happy."

Janis attempted to record the condition of this road segment, concerned she
would not be able to read her own scrawled notes as a result of pot hole-in-
duced vibrations. "Based upon this road surface, I'm starting to wonder if our
tires will even survive, let alone sensitive electronics. See, those State Department brochures were right," she chided.

The gulf city of Tampico was their first night's stop in Mexico, mid-way
between the Rio Grande and their meeting place. This made it a two-day road
trip from the border to the "black" rendezvous in Vera Cruz. The hotel billed
by North as five-star had seen better times. It was a large complex located on
the south side of town with a large pool and an ocean view similar to what
someone would find in Miami.

Other than an electrical system that could not power a blow dryer and electric curlers at the same time, it was adequate. After maintenance up-graded
the amperage of the old style screw-in fuses for the *gringos* in *cuarto* 505, all
was well. Most of the people staying there were wealthy Mexicans who enjoyed
the luxury of their own maids and nannies! Mexico was starting to look better
to Janis, even though she had discovered the country could probably swallow
them up if it were not for the traveler's guides they purchased at the border.
Mexico, they found, felt it wasn't necessary to clearly mark its roads, especially
in towns.

Terry had registered according to Cathey's instructions. The registry read
Mr. and Mrs. Terry K. Reed. (See chapter end.)

Terry was frolicking in the pool with Duncan when the Mexican waiter approached the pool's edge. "*Señor* Reed?"

"*Sí*," Terry responded.

"There is a gentleman in the bar waiting to meet with you."

Terry got dressed and walked into the lounge. It was 1:30 and he was approached immediately by a rather handsome, swarthy Latino who walked up and said in a rhythmic Hispanic accent, "See any boomerangs lately?"

These were the code words, to which Terry replied: "Mainly in Arkansas, but I guess they're spreading south."

The man smiled. "My name is Maximo Gomez. Come, let's sit by the pool. We have lots to talk about. Our mutual friend, John Cathey, speaks highly of you."

As they strolled toward the pool, Reed studied him. Max was near his own height, around 6 feet, weighing 190 pounds or so. His black hair was short, neatly cut and beginning to recede. Terry guessed he must be in his mid to late forties. He was neatly, expensively but casually dressed, wearing light colored slacks, a loose-fitting Panama "walking shirt," worn on the outside, and sandals. His attire, combined with his accent and tan complexion, made Reed think he'd probably spent most of his life south of the border.

As they were being seated by the pool, Gomez switched suddenly to Spanish. "*Señor Cathey dice usted hable Español, verdad?*"

Reed nodded his response.

Gomez continued, "*Y nuestro amigo dice qué tiene odio para todas Comunistas?*"

"Yes, the only good one is a dead one, unless he owes me money," Reed answered, stealing a line from his old commie-hater, Hungarian mentor, Emery West, and responding in a manner he figured Gomez would appreciate.

Gomez laughed heartily, "I'll use that one in the future." When he laughed, he had an almost innocent look about him, but, as he snapped orders to the nearby waiters demanding immediate service, Terry noticed his expression quickly transformed into a more sinister one: the look of one who could take things *very seriously* if crossed.

Being Latino, Gomez did not want Janis or the family involved at all. It was awkward for Terry, but he suggested that Janis go sight seeing or shopping. "Max" clearly did not want her there.

"One thing you must learn," Gomez said. "Latin men get together without their women around. They have no place in business. This a very good custom, something the *gringos* could learn from, don't you agree?"

The rest of the afternoon was spent sitting under a Paisano umbrella drinking *Agua Quina* and discussing Congress, commies (Gomez thought one was synonymous with the other) the Contras, and the cut-out they were hoping to start. As they exchanged war stories Terry gained information about what "Mexican free trade" was all about. Boastfully, Gomez told him he had lived in Mexico earlier and prided himself on his ability to "purchase" services for the Agency, which included "bribes to Mexican ex-presidents, on down."

From this conversation/briefing Terry learned of the United States government's need to have an "offshore" location for a weapons warehouse and trans-shipment point to support the Contras. This fit like a glove with Terry's plan, which Gomez obviously had been studying.

The part of the plan that seemed to intimidate Gomez, however, was his total lack of manufacturing knowledge. This would become an area of tension between the two men later. For now, Max said only, "I'll learn all about that when the time comes. It can't be too difficult if your commie friends in Mexico

City understand it." He was intrigued with the "commie connection," as he called it, but he warned Reed about "never trusting a communist." He was going along with bringing in the Hungarians only because Cathey wanted to.

"I don't agree with it," he said.

Max boasted to Terry that he had been "hand-selected by the White House" to set up and oversee this operation. He made it very clear that he would be what Terry later termed the HMFIC, "the head mother-fucker in charge." Gomez' constant name-dropping, flamboyant style and what seemed to be a volatile personality led Terry to believe that Gomez had other highly-placed friends besides Cathey. And based on his war stories, if true, he was highly-experienced in covert and counter-insurgency operations.

Terry sensed early that Gomez was not the kind of person he would seek out as a friend. They were being thrust together for "business" reasons and as the day wore on Terry got a sixth-sense feeling about Gomez. He was not the kind of guy that you wanted to "get into your six," a fighter pilot's term meaning an enemy plane getting behind you and out of sight.

In short, at the end of the marathon meeting that included dinner by the pool without the family, Terry felt the "interview" had gone pretty well. The primary thing he felt Gomez could offer was a way to "grease up the system" and more importantly, knowledge of who specifically to "grease."

Terry had informed Gomez that an area of great concern in the business plan was for the front company to be successful in its own right after being given a reasonable period of cash transfusion from the Agency. From what he had learned, sure death for any cut-out would be its inability to "blend in" with the real business world. This meant that a new venture like Terry's would have to run at a profit on its own or competitors quickly would see through the veil.

Mexico had levied a 100 percent tariff on all imported machine tools at that time. What bothered Terry was whether Mexican companies wishing to automate could afford to pay the artificially high price for imported equipment. Gomez had a quick solution to the two-part problem.

He was certain he could "arrange it" so that the tariffs on imported heavy machinery for the new operation would be "eliminated", thereby giving the CIA's company a pricing advantage over its competition and providing it with an instant market. This, both men decided, would be an enticement to a prospective partner.

Together, they worked out a routing for the remainder of Terry's trip. He would stay in Vera Cruz in order to inspect the port facilities available for commerce by ship. From there, travel on to Mexico City for a meeting with government officials and the Hungarians and ultimately wind up with a tour of the west coast ports.

Terry was satisfied, and encouraged. Yet something gnawed at him about "Max." He sensed after the long meeting with the CIA man that under that facade of stone, beat a heart of steel. He would not know until later that he had just been "hired" by the man whose career was built around the murder of Ché Guevara. (See photo section.)

When Terry returned to his room, he anticipated what he was sure would be his wife's reaction. "I know," he said, "We're on vacation and I'm spending no time with the family. But I promise I'll make it up to you tomorrow."

But he was already forgiven. "I couldn't bear the thought of being cooped up in here, so the boys and I went exploring. Duncan will tell you all about the big ships we saw at the harbor, but first, tell me about your meeting," she said excitedly. He began to try to capture for her the personality of Max Gomez. He would write in a letter to Cooper more than a month later: "I'm just now recovering from my meeting with Max Gomez (ha!) a very interesting character."

Gomez left that night, but Terry spent two more days in Vera Cruz inspecting the port facilities and talking to local government officials who had their Mexican equivalent of the Arkansas Industrial Development Commission. Armed with brochures of foreign-built computer-controlled machine tools, he was instantly greeted and invited into local business organizations.

He felt he was truly going in the right direction. It was clear he had something Mexico wanted, state of the art manufacturing technology.

On his way to Mexico City, he visited the Volkswagen Beetle plant in Puebla to do a market analysis. There he learned they had great respect for German and Japanese machine tools and wanted a local supplier.

In the capital, the world's largest city, he met with officials of the Mexican immigration service and government representatives who dealt with foreign corporations. After two days of discussions with them, it was time to renew his acquaintanceship with Bona.

After driving to the northwest perimeter of the city to Naucalpan, where the Hungarian-controlled company Cortec was headquartered, he was in for a surprise. Bona turned on his European charm when he discovered Janis was accompanying her husband. She and the children were waiting outside in the Chevy conversion van, a true luxury vehicle by Mexican standards.

"You have Janis with you? Bring her in! We'll have a celebration. My wife still talks about her and the trip they made to Esztergom [in Hungary]. What fun we had."

While Terry left to bring in his wife and show off his sons, Bona ordered his secretary to break out the best Hungarian wines. It was, he proclaimed, "*fiesta* time, or was it *siesta* time? Who cares which one it is. I love it here in Mexico."

As they sat down to drink and reminisce, Bona almost forgot what time it was. When he finally realized it was late in the day, he exclaimed, "Oh, I almost forgot we must send a car to the airport to pick up Fenue."

George Fenue, Terry's long-lost business associate and the man who had been his host in Budapest five years earlier, was arriving in Mexico. Terry had last seen him a year earlier, at the Chicago machine tool show. They had gone to dinner and had a few "liver shots" (drinks) together.

While waiting for Fenue to arrive, Bona explained he was being "recalled" to "the Motherland." The good news for Terry was Fenue was being promoted by Technoimpex and was taking over operations in Mexico. This was too good to be true, Terry thought.

The Reeds returned the next day to Cortec's offices for another round of partying, only this time without the children who were being cared for by a paid nanny at the hotel. Fenue was present now for the day's festivities and both began discussing business. Fenue confided that the "home office" was disappointed with Cortec's performance to date. Their Mexican business partner, who by law owned 51 percent, was contributing nothing to the company and, at the same time, stealing them blind.

Terry's timing couldn't have been better. He'd caught Cortec in a transitional phase, trying to become profitable. Fenue mused that his country was learning "this democratic and capitalistic shit has a downside, they want you to make a profit." Bona, he said privately, was being recalled since he was of the old way of thinking and just didn't seem to care if the company became profitable. Besides, he added, headquarters had a new assignment for him. Reed could only wonder if that meant Bona was going to apply his espionage talents in a KGB hot-spot somewhere else in the world, or if, perhaps, he was being sent to Siberia for punishment. Probably not the latter, considering that Bona still appeared as sly as a fox.

Fenue was eager to listen to Terry's proposal for a new joint venture. The conversation focused primarily on the machine tool aspects. But that night, while dining at an expensive five-star restaurant in the plush, European ambiance of the district of Mexico City known as the *Zona Rosa*, Fenue began to probe into Terry's real motivation for wanting to move to Mexico.

"You can tell me—we're friends. What is it these silent partners of yours want to gain out of all this? I think there's an easier way to make money than investing down here, especially when you consider these ridiculous tariffs placed on machine tools."

A myriad of thoughts raced through Terry's head. Here he was, dining with someone he was sure was a communist agent. A man he liked, to be sure, but a communist agent nonetheless. And Terry was fronting for the CIA. Another strange alliance? He had looked behind the curtain in Arkansas and seen that American politics was a charade. Was geopolitics a charade, too, he wondered?

Terry chose his words carefully. "What would you say if I told you, hypothetically, that my backers are so connected politically that I could get the tariffs virtually eliminated if we proceed with this joint venture?"

"I would say I was very interested, but then I would ask who these people are. They sound very powerful to me. Almost too powerful. Before I could sell this concept to my people, I would have to know who I'm dealing with... for sure." Terry left it at that. He would have to go back to Gomez or Cathey to see how they wanted to handle this.

All in all, the trip had been a great success so far, in more ways than one. The door *might* be opening for a *real* joint venture, he thought. And Janis was starting to realize that Terry was right, something she always hated to admit. She'd been lied to by her government supplied pre-travel brochures. Only propaganda, she thought, courtesy of the U.S. State Department. Once past the border, she had seen no real poverty, no starving children everywhere, no banditos. They had even driven at night.

And now here she was in the *Zona Rosa* looking at the opulence on display by the Mexican elite. The European architecture combined with the Aztec and Mayan influences to create an aura of fantasy.

What intrigued her the most, having been raised in a midwestern middle class family, was the distinct class system. In Mexico, a little money moved you way up the social ladder. She had discovered that many people here had maids, and nannies and servants. With two young boys and a career, her life in Arkansas bordered on continual chaos. She was beginning to see the world through her husband's eyes. He had always loved the Third World, something she was now beginning to understand. Mexico had a pace and style unknown to Americans. The people seemed happy which was somewhat confusing because of the North American propaganda she had ingested about the supposed poverty there.

As he drove toward Guadalajara the next day, Terry saw endless possibilities developing with Fenue. He and Gomez had only discussed the business aspects of luring an international partner into the joint venture as part of the cover. Their plan was to get Cortec, if possible, strictly as a stockholder in a machine-tool venture. Another idea was now forming. The Agency, through Terry, could set up a franchise to the parent company, Cortec, and attempt to run it autonomously, probably in Gaudalajara.

That franchise division would move the "secret shipments" of arms without the knowledge of the partner. Beyond that, another concept was unfolding, in his mind at least. He had not discussed the possibility with Gomez, but what if the partner became a willing participant in the arms traffic?

Holy shit! He thought. The Hungarians, if they played ball and could be trusted, would provide the new venture with access to East Bloc arms!

The smog and traffic of Guadalajara snapped him out of his deep thoughts, at least for the moment. After taking two days to make the rounds of the various government agencies and dictating his reports to Janis while driving, they struck off for the west coast port city of Manzanillo. Looking at the Mexican equivalent of a Rand-McNally map, the Reeds thought this drive would be a piece of cake.

The map showed a new four-lane highway, route 54, extending from Gaudalajara to Colima near the coast. But they found this road existed only in the political rhetoric of Presidente Miguel de la Madrid, whose family lived in Colima. This had been a campaign promise and, in Mexico, a road can "exist" if you simply put it on the map.

After a tortuous trip on a two-lane winding road filled with switchbacks and jack-knifed trucks, Janis penciled in under her heading marked "Highway Infrastructure, Guadalajara to Manzanillo...non-existent, air freight only." Southern Air Transport (SAT) wins again.

Due to the delay in getting to the coast, they proceeded up Highway 200 to the port city of Puerto Vallarta, situated in the center of a beautiful bay, by-passing Manzanillo, which appeared at that time to be inaccessible by well surfaced road. At Puerto Vallarta, he performed the same exploratory work as he had at Vera Cruz. They spent two peaceful days at a tourist hotel on the bay's north side. Janis played the role of the *Norte Americano turista* and spent the days sipping piña coladas by the pool while watching Duncan play in a tidal basin.

When Terry returned to the hotel after visiting the *comandante* of the Puerto Vallarta International Airport to analyze its cargo-handling capabilities, she was sitting pensively in the shade and informed him, "I've been watching ugly Americans all day. Why is it Americans live a life of misery and then attempt to make up for it by taking frenzied vacations?"

She had spent the day watching tourists from the U.S. with pale bodies arriving at the hotel and wearing clothes just purchased from the hotel's "Banana Republic" clothier shop. They all were caricatures, running up their credit card bills and carrying coconuts filled with anesthesia. Why? What were they running from and what were they searching for?

She had analyzed her own suburban culture and concluded that it was grotesque. What was really going through her mind now was that life could be very different for her and the children if they settled in Mexico. Up until that day, her husband's "pipe dream" of running a CIA proprietary on foreign soil was something she thought of only in the abstract. Why hadn't she taken him seriously? Hadn't he always "created reality" by the sheer force of his will?

"So tell me the truth," she asked her husband. "Do you think you can really make all this happen? Up until today, Terry, I have to confess, this whole thing seemed like a pipe dream of yours. I guess I needed this day off here by the pool to clear my mind. It's really happening, isn't it? You're actually meeting with Mexican dignitaries and the CIA is actually paying for this vacation! It's scary, but I have to admit it's exciting. Is this what you really want to do? Because if it is, what can I do to help?" Her adventurous soul had been tapped.

Terry was somewhat surprised. He hadn't fully realized that he had to "sell" her the way he was trying to sell the Agency. He had assumed all along that she would be a willing participant. But, in any case, he was glad she was now on board.

The trip continued up Highway 200 until taking Route 15 back to Guadalajara. This road surface was considerably better. Janis penciled in: possible for manual equipment, negative CNC(fragile computerized equipment).

Their plan as they checked into a center city hotel was to spend one night and leave the next day for the trip home. But as they dined that night in the peaceful ambiance of Mexico, they both realized that their return to Arkansas meant an immediate resumption of the rat race. It was September 9th.

"Why are we going back tomorrow?" Terry asked her. "I just heard about an area near Lake Chapala that's south of here. If Max decides to put this operation in Guadalajara we should take advantage of this time together to explore the area. Call your office. Have Cherryl cover you for another week. What the hell, the CIA's paying the bills."

The next day they headed for the ancient city of Chapala, 50 miles to the south. The lake is Mexico's largest and within it's waters swims the famous Mexican whitefish. On its northern shore is a string of communities, the largest being the town of Chapala with a string of villages connected by the *carretera* extending west from Chapala. It is an area favored by about 5,000 foreign *pensionados*, mostly American, and wealthy Mexicans who view it as a vacation retreat.

The lush valley surrounding the lake, protected by a mountain range on the north, gives the area a much cooler micro-climate and blocks out the smog from Guadalajara. The ancient Indian village of Ajijic, five miles west of Chapala, was the cultural center of the area. It had strict, but self-imposed, zoning codes that retained its rustic character. There, Janis would learn strollers are worthless on cobblestone streets. No matter, here the nannies carry the children!

They checked in at the Posada Hotel and Restaurant, owned by a Canadian couple, and learned that Chapala Realty, owned by a another Canadian named Richard Tingen, was the place to find whatever you needed.

The following day they went to Chapala Realty to inquire about the essentials, schools, grocery stores, doctors, pharmacies, auto repair shops, etc. They were directed to a woman named Diana Aguilar, an American originally from Southern California who had been raised in Mexico. She informed them, much to their delight, that an opulent life style was possible in Mexico for $600 a month.

They had told her they might be moving to this area and the Reeds spent two days with her driving around in their van, "touring" homes (there you don't just look at real estate). A fast friendship developed with Aguilar, who was 36 and lived with two of her three sons in Ajijic. Her Mexican husband, an accountant who lived and worked in Gualalajara, enjoyed a typical upperclass "Latino" marriage, with each living individual lives and pursuing their own careers. She actually ran the real estate office. Her pleasant demeanor and language fluency attracted Americans who were looking for real estate.

They toured the lake's entire north shore and were shown homes in Jocotepec, Ajijic, Chula Vista and Chapala. Janis, familiar with real estate, marveled at the homes and observed that all had servants quarters, and gardeners—who took care of the pools!

"Forty dollars a month! You can get a live-in maid for $40 a month? We're spending $400 a month just on day care" Janis exclaimed in amazement.

"Forty's actually high," Aguilar noted. "I pay my maid $25. Forty will get you one that's bilingual." Janis was starting to realize something else about living in Mexico, there were a lot of perks.

Tomorrow they would have to return to reality. But that was tomorrow. That night they put that out of their minds and concentrated on the sound of the rain drops tapping on the red tile roof and reverberations of the thunder rolling across the lake. They moved even closer together in the *sarape* they were sharing.

They sat in front of the fireplace of their rustic cottage sipping vintage Mexican wine and recapping the places and things they had found in the last two weeks in Mexico as the torrential downpour washed down the Posada's manicured compound. The magic of Mexico had transformed, and seduced, his wife.

The trip had been a business success in more ways than one. It had been a renewal for the two of them, something unplanned when they started back in Little Rock. Janis had not been part of the black world he had lived in at Nella, nor in any of the other intelligence loops in Arkansas. They had come to realize that the tourists she had found so distasteful at the hotel in Puerto Vallarta were a reflection of themselves and what they had become. Maybe, they thought, happiness and pleasure doesn't have to be confined to only two weeks of the year.

But Terry had had some revelations on this trip. He had been right about Mexico and he knew his wife could now understand how the Third World pulled him like a magnet. She had been able to see the hidden beauty and intrigue through her own eyes. But more importantly, they were a real team again. The critical mass was being reunited.

As they re-entered the U.S. at Laredo, Texas they experienced the only disturbing aspect of the trip. Upon entry, U.S. Customs demanded "proof of ownership" for Elliott. When they produced a passport for the infant, the customs inspector challenged the photo and informed the Reeds of a "child smuggling ring" being run out of Mexico, and suggested that they might be spiriting a Mexican orphan into the U.S. This "GS weenie", in Seal's vernacular, backed off when Terry pointed out that Elliott was an Anglo with blond hair and blue eyes.

"Welcome back to the USA," Janis said wryly. "Isn't it great to be back where you're so wanted?"

He had had to drag her across the border going south and now he had to drag her back north. Janis had discovered there was no need to travel half way around the world to encounter the exotic excitement of the third world. It was only a border crossing away.

* * *

It was now mid-September when they pulled into the driveway in Maumelle. They had fully expected things to be hectic and they were not disappointed. Business at his firm, Applied Technologies, Inc., was beginning to take off.

Why do things always seem to happen in one's absence? It appeared that all the Arkansas industry he had been chasing for months was now chasing Terry for up-dated price quotations for machinery purchases.

Before getting fully immersed in business details, Terry went to see Bruce and find Sawahata. Bruce told him that Sawahata was in Washington, but that the OSI office in Little Rock would remain open indefinitely. Terry called Sawahata on OSI's secure communications and went over the high points of the trip. Sawahata said he was going to be talking with Cathey, who was extremely busy, but would take the time to pass on the positive news about the trip.

Asked by Terry about how to proceed, Sawahata told him to prepare a detailed report and send it to SAT in Miami. When asked about Seal's whereabouts, Sawahata said he was "working undercover on a special project."

"A whole new management team," he said, was being assembled to evaluate the feasibility of the proposed Mexican cut-out.

Terry was confused. Who, he wondered, should he report to with the Nella operation shut down. Sawahata was now just a voice on the telephone and Terry seemed to be supervised by no one in particular.

Terry had been sent to Mexico by Cathey and had been interviewed by Gomez, but he was about to find out another boss had been brought into the Mexican loop. He was ill-prepared for the October 1st telephone call from a man identifying himself as Robert Johnson, who said he was Chief Counsel for Southern Air Transport (SAT).

"This whole thing sorta got dumped on me recently," Johnson confided. "I'm looking at a file that's pretty disorganized, but there's all kinds of reports here indicating you've been the main source of a lot of this data pertaining to Mexico. I'd like to go over it with you in detail. My job is to review this project for legal considerations."

Terry had no idea who this man was. He had never heard this name before and no one had ever mentioned him. He knew that people in Arkansas had not been told about Mexico and Terry began to suspect this might be a pretext call from someone in Arkansas state government seeking to uncover the Agency's future plans.

Terry bought himself some time by saying his report was not yet complete and he needed time to type it and send it on to Miami. The man on the phone said that would be fine. He told Terry to mail it to SAT, in care of Cooper, and he would intercept it.

Unable to contact Cooper by phone, he did as Johnson had instructed. He prepared a recap of the trip's highlights and sent it to SAT on October 2nd. The report also highlighted an interesting development that had occurred since his return. In light of articles appearing in *The Wall Street Journal* concerning trade with Mexico, Terry was confident there was genuine interest within the machine-tool industry as a whole to develop a Mexican market. He, therefore, had put out feelers for other possible investors in the joint venture, not wanting to limit his search to only the Hungarians. He had baited the hook and gone fishing for a company with the proper international connections and he was beginning to feel tension on the line.

This was reflected in the section of the report that read: "For the real good news, I have our Asian connection. The company is named Gomiya, U.S.A. I've had dealings with them on and off since 1980. I know nearly all of the personnel in the U.S. as well as quite a few of the high-level managers in Japan. I spoke to Mr. Frank Fujikawa, the manager of the American division and they are really "up" for expansion into Mexico. All they lack is the catalyst (me) to get things going.

"Gomiya, Japan, is an international trading company with public stock on the Japanese stock exchange. You might want to check them out, but they are my first choice, especially since they are set up for this and willing to 'play ball'. I will be seeing Mr. Fujikawa in Dallas soon where, with your permission, I will go into greater details with him."

With the report, Terry enclosed a map he had drawn of North America and entitled "Proposed Distribution." (See chapter end.) It showed how the "supply pipeline" for the company could be developed to establish tentacles from Mexico to Asia, the United States and Europe. Under this plan, if the cut-out found the proper investors, they would develop a supply network giving the CIA access to weapons worldwide, all of which could be shipped and disguised as machine tools.

But, not knowing for sure if the Agency would implement the Mexico plan, Terry still wanted to seize upon the increased business opportunities developing in Arkansas. Since his return Terry was devoting a lot of time to his own firm. He was no longer associated in any way with McAfee's company, which was on the verge of collapse and total bankruptcy with his creditors seizing its assets.

Terry had established an office in his home and one customer he was developing was in fact, Skeeter Ward. The subject of machine tools had become of primary interest to POM, the Wards' parking meter firm in Russellville. Since Terry was the only machine tool dealer who actually knew the "true application" of the equipment POM needed, he had a built-in advantage over any possible competition. Terry, in effect, had a "security clearance" the others couldn't obtain.

As a result of Terry's applications engineering work with the younger Ward, POM had targeted a brand of equipment built by Mori-Seiki, Ltd. of Japan.

Terry found it amusing when the Arkansas media reported that POM was planning a large expansion of its plant because of new government contracts it had recently received. He knew the source of the "government" work and he also knew that the U.S. Bureau of Alcohol, Tobacco and Firearms would have loved to have known about the "contract".

During the fall months of 1985, Terry settled into a routine that bordered on normality. There were no training missions and there was time for the family. But he was getting restless. He had whetted everyone's appetite with the Mexican venture—including his wife's—but there was no response from the lawyer Johnson.

He was getting positive responses about Mexico from the Japanese and the Hungarians. Janis had purchased a Berlitz course and was studiously attempting to become conversant in Spanish. But the Agency was silent, except for a call from Cooper reassuring Terry that Johnson was, indeed, who he had claimed to be. Not only was Johnson SAT's General Counsel, Cooper said, but also "a stockholder" in SAT, and one of those "Yale lawyer types" who had lately started running the Agency.

Then, suddenly, in late November, Barry Seal, who had seemed to have dropped off the edge of the earth, reappeared. He called Terry, saying he was in Little Rock in order to do some "bankin'" at Lasater's.

"I'm in town and we need to do dinner at our usual place. I've got good news for ya."

As they settled into the corner at SOB's, Terry's curiosity had the best of him. He noticed Seal had put on a lot of weight and seemed to have aged considerably.

"Where the hell you been. I figured the Bermuda triangle must have just swallowed you up. Or was it something I said?" Terry joked to get the conversation started.

Seal told him only that he had been "undercover" and apologized for not keeping in touch, "Let's not talk about 'old business'. Let's discuss new business. I got some inside knowledge that not only affects you, but is gonna affect Arkansas...in a big way. The good news is the Agency wants ta do your Mexican venture. You've got Cathey really excited. The bad news is I've been out of the loop so long, you need to bring me up ta speed so I can get involved in this project in order to help you."

Terry started from the top. It was napkin time, once again. He recapped his Mexican trip and outlined the proposed arms supply network. When he came to the part about Max, Seal started laughing uncontrollably, leading Reed to realize he had earlier encountered Gomez.

"What's so funny?" Reed asked.

"So, you met the Super Beaner....the infamous commie-hater." Seal continued laughing.

"Goddam it, why didn't Cathey warn me about this guy? I can't tell if he would be a good manager for this operation, or if he just wants to use it to get at the Hungarians and personally strangle Bona to death. It would have been a real great vacation except for that meeting. I think Max ate one too many worms from the tequila."

Seal turned the conversation away from Gomez and to the Arkansas oligarchy. "The Agency's gettin' real pissed at these guys here. Talk about outgrowing their britches, they're stealin' fuckin' money from the Company. Terry, that's like robbin' the Mob, it's somethin' ya just don't fuckin' do. I guess Bill Clinton and his gang have been workin' on a lot more than their 10 per cent cut. The decision has been made ta pull the plug on the whole fuckin' deal."

"You mean they're shutting down Operation 'Centaur Rose'?"

"Yeah. This worked out real great up here and we all proved it could work. But the Agency's got much bigger plans for Mexico, bigger plans than are included in your proposal. Terry, they want to build whole fuckin' guns down there... from scratch, usin' your machine tools. Shit, man, you've really opened their eyes on this manufacturing stuff. I even brought along some blueprints on the first weapon they want ta build down there."

Seal had discussed Agency interest in perhaps expanding the Mexican operation from one of simply housing and transporting weapons to actual manufacture. From what Terry was hearing, a decision had already been made to include manufacturing in the overall scope. Terry liked this. Subsequently, the program would be refined into two phases. Phase I was the original "offshore" front company getting established in Mexico and Phase II would be utilization of machine-tool equipment being imported to actually build weapons. High technology for Mexico was on its way.

Seal produced a full set of drawings for a weapon that could fire plastic explosive cartridges, a weapon reserved for military use only. But the Agency had decided it was what every right-wing Third World country needed. It would be a good weapon to begin building their offshore manufacturing concept around due to the pent up market for it. The CIA had even done its own marketing analysis.

"Now keep this quiet," Seal cautioned. "It's real sensitive info and these guys here haven't been notified. But Bob Nash is in deep shit. That nigger is gonna have trouble swimmin' with all that chain the Agency is gonna wrap around him. Yessirree, things are gonna get reeeeal interestin' around here. And Governor Bill's gonna learn who's in charge...the hard way. He'll be lucky ta get elected as dog catcher after they're through with him."

Getting back to Gomez, Seal said, "We gotta tolerate him for now. He may appear like a loose cannon, but what's important for both of us is for you ta take them up on their deal, get your butt down to Mexico and be in position ta receive me once I help blow the lid on the whole Arkansas operation."

"How you gonna do that?"

He swallowed his last oyster and said: "Let me worry about that. That's my job."

The rest of the time was spent with Seal telling Terry about a secret meeting he was trying to arrange between his CIA handler and Gomez. As a result of his "undercover operation", Seal said he was "real hot" and wanted to set in place special security for the meeting.

"Remember how to piggyback?" Seal asked. "I think this is an appropriate time to use this procedure for somethin' other than carryin' cash."

On the napkin, he drew a flight plan for a "pre-canned" piggyback mission and codes to be used over the phone when he would call Terry's house.

"I'll refer to my handler as my brother. I'm tryin' ta get this meeting set up ta take place out of the country for security reasons. We won't be gone long, they'll miss me up here if I'm out of the country more than a couple a days. Just be prepared for my call and don't say anythin' stupid over the phone. It's not secure."

"Can you give me an idea where we're going?"

Seal winked. "I'll take you for a trip on the darkside."

1.   North Testimony, Iran-Contra hearings, 100-7, part 1, at 78-79.

MESA	MESERO	PERSONAS	CUARTO	CHEQUE
			505	N° A 2750

HOTEL MOCAMBO, S. A.
Reg. Fed. de Caus. MOC-820320-001

ALIMENTOS FOODS	1,020
IMPUESTO TAX	153
SUB-TOTAL	1,173.=
PROPINA TIP	300
TOTAL	1473

FECHA DATE 8-31-85
NOMBRE NAME REED TERRY
FIRMA SIGNATURE

HOTEL MOCAMBO, S. A.
Reg. Fed. de Caus. MOC-820320-00

CARGO

Veracruz, Ver., a 31 de Agosto 19 85

MESA	MESERO	PERSONAS	CUARTO	CHEQUE
			505	N° A 2750

1	Coca Cola	100
1	Tequila	280
1	Vodka	320
1	Vodka	320
		1020.00
		153
	GARGO	1473

CORTEC S.A.
MAQUINARIA INDUSTRIAL

LIC. JOZSEF BONA
DIRECTOR GENERAL

OLMECAS N° 2 ESQ. RIO TOTOLICA
FRACC. PARQUE INDUSTRIAL NAUCALPAN
53370 NAUCALPAN DE JUAREZ.
EDO. DE MEXICO

TELS. 576-0337 38 Y 39
576-4648

TELEX. 017-73-952 CORTME

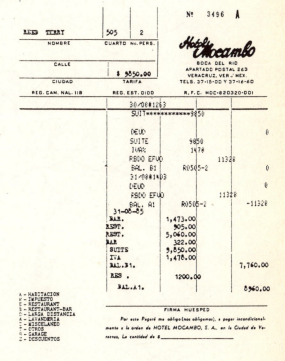

N° 3496 A				
REED TERRY	505	2		
NOMBRE	CUARTO No. PERS.			

Hotel Mocambo
BOCA DEL RIO
APARTADO POSTAL 263
VERACRUZ, VER., MEX.
TELS. 37-15-00 Y 37-16-60

CALLE — $ 9850.00
CIUDAD — TARIFA
REG. CAM. NAL. 118 — REG. EST. DIDO — R. F. C. MOC-820320-001

30/08#1263			
SUIT***********9850			
DEUD			0
SUITE	9850		
IVA%	1478		
RBDO EFVO		11328	
BAL. B1	R0505-2		0
31/08#1403			
DEUD			0
RBDO EFVO		11328	
BAL. A1	R0505-2		-11328
31-08-85			
BAR.	1,473.00		
REST.	905.00		
REST.	5,060.00		
BAR	322.00		
SUITE	9,850.00		
IVA	1,478.00		
BAL.31.			7,760.00
RES .	1200.00		
BAL.A1.			8960.00

A – HABITACION
I – IMPUESTO
E – RESTAURANT
B – RESTAURANT-BAR
D – LARGA DISTANCIA
A – LAVANDERIA
I – MISCELANEO
T – OTROS
R – GARAGE
Z – DESCUENTOS

FIRMA HUESPED

Por este Pagaré me obligo (nos obligamos), a pagar incondicionalmente s la orden de HOTEL MOCAMBO, S. A., en la Ciudad de Veracruz, La cantidad de $_____

CONSULTING

UNIQUE performance oriented indiv. seeking a special position in too level management or key exec. position in an aggressive company that is either developing or wishes to rapidly. My exper. and expertise are as diversified as my talents and interest. I am a 36 yr. old self-starter with international and domestic mkting. exper. who functions well under pressure. Exper incls: 1. Intl. trading/mktng. 2. High level financing and contract negotiation. 3. Major capital expenditure planning. 4. Manufacturing techniques of a wide range of products including most oil field components. 5. Familiarity with state of the art computerized machinery and robotics. 6. Co. and product line start ups. 7. Comml. pilot with jet rating. I am a team player who is a free thinker and new idea person seeking a challenging position that will allow me to apply my full range of talents. I am a family man who loves travel, especially international; and am willing to relocate world wide. Act fast, I'm 1 of a kind. Mr. T. Kent Reed, 809 Bowman Rd., Little Rock AR 72211, 501 224-3600. P.S. I'm used to making money.

14-1. Receipt. lower right, from hotel in Vera Cruz, Mexico, where Terry Reed first met "Maximo Gomez" along with newspaper ad., lower left, that Reed and Seal wrote and placed in Denver Post. Above right, is Jozsef Bona's business card.

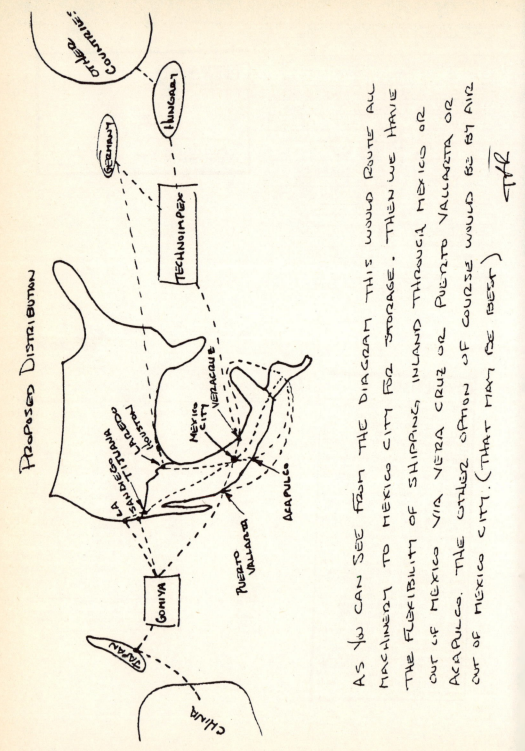

14-2. Distribution diagram explaining the concept of Machinery International drawn by Reed after fact-finding trip to Mexico.

CHAPTER 15

TRIP ON THE DARK SIDE

It was Friday evening, December 13, 1985, just 11 shopping days until Christmas. Barry Seal couldn't know he had little more than two months left to live and his telephone voice was filled with excitement.

"Glad I caught you, Santa Claus! It's time for the trip to my brother's place. I've checked winds aloft and they're predicted to be one-niner-zero degrees at thirteen thousand five hundred feet. We should plan on leaving from my place day after tomorrow at 1400 hours. You may want to bring a RON (remain over night) kit and remember, there's no phone at his place. You'll want to remind Janis, so she's not trying to contact you there."

"Sounds good to me. Will I need a hunting license (a coded reference to a passport requirement) where we're going?" Terry asked.

"Yeah, but I'll take care of that. This trip's on me, and my brother is really anxious to meet you. I'll call my brother and tell him we're coming. Adios Papa Bravo," Seal ended, as usual, with a chuckle.

This cryptic conversation set in place a pre-planned sequence of events that Seal and Terry had devised at SOBs, a week earlier. All Terry had to do was remove "one's" from each of the coded elements of the message. Ever since the FBI/McAfee event that had led to Aki Sawahata's problems, Barry didn't trust Terry's home phone. Seal and Terry felt that McAfee was mentally disturbed and he had probably listed Terry as being a "known associate" of Sawahata. Therefore, they had worked up a way to relay coded flight plan instructions for their secret trip to Panama.

As Seal spoke, Terry jotted down some specially coded details on a telephone note pad:

190 degrees-1 = 90 degrees
13,500 feet-1 = 3,500 feet
1,400 hours-1 = 0400 hours
day after tomorrow = tomorrow

To decode Seal's information, Terry merely had to remove "1" from each item. This meant Terry was supposed to be waiting to intercept Seal's plane on the 090-degree radial of the Monticello, Arkansas VOR (navigation fix) at 3,500 feet at 4 AM the following day.

"His brother" was Seal's reference to a CIA handler who was setting up the meeting in Panama. His reference to a RON kit was his way of advising Reed they might be gone more than one day. The lack of a telephone at his brother's place meant for Janis to understand there would be no way for Terry to be contacted by phone while he was out of the country. "Papa Bravo" was to be decoded as P.B., or simply a cryptic way of "calling the play"—or piggy-backing. Terry would have to tell Janis he wouldn't be at the dinner table for a few days, something routine for a spook's wife.

Seal's voice had exuded excitement and Terry was sharing the feeling. Ever since his return from Mexico four months earlier, Terry had been "consulting" for the Agency and developing an in-depth business plan that would utilize a machine-tool proprietary as a cover for a weapons transshipment operation in Mexico. Operation "Centaur Rose" in Arkansas had proved to be a successful prototype of what the Agency wanted to develop and expand upon, either in Mexico or some other "offshore" location.

The CIA had decided that operating outside United States borders would reduce the nuisance factor that had come into play in Arkansas, where "snoopin' and meddlin' " by the local law enforcement groups had resulted, as in Mena, in too many prying eyes. This problem had been compounded by a major turf war which had developed between federal agents who held diametrically opposing views of who Barry Seal really was.

Perhaps in hindsight, the "drug cover" given the operation had *not* been an excellent idea. In theory, it was to have been a way to allow the FBI to be the "controlling" investigative body, giving the appearance of leading an investigation *against* the operation. This was to provide federal security, thereby keeping state and local law enforcement out.

With this carefully orchestrated disinformation program, if an outsider later read the FBI's case files on Mena, they would appear to be the result of a criminal investigation. But, in reality, the FBI had been using its vast resources for containment and cover-up; the equivalent of a shadow shadowing a black operation.*

But the Agency-selected counter-intelligence F.B.I. agents assigned to Jade Bridge and Centaur Rose had lost control, and it had become literally, a law enforcement feeding frenzy. This had forced the Agency to assert its control with the Justice Department, as well, to prevent arrests and prosecutions.

Believing Mena to be a major drug-smuggling mecca because of Seal's cover as a trafficker, a state police investigator would later testify that stake out operations at the Mena airport by a joint task force included even agents from the Arkansas Game and Fish Commission. Nothing had been accomplished, because they did not realize that the CIA used Seal as a diversion to distract them from what was really happening at Nella, just under their noses 12 miles away. And, by the time the stakeout even began, the training operations at Nella had already been shut down and some of those involved at Nella were being groomed for bigger and better opportunities in Mexico.

* * *

Mexico had been *"numéro uno"* on the agenda at the meeting at SOBs as Terry and Seal renewed their friendship after several months of not seeing each other.

---

*   This became evident from an FBI Teletype provided to Terry Reed through federal court discovery in 1993. The the three-page report dated August 18, 1987 and marked "Secret in its entirety," proves the FBI was *alerting* the CIA and DEA that the residue of the Mena operation was in jeopardy of being exposed by the media. This document identifies Barry Seal as a "CIA operative."[1]

Seal, like Terry, had been very busy with other things. Terry wasn't aware of the fact that Seal actually had been put into the federal witness protection program and had become the government's chief witness in a series of high profile drug trials reaching from Las Vegas to Miami. He had proved to be one of the best undercover agents the government had ever developed and was an extremely effective witness.

His testimony helped convict Norman Saunders, the Chief Minister of the Turks and Caicos Islands, whom Seal had ensnared on tape while giving Saunders a $20,000 bribe to protect drug trafficking in his tiny island nation. During this time, Seal had been kept under wraps in Miami, and sometimes in an underground one-room cell for his own protection. This was the ultimate hell for a man who hated confinement of any kind.

Terry did not know any of this when he met with Seal that December night in 1985 in Little Rock, but it was clear from the onset of the meeting that Seal was anxious for a change of scene.

"Goddam! You must have hit a nerve with that business plan of yours," Seal had proclaimed. "You've really got these people's attention, which ain't easy to do. I think if we handle this right, this is something we could work on together—and out of this fuckin' country! I don't know about you, but I'm gettin' real fuckin' tired of the U.S."

It was apparent from Seal's comments that he had been in touch with the people at SAT or someone reading Terry's confidential reports.

"So you've been in touch with Johnson?" Terry asked. "I was afraid my reports were going into some black hole in outer space. I've been getting no feedback and was beginning to wonder if they were interested at all."

"This is way beyond the interest phase. Not only do they wannna pursue this ASAP, but their plans down there could make 'Bridge' and 'Rose' and Mena appear as small as the tits on a Vietnamese hooker."

Seal was still chuckling as he began to sketch out an operation on his napkin that would possibly be located in the center of Mexico. The map was familiar. It looked just like a diagram Terry had sent to Johnson.

"That looks just like the routing diagram I sent to Johnson. Where arms could come in from all over the world, 'cool off' and be transshipped back out of Mexico."

"Well, if that's the case, I guess John Cathey and my handler are takin' credit for your work product. 'Cause this is what they're interested in. And what interests me is they're gonna need somebody ta move all this shit. So, Captain Reed, let's just retire to Mexico and live the life of fuckin' Riley down there. You can teach me Spanish and I'll teach you how to fly a 130. Deal?" He paused and gulped down a soda, then continued. "Let's start right now. How do you say 'I want a blow job' in Spanish, anyway?"

Terry picked on Seal's mention of a "handler" other than Cathey, and was glad to hear Cathey was looking at his reports. "Who's this other guy you are referring to?" Terry asked.

"He's my main man out of the country—Leroy. He's tryin' to set up a meetin' between you, me and this Gomez character you met in Vera Cruz," Seal answered. "Can you get away for a meetin' to discuss all this, face-to-face, if I can get it set up? They're wantin' ta act on this real fast. And you and I need to take advantage of that. And this time, you're through workin' for peanuts. I'll do all the talkin' when it comes ta money. Fuckin' GS weenies! This is really gonna cost Uncle Sam, an' this time you'll probably get *your* jet."

It all sounded good. Finally, Terry thought, it was payoff time. The hours sweating in the cockpit with the students at Nella were behind him. He had begun to feel at last that he'd made the right decision passing up Bill Cooper's offer to move to El Salvador and join the Enterprise there as a flight instructor.

The door to the good ole boy club, he felt, was finally opening. Apparently, he had been doing things right. Maybe the life of a foreign asset, something he had always coveted since Asia, was now attainable.

The remainder of the meeting was devoted to outlining the needed codes for a piggy-back operation. In addition to the normal piggy-back procedures, which were to be conducted in matching 400-series Cessna aircraft, Seal said that, after the aerial "swap," the two men would rendezvous at Love Field in Dallas, where Seal would have his Lear serviced and ready to go. The Lear, he said, would be used for the balance of the trip south. It was clear Seal was seriously concerned about security, which puzzled Terry.

"If we're going to have a meeting with the Agency, why all the added security of a piggy-back?" he asked. "Who are we trying to avoid?"

"The other fuckin' Feds," Seal snarled.

* * *

At precisely 0400 hours, Terry was holding in the standard right-hand race track holding pattern on the 090-degree radial of the Monticello VOR looking for the green and red navigation lights of Seal's Cessna which should be approaching from the west at 3,500 feet. He was monitoring Memphis Center frequency on his No. 1 radio, waiting to hear Seal's voice report to Air Traffic Control as planned. His No. 2 radio was set to their secret, or discreet frequency of 122.97. That would be used for private air-to-air communication between the two Cessnas throughout the piggy-back maneuver. ATC on the ground would be unaware the two men would be communicating air-to-air or plane-to-plane.

Aircraft radios are normally wired in such a way that the pilot can only listen to one radio at a time in order to avoid confusion. But Seal's planes were custom-wired with avionics packages courtesy of Ultra-Sonics, Inc. of Columbus, Ohio, and Homer (Red) Hall, Seal's avionics expert, thus allowing both radios to be monitored simultaneously.

At 0402 hours, Terry heard Seal's voice transmitting on the normal ATC Center frequency.

"Memphis Center, this is twin-Cessna November six-niner-eight-eight-niner, level at three thousand five hundred trackin' inbound on the two-six-five degree radial of the Monticello VOR showin' twenty DME, squawkin' twelve hundred."

Seal's position report to the center included a precise location in mileage from the ground navigation fix, which was the 20 DME to which Seal had referred. The 1200 code was a frequency set into Seal's transponder indicating the aircraft was on a visual flight plan. Aircraft on a visual flight plan need not communicate with the center. But Seal had established radio contact for identification purposes and to create a record of entering and leaving the center's airspace. What the center would not be aware of was that while Seal's plane was under their control, another plane would take its place. The plane initially "handled" by the center would depart undetected and the rendezvousing aircraft, or Terry's, would proceed on Seals' original flight plan. One plane takes another's place, but no one other than the two pilots is the wiser.

"Roger, twin Cessna eight-eight-niner. What can I do for you?" the ground controller responded.

"Center, how do you read my transponder?"

"I am painting you eighteen DME from the fix, ground speed one-four-zero knots, squawking one-two-zero-zero, level three thousand five hundred feet. What else can I do for you twin-Cessna eight-eight-niner?"

"Oh, nuthin'. It's just that my transponder light appears to be intermittent, and I was wonderin' if y'all were paintin' me OK."

The light Seal referred to was an indicator on his transponder that lights up each time the center bounces a radar beam off of the airplane. This is referred to as having your transponder "interrogated." There was nothing wrong with Seal's transponder, he was simply establishing radio contact with the center in order to establish a record of his arrival and departure from their "window" of controlled air space.

"Everything looks fine here, sir. But, would you like a transponder check?" ATC replied.

"Yeah, that'd be great."

"Roger, twin Cessna eight-eight-niner, squawk ident."

At which point, Seal pushed the ident button on his transponder causing his radar blip to "blossom" or enlarge on the controller's radar scope. This enabled the controller to distinguish it from other aircraft on his screen.

At the same time, Seal also switched his transponder from the altitude reporting mode, mode C as it is called. ATC would no longer be able to determine the plane's altitude.

Terry, of course, had been silently monitoring this radio transmission between Seal and ATC and had used Seal's position reporting to locate the approaching aircraft visually from its navigation lights. Terry's plane had no lights on and was at minimum terrain clearance altitude below the surveillance envelope of the center's radar. The center was totally unaware of Terry's presence.

He had been maneuvering his plane to intercept Seal's flight path. This had been accomplished easily because Seal ran his engines at 55 per cent of their maximum power and Terry had used this time to assure himself visually that Seal had not been followed. If this had been the case, he would have alerted Seal on their discreet frequency and the mission would have been aborted.

"I'm below you and almost in position, your tail is clear. Stand by for a hack," Terry told Seal on the discreet frequency while Barry was faking the test of his transponder.

"Twin Cessna eight-eight-niner this is center. Sir, your ident looks fine, but I've now lost your Mode C. It does appear you have an intermittent problem of some sort," ATC said.

"Roger, center. I'm dual transponder equipped and when I get time in a minute, I'll switch over ta the other one and we'll see what she does."

"Roger, twin Cessna, whenever you're ready."

By disabling his plane's altitude reporting capability, Seal's transponder now no longer would tell ATC his true altitude. This would be important because Terry's plane soon would make an abrupt climb to Seal's altitude and once directly behind him, Seal would turn his transponder completely off and dive his plane for the deck. His electronically enhanced radar blip would completely disappear from the scope.

At precisely the same moment, Terry would switch on his transponder and squawk an ident mode. Terry's large radar return that would suddenly appear on Center's screen would mask any secondary return generated from Seal's plane during his diving maneuver away from Terry.

Terry was now in place below and behind Seal and gaining air speed as the distance between the two planes decreased.

"Thirty seconds to hack," Terry said to Seal. Then, "twenty." Then "ten, nine, eight, seven, six, five, four, three, two, one, hack."

Seal had now synchronized his clock with Terry's, and knew that he now had exactly one minute until Terry's plane would be in position directly behind him and slightly below. Without causing a mid-air collision, it would be Terry's job in this dangerous maneuver to get his airplane close enough to Seal's in order "to count the rivets" as Seal had taught him. It required the same flight precision demanded of the aerial stunt teams and each pilot was entrusting his life to the other.

It would be up to Seal then to execute a right-wing over, or half of a split-S course reversal maneuver taught to fighter pilots to dive in on unsuspecting targets below. This would separate the two aircraft as quickly as possible.

Seal and Terry's eyes were both locked on their cockpit clocks as the second hands approached 12. At ten seconds til, Terry began the count down, "ten, nine, eight, seven, six, five, four, three, two, one, *execute*." At precisely that second, Terry switched on his transponder, which had been off, pushed the ident button and turned on *his* Mode C, or altitude reporting capability.

Seal switched *his* transponder completely off and at the same time abruptly turned his plane beyond 90 degrees of bank angle and dove for the surface in the reverse direction.

If all had gone well the controller on the ground would never see more than one radar blip. For all he knew, he had only assisted one airplane with a transponder problem.

"Twin Cessna eight-eight-niner, this is Center. I'm painting you now at ten miles east of the fix, tracking outbound on the zero-niner-zero degree radial squawking ident and your mode C is now operational, showing you at three thousand five hundred feet. It appears that this transponder is a good one."

Seal, not Terry, now replied to ATC so that the controller hears the same voice.

"Roger center, thanks for the assistance. I'll be seein' ya."

"Good day, sir and have a nice flight."

The switch had been flawless.

Seal continued to fly at low altitude to Dallas Love Field below radar detection. There he landed and waited for Terry as they had earlier agreed. Terry continued flying on to Seal's original VFR flight-planned destination, Greenville, Mississippi airport, pretending to be Seal.

Once on the ground and sure that no one was following him or, even more important, that no one was waiting for him, Terry flew back to Little Rock and landed at Adams Field. It had already been a long morning and the sun was just beginning to rise as Terry boarded a Southwest Airlines flight at 6 AM for

Dallas' Love Field. There, he took the shuttle bus to the general aviation side of the field and rendezvoused with Barry.

Their plan was to be in the air at 0800 hours in Seal's Lear jet N 13SN heading south.

All went flawlessly, and, as Terry's bus pulled into the general aviation parking lot on the north side of Love Field, he could see Barry overseeing the refueling of the Lear. The twin Cessna he had flown in to Love was tied down on the transit parking ramp. Terry hoped all this hocus-pocus of the piggy-back flight had been worth it. He knew Seal was security conscious, but it was still amazing the lengths he would go to ensure there was no tail. It was 7:30 AM.

"Your left engine on the Cessna is losing some oil," Terry said as they boarded the Lear and buckled in. "You better get it checked out when we get back."

"How do ya know?"

"Because it deposited residue on my windshield when I was tucked in behind you."

"Jeeesus Christ! You must have been awful close to me."

"Hey, you're the one who said get close enough to count the rivets. There's exactly 26 holding on your tail hook," Terry laughed.

The Lear's engines spooled and it started its take off roll at exactly 0800 hours as planned. As the airspeed rose to 125 knots indicated, Terry rotated the aircraft as Seal in the right seat called out "V-1, check, cross-check, positive rate, gear up, turn and burn."

Terry banked the plane to the south as Seal briefed him on their planned 400-mile trip to Brownsville, Texas, where they would take on fuel and file a phony flight plan to Campeche, Mexico, a city on the western side of the Yucatan Peninsula. Seal told him they would file all the flight plans in Emile Camp's name and in his honor, since Barry had Emile's pilot's license and voter registration card from Slidell, Louisiana.

"Here's your huntin' license. You file the flight plan in Emile's name once we get to Brownsville, and then we'll cancel once we're in the air over Mexico."

"Oh, we're not goin' to Campeche?"

"No. We'll be flyin' direct to Ilopango (in El Salvador) for fuel and then on to Howard Air Force Base in Panama." Terry was excited.

Terry knew that Mexican Customs would not be a problem. Jets entering Mexican airspace do not have to clear at the port of entry, which in this case would have been Matamoros. Had they been flying a propeller-driven plane, they would not have been able to penetrate Mexican airspace as they crossed the Rio Grande coming out of Brownsville and "just keep on truckin'" as Seal had said. Flying jets certainly had its advantages. Terry knew they would not need Emile's identification unless an emergency forced them to land in Mexico since there would be no identification inspection by the Mexican Federales prior to leaving the U.S. He could tell Seal was an expert at exploiting the world of regulations and had done this many times before. He wondered if there was a loop hole in the rules Barry wasn't aware of?

"Keep this thing below eighteen thousand and we won't even file this leg," Seal said as they departed Dallas airspace.

All clever choices, Terry thought. By staying below 18,000 feet there would be no legal requirement to file a flight plan to Brownsville. The only punishment for not climbing to a higher altitude would be that the Lear's model CJ610-2 GE engines would suck fuel like crazy at this lower altitude.

"Don't worry about the fuel burn," Seal said. "This trip is on Uncle Sam."

After the brief hour trip to Brownsville, Terry (now Emile Camp) went inside the general aviation terminal to check weather and file their phony flight plan to Campeche. He felt a little uneasy using a dead man's pilot's license number. But, as Seal had joked earlier, "Emile won't mind. Where he's flying they don't need licenses."

After filing the plan, Terry joined Seal on the ramp where he was chewing out the "line boy" for not topping off the tanks completely.

"Son, the next time someone tells ya ta fill his fuckin' airplane...I suggest ya do just that...all the way ta the fuckin' top. Know what I mean? A friend of mine ran outa gas and died. A pilot can't burn air for fuel. So get your ass ova' here and top this baby off. I bet she'll hold another five gallons per side. And don't forget the Prist this time." Prist is a fuel additive used to prevent the growth of algae in fuel tanks when flying in humid and tropical climates.

Terry had grown to respect Seal's demand for perfection when it came to the world of aviation. He, too, knew that a pilot couldn't assume anything had been done properly when it came to servicing an airplane.

"Aviation is very unforgiving," he could hear his instructor-examiner John P. Brown saying from his training days at Mizzou Aviation in Joplin. And to prove it, on a wall behind Brown's desk was a picture of an old plane impaled upon and still stuck in the only tree that was visible for as far as the eye could see. A monument to what can happen anytime a pilot drops his guard...for any reason.

"Most aviation accidents can be prevented while still on the ground," he could hear the looming, somber, and often intimidating Brown still saying. Terry admired Seal for living by this rule, even after all the flying experience he had amassed. He may be a "calculated risk taker", but he certainly knew how to "reduce" the risks.

The white Lear was airborne and heading south at 10 AM with "Emile Camp" at the controls and Barry Seal on the radio. Once on their flight plan, and in Mexican airspace, at a cruising altitude of 35,000 feet, Seal went to the rear of the aircraft, grabbed two pilot map cases and dragged them to the front. These were the same type of cases Terry had seen earlier in Seal's Aero Commander that blew the engine in Texarkana. Inside were custom aluminum boxes containing sophisticated electronics, some of which Terry recognized.

"GNS-500s. Damn, those things used to cost a half-million apiece and you've got two?"

"Nuthin' but the best when you're workin' for Uncle." Seal quipped. "And these ain't your normal 500's. They're modified ta do "special" things. With these babies, we can not only pinpoint our position via satellite within about 10 meters, we can find the window to the Bermuda Triangle. That takes accuracy, son."

GNS-500s are navigational radios that continuously read the aircraft's position in latitude and longitude via digital readouts. This, coupled with their capability of storing and processing complex flight plans and denoting wind speeds at various altitudes, and determining ground tracks would give the jet the ability to fly without making contact with ground controllers. Earlier in his aviation training, Terry had attended an advanced navigation class in St. Louis, which taught the operation of this system, but he never thought he would see two of them worth more than $1 million in the same portable box. This was the same type of sophisticated navigation system aboard the Korean 747 airliner, Flight 007, shot down by a Soviet MIG in September, 1983. That aircraft had only one GPS (Global Positioning System). Seal had two to guarantee pinpoint navigation accuracy.

Under the control panel on the co-pilot's side, Red Hall had installed a secret power buss that Seal accessed with a jumper cable to power the GNS-500s. With another jack, Seal connected the antennas, hidden within the fuselage of the plane, to the radios in the box making everything operational.

Terry sat in awe as he watched while Seal remove a piece of paper from his shirt pocket and punched in the coordinates of the entire flight plan.

"OK, I'll just hook up the ground and satellite communications equipment in this other box and it'll be time for us to 'disappear,'" Seal chuckled.

As he opened the second box, Terry saw an array of electronics and radios with ultra-high radio frequency ranges totally foreign to him. On a sticker in the middle of the control panel was a service note, saying: "Direct all service inquiries to Summit Aviation, Middletown, Delaware."

Once power was supplied to these radios, Seal pulled a microphone from the box, smiled at Terry and said: "Now you're gonna know what it's like to fly into the Bermuda Triangle and just fuckin' disappear."

What Seal was preparing to do was to "blind" a Department of Defense satellite designed as a sentry to give advance warning of incoming hostile weapons systems. This would provide a window through which the Lear could fly through undetected. At the same time, Seal said, secret military surveillance tracking stations manned by U.S. Army intelligence personnel would emit large bursts of energy to jam the U.S. and Mexican ATC radar.

Terry felt he was seeing the results of all the Star War countermeasures technology. This, he now realized, was how Seal's Operation Jade Bridge aircraft, codenamed Dodger, had been able to enter and leave the United States without being detected. If there had ever been a doubt in Terry's mind about who Seal was, and how high he was connected, it had been put to rest forever. Seal got his flight plan authorizations not from someone on the ground, like most pilots, but from satellites out in space.

"You get ready to switch transponders to standby. I'll call our guys in Cuba on a secure frequency," Seal said to Terry.

"Sea Spray, this is Lear one-three Sierra November, thirty seconds from the window. How do you read?"

"Loud and clear, Lear," came the voice from the ground. "We've been expecting you. We're showing you being handled by Mexico City Center squawking zero-seven-four-two, level flight level three-five-zero (35,000)."

"That's a Roger. Give me a hack for the trip on the darkside. We're ready to go."

"Ten, nine, eight, seven, six, five, four, three, two, one, hack."

Seal had zeroed the LED clock on the dashboard of the Lear and pressed the 'ON' button as the controller called "Hack."

He turned to Terry, "When that clock reads 30, switch both transponders to standby, hit the speed brakes and let's dive this bitch to the deck. Use your emergency decompression check list."

Seal immediately went to Mexico City Center frequency, "Mexico City, this is Lear one-three Sierra November requesting hand-off to Campeche approach."

The Mexican ATC authorized Seal to leave his frequency and go to Campeche's, thus terminating Mexico City's service.

Thirty seconds later the ground controller announced "your portal time is sixteen forty-five zulu. You're black." Terry saw that the transponder "interrogation" light was no longer working. As the Lear buffeted with its speed brakes extended and its altimeter indicating 20,000 feet per minute descent, Seal got on the radio to Campeche approach and said: "Campeche approach, we are Lear one-three Sierra November, cancel our flight plan to your destination. We are goin' somewhere else."

At this point, they no longer existed as Lear 13SN heading for Campeche from Brownsville. Now, they were self-navigating under no one's ground control. They would now swing out of Mexican and Cuban airspace by circumventing the Yucatan Peninsula and establish a course of 230 degrees to Ilopango, El Salvador.

Terry leveled the plane out at 10,000 feet and started reviewing the approach charts to Ilopongo, now about 600 miles away. The fuel burn at low altitude was horrible, but Seal didn't care as he had factored in the tail wind component supplied him by the GNS-500s.

Now they were flying "on the darkside" mused Terry and asked Seal about the term. It had a science fiction connotation.

"Yeah, some spook technocrat stole it from 'Close Encounters,'" Seal said referring to the movie. "It was originally conceived as a way to hide the whereabouts and destination of Top Secret military flights, including Air Force One. But once they got it perfected, the Agency saw it had lots of uses." Seal went on to say it was rumored in the spook world that this technique of literally falling off the edge of the earth was used not only by the Agency as a way of hiding agents who became too hot, but by unscrupulous people who paid for such disappearance. Perhaps this was part of the Bermuda Triangle myth, Terry thought.

Seal began connecting and activating portable low-frequency receivers called ADFs (automatic direction finders). These were needed to receive signals from low-frequency transmitters common throughout Central and South America. If these devices had been permanently installed in the plane, the Federal Aviation Administration would have flagged this aircraft as one that operated in that area and would have brought unnecessary outside scrutiny.

At 1300 hours, they landed at Ilopongo and took on fuel from the Salvadoran Air Force, whose armed guards surrounded the aircraft. Cold Cokes and flight lunches were brought out for the two men. No one signed for the fuel and no money was exchanged.

There was no flight plan in—or out. They were handled by ATC as a "special flight." Terry realized that what he had suspected was true: the CIA owned El Salvador just as they had owned Laos.

As the plane taxied out for takeoff, Seal instructed Terry to stop the Lear in the pre-takeoff runup area. He had a little "cosmetic work" to perform before the leaving. Once stopped, Seal got out and removed a Mylar masks bearing the plane's tail-number. Once removed, a hidden number of N83JA was exposed. Upon reentering the cockpit, Seal chuckled, "One last little detail taken care of. The world now figures that the Bermuda Triangle swallowed up 13SN."

Once again airborne, they were headed for their real destination, Panama.

During the flight, Seal lectured Terry on how to "handle the handlers," something he had promised Terry back in Arkansas.

"Now keep in mind, you got somethin' these fuckers really want. It's your reputation and experience in the machine-tool industry. And that's what you have for sale. They want ta build a front nobody will be looking at and you've got the creds ta do that. So don't sell yourself short and don't talk money on this trip. View this as an operational discussion only and don't let Leroy pin ya down on anythin'. That'll all come later. Don't forget, he's a fuckin' bean-counter just like all the rest of the GS weenies. Sometimes he acts like it's his money and not Uncle Sam's. I'll take care of the money discussions later."

"So what do you want out of this, Barry?"

"I wanna a new life. They're gonna need major air transportation capability for this program. I always wanted ta own Air America, maybe this is my chance ta do somethin' like that."

Once on the ground at Howard Air Force Base in Panama, a dark blue Chevy pickup truck bearing a large yellow and black "follow me" sign escorted them to a parking area on the east side of the field.

Leroy was waiting for them inside the terminal, wearing his Panama shirt, sunglasses and bearing that thin, drawn look of someone whose liquid intake far out measures solid nutrition.

"You guys are on time," Leroy said with a relaxed, wrinkled grin. "I love punctuality. The meeting's been moved to Chagres. A couple of the people that are attending don't want to be seen here. I've got us a Cessna parked outside and a pilot that'll fly us over there. It's only 30 miles away."

He pointed out the door to a Cessna 172 bearing North American registration. Terry calculated the number and combined weight of the prospective passengers and pointed out that this would require two trips, at least. Leroy obviously hadn't thought about this.

"Can you fly this little thing?" Leroy said to Seal. "If you can, I'll get rid of the pilot. I'll just pay him to sit here till we get back."

"Well, if I can't, Terry can. We just flew a fuckin' Lear jet. Leroy, I keep tellin' ya, they all fly alike just like all women fuck alike when ya get right down to it. They just all come in different sizes."

Seal flew the overweight 172 to a small, 2,700-foot dirt strip on the banks of the Panama Canal. It was a former U.S. Armed Forces Aeroclub with shelter hangers and a couple of wooden out-buildings. From the building where the meeting was to take place, you could watch the ships on the canal pass by.

The three men walked inside. Max Gomez was impatiently waiting. He immediately pulled Leroy and Seal off to a corner, out of Terry's hearing.

After a short, private discussion, Seal walked away from the other two, returned to Terry and said, "This is a pretty sensitive area we need ta talk about. There's another person present outside who represents another government who may wanna get involved in this operation. This other person would like ta sit in on this meeting, but not be identified for security reasons. You got any problem with that?"

"What's his role?" Terry asked, feeling a little leery.

"He just wants ta leave this meetin' fully informed and then file a report with his boss. He wants ta be sure he hears everythin' straight from the horse's mouth. I got no problem with that if you don't."

Terry shrugged and said, "Sure, we flew too far to fuck up the meeting now. I guess I can't be trusted, yet, with this guy's identity, huh?"

Seal nodded. "Spook shit, ya know...let them play their fuckin' games."

Gomez returned from outside with a man who sat down at one end of the table. Terry had never seen the man before. He was built like Terry, about five feet, 11 inches tall, clean cut and had the aura of a businessman, possibly an attorney. He had the lean, muscular build that gave him the appearance of a distance runner.

Terry was struck by one aspect of his appearance. The man's eyes seemed too far apart, giving his face a somewhat peculiar look. It later became apparent to Terry that the man probably had a glass or fake eye.

Reed was given no information about this man, not even a name. He would not be formally introduced until months later, and would then be told his name was "Pat Weber". This, however, was a code name, and his true identity remained a mystery for much longer. He would become a key and mysterious player in this black game further down the murky road.

Leroy was the first to speak. "Mr. Reed—Terry, if I may—sorry about the security precautions taken to not divulge the identity of our guest. But I'll show you my identification to allay your suspicions."

The CIA credentials laid open on the table were like the ones Terry had seen before in Oklahoma City when he first met John Cathey—"the Eagle, the photo and the whole nine yards." The name on the I.D. was Leroy Tracta and he said he had been Mr. Seal's Agency contact for quite some time.

Terry was relieved that someone had a name and government credentials to legitimize this whole clandestine operation.

It was getting close to evening and Terry felt it was time to get things moving. He had been up since 2 AM, and he was tired. He sat down at the long table with Seal to his left. Tracta was directly across from him. Gomez was across from Seal and "Weber," with a yellow legal pad, taking notes, sat at the far end at Terry's left.

Gomez produced a file from his briefcase, which contained copies of Terry's business plan and correspondence with Robert Johnson of Southern Air Transport in Miami.

"Mr. Reed, it appears you've been very busy since our meeting in Vera Cruz," Gomez said. "Mr. Johnson is extremely impressed with the progress of your feasibility study. It is time to get beyond feasibility and into the reality of developing this front company. That is why we have requested this meeting, and I want to thank you and Mr. Seal for coming on such short notice. We felt it best to arrange for a face-to-face meeting and have Mr. Tracta interrogate...ask you...detailed questions. And he wanted to meet you in person."

Tracta, nodding toward the man with the glass eye, told Terry to view the unidentified man as a possible "foreign investor" in the operation. Tracta was sure that the "investor" would have questions of his own for the purpose of filing a report with his "people."

"An area of special interest in your plan is the concept of multi-national ownership for the machinery company," Tracta said. "Could you start out by recapping your entire concept for the sake of our visitor, and please give special emphasis to the foreign ownership portion of your plan."

Tracta handed Seal, Terry and the unidentified stranger a copy of Terry's plan. Terry noticed that his work product was now laden with "Top Secret" stamps. He knew from his military intelligence days that it probably wouldn't be declassified until 30 years later...if then. The document on top of the pile of papers was a diagram of Mexico that Terry and Seal had discussed at SOBs the week before. This was the key to the plan. (See end of chapter 14.)

The map showed import routes from Asia, the United States and Europe entering either directly into Mexico or from third countries, all converging in Mexico City. From there, export lines to other Latin American nations trading with Mexico were indicated. Camouflaged within this trading plan was the ability to store and trans-ship "large, heavy, crated items" to secret destinations. Right now the interest was Nicaragua, but, in the future, who knew?

Terry then explained his plan in detail, including the results of his exploratory work that led to the now-classified written findings in everyone's hands. Addressing Tracta's request, he detailed the interest he had developed between Hungarian, German and Japanese firms that were expressing interest in joint ownership of a foreign machine tool venture in Mexico.

Now, he felt, was a good time to bring up a sensitive issue. "I suppose I need to address this question to Mr. Gomez," Terry said. "Has the Agency considered having partners involved in this who are *fully* aware of the business of the Company? The reason I ask is that my Hungarian friend, George Fenue, is very curious about our ability to control the tariffs. I think he suspicions who my silent partners are. My imagination runs wild at the thought of international investors who are actually into the loop on the weapons procurement side of the equation."

"Is this, in fact, the case?" Gomez asked with great excitement. "Do you sense a degree of willingness from your communist friends to get totally in bed with us? I mean to really spread their legs?"

"Yes. I've known this guy for several years now. And my sixth sense tells me he wants to get involved. And not only that, I don't believe he'll be able to sell his parent company on the idea of a joint venture unless there's something *really* attractive in this for them."

"Good. I will go take care of this. This is my specialty. It's important for them to see there's someone behind you. You make the introduction for me and I will go see this KGB guy. It will be fun." Gomez had a broad grin on his face. He had better alert Fenue, Terry thought.

He interpreted Gomez's enthusiasm as a "Yes" answer to his question about inviting the Hungarians into the venture. So much for the complexities of geopolitics.

After recapping his written reports, Terry outlined his areas of concern about implementing the plan and focused on areas beyond his control such as Mexican licensing requirements and possibly even favorable consideration, or worse yet, legislation that might be required for 100 per cent foreign ownership of the venture.

As the conversation unfolded, it became quickly apparent that the stranger was not there just to take notes. In fact, he assumed the role of Devil's advocate and began posing detailed questions about obstacles he felt had to be overcome to make the plan totally successful. It was clear that he was, by nature, very calculating and conservative. From his questioning, Reed wondered if his "clients" were as tough as he. He became a foil for Gomez who took the typical Latin view that everything was *"no problema."*

Terry stressed that one major factor in favor of such a venture was that the project was something the Mexican government desperately needed. Mexico's President, Miguel de la Madrid, was publicly embracing the need for foreign technology that would allow Mexico to develop a stronger export market. To do so, the Mexicans would need modern factories utilizing state-of-the-art machine tools.

"Mexican machine tool industry is at this moment an oxymoron," Terry said.

"What's that mean?" Gomez wanted to know.

It was apparent the stranger was now embarrassed for Gomez.

"He means this is something that is non-existent in Mexico," the stranger replied. "And, from what I've heard, this is the major attraction of Mr. Reed's plan. When I file my report, I'm going to emphasize this point as well as to expand upon the joint venture concept."

By his comments it seemed the stranger was favorably impressed with what he was hearing. Terry was beginning to feel this meeting was actually a very expensive job interview.

Seal said very little until Terry pointed out the poor quality of Mexican roads made air transportation vital because of the fragile nature of the electronics associated with computer-controlled machine tools. Terry stressed that large air-cargo shipments coming in from all over the world to fill machine tool orders would disguise the arms dealing, reduce the risk of discovery and virtually eliminate scrutiny. It would be a perfect front.

It was Seal's turn to speak. "With all this air cargo activity, we're gonna need a very specialized carrier that can operate freely worldwide, move sensitive cargo and, most of all, keep its mouth shut. I propose the formation of a small, elite air cargo operation based outa Mexico that would be like a scaled-down version of SAT (Southern Air Transport). I can put all that together for ya and, considering the black ops capabilities in place from Sea Spray*, we'll be able to move undetected throughout this region. The U.S. Army's anti-detection capabilities in the corridors around Panama and the Bahamas are excellently suited for this style of operation."

Tracta had a simple question: "What's this gonna cost me, Barry? With you, that's a question I'm always afraid to ask." He laughed.

Seal answered with a question. "Leroy, haven't ya always got your money's worth from me? I'm a professional, and you know it, and professionals cost money. I've instructed Terry to discuss no money figures today. He's sorta new at this. You come to me later after Terry and I have had a chance ta put a sharp pencil to it and then we'll discuss money."

"Oh shit! Just what I need," Tracta joked. Are you training him how to handle me, too, as you're always boasting?"

Even the newcomer was laughing now.

"How do ya know I said that? Ya got my phones bugged again, Leroy?"

When the laughter died down, Terry had a question. "I'm confused. What is the reporting procedure. I'm from the military and I can't work without a chain of command. With my Agency contact in Arkansas now gone, and with Barry out of the loop there, I feel isolated. Can anyone define this for me?"

Gomez had the answer. "Right now, this is Mr. Cathey's project. View him as the big boss. Mr. Bob Johnson in Miami is like a one-man legal oversight com-

---

*   Sea Spray is an operational code name for a joint CIA-Army program to mask covert flights entering and leaving the American airspace.[2]

mittee. You need to be filing all of your reports with him as this progresses. I will be operations manager for this project...if it's a go."

The three-hour meeting ended with everyone upbeat. Gomez and Tracta both said they would file a joint report to Cathey, who would make the final decision. It appeared all systems were go, only the money had to be worked out. It was still not clear to Terry what the unidentified man's role was. It was obvious he had been cleared for everything, but it was a mystery who, or what, he truly represented. All Terry knew for sure was that he had a glass eye, an accent he could not quite place, and he left with a copy of the business plan, which had by now been stamped "Top Secret."

By now it was dark outside and approaching 8 PM. Terry had not slept for more than 18 stressful hours and the day had been anything but routine. Seal, Tracta and Terry got into the Cessna and flew back to Howard where they spent the night at the bachelor officer's quarters.

Despite his exhaustion, Terry couldn't sleep. This had been one hell of a day. He noticed the light from Seal's room coming in from under the door. He walked across the hall and knocked on the door. Seal was lying on his bed just staring at the idle ceiling fan.

"Barry, tell me about this Gomez guy. Back in the states, you said he was a loose cannon and we had to play ball with him. From what I can see now, he's going to be the guy in charge down here. I can't figure out if he's driven by ideals or greed. Does that bother you?"

Seal seemed pensive and in the mood for a philosophical discussion. "Terry, as a young man I had ideals similar ta yours. I was put into play early on with a group of guys wantin' to liberate their country just as your 'freedom fighters' want ta liberate theirs. Anyone whose ideals drive them has ta be a little bit crazy. Gomez falls in that category. My Agency service has pivoted around a group of ragtag Cubans and now, Panamanians. They just come with this business. They're always on the ragged edge between right and wrong and sometimes they'll pull you in there with them. You just gotta keep your own head screwed on straight and remember why *you* got involved. Don't make *their* war *your* war or you can get into real trouble. But all I can tell ya from an Agency point of view, they're the only game in town, at least on this side of the world. If you wanna play this game, you gotta associate with guys like Gomez. They've turned fightin' commies into their own selfish fulltime profession. You don't know what really motivates them, greed or ideals or hatred. But, I agree with you, fuckin' communism *is* a threat. I may be a wild-ass free enterpriser, but I'm also a patriot."

The following morning after a hearty GI breakfast of SOS (shit on a shingle) at the officer's mess, Terry was still trying to absorb all this. For him, it was still new, this sneaking off to a foreign country to hold intelligence briefings. It made him think of Thailand, watching the GIs walking around the Howard Air Base, seemingly barely able to tolerate their surroundings during the Christmas season, gawking back at him and Seal. It reminded him of how envious he had been in Asia while he watched the civilian spooks come and go as they pleased while he toiled in the strict, disciplined environment of the military. That's just how he must have looked to the spooks who operated in Thailand. Now it was his turn to be the envy of the underpaid grunts.

At the base operations building, Terry had to oversee the Lear's refueling while Seal and Tracta indicated the need for another private meeting. As the two walked away, Terry could hear Seal say, "Well, I'm sorry Leroy, if they feel like I'm blackmailin' 'em. But this is business and I just gotta do what I gotta do..."

At 10 AM, after saying goodbye to Tracta, the two prepared to depart. Terry felt that he would be home for dinner with any luck. He was wondering what new excitement might be awaiting him on the trip back.

It didn't take long for him to find out. As soon as the two were airborne, Seal laid it on him. He was full of pent-up emotion and startled his flying companion as they exited Howard airspace.

Seal began yelling at the top of his voice, something totally out of character for him. Terry had never seen him this euphoric.

"YEE-HAWWWWWW," he screamed. "I'm gonna fuckin' make it. We're gonna do this, Terry. We've got these assholes eatin' outa our hands. YEE-HAWWWWWWWWW. Give me the fuckin' airplane."

He grabbed the control yoke and executed a series of aileron rolls. Terry had never been sick in an airplane, but he was sure he was about to lose his SOS.

"OK, enough of that shit," Seal said after seeming to tire of the aerobatic antics. "You got the airplane, I'll hook up the radios."

Terry sat silently at the controls, trying to figure out what was driving Seal. As Barry emerged from under the electrical panel, after making the radio connections, he abruptly began pounding with his right hand on the dash of the Lear until Terry thought the avionics in the control panel would be dislodged.

"There ain't nuthin' in this world more powerful than good ol' fuckin' blackmail, Terry. And don't let anybody ever tell ya different. Jeeeeesus Christ, I got some good shit on some big people."

"Will you let me in on your party? Calm down, Barry! Tell me what's goin' on."

"Terry, what's most important right now is for ya ta play ball with these guys and get your ass down to Mexico ASAP. You impressed the shit out of Leroy... Robert Johnson, too. I won't be able ta come ta Mexico right now, I've got a little matter ta take care of. But ya get on down there and get in a position to receive me, and I'll be joining ya soon. Goddam, this'll be great. Won't it be fun workin' together and spendin' all their fuckin' money?"

"What this blackmail, you're talking about?"

"Ever hear the old expression, it's not what ya know, it's who ya know? Well, whoever said that just hadn't caught the Vice President's kids in the dope business,'cause I can tell ya for sure *what* ya know can definitely be more important than *who* you know."

"You gotta calm down and tell me what you're talking about, if you want me to know. What's this about the Vice President's kids and dope."

"I don't wannna tell ya too much, 'cause truthfully ya don't have a need to know. But Terry I been workin' with several federal agencies for the past couple of years as ya probably suspicioned. In the course of that business, a person can't help but run across some real *sensitive* information. It seems some major players in the Medellin Cartel, whom I personally know, ran across some knowledge that's very valuable to both the Republicans and the Democratic Party. Real national security stuff. It seems some of George Bush's kids just can't say no ta drugs, ha ha ha ha...Well, ya can imagine how valuable information like that would be, can't ya? That could get ya out of almost any kind of jam." Seal paused for a moment then asked, "Ya ever play Monopoly? The information I got is so good it's just like a get-out-of-jail-free card... ha,ha,ha,ha YEE-HAWWWWW..."

"Barry, are you telling me George Bush's kids are in the drug business?"

"Yup, that's what I'm tellin' ya. A guy in Florida who flipped for the DEA has got the goods on the Bush boys. Now I heard this earlier from a reliable source in Colombia, but I just sat on it then, waitin' to use it as a trump card, if I ever needed it. Well, I need ta use it now. I got names, dates, places....even got some tape recordins'. Fuck, I even got surveillance videos catchin' the Bush boys red-handed. I consider this stuff my insurance policy. It makes me and my mole on the inside that's feedin' the stuff to me invincible. Now this is *real* sensitive shit inside of U.S. Customs and DEA and those guys are pretty much under control. It's damage control as usual. But where it gets real interestin' is what the Republicans will do ta the Democrats in order ta dirty up the people who might use this information against Bush."

"So you've got direct knowledge of the Republicans trying to neutralize some Democrats before they can nuke Bush with this?"

"Hell yeah. I've been part of it. Remember that meetin' we had at SOBs when I told ya ya should play ball with these guys and get your butt down ta Mexico and be prepared to receive me?...Remember in that meetin' I told ya I had a plan to blow the lid off the whole damn Mena deal and shut it down due to adverse publicity? Well, what I didn't tell ya was that project was already in effect, and the Republicans were already trying to neutralize some important people in Arkansas...namely the Clinton family."

Seal took a break to communicate with ground control. When he turned back to Terry, he continued, "Yeah, that day ya explained to me the connection between the Ward family, the Rose Law Firm and the governor's mansion, well....I about shit! Ya see what ya didn't know was I was on a secret mission by none other than the Agency ta sort of....uh, dirty up some people real close to the governor. Now I had been workin' on this through Dan Lasater. Now Dan's a good ol' boy and all that, but he's gotta drug problem, and he's got the balls to be stealin' from the Agency, too. From what I hear, Dan's been doin' a lot of questionable out-a-state investin'. In fact, he's stashin' a lot of cash in a resort in New Mexico.*

"I was told ta exploit that, which I was workin' on. But you come along with this new connection. And when ya told me that Finis Shellnut was the guy at the ranch (where the 'green flights' dropped their money in Arkansas)... dollar signs started dancin' in my head. I saw an immediate way to get some white stuff up some noses around Bill Clinton real fast. Now don't get mad, but that duffel bag I had ya take over to Skeeter Ward wasn't really money."

"I'm afraid to ask what it was," Terry said as he focused on the "little airplane" displayed on the Lear's flight director.

"Let's don't call it cocaine. Let's just call it neutralizin' powder. Least that's the way the Bush family saw it. This is just one family warrin' against another. Just like the Mob."

---

* Lasater was a major investor in a ski resort called "Angel Fire" near Taos, New Mexico, where Gov. Bill Clinton vacationed at Lasater's expense. Lasater later sold the resort to a savings and loan that eventually failed and was taken over by the Resolution Trust Corporation (RTC).

"Goddam, Barry, this is heavy shit! Are you saying you were the source of the cocaine ending up around a lot of important people in Arkansas. Like the ones I've been reading about in the paper. There's a major scandal brewing there..."

Terry sat silently and continued to think. Seal gazed out the window and said nothing.

Already predicting the answer by Seal's silence, Terry asked, Did you have anything to do with Roger (Clinton) and some of those guys in Lasater's firm getting investigated?

"Terry, I told ya when I met ya, I'm in transportation and I transport what the government wants transported. In this case, the Republicans...the Bush family...wanted some stuff transported through Mena and into Arkansas that would end up in the noses of some very prominent Democrats. And yes, I must 'fess up, I've had a hand in that. YEEE-HAWWWWWW! It's not who ya know it's what ya know."

Terry found all this disquieting. Seal had never discussed drugs with him before, and if Barry was telling the truth, he had unknowingly delivered some to Skeeter Ward. Seal was telling him that he had a hand in the major political storm that was brewing in Arkansas. Terry had not bargained for this sort of involvement.

Roger Clinton, the governor's brother, had already been arrested and had pleaded guilty to drug trafficking charges. He was now serving time at a federal prison/drug rehab center in Texas. Rumors abounded that Roger was helping the Feds implicate major figures in the Arkansas financial community for cocaine related crimes. Not only was a federal grand jury investigation getting under way, but panic was already permeating the Arkansas bond business with fears that investor confidence would be shaken if the Feds proved that the bond industry was laundering drug money and its corporate leaders were actually trafficking in drugs.

The Feds were targeting Dan Lasater and people in his firm, most of them friends of Governor Clinton. But George Bush's real target, from what Seal was saying, was Bill Clinton and Seal was the instrument that Republicans were using under the guise of the CIA.

But Terry was thoroughly confused as this began to sink in. Why would the Agency want the bond business investigated since it was the source of the black ops money being "washed" there? He began to wonder how much of this was the Agency's plan and how much was just Seal's personal plan? Seal seemed to be enjoying all this too much. Maybe this was Barry's way of extricating himself out of some unforeseen mess and into Mexico. Terry was beginning to wonder why Seal would be needed in Mexico, since the Agency already had easy access to Southern Air Transport. SAT definitely was in the transportation business in a big way. Remembering Skeeter Ward's statement about Seal "playin'" with everyone further troubled Terry.

It was beginning to sound like Barry was the instigator rather than the tool in this "political sting." Maybe Barry had started out working for the Republicans, but now it appeared he was blackmailing everyone with what he knew. This scared Terry. Where was the Barry Seal he knew and respected? Where was the man who was going to teach him how to "handle the handlers?" If this is what he had meant by "handling the handlers," Terry realized this was a career he wanted no part of. As the two friends sat there in silence, streaking along in the Lear above a layer of clouds, Terry's mood turned to anger.

"Barry, I gotta tell you, I'm sitting here pretty pissed off. This whole thing about putting cocaine up people's noses is not what I'm about. We got thrust together by a guy named John Cathey and, up until today, I thought he had made a great decision in putting the two of us together. But I gotta tell you, I'm having second thoughts about a lot of this. If we continue as friends, you've got to promise me two things. I know the first one goes against the intelligence grain, but you've got to start telling me everything so I can make my own decisions. We're treading into some dangerous territory, it sounds like to me. Ours is getting way beyond a need to know relationship. Second, don't ever put cocaine near me again. If that's what you *have* to do for the Agency, then you go do it and I don't want to know about it."

"Terry, you're my friend and believe me I need friends right now. I'm sorry if I upset you or if I *compromised* your values. It's hard to run across a person with values these days. They're scarce."

The conversation was interrupted by a radio transmission. "Lear one-three-Sierra November, this is Sea Spray. We're painting you direct to Ilopongo, squawking four-six-three-three, level flight level three-four-zero. I assumed you'll be using corridor Whisky Echo, sir, then direct New Orleans after you refuel. Give me your ETD (expected time of departure) out of Ilopongo, and we'll have the window activated for you."

"Roger Sea Spray, this is Lear one-three Sierra November. We've got horrible headwinds at this flight level, and they don't get any better any lower. We'll wanna stay high 'til we get to the ADIZ (a coastal defense alert area), then we'll drop down and pretend we're fling-wing traffic 'til we get inland. Can you arrange all that?"

"Roger, one-three Sierra November, we'll provide the cover out of El Salvador. Just squawk zero-seven-seven-two for identification when you're off Ilopongo and we'll receive you."

The two left Ilopongo at noon after a guarded military refueling, just like on the way down. Then the Mylar masks were reinstalled over the plane's N-number, restoring the Lear's tail number to the one it bore when it left the states. Once airborne and back at altitude, Seal established radio contact with the Army Sea Spray ground controllers who gave him a time hack for reentry into U.S. airspace. This would occur about 200 miles out over the Gulf of Mexico. The Lear then would have to be barely off the water, squawking 1200 and at a speed slow enough that American ATC would not be able to differentiate it from helicopter traffic servicing offshore oil rigs. The Sea Spray service effectively masks the Lear's flight from El Salvador all the way to the ADIZ.

Once safely within American-controlled air space the plane landed at New Orleans for a legitimate fuel stop and then on up to Little Rock where Seal dropped Terry off.

As they sat in the Lear at Little Rock Seal made a vow. "I'm sorry about the deal with Skeeter. I promise I'll never do it again. Captain, you and I have lotsa good times ahead of us. I've taught ya all I can teach ya'. It's time for you to 'solo'."

"When will I see you next?" Terry asked, sensing Seal was cryptically establishing some sort of finality to their relationship. What was all this talk about soloing, he wondered. He didn't feel ready to cut the cord. He felt he still needed Seal's instruction on handling the handlers.

Without being specific, Seal answered, "I don't know for sure. I've got to

216   TERRY REED AND JOHN CUMMINGS

attend a legal orgy in Baton Rouge....a private matter.* Be careful with these guys and I'll see ya' soon down south."

Seal gave Terry a thumbs up, and smiled out of the cockpit window as he started the jet engines of the Lear. It was Terry's last trip on the dark side with Seal, and it was to be his last conversation with him.

Seal taxied out, probably still laughing, not knowing his life on earth could now be measured in weeks.

1. FBI Teletype provided in litigation, LRC-91-414. Date/time group F 182227Z August 87, from FM Chicago to Director Priorty, ATTN: Drug Section. CID. and OI-1, Section, INTD, Little Rock Priority.
2. CIA Base, a computer data base on the CIA, compiled by former intelligence officer Ralph McGehee, Herndon, Virgina, 1992.

---

* The legal orgy Seal had referred to was a deposition he was scheduled to give on Friday, December 27, 1985, in Baton Rouge. In the presence of his attorney, Louis Unglesby, he was grilled by Assistant U.S. Attorney Bradley C. Meyers, IRS Special Agents William C. Duncan and Jerry Bize, and Arkansas State Police Investigator Russell Welch, from 1:18 PM to 3:30 PM. The purpose of the questioning was centered primarily around the cash that was turning up in Arkansas' banks around Mena as a result of Seal having paid for work done to DEA and other federally owned aircraft. This reckless questioning of Seal, under oath, administered by the IRS, clearly showed the difficulty the Agency was experiencing in controlling the security for operations "Jade Bridge" and "Centaur Rose". With the operations either shut down, or by this time moved, what the IRS perceived as a money-laundering of proceeds from narcotics trafficking was still bringing unwanted scrutiny. By reading the transcript of the proceedings, one can clearly see Seal handled himself extremely well that day in keeping the Agency's dirty secrets.

CHAPTER 16

A DATE WITH DEATH

What a long day it had been. The exhausting trip from Panama had answered a lot of questions, and yet created a lot more. Terry stood by the terminal at The Little Rock Air Center and watched Seal taxi out for takeoff.

When the white Lear jet's strobe light became only a distant twinkle moving southeast, he paused to think about the man who had become his personal instructor in dealing with this dark and Byzantine world.

He had seen a transformation in Seal over the course of the past two years. He had gone from a confident businessman, seemingly well-established in Baton Rouge, to a man unsure of his future. Terry wasn't sure his friend could any longer control the forces with which he was dealing.

Though still cocky, and often arrogant, Seal was beginning to react rather than act, and seemed to be holding something back. And, indeed, he was. Seal had not told Terry everything on their long trip back from Panama.

Terry didn't know about the previous five months of Seal's life. Seal had become the most important informant in the history of the Drug Enforcement Administration and had tied the Sandinista government together with the Medellin Cartel. As a result of leaks from Oliver North and the White House, the Cartel had put a $500,000 price on Seal's head. In addition, Seal had handed the DEA three of the best drug cases it had ever had, testifying as the government's chief witness. The DEA was winning plaudits from the White House over the Sandinista "sting", but Seal had been left twisting in the wind. While he was undeniably a major asset for the DEA, he was now a major liability for the CIA and George Bush because of the knowledge he had confided to Terry about Bush's sons.

Now Seal just wanted to escape and start life over somewhere else. But that was not going to happen.

Terry wanted to escape, too. Even though he felt there was a genuine opportunity for him in the Arkansas business community, he had made a near-deathbed vow to make his life count for something beyond making a good living. And most of all he, like Seal, had become addicted to adrenalin.

The black ops world, he believed, had built a foundation for him in Arkansas and he could use it to go in several directions. One would be to remain where he was and build up the network of important people with which he had been dealing. He was orbiting in both high social and political circles. Terry also had accumulated a lot of inside knowledge about the secret CIA-state connection and who the hidden players were, which could be of immense value in the future.

Terry was being drawn toward Mexico, but, if he did go he would be turning his back on unknown business opportunities in Arkansas. From his initial sponsorship into the power structure of Little Rock, he felt, he was beginning to stand alone as an individual and a respected businessman. Janis felt that they were finally putting down roots .

There was vacillation, fed by a nagging feeling of uncertainty, but he kept it to himself. After returning home from his flight with Seal, he spoke positively about the trip. He and Janis sat up late that night and reconstructed what had occurred in Panama. This excited her. Mexico was now beginning to looking like a reality.

As Terry immersed himself in his workaday world, he continued to put the Mexican plan in place. He was now dealing exclusively with a man whom he had yet to meet, but who was a major decision-maker in the new operations, Robert Johnson. Johnson sounded friendly, articulate, and knowledgeable on the phone, a man accustomed to plowing his way through bureaucratic red tape.

By mid-January, 1986, the foreign ownership element of the plan was coming into focus. After lengthy discussions with Johnson and the potential investors an equation of ownership had been established. Rodriguez had in fact visited George Fenue, Terry's "commie friend" in Mexico City.

Terry believed he was discovering what he had long suspected, that enemies can become friends when there's a mutual benefit. It was the old "the enemy of my enemy is my friend" story, he surmised, only he couldn't figure out who was the common enemy of both the CIA and KGB. It must be the American Congress, he and John Cathey speculated, in reflecting on their ongoing hatred of that body. Not only had the KGB seen the capitalistic opportunities hidden within the joint venture, but so had "the Harbor Bombers," who Terry endearingly called the Japanese. Johnson's research had uncovered that Gomiya, the Japanese company targeted by Terry as an investor, had strong trading ties with communist China. The CIA knew about these ties, but Gomiya's *American* management didn't.

Johnson informed Terry that Gomiya was actually exporting restricted computer technology to China. They were doing this by selling computer-controlled lathes built by Dianichi of Japan through Gomiya's communist trading partner. Just like Toshiba, Terry thought. Was this another shining example of Japanese honor, he wondered?

A sensitive morsel of information revealed by Johnson was that Frank Fujikawa, the Japanese "HMFIC" for Gomiya U.S.A., had helped set up the illegal trading link. Armed with this intelligence, Terry approached Fujikawa privately in Dallas about a "hypothetical" situation. What could be done, he asked, if the new joint venture company in Mexico had a need to establish a secret trading tie with Peking?

He confirmed once again that the bottom line for these corporation's morality was the bottom line. By dangling the clout of the CIA's backing of the new company, the potential investors now had to be fended off. It was, Terry discovered, like trying to hand-feed a cheeseburger to a lion.

Fujikawa was on board, with a passion.

By January 21st, 1985, Terry put all of this into writing so that everyone understood the arrangement. (At about this same time, Oliver North was putting into play other key people such as retired Air Force General Richard Secord as part of the "Enterprise.")

Reed's project was now going beyond talk and into legalities, which was Johnson's speciality. Terry recapped the proposed stock ownership for the new company, which would be incorporated in America as a holding company and called Machinery International, Inc. Its only holding would be a Mexican company called *Maquinaria Internacional, S.A.*

Stock, to be sold only in the name of Machinery International, would be issued as follows: SAT: 55 per cent; Reed: 25 per cent; the Hungarians: 10 per cent; and the Japanese: 10 percent. Johnson had devised a plan to further insulate the company's true ownership. All potential investors were instructed to form new corporations to hold the stock of Machinery International, Inc. That way, if anyone was able to penetrate its corporate veil it would find only that its owners were other corporations.

Terry learned that's the type of business charade the CIA used. Like a cat, the Agency was covering its own dirt so it could not be easily tracked. And Fujikawa saw another advantage of doing business with the Agency. With a big toothy grin, he added, "It's nice to be in joint venture with people who can *eliminate* competition." Based upon Terry's prior knowledge of Fujikawa's free-wheeling business ethics, he probably actually hoped to have the Agency kill selected competition.

Fujikawa had received a private visit from Gomez, whose job was to scout and do a "final interview" with all the potential investors. During their meeting, Max brought up the capitalization requirements for the new off-shore venture. Gomez, in a prior discussion with Terry, had pointed out that there would be a financial price to pay for what he called the "privilege" of working with the Agency. Johnson had moderated Gomez's language to more business-like terms of "placing value on the stock." At the Fujikawa-Gomez meeting, the Gomiya executive was informed that 10 percent of the company would cost $250,000. Johnson told Fujikawa to view this as "good faith" money from the Japanese side. The Hungarians, after all, were capitalizing their stock with their already operational facilities in Mexico along with their business licenses. As January came to a close, Terry and Johnson were ecstatic about how quickly the venture was coming together.

There was one unexpected development, however, one that would eventually cause Terry legal grief. Fujikawa, like many Japanese managers, was simply a company man, a "salary man" as they call it in Japan. He saw this "new venture" as a golden opportunity to go into business for himself, something very few Japanese even dare to think about. He informed Terry of his plans to "fruck company big time" and secretly "collateralize" his new company, "Okami, LTD" with Gomiya's corporate funds. From this plan, he said, he would eventually end up owning Okami himself.

When Terry pressed him for the details of the scheme he responded, "do not want to discuss on phone. We can talk on trip to Japan."

This was reflected in Terry's letter to Johnson on January, 21st, when one paragraph of it read: "A new twist to the program, though, is that Mr. Fujikawa of Gomiya has indicated he may like to use Gomiya's name initially but eventually do the Japanese procurement side *on his own*. I informed him of the necessity of forming a new corporation if that's the case and also of his being able to "carry his own weight" in the new company. Anyway, I'm going to Japan next month with him and he and I will discuss it in great detail, especially the need to have access to the Chinese market."

Fujikawa later privately told Terry that he had a plan to "temporarily divert" the needed $250,000 from Gomiya's receivables in the U.S. division, and then cover the short fall through a "bad debt write-off procedure" with the parent company out of Japan. If all went as planned, he said, he would be tricking the "fat" part of Gomiya's international trading company to cover his "skinny" venture with the Agency.

He closed the conversation by saying, "It is time I start acting like you '*gaijins*', and take care of Frank first. I work for company many, many years and they do not appreciate my effort and sacrifice."

Terry was beginning to feel there might be some hope for America after all, and eventually the Japanese onslaught into our market place might be stemmed. It sounded like American capitalistic selfishness was starting to undermine and corrupt the Japanese value system. If Fujikawa was typical of Japanese managers after extended tours of duty in the U.S., eventually the Japanese firms would have the same problems as American ones, namely constant management turn-over. Little did Terry realize that Fujikawa was only hedging his bet with his crafty and complex plan, and that eventually Terry's firm, Applied Technologies, Inc. would pay a heavy price for his Japanese colleague's capitalistic endeavors.

But capitalistic endeavors of his own were on Terry's mind on February 19th, and it was an upbeat day at Applied Technologies. New machine-tool business was pouring in and Terry was preparing for a quick trip to Japan to close a large sale to a firm in Texas. He would be traveling with Gomiya management and visiting Gomiya's headquarters in Osaka. This would solidify his relationship with his potential new partner, since Fujikawa was going along. During twenty-four hours in a jumbo jet, a lot of CIA business could be discussed.

Wednesday, February 19th, 1986, may have been a red letter day for Terry, but it turned out to be the last day of Barry Seal's life. His blood, along with pieces of flesh and bone, were splattered all over the interior of his car. For some unknown reason, Seal had tried to contact Terry by phone at his home in Maumelle shortly before his death. This still haunts him. Perhaps Seal was reaching out for help only hours before his "termination."

The Baton Rouge police report, in cold official language, described what happened to him that day:

"Autopsy determined the cause of Seal's death to be multiple gunshot wounds fired by an automatic weapon," the crime report said. "Three rounds entered Seal's upper torso and four entered the left head. Some 15 rounds were recovered at the murder scene. One round traveled from inside the car through the roof. A portable (metal) sign approximately 120 feet away was hit by three projectiles, two of which exited the rear of the sign."

Seal's two assassins had ambushed him outside a Salvation Army Halfway House to which Seal had been committed by U.S. District Court Judge Frank Palozola, who had sentenced Seal December 20, 1985, shortly after returning from Panama with Terry. This nighttime confinement, ordered by Palozola, had been viewed by Seal as a double cross by the government. By now, the Internal Revenue Service had slapped Seal with an incredible $29 million jeopardy tax assessment, and stripped him of most of his property, including his airplanes. This assessment was based on his voluntary testimony to The Presidential Commission on Organized Crime, a year before his death, about

profits he said he made moving drugs for the Cartel while working undercover for the U.S. Government. He testified as an expert witness to demonstrate how deeply he had penetrated the Cartel, and on the level of sophistication of the modern-day drug trafficker which included the use of Defense
Department navigation and communication equipment designed for use in
nuclear war.[1]

His attorneys had worked out a plea agreement. The government guaranteed Seal that he would serve no more time in Louisiana than he had received
for his conviction in Florida. Because of his cooperation with the DEA, the
judge in Florida had resentenced Seal to the short time he had already served,
a matter of days. This meant, Seal thought, that he would walk out of the
Baton Rouge courtroom a free man. But Polozola had other ideas. Seal and his
attorneys were shocked when the judge ordered him to spend the next six months
reporting to the halfway house and to remain there from 6PM to 6AM each
day.

The judge also told Seal he could not leave Louisiana, even to work for a
government agency, without the court's approval. "I don't care if it is the Drug
Enforcement Administration. I don't care if it is the CIA, I don't care if it is
the State Department, I don't care it if is the U.S. Attorney, I don't care who it
is, you don't go any place, any place, without getting my written approval in
advance," Polozola told him.

Seal's attorney, Lewis Unglesby, told Polozola his ruling was tantamount to
a death sentence. Now the Medellin Cartel would know exactly where, and
when, to find Seal. And it did. A month later, outside the halfway house on
Airport Road, Seal died.

When Seal pulled up in his car to check in for the night, the two Colombian
hitmen sent by the Cartel, with MAC-10 and Uzi submachine guns equipped
with silencers, were waiting near a clothing donation bin. One of the assassins
fired into Seal's Cadillac at point-blank range. Seal's skin was festooned from
the car's ceiling.

Seal was buried three days later. He had written his own epitaph in the
family Bible which was read at his funeral: "A rebel adventurer the likes of
whom, in previous days, made America great."

Terry was not informed of the death until weeks later, and the government
did not allow federal agents to attend his funeral.

Seal had been an asset, but assets can become liabilities. To an accountant,
a liability is a red number on a spread sheet. To George Bush and the top
echelons of the CIA, Barry Seal had become a lot more than a red number.
They couldn't just offset this liability. This one had to be erased. Seal knew too
much. He had already told Terry about his plans for "blackmail." His expertise in handling handlers had not gone unobserved by his handlers, the "GS
pukes" as he called them. He perhaps had underestimated his handlers and
had come to feel invincible.

"What you know" can be power, Seal had said to Terry. But, unfortunately,
that same knowledge can also turn you into a liability. Seal knew what had
happened to other people who screwed the Agency. Somehow, he never thought
it would happen to him.

Whatever the case, Terry would now be going to Mexico alone.

Reed left for Japan the morning of the 24th of February at 8 AM without
knowing of Seal's assassination in Baton Rouge. Janis received a phone call an

hour later from Aki Sawahata, who said he urgently needed to reach her husband.

"It is very important I talk to Terry-san," he said. "I have bad news for him."

Janis said she would try to intercept Terry in Seattle if that's what Aki wanted.

"No, that will not be necessary. I do not wish to spoil his trip to Japan. Bad news can wait, so please do not tell I called. Please tell him to call me through Bruce after he returns."

Terry returned on March 7th to learn of Sawahata's call. He called OSI's office and asked Bruce if he knew what the bad news was that Sawahata had referred to in his conversation with Janis. Bruce asked him to report immediately to the office, where Terry received the shocking information.

"What do you mean, Barry's dead? He didn't crash did he?

"No. He was shot to death in Baton Rouge."

As Terry stood there and absorbed what he had been told, his emotions ran the gamut. After learning Seal had been killed nearly three weeks previously, there was no action he could take now. He couldn't even truly grieve. The funeral was over.

It came to him that he had now lost two friends, Emile Camp and Barry. Death in this "war" had now touched him more closely that it had during the Vietnam War. Arkansas was a dangerous place, he began to realize.

Bruce informed him that, because of Seal's death and other "new developments" that he could not explain, the OSI office would be soon closing. Sawahata, he said, was out of the country and unavailable.

Terry had had a premonition about Seal since the flight to Panama. Barry had been acting erratically during the trip and he had felt sure that Seal was dealing with something way beyond his control. The whole idea of blackmailing political groups, presidents and governors frightened Terry. From what he had learned through Seal about knowledge being power, he was beginning to suspect that same knowledge could be lethal.

"Bruce, tell me all you know about the killing. This is extremely important to me. I've GOT to know what happened. I'm getting involved up to my eyeballs with the Agency and my family's a part of this, too. I can't risk their lives. Is there an Agency investigation?"

Bruce told him that the assassins had already been arrested in Louisiana and as far as the Agency knew it was just as the newspapers were saying, Seal had been murdered by the Medellin Cartel to keep him from testifying against them. But the Agency was conducting its own investigation.

Seal's connection to the Cartel was news to Terry, who had been compartmentalized from this aspect of the operation. Terry could barely believe what he was hearing while being briefed by Bruce about the "other side" of Barry Seal's work for the CIA and all of Seal's legal problems. He was also unaware of the television special, "Uncle Sam Wants You," which Seal had orchestrated to prove that he really was working for the DEA and not a drug trafficker.

Terry recalled the conversation on the trip from Panama when Barry had mentioned only that he had received information from people "I personally know" within the Cartel. There had been no further mention of that and Terry presumed that Seal would have told him more if he had a need to know.

But, as Bruce continued, Terry was now discovering a dark side to Seal, the man who had led him into the dark world. Unlike the military, the civilian intelligence world is populated by people who wear no uniform, no rank and no name tag. They give you a name, but they can be someone else. Who else, he wondered, was he associating with now who had a hidden side?

As he and Bruce ended their conversation, Terry had many questions but Bruce had few answers. Bruce advised him to continue on his present course and continue his dialogue with the Agency concerning the Mexico venture.

For the time being, he would have to accept what he was being told and what he was reading about Seal's murder. But Terry's thoughts now were about his family. He decided to undertake his own investigation and proceed cautiously. For now, at least, he would stay on the path that he hoped would lead to Mexico.

He was worried. He had no evidence, yet he felt some powerful people in Arkansas had the most to gain from Seal's death. If anyone in Arkansas was involved in the murder, he was sure the Agency would unearth it. Bruce had told him the CIA was very upset about the loss of Seal. "He was a good agent," Bruce said. But Terry wondered about the sincerity of the CIA's investigation.

That night he took Janis and the boys to SOBs. The children loved the ragtime band, and for Terry, this was a kind of farewell. While driving home that night, he was mentally preparing his answers for the questions Janis was sure to have, once he shared "the bad news."

He didn't want to upset her unnecessarily, so he told her only part of the truth, that Barry "died in his car," leaving her to infer he was killed in an auto accident. She was shocked and upset because she, too, had wanted Seal to be part of the Mexico venture. She knew how close the two men had become and she was looking forward to meeting Seal's wife and forming a new "spook support group" like the one she had known in Oklahoma.

On March 16th, 1986, Ronald Reagan went on television to address the nation and apply pressure on Congress for aid to the Contras. The Reeds watched as Reagan displayed the undercover photos Seal had taken in Managua.

"Every American parent will be outraged to learn that top Nicaraguan government officials are deeply involved in drug trafficking. There is no crime to which the Sandinistas will not stoop. This is an outlaw regime."

There was no mention of Barry Seal.

But in Washington, the push for Contra funding was falling on deaf ears and reports were beginning to leak out about the secret resupply operation called "The Enterprise" now being run by Secord. North was informed in a memo from the field that "what you had hoped to remain quiet is now being discussed openly on the street."[2]

It was now becoming obvious that the war was only a business for Secord and his partners. Pressure was building within the inner circle of aides close to President Reagan for a *long-term* solution, not only to keep open the supply lines to the Contras, but to create a new, perhaps foreign-owned, entity that would bypass Congress altogether.

Toward the end of March, Terry had satisfied all the prerequisites of the Mexican plan. From his point of view he had done all he could do as a consultant. Whatever happened next would be in the Agency's hands.

"Any further participation on my behalf in my present capacity would be a waste of time and money," he told Johnson in a telephone conversation. "If Max Gomez is taking care of the areas you tell me he is, we can proceed no further on this, in my opinion, unless we implement the plan. There will certainly be problems we haven't thought of, but as we said in the Air Force, it's time to kick the tires and light the fires, or go to the officers club and just get drunk."

At that point, Terry considered the plan dead unless he heard to the contrary. He was busy, had closed two major factory automation projects, and was reluctant to take on any more Agency obligations.

He had to prepare for the possibility that the Mexico plan would be dropped. And something else was on his mind, too. Maumelle, where he lived, was a planned community built under a federal program by the Department of Housing and Urban Development. There was talk of it being annexed by the City of Little Rock, which most of the homeowners there were organizing to fight for fear it would drive up their taxes.

The Reeds had attended several meetings where incorporation of Maumelle was discussed. If that occurred, a new city government would be needed and Terry was toying with the idea of running for mayor. Under the HUD plan, Maumelle was to have been a self-contained community allowing the residents "to live, work and play" without having to go anywhere else. It was possible to live and play there, but work was a commuter drive away. What little industry had developed within a the self-contained industrial park was storage and receiving oriented, offering no high-skilled employment. Through Terry's Japanese contacts he had located a large Japanese machine-tool firm looking for a home in the U.S. Recruiting this firm and bringing it to Maumelle, he felt, would be a great foundation for a mayoral campaign.

All of this was on his mind the day John Cathey called him at his home office.

"We just had a meeting about the new plan. I've got great news for you. How would you like to head up this project for us?"

A shot at the "big time" was about to come true. Terry felt the next words out of his mouth would change his life drastically, and forever. And he was right.

Terry was happy and, at the same time, sad. Finally, his machine-tool business was at a point where it could stand alone and support him in style living right where he was. His firm, Applied Technologies, Inc., was now being courted by out-of-state suppliers instead of the other way around. He had even been looking for warehouse space in anticipation of becoming an inventory stocking dealer for several lines of new equipment. But, as he listened to Cathey, he envisioned his life as a foreign asset. He could actually enter the world of James Bond!

"Terry. Are you there? I need an answer," Cathey pressed.

"John, would Curtis LeMay have nuked Hanoi?" he asked Cathey. With those seven words, he had changed his life forever.

"Great. I'm going to make a call to Bob Nash. We need to have a major meeting in Arkansas and I want him to attend. We've got a lot of old ground to cover and we'll take that opportunity to 'swear you in' and discuss the fine points of the new plan."

"We? You said 'We', is somebody coming besides you?"

"Yes, but I don't want to discuss it over the phone. Go see Nash tomorrow. He'll give you details on the whereabouts of the meeting. Welcome aboard."

Terry called his wife after hanging up. "Honey, let's do lunch! I've got great news! You need to master your Spanish!"

At that moment, all thoughts of Seal had vanished from his mind. They met at a Mexican restaurant near her office where Janis expressed both excitement and concern at the thought of relocating in Mexico.

"Are you sure you know what you're doing?" she asked, appearing to need his reassurance. "We've both talked about doing this for a long time and the thought does excite me. But Terry, this is a big decision. We'll be turning our backs on a lot of serious opportunity right here in Arkansas."

"Janis I need to attend this meeting. I'll learn a lot more while I'm there. I'll talk to Nash tomorrow and find out where it is. *Besides what's the worst that can happen?*" He had bought himself some time. He too still had some doubts about "cutting the cord" to their way of life in Arkansas. He wanted to bring up the subject of Seal's murder at the meeting. The answers he received would have a big bearing on his decision. He had not been completely truthful with Janis about Barry's death and that bothered him.

The next day, at Fu Lin's, Nash outlined the details of the meeting, as he understood them. But he had more questions than answers. Terry sensed that Nash was unaware of the complete agenda.

"What's this meeting all about?" Nash asked. And he was particularly curious about what Terry had been doing since the training at Nella had shut down in August.

"Bob, I'm not being flippant. But honestly, you don't have a need to know." Nash seemed irritated and extremely nervous at the answer. Clearly, the entire Mexican plan had been put together without the knowledge, or input, of the Clinton administration in Arkansas. Maybe, Terry thought, the Agency was getting ready to show Clinton "who's in charge" as Seal had put it.

Terry now knew a lot of things that Nash didn't. He was recalling what Seal had said about Nash at the last meeting at SOBs, about Nash stealing Agency money. He was beginning to wonder just how many people were coming to this meeting— and for what purpose. Nash had imparted no information about that and was obviously in the dark himself. Nash's entire demeanor had changed. He reminded Terry of Seal on the flight back from Panama. He seemed to be reacting from uncertainty rather than knowledge.

Nash informed Terry that Cathey would pick him up at his Maumelle home late Friday afternoon and would transport him to the meeting. As they read their fortune cookies, Nash asked what Reed's said. He smiled and replied, "It says I've got travel in my future. What does your says Bob?"

"Oh nuthin'," he said glumly, tossing the slip of paper into the ashtray. As Nash went to pay the tab, Terry retrieved Nash's fortune and read it. It was the same as Reed's: "There is travel in your future." Apparently, the thought of travel didn't fit in with Nash's career plans.

As the two men departed the restaurant Terry was thinking about what Seal had said. "Yessirree, things are gonna get reeeeeal interestin' around here."

1. *Arkansas Gazette*, June 27, 1988, Page 1.
2. Robert Owen testimony, *Iran-Contra Hearings*, 100-2, at 405-06

Nothing works against the success of a conspiracy so much as the wish to make it wholly secure and certain to succeed. Such an attempt requires many men, much time and very favorable conditions. And all of these, in turn, heighten the risk of being discovered. You see, therefore, how dangerous conspiracies are!

—Francesco Guicciardi, 1528

CHAPTER 17

NEW COVENANT

The men alighted from the three waiting cars as the governor's van rolled into position and turned off its headlights. The van's front seat occupants stepped out and took up security positions.

The van's driver positioned himself in front of the vehicle, installed his earphone and spoke distinctly into his attached boom microphone to the unseen recipient of his communication. He then racked the bolt of his Uzi and said: "C-1 security to Robinson Ready Team, we're in position and on duty. How do you read?"

From a receiver still on in the van, the somewhat static-laden response returned immediately from a monotone, no-nonsense voice. "Loud and clear, C-1. Perimeter secure, 12 in place. The door is closed. Radio to me to reopen."

The governor's chief of security, Lieutenant Raymond Young of the Arkansas State Police, had already advanced to the side of the vehicle and opened the door in preparation for the passengers to disembark. The five waiting men were clearly taken aback when Governor Bill Clinton stepped from the vehicle with his aide, Bob Nash, and led the entourage into the World War II ammunition storage bunker that would serve as the meeting place.

In a low tone, Cathey turned to Terry and said: "Shit! I was afraid he'd show up. That'll certainly upset our agenda. I'm glad Johnson is here. He'll be able to handle him."

The waiting group of five had expected Nash, but not his boss, Arkansas' Commander-in-Chief, Bill Clinton. By his mere appearance, Clinton was risking exposure of his involvement in unauthorized covert operations. But he seemed desperate.

The meeting had been called at Camp Robinson, an Army facility outside Little Rock, to get some problems ironed out. In addition to the governor and his aide, the "guest list" included Max Gomez (Felix Rodriguez), John Cathey (Oliver North), resident CIA agent Akihide Sawahata, Agency subcontractor Terry Reed—and the man in charge, the one who would call the shots. He called himself Robert Johnson.

Johnson had been sent from Washington to chair this very delicate operational briefing that would hopefully extricate the Agency from its entanglement in what was becoming a messy situation in Arkansas.

A lot of loose ends were yet to be tied up.

It was a rendezvous that would change the complexion of the secret American policy in Central America and would outline the impending "Operation Screw Worm" in Mexico.

The oscillating sound signaled that the hand-held electronic metal detector had been activated as it passed over Gomez' left, upper torso. Young, who was performing the weapons search of each individual entering the earthen and concrete bunker, stepped back to receive what was obviously a concealed weapon. Reluctantly, Gomez produced a customized black polymer housed, nickel-plated slide, Glock 9MM pistol.

Without breaking his glaring, eye-to-eye contact with Young, and without blinking or looking at the weapon, Gomez deftly and, as if in one rehearsed motion, removed the magazine, racked the slide to the rear position ejecting a live round to the ground, and surrendered the weapon....grip first.

"Take good care of this," he snarled. "This is a special gun. It was a gift from the Presidente of El Salvador and I feel naked without it."

The piercing stare of Gomez' eyes forced Young to stutter: "Oh, yes, yes sir. Ya' can trust me. It's only a formality anyway. It'll be right here for ya' when ya' leave."

Cathey and the undercover resident CIA agent, Akihide Sawahata, voluntarily surrendered their government-issue .357 magnum revolvers without the pompous ceremony that had preceded them.

On that March night in 1986, seven men entered the earthen and concrete ammunition storage bunker at Camp Robinson while Young stood outside on guard. The bunker, dimly lit by a series of one-bulb fixtures suspended near the ceiling, emitted a musty and damp odor. The principals sat down around the gray, government-issue metal tables and chairs while Cathey began the briefing.

"Governor Clinton," he said switching to his toastmaster tone, "I'm glad you could attend tonight's meeting with us. We're both surprised and honored. Bobby (Nash) didn't inform us you would be attending...However, let's get down to it. I know you've previously met some of the people here, but, for everyone's convenience, I'll just go around the table."

Terry could tell by the hypocritical change in Cathey's behavior how Nash and Clinton were viewed as outsiders and the formal tone of voice had been solely for their benefit.

Nash, Cathey noted, was Clinton's top economic aide and the state's liaison officer with the secret intelligence operations "Centaur Rose" and "Jade Bridge" that had been carried out, undetected, at the Mena Airport in Western Arkansas.

Next came Gomez, whom he described as the Agency's man to be in charge of planned operations in Mexico.

Sawahata, who had been the Agency's resident field agent in Arkansas for operations at Mena, would now serve as the transition officer until things in Mexico were fully operational.

Terry Reed was introduced as the man who had worked in both Mena operations and was now being put in charge of setting up a proprietary operation in Mexico. Terry viewed this meeting as his initiation into the inner circle. But this impromptu appearance by Governor Clinton, however, would expose Terry to yet more things that he had no "need to know." It would also confirm his suspicions that operations in Arkansas were being run with Clinton's full knowledge.

Cathey described himself as CIA operations officer for "Rose" and "Bridge" who was now "transitioning over" to the job of operations officer for Mexico.

"Gentlemen," Cathey said, "this meeting is classified Top-Secret. The items discussed here should be relayed to no one who does not have an operational need to know. I repeat Top-Secret. There are to be no notes taken."

Then, Johnson rose to speak. He was the only person attending the meeting that Terry did not recognize. Up until now, he had only been a voice on the telephone. He was taken aback with how young the bespectacled, cherubic-looking man appeared. From the sound of his voice, Terry had expected an older man. His boyish and overly-serious look reminded Terry of fast-track junior officers he had seen in his Air Force days. But his aloof, yuppie demeanor made Terry think of him as akin to the "bond daddies" he associated with in Little Rock and as someone who would be only a message-carrier back to men with the real power in Washington. Even his impending introduction did not convince Terry he was truly the man entrusted with decision-making authority for this sensitive project.

Johnson, Cathey said, was the personal representative of CIA Director William Casey and had been sent to chair the meeting. Casey was too important to show his face, Terry assumed. But he felt honored, and yet surprised, to find he'd been dealing with someone so closely connected to the Director of Central Intelligence, the top of the intelligence pyramid.

"Thank you," Johnson said. "As Mr. Cathey mentioned, I am the emissary of Mr. Casey, who for obvious security reasons could not attend. We are at a major junction of our Central American support program. And I am here to tie up a few loose ends. As you are all aware, the severity of the charges that could be brought against us if this operation becomes public...well, I don't need to remind you of what Benjamin Franklin said as he and our founding fathers framed the Declaration of Independence..."

Cathey interrupted. "Yeah, but hanging is a much more humane way of doing things than what Congress will put us through if any of this leaks out." This marked the only time during the briefing that laughter was heard.

"This is true," Johnson replied. And therefore Governor Clinton I'm going to find it necessary to divide this meeting into groups so that we don't unnecessarily expose classified data to those who don't have an absolute need to know. We can first discuss any old business that concerns either "Centaur Rose" or "Jade Bridge", and I think that you will agree that afterwards you and Mr. Nash will have to excuse yourselves..."

Clinton was visibly indignant, giving the angry appearance of someone not accustomed to being treated in such a condescending manner.

"It seems someone in Washington has made decisions without much consulting with either myself or my aide here, Mr. Nash. And I'd like to express my concern about the possible exposure my state has as you guys skedaddle out of here to Mexico. I feel somewhat naked and *compromised*. You're right, there are definitely some loose ends!"

Based upon his comments about Mexico, Clinton already knew of the Agency's plans to withdraw from Arkansas. And he was not happy about being left out of the decision-making loop.

Nash interjected. "Sir, Governor Clinton's concerns are that there may be some loose ends cropping up from the Mena operation in general. As you know, we have had our Arkansas State Police intelligence division riding herd on the project. And that has been no simple task. Even with some of our ASP officers undercover over there, we couldn't have gained any real inside knowledge had

it not been for Mr. Reed's ability to report it directly to me. This thing about
Barry Seal getting Governor Clinton's brother involved is what's got us all upset. I mean, as we speak, there's an investigation going on that could spill over
onto some very influential people here in Arkansas, and people very close to
the governor personally..."

Johnson looked like he was getting irritated. Clinton had not been scheduled to be there and his original agenda now was being discarded.

"Hold on!" Johnson shot back. "Calm down! Mr. Casey is fully in charge
here. Don't you old boys get it. Just tell me *what* has to be taken care of, or *who*
needs to be taken care of, and I'll fix it for you!"

Johnson boasted to the group that Attorney General Edwin Meese, by arranging the appointment of J. Michael Fitzhugh as U.S. Attorney in Western
Arkansas, had effectively stonewalled the ongoing money laundering investigations in Mena where the Contra training operations had been centered. It was
his impression, Johnson said, that everything was now "kosher" and the "containment" was still in place. Operations "Rose" and "Bridge" had not been
exposed because federal law-enforcement agencies had been effectively neutralized. But Johnson said he was now concerned that the "drug" investigation
there might expand beyond his control and unmask the residue of black operations.

Now the meeting was starting to turn into a shouting match, Terry quietly
observed that Clinton appeared on the verge of losing his well-rehearsed, states-
man-like demeanor. Stopping investigations around Mena had helped the CIA
and its bosses in Washington, but it had not solved any of the governor's local
political problems. And these same problems were threatening to unveil the
Mena operations.

It was the spring of 1986, just over a month after Barry Seal's assassination
in Louisiana. Clinton was facing a very tough and dirty reelection campaign.
His Republican opponent was certain to be ex-Governor Frank White, the only
man who had ever defeated Clinton. The newspapers were filled with stories
about Clinton's brother, who had been convicted and served time from federal
drug trafficking charges, giving White the dirt he needed to launch a serious
and damaging political attack.

Roger Clinton had "rolled over" and turned informant, enabling the Feds to
begin an investigation of investment banker Dan Lasater, a close personal friend
and campaign contributor of Clinton's. This investigation, it was clear, could
spill over into Lasater's firm possibly exposing CIA money-laundering and other
possible illegal activities. [1]

The investigation of Clinton's brother had been carried out largely by dis-
loyal state police officials who were backing White, and without Clinton's knowledge, when the inquiry was first initiated. Terry wondered whether a "coup"
was building? Clinton was clearly in big political trouble and his demeanor
now was not the cool and composed man people saw on television. Perhaps the
CIA and the Reagan administration wanted another "presidente," a Republican one, in its banana republic?

Rumors were also running wild that the bond underwriting business, in which
Lasater was a major figure, had been used to launder drug money. In addition,
candidate White had another big issue to run with. He would charge later that
Clinton was directing choice state legal work as bond counsel to the prestigious
Rose Law firm, where his wife, Hillary, was a senior partner. And Clinton had

to be fearful that exposure of the Mena operations would be the death blow to his reelection hopes. And, if that weren't enough ammunition, the governor was also facing a possible state budgetary shortfall of more than $200 million.

By his comments, the governor's political problems and his potential exposure were clearly on his mind. Clinton showed his contempt for the young man from Washington as he lost his composure, jumped to his feet and shouted: "Getting my brother arrested and bringing down the Arkansas bond business in the process isn't my idea of kosher! You gents live a long way from here. Your meddling in our affairs here is gonna carry long-term exposure for me! I mean us. And what are we supposed to do, just pretend nothing happened?" He was angry.

"Exactly, pretend nothing's happened," Johnson snapped back. "It's just like the commercial, you're in good hands with Allstate. Only in this case, it's the CIA." Johnson paused, took a deep breath, and continued. "Mr. Clinton, Bill, if you will, some of those loose ends you refer to here were definitely brought on by your own people, don't you agree? I mean your brother didn't have to start shoving Mr. Seal's drugs up his nose and your friend, Lasater, has been flaunting his new wealth as if he's trying to bring you down. We're having to control the SEC and the IRS just to keep him afloat.

"Our deal with you was to help 'reconstruct the South,'" Johnson sniped, using a term Southerners hate, since it reminds them of the post-Civil War Yankee dominance of the South. "We didn't plan on Arkansas becoming more difficult to deal with than most *banana republics*. This has turned out to be almost comical."

"Bobby! Don't sit here on your black ass and take this Yankee shit!" Clinton yelled at Nash in an appeal for support. "Tell him about Seal bribing those federal agents!" It was getting to resemble a verbal tennis match as volleys were being lobbed, each one with more intensity. From the comment about Seal, Terry concluded that Clinton did in fact have his own intelligence network, too.

"Why, Mr. Clinton, with racial slurs like that, the federal government could terminate educational busing aid here," Johnson wryly shot back. "I thought Arkansas was an equal opportunity employer!"

Nash touched the governor's arm, coaxing him back into his chair.

Johnson continued, "The deal we made was to launder our money through your bond business. What we didn't plan on was you and your token nigger here to start taking yourselves seriously and purposely shrinking our laundry."

"What do you mean by shrinking the laundry?!" Clinton asked still shouting. By now, Clinton's face was flushed with anger.

To the CIA, Arkansas had to be a money-launderers' heaven. To understand why, one must realize that intelligence agencies have the same problem as drug traffickers. To launder cash, a trafficker must either find a bank willing to break the law by not filing the documentation required for cash deposits or go offshore, where reporting requirements are less strict. Like traffickers, once offshore, the CIA must use wire transfers to get their money into the U.S., but at great risk of detection.

The trafficker, having broken the law to make his money, has no legal recourse if his banker double-crossed him. In other words, it's an insecure investment, which pays low interest, if any.

Arkansas offered the CIA something money launderers are rarely able to achieve, a secure business environment containing a banking industry where vast amounts of money move around unnoticed as part of the normal course of business. Through its substantial bond underwriting activities, the state had a huge cash flow that could allow dirty and clean money to co-mingle without detection. All they were lacking was the "dirty banker" to cooperate with them by ignoring the federal banking laws.

And that they found within the Clinton administration. This "banker" was none other than the Arkansas Development and Finance Authority, or ADFA, which was a creation of, and directly under the control of, the governor's office.* Its official mandate was to loan money to businesses either already in or coming to Arkansas in order to develop an industrial base for new jobs that Clinton had made the centerpiece of his administration. ADFA, was in effect, a bank making preferred loans.

But, from what Terry had learned from Seal and Sawahata, that was not all ADFA was doing. ADFA, in effect a state investment bank, was being "capitalized" by large cash transfusions that the Agency was taking great pains to hide.

"No paper, no trail," seemed to be the dominate doctrine of the Agency's activities since, by design, cash dropped from an airplane in a duffel bag is not the standard way of transferring money.

ADFA was designed to compete for the profits generated by the bond issues necessary to industrialize Arkansas. The old Arkansas Industrial Development Commission that Clinton had inherited had no money of its own and was forced to send prospective clients seeking industrial development loans to the established, privately-run investment banking industry in Little Rock. The state could be very selective in its referral business, however, and those who received the state's business stood to profit handsomely.

This insider referral business was alive and well when Terry moved to Arkansas and he saw Seth Ward's son-in-law, Finis Shellnut, jockey for a position to reap these profits by going to work for Lasater, who was getting the lion's share of the secret sweetheart deals.

Before ADFA's creation, the state sent preferred business directly to investment banking firms like Lasater's. All that was needed for money-laundering was the firm's silence and a source of cash, which, in this case, the CIA provided. The heads of these firms were a coterie of wealthy and well-connected people who got even richer by doing what comes natural in Arkansas, "The Natural State" as it's called.....dealing incestuously under the table.

Arkansas desperately needed new businesses—and so did the CIA. It had plenty of black money, but that alone was not enough. "You can't kill an enemy by lobbing dollars at him" was the phrase Cathey had used with Terry to explain the CIA's dilemma of having the monetary resources to fund the Contras,

---

* ADFA had been the center of major political controversy by that time. Some members of the Arkansas financial community charged that ADFA had been a "money cow" for years for Clinton and his political supporters. State records showed that ADFA private activity bonds totaled more than $719,000,000 between 1984 through 1991, while creating only 2,700 new, mostly marginal, jobs paying an average wage of only $15,000. ADFA, at the same time, had proved a bonanza for investment banker, Jackson T. Stephens. As head of Arkansas' largest investment banking firm, Stephens & Co. made at least $3 to $5 million in bond underwriting fees between 1985 and 1991. Stephens helped underwrite 60 state bond issues worth $18.82 billion. In addition, more than $100,000 was paid by ADFA in legal fees to the Rose Law firm.[2]

but no legal way to deliver it directly. The Agency was barred by Congress from converting the cash into weapons and training the Contras needed on the battlefield, at least not through traditional Department of Defense suppliers.

Under Director William Casey's plan, the CIA needed other companies that would be a source of secretly-produced weapons that would find their way into the hands of the Contras. These *selected* businesses needed payment to perform these services for the CIA, and that cash came to them conveniently in a legal and undetectable manner, through ADFA, in the form of industrial development loans backed by tax-free development bonds. The CIA should have been showing a profit through accrued interest on their secured investments. But a problem had arisen. As Johnson had said, the "laundry" was shrinking.

And Johnson was not happy about that as evidenced by the way he was firing back at Clinton. It was apparent that Johnson knew Clinton and his people had not abided by his agreement with the Agency.

"Our deal was for you to have 10 per cent of the profits, not 10 per cent of the gross," Johnson sternly admonished Clinton.

"This has turned into a feeding frenzy by your good ole boy sharks, and you've had a hand in it, too, Mr. Clinton. Just ask your Mr. Nash to produce a business card. I'll bet it reads Arkansas Development and Finance Authority. We know what's been going on. Our people are professionals, they're not stupid. They didn't fall off the turnip truck yesterday, as you guys say. This ADFA of yours is double-dipping. Our deal with you was to launder our money. You get 10 per cent after costs and after post-tax profits. No one agreed for you to start loaning our money out to your friends through your ADFA so that they could buy machinery to build our guns. That wasn't the deal. Mr. Sawahata tells me that one of ADFA's first customers was some parking meter company that got several million in...how shall we say it...in preferred loans.

"Dammit, *we* bought a whole gun company, lock, stock and barrel and shipped the whole thing down here for you. And Mr. Reed even helped set it up. You people go and screw us by setting up some subcontractors that weren't even authorized by us. Shit, people who didn't even have security clearances. That's why we're pulling the operation out of Arkansas. It's become a liability for us. *We don't need live liabilities.*"

Terry was fighting to control his open astonishment at what he was hearing. He didn't understand all the subtleties of this black financial maze constructed by the CIA and implemented through the State of Arkansas. But Bill Clinton, it appeared, was finding out the hard way that accounting procedures the Agency utilized were the envy of the business world. This meeting had turned into a bean counters' seminar with discussions of post-tax profits seemingly running into the millions. But Terry didn't need to be an accountant to grasp the significance of what was occurring. It sounded to him like the Clinton administration had been caught with its hand in the till and Clinton personally was learning there were no free rides with the CIA.

Johnson's worry was centered on security. He had referred to the CIA's buying and relocating to Arkansas an existing arms manufacturing firm, Iver Johnson's Arms, Inc., which had been based in New Jersey. But what the Agency had hoped would be a very secret operation to build weapons for the Contras had now been gobbled up as part of Clinton's industrial plan, and had now become an open secret among Clinton cronies.

These insiders, learning through a security leak what Iver Johnson's Arms,

Inc. was really doing, had demanded a piece of the action for themselves and had blackmailed their way into this black operation. POM, a parking meter manufacturer in Russellville, Arkansas, was an example of a company that had leveraged its way into the underground arms manufacturing loop. Terry concluded the people running these companies must be the "good ol' boy sharks" that Johnson had referred to.

The weapons clique was composed of five companies situated around Arkansas, at least two of which had received state-backed loans for the machinery necessary to perform the CIA work. This total lack of security and intelligence professionalism was apparently the reason the CIA was preparing to extricate itself from Arkansas and set up operations in Mexico.

The primary "loose end" that Johnson could not tie up was the investigation of Roger Clinton and his friends brought on by his drug problem. His arrest had brought widespread attention to powerful people in Arkansas who were involved in the CIA's operations. In addition, close Clinton political allies, including a state senator, had become targets of the drug investigation.

Terry mused as he absorbed what he was hearing. He realized for the first time the impact of what he believed was Barry Seal's secret plan to expose and shut down the Arkansas operation. Terry reflected how three months earlier Seal had confided to him his disgust with the people he was working with in Arkansas and revealed the secret plan to bring these operations in Arkansas to an end. Had the CIA known about Seal's plan, and helped implement it to dump Clinton and vacate Arkansas?

Terry wondered.

Or, was the Bush family and the Republican Party playing games with Clinton and his friends? True banana republic intrigue. The place was primitive, but the politics were not.

Clinton had paused for a moment to ponder Johnson's words. "What do ya' mean, live liabilities?" he demanded.

"There's no such thing as a dead liability. It's an oxymoron, get it? Oh, or didn't you Rhodes Scholars study things like that?" Johnson snapped.

"What! Are you threatenin' us? Because if ya' are..."

Johnson stared down at the table, again took a deep breath, and paused. It appeared he wanted to elevate the tone of the disintegrating exchange.

"Calm down and listen," Johnson said. "We are all in this together. We all have our personal agendas...but let's not forget, both the Vice President and Mr. Casey want this operation to be a success. We need to get these assets and resources in place and get them self-sustaining and prospering on their own while we have the chance. This is a golden opportunity. The timing is right. We have communists taking over a country in this hemisphere. We must all pull together and play as a team. This is no time for lone wolves. Mr. Seal is an example of what happens to lone wolves. They just don't survive in the modern world of intelligence.

"I'm not here to threaten you. But there have been mistakes. The Mena operation survived undetected and unexposed only because Mr. Seal carried with him a falsely created, high-level profile of a drugrunner. All the cops in the country were trying to investigate a drug operation. That put the police in a position where we could control them. We fed them what we wanted to feed them, when we wanted to feed them; it was our restaurant and our menu. Seal was himself a diversion. It was perfect until your brother started free-enterprising and now we have to shut it down. It's as simple as that. Mr. Seal was a good agent and it's a shame he's dead. But, hopefully, our new operation will build on Seal's success in sustaining our Contra support effort while goddamn Congress dilly dallies around as the Russians take over Nicaragua."

Clinton just glared back. "That was a good sermon, but what can you specifically do to end this investigation concerning my brother and the bond business?"

"Your brother needed to go to jail," Johnson said staring at the governor. "As governor you should intervene and make things as painless as possible now. As far as the money investigation goes, Mr. Meese is intervening right now. There will be no money investigation. The U.S. attorney's office (in Little Rock) is 'getting religion' as we speak.*

"There may be nothing we can do about your friend Lasater's drug problem. I suggest that he and everyone else caught with their pants down take the bad along with the good and do a little time—as your brother has. It's a shame. But bartenders shouldn't drink. If some of our people are going to be in the drug business as a cover, they should do as Mrs. Reagan says and 'just say no'."

Johnson had applied the balm and now the massage began. "Bill, you are Mr. Casey's fair-haired boy. But you do have competition for the job you seek. We would never put all our eggs in one basket. You and your state have been our greatest asset. The beauty of this, as you know, is that you're a Democrat, and with our ability to influence both parties, this country can get beyond partisan gridlock. Mr. Casey wanted me to pass on to you that unless you fuck up and do something stupid, you're No. 1 on the short list for a shot at the job you've always wanted.

"That's pretty heady stuff, Bill. So why don't you help us keep a lid on this and we'll all be promoted together. You and guys like us *are* the fathers of the new government. Hell, we're the new covenant."

Clinton, having been stroked, seemed satisfied that the cover-up was expanding to, at least, protect the bond business. Like Lyndon Johnson, Clinton had learned that politics is the "art of the possible." He had not gotten everything he wanted, but he was at least walking away whole.

It appeared to Terry that Johnson had won the debate. Clinton and his administration had no grounds to complain about the Agency terminating its operation. Too many errors had been made. The young governor seemed to recognize he had lost, for now, and didn't want to continue the argument in front of the others.

"Bobby, I guess you and I should excuse ourselves," Clinton said while turning to his aide. "These gentlemen have other pressing business and besides, we don't have a need to know...nor do I think we want to know."

---

*   And indeed, the federal prosecutor had become a believer. With much fanfare, U.S. Attorney George Proctor announced the following October the indictments of Lasater and others close to Clinton on minor drug charges involving recreational use. Because of later guilty pleas no politically-embarrassing trials were necessary. No other charges were brought and Proctor shut down the investigation, saying there was no evidence of illicit activities being linked with the bond business, which had been widely rumored in the media for months. The "containment" continued and the investigation was limited to the casual and "social use" of narcotics, with Proctor proclaiming: "The case illustrates that the law not only prohibits the selling of cocaine for profit, but it also prohibits one person giving cocaine to another." And that was that.[2]

When Clinton exited the bunker, Terry took a moment to absorb what had happened. Clinton had been treated badly in front of the others. Terry had certainly underestimated Johnson, the man he had sized up initially as a mere errand boy for Casey. His youthful demeanor had been misleading. He was clearly a skilled hatchet man. But Terry felt somewhat embarrassed for the governor. Johnson had effectively neutralized the governor of Arkansas' argument by simply changing the subject, and what a subject it was!

Was he hearing that the presidency is offered to a few groomed men, men groomed by the CIA?

Who was this guy, "Johnson," who so easily manipulated Bill Clinton? He made Bill Clinton, on his own turf, appear to be under the control of an invisible force. Up until now, Terry had known Johnson only as the lawyer for Southern Air Transport. He was obviously a lot more than that. He was beginning to take on the mannerisms of a Viceroy and Clinton was certainly showing his obedience to authority and paying the price for fealty. Clinton was *compromised*.

Who was this Johnson, really? It would be eight more years before Terry would finally find out his true identity and how highly connected he was.

When Clinton and Nash had gone, the mood changed dramatically. A mood of familiarity returned and only the brotherhood remained. Gomez was the first to speak. The man who was to be in charge of the new operation in Mexico was indignant.

"Presidente Clinton," he said with disgust in a thick Hispanic accent. "Why is it I have more respect for the enemy I've slain on the battlefield than I have for that yuppie kid governor. I've seen everything now. Republicans conspiring with Democrats. Isn't that similar to capitalists trusting Marxists?"

Johnson restrained himself as if wanting to chastise Gomez for not showing proper respect for Clinton in front of the others. "You need to realign your thinking about black and white, good and bad, us and them. Under our new plan we all get along for the advancement of the common goal."

Gomez spit contemptuously on the concrete floor. "Sounds like Mao Tse-tung or Lenin philosophy to me!"

Cathey stepped in. "Let me apologize for Max and the rest of us cold warriors here. We're a product of our training and old hatreds die slowly, if ever. But what we must all come to understand is that communism is our common enemy and not our dislike for one another. We are all hand-chosen by the highest office in the land to be entrusted with this mission. We should all feel honored to be here. Our objective is two-fold. One, to rid this earth of the evil communist element we've been trained to seek out and destroy. The other is to set in place a true self-sustaining and modern black operations division worldwide, as Mr. Casey has envisioned..."

Johnson interrupted. This was no time for a marathon speech, something Cathey appeared on the verge of making. "That, John, should be my lead in for the briefing on the Mexico operation. I remind you gentlemen, this is a top-secret discussion. Centaur Rose and Jade Bridge are transitioning to Mexico. The new code name is *Screw Worm*."

1. *Arkansas Democrat*, Sept. 18, 1986
2. *Washington Times*, April 10, 1992
3. *Arkansas Democrat*, Oct. 25, 1986

Memorandum

To   :   DIRECTOR, FBI (66-18090-25)   Date   1/31/91
         ATTENTION: RECORDS MANAGEMENT DIVISION
                   RECORDS SYSTEM SECTION

From :   SAC, LITTLE ROCK (66F-879)

Subject: MISSING FILES AND SERIALS

     In accordance with Bureau instructions, the Little Rock division is reporting the following serial(s) missing from the below captioned file.

     A search for this serial(s) is continuing and the Bureau will be advised when/if located.

LITTLE ROCK FILE: LR 12B-283

CAPTIONED: FRED L. HAMPTON;
                      ET AL;
                      DRUG MATTER
                      OO: LITTLE ROCK

SERIAL(S) NUMBER: 2 - FD-350 with Arkansas Democrat Newspaper
                      article dated 4/25/83 charged to SA Tom Ross
                      on 5/2/86.
                      112 - FAA Registration history for Piper Navajo
                      113 - FAA Disclaimer - Cessna
                      114 - FAA Application - Adler B. Seal
                      115 - FAA Suspense file - Jerry Harvey
                      116 - FAA Conveyance Adler B. Seal
                      117 - FAA Registration - Cessna
                      112 thru 117 charged to SA Tom Ross 4/7/86

2 - Bureau
2 - Little Rock
   1 - 66F-879
   1 - 12B-283
HEH/heh
(4)

17-1. Internal FBI memorandum obtained through Federal court discovery by Terry Reed and Robert Meloni showing key Mena files "missing." Indicates that Special Agent (SA) Tom Ross, the man who was Seal's contact, was the one covering the Agency's trail by conveniently "losing" materials.

1. PROGRAM CODE	2. CROSS FILE RELATED FILES	3. FILE NO. GJ-87-0001	4. G-DEP IDENTIFIER IC1-C1
5. BY: S/A Larry T. Carver AT: Little Rock, Arkansas	☐ ☐ ☐ ☐ ☐	6. FILE TITLE EVANS, Joe	
7. ☐ Closed ☐ Requested Action Completed ☐ Action Requested By:		8. DATE PREPARED October 28, 1986	

9. OTHER OFFICERS:
ASP Lt. Finnis DuVall

10. REPORT RE:
Interview of Brewer BELL

DETAILS:

1. On 10/23/86, Drug Enforcement Administration (DEA) Special Agent (S/A) Larry T. Carver and Arkansas State Police (ASP) Lieutenant (Lt.) Finnis DuVall interviewed Brewer BELL concerning his knowledge of activities of a rural airstrip in Scott County, Arkansas owned by Fred HAMPTON. The farm on which the airstrip is located has been the object of a DEA/ASP investigation in 1983 and 1984 as a possible smuggling field for the Barry SEAL Organization.

2. BELL stated that he never went on the property and never met HAMPTON or anyone connected to it. BELL is a former Navy pilot and said he has seen small aircraft come and go from the airstrip. BELL stated that on one occasion he saw a small airplane land on the strip, which was close to his farm. According to BELL the airplane left and he heard a helicopter leave the area of the strip. BELL stated that he never saw the helicopter.

INDEXING SECTION:

1. HAMPTON, Fred - NADDIS 1484882

11. DISTRIBUTION:	12. SIGNATURE (Agent)	13. DATE
REGION ASP (Lt. DuVall)	S/A Larry T. Carver	11/12/8_
DISTRICT	14. APPROVED (Name and Title)	15. DATE
OTHER HQS, ARI & OC	Gary G. Worden, RAC	1/12/16

DEA Form · 6
(May 1980)

DEA SENSITIVE
DRUG ENFORCEMENT ADMINISTRATION
This report is the property of the Drug Enforcement Administration.
Neither it nor its contents may be disseminated outside the agency to which loaned.
Previous edition may be used.

17-2. DEA report showing how law enforcement agents were unable to look <u>beyond</u> Seal's cover as a drug trafficker. His cover worked. Right under the noses of the police had been Contra training activity which had been conducted at the rural airstrip described above.

CHAPTER 18

WITHDRAWAL SYMPTOMS

Bill Clinton had been pacified, and subdued—for the time being at least. With this distraction behind him, Robert Johnson was anxious to get on to the new business. But there was still a lot of old business—loose ends—to be dealt with.

Akihide Sawahata wanted to make sure that Johnson grasped the significance of the overall money problems. Even though the federal prosecutors in Arkansas had "gotten religion," as Johnson had put it, and had been brought into line, the tenacity of some of the field investigators had been underestimated. They were refusing to be stonewalled. They *really* had religion and they refused to shut their eyes to what was happening.

"With Governor Clinton gone, Mr. Johnson, I would like to express concern about some loose money ends right here in Arkansas," Sawahata said. "Some unfinished business concerning 'Rose' and 'Bridge'. We have overzealous IRS-CID agent taking his job too serious. He is still pressing for indictments on money-laundering in the Mena area, and also pressing the U.S. Attorney to seek indictments against our assets at Rich Mountain Aviation and the local banker. He just won't back off!"

Sawahata was referring to Bill Duncan, an IRS investigator who had been sent to Mena after the Drug Enforcement Administration tipped the IRS about what appeared to them to be massive laundering of drug profits there. As usual in government, no one was really in charge and the right hand apparently did not know what the left hand was doing. Or did it?

Duncan did find evidence of money laundering involving officials of Rich Mountain, the fixed base operation at the Mena airport that Barry Seal had been running as a CIA front company. Try as Duncan would, however, the federal prosecutor was refusing to present the case properly to a grand jury sitting in Ft. Smith, Ark.[1]

Duncan would later say that his investigation was probably just a diversion and that what he was really doing, without realizing it at the time, was protecting the Mena operations. The CIA, by helping to place him there and feeding Duncan what they wanted him to know, could watch and oversee what he was doing and be assured that his activities would preempt any other investigations.

They apparently and mistakenly thought Duncan's behavior would be predictable. That he would confine his evidence to within the law enforcement and federal judicial system. But he didn't. Now, through frustration, he was allowing his close associates to leak information to the media about the inexplicable stonewalling he was encountering with the prosecutor. Duncan felt he and other investigators had been put in harm's way. That was a correct assumption. He had been assigned, without his knowledge, to investigate an Agency black ops program that was employing Cuban exile criminal elements who were conducting political assassination training. At the same time, the operation carried with it a high-profile drug cover that could have easily produced a shootout between law enforcement agents unknown to each other.

The worst part, Duncan now says, was being kept in the dark. "If they had told me to stop, I would have," he told one of this book's authors. "But all I heard was 'sic 'em Fido.'"

This was nothing new. It's an old Agency technique to manipulate other federal agencies without them knowing they were being manipulated. It's what they do best. This is what Johnson had meant when he said "We fed them what we wanted to feed them, when we wanted to feed them; it was our restaurant and our menu."

The American public is led to believe that this is done only outside American territory because the CIA, by law, can only conduct operations on foreign soil. But in Arkansas, the Agency was applying their usual banana republic tactics on their own citizens. But Duncan still had to be contained. He was like a fly annoyingly buzzing around an elephant's ear.

And they thought they had a strategy for this. "Does this guy have a boss?" John Cathey asked. "Go tell his boss to have him back off. Tell the boss 'national security' and all that good stuff...a high level federal matter."

Sawahata answered back. "Yes, boss' name is Paul Whitmore and his office is right here in Little Rock. Problem is we have contacted him already. He also determined to expose money laundering which he thinks is from drug proceeds."

"Jesus Christ!" Cathey said. "Just what we need. A couple of dumb-ass GS types out to get promoted. What's the field agent's name?

"Bill Duncan," Sawahata replied. "And his friend Russell Welch, an ASP (Arkansas State Police) officer are nirvana-bent on exposing all this. I'm afraid with Seal now gone, their attention will now focus on these other people and apply pressure until someone breaks."

Cathey decided it was something he would have to handle personally when he returned to Washington.

"I'll call Revell and see if they can't fix it," he said.*

Sawahata wanted to know what Cathey was planning.

"We'll toss 'em a bone," Cathey replied. "Maybe we'll have them promoted and transferred out of the field, at least the IRS guys, that is. The ASP officer? That's another story. You'd better contact Colonel Goodwin and have him sit on this guy. Maybe our FBI agent over there can help with that."

Cathey was referring to Col. Tommy Goodwin, the director of the state police. Welch was the resident state police investigator in Polk County where Mena is situated.

Whatever Cathey did back in Washington, coupled with the containment by the U.S. attorney in Ft. Smith, it worked. Duncan and Welch were testaments

---

* This is believed to have been a reference to Oliver (Buck) Revell, then an assistant director of the FBI and a person that North would later turn to in times of crises when the Iran-Contra affair began to become public knowledge. Author Terry Reed has documents showing Revell was being briefed on Mena.[2]

to that. Regardless of reams of incriminating evidence, no arrests or prosecutions ever resulted from the countless man hours spent investigating Mena.

Duncan later testified on June 21, 1991 that he had lined up 20 prospective witnesses and the U.S. Attorney called only three before the grand jury. Two of these witnesses, Duncan said, were inexplicably not allowed to furnish any evidence to the grand jury.[3]

One was a vice president of the Union Bank of Mena, who, Duncan said, had conducted a search of the bank's records and provided "a significant amount of evidence relating to the money-laundering transactions...he [the banker] also was furious that he was not allowed to provide the evidence that he wanted to the grand jury."

Duncan said that the deputy grand jury foreman subsequently told him that the jurors "were not allowed to hear" the evidence. The juror also told Duncan that the U.S. Attorney J. Michael Fitzhugh refused the Jury's request to bring Agent Duncan in to testify, telling them Duncan was in Washington "which was not the truth."

When Duncan complained about Fitzhugh's actions to his superiors, including local IRS CID (Criminal Investigation Divsion) chief Paul Whitmore, Whitmore went to Fitzhugh to check on the allegations. Fitzhugh eventually wrote Whitmore telling him not to come to his office complaining, saying that it was "unprofessional behavior."

Whitmore called the entire matter "a cover-up." No indictments were ever returned and, to this day, no one connected with the Mena operation has been charged with a crime——a testament to the CIA's long-standing efforts to pervert the justice system. And so the government-sanctioned cover-up goes on.

Welch, of the Arkansas State Police, later also provided further corroboration about the cover-up. In a sworn oral deposition given the Arkansas Attorney-General's Office on June 21, 1991, he said that two FBI agents, Floyd Hayes and Tom Ross, came to him sometime in 1987 to discuss Mena. They told him that a CIA source of their's at the Hot Springs airport had received a phone call from the CIA in Miami saying the Agency had "something going on at the Mena airport involving Southern Air Transport" and the Agency didn't want the FBI "to screw it up like (they) had the last one."[4]

The "last one" was an obvious reference to the Nella operation, giving an outsider the definite impression that the FBI was involved in the overall security program for the Agency's operations. It was, after all, an FBI Special Agent that Terry had seen Seal hand a parcel to outside the Mena airport the previous fall when Seal went to "slop the hogs."

FBI agent Ross even showed Welch a classified FBI inter-office message to prove to him officially that an ongoing CIA operation would be in jeopardy of being *compromised* if Welch continued investigating.

Welch told author John Cummings that Ross now denies ever having had this conversation or showing Welch the secret FBI telex divulging CIA activity at Mena. Author Terry Reed has obtained under court discovery the secret FBI telex Ross had in his possession when he was cautioning Welch not to *compromise* the operation. (See chapter end.)

The message dated August 18, 1987, clearly outlines the government's concern about pending media exposure of not only the airport, but refers to Barry Seal as a "CIA operative."[5]

Duncan also revealed that Ross became his shadow during the IRS investigation. "Ross...would suddenly appear on the scene," Duncan said, whenever he was about to conduct a critical interview.[6]

Sawahata shifted to money problems. "What about bribe money?" he asked. The others stared at him with confused looks on their faces.

"You mean the stuff that ended up in EM's personal account?" Cathey queried.

Johnson, by now totally confused, asked both to "cut out the code talk" and spell out to him what they were saying.

"Well, Bob, this is a little embarrassing," Cathey acknowledged. "It seems that Barry Seal, God rest his soul, had a very unique trait of being able to *compromise* damned near everyone he came into contact with. I attribute it to good intelligence training, but he had this knack of paying people 'commissions' as he liked to call them. And during his period in Arkansas, I guess he bribed...uh...paid commissions to damned near everyone over there."

Cathey noted that this normally wouldn't have been a problem since intelligence operations are built on bribing all kinds of people. "In fact, as you know, that's right out of the agent's handbook, Bribes 101."

But Seal, he said, was doing something different and quite unorthodox. He was paying bills and bribing people with dirty money. Seal wasn't laundering the money before using it for bribes and this left an embarrassing trail that Duncan was following. Sort of like the stones that led Hansel and Gretel out of the forest.

Cathey said one source of Seal's dirty money came from the DEA, part of which had been confiscated in drug raids in Florida and used to operate Rich Mountain and procure what he called "aviation services" for the Agency.

"He was using this dirty, or marked money if you will, to buy influence from high-ranking officials," Cathey said. "We don't know if Seal was just having fun or if we were setting some of our people up. But anyway his activities were putting this IRS agent, Duncan, on a very compromising and embarrassing trail."

Where does this trail lead?" Johnson asked in a slow, deliberate tone after listening with rapt attention. He seemed almost fearful of the answer.

Somberly, Cathey replied: "Oh......right to Ed Meese's personal bank account as well as to several FBI, DEA, FAA and Customs officials."

Because he uncovered this alleged bribe concerning Attorney General Meese, Duncan invoked the wrath of his IRS superiors in Washington. Duncan testified at a Congressional hearing in 1989 that the IRS wanted him to perjure himself before another Congressional committee if they asked him about his knowledge of any Meese payment.[7] Duncan resigned from the IRS in 1989 because he did not want to be part of an organization that wanted him to lie under oath.

Duncan confided to author John Cummings that a confidential source of Welch's told him that Seal bragged on several occasions about bribing Meese with sums of money running into the hundreds of thousands of dollars. Meese's identity was revealed in closed session testimony Duncan gave before the House Subcommittee on Crime in 1988.

"Goddam," Johnson snapped as he referred back to Seal. "Seal's still gonna have the last laugh in this if we're not careful. It wasn't enough for him to get the governor's brother addicted and bring down half the Arkansas elite in a drug investigation. Shit! What was wrong with this guy? He bought off the Attorney General? What the hell for?"

"We thought maybe you could answer that," Cathey said to Johnson. "But it seems Barry had a death wish. That only makes about four federal agencies, a governor, an attorney-general, at least two foreign governments, the Medellin Cartel and 50 or 60 individuals that had motive to kill him."

Terry could understand the confusion in the minds of Cathey and Johnson as he sat and listened. He had seen first hand the complexity of Seal's thought process and behavior. Seal had been through too many handlers, too many objectives and, clearly, had an agenda of his own. If these were the people investigating Seal's motives and his death, it was clear they had no simple answers. What confused Terry was why Seal would purposely bring attention to a successful covert operation? The men sitting with Terry in the bunker wanted the program to be a success. Was Barry being controlled, not just by these men, but by the Republican Party and the Bush family as well? He recalled Barry's conversation about transporting "some stuff" through Mena and into Arkansas that would "end up in the noses of some very prominent Democrats." Was it possible the Vice President of the United States would jeopardize a CIA operation just to retaliate for his own family's behavior and "dirty up some Democrats?"

Terry knew now why the Arkansas operation was being shut down. It was out of control. There had been too many cooks and the chef took the secret ingredients to his grave. There was no other way to say it: The recipe was now fucked up!

Representative Bill McCollum (R-Florida) would later write a new epitaph for Seal. Referring to the knowledge he gained during Congressional hearings on Seal's death, McCollum would say: "Barry Seal was a tough informant to handle, and he would have become even tougher. In short, the DEA had a monster on its hands."

Terry spoke for the first time. "I'm glad you brought this up, John," he said to Cathey. "This Seal killing really bothers me. People having motive is one thing, but opportunity and means are two others. I'm not buying this Colombian hitman story. I grew to know Barry quite well during Rose and Bridge and something still doesn't fit. From what I've read and been told, Seal was under some sort of house arrest when he was killed. Can you explain that for me?"

Cathey answered: "It was part of his ongoing cover. He was placed there (in a Louisiana halfway house) by a pissed off do-gooder judge who hadn't gotten the word from our guys. We were in the process of getting him out of there without blowing his cover when he was hit. You know the rest. Like the papers say...some Colombian hitmen. We guess Seal must have been trafficking on the side. He certainly had opportunity and he must have crossed someone down there. We're still checking it out."

Cathey was lying, but Terry had no reason at the time to suspect otherwise. He did not know at the time that Cathey was really Oliver North, and it was North who helped leak the information about Seal to the media, and blew Seal's cover. So Cathey could not honestly answer, fearful that Terry would see that agents are expendable under the right circumstances.

"But what about those photos on television that President Reagan was showing?" Terry asked, referring to what he had seen on TV. "Wasn't that The Fat Lady the photos were taken from?"

On March 16th, a little less than a month after Seal was murdered, Reagan went on television and revealed the secret photographs taken by Seal showing

Cartel officials helping load drugs aboard Seal's plane, a military C-123 called
The Fat Lady, which had been outfitted with cameras by the CIA. Seal was
given no credit and was never mentioned by the President despite his undercover activities conducted at great peril.

"Yes," Cathey said, responding to Terry's question about the plane. "But
you've got to keep in mind Seal had a multi-mission, if you will. His drug cover
gave him the ability to move around freely in several areas for us. It's very
unfortunate, but someone at DEA or the White House level made the decision
to use the photo, or they just plain old fucked up. I suspect that Reagan didn't
even know what he was doing that day. That guy's scary. Just wind him up, give
him some props, point him towards a teleprompter and it's action on the set.
You know what I mean. If it wasn't for Bush and Casey and guys like Johnson
here, I'd be really frightened."

In hindsight, once Terry discovered that Cathey was actually North, he realized that North had been feeding him lies about his knowledge of how the leak
was made that led to Seal's death.

Terry was surprised to note that Ronald Reagan's name had been strangely
missing from all this. Only Bush and Casey's names were being discussed in a
respectful tone. But Terry was no fan of Reagan's, and had always assumed he
was only a puppet. Maybe he was discovering who *really* ran the White
House....Bush and Casey.

Terry was still dubious about what Cathey was saying regarding Seal, and
Johnson quickly picked up on that. Now Johnson was applying the balm to
Reed. Johnson shifted quickly to the need for trust.

"Mr. Reed, if I could add," Johnson began. "I'm aware of your friendship for
Mr. Seal. He always spoke highly of you and he is a main reason you're going
to Mexico for us. He was your sponsor, as we say in the Agency. We viewed
Barry as we view you now, an asset to our activities, an asset to our common
objectives, an asset to our national agenda, an asset to our foreign policy. This
has to be a relationship built on trust, however."

Johnson apparently felt the need to stress the difference between Terry's
structured Air Force intelligence service and what he would now be doing,
outside that structured environment, as an asset in charge of a proprietary
CIA front company.

"At the CIA, we're under constant monitoring and scrutiny. We're structured and regimented. Christ, we're a government agency, understand? And
there'll be times we will have to insulate you from certain information in order
to not *compromise* ourselves." He was defining what spooks call a deniable
link, but he was also effectively diverting Terry from pressing further about
Seal.

"You were in Air Force Intelligence. As you know, the government side is just
a chicken-shit outfit full of rules and regulations. But *your* side, that's different. The side you and Barry come from. You're the operational side of the CIA
as Bill Casey and others before him envisioned, you're deniable. You can move
around unobserved and undetected. You can hold meetings like this without
20 idiots armed with machine guns guarding you. Understand?"

Johnson added that Seal had become a liability by violating the basic rule
of trust, one that controls assets. By doing so, he said cryptically, Seal had
grown outside the Agency's control by trying to go into business for himself in
Mexico, an allusion perhaps to the Agency's fear that Seal was trying to force

himself on the Mexican operation with his "small Air America operation" duplicating Southern Air Transport. To support the premise that Seal was possibly going into business for himself, Terry recalled how Seal originally had sworn Terry to secrecy about plans for weapons manufacturing in Mexico. Manufacturing had not been part of the plan Terry had originally drawn up for Johnson. Maybe Seal had learned enough about weapons manufacturing from Terry and was planning to go into production without the Agency...or with *someone else.*

"It's very unfortunate about Barry's death, and we had nothing to do with it," Johnson assured. "These problems have a way of taking care of themselves."

What did he really mean by that, Terry wondered. Had they conveniently allowed Seal to be murdered? In any case, Terry got the message. He would be trusted as long as he was not caught going his own way and screwing the Agency. It was becoming, from what he had read, like the Mafia whose rules were simple: you don't go outside the organization and freelance without prior approval of the bosses.

Maybe Barry's fate was proof of the underworld saying: You live with the Mob, you die with the Mob.

But Terry persisted with his questions. He still wanted to know why the Agency had allowed the IRS and the Arkansas State Police to question Seal under oath on December 27th, 1985, just two months before his death. Bruce, at OSI in Little Rock, had informed him of this interrogation, flabbergasted that the Agency had allowed it. "Isn't that just inviting problems to allow an agent to be scrutinized...that way?" Terry asked Johnson.

Cathey intervened. "Barry handled himself quite well with that legal orgy you're referring to. And, yes, it's unfortunate that happened. Remember the old saying in the military, there's always someone who doesn't get the word. Well, in this case, that someone is that IRS agent, Bill Duncan."

Gomez jumped into the conversation. "There's another way for people like this guy Duncan to 'get the word.'"

This upset Cathey. "Now Max, with talk like that, Terry might get the wrong idea. We're not like the Mob, Maximo. We don't kill people. So explain that last comment for the benefit of Terry and the group."

"Like we say in Cuba, the most precious gift a person can receive is a gift of the rest of his life," Gomez responded, with laughter filling the bunker. "I simply meant that a direct warning in many cases takes care of problems like these...sometimes."

Terry's gut drew in as Gomez' eyes twinkled in the reflection of the enameled military lighting suspended from the ceiling above. He got the distinct feeling that Gomez would truly enjoy dealing with those occasions he had referred to when a threat didn't work to scare someone off.

Johnson tried to reassure Terry. "Don't let this kind of talk upset you. We need to get this conversation back on track, gentlemen. Do these answers take care of this Seal issue?"

"I guess so...for now," Terry answered halfheartedly. He let it go at that. From what he had heard a lot of people had a lot of reasons to kill Barry Seal. But, as far as anyone here seemed to know, it had happened just the way the police in Baton Rouge were saying. Never the less, he was assured the investigation of Seal's death was continuing.

Sawahata then turned back to where he had started by saying "I am real glad the governor is not here to discuss our BIG problem. The papers are full of it. State has big money problems."

Johnson shook his head, "What's this, another loose end?" It looked like Johnson didn't have a realistic understanding of all the problems, which, like an Arkansas diamond, had many facets.

Sawahata knew all too well that Johnson's simplistic reassurances to Clinton about the impending phase out of the Mena operation were, to say the least, misleading. Containing an investigation was one thing, but shoring up a state's finances was quite another.

Economic chaos in the Arkansas bond business could ensue unless a new source of "bridge capital" was found right away to shore up the freewheeling lending policies of Clinton's aggressive industrial recruitment program.

"Yes," Sawahata answered. "And this could cause long-term problems for our other operations in Arkansas. This state has terrible budgetary shortfall with the closing of Rose and Bridge. Governor Clinton has real problems on his hands. Our operations transfused over $250 million into his economy in less than two years...and his people stole...er, diverted...from us another $75 to $100 million."

Sawahata felt compelled to spell it out. Johnson seemed to grasp Clinton's addiction to this money, but not the magnitude of it and the danger that could ensue from all the loose financial ends. The state's "habit" now required "fixes" totaling hundreds of millions of dollars annually to support the economic growth package Clinton had promised his electorate, not to mention meeting the financial obligations for which he was already committed. For Arkansas to go without the black money would be the same as a junkie trying to go "cold turkey." The state would face serious withdrawal symptoms.

Johnson quickly grasped the political implications with the gubernatorial election just eight months away. "Is he in danger of not being reelected over this money issue?" Johnson asked.

"I do not know, but Bob Nash tells me they are having to access funds from First American in Washington in order to cover the commitments they made for industrial development, based upon our cash flow into their economy."

"You mean they are borrowing our money from First American in order to make up for their cash shortage?" Johnson was clearly startled.

"Exactly. And this cannot go on forever, as you know, without causing audit problems from bank examiners," Sawahata told him.

Johnson, in astonishment, replied, "Mr. Casey and Mr. Clifford wouldn't like that." The last name seemed to slip from his mouth as an afterthought.

"Mr. Who?" Sawahata was puzzled by the second name. He reacted as if he had not heard of "Clifford" before.

"Oh, just another guy who's got his butt sticking out over our banking business," Johnson said, dismissing Aki's question and getting onto his own. "But I'm curious, how did Mr. Clinton and company gain access to our funds in First American?"

"Through bond business here in Arkansas. It seems this was brainchild of Mr. Dan Lasater. But with Mr. Lasater out of way, state has implemented the plan through biggest firm here in Arkansas, Stephens & Co."

"Let me get this straight," Johnson said. "Clinton needs money in order to keep his promises to bring industry to Arkansas. So, Stephens issues a municipal bond or whatever and our bank, First American, buys or underwrites the goddam thing. So our offshore money is laundered right here in Arkansas through legitimate industrial loans, and Clinton benefits?"*

By "offshore" Johnson was referring to CIA money held in foreign banks to disguise the fact that it was money used to fund intelligence operations. This was a Cold War technique designed to prevent the money's source from being traced back to Washington. Oliver North and the others had learned that this was an ideal way to move money to the Contras without congressional investigators finding out.

"That's about it," Sawahata replied.

"Goddam. Clinton IS presidential material, isn't he?" Johnson chuckled. "And I thought the South lost the war!"

It now became clear to Terry as he sat and listened that the money delivered by Barry Seal's "green flights" and the profits from black operations in Arkansas had built the "laundromat" that was now permanently in place under the guise of the Arkansas bond business. Having run short on "laundry," Clinton and his friends had tapped into other sources of "dirty money."

The public would learn years later of the tenebrous connection between Stephens, First American Bank and the Bank of Credit and Commerce International, later to have its acronym, BCCI, emblazoned in headlines throughout the world. CIA Director Robert Gates labeled it later as the "Bank of Crooks and Criminals Inc.," but admitted to its extensive use by the Agency.

And Jackson T. Stephens, the chairman of Stephens & Co. in Little Rock, who would later be identified as the one who helped BCCI gets its financial foothold in America, had replaced Lasater as the state's investment banker of choice to attract new capital.[9]

Through these discussions in the bunker, Cathey was realizing the urgency in helping Arkansas find new investors to replace the BCCI money, before federal bank examiners launched an investigation that would lead to Arkansas— and, more importantly, the Agency. This was especially important since state investigators in New York would later charge that First American Bank and Trust in Washington, owned by First American Bancshares, had hidden ownership ties to BCCI. [See *The New Republic*, April 4, 1994, The Poisoned Rose.]

This allegedly secret tie was vehemently denied by its chairman, former Defense Secretary and Washington power broker Clark Clifford, and his partner, Robert Altman, both of whom were indicted in New York in connection with that banking tie.

The full impact of the money debacle seemed to impact Cathey as he said: "Let's not take this money thing too lightly, Bob. We'd better do something to cushion the blow economically, so that Clinton can try and wean himself off of our First American money. That can't go undetected very long, even if he is successful in bridging the shortfall through savvy bond investments."

"Yes," Sawahata answered, "and now with his friend, Dan Lasater, under investigation and out of way Clinton will not have his expertise to fall back upon. But I am curious, Mr. Johnson, what other money is there that can be diverted to Arkansas that will not come leaving trail?"

*   In the Fall of 1990, the Internal Revenue Service began a statewide investigation in Arkansas, saying it believed the state had become a magnet for dirty money. An IRS spokesman, Phil Beasley, said information compiled by the Federal Reserve Board and the FBI showed a 210 per cent increase in cash surplus in Arkansas in 1988 and 1989 alone.[8]

An interesting question. Just what other money might have been diverted through the Arkansas investment banking business will never be known because of Robert Johnson's efforts in aborting the then ongoing federal investigation in Little Rock. This was just the type of behavior that George Bush's Attorney-General, William Barr, was accused of by Congress during the ensuing BCCI scandal when the Justice Department contained its BCCI investigation to one area of the country, Tampa, Florida.[10] By not allowing the inquiry to expand where federal agents saw its tentacles reaching, BCCI's ties to intelligence was suppressed.

Gomez, even though Sawahata's question had not been directed to him, had an answer. He had extensive connections within Latin America that he had obtained either through bribes or previous operations.

"I can talk to my people in Panama," Gomez said. "I'm sure they would love to replace First American and become Arkansas' sugar daddy. They're always looking for good 'Third World' investment opportunities. Maybe they want to buy stock in Arkansas. I'm sure they will be interested, especially considering the capabilities that are in place thanks to Mr. Seal's and Terry's efforts."

"Excellent idea, Maximo," Cathey chimed in. "I'll go with you to see Noriega's people. If we're successful, Aki, you can brief Nash that there'll be a new 'investor' for Arkansas, which means he can begin curtailing his bond underwriting through First American. And Terry, for the record, exactly what capabilities are in place here as a result of Rose. Just what do we have to sell [to the new investors]?"

Terry, having the most direct knowledge of the "assets" in place in Arkansas during the past two years, then began his briefing on what they were. And they were substantial.

"Just about any high technology manufacturing expertise needed to produce high-quality, world-class weapons components up to .50-caliber at the present time," he said. There was metal-casting capability for both ferrous and non-ferrous materials. The company providing that service had a wide array of computerized modern design and testing equipment.

"We have non-destructive testing equipment, which includes X-ray, magnetic particle inspection, finite element analysis and state-of-the-art CAD (computer-assisted design) capability," Terry continued. "We also have a wide range of modern machining options to include computer numerical controlled (CNC) machine tools, plus metal-treatment and plating capabilities.

"In the electronics area, there is the sibling of the Albuquerque-based, military-approved facility located in Piggot, Arkansas, that has automated circuit board manufacturing and enclosure capability. As I understand it, they're making perfect copies of stinger circuit boards."

Terry had given a detailed explanation of the high-grade weapons manufacturing facilities that had been secretly put in place in Arkansas to support Operation Centaur Rose. He had described decentralized, modern manufacturing factories possessing in-house, computer-controlled capabilities to produce untraceable weapons parts or components.

This enabled the Enterprise to bypass the traditional arms suppliers who must document and serialize certain parts they produce. Without such controls, federal agents would have little way of discovering their manufacture.

The Agency had thought of nearly everything, including a method of secure transportation. "No paper, no trail," Seal had said in describing the operation to Terry.

Terry continued. "All of this combined with the secure waterway transportation system afforded by the Arkansas and Mississippi Rivers, which are controlled by the U.S. Army Corps of Engineers, and I would say to a potential investor we've got a complete, turnkey weapons manufacturing capability for anything short of nuclear weapons." Terry smiled.

Cathey mused and said: "How do you know Clinton doesn't have that, too? It sounds like you've done too good of a job, Terry. Considering the nuclear reactors here that could breed fuel, we had better add Arkansas to the list of Third World countries that could produce a nuke."

So it was all in place—weapons, transportation and the money to finance it all. But it had been jeopardized because of unprofessional behavior and greed.

Sawahata understood that the ability to handle "questionable" financial transactions would be the best selling point of all. "John, besides what Terry just explained, I think Noriega's people will be most attracted to money-laundering aspect. Under Bill Clinton's leadership, Arkansas has set in place permanent money-laundering industry concealed as their everyday municipal bond business. They do not care where funds come from. In fact, dirtier is better."

Regardless of the method used by the money-launderer, the common denominator is finding a bank or financial institution along with people in a position of power who are willing to break the law and not ask questions. Money laundering, by definition, involves co-mingling clean and dirty making both indistinguishable. Arkansas offered this environment under the umbrella of its cooperative bond business.

All that was lacking was a way of consistently and inconspicuously moving large amounts of money offshore to be deposited as collateral against loans generated for industrial development. Once this activity was underway, occasionally dirty money could be substituted by the Agency for clean money without drawing attention to it.*

---

*   A federal financial investigator consulted by the authors said the millions of dollars that Seal was dropping each week could easily have been laundered and disguised, leaving no clue as to its source, if the right people—bankers and organizations worked together and kept their dealings to themselves.

All that would be required, the former investigator for the Securities & Exchange Commission said, was "cooperation" among a triad of key financial services willing to enter into a white collar criminal conspiracy to work together for their mutual gain. And such a triad was already in place in Arkansas: ADFA, investment banker Jackson T. Stephens, a stockholder in several Little Rock banks, and Dan Lasater, then the CEO of Lasater & Co., a brokerage firm specializing in bonds.

These three institutions could share top management or simply operate autonomously if the proper amount of "trust" existed among these key conspirators. The Arkansas banking, investment banking, bond business and state development authority does, in fact, orbit around a coterie of very small and centralized power base, in many cases sharing the same boards of directors.

The most likely scenario the investigator outlined, would work as follows:

1.   A trusted courier (such as Lasater) deposits the cash in a bank or banks (like Worthen) under various corporate names. No federal banking attention is drawn to the deposits since the banker (like Stephens) waives the requirement of filling out the CTR's.

2.   ADFA attracts a "preferred client" (CIA Proprietary) in need of a "loan." This client can be a firm or individual from within the state, which is involved with this secret group (i.e. POM and MRL) or even an out-of-state corporation (i.e. Lasater's Angel Fire

One such case in point is the record of the Arkansas Development and Finance Authority (ADFA) depositing $50 million offshore with the Fuji Bank, Ltd., in the Cayman Islands on December 29, 1988. This was a very strange transaction indeed, for an organization chartered and founded on lending money for investment and development *within* Arkansas, not for moving large sums of funds offshore.

Fuji Bank's name reappears as being the bank that purchased the industrial development loan of POM Inc., the parking meter company in Russellville, Arkansas, owned and operated by the Ward family. Oddly, the underwriter, or issuer, of this loan was initially an out-of-state bank in Memphis, named First American, the same name as Clark Clifford's bank, First American Bancshares in Washington.

By purchasing the loan from First American Bank of Memphis, Tennessee, Fuji effectively retired the loan and the Ward family presumably continued making their payments directly to Fuji. This was curious behavior on behalf of POM since they were giving up a long-term, fixed rate, low interest loan issued by ADFA, which had a guarantor, the bank in Memphis, to back it up. Curious behavior, indeed, to forfeit a loan that has a co-signor, since this action would normally reduce a company's line of credit. Unless, of course, the objective was to move the loan offshore, where repayment ledgers are nearly impossible to attain. Webb Hubbell, Hillary Clinton's law partner, was POM's corporate attorney at the time.

ADFA, being a state authority, is not legally required to publicly divulge its records. And therefore, the millions of dollars that flow through the Arkansas agency's coffers can be shrouded in secrecy, just like the money that flowed offshore in the ADFA "investment" just cited. One possible reason the money

project in New Mexico), since ADFA's charter allows it to underwrite business outside of Arkansas.

3. The financial banking firm (Stephens & Co.) announces it is seeking capital to underwrite a bond issue to develop the money needed for the "loan." The bonds will be guaranteed by the state since ADFA will be the issuer, thereby eliminating the SEC scrutiny of the "buyers" (Lasater's fake corporations) of the bonds, and reducing or eliminating the collateral requirements needed by the "client".

4. Lasater announces that he has "sold" the bonds to various customers (Lasater's fake corporations which have large cash reserves on deposit at the Stephen's bank).

5. ADFA handles all the paperwork and contracts at the time of loan "closing", becomes the guarantor (co-signer) of the loan, and retains the right to "sell" the entire loan package to another financial institution in the future, if it wishes.

6. Lasater's customers (his fake corporations) issue checks to Stephens & Co. earmarked for this bond issue. Stephens issues a check to ADFA in order to buy the bonds for Lasater's customers, after deducting commissions (clean money) on the transaction for his firm (Stephens & Co.) and Lasater's (Lasater & Co.). The bond certificates are then issued and are held by Lasater's "customers" as security and collateral.

7. ADFA issues a check to the "client" (the CIA proprietary) and it builds or buys whatever it needs in order to comply with the conditions of the loan.

8. The "client" puts the purchased equipment to use and creates a positive cash flow as any legitimate business would and makes monthly payments in order to retire the bonds. The principal and interest received by the lender (Lasater's customers) is clean.

9. At any point during the life of the loan, ADFA is free to find a "buyer" for the entire loan package, retire the debt owed to Lasater's customers and distance itself from the "client's operation" if the CIA wants to "sell off" the assets.

was deposited in the Cayman Islands was to set up a laundering process similar to that provided by Panamanian banks.

Panama, then under the leadership of General Manuel Noriega, was the main country of choice for drug traffickers wanting to hide their money. But even safely in Panamanian banks, there was still the problem of moving the funds, particularly into the United States. But Arkansas offered its own version of what bankers' slang calls "the Dutch sandwich."

The Dutch sandwich is a method perfected in the Netherlands Antilles, a small group of Caribbean islands off South America, and is a legal tax avoidance maneuver in the Antilles.[11] There, funds, dirty in this case, remain offshore on deposit and are used only as collateral to back legitimate loans in the United States.

Legitimate loans are what Arkansas needed to underwrite industrial development bonds at low interest rates to attract business to the state. If Arkansas allowed the CIA to guarantee its loans by collateralizing its industrial bonds with dirty, off-shore money, the interest from the loan which is repaid in the form of clean money by the borrower, has in reality accomplished the goal of generating clean money from dirty money.

Arkansas, in effect, could become the "cooperating banker" in the equation. The owner of the dirty money would get back clean money from the stateside loan's interest. In this case, the stateside bank, a bank like First American, supplied the up-front cash through CIA sources.

This apparently was what Sawahata was referring to when he said "the dirtier, the better." Sawahata then continued: "I suppose if you have to launder money, it is very secure way even though there is risk, considering the fact that a high per cent of out-of-state businesses Arkansas recruits fail within the first few years of being transplanted. But, when it pays off, it pays off well...you get back clean money plus tax-free interest and no one in Arkansas asks questions...at least not at state auditor level."

Sawahata noted that the state gets the high-risk venture capital it needs to grow and the investor can't complain when he loses his money in what appears to be the normal course of business. But to offset this risk, the "investor" could even attend the bankruptcy sale if a business failure occurred, and possibly buy back his undocumented, and hidden, assets wholesale.

Through possible combinations of laundering CIA money, either off-shore, domestically, or by direct infusion into the lending system, the Clinton administration had evidently developed an insatiable appetite for money that could only be compared to that of the plant from outer space in the movie *"The Little Shop of Horrors"* which continally said, "Feed me, feed me."

"So far," Sawahata continued, "they have gone through all Mena black money that started it all. Now, they are laundering First American's black ops' proceeds and we are going to help them attain Panama as client? What a deal for Arkansas! Money-launderer's nirvana!"

Johnson expressed hope the "loose ends" had been dealt with through the possible solutions that had been tabled. Maybe, he suggested, they could get on with the original purpose of the meeting.

"Terry, it sounds like we've selected the right person for our Mexican operation. From your correspondence with me, as you developed your business plan and strategy for us down there, I could tell you were a star at this game, which brings me to the major reason for coming.....your initiation. So before we go any further with this briefing, I'll ask Mr. Sawahata to excuse himself if he's finished with all the loose ends of 'Bridge' and 'Rose'. The remainder of this meeting will focus on 'Screw Worm' and frankly, Aki...."

"I know, I do not have need to know," Sawahata said. "Intel 101. Yes, I am finished for now, but I would like to say goodbye and good luck to *Weta Okami*. It has been pleasure." Sawahata shook Terry's hand and then walked toward the bunker door.

The sanctity of the "initiation" began to set in.

Terry was beginning to feel a little panicky. Butterflies! Just like before an FAA check ride, he thought.

With Sawahata in the process of leaving, he was now looking at the faces of men he didn't know well. Of those left, Cathey was the only one with whom he had any real familiarity. Feelings akin to those of religion that he had long ago abandoned were starting to rekindle within him. He was convinced that he was entering into a patriotic brotherhood of honorable men. A secret society.

Terry had to push his doubts about Seal's death out of his mind. It was time of decision. He felt there would be no turning back.

It was all falling together, he thought. All knowledge gained from Air Force Intelligence, combined with his skills and experience in the business world were coming into play. His reward was in sight. There *was* a secret world of sponsorship for patriotic men like him. Doing things the hard way was paying off. He was glad he'd made the right decision to serve his country in time of war. Surely, that was a prerequisite for joining the inner circle.

The thought of being expendable had not entered his mind.

1.   Testimony of William Duncan, July 29, 1989, *House Subcommittee on Commerce, Consumer and Monetary Affairs, Washington, D.C.*
2.   Confidential FBI telex dated 7/26/84 from Little Rock FBI Field Office to Assistant FBI Director Oliver Revell, obtained by Terry Reed under court discovery, LRC-91-414.
3.   Duncan, *Deposition given the Arkansas Attorney-General's office*, June 21, 1991, Page 6.
4.   Ibid. Testimony of Russell Welch, pp. 35-36
5.   Classified FBI AIRTEL, Date/time group: F 182227Z AUG 87
6.   Duncan, *Deposition given Arkansas Attorney-General's office*, June 21, 1991, Page 21.
7.   Duncan testimony, *House Subcommittee on Commerce, Consumer and Monetary Affairs*, July 29, 1989, and executive session of *House Subcommittee on Crime*, February 26, 1988.
8.   *Arkansas Democrat*, November 14, 1990.
9.   *Arkansas Gazette*, August 14, 1991, and *The Wall Street Journal*, July 7, 1993.
10. *New York Times*, November 13, 1991.
11. TIME magazine. December 18, 1989, p. 50.

F(?) 182127Z AUG 87

FM CHICAGO (12-0)

TO DIRECTOR PRIORITY

(ATTN): DRUG SECTION [CIO, 01-1, SECTION INTS]

LITTLE ROCK PRIORITY

    ET

  SECRET

THIS COMMUNICATION IS CLASSIFIED "SECRET" IN ITS ENTIRETY. INFORMATION CONCERNING POSSIBLE DEA AND/OR CIA OPERATION.

ON AUGUST 6, 1987, SA FRANCIS MARROCCO WAS ADVISED BY CONFIDENTIAL SOURCES, WHO HAVE PROVIDED RELIABLE INFORMATION IN THE PAST, OF THE FOLLOWING:

BOTH THE NEW YORK TIMES AND THE TELEVISION NEWS SHOW WEST 57TH STREET ARE PRESENTLY PREPARING STORIES REGARDING ALLEGED CIA ACTIVITIES AT AN AIR FIELD IN MENA, ARKANSAS.

THE ORIGINAL INFORMATION DATES BACK TO A PILOT, BARRY SEAL, NOW DE-CEASED, WHO IS PURPORTED TO HAVE FLOWN GUNS TO SOUTH AMERICA FROM MENA AND DRUGS BACK INTO THE UNITED STATES. THE INFORMATION INDICATES THAT SEAL WAS AN INFORMANT FOR THE DEA AT THE TIME BUT ALSO WORKING AS AN OPERATIVE OF THE CIA. DURING THE PAST FEW YEARS, THE ACTIVITY AT THE AIRSTRIP HAS AROUSED THE INTEREST OF LOCAL LAW ENFORCEMENT WHO THEN ATTEMPTED TO CONDUCT SOME INVESTIGATIONS BUT WERE BLOCKED BY THE U.S. ATTORNEY. IN 1986, SEAL WAS GUNNED DOWN IN BATON ROUGE, LOUISIANA. THIS WAS PURPORTED TO BE A HIT BY COLOMBIAN DRUG DEALERS.

EVEN WITH THE DEMISE OF SEAL, ACTIVITY AT THE AIRFIELD CONTINUED. THERE IS CONTINUOUS TRAFFIC FROM C-130 AIRCRAFT BELONGING TO HERC AIR-LIFT CORPORATION. FOKKER AIRCRAFT OF ANTWERP, BELGIUM, HAS SET UP SHOP AT THIS AIRSTRIP AND IS PURPORTED TO BE INVOLVED IN OUTFITTING AIRCRAFT WITH VERY HIGH TECH GEAR.

ANOTHER COMPANY, GOODNER BROTHERS, HAS ALSO SET UP BUSINESS AT THE AIRFIELD. GOODNER BROTHERS REPAINTS AIRCRAFT. GOODNER IS RUN BY GEORGE REEB, WHO CLAIMS TO BE FROM MARYLAND. SOURCES ATTEMPTED TO VERIFY GOODNER'S BACK- GROUND BUT WERE UNABLE TO DO SO.

SOURCES FURTHER REPORTED THAT ONE OF THE AIRCRAFT RECENTLY OUTFITTED BY FOKKER WAS SIGHTED IN AN EAST BLOC COUNTRY.

TWO AIRCRAFT BEARING "N" NUMBERS, N239MA AND N243MA AND THE CHICAGO AIR LOGO WERE SIGHTED AT FOKKER AND ARE AWAITING OUTFITTING. (CHICAGO AIR RECENTLY DECLARED BANKRUPTCY IN CHICAGO AND IS BELIEVED TO HAVE SOLD THEIR AIRCRAFT.)

ABOVE BEING FURNISHED TO FBIHQ FOR INFORMATION AND DISSEMINATION TO CIA HQ AND/OR DEAHQ AS DEEMED APPROPRIATE.

LITTLE ROCK IS REQUESTED TO PROVIDE CHICAGO AND FBIHQ WITH ANY INFOR-MATION CONCERNING THIS MATTER.

PT

18-1. August 1987 "Secret" report alerting the FBI, DEA and CIA of pending media inves-tigation into Mena which lists Barry Seal as a CIA operative. Above is a reconstructed copy, since original is barely legible.

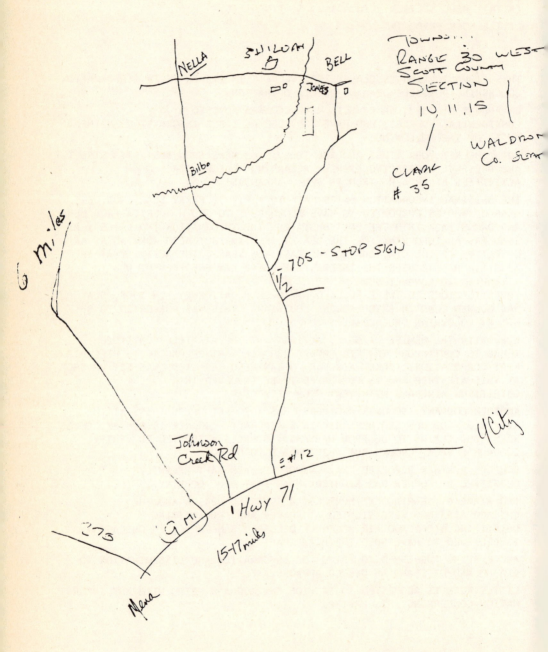

18-2. Hand drawn sketch of the location of the Nella strip. This diagram, which denotes mileage, was used to develop a "homemade" visual approach to the field to be used in marginal weather and during low visibility conditions.

JOE H. HARDEGREE
Prosecuting Attorney

8th Judicial Circuit West
Polk and Montgomery Counties
State of Arkansas

August 21, 1987

507 Hickory Street
Mena, Arkansas 71953
(501) 394-4275

Mr. J. Michael Fitzhugh
United States Attorney
Post Office Box 1524
Fort Smith, AR 72902

     Re: Local/State Criminal Investigation of
            Drug Activity at Mena Airport

Dear Mr. Fitzhugh:

In my capacity as Chief Deputy Prosecutor for the 18th Judicial
District-West, which is comprised of Montgomery and Polk
Counties, information has come to my attention regarding illegal
drug activity at the Mena Airport in Polk County. I have been
further advised that your office has been informed of this
activity, but that it is uncertain whether there is going to be a
federal level prosecution of this matter.

The information I have received, in my opinion, certainly
warrants a prosecution of the participants. I would appreciate
it if you would advise me by September 10, 1987 whether there
will be any further federal-level investigation/prosecution of
this matter. I need to receive some type of positive indication
by that date that there will be federal prosecution because if
there is not, I intend to pursue the matter on a state level; and
if there is any further delay, prosecution by the state could be
hampered by statue-of-limitation problems.

I thank you in advance for your prompt response to this inquiry.

                      Respectfully,

                      Charles E. Black
                      Deputy Prosecuting Attorney

CEB:vb

**18-3. Letter from Polk County Prosecutor Charles Black to U.S. Attorney J. Michael Fitzhugh,
trying to nudge him and the Justice Department into action.**

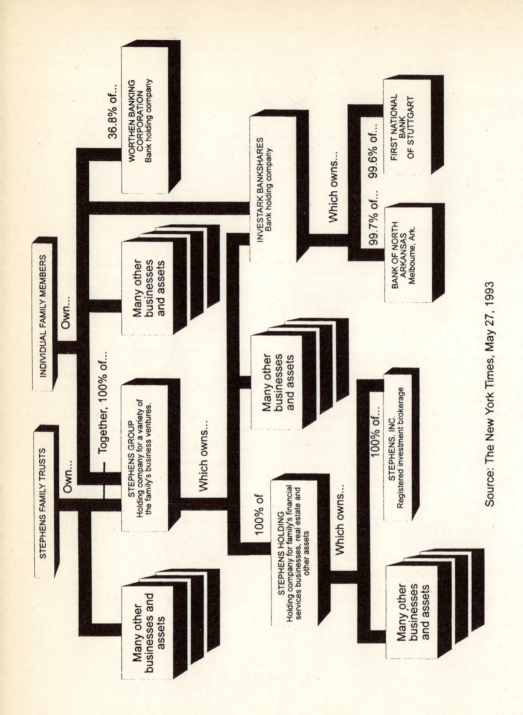

18-4. Dichotomous key showing tangled financial empire of Arkansas' Stephens family.

CHAPTER 19

OPERATION SCREW WORM

As Akihide Sawahata approached the bunker's large metal exit doors, his footsteps echoed from the concrete floor. His knock on the plate steel door, signaling his wish to leave, reverberated as if it had come from a hollow steel drum.

The returning echo following the arched roof was reminiscent of the acoustics of a church's vaulted ceilings.

A faceless guard opened the door. As Sawahata started to step out into the chilly night air, he paused, turned and focused on Terry, saying: "I guess it's *sayonara* time. Goodbye, Terry-san."

He felt alone now that Sawahata was gone. It was time to decide his future. One chapter of his life was ending. Another was about to begin.

Terry thought, as the door slammed shut, his time was at hand. He was about to join the cabal. The other three men took up new positions at another table, facing Terry as if sitting at a tribunal. It was a change from business as usual into a solemn ritual. The bunker took on a hallowed atmosphere, and he felt was taking a sacred vow, like that of receiving knighthood.

He had been found worthy of acceptance to the Round Table where he would live under unwritten rules and, he hoped, be judged an equal.

Cathey was the first to speak. "Terry, you're now crossing the line few operatives...assets, if you will...are ever given the opportunity to do. You understand this is a honor, and we feel confident you won't let us down. You've proved yourself time and time again. You are, in fact, a star. So, from this point on, you will be known by your code name, *Señor Estrella*. Congratulations."

With those flowery words, Terry was initiated. In the darkened room whose lights cast long shadows over the faces of the three other men present, he felt as if those in a position of sacred trust were placing their faith in him. This was an appeal that went to the core of his being. It was not only a position of honor, but just as much an obligation. He was to protect the core of American values.

He felt he had been part of a sacred ritual, but he did not realize then that there was a *Judas* among them.

Turning to Cathey, Robert Johnson and Max Gomez, he said: "Thank you gentlemen, I feel deeply honored. I will do everything in my power to make 'Screw Worm' a success and to represent our country with honor and professionalism."

Johnson continued the briefing: "Terry, as you know, from this point forward you will be in the gray zone, a no-man's land in which assets operate. You have no written contract to protect you, nor to hinder you. You can move freely. We will always be near you, but yet you must be kept at arm's length for built-in deniability—for your protection, as well as ours. We will be your shadow in Mexico and Max will see to it that maximum allowable security will be provided for you and your family. But yet we will not be in a position to directly or overtly intervene in an emergency for fear of exposing your cover."

"Beyond the three of you who else, in country, will know of 'Señor Estrella' and what his mission is?" Terry asked.

"From an Agency operational level, only our local handler in Ajijic and the consul-general in Guadalajara," Johnson answered. "Others may have to know that you are somehow aligned with the State Department and getting preferential treatment, as is not uncommon for U.S. businessmen being supported overseas by our government. But only those two individuals know exactly of your, and our, true objectives."

Later on, only 12 names—"The Dirty Dozen"— surfaced in the Iran-Contra scandal as having detailed knowledge of the affair. By design, Terry began to realize how small the circle was of those "in the loop."

Cathey had an additional concern, "And Terry, that brings up another point. I know you told me your wife knows generally what's going on here in Arkansas up to now. But, from this point forward, you should begin limiting her knowledge of details that may *compromise* her or put her at risk."

Johnson then revealed what Terry had already assumed. The Agency had done an extensive background check on his wife and her family. Johnson said his wife had been cleared for a "general operational knowledge" on a "need to know" basis.

"But it's important for you not to forget, we're investing a great deal of time and money in you," Johnson stressed. "And we wouldn't want to jeopardize the whole operation by a mere marital dispute. Spouses have been problems in the past, not saying that yours will be. I've been told you have a very stable family relationship."

Gomez had another point of view. It was clear by this time that a subtle friction was already developing between him and Terry. Only later did Terry realize that Gomez didn't hold most Anglos in high esteem.

"That's where we Latinos make much better agents than you gringos!" he said reflecting his Latin macho attitude. "We don't tell our wives fucking shit!"

"You guys just tell your secrets to your mistresses in order to impress them," Cathey shot back, shaking his head and laughing. "Some security!"

Johnson stepped in to head off any more racial comments and to soothe ruffled feelings. After referring to Gomez as the "field *jefe*" for "Screw Worm," he asked for an up-to-date operational briefing about Mexico, which ended the squabbling.

"Well, at the present time all should be in place to receive Mr. Reed and start up the operation within 60 days...by May at the latest," Gomez replied.

Terry said he needed more time to phase out his regular business in Arkansas without bringing attention to what would appear as a too-rapid departure.

"There are ongoing automation projects both here and in Texas that require my involvement. I can't go that soon," Terry said.

"He's right, Max," Cathey said. "Let's move slow on this, so it appears that Terry is just making a career move. That way his present customers and suppliers won't get jumpy or suspicious on us. We have all worked too hard in order to develop this multi-national front for Machinery International and we don't want to blow that cover. It's excellent for our purposes."

Terry had been successful in attracting two other companies, one Japanese and one Hungarian, into this operation to make it a real multi-national joint venture. *Maquinaria Internacional, S.A.*, was the selected name of the company Terry was setting up to front for the gun-running operation. Headquartered eventually in Guadalajara, it would serve as a legitimate import-export machine tool trading company.

For now, at least, the new company would use Cortec's warehouse facilities in Mexico City and Reed's operation would serve as a "satellite" or franchise operation based in Guadalajara. Robert Johnson had liked the idea of remotely locating Reed's warehouse away from Cortec, not only for security reasons, but for giving the business the appearance of being one that was expanding from an already established firm.

From the onset, Seal had told Terry the Agency's attraction to him was his ability to move around in international trading circles that included German, Japanese and Hungarian companies. This would give the operation firm business "roots" and a true multi-national flavor.

Front companies, or proprietaries as they are called, must not only *appear* as legitimate businesses, they have to *be* legitimate so as not to be exposed. Carrying out seemingly real operations requires real businessmen who speak the "language" and understand the intricacies of the front business they are carrying on.

Even in a dark world, some things must be opaque or their true function will quickly become transparent.

Gomez did not wait long to respond to Cathey's fear of going too fast for Terry's investors, adding fuel to the existing tension.

"After my visits to Reed's commie friends in Mexico City, the Hungarian KGB assholes, I don't think anything we do can scare them off. They know opportunity when they see it. I've been able to buy off more mother-fuckin' Mexicans in the past five months than those Russian influence peddlers have in the past three years. This is a good deal for them and they know it."

Gomez's prejudice highlighted a problem that plagued the operation from the beginning. "Reed's commie friends," as Gomez had put it, were legitimate Hungarian businessmen operating a machine-tool company named Cortec in Mexico City. This is what made the plan attractive to the CIA. But Gomez couldn't overcome his continually-professed hatred of anything "communist." Terry was beginning to view Gomez as something akin to an Air Force guard dog that can never be retrained to become anything more than a killer.

Terry had informed the Agency earlier that one of the Hungarians was indeed KGB, something he had been told earlier by the FBI. But the CIA found this attractive and intended to use this as a conduit for disinformation and, possibly, as a source for obtaining weapons from Eastern Europe.

The "buy offs" Gomez was referring to were bribes he had been paying high-level Mexican government officials to insure total foreign ownership of Machinery International, something rarely allowed under Mexican law. It was essential to the CIA plan because the Agency wanted to be certain that no Mexican partner would be brought in, as is normally required. There could be *no* security leak.

Stepping in again as mediator, Johnson replied: "That may be true Maximo

but, for Terry's sake, let's go slow on this. We've waited too long for an opportunity like this just to blow it through impatience. Don't you have a sufficient
stockpile of weapons in place in country to carry the Contras through until
summer?"

"With all the disorganization down there, I don't know," Gomez admitted.
"These guys you brought into the supply side of this, John, are just not professionals in my professional opinion."

(Rodriguez would later testify in Congressional hearings that the resupply
operation was being run solely by profiteers "and not patriots." They were, he
testified, "unprofessional.")[1]

"If worse comes to worse," Johnson replied, "I can get Southern Air Transport to fly some missions direct to Honduras or El Salvador, but I don't want
to. It's too risky. That's the beauty of 'Screw Worm.' Once this front is set up in
Guadalajara the pressure will be taken off. We can control things in Mexico
and no one will be looking there. Terry's facility can warehouse several months
of munitions and supplies, with the ability to bring in weapons from all over
the world through this multi-national appearance. That's why 'Operation Screw
Worm' is so important to Mr. Casey's plan. Max, you can control things in
Mexico for us? Over the long haul, I mean?"

"By this time next year, I'll have Mexico wanting to apply for statehood in
the U.S," Gomez said. "I'll have them all speaking English as their *native*
tongue...I'll be the true *Conquistador* of Mexico. I will make Cortez appear as a
coward."

Cathey had had enough. "Calm down, Maximo. I'm sure you could do all
that...with enough bribe money. But, in the meantime, please brief us on the
operational consideration of 'Screw Worm,' OK?"

After a piercing stare at Cathey, and a long pause, Gomez returned to the
agenda. "I have been in touch with my good friend at the DFS (the Mexican
CIA) in Mexico City, Mr. Jaime Bravo. He is taking care of security at both
facilities, the Hungarians' warehouse in Mexico City as well as the warehouse
at the Guadalajara Airport. By working through his people in the Mexican
Army, he can station DFS agents within pissing distance of all our materiels. It
will be secure.

"My good friend, Capitan Raul Fierro, the ex-commandante of the
Guadalajara airport will be in charge of operations. He's connected with the
Mexican FAA and can fix *anything* as it pertains to flight plans, documents et
cetera."

Cathey liked what he heard, but he was still worried. What about flight
records maintained by the Mexican air traffic control system?

Specifically, Cathey wanted to know: "Now, are you sure that if one of Southern Air Transport's planes delivers a load of guns to Terry's facility that Fierro
can fix the international air traffic control system so that there is no permanent record of that flight? Either from its origination as it penetrates Mexican
air space or to its destination at Guadalajara?"

"Señor Fierro said to tell you he has a brother who provides this same security service in the Bermuda triangle," Gomez joked. "What flies in never flies
out, at least not from ATC point of view." That took care of Mexican
airspace. With everyone still laughing, another problem occurred to Johnson.

"What about our own satellite reconnaissance?" he asked.

Cathey had the answer to that. "The same procedures as we used for Dodger sorties. We will have them blinded just as we did for Seal's departures and penetrations. The military's satellite coverage is from the equator north all the way into the U.S."

"But I'm curious." Johnson said. "I've never understood how Seal got back in. Taking care of the defense system is one thing, but what about American ATC? Don't these two systems overlap?"

"Sea Spray is the coordinator," Cathey replied.

"For the purpose of my report, remind me what Sea Spray is?" Johnson requested.

Cathey explained the technical details of Sea Spray, itself a black joint Army-CIA unit that provides "cover" for covert ops flights to enter and exit American airspace undetected, and added "Terry knows how it works. He went on a Sea Spray flight with Seal down to Panama, remember, Max?"

Gomez nodded.

"Beautiful," Johnson said. "The flights just never happen."

Satellites in orbit provide the primary defense network that protects American coastal airspace. By "blinding" those satellites, Cathey was referring to the Defense Department's ability to selectively turn off their detection capability. This had to be done in order to prevent a triggered response from the military whose mission is to intercept unauthorized incursions into U.S. airspace.

Southern Air Transport's aircraft, which would be carrying the weapons to Guadalajara, would be exiting and entering United States airspace without flight plans. For such black flights to come and go, avoiding detection and interception by the military, certain select air corridors would momentarily be "established", allowing penetration without detection.

Electronically, a "hole" is temporarily created in the defense network. This was how Barry Seal was able to fly weapons south from Arkansas for so long, seemingly without interference. The same was true for return flights, when Seal and others were hauling drugs.

Gomez said that he was going directly to Miami after the meeting in order to brief the "black operations" commander at Southern Air Transport about the procedures their air crews would need to use.

"Mr. Fierro has developed a system for penetrating and departing Mexican air space while on a 'Sierra Whiskey' mission," Gomez added.

"Sierra Whiskey?" Johnson asked.

"Screw Worm," Gomez replied.

"Oh yeah, Army talk," Johnson confirmed, appearing a little embarrassed. Reed guessed he hadn't been in the military and didn't know the phonetic alphabet.

Since he had to separate and safeguard the shipments after they arrived at the facilities in Mexico, Terry expressed concern about flights where legitimate machine tools would be arriving and how he would be informed as to which flights were which.

Gomez said the legitimate flight plans would be processed in normal fashion that would be labeled "negative Sierra Whiskey." He went on to say that Fierro's people typically would know 24 hours in advance of the arrival of black flights and they would nearly always be at night. All Terry had to do, he said, was to have his warehouse ready to receive cargo.

"How does Terry know when to ship black cargo that he has been warehousing?" Johnson asked.

"His local boss in Mexico, Mitch Marr, will alert him," Gomez answered. "He's in charge of that. I will communicate to Mitch by a secure system and he will then inform Mr. Reed...or Señor Estrella, that is. They will be living in the same village south of the airport."

The problems arising from air operations seemed to have been addressed. Now they turned to licensing aspects of Machinery International.

"What about all the necessary business licenses Señor Estrella and Machinery International will be needing," Johnson asked as he appeared to be checking off a list in his pocket-size day planner. "Where do we stand on all that?"

"I've already greased the wheels in Mexico City and they are just waiting for the green light," Gomez boasted. "Señor Estrella will have to appear personally before several *personas muy importante* in Mexico City. I can't do anything about that. That is just a Latino formality."

The meeting was winding down. It was time now for a Cathey pep talk. "Good, gentlemen. Let's all make Phase I of Screw Worm a gigantic success. I would like for the brass upstairs to hear nothing but glowing reports on this operation so that we can implement Phase II of the plan as soon as possible. So, Terry—I mean Señor Estrella—What is your commitment date to move...when can you be in place so that we may get started?"

"Let's do it the government way. I'll be in place the first day of fiscal year 1987 (meaning July 1, using the military fiscal year system)," Terry said.

Everyone was finished but Gomez. "I would like to add something, a personal message to Mr. Reed. I am a professional agent. I have spent my whole adult life involved with the CIA in one way or another. I know that you come to this operation with high qualifications technically, but, from an intelligence point of view, I still consider you an amateur. This is my operation and you are a key player...but don't screw this project up by playing like a spy. You are to be an American businessman conducting high-technology trading in Mexico, period. Just go about your business, and leave the spy work to us professionals. You provide the cover and we pay the bills, it's just that simple. *Comprende?* Don't play spook and don't cross us."

Cathey again felt the need for moderation. "What Maximo is trying to articulate, Terry, is that it's our job to handle the dirty end of the business. Your job is to attend to the clean end. A good asset always remembers who he is and what his mission is. It's imperative you do not compromise our agents and our methods. This will take a lot of self-control. But try to turn a blind eye to our side of the operation and do not delve into areas in which you do not have an absolute..."

"Need to know," Terry said finishing the sentence. "I know, Intel 101."

Johnson now was closing down the meeting. "Gentlemen, this concludes our operational meeting. Señor Estrella, with Mr. Seal gone you can continue reporting directly to me at SAT, just as you have been doing. Keep us informed of your progress to move to Mexico."

There was one more small piece, or so it seemed then, of unfinished business for Terry, a small detail that would come back to haunt him. He had been maintaining a hangar at the North Little Rock Airport at Agency expense. He thought he would not be needing it now as he moved on to Mexico.

"One question. With the Arkansas operations all but shut down, will the Company have any further need of me maintaining the hangar, once I depart for Mexico?"

"Good point," Johnson said. "Yes. Keep it rented, leased, whatever your arrangements are. The SAT maintenance people are always in need of secure storage facilities, safe hangars if you will, especially considering all of our flight activity here in the central U.S."

Gomez was now thinking of something beyond the meeting. "So Señor Estrella, where does a good-looking Latino ladies man go around here in order to surround himself with these southern belles I keep hearing of. It's still early and I don't go back to Miami until tomorrow."

Cathey had the answer. "Maximo, for a guy like you, I would suggest a place on the Arkansas River not far from here called 'Snug Harbor.' The women there are accustomed to servicing all of the different racial elements stationed here at Camp Robinson. But, on second thought, I don't think they'll fuck Cubans!"

"You wouldn't say things like that if I had my weapon! Speaking of which, where's my Glock," Gomez snapped back with a smile. "I feel naked without it!"

The four men left the bunker and joined the security force outside. Cathey volunteered to drive Terry back to his home on the golf course in nearby Maumelle.

Terry would think about this night for long time.

1.   Rodriguez testimony, *Iran-Contra Hearings*, 100-3, at 302-06

CHAPTER 20

MEXICAN HANDOFF

Terry was quiet on the ride home. John Cathey, who was driving, sensed something was troubling his passenger.

"What's wrong? Are you upset because we didn't go with Max to 'Snug Harbor?'" Cathey asked, trying to inject a little humor and draw Terry out of his funk.

"No. It's...I gotta be truthful with you. I still have to sell this idea to Janis."

"I thought she was totally on board!"

"She is, based on my deceit. I haven't been totally truthful with her. She's not aware of the circumstances of Barry's death. And, John, I'm gonna go home and tell her everything. It's just not fair for me to ask her to give up her life here in Arkansas and move to Mexico on a decision based upon half-truths."

"Well, all I can tell you is, I'm counting on you. We've gone with you a long ways on this program. This was your idea, whether you realize it or not. Call me as soon as both of you make up your minds on this. I've got to know, one way or the other."

As the car's headlights illuminated the lawn of Terry's new house at 32 Club Manor in Maumelle, its serene setting wasn't helping him to cut his ties with the community he now felt part of.

The light was on in the upstairs bedroom as he got out of the CIA man's car. "I'm not gonna tell anybody about your indecision for 72 hours. Then I'll be obligated to alert them," Cathey said in parting.

"Thanks."

The sedan pulled away form the house leaving Reed alone with his thoughts and his problems. Damn! He didn't feel any happiness and it was his own fault. He had just been "sworn in" to what he thought was an elite brotherhood. A once-in-a-lifetime opportunity to work undercover as a secret intelligence agent in a foreign country lay before him. What the thousands of Walter Mittys would pay to trade places, he could only speculate.

But on the opposite side of the scale was Janis, the mother of his two sons and the woman he had vowed to love forever. He had lied to her. He had let her down; he had let himself down. He had to confront her with the whole truth.

"So tell me how it went," she said, peering through her reading glasses. She put her book aside to give him her full attention. "Who all did you meet. Is it real? Do they really want you to go?" The questions came tumbling out.

He now had to dampen her enthusiasm and the answer came as fast as the questions. "Janis, I've let you down and you don't even know it. I'm sorry I lied about Barry's death. He died in his car all right...from multiple bullet wounds. He must have got in way over his head. All I know is, he died a violent death. And I've led these guys on as if you're 100 percent behind me. And now I've got to back up and deal with reality. The reality is this could be a very dangerous business and I've got you and the boys to think about. I'm willing to abide by your decision if you want me to pull the plug on all this."

She was furious. It was not only that he had lied, she said, but he had not trusted her enough to be honest. Now, he was tossing the problem in her lap, putting her in the position of a spoil-sport that would wreck his opportunity. If she said "No," he would rebuke her all his life.

It was a long and tormenting night. After telling her *everything*, including all he knew about Barry's murder, an assassination as she saw it, the decision was made for him. He realized as he was describing the gruesome details, as he understood them, that this flirtation with danger should not have gone this far. It was no kind of life for a family.

"Terry, Barry Seal was *assassinated*," Janis lectured. "You need to accept that and quit referring to his death a *murder*. I know you weren't doing anything wrong, but you were around Barry so often that whoever killed him probably thinks you were in on his activities, too. You may be next. They would love to get you out of the country where it would be easier to kill you. And maybe me too."

He awoke early the next morning. As he surveyed the bedroom his sleeping wife had so tastefully decorated, he realized she was right. They were giving up too much security to leave Arkansas for the unknown. His cooling-off period had given him a new focus. He called his attorney, Mark Stodola at his new office. He was now the Little Rock City Attorney and a political-wannabe who had run unsuccessfully for county prosecutor.

"Can I take you to lunch?" he asked Stodola. "I need some advice on running for office."

Over lunch, Terry outlined his hope of running for mayor of Maumelle. Stodola said he would contact a "political handler" named Buddy Vilines, a former Little Rock mayor. Vilines, Stodola said, had been the mastermind behind several political upsets. Terry left convinced that Vilines was on the inside of the political fast track and looked forward to meeting him.

The following night, he dined, no, drank, with Vilines, a man with a hollow leg at the Faded Rose, THE political hangout in Little Rock. Vilines drank multiple whiskey sours starting with happy hour and all through dinner. He seemed impressed with Terry's plans for bringing foreign industry to Maumelle.

"If you can deliver, or even come close to deliverin' on your promise of a new factory in Maumelle, I'll be your campaign manager," Vilines told him. He then gave Reed—on a paper napkin—a cost-per-vote analysis. "I'm glad Stodola sent you my way. This could be fun. You know Bill Clinton is makin' a lotta noise right now about his upcomin' trip to Japan to recruit industry. We can steal his publicity. It's a good idea."

Janis was excited when she heard about her husband's plans to enter the political arena. She got the nominating petitions and began collecting the prerequisite signatures he would need to get on the Democratic primary ballot.

"Are you sure this is what you want to do?" she asked. "You're not doing this just to put excitement in your life since you're not going to Mexico?" He told her no.

He lied. In fact, he genuinely dreaded informing John Cathey of his decision. He scheduled lunch with Bob Nash instead. Nash and Clinton had left the bunker meeting with a *compromise* settlement. Reed felt it politically advantageous to inform Nash of his decision to stay in Arkansas. He still was having ambivalent feelings. He was trying to convince himself he was more an Arkansan than part of the cabal he had joined in the bunker. In hindsight, he was unhappy about the cavalier way Nash and Clinton had been treated by the men from Washington.

"You need to inform your people that I'm not going to Mexico," Reed told Nash as he spooned his egg drop soup at Fu Lin's. "I have new plans." Reed told him of his desire to stay in Arkansas where he saw great opportunities in the machine-tool business. Besides, he said, he was planning to run for office and there was a possibility of attracting a Japanese company to Maumelle.

"Why this sudden change of heart?" Nash asked.

"To tell you the truth, Bob, this Barry Seal death has strongly influenced my decision. I just can't get it out of my craw that there's a lot more to his death than we all have been told."

Nash sat silently, looking at Reed. "This'll really be a disappointment to our friend," Nash said, referring to Cathey. "Have you informed him yet of your change of mind? You know he's already factored you into his plan."

Reed told Nash that he had not informed anyone up to now. His primary reason for not going, he said, was concern for his family's safety in Mexico. But there were other considerations, too. There was the burgeoning media coverage of the drug trial of Hot Springs attorney Sam Anderson Jr. The trial was bringing Roger Clinton's name back to public attention. Roger, who had pleaded guilty to drug trafficking charges, had turned informer and was the government's star witness against Anderson.

This scandal was certain to spread, if it hadn't already, into Dan Lasater's bond firm, which handled millions in state bond business along with Seal's money and the "deposits" from the green flights.

All of this renewed media coverage about Roger was generating haunting thoughts of Seal's comments about being involved in a Republican-backed sting operation to bring down some major Democrats. He was certain that somehow Seal's name would surface in all of this and that other motives behind his death and connection to Arkansas would be revealed. He couldn't be sure how much Nash knew about this.

"I still have unanswered questions about what all Barry Seal was doing here. You and I both know Barry was doing a whole lot more that just flying 'green flights' into the Triple-S," Terry said.

"What are you referring to?"

"Well since Barry's dead now, I guess he won't mind me talking about it. But he alluded to being the source of the drugs that are bringing down some important people here. I guess you know all about that." It had been discussed by the governor himself, in a round-about way, during the bunker meeting at Camp Robinson. *("Gettin' my brother arrested and bringin' down the Arkansas bond business in the process isn't my idea of kosher.!")*

Nash shot back. "You weren't involved in any of that, were you? 'Cause Bill is really pissed. And if you were, it'd be my advice not to plan a political career in Arkansas. In fact, if I were you, I wouldn't plan any career in Arkansas."

Terry shook his head. "No. I wasn't involved in any way...that I know of. I was aware of some mutinous planning by Seal, but I thought it was only against the Agency. It certainly didn't involve Roger, Lasater or anyone else close to Bill. What I did learn was strictly after the fact stuff. Bob, I've *never* had anything to do with drugs."

"That's good. I'll tell Bill. I've got to call Cathey on something else anyway. Do you want me to tell him about your decision not to go?"

"Yeah, I'd really appreciate that. It's a call I haven't been looking forward to and I have no way to contact him directly anyway."

"I'm sure he won't be happy. But you know the Feds, they're never happy anyway." Reed felt they parted as friends.

Whatever Cathey's reaction, Reed's news would certainly not sit well in the governor's mansion. Terry Reed had been an eyewitness during the secret Camp Robinson meeting when the CIA, through Robert Johnson, gave the 39-year-old Bill Clinton his marching orders. Now Terry, who had been privy to unauthorized Contra operations and money laundering in Arkansas, was not going to Mexico. Instead he was planning to stay in Arkansas and attempt to build a political power base there just as a major political scandal was unfolding. He would be an on-going threat to Bill Clinton, who was already in trouble.

Because of his Agency connection, Terry had inadvertently amassed a lot of political dirt. Locked in Terry's head, which had a tremendous capacity for detail, were enough dark and dirty secrets to send half of the Arkansas oligarchy to prison. Clinton didn't need another loose end in Maumelle. The phone lines between Little Rock and Washington had to be buzzing about Reed's decision to stay.

For the next three days, Terry kept waiting for the phone to ring with an irate John Cathey on the other end. The call never came and it was beginning to eat at him that he had not told Cathey personally of his decision. But what was really tearing at him was whether he had really made the right decision about staying in Arkansas?

He endured a hectic week wrestling with all the turmoil of his decision and trying to get in the groove of his machine-tool activity. How could he ever live the life of a mundane surburbanite, even as a small town mayor, with the secrets he had acquired in the spook world. Janis knew by the look on his face that he was "faking it" with being content about his decision.

Twice she had broached the subject of his decision. Had she been responsible for it, she had asked? Both times, he assured her that was not the case.

He lied.

It was a Saturday afternoon, April 19th, 1986, and Terry was in the garage for a self-imposed therapy session. Restoring the 1967 Corvette he had purchased was actually therapeutic.

Janis leaned through the doorway holding the receiver of the hall phone. "I've got Cherryl Hall on the phone, she wants to know if we want to go with her and Wally tonight to a new Mexican restaurant."

The last thing he wanted was to be reminded of Mexico, but he knew Janis wanted to go out for the evening.

"Sure. Why not? It'll get my mind off things." What the hell, he thought, there'd be a price to pay if he didn't.

As he continued reassembling the Corvette's engine, all he could think about was how he wished he would be going to dinner with Barry Seal or someone else with which he had something in common. He knew Barry liked engines. If he were here, they'd both be "shootin' the shit" and discussing such things as the compression ratio of a 327 cubic-inch, small-block Chevy engine.

Wally Hall was just not his type. It wasn't that he disliked him, they simply had nothing in common. Terry knew the evening would be occupied with idle chit-chat centered on what jock could jump the highest, who'd elbowed who, sports injuries, coach gossip and, of course, which star athlete was servicing the wife of some Arkansas power broker. Yup, he thought, that about sums up Wally Hall, the famous Arkansas sportscaster who was sports editor of the *Arkansas Democrat*.

His wife, Cherryl, now, that was something else, he decided, as he torqued the cylinder head bolts. Cherryl and Janis had become rather close friends, but it was a "friendship" founded on convenience. They worked together in real estate, had joined the same firm at the same time and had a child the same age. Cherryl, for some reason, had decided to share with Janis all the intimate, blow-by-blow minutiae of not only her present extra-marital affair, but also the details of her previous criminal charges stemming from drug addiction while living in Virgina Beach.

Wally was totally in the dark about his wife's jaded past and her current sexual indiscretions, making it a pain for Terry to try to remember what he could and couldn't say around the Halls for fear of bringing up something he...or Wally... wasn't supposed to know about. Yeah, it was sure to be a hell of an evening.

Shit, Barry, it's all your fault. I miss you. If you hadn't gone and got yourself riddled with bullets, Janis wouldn't have turned on me and we could all be in Mexico tonight havin' fun, he thought to himself while carressing the body lines of Zora Duntov's creation.

But Terry made one of those marital *compromises* a wise husband makes. His wife wanted to go. That night, the four of them drove to Juanita's restaurant in the Reeds' van. Terry was at the wheel making idle conversation with Wally, seated in the front with him. The two wives were laughing in the back drinking pre-prepared margaritas as part of their mood adjustment. His thoughts were not on Wally's gossip about basketball coach Eddie Sutton leaving Arkansas and going to Kentucky.

He needed some adrenalin, he thought. Damn, it had been a long time since the Contra "graduation." He needed a "fix." He was certain he had made the wrong decision, *but he couldn't admit it.*

And little did he know that Janis in the back seat was thinking the very same thing. She and Cherryl's conversation had gravitated to a discussion of the Montessori school system where their children were enrolled. Is this all there is to life, she thought, as she listened to Cherryl worry about the school letting in black children. She had forced Terry into making the wrong decision, *but she couldn't admit it.*

It was what marriage is sometimes all about, pursuing a course each thinks the other wants and which makes neither happy.

"My God, look at the crowd! They're standing outside just to get in," Reed said looking for a place to park a block away. The sight turned Terry off. Here was Little Rock's "Who's Who" all fighting to get into what was now becoming the new "in-place," where one would go to be seen and dine on Tex-Mex food.

"Whose idea was this?" Reed asked of no one in particular. "Let's go to SOBs, at least they've got a band there."

1a. Cadet Lt. Colonel Terry K. Reed (sabre drawn) ,1966, with award winning ROTC Company Alpha, which he commanded.

1b. Harry S. Truman, 1966, receiving sabre from Reed's R.O.T.C. unit. Photo courtesy of Truman Library.

2a. Emery (Veda) West, 1981, the F.B.I.'s Hungarian technology transfer asset in Oklahoma City.

2b. Terry Reed (left) in 1981 with Hungarian KGB asset George Fenue at height of F.B.I.'s technology transfer "monitoring."

3a.   Barry Seal 1984 testifying before Presidential Crime Commission.
3b.   Barry Seal, late 1985 outside Federal Court house, Baton Rouge, Louisiana.

4a.   Hangars used for C.I.A. black operations at Mena Airport.

4b.   Panoramic view of "field" near Nella, Arkansas, prior to construction of the C.I.A.'s clandestine training base.

4c.   Oliver North (left) dressed as he appeared when undercover as C.I.A. agent John Cathey.

5a. C.I.A. asset Fred Hampton, Jr. and man who ran Barry Seal's airplane maintenance operation in Mena.

5b. C.I.A. asset Joe Evans, Barry Seal's chief aircraft mechanic.

6a.   Terry, Elliott, Janis & Duncan Reed, 1985, shortly after C.I.A. funded fact finding trip to Mexico.

6b.   Terry Reed (with sunglasses), Mena, Arkansas Airport, 1984, during C.I.A. Operation "Jade Bridge".

7a.   "Parking Meter Factory" in Russellville, Arkansas where C.I.A. weapons parts were secretly manufactured.

7b.   Webster (Webb) Hubbell, Hillary Clinton's former law partner, corporate attorney for POM and now number 3 man in Clinton Justice Department. Photo courtesy of Arkansas Democrat Gazette.

7c.   Seth Ward (left), owner of POM with friend Joe Ida. Ultra light in background.

CAPT. BUDDY YOUNG
Arkansas State Police
Director
Governor's Security

8a. Raymond "Buddy" Young, Bill Clinton's former security chief and man who guarded the "bunker" meeting, posing in front of Arkansas State Capital Building.

8b. Bob Nash, Clinton's Chief Economic Advisor and Liaison to the C.I.A.'s operations in Arkansas. Now with the Clinton Administration in D.C. Photo courtesy of Arkansas Democrat Gazette.

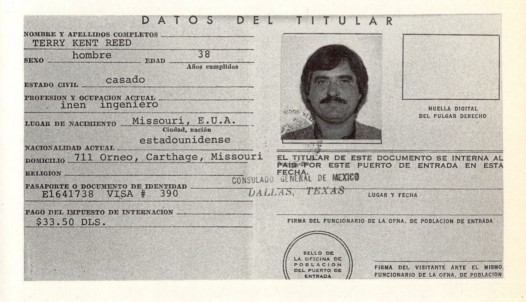

D A T O S   D E L   T I T U L A R

NOMBRE Y APELLIDOS COMPLETOS
TERRY KENT REED

SEXO hombre   EDAD   38
                     Años cumplidos

ESTADO CIVIL casado

PROFESION Y OCUPACION ACTUAL
inen ingeniero

LUGAR DE NACIMIENTO Missouri, E.U.A.
                  Ciudad, nación
                  estadounidense

NACIONALIDAD ACTUAL
DOMICILIO 711 Orneo, Carthage, Missouri

RELIGION

PASAPORTE O DOCUMENTO DE IDENTIDAD
E1641738 VISA # 390

PAGO DEL IMPUESTO DE INTERNACION
$33.50 DLS.

HUELLA DIGITAL
DEL PULGAR DERECHO

EL TITULAR DE ESTE DOCUMENTO SE INTERNA AL PAIS POR ESTE PUERTO DE ENTRADA EN ESTA FECHA.

CONSULADO GENERAL DE MEXICO
DALLAS, TEXAS   LUGAR Y FECHA

FIRMA DEL FUNCIONARIO DE LA OFNA. DE POBLACION DE ENTRADA

SELLO DE
LA OFICINA DE
POBLACION
DEL PUERTO DE
ENTRADA

FIRMA DEL VISITANTE ANTE EL MISMO FUNCIONARIO DE LA OFNA. DE POBLACION

9a.   Terry with co-pilot Duncan Reed at Guadalajara Airport, 1987, during Operation Screw Worm.

9b.   Mexican working papers for "Sr. Estrella".

10a. Then Vice-President George Bush and Felix Rodriguez/Maximo Gomez circa C.I.A. Operation "Screw Worm".

10b. A young Felix Rodriguez with Ché Guevara in Bolivia, just prior to Guevara's execution.

11a. Terry and Janis in Mexico, 1987, showing results of "undercover" work. Janis is carrying baby Baxter.

11b. Janis and Terry partying in Mexico with Patrick Juin, witness to "divorce meeting" with Felix Rodriguez.

12a. Terry and Janis Reed shortly after their marriage in 1981 when Terry was performing "monitoring" services for the F.B.I.

12b. Janis Reed and children while Terry was working undercover in Operation "Screw worm", Ajijic, Mexico, 1986.

13a. Assistant U.S. Attorney Robin Fowler, the man who led the government's merciless attack on the Reeds...and who was defeated!

13b. In-processing into Criminal Justice System August 1988, courtesy of Mr. Fowler's Grand Jury proceedings.

13c. Terry and Janis Reed 1989. Packing for Federal Court odyssey with court documents loaded on roof.

14a. Steve Clark, former Arkansas Attorney General and man who would be Governor had he not threatened Clinton's political future. Photo courtesy of Arkansas Democrat Gazette.

14b. John Wesley Hall Jr., the Reeds' former Attorney and man who assisted Time Magazine in preventing the Reeds' civil suit from going to trial during the presidential election. Photo courtesy of Arkansas Democrat Gazette.

15a. William C. Duncan, former IRS criminal investigator and man whose Mena investigations were stonewalled by the Reagan/Bush White House.

15b. Russell Welch, Arkansas State Police investigator in Mena whose inquiries about C.I.A. activities were stonewalled by the F.B.I.

16a. Reed's refuge and "secret communications headquarters" in Bernalillo, New Mexico.

16b. Clark Ronnow, man who befriended the Reeds and gave them asylum after Time magazine's vicious attack.

"No," Cherryl said," we have to go here, everybody in the office is just raving about this place." Terry was outvoted 3-1.

Before elbowing their way through the Corona drinking crowd that spilled out onto the sidewalk, Reed noticed a dark-colored van parked directly in front of the screen door, which served as the entrance.

I've seen that van before, Reed thought to himself, and then shrugged it off as he searched for the right person to bribe for a table. The women remained outside, while Wally accompanied Reed to the maitre d'. Terry pressed a $20 bill in his hand and said: "We're the Reed party of four. I hope the wait won't be long."

As they returned to their wives with four bottles of beer, Wally said for everyone to hear: "Shit! I can't believe it. Terry just bribed that guy $20 and the maitre d' said we'd only have to wait 15 minutes." Janis threw him a dirty look. He shrugged and said: "Hey, I couldn't help it. I've been practicing for Mexico by bribing people. This looks like Mexico to me, or at least as near as I'll ever get."

Cherryl was impressed. Wally never bribed anyone. She admonished him that he probably didn't even know how. They were ushered in past the throngs of people, and seated in the back on the west side of the packed restaurant. In the southeast corner of the main dining area was a large, rowdy group of people seated around several tables put together to form one large one.

The Reed party ordered their Tex-Mex gringo food and passed the time in meaningless conversation. This was very much like the vacation scene in Puerto Vallarta, people trying to offset their week-long misery with two hours of drunken merriment. Why couldn't people live a life that makes them happy most of the time? Why did people find it necessary to group together and make fools of themselves on the weekend? It rekindled his thoughts they shared in Mexico. He didn't want to be like these people, yet here he was, with them, instead of in Mexico. By the strained look on her face, he knew Janis was sharing the same feeling.

When the check came, Wally placed the cash Terry had laid on the table in his pocket and pulled out his company credit card, saying: "I hope you don't mind if I take your money. I need some cash for the weekend and this way I won't have to use the money machine. I'll just put the whole bill on my credit card." Reed shrugged, figuring the newspaper had probably just bought the four of them their dinner and Wally had actually turned a profit by pocketing the cash. Terry hadn't noticed a man approach their table. He looked up and saw Bob Nash standing beside him.

"I noticed you were just finishing with your dinner. Bill would like to talk to you outside," Nash said.

"Bill?"

"Yeah, he's right over here in the corner... Oh, here he comes now."

Reed turned around in his chair to get a better look and saw Bill Clinton walking away from the unruly group in the corner and toward Reed's table.

Clinton made eye contact with him and sauntered by without stopping.

"Hi!...Bye!" was all he said as if speaking to no one.

The young governor continued walking until he reached the exit. It was easy to see by his glassy gaze and relaxed posture that he was under the influence.

Nash shrugged his shoulders and conjured up an apologetic expression, "I guess that means we're going."

"I hope you'll excuse us," Nash said to Janis and the Halls. "I'm sure we won't be gone long."

Terry excused himself from his wife and the wide-eyed Halls.

Outside, Clinton was already seated in the parked security van with the side door open. A man and a woman stepped out of the van as Reed and Nash approached and the governor told Nash: "Bobby...I'd like to talk to him privately." Reed stepped in and Nash closed the door. Standing guard outside the restaurant watching the van was Arkansas State Police Lieutenant Raymond (Buddy) Young, the governor's chief of security. This was the same vehicle he had witnessed Clinton arrive in for the Agency's meeting at Camp Robinson.

Clinton was comfortably seated in a plush, swiveling captain's chair on the streetside of the van and Reed took the one opposite him on the curbside with his back to the van's side door, which was now closed. His eyes scanned the interior of what was really a mobile command post equipped with an array of electronics that included a computer terminal. It was a much scaled-down, wingless version of Air Force One, he thought.

The governor's invitation had come as a surprise to Terry. He would be even more surprised by what he was about to see and hear.

"Bobby says you've got a problem about going to Mexico because of the deal with Barry Seal," the glassy-eyed governor began. By this time, the smell of marijuana was unmistakable.

Clinton paused for a moment as if trying to sort out his thoughts. "I can see your concern. I understand Seal was a friend of yours. His death does appear suspicious. And Bobby says you got a feeling somebody here in Arkansas may have had a motive to kill him. But nobody here had anything to do with that. Seal just got too damn big for his britches and that scum basically deserved to die, in my opinion..."

With that, Clinton got up from his chair and went to the back of the van, returning with a half-smoked joint. He reseated himself. He took a long, deep drag. After holding it in until his cheeks bulged, he then exhaled slowly and deliberately.

He extended his arm and offered the joint to Reed. Terry shook his head and gestured, no thanks.

"Go on, I'm the commander in chief here; you won't get busted," the governor said with a straight face while exhaling. Reed felt uncomfortable with a cop standing right outside the van and he sure didn't want to cloud his mind with anything more that the two beers he had already consumed in the restaurant.

"No, thanks. I just want to get all of this straight. You're saying that Seal's death, from what you know, is just as the papers say, he was killed by some Colombians because of his connection to the Medellin Cartel?"

"Yeah. And I think you're makin' a big mistake by passing up the opportunity to go to Mexico for Cathey. It sounds attractive to me. I wish I could go in your place. Terry, these guys are counting on you and they're leaning on me to get you to go. I'm not standing in your way. I just want to tell you that if you wanna still go to Mexico, you'd be leaving here with my blessing. There's no hard feelings about anything that happened here. I wanted you to hear that coming from me."

Clinton took another deep drag, held it and exhaled. In a raspy voice, with smoke still coming from his mouth, Clinton added, "Sure you don't want some of this? This is good shit. We sure do grow lotsa good things besides watermelons here in Arkansas."

"Thanks, again, but I gotta get back inside with my group before they wonder what happened to me."

"So what's your decision, you gonna go or aren't ya? I gotta tell Cathey somethin' ASAP to get him offa my ass. It's ridiculous, but he's holdin' me responsible for your vacillation."

"Tell him I'm goin'."

"Good."

Terry walked back toward the restaurant entrance and could hear Clinton calling out to Nash. "Bobby, get 'em rounded up. I'm ready to go."

How could Terry know then he had just witnessed the future President of the United States smoking a joint and inhaling with expertise.

As he rejoined his wife and friends, Terry felt elation beginning to bubble up inside him. He had spent a miserable evening with boring company and had just left a man close to his age, who was the governor, and who should be on top of the world. Yet this same man had just expressed the desire to change places with Terry. Nobody's really happy, he decided. Like Grandpa said, "The grass is always greener..." Somehow the thought of grass seemed fitting..

He had needed a "fix" and the adrenalin was now flowing. Yes, he was going!

Back at the table, Cherryl, always nosey, was champing at the bit and demanded to know what had just happened. "I didn't know you knew Bill Clinton. What's that all about? Where'd you go?"

Ignoring the question, Terry turned to Janis and smiled. "We're going to Mexico."

Oblivious to their dinner guests, she asked, "Are you sure you're making the right decision?"

"Yeah. *What's the worst that could happen?* We're off on an adventure."

On the drive home, he had time to think about what had happened in the governor's van. With all things considered, and even having inside knowledge of the source of "capitalization" of the governor's industrial plan, Terry still liked Clinton. He and Janis had found it refreshing to live in a state that was ruled by someone of their generation. Clinton was doing a lot of good things for Arkansas and was taking it from the "corn cob pipe and moonshine" image of its past to its proper place in the industrialized world.

But he couldn't help but feel let down by the hypocrisy demonstrated by Clinton having the courage to smoke a joint in his presence and yet not possessing the strength to campaign openly to reform marijuana laws. When, he wondered, was someone from his generation going to stand up and tell it like it is to the voters.

Throughout the state that night, Terry was sure, kids were being busted and their lives destroyed for the possession of a few joints of "Arkansas' finest."

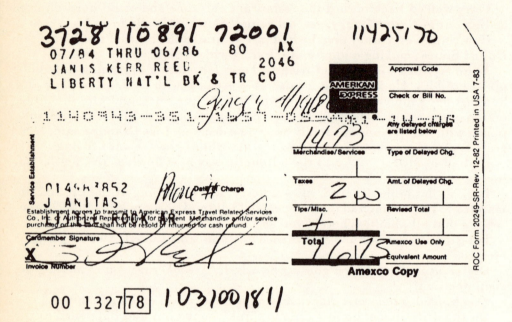

20-1. Bar bill from Juanita's Restaurant on the night Terry Reed met with Bill Clinton.

BOB NASH
SENIOR ASSISTANT FOR ECONOMIC
DEVELOPMENT

STATE OF ARKANSAS
OFFICE OF THE GOVERNOR

BILL CLINTON
GOVERNOR

STATE CAPITOL BUILDING
LITTLE ROCK, ARKANSAS 72201
501/371-2345

OS International U.S.A. Inc.

Aki Sawahata
Vice President

OS International, Inc.
Ichikawa Bldg. 27-2,
1-Chome, Takadanobaba,
Shinjuku-ku, Tokyo 160, Japan
03-208-0314
TLX 232-4424 OSINTL

OS International U.S.A. Inc.
1217 Rebsamen Park Road
Little Rock, Arkansas 72202
501/661-1023
TLX 757901 OSIUSA

Dean Mangum
VICE PRESIDENT

Lasater & Company
INVESTMENT BANKERS

312 Louisiana Street • Little Rock, Arkansas 72201 • 501/376-0069
National WATS: 1-800-643-8072 • Arkansas WATS: 1-800-482-8496

J.A. MATEJKO
Manufacturing · Engineer

Iver Johnson's Arms, Inc.
2202 Redmond Rd. Jacksonville, Arkansas 72076
(501) 982-9491

20-2. Reed's decision to move to Mexico meant he would no longer be orbiting in the same circles as Bob Nash, Aki Sawahata, Dean Mangum, and Tony Matejko. Little did Reed know, however, that his sheer knowledge of "Jade Bridge" and "Centaur Rose" as he transitioned to "Operation Screw Worm" would make him a liability to powerful people in Arkansas.

CHAPTER 21

ESCAPE FROM 'FREEDOM'

In a 1984 Chevy conversion van, loaded to the ceiling with all the Reeds' "important, have-to-have, can't-live-without, absolutely-essential stuff," Terry, Janis and the two boys sat waiting for the United States Customs agent to raise the barrier allowing them access to Mexico.

It was June 15th, 1986, a day they thought would never arrive. The mystique of a secret agent's life lay just across the meandering stream called the Rio Grande.

Presidio, Texas, which advertises itself as the onion capital of the world, was both their port of debarkation and their springboard to happiness, or so they thought. Across the river lay the sweltering and dusty Mexican town of Ojinaga, one of the typical "arm-pits" strung along the border.

It was early Sunday morning and they were the first car of the day to pass southward through the checkpoint, catching by surprise the U.S. Customs agents who had to rouse themselves and raise the barricade.

Terry had honked the horn, thinking the booth was unmanned. The confused, young agent walked out with a mirror mounted on wheels and rolled it underneath the van to inspect it for contraband. "Excuse me, we're going *into* Mexico, not coming out," Terry reminded the still groggy agent. An embarrassed GS weenie, as Seal would have called him, raised the barricade and they made their escape.

Fifteen minutes later, after bribing Mexican Customs Officials in exchange for expeditious and hassle-free passage, they were on their way, and free at last, dodging the potholes on Mexican Highway 16 enroute to Chihuahua. Janis was in the back comforting the children and breaking out the toys she had packed to occupy them for their journey. They were a full 30 miles inland and avoiding cattle roaming the road when it finally hit them—they had done it, they had escaped the American rat race—at last.

Everything was now a blur from this point back to that night two months earlier at Juanita's restaurant when Bill Clinton had personally taken the trouble to encourage Terry to join the operation. This gesture had removed Terry's fears about any sort of ill will or retribution coming as a result of confusion that he may have been part of Seal's dirty-tricks campaign.

John Cathey and Robert Johnson were relieved that both Reeds were now 100 percent on board. Besides putting final touches on the business plan with Johnson, Terry began interfacing with Gomez in anticipation of his "handoff" from the States to Mexico. The itinerary had been difficult to plan due to machine tool business that Terry had to clear up before leaving. The cover story for Terry's departure was an expansion of his machine-tool business to Mexico and to test the Mexican market for factory automation.

In addition to contractually transferring maintenance obligations that Applied Technologies had with clients in Arkansas and Texas, Terry had been busy "mothballing" the firm just in case Mexico didn't work out as he hoped and he wanted to return. Janis had frantically shut down her real estate activities in Little Rock just days before the moving van arrived to transfer their household goods to storage. Then there were the usual goodbyes to friends and associates and the calls from well-wishers who couldn't believe they were actually taking children to Mexico considering all the disease and filth they had heard were there. Janis and Terry knew this was a myth perpetuated by ill-informed non-travelers, but didn't wish to correct these misconceptions for fear that too many gringos might move there and destroy the paradise they had discovered.

Janis and the children had departed Little Rock on June 1st to visit her parents in Kansas City while Terry had gone to Texas to oversee a large machine-tool installation. While in Texas, Gomez called him with the itinerary for Mexico and he was told to be at the Hotel Playa Conchas Chinas in Puerto Vallarta by June 21st. It was a remote hotel on the outskirts of town, he was told, and it was frequented primarily by Mexican tourists.

A man by the name of Mitch Marr, he was told, would find him and rendezvous with him there.

"Why meet him in Puerto Vallarta? Aren't we going to set this up in Guadalajara?" Terry had asked Gomez.

"There is a very large gringo element in Guadalajara," Gomez explained. "That's a bad place to meet....someone who knows him might see the two of you together there. Remember, you and Mitch are never to be seen together in public. Mitch wants to meet you in PV (Puerto Vallarta) and spend some time with you, you know, get to know you. He'll be your handler and, I'm sure most important to you, your money man. Besides, this trip is on Uncle and Mitch wants to take advantage of the scenery, and the women, at the beach."

The Reeds had planned a leisurely trip to PV, which included a stopover at several cities they had never seen. They had factored in several days for the trip from the border to their destination and the second night "in country" was spent in Durango, home of the large Hollywood movie set where John Wayne and other western stars filmed some of their best.

After finding "*el centro*," they purchased a brochure on the city and discovered Pancho Villa was assassinated right across the street from where they were parked. They decided anyway to spend the night in the very room the assassin had taken.

The foreign intrigue began to remind them of their honeymoon in Budapest. Janis was very amorous that night. This was, after all, Mexico with its endless, night-long street sounds mixed in with *Mariachi* music and laughter. Both were starting to settle in together and the aura of pending danger, coupled with cutting the chord to the life she had known, excited her.

Then, the next day, on to Mazatlan on the Pacific Coast, after first crossing the famous gorge of El Diablo Canyon. In Mazatlan, they found a very Mexican beach hotel, away from gringos, and checked in for the night to watch the sun set and take on a supply of margarita mix. They were, after all, on vacation, and tequila was why Mexico was famous. Jose Cuervo was only three U.S. dollars a bottle.

They quickly discovered they were not only in the tropics, but it was also the tourist off-season, due to the sweltering heat and the summer invasion of insects. The humidity was unbearable and only the poorest Americans *turistas* were showing up now causing the hotels to virtually give the rooms away. For every minus there is a plus.

They had been out of the U.S. for three days and still having difficulty dealing with having no phone and no schedule. Work habits die hard for gringos. Even though there was nothing to plan, Janis kept her daily planner up to date and attached her yellow Mexican automobile insurance policy sticker with a phone number to call in case of accident. They hadn't yet discovered that only gringos believed in and were required to have insurance. The entire industry was one that Mexican's not only avoided but ridiculed classifying it as a "Yankee" problem and creation, not one of theirs.

The following day brought them to Puerto Vallarta, their destination, a day ahead of schedule. After asking directions, they discovered the hotel they were seeking was situated on the far south limits of the cove that defines the port city. The southern area geographically shared nothing with the central city and the hotel row on the north, built on flat coastal terrain.

This area had steep cliffs and was much more private and exclusive, reserved more for wealthy Mexicans and foreigners who wanted to avoid the tourist element. The hotel was built on the side of a cliff and had 40 "junior suites" that extended down to beach level from the lobby level, which was the top floor.

On the 21st, a Saturday morning, the phone rang around 9 AM in the Reeds' room. The desk clerk, in his best English, told Terry, "Your friend is waiting for you at our Oceanside bar. He requests for you to join him for *desayuno*." Terry would soon find why Marr rhymed with bar.

He left his sleeping family and went to join his new "handler" at the surfside bar. There, under the shade of palapas, the Mexican beautiful people were taking breakfast by the beach, most enjoying fruit or a continental breakfast. From among the beautiful bodies attired in coordinated beach wear, Terry searched for a person he had no face to hang on. Unlike the movies there were no whispered code words, no passed notes. Marr spotted him first. In a loud voice, he beckoned "Terry! It's me Mitch! Come join me over here."

Marr was easy to find. Besides shouting, he was the only one wearing an iridescent tank top, Bermuda shorts, and tennis shoes.

Terry joined Marr at a small table nearest the bar. He would soon learn why Marr had selected this strategic location. Once seated down wind, he got the aroma of stale booze. Marr was a man in his late 50s, sporting a flat-top haircut with closely cropped sides. His full head of hair, which showed no signs of receding, was salted with gray and joined what appeared to be a two-day growth of beard. He was about six feet tall and had a burly chest above his sagging middle.

Mitch was one of what the media later called the "over-the-hill gang." Like Bill Cooper, Marr was ex-Air America, men long thought to have been put out to pasture. But Terry was learning that old CIA men never really retire, but become "dormant," to be recalled, recycled and used again. For Mitch, it'd been a long time between secret projects and government-paid expenses.

"I got here day before yesterday," Marr belted out once Terry was seated. "Thought I'd come on down early an' check out the broads at the beach. It's hotter'n shit this time a year, but a lot of the classy Mexican cunts come down here in the off season and run around half fuckin' naked. They leave their fag Latino lovers at home and come down here in pairs and a lot of 'em wanna fuck around. You're gonna like it here, Reed."

He paused long enough to down the remains of what appeared to be a screw driver. "Coop's told me all about ya. Ain't this great? Startin' up Air America again. Fuck, I was about to go crazy in retirement down here 'til all this shit blew up down south. Goddam, let's order a pitcher of bloody Marys and drink to communism and Daniel Ortega."

Terry was observing the results of too many years with not enough to do in "Margaritaville," as he would later call it. He knew he would like the life here, but only if he stayed busy and didn't end up a drunk like Marr.

"So, you still doing any flying down here?" Terry asked.

"No, flyin' brings too much attention to me. I've sorta grounded myself for security reasons."

Terry would learn later that was a lie. Marr was grounded, but not of his own volition. He simply couldn't pass the pilot's physical anymore, and he had lost what a pilot calls "his edge." The booze had gotten him.

Terry didn't realize that morning, as Marr "inhaled" his *huevos rancheros* while washing them down with bloody Marys, just how bad Mitch's drinking problem was. The two men spent several hours while Marr gave Terry his operational briefing while consuming the bulk of the pitcher.

"You met Diana Aguilar from Chapala Realty when you were here last September," Marr said between swallows of the bloody Mary. "I've had her lookin' for a house close to where I live for ya and the family. After this trip, we should not be seen together in public unless it's at a fiesta or some gringo shindig like the ones that go on at the Lake." He was referring to the Lake Chapala area south of Guadalajara.

"I believe Aguilar had lined up several homes to show your wife and is expectin' ya to call her once ya arrive in Chapala. Gomez said you'd be needin' a phone for business reasons and the problem is none of the one's she's targeted has one. A phone stays with a house an' is just passed on from one occupant to another. It's damn hard to get a phone down here. Last time I checked, the waitin' list for a new phone number is over a year. And only then after ya bribe some motherfucker about 500 bucks. You'll soon learn that greenbacks make anything possible down here."

Again, it was napkin time. As they talked, Marr sketched a map of the village of Ajijic showing where he lived. "I don't have a phone either, so, if we need to communicate directly, ya can walk over to my house, at night. I'm normally at home then. Don't drive. I don't want the neighbors to see your car near my home. We'll only have reason to see each other a couple of times a month once things get set up. It's my understandin' you'll just be comin' to me for money, and for monthly progress reportin' which I'll just pass on to Gomez."

"How do you communicate with him if you don't have a phone?" Terry asked.

"Say, you know better than to ask questions like that! You just do the reportin'. Communication's my problem."

Marr, he learned, was going to play strictly by the rules, at least for now. Marr would be Terry's only communication link to the Enterprise, as Oliver

North and Richard Secord called it. For security of the entire operation, Terry was being insulated and, as he would find, isolated as well. He had learned as far back as the Air Force Intelligence School in Denver that you can't *compromise* what you don't know, no matter how much someone would try to extract it from you. And, for now at least, he realized his linkage to the intelligence world started and stopped with Mitch Marr.

What a scary dilema, Terry thought, as he watched the ex-Air American cowboy woof down the last of the refried beans and fart loud enough to attract the attention of the "classy Mexican cunts" sitting near them. Marr certainly wasn't as well preserved as Bill Cooper, for whom Reed had nothing but admiration. Oh well, maybe he was seeing Marr on one of his bad days. We all have those, he rationalized.

The reality of what was happening began to make Terry feel a little claustrophobic. To the world, Terry was to appear as an entrepreneurial-driven American businessman. Only he and his wife would know the deep, dark secret about their sponsorship into the Mexican business community. From what Marr was telling him, only this CIA retread could attest to Terry's secret linkage. For this reason, Terry decided to confirm what he had been told during the bunker meeting back in Arkansas. "Up in the States, I attended a meeting with Gomez, Cathy and Johnson in which I was told the American consul also knows of my true mission. Is that so?"

"They told ya that!" Marr said somewhat taken aback. "I didn't think ya were supposed ta know that. But hell, if they told ya that, I guess ya know already. Yeah, his name is Daniel Darrach. What else did they tell ya?"

"Only that I was to turn to him only in an emergency."

This made Terry more comfortable, knowing that someone officially linked to the State Department would be on hand if something went wrong.

"But ya shouldn't be goin' there and talking to him or anythin' like that. He's only there, like they said, for an emergency," Marr stressed. "I'm the *only* guy you're supposed to be havin' official contact with. Understand?"

Reed nodded.

The balance of the conversation at the beach that morning consisted of an outline for a trip during which Marr would introduce Terry to the people selected to provide the services he would need in order to operate as a businessman in Mexico.

"When ya get ready, I'll take ya to the Guadalajara Airport an' introduce ya to Commandante Raul Fierro. He's an old buddya mine and we go way back," Marr boasted. "He ain't the real commandante anymore, but ya still gotta call him that or he'll get offended. He's big on respect. You'll find his family is the Mexican equivalent to the Wright Brothers, Lindbergh and Chuck Yeager all rolled up into one. His brother flew an airplane nonstop from Mexico City ta New York and somehow these fuckin' Mexicans think that compares ta Lindbergh's flight over the Atlantic. No one's ever confirmed if he even fuckin' did it non-stop, or over *any* fuckin' water for that matter."

"So does Fierro know what I'm doing here?" Terry asked, trying to probe deeper into the command structure in Mexico.

"He knows enough, and another guy in Mexico City named Jaime Bravo, who's with the DFS (the Mexican CIA) will take care of all the flight plans in an' out, or at least that's my understandin' from Gomez. Remember, you're not supposed to be pokin' your nose in ta areas ya don't belong. Gomez told me ta remind ya not ta be playin' like a spook...just run the fuckin' company."

"You've mentioned Gomez several times today, you know him pretty well?" Terry asked again.

"Yeah, but he's one of those guys you'd like ta forget sometimes. We all go back to SEA (Southeast Asia) together. Back when killin' commies was legal, uncontrolled and fun. Weren't no limit on 'em then. I always liked killin' slant-eyed commies the best. Somehow I just never cottoned ta killing the ones with round eyes, though. They seem a lot more human."

It was apparent from Marr's comments, and what was not being said, that Mitch had seen a lot of action in Southeast Asia. He would later learn Marr had been in Korea as well as Vietnam and Laos.

Marr looked pensively at the water lapping over the beach next to them, and added: "Some of us have grown up since then, though. But then there's Gomez, he'll never change. He's made commie-killin' his life's occupation. Nah, me an' Coop, we see through it all now that we're older and wiser. We're just in it for the money and adrenalin. Adrenalin keeps ya young."

This lapse into personal philosophy and war stories was a sign that the endless Bloody Marys Marr had consumed during the past two hours were starting to take effect. It was 11 AM and the *palapas* could no longer insulate them from the heat.

"Say, it's gettin' fuckin' hot," Marr said." We don't have ta cover all this shit in one day, ya know. Why don't we knock off 'til tonight when the sun goes down? One good thing ta remember is there's no hurry down here, 'specially when the 'Company's' payin' the bills."

Terry suddenly heard Janis shouting from the balcony above them and waving: "Is it OK if I come on down and join you? These kids are driving me crazy cooped up in this room."

She and the children, dressed in their bathing suits, joined the two men. Duncan, their oldest, ran to the coral-rimmed tidal basin while the younger, Elliott, now 13 months, contented himself with playing in the sand.

Terry took the opportunity to introduce Janis to his new CIA handler. She was not impressed. He represented all the attributes of the male stereotype who looked at women as decorations and something to be tolerated in exchange for sex. Something better rented when needed and not owned. Based on her initial conversations with him, she could tell Mitch was not someone with whom she wanted to socialize.

She was definitely not offended when Marr told her they could not be seen together in Ajijic. "It's real unfortunate I won't be able ta introduce you ta the little lady," Marr said referring to his wife. The term made her cringe. "She needs a new friend, someone ta keep her occupied and offa my ass." He laughed.

Janis winced. He was not the type of "spook" she was used to seeing. It was only 11 AM; he was already drunk; and no party was going on. She also found his words offensive and his macho, condescending attitude toward women insulting. And Terry found the situation uncomfortable because he had to make excuses for someone he had only just met and would be dealing with on an ongoing basis. She learned quickly that spies come in many styles and varieties and this guy was certainly not like Joszef Bona or Wayne Barlow back in Oklahoma.

After making his excuses about the heat and leaving the table with plans to meet that night, Marr staggered off to his room and left Terry to defend his unprofessional actions.

"Hey, Janis, we all get drunk occasionally. The guy said he's been waiting here for two days and he's obviously been relaxing a little too much and vacationing on the CIA. I'm sure he has a good side to him, otherwise he wouldn't be in charge of this project at this level."

"I don't know. There's something about him I don't like," Janis said apprehensively. "He seems like the kind of guy that would stab you in the back if he had to. I do want to meet his wife, once we get settled, in order to learn more about him."

She got no argument. Such information would be helpful to Terry, as well.

After a day of frolicking in the surf, and admiring the golden brown bodies of the Mexican "cunts," as Mitch referred to them, Terry decided it was time to prepare for the evening meeting with Mitch. The family retired to their room to shower and dress, waiting for Marr's call. The call never came.

A check of the front desk revealed that no one by the name of Marr was registered there, Either Mitch was using an assumed name or was staying somewhere else. Terry figured that was just spook caution. But, regardless of the reason, being stood up was something else, something that bothered Terry. And this made Janis even more suspicious.

"I'll bet he's dead drunk somewhere and doesn't even know what time it is," she said in a chiding tone as they headed out on their own for dinner. Nor did she appreciate Terry's idea of humor when he said: "Maybe some commie assassin got to him."

They dined that night at a place named Le Bistro, which was situated near the river that flows though Puerto Vallarta and turned out to be the No. 1 "action spot" in town.

The continental atmosphere, the gourmet food and the romantic setting peopled by mostly upscale Mexicans helped compensate for his wife's uneasiness with Marr. Having subcontracted the children's care that evening to the hotel nanny, they both settled into what they envisioned more to be the life of a CIA asset with his family in a foreign country. Later that night, as the sound of the pounding surf echoed up the cliff and into their suite, Janis had to take special care to touch only the areas of her husband's sunburned anatomy that had been shielded by his swim trunks. The pleasure and the pain off set each other.

Early the next morning, an apologetic and still-unshaven Mitch Marr summoned Terry back to the breakfast bar by the beach. "I guess it's a combination of the heat and the remnants of Montezuma's revenge. I took some medicine that wiped me out for the night. But I'm feelin' great today, so let's get on with the details. Hey, waiter, give me and my friend a pitcher of screwdrivers."

Terry nursed one glass, while Marr quickly emptied the multi-liter pitcher. It was becoming pretty apparent the type of guy with whom Terry was dealing. Since Marr was having some "hair of the dog," Terry decided he had better get this meeting over with quickly and get the important points out of the way before Marr needed more "medicine." Not the least important topic was Reed's need to get in touch with William Cooper.

"Do you have a way of contacting Cooper?" Terry asked. "He and I still have a little unfinished business up in the States." The Charlie Cuatro was still where Terry had buried it in Little Rock. Terry revealed the C-4 situation to

Marr and that Mark McAfee's building was going to be auctioned off in the fall. Someone, he said, had to remove the explosives before the new owner moves in and increases the chance of the C-4 being discovered.

"I'll be making weekly trips between here and Texas for the next six to eight weeks in order to finish up a factory start-up I'm involved with. I'd like you to help me take care of this matter before I get permanently situated down here."

"Yeah, I can contact him for ya," Marr replied as he downed another screwdriver.

Marr said Terry's concerns would be relayed to Cooper and, in fact, indicated that Cooper would be flying in and out of the Guadalajara airport from time to time. Marr said he was planning to have an Air America old flyers reunion when circumstances permitted.

After a discussion of finances dealing with the methods of payments, disbursements, accounting and draws for the new operation, Marr handed Terry an envelope.

"Don't open it and count it here, but there's ten grand here. That ought ta take care of ya for a couple a weeks, at least until I get back from a trip ta Washington. They want ta talk ta me about all of the chicken shit aspects of this operation. Remember, if ya wanna be reimbursed ya gotta have receipts."

(As Marr was heading to Washington to discuss "chicken shit" details, there was good news and bad news for the Enterprise. With Congressional elections five months away, the White House apparently had twisted enough arms to get the House of Representatives to reverse itself and approve, after a vote of 221-209, a $100 million appropriation for *military* and humanitarian aid for the Contras. It was a major victory for Reagan, reversing as it did the most recent Boland prohibition on military aid. The bad news was that North and Rodriguez were at each other's throats again. It was clear from what Terry had heard during the bunker meeting near Little Rock just a few months earlier that their personal animosity toward each other could not be contained. But this time, North in the presence of former Air Force Colonel Robert Dutton, another operative who had been activated for the operation, accused Rodriguez of talking about secret information over open phone lines. Rodriguez countered with the same charges against Dutton and William Cooper. This behavior resulted in internal power struggles based on conflicting ideology, animosity, jealously, and greed. It was beginning to show there was no real chain of command holding the operation together. The "commie killers" were turning on, and devouring, each other.)[1]

Marr continued with his instructions for Terry while he was away in the States.

"All you need ta do is get settled into your new house and begin scoutin' around for a suitable attorney, et cetera. Gomez tells me that you and Johnson are takin' care of all the business paperwork up in the States...so I don't have ta fuck with any of that, I hope. I don't like fuckin' paperwork unless it's green and has pictures of Benjamin Franklin," Marr joked, making reference to hundred dollar bills. It was flash-back time.

"Did Coop ever tell ya the story of the time I flew a DC-3 loaded with Meo tribesmen and $10 million in gold bouillon out of a 2,500-foot strip built on a cliff over lookin' the side of a Karst mountain near Tchepone on the Plain of Jars in Laos while gettin' hit by over 50 rounds of 23 MM ack-ack fire?"

The day's business, obviously, was over. Marr was slipping off into one of his "there I was at 10,000 feet with both engines on fire" stories.

Terry could have listened all day.

That night Reed made the mistake of calling Texas and checking on the status of his machine-tool installation in progress there. He learned to his dismay that his presence was needed there immediatly. He made plans for Janis and the children to remain in PV until he could return by air.

Deplaning from AeroMexico Airlines after returning four days later, he was greeted by a sunburned, very relaxed, beautiful woman wearing a strapless sun dress and being escorted by two handsome young sons.

She had enjoyed some "quiet time" with only herself and the children, to become immersed in her own thoughts and adjust to the time warp separating the Mexican and gringo cultures. In her bag was a newly purchased, must-read book entitled *Distant Neighbors* analyzing the chasm that separates the cultures of the U.S. and Mexico. She was trying to understand what made this nation of twenty-five million people so different from the chaotic environment she had just left.

She watched Terry clear customs and saw a man in a business suit and carrying a briefcase, the modern American's battle dress. As Duncan, dressed in his surfer outfit, rushed to greet his father, Terry felt he was viewing a family that in four days had become foreign to him. It was unnerving to see how fast his family had shed their Yankee look and attitudes.

Terry truly hoped that what lay ahead was a life that would give him the one thing he had not had in the U.S., ..time...time...time to spend with his family. He no longer wanted to subcontract the care of his children to a day-care system that had turned into an industry.

He hugged her, kissed her and while Duncan embraced his leg he spoke softly, "You sure you're up for this? We can turn back now. I don't ever want to hear I made you do this."

He needed the assurance from Janis that she was still a consenting adult participant in the cultural shift underway.

"Hey, what's the worst that can happen?" she said using his favorite line and grinning. "Let's get you out of those funny looking clothes and go find our new home."

1.   Rodriguez testimony, *Iran-Contra hearings*, 100-3, 221-22, 275-76; North testimony, *Hearings*, 100-7, 302-06, 333-35.

REG.FED.de CAUS.REGM-240417 REG.EDO13861CAM.COM.131.

HOTEL
Playa Conchas Chinas.
CALLE CAPRICORNIO NO.40.

Nº 2963

Tel.2-01-56.   PUERTO VALLARTA, JALISCO. MEXICO.

·502   REED TERRY (2) DVS.   JUN/18/86
        RV/DIRECTO   E.P.   JUN/20/86
        CON CREDITO
C   CLIENTE PAGA DIRECTO CON AMERICAN EXPRESS OPEN

R OBSERVACIONES	FECHA	CLAVE	CONS.	CIO.	IMPORTE.
	JUN18	RS	1230002		
* 40 SUITES	JUN18	DL	1227000		
* OCEAN VIEW	JUN18	RA			
* RESTAURANT " EL SET "	JUN18	DL	1231000		
* KITCHENETTE	JUN18	RS	1240000		
* AIR CONDITIONED	JUN19	BL	1241000		
* MUSIC					
* TELEPHONE	JUN19	LD	1242000		
* ROMAN TUB WITH MASSAGE	JUN18	LD	1242000		
* POOL	JUN18	LD	1243000		
* PRIVATE BEACH	JUN18	DL	1241000		
* ATTENDED BY IT'S OWNERS	JUN18	LD	1251002		
SUMMER RATES: MAY/01-DEC/15	JUN18	LD	1251002		
SINGLE DOUBLE TRIPLE	JUN18	DL			
STANDAR.: $ 28 ! $ 35 ! $ 42					
SUPERIOR: $ 35 ! $ 42 !	JUN19	RA	1251024		
DELUXE..: $ 42 ! $ 50 !	JUN19	DL	1262000		
TVL. AGENCY COMISSION = 10 %	JUN20		1257000		
TAX INCLUDED * TEL.: 2-01-56	JUN20	DL	1260000		

No.de Personas	Precio-Rate.	Plan
2	$ 15,250 00	E.P.

| | JUN20 | RA | 1251000 | | |
| | JUN20 | DL | 1270000 | | |

Debo y pagare incondicionalmente en esta plaza, o en otra que se me requiera de pago
el dia de   de 19   a la orden de HOTEL PLAYA CONCHAS CHINAS. valor
recibido a mi entera sastifaccion.   FIRMA-SIGNATURE.
Regardless of charge instructions the undersigned guest acknowledgest the above as a
personal indebtednes.

21-1. Hotel bill from Puerta Vallarta where Terry Reed first met his CIA handler Mitch
Marr.

AEROVIAS CASTILLO

PASAJE · CORREO · EXPRESS
VUELOS ESPECIALES

Cap. P. A. Manuel Castillo M.

AV. FRANCIA No. 1886
TELS. 12-56-58
12-86-61

89-00-01

AEROPUERTO CIVIL
TEL. ~~12-50-25-66~~
GUADALAJARA, JAL.

P. A. GERARDO MEJIA RODRIGUEZ
COMANDANTE DEL AEROPUERTO

89-02-84

AEROPUERTO FEDERAL
TEL. (682) 2-29-58

LA PAZ. B. C. MEX.

CAP. RauL FIERRO
TeL. 89-03-93-OF.
91-373-6-10-67.

 GESTORIAS AERONAUTICAS Y SERVICIOS

RICARDO LOPEZ ALCANTARA

AEROPUERTO INTERNACIONAL MIGUEL HIDALGO TEL. 39-~~35-35~~ *37 13*
EDIFICIO DE AVIACION GENERAL GUADALAJARA, JAL

21-2. As a result of Reed's introduction to Mitch Marr, he would now be "put in play" with the above CIA connected Mexican Nationals. A new layer of "black" players.

CHAPTER 22

MARGARITAVILLE

"Home" for the Reeds was now less than a day's drive through the layers of Mexican climate. From the steamy, tropical coastline upward and through the high desert elevations and into the cool micro-climate formed around Lake Chapala.

It was Mexico's rainy season and the foliage on the mountains that provided the backdrop to Chapala and Ajijic was a sharp contrast to the smog-laden air of nearby Guadalajara.

They departed Puerto Vallarta on June 27th, 1986, and arrived in Ajijic the same day. After checking into La Posada, they contacted Diana Aguilar, as Marr had instructed. After two days of searching, they found the house they wanted, one just off the square at #57 Calle Hidalgo, which was being vacated by a congenial male couple who were part of the large gay community there. As is often the case, this artistic pair were drawn to this romantic, isolated and naturally beautiful area.

Strangely, the macho Mexican culture made less ado about homosexuality than America, causing many to "flee South" where they lived openly in their relationships and seemingly were accepted by the Mexican community.

The expensively-furnished house was on a cobblestone street which fed into the *Zócalo* (town square) and had once been converted into a private art gallery. From its exterior, the walled compound gave no hint of the opulence hidden inside. A large palm tree rose from the lush manicured lawn and provided a perfect, shaded playing area that could be viewed from inside the glass-encased house. A *casita*, or guest house, was included in this single-story, stone and glass L-shaped home with a secure off-street parking area. All of this third world elegance came at a "grossly-inflated" rental price of $350 a month.

By July 4th, the Reeds were ready to celebrate their house-warming, with the help of their new day maid named Concha, a woman in her mid-30s, with six children of her own and two foster children.

It was fitting that the Fourth of July, the day America celebrates its independence, was being celebrated by the Reeds in a foreign country from which Terry hoped freedom for Nicaragua would be spawned. *Congress be damned!* There would be victory this time whether they approved of it or not. Terry Reed and John Cathey would make it so. He felt elated that he was part of something, a cabal about which only a few knew. It was time for Terry to cash in, believing the members of the Cabal had singled him out to collect his reward for what he had suffered in Southeast Asia. That's what he thought, anyway.

That evening, as the colorful hand-made firewheels spun in Terry's front yard, he felt light years removed from the July 4th just a year earlier when he was training Contra pilots in Arkansas. He thought of his students, probably jettisoning cargo over some battle-riddled area of Nicaragua. And he hoped for their safety on that night of the celebration of freedom.

In addition to getting his household in order in the early part of July, Terry had gone to Mexico City to visit with George Fenue, his soon-to-be Hungarian partner, to discuss the types of machinery likely to be preferred by Mexican customers.

Marr had quietly returned from his trip north and found Terry mired in decision-making concerning compliance with Mexican laws as they related to the new company. Marr arrived discreetly at Terry's house one evening in mid-July and invited him back to his home for a secret operational meeting. The two men departed separately for Marr's house so as to not be seen together in public.

Terry seated himself in Marr's favorite room, his den. It contained his essentials: an overstuffed, rattan papa-san chair from Southeast Asia, a fully-furbished wet bar and his Sony Trinitron large-screen TV. Recessed into the masonry wall was a major collection of mostly pirated videos of *Rambo*, John Wayne, Clint Eastwood, and *Rocky* movies including *anything* that pertained to Vietnam or martial arts. Enshrined in a special place was the video tape of *Apocalypse Now*. He had even recorded the film's sound track on an audio casette, which he later loaned to Terry, so that he could listen to it in his car.

"So what are you drinkin'? Have you discovered Mexican white lightening yet?" he asked as he produced a plastic milk carton from the refrigerator. Scrawled on the side with a black marker was "1982."

"It's worth livin' in Mexico just for this. It's green tequila bought right at the factory and personally aged by me. I've got all the years aging, goin' back to 1975. 1982 was a very good year, however. So I chilled this just for us. Maria! *Tome dos limónes, por favor*."

The Mexican maid appeared with two limes, two tumblers and a jigger of salt. It was obvious she had served her master his liquid drug paraphernalia many times before. Her silent actions were so rehearsed as to be almost mechanical.

She filled both tumblers to the brim with the aged green tequila which had been purchased at one of the factories in the City of Tequila, north of Guadalajara. The fiery Mexican drink, which comes from the fermented juice of the tequila cactus, is something akin to rocket fuel. Tequila could be bought there in bulk at a certain time each year for approximately $1 per gallon as the maturing product is moved from vat to vat. It was part of an annual pilgrimage for the American expatriates living in Mexico. It was a way to lay in a 12 month supply cheaply and was another fringe benefit of living south of the border.

While Terry was busy biting his *limón* in preparation for the taste test, Marr was preparing the entertainment.

He thumbed his remote control to activate the video tape of *Apocalypse Now* already loaded in the VCR, as he emptied half his tumbler in one gulp. The previously queued tape was strategically wound to show the invasion scene with Robert Duval as commander of the Air Cavalry Unit attacking a Vietnamese village by helicopter at sunrise as loudspeakers blared the music from Wagner's *Ride of the Valkyries*.

Terry coughed as he swallowed the tequila in his glass. Suddenly his attention was drawn to Marr, who was mouthing the dialogue of the entire battle scene being played out on the giant screen. The sounds of war shrieking from the dual speakers reverberated off the arch-brick ceiling causing Marr's eyes to glass over as he joined Duval in saying his famous line: "I love the smell of napalm in the morning."

Marr switched off the movie, drained his tumbler and said: "Goddam, I miss 'Nam. They don't make scenes any better than that, do they? Sure wish you and I could hang out together. I've got lotsa war stories I could share with ya. It gets pretty lonesome down here between wars. An' that bitch of mine is drivin' me fuckin' nuts. She just don't understand me. Know what I mean?"

Terry viewed the whole scene with a mixture of humor and sadness tinged with respect. He also felt somewhat uneasy in that he could remotely identify with Marr....wondering if he could be seeing himself years from now. He had observed that seasoned combat flyers like Marr often substitute alcohol for the adrenalin high they can no longer experience. They couldn't kick the habit from the rush their own bodies created, and at this stage in their lives, instead ingested foreign chemicals.

Adrenalin's repeated and controlled rush not only raises one's threshold of fear, but also lowers one's threshold of boredom. It may enable a person to deal with fear and stress, but it's as addicting as tobacco, Reed knew from his previous two-pack a day habit.

For now, Terry put this thought out of his head and felt thankful to see a fate he wanted to avoid.

"Yeah, Mitch, that's a great movie. Duval's a great actor. But it's getting late and I don't think you asked me here just to look at a movie, did you? By the way, where's your wife? I was hoping to meet her."

"Ah, we're not gettin' along right now," Marr responded in a low, melancholy tone. "She's up in the States visitin' her grandchildren. Besides that's the best place for her right now with all the action we got goin' on down here." He paused and then continued in an upbeat way. "And guess what? I think Coop is comin' over for a visit next month."

"Glad you brought up his name, " Terry interjected. "I mailed him a letter while I was up in the States and haven't heard back. I'm hoping to rendezvous with him in Arkansas sometime this month. He mentioned to me he'd probably be attending his daughter's wedding this summer. Has he said anything to you about that, 'cause that would be a perfect time for him to pick up the Charlie Cuatro we talked about?"

"Yeah. I saw him while I was in Florida," Marr noted. "It's my understandin' he'll be attendin' the wedding. It's a big occasion for him. His last kid living at home is finally leaving. I nearly forgot, he said ta tell you ta pencil in July 31 as a target date to meet in Little Rock."

Terry was relieved. Finally, he would be able to resolve this problem.

Marr continued, this time on the business arrangements and partners. "And Johnson wants ya ta meet him and your Jap friend Fuckikawa in Dallas around the same time. He wants ta talk ta you about the stock issue and all that business stuff. So if you can make it, I need ta know soon so I can relay the info."

"Tell them I'll be there".

The remainder of the evening centered on the plans for Terry to meet Raul Fierro, the Mexican contact, at the Guadalajara Airport and to deal with problems that had arisen as a result of the American Drug Enforcement Administration (DEA) moving its aircraft maintenance to a company called *Aviacion del Pacifico*, which was situated next to the warehouse Fierro had selected for Terry to house the machine tool company.

"In some ways, that's bad. You'll have to be awfully careful not to *compromise* yourself or our mission to these beaner flyers the DEA is usin' down here. Ever since that Camarena shithead (DEA agent Enrique 'Kiki' Camarena who was kidnapped and murdered along with his pilot a year earlier) got greased down here, the DEA has been on red alert about Cartel sabotage to their airplanes. They trust this cat nicknamed *Gato*. His real name is Ricardo de Veal; he runs the maintenance for *Aviacion del Pacifico*. His chief mechanic is a Mexican by the name of Pablo Ponce. Pablo used to fly Agency missions down here until his brother cracked up doin' the same. He sorta retired from flyin' after that. You know, lost his nerve. He's still a good mechanic, though. He used to work on my 123.

"So you'll have Feds, if ya want to call them that, crawlin' all over the place right next to your facility. But it's been my experience when you're dealin' with these card-carrying government types, the best place to be is right under their noses. They never think to look right there. So we'll go out there tomorrow and talk to Fierro. I won't be hangin' around with ya once the introduction is made."

"Is it safe for you to be going to the Guadalajara Airport? What if you get spotted out there?" Terry asked recalling the "never to be seen together" rule.

"No one out there will think nuthin' of it, " Marr said with a shrug. "I hang out there a lot. I know all the pilots in Mexico, foreign and Mexican. You forget, I flew C-123s out of Guadalajara for six years for the Agency."

Terry had learned from Marr's discussions at the beach that several of Air America's old crews and aircraft had been reassigned to Mexico when the CIA cut back operations in Southeast Asia. Marr had been based at the Guadalajara Airport since 1973 and had been involved in a program, also called "Screw Worm," to secretly photomap portions of Mexico using state-of-the art infrared surveillance equipment to pinpoint poppy fields grown for heroin production.

All of this had been done by the CIA without the Mexican government's knowledge under the cover of a United States Department of Agriculture program to eradicate a parasitic worm that attacks cattle. This was one way the Agency could retain the pilots and planes that had been used by Air America during the Vietnam war without Congressional knowledge.

The codename "Screw Worm," Marr told Terry, was being resurrected for the new operation now being started in Mexico, as a way to further disguise the arms transshipment program. If the name was heard by *compromising* ears, they would probably think it was only a reference to the old operation and not suspect there was a new one.

They wound down with a plan to meet the following morning near the base of the VOR transmitter (a ground based navigation antenna building) centrally located near the airport terminal. As the maid opened the squeaky wrought iron gate to let Terry out of the compound, Marr had restarted the VCR and Terry could hear Duval screaming amid the mortar explosions: "Lance, get me my surfboard...sure the beach is secure...Charlie don't surf."

"*Señor Mitch es muy loco*," Maria said as she chuckled at the door.

The next morning, at ten-hundred hours, the two men met at the designated spot and Marr took Terry to the general aviation terminal that houses *Aerovias Castillo*, a fixed base operator, and the pilot's lounge.

When the two men entered the combination lounge and flight-planning room, "Comandante" Fierro was already regaling a group of airline pilots with one of his famous flying stories—something pilots call "hangar flying." Fierro was not only the scion of Mexico's premier aviation family, but had become the *padron* of the Guadalajara Airport. Though he was no longer in charge officially, he nonetheless was the man without whose approval nothing moved or happened.

The group of uniformed, off-duty pilots from various international airlines stood captivated around Fierro as he talked about shooting an instrument approach while flying an ice-laden 707 through a mountainous pass in the Andes on one engine. Out of respect, Marr waited for the group's laughter that signaled the end of yet another tale that always improved with age. Aviation, by Fierro's macho interpretation, was a Latino invention.

When the story ended, the time came for Fierro to switch from entertainer to store owner and sell supplies to the waiting aviators. Fierro's concession stocked not only the usual array of pilot necessities such as charts, plotters, flashlight batteries, flight computers and Rayban sunglasses. His glass display case that served as a check-out counter contained a well-stocked supply of miniature bottles of liquor.

To Terry's shock, many of the Mexican and Latin American airline pilots were popping the caps and downing several shots of whiskey as they charted their next flight. Aviation rules in the Third World appeared to be a lot more lax. There clearly was no rule here about time restrictions between "bottle to throttle."

From the *embrazo* Raul Fierro and Marr exchanged, they actually were the "blood brothers" Marr had said they were. They were about the same age, and as they hugged, Terry could see that Fierro had the same stocky build as Mitch, though he was slightly shorter. His light complexion tone suggested to Terry that he was of the Mexican ruling class, meaning someone of Castillan descent. He, too, had a full head of dark hair peppered with gray. A relaxed demeanor and cherubic face radiated the quiet confidence of someone who didn't need to demand respect....since he knew he was going to get it.

"Raul, this is my friend from the States, Mr. Terry Reed," Marr said as he introduced them. "He's the one you've been waiting for."

Fierro seemed apprehensive, looking around as if to see who might be watching. He quickly ushered the two men down the hall to his office. The rather functional office whose walls were adorned with framed mementos and photographs of Fierro and his family shaking hands with dignitaries contained a singular gray metal U.S. government issue desk, around which the men seated themselves. Terry was somewhat surprised at Fierro's tact. Instead of an operational briefing, Fierro launched into a lengthy personal interview that included extensive questioning about Terry's family, background and religion.

"So Mitch tells me you, how do you say...cut your teeth in Southeast Asia, supporting Air America and fighting communism," Fierro said in his soft-spoken, broken English that reflected his *padron* bearing. "And did you work with my good amigo, Maximo Gomez, while over there?"

Fighting communism, there were those words again. The common thread that seemed to tie all these people together, the reason—or the excuse—for all their actions.

"No. I didn't work with Mr. Gomez or with Mitch while in the Air Force over there," Terry replied. "The man I knew best who worked for Air America out of Laos was Mr. Bill Cooper, who is presently based in El Salvador as I understand it."

"You know Guillermo!" Fierro shot back. "He is one of my other best *amigos*. We go way back together. Guillermo is the only gringo I know of that can tell a better flying story than myself, and he certainly doesn't let the truth limit them."

The ensuing laughter broke the initial tension and now Fierro had found a common link with Terry, namely their joint friendship with Cooper. Fierro had seemingly found his personal comfort level with Terry. Everyone was now relaxed and Terry felt he was being accepted into the Mexican fold. His bona fides had been established and he was being handed off with the usual ritual, but this time it was spiced with a Latin flavor. Terry had apparently met the test.

"You come back *mañana en la tarde* after *siesta* and I will make the necessary introductions for you here at the *aeropuerto*," Fierro told him. "You will need a flight line pass for your *coche* and I will show you the *complejo industrial* I've selected to house your new company. And Mitch, it is my understanding you are not to be seen with Mr. Reed, so I don't think you should leave here together."

"Sure, but on the way out, I need ta buy a six pack of those little miniatures from ya," Marr said. "Just for the 'flight' home, if ya know what I mean."

When Terry returned home that day, he found a 1978 red Ford LTD with Texas license plates parked in front of his house.

Upon entering his living room, he was struck by the presence of a stunning, statuesque Latin beauty in her mid-20s with long flowing black hair and dark eyes. Janis introduced her as Patricia Juin, a Colombian who now lived on the lakeshore and who was married to a Frenchman named Patrick. Janis and Patricia shared something in common. Patricia's daughter, Joana, was the same age as Duncan. The two children were happily playing in the yard as their nannies watched over them.

Judging from the smiles on the faces of the two women, and from the half dozen or so empty miniature Corona bottles and the lunch leftovers still sitting on the table, it was obvious they had established an instant informal friendship.

"Terry, this is Patty Juin, she lives right here on the lake, two miles down the road and you won't believe what her husband does.... He flies Ultra-Lights and a hang glider and Patty says he's setting up a company to give tourists Ultra-Light rides from hotels on the beach."

Terry extended his hand, but instead Patty caught him off guard by leaning over to be kissed on the cheek, a traditional Latin response among close friends. Terry kissed her perfunctorily, but this custom was something that always bothered him about the Latin culture. They just didn't do this in Missouri.

The striking woman with a naturally tanned complexion had already decided that she liked Janis, and therefore, Terry, because, to her mind, they were not like most of the Americans she had met there. Those gringos were older, retired and symbolized the stereotypical ugly American. Many had become alcoholics since they spent most of their time socializing, entertaining....and drinking. Live cheap and drink, was how it looked to her.

In the Reeds, she told them both later as their friendship blossomed, she saw the type of people with which she had always wanted her family to associate. She wanted her daughter to speak English without an accent and, in one afternoon of playing with Duncan, that process had already started. Janis had explained that Terry was a businessman there to advance Mexican manufacturing technology, something that intimidated, yet fascinated her.

"Oh we are so glad to see people like you moving down here," she gushed. "Diana Aguilar is a friend of ours and she told us all about your business plan here in Mexico. I can't wait for you to meet Patrick. He'll be home tomorrow and I've invited you all over for dinner. We live on the lake and have a pool the children can play in."

While engaged in conversation with her, Terry was struck by her bearing—aristocratic without pretentiousness. Patty Juin displayed all the positive aspects of the Latin culture, and none of its negatives. She was bilingual, intelligent, demonstrated a knowledge of the world and was someone who could really teach the Reed family the inner workings of the Mexican culture.

He was hoping they had found a mirror family to ease them into their new lifestyle. And if they could contribute to the Americanization of the Juin family, it could evolve into the perfect cultural exchange program.

The best part of all was the fact that Janis now had linked up with a young, female friend she could relate to and who would help her assimilate into their new lifestyle. And even better for Janis, they would soon discover Patty didn't allow Patrick to smother her with his Latin machismo dominance they already noticed was prevalent in most male-female relationships.

The day following, after Terry had spent the afternoon with Fierro and being shown around the airport, he took his family to dinner at the Juins' home situated on the *carraterra* midway between Ajijic and the lakeside village of Jocotepec. The two-story, salmon colored, masonry house on the lake had an attached *casita* and conveyed a subtle elegance. By Mexican standards, it was opulent. And not only did it have an unobstructed view of the mountains on the south shore of Lake Chapala, it had another characteristic to which the Reeds were unaccustomed. It was fully paid for. The Juins, not a bank, actually owned it. A strange concept for Americans to deal with.

That night the Reeds and the Juins became a tight foursome. Terry and Patrick Juin found they each had a common goal. Each strangely was searching for something they believed existed only in the other's culture—true happiness.

Patrick thought he saw in Terry a man about the same age who was launching a business in his adopted country, Mexico. Patrick harbored ambitions of starting a business exporting Mexican manufactured goods to the U.S. As the evening wore on, both realized each viewed the other man's country as his golden opportunity. Neither could see the down-side in the other's culture. Here was a classic example of how the grass is always greener on the other side.

Patrick Juin was an interesting person. He had a European outlook and features to match. Born the son of a French couple, Juin's father had started his own firm in Mexico to market famous French perfumes. Patrick was born in Venezuela and, at one time, held triple citizenship, but had voluntarily given up his Venezuelan citizenship and had tried to renounce his French citizenship, which is impossible under French law and custom.

After an earlier, unhappy marriage, which produced two teenage daughters now living in Mexico City, Juin told the Reeds he underwent a personal metamorphosis, working as a musician and becoming a drifter searching for something he could not define. He found the answer while wind surfing off the beach at Puerto Vallarta. Patty, the daughter of a wealthy Colombian family, was vacationing there, too. Patricia, he said, represented to him Eve when Adam first saw her, someone he could mold to his liking. Their love had produced one child, a daughter who was the best of both cultures.

During dinner, Patrick told the Reeds he had just sold a jewelry business in Ajijic that catered to foreign tourists and was about to launch the Ultra-Light project. As the night wore on, he sat with Terry by the pool pointing out the features of the heavens as seen from south of the Tropic of Cancer. Their talk centered on aviation, Ultra-Lights, the modernization of Mexico, the decay of the United States, and the meaning of life. Through Juin's eyes and experiences, Terry would get a condensed and practical education on Mexican culture and Latino attitudes.

Throughout the remainder of July, Janis adapted quickly and easily to the land of *mañana* and life on the shoreline of Lake Chapala. Her biggest domestic problem was "maid management" or how to stay in charge in your own house and not end up working for your hired help. Terry, having once lived on the local economy in Thailand, had become knowledgeable about servants and the Third World mentality when he lived off the base.

She refused to take his and Juin's advice to be "non-friendly" to servants and establish the necessary class lines. This led to a constant turnover of domestic help until Janis finally mustered up the correct "game-face" and attitude to supervise the "professional maids" who were abundant in the area.

Every day brought a new discovery. Janis found delight in probing the area's large art community, discovering the region's posh hideaway hotels, endless artisan gift shops, and more importantly, the interesting people who in actuality were mostly misfits and malcontents. Terry, on the other hand, had to immerse himself in the business of setting up a company.

Marr arranged a meeting with a local *abogado*, an attorney named Arturo Velazquez Lopez, who Terry was told had done work for the Agency in the past.

"He's connected and he knows how to keep his mouth shut," Marr assured Terry. "He's expecting you. Don't talk about anything *we're* doing, only discuss the business aspects of your licensing with him. He'll keep ya straight when it comes to Mexican law."

It was late July when Marr told Terry it was time to travel to Dallas for a meeting with Robert Johnson of Southern Air Transport and Frank Fujikawa of Gomiya, USA Inc., the Japanese investor in the Mexican operation now called Machinery International, Inc., on the American side of the border. On the same trip, he would link up with Cooper in Little Rock to recover "the storage item."

Terry left Guadalajara early on July 31 aboard American Airlines flight for the planned afternoon meeting in Dallas. He was told the meeting to spell out Fujikawa's contribution to the project would take place in a rented conference room at Dallas-Ft. Worth Airport. Fujikawa, in typical Japanese fashion, wanted to meet face-to-face with the operation's top man, Johnson, before finally committing himself. Terry's presence was requested to answer any questions that Johnson could not, and was designed to give Fujikawa a "comfort zone" prior to consummating the deal.

Fujikawa, he was told, had recently inspected the Hungarian's facilities in Mexico City, and Terry took with him photographs of the facilities now ready to be leased at the Guadalajara Airport. Key to the plan, he also had important Mexican client information provided him by the Hungarians, showing projected sales to industries presently operating in Mexico. All projections showed Mexico with a pent-up demand for high-tech manufacturing equipment as well as the government's burgeoning desire to develop an export economy.

That year, 1986, tourism dollars had for the first time exceeded petro-dollars on Mexico's GNP spread sheet. Elements of the De La Madrid government were pressing hard for immediate expansion of tourism to bring in more hard currencies desperately needed to prevent default on Mexico's massive international bank loans. Brazil had already declared a "moratorium" on interest payments on its billions in loans from world banks.

But the group Terry had been dealing with in Mexico City represented a consortium of Mexican banks and businessmen pressing the government equally as hard for legislation, tax and banking law changes, to help establish an export economy. This group's views dovetailed right into the Agency's plans and Terry was excited about the future.

No one, including Johnson, Fujikawa or Reed, could have predicted how far the slipping peso would eventually fall. While Terry was flying to Dallas that morning, there already had been a devastating 23 per cent drop in one week during June. But the Mexican government was declaring that the "monetary adjustment" was over, and the nation's financial condition was stable. This did not provide much solace for the individuals and companies that had converted their strong currencies into pesos and had lost 50 percent of their value over a period of a few months.

After clearing U.S. Customs in Dallas, Terry called Johnson's office in Miami and discovered a glitch in their schedules. Bill Cooper, Johnson told him, had already attended his daughter's wedding and had departed Reno, Nevada, enroute to Little Rock. Cooper had expressed dismay at having no way of contacting Terry directly, but was requesting his assistance immediately in Little Rock. Johnson told Terry to go on to Little Rock and he would see Fujikawa alone, hopeful that Terry could make it back to Dallas before the meeting was over.

Terry flew on to Little Rock, confident he could return with knowledge that the C-4 problem had, finally, been resolved. Upon landing, he rented a car at Adams Field, drove to the North Little Rock Airport and found Cooper waiting in the city terminal.

"I guess Johnson was able to getta hold of you, but I think we need to wait until dark if we gotta go dig this stuff up at your friend's warehouse," Cooper cautioned.

Terry agreed and both men killed the day by going to the Jacuzzi Corp. in Little Rock, one of Applied Technology's accounts, where he supervised a machine tool installation that was underway.

After dark, the "grave robbers" went to what had been McAfee's warehouse and spent a half-hour digging up "Charlie." Back at the North Little Rock Airport, they loaded it aboard a Maule plane Cooper had flown in and parked near Terry's hangar. The Maule, he had said earlier, was another new plane destined for action in Central America. Cooper departed the North Little Rock airport at around 10 PM, establishing a course of approximately 120 degrees, heading southeast.

Terry breathed a sigh of relief. At last, he could clear his mind of this troubling issue and get on with his business in Mexico. He closed and securely locked the door of the hangar that now housed an Ultra-Light, a monument he had saved to remind him of his near death, and several file cabinets containing mostly business records. He went from there to a motel and left for Dallas the next day.

In Dallas, he caught up with Fujikawa, who had stayed for other business. He told Terry the meeting with Johnson went without a hitch and he was ready to close the deal. The money was ready, he said, and just waiting for Terry to tell him where and how to deliver it. All was well.

He returned home and told Marr that Cooper was, in fact, going to try and visit Guadalajara for an Air America reunion. Hopefully, he would be bringing another friend of Marr's by the name of John McRainey*, (See chapter end.) and possibly some others. Marr was ecstatic. The resurrection of the "over the hill gang" was in full swing and Marr began immediately making plans.

"That's great news! I'll go down to Chapala Realty tomorrow and attempt to getta hold of the bitch by phone," Marr said referring to the real estate office as telephone central for Americans there and a way to contact his wife. "She's still up in the States visitin' the kids and that's right where I want her to stay. I don't want her down here fuckin' up my party. You're gonna love these guys, Terry."

The first few weeks of August Terry spent shuttling between Guadalajara and Mexico City, visiting potential clients with Fenue. Fierro was working out the final security details on Reed's new airport facility. It was scheduled to be turned over to *Maquinaria Internacional, SA*, by the first of September, if the attorney could finish the paper work in time.

Terry was learning that Mexico's centralized bureaucracy made legal affairs move at a snail's pace. No document was complete unless it was affixed with enough official-looking seals to obliterate its contents. It seemed bureaucracy was a problem no matter where you lived.

The Reeds' immigration problems had been ironed out. Terry had been given a temporary business visa, which allowed him to do marketing analyses and set in place all the necessary elements for the planned transition to 100 per cent ownership of the Mexican corporation by the U.S. corporation. At that time, this was prohibited by Mexican law.

As far as anyone could tell, he was an American deeply involved in creating a venture to import machinery, something the country desperately needed, and a company for which the government would make an exception to its owner-

---

*   From an organizational chart later supplied to the Iran-Contra congressional committees by Retired Air Force General Richard V. Secord depicting the Enterprise's reporting structure, one could find directly under the name of W. Cooper, Manager, C-123K/C7A/Maule AC, the name of J. McRainey. His title was noted as Operations Director, C-123K/Maule AC, another of the now activated Air America "Over the Hill Gang."[1]

ship rule. This was humorous, in a way, because when comparing the list of companies to which this exception had been granted, one would find the likes of Ford Motor Company, Goodyear Rubber Company, Dupont, RCA, and then....*Maquinaria Internacional.*

In the third week of August, he received an oral invitation from Marr to attend the official Air America reunion that was to take place at Marr's home...without the "bitch's" presence.

"I'm goin' out ta the airport to pick up Coop and McRainey today, Fierro says their plane is due in around noon," Marr informed him. "Why don't you come on by the house after dark tonight. We'll down a few and talk about the good old days in 'SEA' (Southeast Asia)."

That night, as Terry walked under the Roman-style stone arch that defined the entrance into Marr's posh subdivision, he was hoping his new Nissan pickup wouldn't be stolen from the shoulder of the highway where he had left it. He was being cautious because Marr was violating a key rule by even inviting Terry to the party, and he did not want his 1985 orange, four-door Mexican-made pickup seen in Marr's neighborhood.

As Terry approached Marr's compound he could hear the VCR blaring away, but this time it was John Wayne's voice coming from the sound track of *The Flying Leathernecks.* By the sound of the laughter echoing from the den area of Mitch's house, it was clear that the party was in full swing.

Terry rang the claxon and a voice boomed back, "What's the password?"

"Sierra fuckin' Hotel!"*

Terry's response brought Marr quickly to the door and ushered him in. When the door closed behind him, he felt as if he had stepped back through time and walked into the lounge of the Chiroen Hotel, Air America's hangout in Udorn, Thailand. Only the Thai hookers were missing. But the talk had already turned to what carnal adventures might lie ahead in Guadalajara later.

Cooper introduced Terry to John McRainey, another ex-Air America pilot who was flying C-123 air supply missions for former General Richard Secord's "Enterprise" based in El Salvador. The slender, stylishly-dressed McRainey was tanned and fit, giving the outward impression of being a conservative businessman, a banker or maybe a corporate attorney. Also present were two Salvadoran Army officers in civilian clothes and two contract American aircraft maintenance personnel. Terry would learn through conversation that the whole group was shuttling an old, previously mothballed C-123 to El Salvador to join the Contra resupply operation. They had flight-planned their route through Mexico to stay over land, considering the unairworthy condition of the plane, which had not been flown since the mid-70s.

"Cooper's told me all about you. You're one of the guys that was training beaner pilots up in Arkansas for the Agency," McRainey said as he approached,

---

* Sierra Hotel was a term used by pilots in Vietnam. To understand this, you must understand the use of the phonetic alphabet by the military to prevent miscommunication by radio. Each letter has a word such as A for Alpha and Z for Zulu. S is "Sierra" and H is "Hotel". What the pilots must relay to each other during an air strike is the level of destruction of a target, or bomb damage assessment (BDA) reports. When a target was destroyed by a direct hit in Vietnam, the pilots for a time were yelling "Shit Hot" to signify total destruction. The politicians were becoming upset at such ungentlemanly language and that forced the pilots into code talk. "Shit Hot" was refined to "Sierra Hotel."

acting openly friendly. "Can't believe you survived it all, considering the level of skill you had to start with. I got involved in a similar situation training Laotian pilots. Wasn't fucking Vietnamization a great program? Let's all toast to the *hèn-nhàts* (Vietnamese for cowards) we defended, and to Richard Milhous Fucking Nixon!"

As the tumblers clinked together and slopped portions of their contents onto the floor, Cooper added, "Here's hoping Daniel Ortega butt fucks Henry Kissinger before WE kill him."

Terry looked around him. He realized that what he saw in Marr's den defined the term "Post-Vietnam Stress Syndrome (Its official name is Post Traumatic Stress Syndrome). But this group didn't suffer from the mental condition that the psychiatrists have defined, an illness in which veterans have frequent, stress-related, flashbacks triggered by an ordinary event, that reawakens some wartime experience. Nor was it their inability to control their reactions to these flashbacks which renders them unable at times to cope with the stress of everyday civilian life.

These men, Terry observed, were like himself. They were not the kind to walk into a schoolyard and kill a dozen Oriental children. They were combat veterans locked in time, suspended in an anti-climactic state of not having been allowed to complete the mission for which they were trained. Society had taught them they were males and their mission was to defend their nation and its way of life, if called to do so. They were called, but for all the wrong reasons, and then not given the go-ahead to do what their training had prepared them for. They came home defeated and in many respects could be compared to impotent males who never had the psychological satisfaction of knowing they had fully consummated their "marriage" with their own society.

He found humor laced within the stories and enjoyed the camaraderie of these "men of men," who had risked their lives and were not like Bill Clinton and other modern leaders, men who sat back and debated the morality of it all at Oxford— after the fact—and after the shooting had started and the body bags were coming home by the thousands.

These men at Marr's house were known commodities, tried, proven, tested and could be counted on when the going got rough.

But Terry found sadness in a lot of this as well, since their bond was built on mutual failure: Their inability to win and come home victorious. These veterans found it hard to accept that they had been manipulated by the likes of Nixon and Kissinger and that they were, truly, expendable... and for what?

Détente, they once again concluded. The reason, they each decided in their drunken soliloquies, had to be Nixon's obsession with being the president who "recognized China."

"Nixon couldn't figure out if he wanted to marry and make love to Mao Tse-Tung, or to fuck him to death and shit on his grave," John Cathey had once said. "We need leaders that know what they're doing, where they're going, and define the role the military plays in all this *detente* shit."

That about summed it up as the Over the Hill Gang toasted Ho Chi Minh: "To a better man and leader than anybody we had on our side....'least he was there to win."

Here was a roomful of intelligent men burying their problems with alcohol and living in the past. Terry hoped he wouldn't end up like the men he was watching. What seemed apparent to him was that these men could share their feelings only with one another. And this made him sad. One thing for sure, he had the comfort of knowing he had a wife he could talk to.

He was jarred from his thoughts by the arrival of Raul Fierro, who couldn't resist any kind of reunion with story-telling combat aviators. Each took the floor in turn to regale the others in one-upmanship, hyperbole and just plain bullshit. As each man spun his tale, Mitch broke out the milk containers with the 1975 tequila, his oldest and best.

As each container was drained, the subject of conversation turned to the current war, the one that had brought them all together. Terry felt a sense of uneasiness because Marr was the only one who had been cleared to know his true role or mission in Mexico. All the while, Terry was hoping the conversation wouldn't turn to Machinery International's role in all of this, especially in front of the "outsiders" present.

Marr asked McRainey: "So how you guys doin' down there? How many sorties a day are ya flyin' and what kind of tonnage are ya puttin' on target?"

"We're not doin' too good, Mitch," McRainey answered. "I'm glad our pay isn't tied to our performance. We're all gettin' older and slower and so's our equipment. It's a hell of an undertaking considering what we've got to work with."

The fact was that during this period in the summer of 1986, the air resupply operation was floundering, Felix Rodriguez would later claim when testifying before a Congressional committee that the Enterprise flew only one successful mission during July and August of that year.

"Goddam Mitch, you ought to be down there flyin' with us," Cooper said. "It's just like old times. They're puttin' pressure on us from Washington to get fully operational by the first of the year and we could use another skilled 123 pilot. I've got my hands full just keepin' this old iron in the air." This was a reference to the antique aircraft being retrieved from "bone yards" in the desert where surplus military aircraft had been stored as well as those being "borrowed" from military museums. Barry Seal's C-123K that had been used in the Sandinista "sting" was but one example of an old Air America war bird conveniently finding its way into civilian hands when the CIA deemed it necessary.

"Yeah, I'd love ta go but the Agency needs me here right now," Marr replied. He lied. He knew why he had not been recruited to fly, and so did most of the people at the party.

"That's not your problem Mitch, we know why you're not flyin' with us," an inebriated McRainey injected, in an obvious reference to Marr's problem with the bottle. The room went silent.

Cooper defused what was about to become an uncomfortable situation by injecting: "Yeah, Mitch, we know you're not flyin' with us because of your wife. Some of us know how to control our women. Can't believe that the Mitch Marr I knew in Asia has now settled down answering to only one woman... and being pussy-whipped besides!" The roar of drunken laughter broke the tension.

"Pussy-whipped my ass, I'll show ya. Let's go ta Guadalajara and fuck some of them fine Mexican cunts. Line 'em up. I'll show ya," Marr slurred.

Fierro suggested they all leave for Guadalajara where he could arrange for the local DFS (Mexican CIA) commandante to take over a "private club" for the night's entertainment. Terry knew he could not be seen in public with these people and was surely passing up a memorable night, and can now only imagine what it must have been like.

Before leaving they all decided to hoist one more tumbler of Marr's high-octane libation in memory of the men left behind in Southeast Asia. The thought of prisoners of war and the knowledge of what happened to many of them saddened Reed. It angered him that he was silenced by a sworn secrecy statement and couldn't share this classified information with them.*

What a depressing way to end an otherwise interesting night.

One key player in all this was not there. Felix Rodriguez was back in El Salvador creating some mischief. Oliver North would later claim that Rodriguez' ego was getting out of control. At the same time, Rodriguez was aligning himself with the Nicaraguan rebels and trying to freeze out Secord and the others dealing with North. Rodriguez claimed in his book, *Shadow Warrior*, that the Nicaraguan rebels were being "screwed" by Secord, who was simply trying to sell the whole supply operation to the CIA for a quick profit.[2] This was unquestionably true, but what was Rodriguez' motive in all of this?

Terry believes today that this was part of a power struggle based along racial lines. Rodriguez wanted to control the aerial operations and its assets so that he and his Salvadoran military friends could profit personally from other business ventures that Terry would discover later.

It was more of his trademark smoke, mirrors and "war on communism", used to hide his greed and true motives.

Rodriguez admits he even went so far as to meet with the rebel leadership and act as their champion in the tug-of-war over who really controlled the resupply aircraft and the operation's assets. This clearly was mutinous behavior since Rodriguez was not in charge, nor empowered with the authority to do so. So why was he generating all this turmoil? Was it because he saw himself as HMFIC in the Nicaraguan War? Or was he operating under secret instructions to do so? Did someone want the Enterprises' spooks pushed completely out of the operation so that it could be conducted more as the Vice President saw fit? After all, didn't Rodriguez have the ear of then-Vice President Bush's closest advisor, Donald Gregg?[3]

Rodriguez made the puzzling admission that he persuaded the rebels to put armed guards on the resupply aircraft to keep the Anglos working for the Enterprise from "making off" with them. But where would they have taken them? All this back-stabbing and in-fighting was part of a power struggle that created an environment of an accident waiting to happen. And that's exactly what happened.[4]

But Terry knew none of this in the summer and fall of 1986 in Guadalajara. To him, all looked well and everything was falling into place. By early October, Terry was up and going with *Maquinaria Internacional*. Even though the Mexican corporation's ownership had not yet been approved by the Mexican government, he was using the license of Fenue's company, Cortec, to get business started.

Things looked so permanent Reed signed a lease on a larger and more family-style home situated directly on the shore of Lake Chapala and the family was preparing to celebrate Duncan's fourth birthday in a very Mexican way.

---

* Reed kept this information to himself until August 3, 1992. He offically revealed the sacrifice of the POWs during an oral deposition in a Freedom of Information suit: John Cummings vs. Department of Defense, in the United States District Court for the District of Columbia, 91-1736-GAG.

There would be *pinatas, mariachi* music and authentic Mexican food served by the maid; and the guest list was growing.

On October 4, Janis savored her new-found lifestyle that allowed her the time to bake the birthday cakes depicting the Sesame Street characters, Bert & Ernie. How could the Reeds know they were 24 hours away from disaster?

Since the Air America reunion at Marr's house two months earlier, the "over the hill gang" was getting their act together. By mid-September, the antiquated pilots and their planes were proving they still had "the right stuff." On September 13, 1986, they had managed to put five planes in the air simultaneously and, on one flight alone, 10,000 pounds of supplies had been dropped deep into Nicaragua and into the hands of "freedom fighters" trying to establish a toe-hold in southern Nicaragua.

Bob Dutton, who was reporting to North from the field, said more than 180,000 pounds of supplies had been dropped successfully. But in the Reagan administration's rush to accomplish the aerial delivery effort, there were lapses in security that would soon impact on the Reeds and *compromise* the Enterprise's operations.

Their lifestyle in *Margaritaville* would literally come to a crashing halt.

October 5th, 1986, was a cool night on the north shore of Lake Chapala and the Reed family was just preparing for a sweater-weather barbecue when the claxon rang at the compound's front gate.

It was a strangely sober, and somber, Mitch Marr standing outside the iron gate. "I guess you heard the news? Hasens fucked!"

"What do you mean? I don't get it," Terry responded. "And besides, aren't you breaking your own rule by being here? You said we were never to be seen together. And this is a very public location," Terry said, referring to the home's street-side entrance that was in view of the *zócalo*.

Marr spoke slowly, coherently and very low-key as he went on: "After tonight, nobody may ever give a fuck if we're ever seen together, alive or dead."

A confused Terry just stared at him, wondering what on earth was going on. "What's the matter, Mitch? And what does Hasens fucked mean?"

"His name is Hasenfus. He was 'the kicker' on the plane—you don't know, do you?" Marr began to realize. "I forgot, you don't have satellite TV..... COOPER'S DEAD! He got shot down."

After a long pause, Marr sighed and continued. "Some commie shit put a heat-seeker up his ass and his 123 went down in flames. He died with his boots on, though. That lucky shit! He always did have all the fun."

While reeling from the shock of the statement about Cooper's plane, Terry began to analyze Marr's comments. It was obvious, based on what he was saying, that what Terry had suspected about Marr was true. He was envious and miserable. Envious of the men still flying under fire and wallowing in his retirement lifestyle that he blotted out with booze. Here he was, wishing he could die in combat with honor like Cooper just had.

After another pause, Marr turned to a briefing mode.

"But I guess this guy named Hasenfus survived the crash, and the commies got him. I thought you knew him, too."

Though Terry didn't know it at that moment, words like Iran-Contra and Irangate were being written by newspaper editors everywhere. As Hasenfus was being pulled out of the jungle on a leash by a Sandinista soldier, political shock waves were beginning to reverberate around the world. Back at the White House, damage control was already under way.

There would be a flurry of questions about why a C-123 military cargo plane registered to a CIA proprietary in Miami had been shot down that day in Nicaragua with gringos and guns aboard.

There were, of course, responses from Washington.

President Ronald Reagan said: "There is no connection with that [between the U.S. and the shootdown] at all." *He lied.*

Vice President George Bush said: "This man [Hasenfus] is never—is not working for the United States Government." *He lied.*

Assistant Secretary of State Elliot Abrams: "Let me repeat flatly that there was no U.S. government involvement in this...direct, indirect, provision of material financing, whatever you want to call it...none." *He lied.*

Eugene Hasenfus, the survivor and now a prisoner in Managua, told it somewhat differently. "I worked for the CIA, who did most of the coordination of these flights." *He had a rope around his neck. He told the truth.*

The covert supply operation had turned overt, and Oliver North was heading for the shredder.

1. Testimony of Richard V. Secord, *Iran-Contra Hearings*, 100-1, p 446.
2. Testimony of Bob Dutton,. *Iran-Contra Hearings*, 100-3, at 219-20.
3. Ibid. 221-22, 275-76.
4. Deposition of Donald Gregg,5/18/87 at 28-31; Rodriguez testimony, *Hearings*, 100-3, 311, 349-50.

CHAPTER 23

ON ICE

Mitch Marr told Terry that "Operation Screw Worm" was on hold indefinitely, if not permanently.

"So what am I supposed to do?" Terry asked. "I've got my whole family here. I'm set up and in place. I've signed a lease on a new home. I have to move tomorrow. I'm ready to go."

"Take a vacation," Marr advised. "Drive around Mexico. Get ta know the country. Enjoy, good bourbon is only two bucks a bottle here. I'll authorize ya some expense money 'til these guys figure out what they wanna do, for sure."

Marr then turned and walked away, leaving Terry in shock and disbelief to mourn Cooper. He needed to find a newspaper or something to confirm what he had just heard. It wasn't that he didn't believe Marr, he simply couldn't accept what he had just been told.

The training in Arkansas had been undertaken for the sole purpose of avoiding the type of catastrophic exposure the Hasenfus incident would now reveal. "They had better be beaners," Barry Seal had said when talking about the necessity to quickly train Latin pilots for the aerial resupply operations. What had gone wrong? And why weren't "beaners" piloting the plane?

From what Marr had said, there was an American survivor to interrogate. Cooper had mentioned the name Hasenfus back in Arkansas thinking it was someone Terry might have known back in Southeast Asia. The blood had drained from Terry's face. He walked back into the kitchen where Janis was practicing her kitchen Spanish with the maid.

"What's wrong?" she said, immediately realizing something had happened. "You look like you just saw a ghost!"

"Bill Cooper's dead!" The words did not come easily. "He was shot down, from what Mitch just told me. I'm gonna jump in the car and drive out to Patrick's house and see if I can't get something on satellite TV from the States. The papers probably won't carry this until sometime tomorrow."

At the Juin house, he learned from the maid the family had gone to the beach. He was asked inside and turned on the TV to watch the American news reports. It had happened all right. It was the usual media feeding frenzy, interviews with State Department spokespersons and reporters having endless consultations with each other.

A United States "military" plane had been shot down and Daniel Ortega was claiming it contained weapons and CIA personnel. It was worse than Mitch had told him. This was proof, Ortega had charged, that Reagan was "lying to the American people and Congress about his true, aggressive intentions...it is clear the U.S. intends to invade...The United States clearly does not want a negotiated peace." An emergency meeting of the United Nations Security Council had already been demanded by Nicaragua.

As Terry drove home, he activated his pilot's checklist mentality and was contemplating his possible exposure from all this. What, if anything, did Hasenfus know about him and "Screw Worm?" Had Cooper told him anything?

"*What's the worst than can happen*" was no longer just a rhetorical question for Terry. He was now adding things to that list of unpleasant possibilities. For now, he needed to reassure his wife, get some rest, and analyze his liabilities and options. The ensuing 24 hours would decide a lot of things.

The next day was still moving day. Diana Aguilar showed up early with the Mexican helpers and the moving truck to relocate them to their new house at #20 Linda Vista, a picturesque lakefront property that literally meant beautiful view.

The family had looked forward to moving day with eager anticipation. The new house Diana found for them was much larger and comfortably suited to the family's life style. There were even quarters for a live-in maid. Unfortunately, the shoot down crisis was robbing them of the happiness and excitement they had anticipated.

Moving did indeed turn out to be exciting, but for all the wrong reasons. Diana Aguilar was in a total buzz about the Hasenfus affair. As she poured herself a cup of coffee, she highlighted what she had witnessed on her TV and was clearly relishing in the knowledge that the U.S. got caught with its pants down. Aguilar, a Californian, had lived in Mexico for most of her adult life, and had adopted the Mexican view that the United States was, as the Ayatollah once said, "The Great Satan". Her philosophy represented that of most of the expatriates and artists living in Mexico who had adopted a left-wing attitude toward America: the United States was a meddler and trouble-maker in Latin American politics that sided with the oligarchies to keep the poor people repressed and in line.

They did not like the Sandinistas, but they felt the U.S. should stay out of Nicaragua and let the Latin Americans deal with their own problems. After having spent several months in Mexico and listening to these views, Terry was beginning to agree with them. He saw no contradiction in this because he believed his efforts would result in the anti-communist Nicaraguans having sufficient weapons and skills to force Ortega to the negotiating table.

"Where do you keep the Kahlua?" Diana asked as she rummaged through the kitchen cabinets. "I need to calm down. They finally caught this damn Reagan doing what we Mexicans knew he was doing all along. I hope this time the American people crucify this son-of-a-bitch. It seems like all *you* Americans want is war, war, war."

"The Kahlua is in the cabinet to your right. And Diana, you talk like you're a Mexican. Aren't you still an American, or have you been down here too long?" Terry asked, wanting to pick a fight. "Come on, let me teach you about the balance of power and how we'll never be able to co-exist in peaceful harmony as you ex-hippies all think."

He knew that would get her going. What the hell, he felt like a good argument. At least it would get his mind off things. The Reeds and Diana moved to the garden and engaged in a heated debate as the Mexican workers lethargically loaded their belongings onto the truck. Terry and Janis had decided to continue with their lives as if nothing had happened, just taking one day at a time. Anything else, Terry was sure, would bring attention to himself.

Before sunrise that day, he had visited Marr to confirm their earlier understanding, namely that Terry's personal overhead would be covered by the Agency as the CIA, Washington and the world began coping with the political shock waves that were sure to come.

So far, Marr was convinced that Hasenfus knew nothing about "Screw Worm" and could not *compromise* their upstart operation regardless of how tough the interrogation in the Managua prison might be.

"I know this guy," Marr had said. "He's a pretty tough cookie. He may tell 'em a little. I would. Ya just need to sit tight and, like I said, take an extended vacation on Uncle. I've already talked to Gomez, who's talkin' to Washington and they figure any kind of abrupt change in your behavior might bring attention to ya. Go on about yer machinery business in a very low-key nature. Don't be signin' any legal agreements beyond what you've committed for already. Tell your Jap and commie business partners that we're gonna go slow on this for awhile. I'm sure they'll understand. Here's ten grand more and there's more where that came from. I'm gonna be leavin' for the States for awhile, so I won't be here. If there's an emergency, do as you've been told and go see Darrach (the American consul in Guadalajara), but don't use the front door at the embassy. Just give your code name to the guard and they'll let ya in."

This had made Terry nervous. "Where are you goin' Mitch? You're not gonna leave me here all alone, are you?"

"Terry, there's no use shittin' ya, I got a drinkin' problem that I gotta take care of," Marr said with resignation in his voice. "My wife's not comin' back down here unless I dry out. She's checkin' me into one of those damn clinics up in the States. It's probably best. I need ta get my head screwed back on straight so I can be useful to you and the Agency. I don't mind tellin' ya, Coop's death has brought me back down to earth. This is pretty serious fuckin' business at times. I guess we all need ta be reminded of that occasionally."

Terry realized that some good had already come out of Cooper's death, a positive for every negative, as always seemed the case. Marr was now going to dry himself out and, if the operation did continue, Marr would hopefully become more professional and shun the party mode that had developed by the reactivation of the "over the hill gang." An old comrade had died and now an aura of seriousness was starting to develop. Terry had relayed Marr's instructions to Janis before Aguilar arrived that morning.

She was still going strong as she sat and drank the Kahlua. "Well, considering who you used to work for, I would expect you to have nothing but an American warmonger view on this," Aguilar said referring to her knowledge of Terry's military background.

"Diana, cork the Kahlua," Terry told her. "You've had enough and we're not going to solve the world's political problems sitting here arguing on a beautiful morning in Ajijic. Besides, we gotta be moved out of this house by tonight, and at the rate these guys are moving, the *new baby* will be here before they're finished. Let's get on with it."

The romanticism of Mexico had definitely drawn Terry and Janis closer together than they had ever been. The EPT test Janis had taken showed positive; she was pregnant. They were ecstatic, there was going to be three little "Reedlets". Terry only wondered why James Bond was never confronted with this issue?

Terry viewed the up-coming birth as his final contribution to the world's population, and hadn't realized that getting Janis pregnant was a Latino sign of being genuinely *macho*. The gardener, Geronimo, now held Terry in true esteem. He had become one of them. Now they would call him *padron*.

One of the first tasks after moving into the new house was to find the right obstetrician for Janis. After much consultation with the aristocratic women the Reeds were beginning to socialize with as a result of Terry's business dealings, she was referred to Dr. Roberto Lopez Ramirez. He was a Caesar Romero look-alike who had been educated in both Mexico and the United States. His practice catered not only to the upper crust Mexican women, but Americans traveling to Guadalajara to give birth there, as well. There, they would be assured of more personalized care at a fraction of the inflated American cost.

Janis, at first, was apprehensive about having her baby born in Mexico. But Lopez' charm matched his professionalism and she was soon at ease with him and the Mexican medical system. He personally took her on an escorted tour of the Mexican-American Hospital to overcome any preconceived notions about "Third World" medicine.

Also, Terry selfishly saw future business advantages of having a Mexican-born child. As a Mexican citizen, the child could own land outright, which foreigners such as himself could not do at that time and, more importantly, own one hundred per cent of a Mexican corporation. The child some day, he told his wife, could be his joint-venture partner and their legitimate tie to Mexico.

Terry decided to use this time to do a first-hand market survey and acquaint himself with the rest of the country. This down time could be spent analyzing Mexico's manufacturing base while also exploring Mexico more fully through a native's perspective.

Because the Juins were friends and seemed to have a flexible schedule, they seemed the perfect couple to help the Reeds discover the real Mexico. But before beginning their odyssey, proper transportation was needed. It was now mid-October and the Reeds decided to travel to Kansas City and purchase a motor home to serve as their "land yacht".

The visit to Missouri served a dual purpose; the children visited with their grandparents while the Reeds picked out the new motor home. They then "set sail", bound for Guadalajara by way of Albuquerque, New Mexico. Terry wanted to visit John Desko, his old comrade from Task Force Alpha whom he hadn't seen for more than a year. Terry still considered John his only true friend since their bonding traversed divergent experiences shared in the Southeast Asian war.

Terry had a reason beyond friendship for wanting to see Desko. There was a possibility, considering the non-stop headlines being generated out of Washington about the fallout from Cooper's crash, that the Agency would wash its hands of "Screw Worm" and force Terry to make a decision about his future.

Southern Air Transport had become the center of two major investigations, one by the Federal Aviation Administration and the other by U.S. Customs. Cooper's photo ID card, found in the wreckage by the Sandinistas had been issued by SAT, a CIA proprietary in Miami. The FBI also had joined in the investigation and Oliver North, whom Terry still did not know was John Cathey, was intervening with the Justice Department to have it stopped.[1]

For Terry's part, he could not understand why Cooper would be carrying something so sensitive. It was totally out of character for a seasoned spook veteran like him. Air America planes, and particularly their crews, had been completely sanitized for Agency work in Asia. It just didn't add up, and Terry was beginning to sense something very, very wrong with all of this.

The S.O.P. (standard operating procedure) for "deniable flights" called for the following: all data plates showing aircraft serial numbers were removed so that they could not be traced to a particular federal agency; the crews carried no ID at all; even their flight suits were sanitized and bore no rank or insignia; and only basic maps and charts were carried and these were destroyed at the first sign of trouble.

If positive identification had to be made of a downed airman, the official identification records known as SAR (search and rescue) cards, were retrieved from the pilots' home base. This classified card contained very personal information, such as maiden name of mother, first automobile owned, etc., and was used for "authentication purposes" if positive I.D. had to be confirmed by radio communication during the SAR process. The flyers' dental records and X-rays were also available for identification of their bodies, if it came to that.

It continued to haunt Terry. Could Cooper have been that sloppy? Daniel Ortega had been smart enough to reveal the SAT I.D. card to the American media. They did the rest, and the feeding frenzy was under way. The predators could smell the raw meat.

Janis and Terry, though, were far away from the escalating tumult in Washington. They were mobile and free to roam. They had fallen in love with Mexico and its lifestyle and each other all over again, and desperately wanted to stay there and live successfully off the local economy.

Terry was developing an idea about being the middleman, or manufacturing broker, in bringing together American retailers with Mexican manufacturers. This concept was just developing along the U.S.-Mexican border and Terry was already discovering the diverse manufacturing base located deeper inside Mexico that was anxious to find American partners to market their products or services. When the Reed motor home pulled into Albuquerque that day, Terry was thinking of the various products Desko needed on a daily basis to supply his company.

"No, I'm *not* going in there," Janis said to her husband as their motor home came to rest behind Desko's warehouse. "That place gives me the creeps. Every time I go in there, I'm afraid the place is gonna blow up or I'll be raped by some Hell's Angel biker who's shopping in there."

"Oh, come on and get out of the car, Janis," Terry coaxed. "You know he's my best friend and he's a hell of a nice guy. Quit exaggerating about all the evil equipment John sells. Most of it's police equipment and besides, I like this stuff, too."

"Post-Vietnam stress syndrome, here we go again," Janis said under her breath but loud enough for her husband to hear.

As they walked toward the door, Terry spotted Desko's pristine, white 1978 BMW R-100 RS parked next to the owner's custom Harley-Davidson Sportster. And then there was the 1000 CC ragged-out Suzuki that one of the female employees, Allie Helmer, rode.

"Good, the gang's all here," Terry said to Janis who was still wearing a frown but reluctantly following with the children in tow.

"Raquel is the only reason I'm going in there," she snipped referring to the owner's daughter. Janis considered her the only sane person inside.

Upon entering the Quartermaster Sales' facilities on West Menual in Albuquerque, one is struck by what looked like a Hollywood prop room for an S&M movie. The first thing that catches one's eye is a giant map of Southeast Asia hung from the ceiling and emblazoned with six-inch high words: "Kill Jane Fonda, Pinko commie Bitch."

Adorning the walls near the ceiling is a selection of posters advertising weapons and SWAT team gear, most being draped across dominant, and barely-clad, Amazon females holding weapons of death and destruction. These combined with posters of heavily-modified Harley-Davidson motorcycles depicting women wearing skin-tight leather established the mood of what adventures might lie ahead for the adventuresome customers.

High above the counter was a sign that said: "No more Vietnams. And don't forget the POWs. We'll never rest until they're all accounted for."

This was a veritable supermarket for survivalists. In addition to accommodating walk-in customers, the store catered, for the most part, to mail-order markets and distributed SWAT team paraphernalia to police departments and to federal agencies all across the United States. Although not primarily a gun shop, one could purchase any and all gun accessories known to man: night-vision scopes, laser sights, magazines, ammunition, holsters, belts, bandoliers, stocks, flash suppressors for gun barrels, and bayonets. Popular sellers were self-defense items: brass knuckles, nightsticks, mace, and taser and stun guns. In addition was a complete line of clothing that included camouflage and black fatigues, boots, hats, body armor, bullet-proof vests and "industrial strength" camping equipment.

"Hey guys, what are you doing in town? I was afraid that Mexico had swallowed you guys up," John Desko said as he looked up from his desk. Grinning, he picked up Duncan and gave him a big hug.

"John, does GI Joe really live here like Daddy said?" the awe-struck little boy asked.

"Gosh, Duncan, you just missed him. Hey, this calls for a celebration," he yelled to Allie, a 90-pound woman who was wearing one visible pistol on her hip and a second one tucked inside her boot. Allie ran the shipping and receiving end of the company's thriving mail-order operation.

As he locked the door to the shop, he told Allie to pull out the large plastic garbage bin and start icing down the beer.

"It's party time. I'll go tell Bob you're here."

Bob Provance, the owner, was a man whose biker image belied the real person. Beneath the pseudo-biker look, which normally included a healthy growth of hair and beard, a bandana, Levis, T-shirt, leather vest, motorcycle boots and a chromed chain belt, beat the heart of an astute businessman and close friend of Desko's. He had found that the many Walter Mitty civilians of the world harbor a craving for military paraphernalia. And Provance was no stranger to operating most of the equipment he sold.

In actuality, he was a highly decorated Vietnam veteran who served with the U.S. Army's elite "Black Tiger Division" in Nha Trang, South Vietnam. Provance saw ground action while performing in a combat role with the 44th battalion,

4th training brigade, his company commander being the famous Captain Gerald Devlin.

Both Desko and Provance worked hard to project the image of survivalist oriented, soldiers of fortune. But Terry knew that beneath the facade were two men who had discovered a way of making a good living doing what they really liked, namely purveying to the world of "mercenaries." And, they had the added benefit of keeping themselves surrounded by guns, the latest in expensive toys.

Provance, happy to see the Reed family, pulled the blinds, locked the doors and put the "closed" sign outside. It was time to party.

"Terry, stop him, stop him," Janis screamed, trying to get her husband to rescue Duncan who had just pulled the pin on a hand grenade sitting on Desko's desk.

"Calm down, Janis, it's just a joke!" giggled Raquel, Provance's 22-year-old daughter, who was a quintessential wholesome and "normal"-looking woman.

With that, Desko picked up the dummy grenade mounted on a wooden board that said: "Complaint department, please take a number." Duncan was by then holding the red tag attached to the grenade's pin, which said "No. 1."

Provance laughed. "This is our hottest mail order item this year, Janis. It's only a joke. Get it? We don't sell explosives. Have a beer and tell me about Mexico!"

Janis breathed a sigh of relief as the Reed's were toasted by this engaging group of characters. Desko then whipped out his latest creation. He had seized on the marketing potential of the front-page news by using it on his latest bumper sticker.

"Whatta ya think, Terry, want one for your motor home?" Desko said holding it up. It read: "Free Hasenfus/Kill Ortega." Terry wished he could confide in Desko the truth about what he was doing in Mexico. By doing so, he would become an instant hero to the Quartermaster Sales gang. Bob would probably have closed for the remainder of week, and done some serious partying.

As Janis observed the comraderie between these Vietnam veterans, she felt a slight jealousy since these men seemed to be able talk in their own special code. Much of their feeling and communication was in what was not said. She was reminded of a line she had heard in a movie whose title she had long forgotten. "Women never get to share anything so important as a war," the heroine had said.

If she didn't know these men, which included her husband of five years, she would think she was watching the road company of *The Dogs of War*, a movie about mercenaries. It disturbed her to think that before falling in love with her husband, she had viewed most Vietnam veterans as "sickos," and not as they truly were: Men who had been done an injustice by their country, and especially their leaders.

As the conversation shifted to gun control and the National Rifle Association's view of it as a "communist conspiracy to disarm Americans," Janis and the children gravitated toward Allie, who was opening soft drinks for the children.

"What kind of gun you carryin' down there in Mexico Janis?" Allie asked her. "We just got in a good selection of used Smith & Wesson .38-caliber airweight specials. They make great girl guns, especially if you have the hammer shaved like mine so you can carry it in your boot. Make Terry buy you one."

"Allie, just being around guns makes me nervous," Janis told her. "I'll leave all that up to Terry. My role in life right now is packin' diapers and wet wipes, not pistols. It's still sort of a secret, but I'm pregnant again. We're going to have a Mexican baby."

"Hey guys, Janis says she got pregnant by a Mexican!" Allie blurted out across the shop.

A now blushing Janis had to explain to the group what she meant.

The women then turned their conversation to the subject of life in Mexico, the men focused theirs on the business purpose of Terry's visit. Having discovered the textile industry of Mexico, Terry was telling Desko and Provance about the significant cost savings they could experience by having their most popular clothing items custom-manufactured in Mexico.

They requested quotations for comparison and agreed to consider Mexico as a source in the future, if things were as Terry claimed. With business matters out of the way, the talk turned to fast motorcycles, fast cars, and fast women. All three men were happily married, but a private discussion of women was somehow mandatory.

Provance took the opportunity to produce his latest bumper-sticker creation that read: "If it has tits or wheels, it will cost you money." Janis found no humor in it.

The Reeds accepted Desko's invitation to spend the night at his home. Over dinner and considerable reminiscing, the old friends agreed that they would meet again in Mexico the following summer, provided the Reeds were still living there.

Later, as Terry drooled over John's immaculate 500-CC Penton dirt bike in his impeccably clean garage, John asked, "So what kind of firepower are you carryin' to neutralize the *banditos* down there?"

"I was hoping to come by your shop in the morning and buy a couple of items before leaving town," Terry replied.

"Come on down. I'll get you fixed up with whatever is necessary".

The next morning, Terry met with Desko to make his weapons purchases. He selected a nickel-plated 9 MM Smith & Wesson for himself and, per Allie's suggestion, the airweight special for Janis. That, along with several boxes of ammunition and a selection of survivalist-oriented items, gave Terry a more warm and fuzzy feeling for what dangers might lie ahead while camping in Mexico.

Yup, he and Desko again agreed: That's why they had fought the Vietnam War; to protect the American way of life, which included owning guns.

With the motor home now loaded for the trip south back to Mexico, Desko's wife began to get teary-eyed, while standing on the lawn in front of her manicured suburban home. "We're gonna worry about you guys traveling on those dangerous roads down there. We'll pray for you. You let us know if we need to come rescue you. I won't come, Terry, but I'll send Bob and John."

Desko stood on the opposite side out of view of his wife, rolled his eyes and shook his head. After having spent an entire year on a remote jungle air base with Terry, he knew Terry would not be exposing his wife and children to needless danger.

"No shit, if you do have any problems down there, call me," Desko said reassuringly. "I'll call in an air strike. Just let me know what kind of ordnance you want delivered. Better yet, me, Bob and the gang would love to live out *Let's Go Get Harry*, [the movie in which a group of friends rescue a kidnapped American from foreign terrorists]."

"Mai pen rai, kuip," Terry answered in Thai, which means "don't sweat it."

During the four-hour trip on I-25 to the border, Terry mulled over the meaning of the special relationship he shared with Desko. It was just one of those automatic things. You didn't have to work at it, it just happened. It did give Terry a sense of security knowing he had a friend like Desko.

After motoring through El Paso, the usual Third World harassment by the Mexican customs inspectors now awaited them. In the customs booths were men dressed in tight and unkempt dress resembling bus drivers' uniforms and bedecked with medals for unknown achievements.

The Reeds wondered what these medals were for. Had Mexico won a war? Not that they could recall. Terry concluded that they were probably rewards for gringo-baiting and bribe-negotiating. As their motor home waited on the Rio Grande bridge to clear Mexican customs, Terry appreciated the nooks and crannies a motor home afforded in which to conceal the newly purchased handguns. He had not confided to Janis they were hidden in the R.V.'s waste tank for fear of making her more nervous. Border crossings always had that effect on her, even when they had nothing to hide. They cleared customs with no problem despite the hidden booty and the Hasenfus bumper sticker.

The motor home was an instant hit in Mexico, but the bumper-sticker had to go.

Immediately upon returning to Ajijic, Terry went by Marr's house for an update on the crisis. The Marrs weren't there, but Maria, the maid, informed him that *"Señor Mitch es muy enfermo en un hospital en Los Estados Unidos. No se cuána regressar"* (Mitch was sick and in a hospital in the U.S., and she didn't know when he would be returning). Terry knew what that implied.

Feeling like he was now "flying blind" and on auto pilot, and with no new instructions, Terry decided it best to "drive around Mexico and get to know the country" as Mitch had suggested.

The Reed's began mapping a practice camping trip to the Pacific Coast, to familiarize themselves with the motor home and get accustomed to guiding the large vehicle over the narrow roads which were normally jammed with heavy truck traffic. They set off with the maid on a planned round-robin trip with two stopovers, to return to Ajijic several days later.

"You never fly into combat in untested equipment and untested skills," Terry always cautioned. To Janis, just packing the proper items for two small children to live in Mexico's radically diverse climates was a major undertaking.

Terry had come to have nothing but respect for Mexican drivers, who displayed courtesy and unquestionable skill in maneuvering their vehicles over less than desirable roads. In the short time he had been there, Terry had grown to sincerely believe that the State Department was spreading disinformation concerning Mexico's interior. The U.S., he was now sure, didn't want Americans to discover what a paradise it truly was.

The propaganda about crime, hunger and economic collapse was simply not true. Instead, he and Janis had discovered a country with a true national identity no longer found North of the Border. Milk, tortillas and medicine, basic human needs, were subsidized and guaranteed by the government. That, he believed, was why the people appeared so passive and content, displaying no threat of an armed revolution.

The Reeds were discovering first hand that the American system seemed to be driven by one evil catalyst—CREDIT. The pressure Americans felt for their daily, aggressive performance could be summed up by the words of one bumper-sticker Patrick Juin loved to sing: "I owe, I owe, it's off to work I go."

Juin had invited them to join him and his family at a beach hotel north of the resort town Manzanillo near the quaint village of Boca de Iguana. Prior to arriving, all the Reeds knew was that Patrick was a friend of the hotel's owner and the Juins were living there for the tourist season.

The Juins had moved to the beach in order to run their new business of giving gringos a bird's eye view of the incredible coastline from Ultra-Light flights. The Reed's were not expecting what they would soon find.

As their motor home pulled off the main coastal highway and lumbered down the unimproved dirt road through the palm groves and toward the beach, Janis feared they were getting lost. "This can't be right. Patty said they were living in a five-star hotel that has 200 rooms. The holes in this road can swallow up a small car."

Thirty minutes and five miles later, the ocean finally came into view. Nestled among the coconut trees was an eerie, dated, Third World-type hotel complex that had the appearance of being abandoned and in desperate need of maintenance. Parked under the covered entrance where a doorman normally would be standing were the Juins' two vehicles and three Ultra-Light aircraft with their wings folded.

Abandoned described it, all right. What the Reeds learned was that the hotel belonged to a wealthy Mexican businessman who had built it some 20 years earlier. The hotel had been shut down and Juin was providing security from vandals by living there, thereby giving him a cost-free base of business operations.

The hotel was to have been the prototype for a number of resort "sex hotels" the owner planned to build in the world's most beautiful places. His plan was to take the Club Med environment one step further and eliminate the haunting fear of every male vacationer: *Am I going to spend all this money and not get laid?*

His master plan was to build a plush, elegant five-star romantic setting situated near, but not directly in an already popular tourist location. Male vacationers there could not only escape the pressures of society, but create a hedonistic society of their own, without the stigma of having to negotiate with a prostitute. After having previously selected their female companion from the hotel's photo "menu," which would have been mailed in advance to the prospective vacationers, they were guaranteed not only that their nagging question be truly answered in the affirmative, but that they could also put a face on their fantasies. All this at a packaged price that included airfare and baggage handling. The creator of the resort had thought of everything.

Juin was not sure why the hotel had failed, but his wife Patricia suspected it had something to do with the developer's spouse discovering the hotel's existence. Both Patrick and Terry concluded that the hotel's failure had surely set back societal advancement by light years. So much for *machismo* idols.

As the adults sat in the gargantuan lobby drinking their Bohemia darks, sunlight flooded through the massive domed skylight onto its marble floors where the children were racing their tricycles from one end of the lobby to the other.

"Mommy, this floor is a fast race track! Can I ride my trike inside when we get back home?" Duncan asked, leaving skid marks as he came to a halt in front of his parents."

After explaining that this wouldn't be acceptable behavior at home, and watching her 4-year-old do a wheely across the lobby toward the marble inlaid fountain, Janis realized she was getting accustomed to out of the ordinary sights. She decided to just take it all in stride. This was an adventure.

Patrick explained the details of his new business and introduced Terry to his Ultra-Light pilot employees, one an American and the other a Frenchman. The new business concept was simple and highly lucrative. From the hotel's sand-packed runway, he could service other tourist hotels up and down the coast, which included Fiesta Americana, Club Med and Las Hadas. For $10 U.S., you got a 15-minute ride over the ocean and surrounding countryside. Juin would be making money for something he would be doing anyway, relaxing at the beach and flying his Ultra-Lights. When Juin learned that Terry's "silent partners" were reassessing their business commitment in Mexico, allegedly due to the peso devaluation, he begged him to become his partner so that he could expand and service the entire coastal tourist trade. Terry found the offer tantalizing.

Later that evening as he grilled *huachinango* (red snapper) over the open fire on the beach, basting it with fresh lemon and garlic, he watched another of Pacific Mexico's intoxicating sunsets as his children frolicked in the surf. But a nagging thought disturbed his reverie.

"What are you thinking?" Janis asked as she approached in the diaphanous dress she was wearing over her bathing suit. Pregnancy had not yet changed her appearance, but had added a glow to her complexion that accentuated her sensuality.

"I wish I had the ability to slow down and try out a lifestyle like this....but I don't," he replied sadly. "I just know it would drive me crazy after awhile. I guess I'm just driven to be successful. Let's pack up in the morning and get back to Guadalajara's pollution before I begin to like it here."

"I'll bet you'd stay if this hotel was still operating," she said with a grin.

The following day, they headed toward their next destination, leaving the Juins with the understanding that the two families would soon make a motor home trip together through some of Mexico's more remote industrial areas. The Juins said they would be returning to Ajijic by Halloween to attend the annual private masquerade party hosted by a mysterious and wealthy Mexican woman who was an heiress to a department store fortune. Mexican custom allowed the Juins to invite the Reeds even though they had not gotten a direct invitation from the hostess.

When they reached home, Terry returned to Marr's house for a status check. Maria informed him she had no news about Señor Mitch. Terry felt uneasy. The Mexican papers were now filled with speculation about the Yankee scandal that was developing in the U.S. Strangely, the American media seemed to have lost their initial enthusiasm in covering the story, but Daniel Ortega continued to receive extensive coverage in the Latin American press as he raged on about the Yankee imperialist pigs.

Terry felt sure "Screw Worm" was doomed and that he had better start firming up his own personal business plan for Mexico if they wanted to remain there without the Agency's assistance.

For the Reeds, each day was becoming like another chapter in a book and they were becoming as close as the pages. They were not only discovering the true Mexico, they were learning to have old-fashioned fun.

But to off-set their more relaxed lifestyle, Janis had encountered a problem in Mexico that was driving her up the wall. She was discovering that controlling a Mexican maid was a fulltime job. It was late October and she had just fired the third maid since arriving in June. This one had run up a $400 phone bill to her cousin in California. Janis decided this time she was going to take the Juins up on their offer of letting them conduct the job interviews.

Managing a domestic staff was the least of Oliver North's problems, though. He knew that he had to create some sort of diversion of his own, and fast. And it was not the diversion of money to the Contras from Iranian weapons sales that then-Attorney-General Edwin Meese referred to three weeks later in his White House press conference.

The real diversion ended up intertwining a major foreign policy initiative with the scandal that was erupting and had to be contained. What better way to contain it than to shroud it in secrecy and blend it with true national security interests? Putting a humanitarian edge on it and masking the scandal behind the release of the American hostages in Beirut was a stroke of genius by the CIA.

After all, who could denounce such a morally correct mission?

North was working overtime with the White House. He was on his way to Israel trying to work out the problems connected with another secret shipment of arms to the Iranians. His trips coupled with increased hostage negotiation activities became the foundation for grafting the illegal Contra support operation to national security interests in the Middle East. From this, the term Iran-Contra was invented. And the media later signed on, taking the bait, hook, line and sinker.

By Halloween, Terry was beginning to breathe a little easier. It had been nearly four weeks since the shoot down and maybe this would all blow over despite the fact the previously slumbering American media, which was getting its information from a Beirut weekly, was pressing hard now for more details. But Terry was amazed that so far nothing had surfaced at all about Arkansas' involvement. Was the investigation at a dead end?

Arkansas, he knew, was where all the trails would lead if someone was smart enough to follow them. He was fearful that perhaps some of the weapons on board the Cooper plane might be traced to factories in the Hog State. Weapons without serial numbers should create serious questions if the Nicaraguans were smart enough to know what to look for. And not only had there been pilot training in Arkansas, Terry knew that somewhere in Rich Mountain Aviation's maintenance records in Mena there had to exist a paper trail showing repair work performed on aircraft used for the Contra program. And what about the hundreds of millions of dollars in cash that Seal had dropped on Arkansas?

What if investigators began following the money trial between the "drop zone" at the Triple-S Ranch outside Little Rock and into the Arkansas Development Finance Authority by way of Lasater & Co? These undocumented transactions and unexplained injections of cash into the Arkansas financial community could spell imminent disaster for everyone involved.

Terry's memories of Watergate centered on Deep Throat saying: "Follow the money."

And how was CIA's Hasenfus holding up? By now he had a team of American attorneys and was starting to change his story and play down his connections to the U.S. Government.[2] This would certainly test CIA's ability for scandal containment and damage control. The federal spin doctors had to be working overtime.

Terry speculated that if the Agency could masquerade the whole tawdry mess as a national security matter, they might just pull off the deception. It certainly seemed their only option.

* * *

On that Halloween afternoon, his attention was focused as well on his costume for the masquerade party that night. The Juins were back in town and the four of them had a date to meet for an evening's celebration, Latino style.

The Reeds had decided to go all out and get absurd with their costumes and had created "his and hers" potted palms as their theme. The look was achieved by attaching eight foot palm fronds to the interior of a bottomless wicker basket, large enough to be worn around the legs, with feet protruding, thereby allowing the wearer of the "plant" to walk around.

As Terry put the final touches on the costumes, Janis was having difficulties of her own. She was furiously clearing out the personal effects of the newly-hired, live-in maid. She had just discovered the children riding their trikes around the swimming pool while the maid was preoccupied in an intimate conversation with her boyfriend through the back fence. She was history!

After making last minute babysitting arrangements with the Juin's maid, the four adults finally arrived at the picturesque estate near the lake. The Reeds were taken aback by the hostess' live giraffe, a member of her menagerie. The hostess, in true aristocratic Latin tradition, did not attend her own party until nearly midnight.

When the orchestra arrived around 8 PM and the professional sound equipment normally found in recording studios was being set up, Terry was beginning to realize he had never before been to a real party.

The guests, dressed in extravagant costumes that looked as though they had been rented from a Hollywood studio wardrobe, outgrew the capacity of the elegantly decorated home and began spilling out into the courtyard and onto the lawn. A live band provided the music and, during breaks, blasted the entire valley with a recording of Latin America's idol, Franco, singing the song of the year: *Todo La Vida.*

The merriment, drinking and dancing continued non-stop until the Reeds realized they had reached the limit of their endurance. There was a ritual that usually preceded a party like this, one with which the Reeds were not familiar. The practical thing to do in order to survive this type of revelry, they were told, was to sleep until 6 PM the day of a party, arrive around 10 PM and indulge until sunrise. The next day should be spent sleeping. You lose at least 24 hours when you party properly, Juin would tell them.

At 2 AM, just as the mobile *tacito* cart, the Mexican equivalent of a New York hot dog stand, and its owner arrived to begin serving food to the 300 people, the award for the best costume was given to the Reeds, to the dismay of many partygoers who had outspent them, but had lacked true originality.

November dawned for Terry with a hangover, from the party and from the Hasenfus incident. He had to come down to earth and attend a business meet-

ing November 4 with Fenue in Mexico City. Gomez already had met with Fenue
a number of times and Fenue and his company, Technoimpex, had been clued-
in on the capitalistic, profit-making opportunities ahead. The Hungarian knew
that the machine-tool company was to be a front for weapons shipments and
that things right now were on hold because of the Hasenfus incident.

Fenue had no knowledge of how connected Terry had been to the pilot who
had been shot down and killed or about his true activities back in Arkansas.
Fenue knew basically that Terry was running a cut-out for the CIA just as
Fenue was running one for the KGB. Strange bedfellows, he thought, they simply viewed each other as peers.

But the two men agreed that this time should be used to mutual advantage
and to continue developing their joint marketing analysis, at least through the
first half of November. That way, if by chance all systems became "go", they
could launch into the actual sales activity phase.

Just as the Reeds and the Juins were preparing for their first joint motor
home trip, Mitch Marr reappeared in Ajijic, dried out and seemingly ready to
get down to work. He relayed to Terry in their meeting that there had been
discussions in Washington about getting "Screw Worm" back on course and
gearing up for weapons shipments. Marr kept saying everyone was "cautiously
optimistic" that the Mexican operation had not yet been *compromised* by the
shoot-down and the ensuing investigations. Marr expressed the belief that the
Reed's front operation was now a *necessity* if the Contras were to continue
being supplied. He knew for sure that all re-supply activity out of El Salvador
had been curtailed, he told Reed.

Marr was confident, based on his talks in Washington, that the Agency needed
a new source of arms delivery to be developed and put into place regardless of
what Congress did with their yo-yo actions towards the Contras. He said Cathey
had told him that CIA Director William Casey had invested too much time and
money on preparing the ground work for "Screw Worm" to abandon it now.
The Agency, Cathey had told Marr, was working on a secret plan that hopefully
would contain the scandal and divert media and congressional attention away
from Mexico. Marr told Reed to continue with "whatever you're doing" until
further notice. "Don't worry, the expenses are on Uncle".

It was great to actually meet the real Mitch Marr. This one was articulate,
much less vulgar and behaved more like a "take-charge pilot type".

It was unnerving and saddening to discover through Marr that Bill Cooper's
remains had still not been laid to rest. Marr told Terry it was driving Cooper's
wife and daughters crazy not having a proper funeral, but, for some strange
reason, the State Department would not release the corpse to the family.

Terry drew more expense money, and set out with the Juin family on a small
fact-finding trip to Cuernavaca. After visiting several industries that included
the Nissan truck factory located there, the two families returned by way of the
Mexican resort area of Valle de Bravo, west of Mexico City. The breath-taking
beauty of this area, where Juin had once lived, further convinced the Reeds
that they had found their hidden paradise. He now hoped the State Department would continue spewing out its misinformation and propaganda so that
not too many ugly Americans would discover their secret and screw it all up.

Even though Terry had lived abroad before and Janis had traveled extensively throughout Europe, both were just beginning to see their country from
another perspective. Through the eyes of the Juins and others, America's arro-

gance and dictatorial policies toward Third World countries were just coming into focus and the Reeds didn't like what they were seeing.

In many respects, Mexico was taking much better care of its social problems and had retained and was building upon a very unique institution being discarded by Americans—the family. By the U.S. Government trying to force American attitudes, values and way of life upon Latin America, the Reeds were beginning to wonder if this wasn't, in fact, a giant step in the wrong direction. The Mexican people, for the most part, seemed truly happy, content, and did not rely upon the government to cure their ills. They turned instead, inward, to family, church, friends and the Community, like the days in America when Terry was young.

It was simple—Patrick reminded him once again. America's problems centered around their Yankee aggressiveness based on over-extended credit and that leads to "I owe, I owe so it's off to work I go." And yet, strangely, that's the kind of life Patrick's wife yearned for. It was at times a peculiar and argumentative group, motoring around Mexico, analyzing the world's social ills.

With the rule in effect that all four would speak only Spanish to one another half the day, and English the rest, it was turning into a cultural exchange on wheels and both families were pleased to see how quickly the children were learning each other's language.

Upon returning to Ajijic, Marr had good news for Terry. "Gomez wants you ta be in Mexico City for a meeting he has set up for December 4th. Meet him at the Hotel Century in the Zona Rosa. The address is Liverpool, number 152. You'll like it there. It's a spook hangout.

" And, Oh yeah, he said ta bring the Jap's money," Marr instructed, referring to Frank Fujikawa's "capitalization" of Machinery International, Inc.

By this time, Attorney General Meese had set in place what Marr had referred to earlier as Casey's "secret plan" to contain the scandal and divert attention away from Arkansas and Mexico. Meese, at a White House news conference on November 25th, 1986, had revealed what he said was "the diversion."

Meese said funds from the sale of U.S. weapons to Iran were being diverted to aid the Contras. The investigation was continuing, but a National Security Council staff member by the name of Marine Lieutenant Colonel Oliver North had done this all alone. Somehow, Meese indicated, North had taken over the entire government bureaucracy without anyone else noticing. Incredibly, just about everyone bought it.

Meese never said specifically if anything was wrong with the diversion and was evasive when pressed by reporters on this scandalous behavior. He replied that the U.S. had no control over the diverted funds because they were "never the property of the United States." But if these funds were not American funds, whose were they? Meese speculated the money belonged to the "party" that sold them to Iran—and that was Israel.

So was the diversion itself a diversion?

"What's to prevent an increasingly cynical public from thinking that you were looking for a scapegoat and you came up with this whopper, but it doesn't have a lot to do with the original controversy?" was a question posed to the attorney-general.

Meese replied he was laying out "the facts", but did not say anything more about the "original controversy" for the rest of the press conference.[3] Nor was he asked.

Meese had thrown out enough peanuts to send the trained monkeys in the White House press room scurrying to pick them up. Somehow they overlooked the fact that this really didn't make sense. And the inquiry ended there. North, of course, knew the truth, though he was not remembered for being particularly adept at uttering it.

North himself remarked later in his book, *Under Fire*, stated: "The diversion was a diversion."

1. Dutton testimony, *Hearings*, 100-3, 239-40, 280; North testimony, 100-7. Part II, P. 105; Deputy FBI Director Oliver (Buck) .i.Revell deposition, 6/11/87. 60-71.
2. *The New York Times*, October 17, 1986.
3. Theodore Draper, *A Very Thin Line*, Hill and Wang, 1991, P. 544-46.

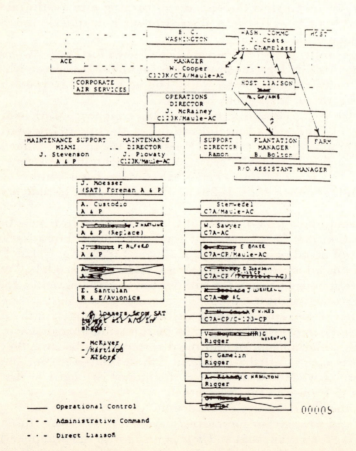

23-1. Chain of command for Richard Secord's "black flight division" within the Enterprise. Had Terry Reed accepted the offer to join William Cooper, a line would probably be drawn through his name too. (Source: House Select Committee to investigate covert arms transactions with Iran)

TRANSMIT VIA:
☐ Teletype
☐ Facsimile

PRECEDENCE:
☐ Immediate
☐ Priority
☐ Routine

CLASSIFICATION:
☐ TOP SECRET
☐ SECRET
☒ CONFIDENTIAL
☐ UNCLAS E F T O
☐ UNCLAS
Date _____

1 FM LITTLE ROCK (I-C)
2 TO DIRECTOR PRIORITY
3 JACKSONVILLE PRIORITY
4 MIAMI PRIORITY
5 PHILADELPHIA PRIORITY
6 SAN FRANCISCO PRIORITY
7 SAVANNAH PRIORITY
8 BT

declassified by ___ 7/27/88

9 C O N F I D E N T I A L
10 ATTN: COUNTERTERRORISM PLANNING AND SPECIAL INVESTIGATIONS
11 UNIT, TERRORISM SECTION, CID.
12 SENATE FOREIGN RELATIONS COMMITTEE REQUEST FOR INFORMATION;
13 NEUTRALITY MATTER - NICARAGUA; OO: BUREAU; BUDED:
14 NOVEMBER 3, 1986.
15 UNSUBS; POSSIBLE NEUTRALITY VIOLATIONS CONCERNING AC-123
16 AIRCRAFT SHOT DOWN BY NICARAGUAN ARMED FORCES ON OCTOBER 5,
17 1986; NEUTRALITY MATTER - NICARAGUA; OO: BUREAU.
18
19 ① - I-C
20 ① - 12B-283
      CLR:jcb
21 (2)

Approved: _____ Transmitted _____ Per _____
                      (Number) (Time)

---

1 PAGE TWO LR I-C C O N F I D E N T I A L
2   RE BUREAU TELETYPE TO ALL FIELD OFFICES DATED OCTOBER 30,
3 1986; AND LITTLE ROCK TELEPHONE CALLS TO SUPERVISOR JOHN COX,
4 OCTOBER 30-31, 1986, AND NOVEMBER 3, 1986.
5   SEARCH OF LITTLE ROCK INDICES LOCATED TWO PERTINENT
6 REFERENCES PERTAINING TO SENATE FOREIGN RELATIONS COMMITTEE
7 INQUIRY AS FOLLOWS:
8 ██
9 ██
10 ██
11 ██
12 ██
13 ████████████████████████████
14   ADLER BERRIMAN SEAL, AKA BARRY SEAL, WAS ONE OF SUBJECTS
15 OF LITTLE ROCK FILE 12B-283 CAPTIONED, "FRED L. HAMPTON;
16 ET AL; DBA RICH MOUNTAIN AVIATION, INC., MENA, ARKANSAS;
17 NARCOTICS; OO: LITTLE ROCK." INVESTIGATION IN THIS PENDING
18 MATTER WAS INITIATED BY LITTLE ROCK IN FEBRUARY, 1984, AND
19 IS IN FOUR VOLUMES. SUBJECTS WERE PREVIOUSLY INVESTIGATED
20 BY NEW ORLEANS AS A 245D MATTER. SEAL WAS MURDERED AT
21 BATON ROUGE, LOUISIANA, IN FEBRUARY, 1986. PRIOR TO HIS DEATH,

Approved: _____ Transmitted _____ Per _____
                      (Number) (Time)

FBI

TRANSMIT VIA:
☐ Teletype
☐ Facsimile
_____

PRECEDENCE:
☐ Immediate
☐ Priority
☐ Routine

CLASSIFICATION:
☐ TOP SECRET
☐ SECRET
☐ CONFIDENTIAL
☐ UNCLAS E F T O
☐ UNCLAS
_____ Date _____

PAGE THREE LR 0-0 C O N F I D E N T I A L

SEAL ADMITTED SMUGGLING LARGE QUANTITIES OF COCAINE FROM SOUTH
AMERICA (COLOMBIA) TO THE UNITED STATES AND TESTIFIED BEFORE THE
SENATE INVESTIGATIVE COMMITTEE. COMMENCING FEBRUARY, 1984, SEAL
OPERATED UNDERCOVER FOR DEA, UNDER SUPERVISION OF DEA SUPERVISOR
ROBERT J. JAURA, STATIONED AT MIAMI, FLORIDA. AT THAT SEAL WAS
"COOPERATING" WITH DEA, MIAMI, HE WAS SUBJECT OF INVESTIGATION
BY FBI, NEW ORLEANS, AND LITTLE ROCK, WHO WERE NOT AWARE OF HIS
DEA CONNECTION.

SEAL UTILIZED THE MENA AIRPORT AND RICH MOUNTAIN AVIATION
FOR AIRCRAFT STORAGE, MAINTENANCE, AND MODIFICATIONS DURING HIS
COOPERATING PERIOD WITH DEA. DURING THE PERIOD LATE 1980 - MARCH,
1983, THE MENA AIRPORT WAS UTILIZED FOR SMUGGLING ACTIVITIES BY
SEAL AND ASSOCIATES.

IN INTERVIEW OF DEA SUPERVISOR ROBERT J. JAURA ON JUNE 2,
1986, AT MIAMI (MIAMI FILE 12B-1392), JAURA ADVISED THAT SEAL
HAD THREE AIRCRAFTS MODIFIED AT RICH MOUNTAIN AVIATION FOR
DEA: A LOCKHEED LOADSTAR, A CONVAIR, AND A C-123-K.

FBIHQ SHOULD NOTE THAT ELECTRONIC MEDIA, LITTLE ROCK,
REPORTED SUBSEQUENT TO CRASH IN NICARAGUA ON OCTOBER 5, 1986,
THAT CRASHED C-123 WAS, IN FACT, THE AIRCRAFT OPERATED BY BARRY

Approved: _____ Transmitted _____ Per _____
(Number) (Time)

PAGE FOUR LR 0-0 C O N F I D E N T I A L

SEAL AND SUBJECT OF NATIONAL ELECTRONIC MEDIA DOCUMENTARY
REGARDING SEAL'S COCAINE ACTIVITIES WITH NICARAGUAN INDIVIDUALS.
BACKGROUND INFORMATION REGARDING THE C-123 WAS PREVIOUSLY
PROVIDED TO FBIHQ, OC SECTION, VIA TELETYPE FROM LITTLE ROCK
DATED JULY 26, 1984, AND CAPTIONED, "FRED L. HAMPTON ET AL."

INFORMATION COPY FURNISHED JACKSONVILLE, MIAMI, PHILADELPHIA,
SAN FRANCISCO, AND SAVANNAH PER FBIHQ.

BT

23-2. FBI four page classified message alerting various Bureaus of pending Senate investigation into the October 5th, 1986 shootdown of the C-123 in Nicaragua. Note the connection that has already developed (by November 3, 1986) between the Iran-Contra scandal and Barry Seal's Mena operation. The common thread: the CIA provided aircraft used in both black operations.

CHAPTER 24

'THE SNAKE THAT WOULDN'T DIE'

Attorney General Edwin Meese was performing his post-mortem on the viper conceived by Ronald Reagan and the CIA.

As he attempted to peel back the epidermis surrounding the Cooper shootdown, he was finding two black cancerous growths that appeared to have metastasized the organs of the Presidency, not unlike what John Dean had described during Watergate when he told Richard Nixon, "There's a cancer growing on the Presidency."

And perhaps even worse, this viper, labeled Iran-Contra, was still twitching and might still be alive.

Secretary of State George Shultz wrote recently in his memoirs: "I feared that, despite the press, Congressional and public uproar, some version of the operation was *still* alive. Those who were responsible for the operation now seemed desperate to vindicate their judgment in the face of overwhelming criticism."[1]

Shultz was deeply troubled in December, 1986. The roof was falling in on the Reagan Administration. The President's dual obsession with keeping the Contras together "body and soul" and trying to free the American hostages in Beirut had blown up in his face. The President was facing serious problems, maybe even impeachment.

But Shultz was learning to his dismay that Ronald Reagan and William Casey were still dealing behind the scenes, and behind Shultz' back, with an Israeli named Amiram Nir, who had been North's link to the Iranians. This is what Shultz referred to when he said he was disturbed by finding elements of the operation "still alive" even after Meese's disclosures to the nation that as much as $30 million from the sales of arms to Iran had been diverted to the Contras.

After Shultz gained knowledge about the depth of the CIA's involvement with Iran, being conducted through the Israeli cutout Amiram Nir, Shultz tried to make Reagan see that his explanations were not truthful with regard to America's dealings with Iran and this was undermining public confidence. Reagan had in fact been trying to swap weapons for hostages while saying at the same time that "the United States will never negotiate with terrorists."[2]

But what did secret dealings with the Iranians have to do with Cooper being shot down over Nicaragua? Shultz, like the rest of America, didn't know there was any connection at all. This signaled to Shultz a total lack of leadership at the top allowing compartmentalization of policies and conflicting goals with no feedback to those in charge of implementing policies, namely the Secretary of State and his department.

"The CIA and NSC (National Security Council) staff, with the apparent support from the...Vice President (George Bush), were still proceeding just as though nothing had happened," Shultz wrote. "Congress was being misled now, a month and a half after the revelation (the Cooper shootdown) first appeared. What was worse, John Whitehead (Deputy Secretary of State) said, 'the CIA has told the Iranians that the State Department is just a *temporary impediment,* (italics ours) and that after it calms down, Cave (a ranking CIA official) and Secord will be back in action. *The President is being ripped to pieces and the CIA is reassuring the Iranians.'"[3]

CIA Director William Casey seemed to be stepping into an apparent vacuum of leadership and seizing *de facto* control of the government. Was some kind of "coup" developing? If Shultz had been getting briefings on this type of behavior going on in another country, he would probably have called it just that....a coup. And as in any coup attempt, at least two factions are involved. Who was behind this coup? Casey had no political ambitions. And if not Casey, then who?

In private meetings that included Reagan, Bush, Casey, Defense Secretary Casper Weinberger, White House Chief of Staff Donald Regan, National Security Advisor John Poindexter, and CIA official George Cave, Shultz was learning to his dismay that the CIA was running foreign policy and possibly controlling the President. Unlike Shultz, they were telling Reagan what he wanted to hear, namely that his goals were correct and he should continue pursuing them despite everything. The end justified the means.

Shultz was discovering this was another real-life example of "The Emperor's New Clothes." He was the only one telling Reagan to his face that he was naked, that he had violated his own stated policy and was lying to the American people and the world by stating the U.S. would never deal with terrorists. The others in the Reagan circle, led by Casey, were telling the President his wardrobe was superb and that deceit was necessary for security reasons to carry out secret policies with which the President had become obsessed.

But, to Shultz, it appeared Reagan didn't fully understand the depths of the CIA's activities in the Middle East and had no knowledge of the two secret operations being intertwined. And he refused to even consider suggestions that he and others had been breaking the law.

Attorney General Meese confided to Shultz during his internal investigation: "Certain things could be a violation of law. The President didn't know about the Hawks (missile shipment to Iran) in November, 1985. If it happened and the President didn't report it to Congress, it's a violation."[4]

Perhaps *this* was part of the plan Mitch Marr had referred to as the CIA's secret way to steer attention away from Arkansas and Mexico. If so, it was working. Oliver North had been successful in weaving the two operations together. He had taken the illegally-generated profits from the arms sales to Iran and diverted them to purchasing arms and supplies for the Contras. Neither action, Shultz was learning, was legal nor were they approved by Congress.

But if a Marine lieutenant colonel and an admiral, National Security Advisor John Poindexter, had been the only ones influencing Reagan, and they had now been fired, why was this monster still alive and breathing. Was Shultz dealing with a hydra-headed serpent? And, if so, where were these other heads buried and likely to surface?

As Terry Reed and his wife checked into the Century Hotel in Mexico City on December 3rd, 1986, as instructed by Mitch Marr, he was carrying with him the Japanese investor's "contribution" to Machinery International, Inc., the company whose job it was to create the new "head" of the serpent. (See chapter end.)

"What are you going to do with all that money between now and until your meeting tomorrow?" his wife asked nervously as the Mexican bellboys unloaded the baggage from their car.

"Nothing special. Just don't be nervous and bring attention to it. Nobody knows I'm carrying a quarter of a million dollars in cash except you. Relax. Let's enjoy this trip. Besides, who would think there's that much money in a plastic, eight-dollar briefcase."

Janis Reed still occasionally marveled at her husband's ability to put on his poker face and pretend nothing was out of the ordinary. She was still in training as the wife of a spook, and was having difficulty dealing with some of the job's requirements.

Marr's instructions to "bring the Jap's money" meant he had to get the money down to Mexico and in cash. Frank Fujikawa's $250,000 had been on deposit in a bank in Kansas City awaiting instructions on the transfer. Fujikawa and Robert Johnson had agreed in Dallas that the Japanese businessman would hand over $250,000 in untraceable cash in exchange for stock in the new American corporation. There would never be any official record of this transaction and the stock would be reflected on the books as issued with "no compensation received." They had agreed for security reasons that the transfer would take place outside the United States in order to throw off any banking trail between the withdrawal of the funds and the eventual redeposit. "No paper, no trail," as Barry Seal had said.

By withdrawing the funds from the bank in Kansas City and physically handing them over to Max Gomez there would be no linkage between Fujikawa's newly-formed holding company, Okami Ltd., and Machinery International, Inc. Thus, the investors could remain anonymous since it was a privately-held corporation requiring no public filings or disclosure. Security and deniability required taking risks like carrying around large amounts of cash.

Further, Fujikawa's company, Okami Ltd., had no corporate or legal ties to Gomiya USA, Inc., the Japanese company that Fujikawa managed in Chicago. "The linkage had been broken", Fujikawa assured Reed and Johnson, meaning there was no trail between the two companies.

After checking into the hotel, the Reeds were beginning to appreciate the digs spooks had become accustomed to in Mexico City. The small and elegant, European style hotel was lavishly furnished with imported marble, and its rooms had sculptured walls with no intersecting corners. Each mini-suite automatically came equipped with a large sunken tub with ornate gold-plated fixtures.

It was strategically-situated on the eastern edge of the *Zona Rosa,* an area of the city with a European ambiance and close to Insurgentes Boulevard, the Mexican equivalent of the Champs Elysee. The hotel itself was on a small uncluttered street that allowed easy access to the Autopista network looping around the world's largest city and within walking distance of the elite shopping district where Mexico City's *Chilangos* (ruling class) lived, played, dined and shopped.

Within the *Zona Rosa* were streets closed to all but pedestrian traffic and lined with scenic gardens, sidewalk cafes and dotted with Paisano umbrellas over tables where Latino beautiful people stylishly dined, flirted, sipped cappuchino or just watched the world go by.

After dining at the *Vagabond Trucha,* a popular seafood restaurant within walking distance of the hotel, Terry and Janis walked to the monument dedicated to the *Niños Heroes,* the hero children of Mexico. At the large traffic circle there, they sat in the park and read the inscription that told the story of young military cadets who defended their academy from foreign invaders.

Terry choked with emotion as he learned that they all committed suicide with honor rather than surrender to the invading forces who had put them under siege. As they were about to be overwhelmed by superior numbers, he read, they climbed to highest point on the wall, wrapped themselves in the Mexican flag and leaped to their death. Why wasn't this story taught in American history, Janis wondered, since it indeed involved Americans? The invading American forces, she was ashamed to read, were under the command of Theodore Roosevelt. How many monuments like this, they wondered, were scattered throughout the world. The term "ugly American" was truly becoming a part of their vocabulary.

The next morning Janis was preparing to spend the day Christmas shopping for the upcoming holidays and for her soon-to-be-needed maternity wardrobe. Just as she was getting ready to leave, their room was buzzed and Terry was informed that the meeting was at hand.

To Terry's surprise, waiting in the coffee shop was not only Gomez but another man he had met before. He was the same man who had sat strangely quiet during most of the meeting in Chagres, Panama, a year earlier. This brought back sad memories of Barry Seal's last days.

Maximo Gomez went straight to the introduction and business at hand. "Señor Estrella, I know you've met this gentleman before, but now I would like for you to understand more about him, who he is and the role he is about to play in all this. But first, *tome el dinero Japonesa, por favor!*"

Terry handed Gomez the briefcase containing the money and, without bringing unnecessary attention of any kind, casually set it between himself and the other man. Terry was sure from the aplomb Gomez demonstrated in taking the money that this was an exercise he had undergone many times before.

After executing the adept maneuver, he introduced Terry to Señor Pat Weber. In reality, "Weber" was the very same Amiram Nir that George Shultz was so concerned about at that very moment. The serpent was still very much alive.

With no discussion at all about the contents or the amount inside the briefcase, Gomez began: "I have good news from north of the border. All systems are go, as we pilots like to say. In fact, in light of recent occurrences, we are going to expand into Phase 2 of your plan immediately, if not sooner!"

Terry was surprised at what he heard as the briefing unfolded over cups of strong European coffee and croissants. The Agency was literally pulling out all the stops. Gomez was requesting Terry not only to return to Guadalajara and immediately consummate all outstanding legal agreements being held in limbo as a result of the shootdown, but to begin implementing Phase 2 of the plan ahead of schedule.

Phase 2, as it was referred to in the business plan provided to Johnson, was the portion dedicated to the manufacturing of weapons and components. But it had been designed to be implemented only after successfully developing the storage and trans-shipment portion, which was Phase 1.

Gomez said it now appeared that "Screw Worm" had not been *compromised* in the two months since the scandal broke. As a result of the shootdown, however, and since "Centaur Rose" was now shut down, the Agency was desperate for "Screw Worm" to come on line...immediately. The need now was to begin quickly producing arms, not just storing and shipping them. What Terry was hearing from Gomez was that the CIA no longer had time to fully develop Phase 1 before cautiously transitioning into Phase 2, which had been the original plan.

"The Contras are rapidly depleting inventories warehoused in Central America," Gomez said. "Even though Congress has turned on the lethal aid valve, it may only be momentarily. That's why it is necessary for you to get down to business with the production phase."

"But Max, I'm just only one guy," Terry complained. "I've been devoting my time with marketing efforts to develop legitimate Mexican clients. And now you're telling me I have to duplicate Arkansas overnight? In a country that has an acute shortage of skilled machinists!"

It took a year, Terry knew, to get the arms manufacturing loop in Arkansas into production and stabilized and that was in the U.S., where raw materials for the weapons were produced to strict standards.

And in Arkansas, the necessary infrastructure had been in place to build upon, not to mention the support they could count on from the governor's office. Gomez was asking him to do something he felt was reckless and way too much of an undertaking to attempt by himself, especially in a Third World country.

"That's why Mr. Weber is here. Pat and his people can make things happen here in Mexico, fast. Almost as fast as I can," Gomez said in his typical braggadocio fashion.

"Pat and his people?" Terry was confused. "Are these machine-tool people you're referring to, people with weapons manufacturing background?"

"Yes," Weber answered. "My people have much experience, not only in manufacturing, but, I think you'll agree...in using them as well." Weber and Gomez both laughed, but the humor escaped Terry.

"*Señor Estrella, I represent the Government of Israel,*" Weber informed.

Holy shit, Terry thought. Who am I dealing with here? His mind flashed back to the Panama meeting. Had the Israelis been part of this plan for more than a year? He could remember "Weber" sitting there in Panama taking extensive notes and later asking detailed questions concerning all aspects of "Screw Worm." And since no one from "his side" intervened as he answered Weber's questions, Terry could only conclude that the government of Israel must have been Weber's "silent investor" all along.

"I can see by the expression on your face, you are accessing your memory data bank concerning what we discussed in Panama," Weber said. "Enjoy your croissant for a moment while you adjust to who I am and who I represent. I would wish the same."

It was obvious to Terry that this guy hadn't just left the *Kibbutz*. Terry didn't know that this man with a glass eye and undefinable accent was traveling in the same circles as John Cathey and had just a few months earlier personally briefed George Bush on Israel's role in acting as a middleman for the United States to establish diplomatic contact with Iranian "moderates" wishing to undermine the Ayatollah Khomeni. Had Terry known all this then, he would have felt even more honored to be involved in such a high-level loop.

Terry was getting a lesson in geopolitics as well as the spy business and manufacturing. He had accepted the CIA's behind-the-scenes liaison with the KGB, but to now be spicing the clandestine recipe with the addition of what he assumed was the *Mossad* made him curious. And he was wondering, did the *Mossad* have this symbiotic relationship with the KGB elsewhere in the world?

What did the Israelis really want out of this triad? For them, weapons export is vital to their existence for two reasons, one obvious, the other less so. First, their battle-proven weapons such as the Uzi submachine gun bring in hard currency. But secondly, and equally important, arms bring the Israelis influence in the countries to whom they sell.[5]

After Weber gave Terry an appropriate amount of time to finish chewing his croissant and his thoughts, he turned to security. "Mr. Estrella, I am fully briefed. Not only on 'Screw Worm,' but your prior intelligence activities as well. You have served your country well and I am honored to be working with a professional. I know you were a friend of Mr. Seal's and I join you in grieving over his death. I am sure Mr. Gomez will agree, you should not share any knowledge concerning my country's involvement in 'Screw Worm' with your wife. There's no need in transferring to her potentially dangerous information. Do we all agree with that?"

By now, they were all chewing Chiclets sold them by a street urchin who was in the process of being run out of the coffee shop's street-side entrance.

"Yes, I agree," Terry answered. "But I am curious. What can you specifically do for me in light of the pressure Max here is exerting? Do your people have plans in getting directly involved in *Maquinaria Internacional*? Just what are we discussing?"

"What you need here in Mexico is what you had going for you in Arkansas," Weber replied. "You need a state government on your side with a governor desperate to make things happen quickly for his impoverished state."

"Do you know such a place?" Terry asked. "One in which your people can exert the same type of influence the Agency did in Arkansas?"

"Yes. Max and I both have friends in high places in the State of Michoacuan. The governor there in many ways compares to the man who was in charge of the State of Arkansas. He has high political ambitions and is willing to, how do you say..."

"Play ball?" Reed guessed.

"Oh yes, that's the expression I was searching for. One of your great American pastimes."

"What are the others?" Gomez asked.

"I know of only one besides baseball...starting wars. That's what you Americans are known for, worldwide," Weber joked.

"This time, we're not only going to start a war, we're going to finish one!" Gomez boasted. "communism *is* going to die out in this hemisphere, at least with all our joint efforts."

"Not if you keep behaving as unprofessional as you were and by allowing such an embarrassment to happen," Weber said chastising Gomez about the

Cooper crash. "Actually, my people are being drawn into this quicker and deeper than we would like, in an attempt to help you keep control of this messy situation."

Gomez now seemed anxious to shift the conversation away from intelligence foul-ups and onto something he did do well, bribe people and arrange meetings. He produced a portion of a topographical map detailing the remote, high-elevation region of north-central Michoacan. He pointed to the City of Morelia which he said had been targeted as home of the new manufacturing complex where the Agency would secretly produce weapons as they had in Arkansas.

"On the west side of town, near the airport, we have selected a piece of land to build a new building to your specifications," Gomez briefed. "We can co-locate the manufacturing with a new technical school the governor wants to build. That will be a way to train the machinists to make the weapons parts. See, that's simple. We've thought of everything."

That's what bothered Terry about Gomez, always oversimplifying. Sawahata and Seal had learned the hard way there was a lot more to any type of close-tolerance manufacturing than meets the eye. But he continued to listen without comment.

With his pencil, Weber traced a route that began at Morelia and continued 50 miles west to the town of Patzcuaro. From there, his pointer went south to the small town of Santa Clara del Cobre and then 10 miles further west to a small lake.

"On the west side of this lake is a small village by the name of Zirahuen. You need to be there on January 5th for a very important meeting with Governor Cuauhtemo Cardenas and others."

The man he was referring to, Cuauhtemoc Cardenas, had high political ambitions that came to him naturally since his father had once been president of Mexico. He later ran for the presidency in 1988. Many say the election was stolen from him by the vote-counting fraud traditionally employed by the ruling party, called the PRI *(Partido Revolucionario Institucional)*. This entrenched political machine has held office for more than 60 years. Cardenas is now the head of a new political party known as PRD *(Partido Democratico de la Revolucion)*, which was gaining popularity and positioning itself for the 1994 election.

"The meeting will be very similar to the one you attended in Panama," Weber continued. "I will make the introductions and you should be prepared to make a presentation to these people...like you did for me in Chagres. I'm sure no one on his staff will be able to ask technical questions, but be prepared to cover all facets of what you will need to make this project happen. Bring your shopping list."

"Where will we meet once I get there?" Terry asked.

"You'll be driving your new motor home?" Weber asked, with Terry now realizing the Agency and the Mossad were keeping track of what he drove.

Terry nodded.

"It's a very small place, we'll find you," Weber said.

Gomez added, "You should go to Morelia first by yourself and take a look around. It's a good size city and I would like for you to see the town through your eyes without the governor's entourage that will be accompanying you later."

For once, Terry thought, Gomez was making sense. From his earlier experience in the States, he'd found it best to always scout around a prospective factory site alone. That way, you get an uncensored view of the area, its people and its problems.

Gomez went on, saying, "Don't take your Mexican friend Juin with you on your scouting trip to Morelia. We don't want anyone getting any idea of our plans for there."

This bothered Terry. Someone had been watching him. Was it Marr? Or someone else? Someone was reporting not only what he was driving, but information about personal relationships he was developing, and Gomez must have been aware of Terry and Juin traveling together earlier to Cuernavaca. He put these feelings aside for now, figuring it came with the job.

Immigration became the topic. Gomez informed Terry that he had been applying some "lubricant" to some key Mexican immigration officials who would now surely expedite Terry's papers allowing him to work legally in Mexico.

For one to appreciate what it takes for a foreigner to be gainfully employed in Mexico, you have to understand why Mexico is protectionist. Having been invaded by foreign conquerors beginning with Cortez, Mexicans say with some irony that they never fought a war they didn't lose. This is why they are distrustful of everyone, particularly *Norte Americanos*.

So laws and a bureaucracy were created to keep foreigners at arms length and in the country only long enough to spend their money and leave. Retirement incomes are welcome, but for Terry to be out aggressively soliciting business in his own name through his own company is normally viewed as a threat to national security. In their view, that's stealing both jobs and income from some deserving Mexican citizen.

Even though he was now "in country", Terry was still running head-first into an invisible wall that kept him in visitor's status and unable to negotiate and close business contracts. This was essential for his company's existence.

The full impact of just who Gomez was lubricating to get over this legal hurdle Terry would not fully appreciate until he later relayed his stories of this trip to gringos in Chapala. They had been fighting unsuccessfully for years to qualify legally to work on the open Mexican economy.

"*Mañana en la mañana,* you need to go to the lobby of the building located at this address," Gomez said as he passed to Terry a small slip of paper and typed on it:

Subdireccion de No inmigrantes
Insurgentes Sur #1388
Casi Esq. Con Parronquia
Horario de 9.00 A 13.30

"Go there before they open officially, around 800 hours. You need to ask for a Señor Iturraldi. He is chief of Mexican immigration documentation. Give him your correct name. He is expecting you."

"What is he going to do for me?" Terry asked.

"Any fucking thing you ask him to do. If you want a Mexican birth certificate for the non-existent children of your children, he will give it to you," Gomez said with a boastful laugh, obviously trying to impress the Israeli participant in these shadowy affairs. "He's on *my* payroll. And you tell me if he gives you any shit!"

"Fine," Reed answered.

The meeting was over.

The following morning, at precisely 8 AM, Terry's taxi pulled up in front of the federal building whose address Gomez had given him. The two Army guards positioned in front of the locked glass doors indicated to Terry somebody had not gotten the word and he'd probably have to wait outside until the building opened. Just for kicks, though, he said in Spanish that he was there to see Señor Iturraldi concerning an immigration problem.

Much to his surprise both soldiers came to present arms, the equivalent of a salute, and allowed him to pass through the door unescorted where he was joined by a shapely Mexican secretary so typical of the lighter-skinned Chilanga women who populate Mexican government offices. She wore five-inch spiked heels, black mesh stockings, a skirt that looked like it had been painted across her slightly plump posterior, and a ruffled blouse that was one size too small. She walked with her shoulders thrown back and her head erect to accentuate a well-endowed chest that kept your initial gaze off her over made-up face.

She exuded an aura of importance as she paraded past the lesser secretaries with darker skin tone and belonging to the working classes. On their desks were antiquated typewriters and piles of yellowed papers stacked on their work areas and beyond. It was an image of Third-World bureaucracy raised to its highest art form.

As the secretary approached a massive door at the end of a hall, Terry's licentious viewing from the rear came at an end. Without knocking, she opened the door and led him into a ornately-furnished office. He concluded the opulent and somewhat gaudy furnishings were probably the fruits of decades of kickbacks, or "commissions" as they are politely called. The Mexican bureaucrat sitting behind the carved wooden desk looked too young to fit the dated Spanish decor. He had to be important since his trademark credenza, which was centered under a huge portrait of Presidente Miguel del la Madrid, held the requisite number of continental telephones. The more telephones, he would learn, the higher the rank in Mexico.

Standing on either side of his desk were huge Mexican flags, giving the whole room the appearance of an altar where some Mayan might sacrifice a virgin to the sun god.

The young bureaucrat sprang from behind his desk, snapped to attention, clicked his heels and bent forward slightly at the waist in order to greet Terry. The only act of deference that was omitted was the kissing of Reed's ring.

"My name is Licensia Felipe Urbiola Ledezma. I am chief of the Department of Immigration for all of Mexico. I am here to serve you in any way I can. Mr. Iturraldi will not be available...I am his superior. When he told me of the importance of your request, I felt it necessary to get personally involved. What may this office and the government of Mexico do for you, Señor?"

Terry outlined his needs and problems associated with the new company start-up, emphasizing the lack of government response to the 100 per cent ownership issue as well as his own working papers, entitled an FM-3.

"*No problema, Señor Reed.* How else can I be of service to you?" the official said as the secretary sashayed from the office to get the papers typed.

When the typing task was finished, he then selected several from among the plethora of official government rubber stamps on his desk carousel and applied them to the document giving Terry his coveted right-to-work documents.

Terry felt a bit uncomfortable. What was the protocol now? Was he expecting the usual "commission" for his services. Here he was, standing in an office whose walls were draped with crushed red velvet, something akin to be inside a coffin, he thought, and he didn't know what was proper or expected. A misplaced bribe to an official at this lofty level could cause embarrassment. Gomez had made no mention of his controlling the chief of *all* Mexican immigration.

"Señor Urbiola, may I pay the fee for your office's services directly to you?"

The official immediately began waving his hands, squinting his eyes and shaking his head if someone had just offered him a jellyfish to hold. Tsk, tsk, tsk!, he said.

"Señor Reed, please do not insult me! There is absolutely no fee required for your immigration papers. It is my duty to service businessmen like you who are helping to advance Mexican technology."

By now Terry had noticed he had been handed only documentation solving his immigration dilemma and when the subject of his corporate problems were raised, that was something else.

"As for the papers for your corporation, you will need to travel to Dallas, Texas, and have them issued out of the country by our consul there. His name is Señor Raul Gonzalez Certosimo, and it is my understanding you have had dealings with him previously. I spoke with him yesterday by phone in anticipation of our meeting and he is standing by to service you and your company's needs immediately."

More confusion. Gonzalez was the same man Terry had been dealing with in the States prior to moving to Mexico. This same man was the one who had told Terry it would be "impossible" to get the proper papers issued until he was in place and residing in Mexico. This, he had said, was the visual sign of *foreign commitment* necessary to demonstrate true intent to the Mexican Government before such a major request could be granted. At that time 100 per cent foreign ownership of a Mexican corporation was a violation of the Mexican Constitution.

"Mr. Gonzalez is now prepared to issue what he previously said he could not? I am confused."

"It is simple. We here in Mexico are controlled by the Spanish order of the *sistema de notario* (notary system). This was set up by Cortez and basically allows each province of Mexico to function under its own rules as long as it stayed generally in line with Spain's wishes. Mr. Gonzalez is now a *notario* and can execute such documents, but *only* on soil he controls. Our building in Dallas *is* Mexican soil. This way, he can expedite your wishes without upsetting officials here in Mexico that may only delay your request."

The term notary, Terry already knew, had a totally different meaning in Mexico than in the U.S. In the Spanish bureaucracy imposed on Mexico by its conqueror, the notary WAS the law, and an extension of the Spanish Crown. Each notary was the chief of a province carved from the vast colony of Mexico and answered directly to Cortez, but in a very loose fashion that basically allowed them to rule their territories as fiefdoms.

Terry was learning that there were notaries placed in Mexican embassies as consulates who could operate as if their diplomatic missions were Mexican states. Terry was about to learn that Notario Gonzalez viewed his consulate as a sovereign state and was being allowed to bypass the Mexico City bureaucracy, and at a handsome profit to himself.

"When will Mr. Gonzalez be prepared to receive me?"

"It will take him approximately 30 days to get all of your paperwork in order. I will notify you by phone when all is ready and it's as simple as that. Like

I said, we are anxious to serve you."

As Terry was preparing to depart, and thinking this all had been too easy, he found out his instinct was right. The official interrupted his departure by saying, "Oh, by the way, Mr. Reed, Mr. Gonzalez' services require lots of paperwork and you must bear the cost of internal expenses generated within his office as a result of your unusual demand."

"Do you have an estimate of cost for these services?"

"Precisely $20,000, U.S. currency. And please, no checks. You may pay Mr. Gonzalez personally."

As he was leaving the immigration building, Terry was musing about the Agency's inability to control their Third World "client states." Even though Gomez prided himself in his ability to buy off anyone in Mexico, it was clear that some of those who had to be bought off were operating outside of Mexico, not under the control of the internal Mexican bureaucracy. He was wondering how Gomez would take this requirement to be stiffed for an additional $20,000, which he was sure was going directly into both Gonzalez' and Urbiola's pockets. Oh well, that was Gomez' problem.

With all of the "official business" out of the way, his attention returned to more domestic-type problems. Being Santa Claus' surrogate and tasked with hauling a Christmas tree tied on top of his car all the way back to Guadalajara from Mexico City presented an immediate one. Also, how were they going to hide all those Christmas presents Janis had bought for the children until Christmas morning?

This was the Reeds' first Christmas in Mexico, and they were learning that, unlike in the U.S., Christmas trees have environmental value. Mexico has very few forests and it's a federal crime to possess a Christmas tree that did not have a federal tag attached to it showing it had been legally cut.

The "official" supply of trees in Guadalajara were ugly and resembled the one in "A Charlie Brown Christmas," a lonely exposed trunk with spindly, wilted branches. Janis had learned while shopping, however, that in Mexico City the *Chilangos* were having American-grown trees air-freighted in to assure their freshness.

Back in Washington, D.C. Christmas trees were the least of the concerns for some people in the Reagan Administration. Meese was asking for the naming of a special prosecutor to investigate possible criminal activities on the part of the Contra conspirators. And high-priced Washington attorneys were getting frenzied calls from those who knew they were obvious prosecutorial targets and whose names were now appearing daily in the media.

1. George P. Shultz, *Turmoil and Triumph, My Years as Secretary of State*, Charles Scribner's Son, New York, 1993, P. 845.
2. Ibid, pP.843
3 Ibid, p.849.
4. Ibid, p. 835
5. Raviv, Dan and Yossi Melman, *Every Spy a Prince*, Houghton Mifflin Company, Boston, 1990, P. 343.

"THE ENTERPRISE"

KL-43

MENA

MEXICO

U.S. Consulate

GUADALAJARA

Felix Rodriguez
Mitch Marr
et al

Maquinaria
International S.A.
Terry Reed

 DRUG AND MONEY SHIPMENTS

 WEAPON SHIPMENTS

 SECRET COMMUNICATIONS

 MONEY TRAIL

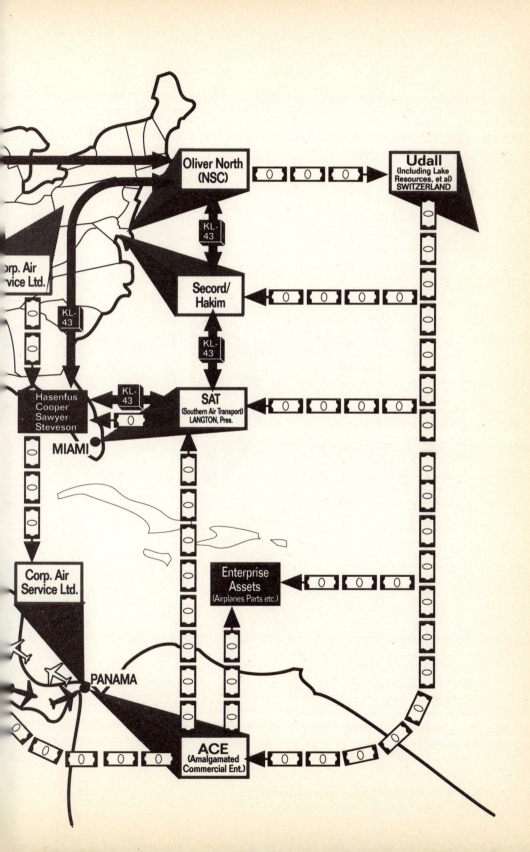

```
12-05  ... (2)17,900      118
12-03       (18:30) HR. (1)
TARJDA.
S/RVA.  ...  CTE.CO  MEXICO FIXION   CUARTO
DIR.  EK U JA.                RATE    ROOM
DIRECCION        RE/SR   F/85278
ADDRESS
R V A  Y  PAGA
```

F A C T U R A

85278

★★★★★
HOTEL CENTURY
zona rosa
Liverpool 152 Esq Amberes Col Juárez
C P 06600 Mexico D F
Telefono 584-71-11

CLERCK   MAQUINISTA   FOLIO
CED EMP EN TRAMITE REG FED CAUS IJE-720610-002 CAM. COMERCIO 079907

REGISTRO DE FIRMA
REGISTRATION SIGNATURE

MEMO

	FECHA DETALLE CUARTO DATE SYMB ROOM	CARGOS CHARGES	ABONOS CREDITS	SALDO BALANCE DUE
	03/12#1152			
	C.E. ***************0			
				8888
5	DEUD			0
6	L.D.	6050		
7	BAL. B1	P1108-0		6050
8	03/12#1304			
9	DEUD			6050
10	HABIT.	17900		
11	IHO.	2685		
12	BAL. D1	P1108-0		26635
13	04/12#1553			
14	DEUD			26635
15	L.D.			
16	BAL. P1			31821
17	04/12#1741			
18	DEUD			31821
19	HABIT.			
20	IHO.			
21	BAL. D1			52406
22	05/12#2005			
23	DEUD			52406
24	S.BAR	1048		
25	BAL. B1	P1108-0		53454
26	05/12#2024			
27	DEUD			53454
28	L.D.	3593		
29	BAL. B1	P1108-0		57047
30	05/12#2146			
31	DEUD			57047
32	HABIT.	17900		
33	IHO.	2685		
34	05/12#2146			
35	BAL. D1	P1108-0		77632

O B S E R V A C I O N E S

```
PAGA CTE.CON AMEXCO FDO. #
3728 110891 73017
A NOMBRE DE: TERRY K. REED.
VENCE: 06-66
```

DEBO Y PAGARE A LA ORDEN DE
INMOBILIARIA JEVI, S. A. DE C. V.

LA CANTIDAD DE $_____

NOMBRE_____

DIRECCION_____

COMPAÑIA_____

FIRMA_____

IT HAS BEEN A PLEASURE TO HAVE YOU AS OUR GUEST WE HOPE THAT YOU
ENJOYED YOUR VISIT THAT OUR SERVICE PLEASED YOU AND THAT YOU WILL
RECOMMEND CENTURY TO YOUR FRIENDS

HA SIDO UN PLACER TENERLO A USTED COMO NUESTRO HUESPED CONFIAMOS
QUE USTED HAYA DISFRUTADO DE SU VISITA Y QUE NUESTRO SERVICIO HAYA
SIDO SATISFACTORIO ESPERAMOS QUE USTED RECOMIENDE AL Hotel Century

24-1. Receipt from hotel in Mexico City where "Max Gomez" and Israeli Agent "Pat Weber" met with Reed when Operation Screw Worm was resurrected.

FORMA C G - 2 - A

SECRETARIA
DE
GOBERNACION

DIRC. GRAL. DE SERVS. MIGRS.
SUBDIRECCION DE NO INMIGRANTES
DEPTO. DE NO INMIGRANTES "A"
SECC. PRORROGAS.

ASUNTO: Se remite F.M.3 que se cita

(NAC. ESTADOUNIDENSE)

México, D.F., 5 de Diciembre de 1986.

SR. TEDDY KENT REED
HIDALGO # 223
CHAPALA, JAL.

82030

EXO:

En atención a las gestiones realizadas con el pre-
sente remito a usted su F.M.3 No. 557470, debidamente anotado en los --
siguientes términos;

"Se concede PRIMERA PRORROGA, de su permanencia en
el país, por una temporalidad que vencerá el día 26 (VEINTISEIS) de Ju-
nio de 1987 (MIL NOVECIENTOS OCHENTA Y SIETE), para el exclusivo objeto
de que continúe desarrollando las actividades anotadas en la página núm
ero 4, de este documento; subsistiendo la prerrogativa de salidas y en-
tradas múlitples, El pago de los Derechos correspondientes, se acredita
según orden de cobro No. A 5300679/615160, de fecha 4 de diciembre de -
1986, expedido por la Caja Recaudadora en Gobernación".

A T E N T A M E N T E
SUFRAGIO EFECTIVO. NO REELECCION
JEFE DEL DEPTO. NO INMIGRANTES "A"

LIC. FELIPE ORIOLA LEDEZMA

DIC. 5 1986

c.c.p.-Depto. de Información y Servicios Legales.-Edif.
c.c.p.-Unidad de Erogramación e Informática.-Edif.

FUL*mlc   s/exp.   102817

SUBDIRECCION DE NO INMIGRANTES
INMIGRANTES JUR / 1986
CASI ESQ. CON PARROQUIA.
HORARIO DE 9.00 A 13.30
MP. ITURRALDI

24-2. A copy of the working papers given Reed by the chief of Mexican Immigration-some-
thing rarely granted foreigners residing in Mexico.

APPLIED
TECHNOLOGIES. inc.

T. Kent Reed
president
Thesis Group member

AUTOMATION SPECIALISTS in

301 N. Shackleford, Suite C201
Little Rock, Ar. 72211
501-851-6353

CNC
FMS
CIM
CAD
CAM
JIT
ROB

· engineering. sales. service ·

February 24, 1987

RECEIPT

It is agreed between all parties below that the transaction described
here-in will be conducted as follows:

1. Terry and Janis Reed agree to give to Richard Tingen
   $20,000.00 (twenty thousand dollars) U.S. currency,
   in cash on February 24, 1987.

2. In return, Richard Tingen agrees to provide Terry Reed
   with a cashiers check in the amount of $20,000.00 (twenty
   thousand dollars), U.S. currency made payable to Terry K.
   Reed or Janis Kerr Reed, to be drawn upon ~~Cullen-Frost~~ INTE
   Bank of San Antonio, Texas.   FIRS

3. The check will be made available for pick-up by Mr. Reed
   on February 27, 1987, at the Cullen-Frost Bank, San
   Antonio, Texas.

Richard Tingen

Terry K. Reed

Janis Kerr- Reed

24-3. Receipt between Terry Reed and Richard Tingen that served as security for the twenty
thousand dollars needed in the form of cash in order to bribe the Mexican diplomatic
official in Dallas.

Providing Support—The Private Network

With funds available from Country 2, North turned to creating a mechanism for providing materiel support for the Contras.

North testified that, at Casey's suggestion, he turned to Retired U.S. Air Force Maj. General Richard V. Secord:

> I approached General Secord in 1984 and asked that he become engaged in these activities. . . .
>
> I went back to him again and at some point in '84, he agreed to become actively engaged. He agreed to establish, and did, private commercial entities outside the United States that could help carry out these activities. It was always viewed by myself, by Mr. McFarlane, by Director Casey, that these were private commercial ventures, private commercial activities. . . .
>
> [I]t was always the intention to make this a self-sustaining operation and that there always be something there which you could reach out and grab when you needed it. Director Casey said he wanted something you could pull off the shelf and use at a moment's notice.

The network, albeit privately run, was created for the purpose of pursuing "foreign-policy goals." According to North: "It was never envisioned in my mind that this would be hidden from the President."

The President has publicly stated that he was kept informed of some of the efforts by private citizens to aid the Contras. Poindexter testified the President "knew the contras were being supported . . . by third-country funds and by private support activity. . . ." There is no evidence, however, to suggest that the President was ever informed about an "off-the-shelf" covert operation.

24-4. Excerpts from Oliver North's congressional testimony describing the "off-the-shelf" operation which CIA Director William Casey hoped would enable the CIA to circumvent congressional restraints. Reed's Guadalajara operation became the central focus of that effort.

CHAPTER 25

PROJECT Z

Santa Claus successfully found the Reed home. Apparently, the letter Duncan had written Santa notifying him of his new Mexican address had arrived at the North Pole in time.

There was a big problem, however. The new German Shepherd puppy Terry and Janis had purchased in Mexico City during their shopping trip had not arrived by December 25th as had been guaranteed. This was the only gift Duncan had asked for, something he had been promised he would get when he turned 4. He was now three months beyond his birthday, and he still was waiting.

But fastened to the Christmas tree, Santa had left a note saying that this year, due to his unusually large sleigh load, he could not carry all the gifts to the children and was having to use Mexicana Airlines to deliver his surplus.

After an excitement-filled morning of exchanging gifts under the tree, the Reed family set out for Guadalajara to greet a flight from the "North Pole" that carried a special passenger. It was a six-week-old puppy with a note attached to its collar attesting it to be an offspring of Santa's own guard dog, whose job it was to protect the reindeer from hunters.

They officially named him "Bavarian Machismo Wolfgang III" (BMW), and affectionately called him "Macho" for short. As he grew, Macho became a full member of the Reed family and the protector of the children, a much more important task than guarding Rudolph.

With the Christmas holidays over, the Reeds began the new year with optimism. The year, 1986, hadn't been the best of years in many ways. Terry had lost two good friends. Barry Seal had been murdered, and Bill Cooper had died with his boots on. Cooper, like Seal, had been a *true* silent warrior for a long time. But due to his photograph having been laminated to the Southern Air Transport identification card he was carrying at the time of his death, he was now famous. His picture and headlines bearing his name were in print throughout the world.

The on-again, off-again project was now back on, for good it seemed, and Terry was in a hurry to put the last elements of his business plan in place. He also felt the added pressure and anxiety of being pushed to rush into the Phase 2 aspect of his plan...manufacturing.

He had notified the Hungarians and the Japanese of Gomez' "all systems are go" response and was spending a lot of time at the offices of Capitan Raul Fierro, *Abogado* Arturo Velazques, and at Marr's house ironing out the legal details concerning the warehouse at the Guadalajara Airport. With any luck, machine tools would be arriving there in February and already local politicians and industry were talking about the new firm, Maquinaria Internacional, and its goal of assisting in the automation of Mexico.

On January 3rd, the Reeds were busy packing their motor home for the 200-mile trip over "improved" Mexican roads to Zirahuen, where the meeting with the governor of the state of Michouacan was scheduled two days later.

Terry had decided to take the entire family and the nanny along in order to share the beauty of the Michouacan region with Janis. He had made two exploratory business trips there in mid-December and was anxious to show Janis the charm and aristocratic elegance of the city of Morelia—the future home of Agency project "Z", as it had been codenamed.

The plans called for finding a hotel room in Zirahuen for Terry, Janis, and the children, thereby allowing the nanny to serve as "night guard" by sleeping in the motor home. At least that had become the drill on the majority of their other excursions since they were finding the term "Mexican campground" was mostly an oxymoron.

Mitch Marr had been unable to provide much advance information about what the meeting would entail, or even who the participants would be. "All I know is Gomez and his Israeli friend will be there with the governor. But you can bet on him havin' his ass-kissin' entourage in tow, it's the Latino way," Marr had said in his usual demeaning way. Then he added, "The agency is giving him a big break by puttin' this factory down there. So don't let him or any of his third world henchmen give ya any shit. You got sumthin' they want and need."

Their road trip took them through the industrial town of Zamora and on to Patzcuaro, a picturesque lakeside town famous for the strange-looking, yet uniquely tasting near-transparent fish indigenous to this lake. The Reeds stopped for a photo session capturing the local fishermen plying their trade with their butterfly nets on the deep blue lake.

But not everything, however, was so picturesque. The bases of the trees of the heavily forested town had been white-washed mid-way up their trunks and converted into gaudy political advertisements. Most bore the letters "PRI" painted in green, red and black, the acronym for *Partido Revolucionario Institucional*, the ruling Mexican political party. This city, the Reeds learned, had become the focal point of a political tug of war between the PRI and its challenge party, *the Partido de Accion Nacional (PAN)*. The balance of the once beautiful eucalyptus trees sported the "PAN" insignia denoting the upstart party's contention for the region.

The high elevation highway extending south out of Patzcuaro took the family to the ancient mining town of Santa Clara del Cobre, famous throughout Mexico for its copperware. The entire town was one gigantic showroom of handcrafted copper items and was riddled with *madre y padre tiendas and fabricas* that convert copper sheeting into a multitude of exquisite articles.

Although now close to the Village of Zirahuen, the Reeds stopped to shop and ask directions since the roads they were now traveling were remote, and as usual, poorly marked. The attitude of the otherwise friendly shopkeeper changed drastically when Janis asked her for directions to their meeting place. The jovial demeanor disappeared.

"*No se,*" she answered curtly as she abruptly turned away. Janis began to feel uneasy and wonder if she had unintentionally offended the woman, or if perhaps they had simply lost their way.

Confused, they sought help from the local *policia* who was sleeping behind the wheel of his patrol car parked on the village square. He was the Mexican version of a stereotypical Southern sheriff and volunteered directions, but only after demanding to know why they were going to Zirahuen.

"*Somos turistas,*" Terry answered. "*Solomente vamos a ir a el campo por campar. Es un bonita lago para pescar, verdad?*" (We're tourists who have come only to camp. Is it true there's a beautiful lake that offers good fishing?)

The police officer must have accepted the answer. After eye-balling Terry's fishing equipment tied on top of the motor home, he gave directions, then added, "*Tiene cuidado alla, es muy peligroso.*" (Be careful there, it's very dangerous.)

Terry shrugged off the warning figuring the sheriff was concerned about the dangers of drowning while boating and fishing. He saw no need to relay the message to Janis.

A short distance south of town they found their turnoff to the west, which the policeman had been told would lead to Zirahuen. They turned onto a well-maintained, cobblestone road capable of handling two lanes of traffic, a stark change from the road they had just left. A few kilometers later, they curiously arrived at a combination guard shack and toll booth. A rope extended from the shack and stretched across the road to serve as a make-shift traffic barrier.

The guard within demanded 350 pesos (about $1 then) before allowing them to pass. Quite a sum in Mexico, they thought, to be this far from civilization. From this vantage point, though, they could now see the edge of the crystal blue lake, surrounded by tall pine trees to the west. Below, in the valley, extending for what seemed forever, was the road leading to the lake.

After a drive of 10 miles, more or less, they were stunned to discover the cobblestone road dead ended at a resort complex. Contained within was a water's edge, improved campground complete with electrical hookups. The RV site they selected was situated on a small hill within view of a large floating dock complex. They found it extremely odd that this campground, the best they had encountered in Mexico, was not listed in either the Mexican or American camping guides.

Someone had spent a great amount of money constructing and maintaining this remote resort complex which was totally void of campers....other than them.

Between the campground and the shoreline were a series of interconnected stone arches, resembling a Roman aqueduct, that stretched for more than a quarter-mile, but served no apparent purpose. There was even a small floating restaurant, bobbing ever so slightly, built up on the main boat dock. Nearby, a chalet-style house was nestled in a grove of tall pines trees, the home of the caretaker, no doubt.

The shoreline near the pier was strewn with small pleasure boats that appeared to be in storage, out of the water for the winter season. Tied to the pier along the dock were several 30 foot launches painted white and bearing red, green and black stripes. Along side them were an array of small pleasure and fishing boats, a few of which contained lonely looking fishermen using single-line poles.

Zirahuen, they were told by the caretaker, was only a few kilometers further south, but the Reeds decided to camp there for the night to avail themselves of their surprising find. It was off-season for campers and basically closed for the winter, so they would have the entire place to themselves.

After spending a quiet afternoon and evening wishing all the while that the nanny had been left behind so they could privately enjoy each other's company, the Reeds bedded down for the night.

At precisely 6 AM, with Teutonic precision, the nearby town's civil defense PA system began to blare *Deutschland Uber Alles* and everyone in the camper, and probably everyone in the surrounding countryside, bolted from their beds. They may have gone to sleep in Mexico, but it sounded like they were awakening in the Third Reich.

Now fully awake, Terry dressed and walked to the village to see what exactly was going on. He was not prepared for what he saw. Around a curve in the road, and built in a cove on the water's edge, were the buildings and houses that defined Zirahuen. The architecture was a conglomeration of Scandinavian and Mexican design, much of it adobe but with wooded peaked roofs. The A-frame style construction of some of the homes, and especially the gingerbread trim of the larger chalet-types gave the village the look of having been transported from the Alps.

Standing in the center of the *Zócalo* was an old man in a military uniform and blowing a trumpet, which apparently was the signal for the village's children to assemble for their march to school.

"Jesus Christ" Terry said to himself. "Am I in Mexico? I was when I went to sleep last night."

The children, many of whom were light-skinned and some even blond-headed, lined up like "Hitler Youth", performing a youthful version of the military's "dress right, dress." The old trumpeter was now substituting the horn he had played for a drum he was wearing. All the inhabitants gathered in the village square to view the old man tap out cadence and lead the children several times around before marching them off to the school.

No more than a half hour had passed since reveille and the village was bustling with activity. This was definitely not typical Mexican behavior. All the shops were now open with shopkeepers busily sweeping the sidewalks, so Terry decided to look around. He heard an unfamiliar dialect of Spanish being spoken, somewhat Indian he guessed, but gutteral-sounding as well. He concluded that these villagers had to be remnants of Nazi Germany who had fled after World War II and settled here. After a tour of the square and with his freshly-purchased bratwurst in hand, Terry walked back to his motor home to share his unusual discovery. And the day had just begun.

Later that morning, Terry took Duncan down to the dock for some fishing. Fishing had been a special time between he and his father and grandfather—a time of conveyance—and he wanted to try to duplicate this type of parental bonding with his children. While preparing their tackle, he joked with his four-year-old companion about the possibility of reeling in Moby Dick.

It was definitely sweater weather, but the warm, noon—day sun offset the cool, mid-day January temperature.

Suddenly there was a flurry of activity on the dock. A team of Mexican workers were giving the official-looking launches a thorough cleaning. A man in a European-cut business suit, wearing sunglasses had arrived and was barking orders to the laborers and communicating with someone via a walkie-talkie he was carrying.

Terry looked around and noticed a large antenna mast adjacent to the caretaker's house and another smaller one on the roof of the dock's restaurant. The workers were feverishly setting the tables inside the launches with white linen tablecloths and fine China, the accoutrements for a formal dinner. He hadn't seen Mexicans of any occupation move this fast since moving there.

Then, with the transformation of the vessels now complete, a second transformation took place before his eyes. With the manual work now finished, the workers disappeared into the restaurant, only to reappear, but now as well-groomed waiters. The work clothes were substituted for attire more befitting catering, and the men were resplendent in white Nehru jackets, black trousers and black patent leather shoes, a sight not seen often in Mexico. They then rigidly began milling around the restaurant, behaving as if they were fearful of soiling their uniforms. It was reminiscent of waiting for inspection in his ROTC days, Terry thought.

With the dock now returned to its original, placid state, Terry and Duncan got back to the serious business of fishing...just in case "Jaws" was out there somewhere lurking.

As the tethered red and white bobber teetered from the ripples of the lake, the reflection from the sun on the water's surface made the fishermen squint. While being hypnotized by the motion, Terry heard a faint whirring noise in the distance. He tilted his head away from the breeze to remove the wind noise from his ear and could hear something intermittently....something that sounded familiar in a strange and eerie way.

Gosh, he thought, do these things really happen? He had discarded all the theories he had read or heard about Vietnam, and the so-called stress-related flashbacks. But now he was sure he was hearing something and looked to his son for reassurance.

But Duncan didn't hear it! The boy, instead, was intently focused on his fishing line, oblivious to everything else. Maybe flashbacks are real, Terry thought. He was sure he could faintly distinguish the sound of helicopter rotor blades. Maybe this Mexican *Oso Negro*, the local vodka, was getting to him.

It was like an audio track stored deep within his memory bank, labeled Thailand, where those very sounds never stopped. There, the Air Force helicopters on continuous perimeter patrol circled the base at low altitude day and night, always on the lookout for infiltrators.

The sound from their main rotors beat the air in an unending rhythm 24 hours a day, providing a background noise that one had to literally, mentally, turn off in order to get anything done. He and John Desko, his close buddy, had jokingly theorized that the CIA was using them as guinea pigs to conduct audio-fatigue testing.

Terry squinted and raised his eyes to peer across the lake from where he *hoped* the sound was originating. From over the distant tree tops, he could now see faint images from his past. It looked as if a group of helicopters were approaching from the east at extremely low altitude.

Shit, I'm not only hearing it, but seeing it, too, he thought. No more *Oso Negro*!

"Daddy, look at the helichoppers!"

Images were coming into focus. Their unsynchronized rotor noises were now echoing throughout the quiet valley and off the water, with the armada now flying toward them in tight formation.

Terry counted four Hughes-500D helicopters in camouflage, escorting a large, white Bell HH-53 helicopter bearing the official Mexican insignia of green and red stripes.

He observed one of the 500-Ds break formation, head directly toward them, buzz the dock at low altitude, and then begin circling the campsite. The once serene setting now converted to one of chaos, as in horror he watched the destruction created by the down-wash of the buzzing rotor blade. The severe turbulence wreaked havoc on the motor home's awning exerting enough leverage advantage on the RV to begin rocking it violently. Janis, with the nanny carrying Elliott, ran from the vehicle in shock, unable to comprehend what was happening as the helicopter simply hovered near by, continuing its "attack" upon the campsite.

Terry grabbed Duncan and ran toward the site, which by now, was in a state of bedlam. The helicopter had descended and hovered only 50 feet off the ground completely engulfing the RV in dust. With the near-hurricane velocity of the rotor-wash now captured under the awning, the vehicle pitched back and forth so acutely that it was in danger of rolling over.

Terry finally drew the pilot's attention, realized it was none other than Max Gomez, and frantically signaled for the aircraft to back off. Gomez, with all the speed of molasses, eventually comprehended what was occurring and landed nearby. With the near-disaster over, Janis comforted the children while the nanny began gathering the litter generated by the copter's wake. The other helicopters had by now landed closer to the lake's edge, a safer and more prudent distance from the motor home, not finding it necessary to duplicate the *machismo* entrance made by Gomez.

Gomez, appearing somewhat humble and embarrassed, got out and signaled Terry to join him. After apologizing profusely for the turmoil he had caused, he escorted Terry toward the group and began identifying the men who were deplaning and assembling. It was very apparent to Terry who the governor was and Gomez had no need to point him out. Cardenas was at the center of an entourage of sycophants who were disembarking from the other helicopter.

"Come, let me introduce you to *Señor* Cardenas," Gomez said as they walked toward him together. "He is a very important man in Mexican government. His father was once *Presidente de Mexico*. But don't forget, he's in our pockets and I am personally paying him lots of Agency money to make this project happen. So think nothing of his attitude of royalty during today's meeting. *He's ours.*"

By this time, Terry had spotted Pat Weber, who had flown in with the Cardenas and was now chatting with him beside the white helicopter. He also recognized another person he had seen before, Leroy Tracta, Seal's ex-handler and the CIA man who had "hosted" the Panama meeting more than a year earlier. All were casually, but expensively, dressed and accompanied by three of Cardenas' political aides who had in tow two businessmen from the City of Morelia. Two fashionably-attired Latin women were the last to deplane. Adorned with jewelry and overly made-up, they were immediately escorted to the restaurant by the man with the European suit and the walkie-talkie.

"Shall I go get my wife?" Terry asked, somewhat confused. He hadn't planned on inviting Janis, thinking it might be a breach of security.

"These are not wives!" Gomez corrected. "You gringos are all alike. You just don't know how to live. One of them is the mistress of *Señor* Cardenas and the other is the mistress of the mayor of Morelia. They only came along for the helicopter ride. Don't worry, they will not be present during any sensitive discussions."

"Isn't it classified just to know who is in attendance?" Terry asked.

"They know better than to say anything. They are *Mexican* mistresses," Gomez informed in his instructional tone. "Their job continually demands they be trusted with sensitive information. The only time you have to be careful is when you replace an old one with a new one...that's when they become a security risk. And then, I've found it's best just to kill them," he boasted in his characteristic macho tone, and then breaking into a grin. "I had you going for a minute, didn't I, *amigo*?"

Terry felt uncomfortable, still convinced that Gomez had been serious. He put these feelings aside in order to focus on the unprofessionalism of it all. Terry shook his head. Who else but Latinos would bring their mistresses to an intelligence briefing?

The group toured the dock while Terry went back to the motor home to change from his fishing garb into more appropriate attire. Walking past the launches on his way back to the restaurant, Terry observed the waiters, now scurrying around putting fresh fruit on the plates in the launches.

Inside the restaurant, Weber escorted Terry to the bar and passed a rather rowdy group which had Gomez as its center. With the women on either arm, he had the cluster of Latinos totally enthralled in yet another braggadocio war story. As Terry and Weber sipped their drinks, the sound of starting engines signaled it was time for Gomez to bring the story to its climax and for the group to board the launches. With the governor now unencumbered, Weber made the introduction.

"Mr. Terry Reed, I would like to introduce you to a very important man, not only in the State of Michoacan but in all of Mexico as well. This is Señor Cuauhtemoc Cardenas, the governor of this beautiful state."

While the two men firmly shook hands, Terry took the opportunity to study the official. He radiated an aura of confidence.

"Mr. Cardenas, I am honored."

"Please don't refer to me as Mr. Cardenas. It is my understanding that we will soon grow to be friends. Let us drop the formalities. Please call me, as my friends do, Lazaro, it was my father's given name."

The young governor, who was about Terry's age, explained the complexity of his name after seeing the relief mirrored in Terry's face for having been relieved of the requirement of continually calling him "Cuauhtemoc."

"I am a descendent of one of Cortez' lieutenants," the governor said. "His name was Cardenas, a family of royalty from Spain. He was a key aide to Cortez during the conquest of Mexico. The other side of my family was Aztec. The family name was Cuauhtemoc, and one of them was a spiritual advisor to Montezuma. And I'm sure you know, of course, my father Lazaro was *Presidente de todo de Mexico.*"

Dutifully impressed and with introductions out of the way, everyone headed for the launches. The women escorted by the man with the walkie-talkie boarded a separate launch. The men all boarded the main launch with most of the servants in a third. One armed helicopter pilot boarded each boat, leaving the others to guard the helicopters. The boats then set a course for a heavily-wooded island set in the middle of the lake.

Terry and Gomez were sitting beside each other at the dining table partaking of their fruit and sorbet served in champagne glasses, when Gomez whispered to Terry under the concealment of the boat's engine noise, "That fucking story about his name, all it means is that one of Cortez' men raped some Indian bitch. And sitting across from us is the bastard descendant of that act of love."

As the boat's captain retarded the throttle, Terry ended his conversation with the Cardenas aide seated across from him and took notice of a well-constructed dock nestled inside a small harbor. Above the dock, he could see a stairway zigzagging up a hill to a large and elegant looking chalet built of stone and glass.

"This is Señor Cardenas' summer and weekend retreat," the aide told Terry. "He only escapes here to relax and to entertain dignitaries." Reed was impressed to be in such company. Somehow all this third world opulence was missing from the State Department's brochures.

The inside of the home radiated a mixed feeling of relaxed formality. A huge stone fireplace was the centerpiece of the understated, yet lavishly-decorated main room overlooking the lake. Persian rugs covered the floor and hand-carved Spanish colloquial furniture had been placed informally around the room. From the art, statuary and the oil paintings visible on the walls, Terry perceived that no expense had been spared in decorating.

Waiters circulated and took drink orders while the guests gathered and chatted informally waiting for the dining table to be prepared for dinner. Cardenas and Tracta talked quietly by themselves, leaning on a bookcase in a corner. From their body language, it appeared they knew each other well, and had much to discuss...privately. Weber moved from group to group and at times joined the governor and the CIA man in their hushed conversation.

After a gourmet meal in the adjoining dining room which was furnished with Japanese-style black lacquered furniture, the time for business had come. The two women were escorted to a launch for the trip back to the mainland.

With the women now gone, and the foreplay out of the way, Tracta took charge of the meeting while the after-dinner coffee was served.

"Señor Cardenas, I'm sure you'll agree opportunity is getting ready to land in your backyard...literally," Tracta began, sounding as toastmaster. "The site you have selected at the Morelia airport is going to need some infrastructure development. Therefore, I'm going to turn this meeting over to Mr. Reed so he can tell you personally what will be required in order to make the project successful and to bring technology to the State of Michouacan."

In order for everyone to understand fully what was required for site development at Morelia, Terry began by saying that air transportation was the centerpiece of this operation. Having been to the Morelia airport during his fact-finding trips in December, he had discovered the runway surface at the rather small facility was in need of repair, and that the length could only marginally accommodate the type of aircraft that Southern Air Transport, meaning the CIA, would be using to service the new facilities. The Mexicans, he assumed, had not taken into account the C-130 and 707-style aircraft that SAT operated.

He told them it would not be feasible, in his opinion, to use the poorly-surfaced roads between Morelia and Mexico City to transport the equipment by truck. He pointed out the fragility of the computers and the sophisticated equipment that would be needed to build the close-tolerance arms components, then offered a remedy.

He explained that two birds could be killed with one stone. Building a new runway at the Morelia Airport would not only solve the road problem, but would also help provide security for weapons shipments in the future. As Barry Seal had demonstrated in the U.S., transporting weapons by air avoided ground detection from roadblocks, weigh stations and nosey police.

Cardenas, at this point, interrupted Terry's briefing to carry on a conversation in Spanish with the mayor of Morelia. After a brief interchange he switched back to English and asked, "How long of a runway do these size of aircraft need to operate?"

Reed estimated that taking into consideration Morelia's 6000 foot elevation they would need at least 7,000 feet of runway to safely accommodate the large, heavy aircraft on a hot day.

"OK. Consider it done. What else do you need?"

"What is done?", Reed asked, somewhat confused by the brief answer.

"We will build a whole new airport, just for this operation, and I will provide you with 8,000 feet just for safe measure. The mayor will begin work immediately."

Terry was impressed with how fast things can be done in the Third World. What would have taken months of planning between federal, state, and local governments and airport commissioners north of the Rio Grande had been accomplished in minutes. Terry ascertained he was dealing with the top level, or the HMFIC.

"I repeat *Señor* Reed, what else do you need?"

"Power," Terry answered. "I need a *constant* source of quality electricity that does not fluctuate in voltage. Power surges wreak havoc on equipment of this type. It will be necessary to build a substation near the new building that has transformers large enough to monitor and control the electricity that powers the new equipment."

This time, the mayor began a brief dialogue in Spanish with one of his aides. He turned to Terry and asked, "He wants to know if 440-volt, three-phase will suffice, and, if so, how many KVA do you need?"

Terry was surprised, and glad, that someone with technical knowledge was there.

"That depends on the type of foundry we build," Terry responded. "If we use oil or gas as a source of heat, we will need less, but I prefer an induction furnace using electricity. And therefore, the KVA requirements can be quite high." Later, Terry learned that the man whom the governor conferred with was the federal representative for the Mexican government's utility consortium.

Within 20 minutes, the money and manpower for a new runway and power substation had been approved. By the expressions on their faces, Weber and Tracta, and even Gomez, were impressed. It was acutely evident that Cardenas was serious about fulfilling his gubernatorial campaign promises to create skilled "jobs for *Michoacuanans*."

On to the square footage and foundation requirements for the new facility. Terry had researched and discovered a history of volcanic activity in the area. In fact, there were still active volcanoes west of Morelia in the state of Colima. He had no personal experience in foundation requirements in this type of geologic region and didn't feel qualified to make recommendations.

After pointing this out, Cardenas assured him that a civil engineer from

Mexico City who dealt with these problems would be assigned to this project. The governor had an immediate answer and solution for everything. Terry liked his style. After a discussion of the types of machine tools that would be needed, the conversation turned to manpower requirements.

Another of the mayor's assistants took from his briefcase an artist's rendering of the technical school complex they planned to build adjacent to the new weapons plant. From among its graduates, they said, they intended to draw a pool of skilled machinists. In addition to that, the instructors who would be recruited and hired would all be "hands-on" engineers themselves and would serve as division managers for the new company. These people would not only be responsible for running the school, but for filling the supervisory slots for the factory as well.

Phase 2, it appeared to all, was a definite "go."

During the trip back on the launch Gomez maneuvered to become the center of attention with some more tales of killing communists. As the story approached its climax, Weber, who was sitting next to Terry, leaned close and whispered, "You see, I told you in Mexico City we had a governor selected who was as desperate as the one you worked with in Arkansas."

CHAPTER 26

BIRTH, LIFE AND DEATH

Dr. Roberto Lopez Ramirez was shaking his head.

"I don't know, I am worried. It is mid-May and the baby's head is so large I would swear it is way past term."

He and Terry Reed were looking at the sonograms just delivered to him by the Mexican version of Federal Express, a foot runner, from the office of Dr. Ricardo Ortiz Amezcua. The obstetrician was still not used to discussing medical details with a patient's husband. Terry had been his wife's coach during her two previous natural childbirths and the Reeds had upset the bulk of the medical community in Guadalajara by insisting that he be part of the pregnancy and birthing process.

That just wasn't done in Mexico. But reluctantly, Lopez agreed and used the Reeds as a "pilot" for what surely was coming as Mexico shed its *macho* mentality and attitudes. Mexican males Terry had met took advantage of the time their woman was in labor to celebrate at the bars with their friends and get drunk while their wives gave birth under sedation. It wasn't fashionable to experience pain, Janis had learned from the Chilangas, the upper class women with whom she had become acquainted.

The pelvic examination was over and as Janis dressed, Lopez was expressing concern at the head size of the baby she was carrying. She was near term and Lopez decided it best to consult a colleague in Houston who had experience delivering "these large gringo babies."

Terry and Janis were still looking at the sonogram negatives when Lopez shocked them by announcing, "Let's go to the hospital and have a baby." He had decided after consultation that a caesarean procedure was in his patient's—and the baby's—best interests.

"Only if Terry can be with me. Otherwise I think we'll just get on an airplane and head back to the States," Janis said feeling a little uncomfortable about having a C-section in Mexico.

Terry reiterated Janis' position and Lopez shook and gave in, "You American males...You amaze me. Why do you want to see all this pain and suffering? Is it because your *gringa* women all control you? Or is it you truly think you are each other's equal?"

Later that night, at 9:30, at the Baptist Mexican-American Hospital in Guadalajara several records were set. On May 18, 1987, Dr. Lopez successfully delivered a nine-pound, 10-ounce baby boy, the largest he had ever delivered. And the hospital had allowed the father to be present in the delivery room, not only during the birthing process, but during the surgery as well. Everyone was pleased.

Two days later, after much discussion, the baby was named Baxter Xavier Kerr Reed Kerr, the second Kerr automatically added by the Mexican Government to reflect the Latin custom of appending the mother's surname to that of the child. Terry now had a future Mexican business partner since being born on Mexican soil to American parents automatically bestowed upon Baxter dual citizenship.

Two weeks later, it was time to document the baby's American citizenship at the U.S. Consulate in Guadalajara. Terry found it amusing that Baxter's American birth certificate was signed by U.S. Consul-General Daniel Darrach, the only American official in Mexico who knew what Terry was really doing there.

For Terry, it was a time to be honored by the Mexican males. He had fathered three sons consecutively, quite an achievement for a gringo, his friend Juin said.

For Janis, it was celebration time. She had been delighted with the care she received in the Mexican hospital. The attention, amenities, and especially the food surpassed her previous birthing experiences. Her first dinner meal after Baxter's birth was catered Chinese food, and she and Terry were touched when Dr. Lopez joined them in her private room to share their food and present them a gift of vintage wine. Not quite like the hospitals in the States, she thought.

And now her friends were giving her a "coming out" party at *La Posada.* It was time for her to catch up since she hadn't allowed herself to indulge in the fine Mexican wines during her pregnancy. Though unheralded outside the country, they are among the best in the world, and as her friends toasted her and her new son, she couldn't have been happier.

On a Friday night in early June, a mysteriously absent Mitch Marr suddenly reappeared with his wife as the Reeds were sitting at the Posada's bar. Certain that the infectious, wailing mariachi music and the drunken dancing would provide the distraction he needed, Terry approached Marr's table and pretended to be admiring some of the local Mexican artwork on the wall.

"Glad to see you're back," Terry said without directing his glance to Marr. "I need to see you immediately."

Marr, without looking up from his drink, said: "What's the matter? Your commie friend has another problem?"

"Yes. But this time he has the evidence we need."

A lot had happened since the meeting at Zirahuen back in January, which, when Terry looked back on it, seemed like a stilted scene out of *Apocalypse Now.* After returning to Guadalajara from that trip, Operation Screw Worm had been kicked into overdrive. Out of nowhere, like *Brigadoon,* the entire clandestine operation that included both Phases 1 and 2 of Terry's plan took form.

Maquinaria Internacional's facility at the Guadalajara Airport immediately began receiving, storing and shipping large bulky and heavy containers that occasionally contained machinery necessary for the legitimate business activities. Mexicana Airline's forklift drivers learned well the path between the Mexican Customs holding area south of the main terminal and Terry's warehouse a quarter of a mile away.

Southern Air Transport C-130s and 707s were eased in and out of Mexican airspace unobtrusively day and night through special flight plans denoting them as "Sierra Whiskey" flights. Raul Fierro, the DFS and CIA's main man at the airport, had assigned all Screw Worm air activity to a person under his control in the flight operations division.

He was Ricardo Lopez Alcantara, who worked for the Mexican FAA, and he personally processed all of the Agency's flight plans to be sure they "never happened." It was, in fact, as Max Gomez had boasted back in the bunker in Arkansas: "What flies in never flies out, at least not from the ATC point of view."

Fierro took all of Terry's problems straight to the top. Customs documentation, restricted area passes, extra security for Terry's warehouse and even hangar space for Terry's private airplane, which he brought to Mexico in April, were all expeditiously handled by Guadalajara's *Comandante del Aeropuerto* P.A. Gerardo Mejia Rodriguez. By the way in which Mejia responded to Fierro's demands and instructions, he clearly was just a puppet *comandante* manipulated by the real boss. And the real boss in Mexico, Terry was learning, was the CIA.

It was interesting for Terry to be on the receiving end of American influence and power, but it was upsetting to see America's foreign policy toward its allies through this perspective. Outwardly we say we support democracy and the American way. Terry was seeing that in reality the CIA was subverting democracy. It behaved in Mexico as if Mexican laws didn't exist. The Agency's and Gomez' ability to "grease the wheels" was undermining efforts by progressive Mexican reformers to achieve true democratic reforms and keep the oligarchy in power. It was an old story repeated over and over again in the underdeveloped Republics in Central America.

Terry observed that the banana republic attitude in Mexico was reminiscent of that in Arkansas. There, through Seth Ward, he had been sponsored into the upper echelons of society and put into play with powerful people. The sponsor for Mexico, however, was not analogous to Ward. It was much more powerful, and Terry could feel its presence everywhere. The undercurrents of power and greed in both places bonded easily with the CIA's objectives. It mattered little to these Mexican rulers that they were giving away their sovereignty, just as Terry had seen the government of South Vietnam do years earlier.

The elite in Mexico behaved like the elite in Arkansas, opposing any change unless they could see a personal benefit for themselves. This "me" attitude began to disgust Terry, forcing him to look inward to re-analyze his own motives. He felt he was beginning to get reacquainted with his old self. He was in fact still the poor boy from Missouri, the great grandson of a mule trader, and the addictive social trappings offered by his CIA sponsorship didn't interest him.

How could these elitists not really care for the millions of poor peasants, their fellow Mexicans? What Mexico needed was a strong middle class society to establish a large tax base, but these people, just as the elitists in Arkansas, suppressed the development of that group fearing it would diminish their power.

But these disturbing observations were put on the back burner as George Fenue, his Hungarian partner, began expressing concerns in early February about what he thought were mis-billings to his company, Cortec, in Mexico City.

Terry had not yet made his trip to Dallas to pay his "processing fees" for his Mexican corporation because the Mexican consul there was vacationing in Europe. This forced *Maquinaria Internacional* to continue using Cortec's pre-established business licenses for importing and exporting purposes as it conducted machinery business in Guadalajara.

Fenue complained of receiving invoices for customs services from his customs broker in Nuevo Laredo at the border for a shipment Fenue and his employees had not sent.

"I have an invoice from my *agente aduanal* for a 500-pound shipment of tooling going to the United States," Fenue told Reed over the phone. "Shall I send the bill to you for payment?"

"I haven't been shipping anything *to* the U.S. It must be an erroneous statement," Terry suggested.

Terry's plan, from conception, had called for procuring *from* the United States hard-to-find and precision items. Nowhere had it included exporting *to* the states. He was aware *Maquinaria Internacional* was *receiving* American-made items via SAT aircraft, but these were weapons and they didn't require customs bills of lading. The CIA leaves no paper trail.

What Terry initially dismissed as an error on behalf of Fenue's customs agent, Andres Mounetow, was anything but. Mounetow operated a customs brokerage firm in Laredo, Texas, with his brother, Alfredo covering the Mexican side of the business in the town across the Rio Grande, Nuevo Laredo. The Monetows adamantly claimed they had in fact handled a single-crate shipment going from the Mexican town of San Miguel de Allende, destined to the U.S. Their records indicated it had been delivered to the border by an overland express truck service out of Mexico City, had cleared the scrutiny of both Mexican and U.S. Customs Agents, and was held in their warehouse on the American side for pickup.

With the crate now gone and signed for by an indecipherable signature, Terry and Fenue were mystified. Reed brought this incident to Marr's attention during an expense reimbursement meeting, but Marr seemed oblivious when told the details. And he, too, attempted to explain the event away as a mistake.

But what haunted Terry was the paper work from the shipment showed the name *Maquinaria Internacional* listed on the manifest with Fenue's export license number. This was strange, he thought. Shouldn't it have mentioned only Cortec, which was Fenue's firm? If the customs broker had made a mistake, *Maquinaria Internacional*'s name should not have appeared at all. *Maquinaria Internacional* had no account with this broker.

But it was early February and Terry was being torn in all directions. With the governor of Michouacan anxious to get his hands into the CIA's pockets, Terry was spending much of his time outlining the details for the new arms facility in Morelia that was scheduled tentatively to be operational by late summer. Between this and getting "Screw Worm's" facilities operating in Guadalajara, he had little time to worry about $300 invoices that appeared to have been issued in error.

The rat-race life he had now built for himself in Margaritaville was quickly becoming the Mexican version of the American bumper sticker. *"Yo debo, you debo, y asi pues trabajar yo voy* [I owe, I owe...]." Patrick Juin gave up trying to keep up with Terry and decided he didn't want to be Americanized after all if this was the type of work schedule necessary for success.

Terry had Japanese problems as well. As he itemized the equipment necessary to be ordered and put on display for the Guadalajara operation, he was

finding that Frank Fujikawa had over-committed himself and was having difficulty getting Gomiya, his firm in the States, to go along with putting large
amounts of consigned equipment in Mexico. This was an integral part of the
plan, and it was agreed that behind the scenes, and with a definite conflict of
interest, Fujikawa was to have used his executive influence to floor plan computer-controlled machine tools in Terry's Mexican facility. But with the peso
in a continuous shallow slide, the Japanese were getting cold feet about investing in Mexico.

This was really straining relationships between Terry, Johnson and Fujikawa.
Meanwhile, the Hungarians were hoping to be part of the Japanese marketing
operations and were starting to view this delay by Fujikawa as a possible breach
of contract. After all, they had a tangible investment in Mexico. They viewed
Fujikawa's vacillation and delay as an opportunity to demand a bigger share
of the company. His communists friends were definitely honing their capitalist
skills and learning the art of the power play.

But the Hungarians were "married" to Terry's plan by now since Gomez
had, in fact, been able to "grease" Mexican customs properly and save them
the heavy 100 per cent duty normally imposed on imported machine tools.
They were actually beginning to turn a profit after years of losses. Fenue was
beginning to appear to headquarters in Budapest as the equivalent of a "corporate turn-around man."

As Terry was stomping out these small fires, he finally received word in late
February from Felipe Urbiola Ledezma that the vacationing Mexican consul
in Dallas was "ready to receive you now." This meant Terry had to lay his
hands on $20,000 in cash for the "licensing fee."

Marr knew Terry would be needing that money since he had reported his
earlier conversation with Urbiola. And Terry still laughed at Gomez' comments
when told of the "processing fee."

"Jesus fucking Christ," Gomez had shouted. "I'm paying these mother fuckers
enough money as it is. For $20,000 dollars, I could grease up Mother Theresa!
But it's Agency money anyway, so what the fuck. No sweat off my mangoes."

"So Mitch, I'm here for the money," Terry told Marr at his house. "I need to
run up to the States, bribe this guy and get my ass back down here. I'm busier
here than I was up there."

Marr seemed ill-prepared for Terry's demand. He also appeared to be sliding off the wagon that night in late February.

"I can't get it together until tomorrow afternoon," Mitch told him. "I'll go to
Guadalajara in the morning. You better come back tomorrow night and by
then I'll have it."

This was the first time Marr had not had money ready and waiting for Terry.
He was extremely curious where Mitch was doing his "banking." Terry rationalized that with pending Japanese problems, and in light of everything else
that had occurred unplanned since arriving there, it wouldn't hurt to know
where Mitch was actually getting the money.

Terry knew that Marr normally used a "taxi" when he went to Guadalajara,
a kind of Third-World limo service provided by Mexican locals who used their
private cars to make a little money. For this reason, Terry was sitting in his
Nissan pickup at a strategic point on the Guadalajara highway early the next
morning hoping to see Marr pass by.

Sure enough, at precisely 9 AM, Marr went by with his Mexican driver piloting him toward Mexico's sprawling second largest city.

All of Terry's suspicions were confirmed when Marr's cab pulled up in front of the U.S. Consulate. Marr got out and walked to a secure area protected by chain-link fence. Heavy security around the building had been put in place since the abduction in broad daylight in February, 1985, of DEA agent Enrique (Kiki) Camarena on that very street.

The armed guards allowed Marr immediate access through a side entrance. Terry stood on the corner eating peanuts and waiting for Marr's exit, and wondering if by chance he too was being watched. Terry knew he was "sort of" violating Gomez' rule of not acting like a spy, but he wanted to make sure Marr exited the building with a parcel. That way he'd be positive this was the source of money since Marr had gone in empty handed.

Sure enough, approximately 15 minutes later, Marr came out carrying a small attache case. Bingo....he had found the bank.

That night, as instructed, he went back to Marr's home and was somewhat astonished when the now inebriated Marr handed him $20,000 in brand new, consecutive-numbered $100 bills.

"So how am I supposed to get this money to the U.S.?" Terry questioned. "I certainly will have a difficult time explaining to U.S. Customs where I got this if I declare it."

"That's your problem. My job is to get you the money. It's your job to spend it. Wanna stay and watch a film?"

A bad sign, Terry thought. He knew Marr long enough now to realize that when he became overly preoccupied with his VCR and war films, his old problem had returned.

But Marr wasn't the only one withdrawing from reality. Ronald Reagan, too, was sitting alone, in the White House and watching old movies. Reagan had slipped into a deep depression when awakened to the fact he really had been trading arms for hostages. As his popularity slipped for the first time in his presidency, he became a recluse watching the films he had starred in during his youth——over and over again while sitting in his pajamas.

"*Aye fucking caramba!*" Richard Tingen exclaimed while looking at the carefully-banded stacks of money that Terry had laid on his desk. "I'm afraid to touch it. Where did you get it?"

"Oh, let's just say I came into it," Terry answered to the young Canadian who was about his age. "Besides, the reason I'm here is Diana (Aguilar) said you help your clientele out with their banking problems, and I'm a client."

It was February 24th, 1987 and Terry was sitting in Tingen's private office in the back of Chapala Realty. Tingen was an interesting man. From what Terry knew, he was a Canadian citizen born of upper middle class parents, and who left college on a summer break to explore Mexico. He never returned. He had been in Mexico more than 20 years, having married a Mexican *chilanga* from the city of Chihuahua and whose marriage had produced three children. Richard was by now bilingual, and many of the retired *gringos* assumed incorrectly that he was an attorney.

Well-versed on Mexican contract law, he had become sort of the pied piper of the north shore since those *gringos* in need of almost any business service gravitated to him. A laid-back individual always sporting a tan, a smile and dressed as if on a perpetual vacation, he had a reputation for solving most problems.

Terry had a problem that morning. He did not want to break American law by transporting $20,000 into the U.S. and not declaring it. His only other alternative was to declare the money and risk the consequence of explaining where and how he obtained it.

"If you'll guarantee me this money's not hot, I have an idea," Tingen said. "I could use some American cash down here for my business and I have money up in the States in my bank in San Antonio. You could give me your cash and I could arrange for you to draw $20,000 out of my bank in the form of cashier's checks. Will that help?"

Terry was relieved. For some strange reason, he just couldn't shake the feeling that something bad was going to happen if he tried to transport the money to the U.S. himself. This way, he wouldn't be breaking the law and Tingen considered his favor offset by the fact he had immediate access to $20,000. The float on the money certainly was in his favor. (See chapter end.)

The trip to the States was uneventful. Terry was given cashier's checks totaling $20,000 on February 27th in San Antonio and the next day he tried unsuccessfully to pay the Mexican official with them in Dallas. But he wanted cash only. The Mexican too knew the Barry Seal rule: *No papel, no huella* (no paper, no trail). The checks were cashed and Raul Gonzalez Certosimo was paid his processing fee...in green backs.

After entrusting the Mexican to do his job, and get the necessary corporation documents to Robert Johnson in Miami and to the government officials in Mexico City, Terry returned to the land of *mañana* just in time to discover somebody in the States once again had a strange requirement to buy Mexican tools.

"I just received another bill from my customs broker" Fenue said by phone from his Naucalpan office. "The shipment appears to be identical to the last one. It was shipped from San Miguel to the border. This time, I want an answer from your people. Who is using our business license number for this activity?"

Terry could tell by Fenue's voice that their friendship was being strained by this mysterious activity. In Mexico City, both men privately discussed their options since Mitch Marr still seemed unresponsive to Terry's demands for answers and an investigation. And Fenue was beginning to feel vulnerable. Both men fully realized that the main export Mexico was becoming famous for was narcotics. What frightened them both was that whoever was doing this had access to their business names and numbers and someone skilled at not leaving a defined trail.

They had investigated the point of origin of the shipments to an overnight express company that specialized in quickly shipping cargo to the border. Shipping costs for both crates had been paid in cash, thus leaving no paper trail to the sender. The invoices from San Miguel simply showed *Maquinaria Internacional* as the sender, with the broker in Laredo as the consignee.

Their suspicions were beginning to zero in on Fenue's customs broker and both were wondering if perhaps they were dealing with a much larger smuggling ring, perhaps with connections to some government official who had access to corporate records. If so, they theorized, there was not much they could do about it. But quietly, and without Terry's knowledge, Fenue decided to get to the bottom of it. What he saw was greater risk than Terry felt at the time. He was still a KGB asset and fearful that one of his new-found business partners, the CIA, was setting him up.

Back at the Guadalajara airport, a major screw up had occurred which demanded Terry's immediate attention. One of the sales of machinery Terry had consummated with a firm in Guadalajara required importing an expensive Okamoto Japanese grinder that was warehoused in the States.

The Conex container, a large aluminum shipping box measuring approximately 10 by 20 by 8 feet, housing the grinder had been mistaken by an SAT crew as containing weapons destined for Central America. They had mistakenly delivered to his facility a container full of M-60 grenade launchers and the grinder was sent on to the Contras.

Oh well, mistakes happen in any business, Terry told himself. But as he was trying to track down his equipment and keep his irate Mexican client happy, Terry was beginning to feel like the little Dutch boy with his fingers in the dike. But he was running out of fingers.

Just keeping everyone satisfied and at bay, was becoming a fulltime job. This multi-national concept looked great on paper, but now that he was dealing with volatile personalities intertwined with cultural barriers and personal differences, his prior life in Arkansas seemed at times attractive.

It was, by this time, mid-March and the decisions about the Morelia airport runway, power requirements, foundation specifications, et cetera, had all been made and there was not a lot Terry could do until the new factory building was completed. Ground breaking had occurred for the new technical school and Pat Weber was taking care of all of the political problems associated with the project.

The first weapon to be produced at the new site had been selected. Weber had told Terry it was a weapon that the Israeli military was hoping to add soon to its arsenal as a close-quarter combat weapon. He said his government and the CIA felt it would be a good initial exercise to be conducted on Mexican soil to fine-tune and test the Mexicans' capability to produce quality firearms. It would require casting, machining, plating and heat treating as well as plastic-injection moulding.

It was a rather crude weapon, Terry felt, but certainly would test the concept from A to Z. He had been informed by Weber that the Israelis would be contributing technical expertise to the project in the form of bilingual technicians. What price was Governor Cardenas really paying for all this *opportunity*, Terry wondered. He predicted one thing for certain—CIA and Mossad favors don't come without strings attached.

On his desk in Guadalajara lay the blueprints for this weapon. It was a shotgun. But this new weapon the Mexicans were going to "cut their manufacturing teeth on" was not your garden variety shotgun. This one appeared *extremely* lethal.

Terry knew from his days in Southeast Asia that, from all the modern weapons the Army had to choose from, the grunts still preferred the shotgun in close combat, especially in jungles where vision is limited. The shotgun, the army proved, was the type of weapon a person could fire under duress and perhaps still hit something, due to the larger "pattern" its projectiles created.

The Agency-supplied blue prints defined a 12-round, semi-automatic shotgun that had been recently developed and was to be marketed as the Striker 12-P. It had an 18-inch barrel and looked similar to a Thompson submachine gun making it short and easy to carry. Its over-all length was only 19.7 inches with the stock folded and 26.2 inches with it extended, and its nine-pound weight made it a shoo-in for the Contras, who desperately wanted this weapon.

Terry was studying those prints in early June when he received a near-panic call from Fenue.

"You need to come to Mexico City immediately!, "he said.

"Can't it wait until next week? I'm awfully busy," Terry said.

"No, get in that airplane of yours and come now. I have something here you'll find very interesting."

Terry wasted no time. He piloted his twin-engine Piper Seneca II, N13LM, out of the smog-layer overlying Guadalajara into the clear air for the trip to Mexico City.

After getting rid of the cockpit workload required to safely get the plane to altitude and out of Guadalajara's ATC control, his mind began to wander. He dismissed his concerns about why Fenue had summoned him, and his thoughts drifted to his favorite co-pilot. How he wished his son, Duncan, was here with him. Duncan loved flying already and he was only four years old. Terry's mind went back to a special day just before Easter when he and Duncan flew the plane from Mineral Wells, Texas, to Mexico.

He had purchased the plane with the idea of using it in his business in Mexico, in order to better service the industrial base that he was finding was scattered throughout this expansive country and, in many instances, in remote regions served only by bad roads. Once the post-purchase inspection was completed and the plane deemed airworthy, he and his son had picked up the plane at a fixed base operator in Mineral Wells early in the morning and planned to rush back to Guadalajara in one day so that Janis wouldn't worry.

"Two people I love will be in that airplane," she had told him by phone before he left Texas.

"Don't worry," he had told her, gently assuaging her concerns.

"What's the worst that can happen?" she fired back. But she knew what the worst could be. She could lose her oldest son and her husband over the remote desert regions of Mexico.

But nothing was lost that day. On the contrary, a lot was found. To Terry, it was as near a religious experience he felt he could ever have. He and his young son, isolated in the cockpit of an airplane, bonded as few fathers and sons ever had. As the four-year-old "pilot," displaying no fear whatsoever, radioed Guadalajara approach, tears welled up in Terry's eyes.

How could be so lucky? And he was so thankful that he had found a special woman to produce this special child.

"November one-three, Lima Mike, this is Mexico City approach painting you three-zero nautical miles west at eleven thousand five hundred, squawking one-two-zero-zero, state your intentions."

The ATC's voice woke Terry from his trance. On the ground at the Mexico City airport, a pacing Hungarian was waiting for him and it was time to become a pilot and land.

"I'm glad you came immediately," Fenue told him. "I'll take you to the warehouse and show you the 'shipment of tools' I intercepted at the border."

On the way to Cortec's facilities, Terry's Hungarian friend told him of how he had alerted his customs brokers to intercept any additional shipments through their facilities at the border. His instructions to them were to seize any future shipments bearing Cortec's name and to hold them for his personal inspection.

Together they were going to review this third mystery shipment. From what Fenue was saying, it was identical in size, weight and packing as the other two and he could only conclude the others had contained the same "tooling" as this one. He had, in fact, intercepted the crate before it crossed the Rio Grande and had personally returned it by truck to Mexico City.

"IT'S COCAINE!" Fenue said, as he and Terry looked into the crate neatly filled with plastic sealed parcels that were now stored in the private rear office of the warehouse complex. "We've already had it tested and it's pure. My people are not in the drug business...at least not here in Mexico," he added. "You need to get hold of your boss and find out what exactly is going on here. I have already told my people and they are expecting an answer. Comrade, I'm afraid our friendship is now on the line. Please.... help me with this problem."

The two men were the same age and were caught in the same web of conspiracy and deceit neither could understand. Why either side would be attempting to embarrass the other was beyond their reasoning since both were *compromised* by their mutual involvement in Screw Worm.

Even though they came from different ideological backgrounds, Fenue and Terry had hoped that their working relationship in Mexico would in some small way bring together their two cultures and countries. They viewed themselves as political pioneers, the equivalent of two young military officers in opposing armies who suddenly realized that the future is in their hands. They had hoped to prove that there was no reason to continue along the same path of hatred and paranoia as their elders had followed. By working well together on this project and laying the groundwork for trust, they had also hoped to prove to their respective handlers that there was no longer the same foundation from which to continue the arms race—the world's preoccupation with self-destruction that had affected them their entire lives. Somehow this project was, in itself, a fragile experiment in cooperation and understanding. They had dared to dream that the intelligence agencies of the world could teach a lesson to their political masters.

But here they were, staring into a crate that contained a substance that could subvert and *compromise* the entire operation. Who would be so foolish? Was it someone who, for his own selfish reasons, did not want the political hatred to end?

Was someone toying with both of them?

As a deniable link to the CIA, Terry realized at this very second, how vulnerable he actually was.

CHAPTER 27

POWDERED MONEY

John Desko emptied the remnants from his third bottle of Bohemia lager, brought up a belch from the depths of his digestive tract and said, "That's some story, Reed. How in the hell did you get in so deep with these guys?"

Firecracker explosions echoed throughout the Lake Chapala valley, signaling that the 1987 Fourth of July celebrations were in full swing. In the backyard of Terry Reed's walled estate just off the Chapala highway, he was violating a cardinal rule of intelligence.

For the first time since graduation from the U.S. Air Force's intelligence school in 1968, he was crossing the line and possibly *compromising* an entire operation by passing on sensitive information to a person who did not have "an operational need to know."

In the weeks prior to Desko and his wife arriving for a vacation in Mexico, Terry had been wrestling with his dilemma. He was overwhelmed with the problems that surrounded him and had made the decision to confide in the one person, besides his wife, that he trusted. It was his old buddy from the days in Task Force Alpha. He and Desko had seen each other through their problems before and he was reaching out to John from the darkness.

He had some hard, and possibly life-threatening, decisions to make. And he already knew what he had to do. He needed to hear Desko's words reinforcing his moral choice. He couldn't turn to Janis yet. He had not told her about George Fenue's discovery for fear of frightening her. The entire intelligence operation he was involved with was, in his opinion, out of control. It had degenerated from the business plan he had developed into a monster that he felt was about to devour him. He needed Desko now, more than he had ever needed him in Thailand.

Through their common interests, common values and their ability to communicate, often without words, they had been able to support one another through in their time of mutual, youthful and stressful disillusionment during the war. They had been misled then and through their use of logic had been able to sort through the misinformation being dumped upon them by elders and superiors to find the morsels of truth they needed to sustain them.

As the smoke rose from the barbecue grill, and the steaks sizzled, Terry shared with Desko all the dirty details of not only Screw Worm but also recapped all of his intelligence work since becoming a civilian. It had been an interesting psychiatric session for the two men while the wives sat out of earshot by the pool watching the children swimming.

Terry's worst fears had come true, and most troubling, he had told Desko, was the behavior of Mitch Marr when he had reported George Fenue's discovery of the cocaine.

"So what are you going to do Mitch?" Terry had asked. "Fenue has the evidence you said we needed to prove our case. This time, I and he expect action. I owe him a hard answer to a hard question. Who in the fuck is shipping cocaine through our company?"

Several days later, Terry had gone back to Marr urgently seeking answers. Fenue had severed all business ties until he and his people were told who was behind those shipments. If it were some lone wolf in the organization, he had said, they could accept that, provided this individual was dealt with. Everyone has people problems, Fenue acknowledged. But if this were some kind of CIA conspiracy to embarrass the KGB, he said their cooperation was at an end. And maybe, they might even retaliate. Terry was witnessing first hand, just how easily wars could get started.

"We know nuthin'," Marr slurred. "Call your commie friend back and demand the truth from his end. We think it's his people that are doin' it—if it's even bein' done. It's still only his word that those crates were bein' shipped up there through his company. How do ya know he's not in the drug business and usin' you for cover? He didn't take ya with him to the border to reclaim that box, did he? Ya can't trust these goddam commies. I coulda told ya that. You and Cathey's fuckin' multi-national business plan. I coulda told ya it'd fail...commie bastards."

Terry was beginning to feel isolated, dealing with a drunk who seemed more preoccupied with "commies" than understanding what was really happening. He always felt that Marr was "in and out of it" with his penchant for the bottle. Now, he wondered if Marr was part if it. And if so, there probably had been no "investigation." Or had there? Could Marr be right? Was Fenue tricking him? Where do you turn for the truth?

All Terry knew was the situation read like a crime novel. A crime had been committed and everyone was pointing fingers at each other, and professing their innocence. One thing for sure, however, Terry was in the middle and felt like a negotiator as all of the participants were walking away from the table. This must have been how Henry Kissinger felt when Le Duc Tho stomped out in Paris. But Kissinger had B-52s to force his return. Terry had nothing. By this time, the Japanese also wanted out of the volatile situation. Frank Fujikawa was living up to the name Marr had given him, "Fuckikawa", and he had sued Terry in federal court in Arkansas in order to distance himself from his involvement in Mexico. By muddying the water between Gomiya and Terry's old firm, Applied Technologies, Fujikawa, he figured, was trying to slow down any investigation that might ensue. Masking the entire Japanese involvement as a "business dispute" was slick, but Terry didn't give Fujikawa the complete credit for the plan's creation. When he heard the name of the law firm Fujikawa had retained, he rationalized that perhaps Frank had "'fessed up" about his Agency involvement to his superiors back in Japan, and now no cost was being spared to implement crucial "face saving" measures.

Gomiya had hired the law firm of Masuda, Funai, Eifert and Mitchell, Ltd., out of Chicago, to blindly build an effective smoke screen in federal court in order to insulate the Japanese firm and Fujikawa's past involvement in "Operation Screw Worm". What Terry found most interesting was that the law firm was none other than the one which had represented the scandalous, treason-riddled firm of Toshiba Machine Company...the Japanese company that had sold American defense secrets to the KGB. He figured they were a foe to be reckoned with since they appeared to be a firm that applied few litmus tests to those they represented. He wondered if Gomiya/Fujikawa had been so nice as to inform the firm's lawyers about the illegal exporting of the Dianichi computer technology to communist China. Probably not. But recalling the words of his grandfather— "Attorneys are like ass-holes, everybody with shit on his hands has one"—he expected this greed-above-ethics behavior.

Terry was wallowing in deceit and deception. He was still recovering from his discovery of the true identity of John Cathey.

What a day that had been. It was fashionable among the American expatriates in Ajijic to oppose the U.S. policy toward Nicaragua. In fact, a small club had developed whose purpose was to keep track of noteworthy events about the "Yankee imperialists" who were subverting the U.S. Constitution and had even printed bulletins highlighting the Iran-Contra proceedings and hearings underway in Congress.

None of this material, however, included photographs of any of the key participants in these "atrocities." So, one could imagine Terry's astonishment when he discovered John Cathey's true identity while attending "an Iran-Contra wine and cheese party" being hosted by the American gay community in Ajijic. The host was videotaping the hearings in Washington and there, in recorded color, was a uniformed Marine Lieutenant Colonel who appeared to be in "deep shit," too. Oliver North appeared to be "reacting" to these events rather than his usual posture of "acting", as Terry had always seen before.

Janis recognized him, too, causing her to nearly spill her vintage chardonnay on the plush Oaxacan tapestry. This shocking experience had followed yet another startling revelation.

Terry sat in the doctor's office of Roberto Lopez Ramirez reading a second-hand copy of the New York Times dated May 28, 1987 while Janis was being "inspected" by the doctor. He turned to page A-12 and received a shock that nearly stunned him. He discovered from a picture and an in-depth profile that he had been working all along with a Cuban CIA agent by the name of Felix Rodriguez, age 45, who had adopted the code name Max Gomez. The article highlighted the results of Rodriguez/Gomez' testimony before the Congressional hearings on the Iran-Contra affair. He still didn't know Rodriguez/Gomez' background sufficiently, so he confronted Marr with the newspaper who then confirmed Gomez was in reality Felix I. Rodriguez, a Cuban exile activist, Bay of Pigs veteran—and professional cold warrior.

It all made sense—now. North had come into his life back in Oklahoma as a CIA agent involved in protecting American nuclear submarine technology. It stood to reason that someone from the National Security Council would be heading up such an investigation, or at least monitoring it closely. Terry was honored to have been dealing with someone of North's stature and ranking within the U.S. intelligence community. Rodriguez was something different, and questionable.

After the dust settled, Terry reported his new-found knowledge about North to Marr and demanded to know if Marr was who he said he was. Was he really Mitch Marr? He swore he was.....for whatever that was worth.

"Lies or lives," were the words uttered by North during the ensuing Congressional hearings. Terry was learning that the operation was heavy on "lies."

Things were coming apart. Business partners in the Enterprise were becoming disgruntled and suspicious of the operation and each other. To make matters worse, the peso had been devaluing horribly, dashing hopes of building a bonafide business. The life of James Bond was truly a fantasy.

As the two men finished their backyard conversation and downed more Bohemia, Terry added, "Well, JD, you're lucky you got out of the intelligence game. I'm in way over my head and I don't know who to reach for."

"The whole situation sounds FUBAR (fucked up beyond all recognition) to me," Desko responded. " I'd get my family the hell out of here if I were you. These guys are playing hardball. And as far as your reaching out for help, you know you can always count on me, but I can't do much for you down here. If you can make your way out of Mexico, and up to Albuquerque, that's my backyard. The desert has a way of just swallowing things up, if you know what I mean. I can arrange that, if that's what you want." Desko had to pause in order to finish his beer, belch once again, and continue. "But I know you, Terry, and that's not your style. In Thailand we always dealt with our problems head on. You gotta reach down deep inside of yourself and find that guy I knew in Thailand. You've made tough decisions before."

Desko was right and he knew it. His old friend from the past was sending him a cryptic message: Terry had to take matters into his own hands if he was to survive, the way he had survived in Southeast Asia. The military's "sheep mentality", as they called it, needed to be continuously questioned. At times, they had found it necessary to disregard orders and policies in order to protect themselves. Without telling him *what* to do, Desko was reminding Terry of what he *had* to do.

Terry recalled one of their dilemmas in Thailand in which it appeared to them the Air Force needlessly put them in harm's way and possibly was going to sacrifice them.

As a result of the Tet Offensive, in which there were more Americans killed by friendly fire than by the VC, the military had changed its policy of giving each soldier a weapon and ammunition. In Thailand, that policy had developed to the point of ludicrousy to where each arriving airman was assigned an M16 rifle, which was kept locked in the armory and made available to them only for cleaning and in emergencies. And even then, they had learned to their chagrin that ammunition for the weapons would not be provided until, in their minds, it would be too late. This ridiculous policy obviously had been decided on by some Pentagon bureaucrat in Washington or by a general basking in Hawaii. To Terry and Desko, who had been raised in a rural survivalist environment, this policy made no sense. If they were mature enough to be there, and to be put in harm's way, why were they not entrusted with the weapons they needed to defend themselves?

Their unit, Task Force Alpha, situated at the perimeter of the base, had been put on Red Alert in the early months of 1970, fearing that North Vietnamese regulars who had crossed the Mekong River into Thailand, were recruiting Hanoi-sympathetic Thais and massing them for an attack. All enlisted personnel assigned to the top secret project had a secondary mission of augmenting the security force for this type of emergency. The first time this had happened Terry and Desko were assigned to a perimeter bunker and, to their disbelief, were left there alone in the dark with no ammo.

In the event of an attack, an armed military policeman with a radio was to call for ammunition to be delivered. As they sat there in fear, peering into the jungle in front of them that night, they swore this would never happen again.

Later, they decided that if their own superiors wouldn't arm them adequately, they would supply themselves from the thriving black market in the nearby town of Nakhon Phanom. There, they illegally purchased four magazines of M16 ammunition, which they taped to their legs under their jungle fatigues when the next emergency came. The security police technical sergeant in the bunker with them took note of their action and exclaimed, "Where in the fuck did you guys get the ammo?"

"We could tell ya, but it's classified. And then we'd have to kill ya," Desko had replied sardonically.

This survivalist instinct is what had gotten them through the war. They were young men being forced to second-guess all their leaders' decisions, whereas those who put them in harms way should have been looking out for the Reeds and the Deskos who were serving their nation. War is a black or white, life or death issue. You don't just "sort of" die and you don't just "sort of" defend yourself. To Reed and Desko, their civilian leaders were playing politics with human lives while Henry Kissinger was playing politics in Paris, being chauffeued in his Citroen, and dining in the gourmet capital of the world.

As the Deskos and Reeds ate their barbecued steak that night, sampled Mexican red wine and prepared to attend Chapala's nighttime fireworks display, little did Terry and Desko know that the next day, July 5th, would be Terry's independence day, the day he would have to take matters into his own hands again, and sever himself from the CIA.

The following day, the phone rang and it was Raul Fierro, the "*padron*" at the Guadalajara airport. Fierro was upset. He couldn't gain access to a cargo shipment being held in Terry's airport warehouse. Terry had changed the locks for security reasons and Fierro's keys no longer worked. On an earlier occasion, Terry had found two Mexican guards who said they had gained access through an open door wandering inside the facility. Terry decided to change the locks and had been unable to connect with Fierro to provide him a new key.

"You got to get out here right away," Fierro said. "There's a bird on the ground. I've got a whole crew standing around waiting to receive cargo. Bypass main security when you arrive, I'll tell the guards to let you in."

Leaving the wives at home, Terry and Desko drove together to the airport in Terry's BMW. Access to the field and through Mexican security was swift. As they rounded the corner of the taxiway that led to Terry's warehouse they saw an L-100, the civilian version of a C-130, bearing a gray and white color scheme and the name of Southern Air Transport. The giant cargo plane, North American registration No. N517SJ, was backed into loading position by the main door of *Maquinaria Internacional*'s facility. Though Reed didn't realize it at the time, this was the same airplane he had seen on May 30th, parked in nearly the same position.

However on May 30th it bore a different registration number, N46965, but had the identical paint scheme, a black band running longitudinal down the fuselage, separating white above the stripe and light gray below it. The number change was discovered in a search at the FAA records center in Oklahoma

City by investigative reporter Jerry Bohnen, who found that tail number N46965 had been surrendered back to the FAA by SAT and replaced by N517SJ.*

Reed and Desko noted that the plane's loading ramp was down, but after circling the plane with the car, they ascertained no crew members were present, so Terry parked 100 yards from his warehouse under the shaded general aviation aircraft parking area.

"Before we go find these guys, JD, I'd like to go inside and make sure there's no mix-up on the cargo they've come for." This was a reference to the earlier foul-up in which Terry's machinery was accidentally shipped south.

From invoices he had received, there should have been another grinder belonging to *Maquinaria Internacional* in one of the containers. To avoid another cargo mix up, both Terry and Desko decided it was necessary to open the two conex containers stored in the warehouse to determine which one to ship.

After breaking the metal band attached to the handle of the container nearest the hangar door, Terry, to his horror, unexpectedly found the "hard evidence" that Marr had demanded.

Desko cooly peered inside the container. He shook his head in disgust. "If these guys can get loads like this in, Terry, the Agency obviously has the DEA and customs under their control."

The two men were looking in disbelief at a load of cocaine that measured at least 10 feet by 20 feet and five feet deep.

The container was filled waist high with green wooden weapons crates with rope handles. They were about four feet long, 24 inches wide and 12 inches high. Two of the boxes, whose label said they held rifles, had shifted in transit, and one had spilled its contents. Clearly visible were at least 12 rectangular parcels neatly wrapped in plastic and sealed with duct tape. From all the movies they had ever seen, the two men were certain the white powdery substance they were looking at was cocaine.

"It's either cocaine or someone is spendin' a hell of a lotta money to air transport sugar," Desko said.

"It's gotta be tons!" Terry exclaimed. "Think this'll be enough evidence for Marr? Fenue certainly had nothing to do with this shipment."

SO MUCH FOR THE WAR ON DRUGS!

Terry told Desko to return quickly to the car. He did not want his friend to become more deeply enmeshed in what they had found. Neither man realized it then, but Desko would become Terry's witness to that infamous day: July 5th, 1987, when Terry knew for a certainty that the CIA was in the drug business....in a big way!

Now Terry knew he had to act. With Desko out of the building, Terry decided to give Marr the hard evidence he had been demanding. What better way than to "store" some *samples* as *evidence* just in case Marr continued to insist that it was only the "commies" who deal in drugs.

---

* The information obtained from the FAA records in 1991 by investigative reporter Jerry Bohnen, showed that both tail numbers associated with L-100 aircraft supporting Reed's operation had indeed been issued to Southern Air Transport in Miami, Florida. Curiously, both had been assigned to the same plane in the summer of 1987. This in effect gave SAT the ability to give one plane the appearance of being two different ones, just as Barry Seal had done to his Lear jet during his covert trip to Panama with Reed. One can then conclude that the plane which Reed saw on May 30, was the same one he witnessed on July 5.

With the *evidence* safely tucked away in a nearby tool box, the Conex container closed and Desko out of view sitting behind the tinted windows of the BMW outside, Terry set out to find Fierro. He figured it would be best just to get the crate out of the warehouse as fast as possible and give himself time to think. He didn't want to create a scene with Fierro on his own turf. *Always pick the time and the place, his grandfather had taught him.*

Terry exited the hangar and went to the flight planning section of aerial operations looking for the crew. He found himself in an entourage of pilots and cargo handlers. In addition to Fierro, Terry recognized SAT pilot John McRainey, whom he had met at Marr's party and who was wearing an orange flight suit. There was another Anglo pilot and two Latino loadmasters wearing sanitized flight suits, whom he did not know. The suits all had the velcro attachment points for name tags and rank insignia, giving them the appearance of being the military issue variety.

Fierro requisitioned two Mexicana forklifts and operators to load the container aboard the waiting SAT aircraft. Noticing that the band of the container had been broken, McRainey asked Terry if there was a problem with the cargo. Terry simply replied that he had opened it to make sure which of the two containers belonged to him, and no further questions were asked. After seeing the cargo safely loaded, and giving Fierro his new keys, Terry watched the L-100 engines fire up and taxi away from his warehouse. He was anxious to lock up his facility and return to his waiting friend, glad that no one had spotted him sitting in the car behind the tinted windows.

"OK, Mitch. This is not my paranoia at work and my 'commie friend' had nothing to do with *this* shipment," Terry began 90 minutes later as he stood in Marr's den. Marr could tell by Terry's demeanor that it was time to put down the tequila and the channel changer and just listen.

After rehashing the events at the airport, Marr attempted to theorize that Terry was, again, witnessing some sort of DEA "controlled delivery" (sting) operation and that SAT was merely the courier for the drugs. It wasn't uncommon, he said, for the CIA and the DEA to work in concert for this sort of black operation. He apparently could see Reed's anger surfacing and that he wasn't buying this line. So he then promised to get in touch with Gomez/Rodriguez and to get to the bottom of things.

Marr's reference to an earlier incident was an occurrence on May 30th, in which Terry inadvertently walked in on what appeared to be a drug transshipment going on at a hangar next door to his facility, where the DEA stored and maintained its aircraft. That incident, which Terry had reported to Marr as well, again involved an SAT L-100 and crew that appeared to be receiving drug cargo from a Mexican-registered Cessna 182RG being operated by the American DEA.

The longer he sat and fumed, the angrier he became. The sight of Marr being drunk again added to his rage. Terry wasn't buying any theories from Marr. He wanted answers.

"I don't mean to sound threatening, Mitch, but I figure 48 hours is long enough to get an answer about the plane, the crew, its contents, and most of all, what the hell was that shit doing in my facility in the first place?"

"Calm down," Marr slurred as he attempted to extricate himself from his papa-san chair. "I'll get with fuckin' Gomez...I mean Rodriguez, and tell him you're pissed. He'll get to the bottom of things."

Marr escorted Terry to the gate of his compound and was shocked to see Reed's car parked directly in front of his house. He was even more shocked seeing Desko sitting there staring at him.

"Who's he?" Marr said somewhat taken aback. "I didn't know you drove here...you're not supposed to be this visible, you know."

"He's an old Air Force buddy of mine, Mitch. Down for the holidays. And about me drivin' here, I figure this is an emergency...don't you?"

As the two men drove off, Terry turned to John and informed, "JD, you just met my handler, Mitch Marr."

It didn't take 48 hours for Marr to report back. But he didn't seek out Terry to relay any answers to his questions.

"The shipment is short two bags...you know anything about that?" Marr queried.

That was it. The trick had worked. Terry had dyed the water and the man who allegedly knew nothing was standing there with dye on his hands. Nothing else needed to be said. Marr had gone for the bait. Terry had not told him about the two parcels he had taken from the container. He had hoped and yet feared he would get this response.

The CIA was dirty.

Instead of Marr giving him the answers he had demanded and giving the illusion of concern about the drugs...here he was standing at Terry's front gate being concerned only about the shipment being shy some cargo.

Now, Terry's nightmare scenario was unfolding and becoming a reality. He recalled his words that night more than a year earlier in Arkansas. *"Hey*, he had said, *"what's the worst that can happen?"*

Now, he knew the answer. And since that day, Terry's life had gone steadily downhill. He felt a swarm of emotion; anger, isolation, the feeling of being used, but, most of all, he felt violated. Patriotism had become a joke. It had become just another word for profiteering. His patriotism had been exploited in Southeast Asia and now it was happening again. The selfishness, greed and illegal activity by a handful of renegade CIA operatives had placed him and his family in peril.

At this moment he could not be certain exactly who was involved in trafficking and how high up the chain-of-command it went. He wanted to reach out for Oliver North, whom he considered the only true professional ever involved in the disintegrating organization. He still trusted North, who, Terry believed, was someone too straight to be involved in drug activity. But North had problems of his own as he prepared for his congressional testimony, and Terry had no idea of how to locate him. North probably couldn't even be approached now that he was insulated by attorneys, Terry reasoned. And would North even acknowledge him now?

How long had America been in the drug business, he and Desko wondered? In Laos, Terry had been aware that certain U.S. military personnel had been arrested and court-martialed for shipping heroin under the guise of "classified material." Now, seemingly alone and helpless, he was smack in the middle of a drug ring and was being set-up to take the fall if anything went wrong. The company documents all bore his name and everything seemed to be disintegrating.

Terry thought there could be no lower point in his life. His foreign business partners wanted out, and their money back. His reputation as an honest businessman was being destroyed.

George Fenue had already walked away to protect his communist-backed trading company. George could not allow his firm to be associated with trafficking. His Japanese partner had sued him and was holding Terry personally responsible for the business losses.

And it was becoming clear to Terry that Rodriguez and company would take the drug profits as long as they could, and then let "the commies" take the fall along with Terry, if the activities were discovered or if anyone got out of line.. Rodriguez, George Bush's good friend, would later write a book entitled *Silent Warrior* telling of his selfless patriotic service to America, even as he was tightening the noose around Terry, and would probably choke and kill him if he didn't go along.

Fate had placed Terry in a dangerous position. Through no fault of his own, he had become a major liability for Rodriguez. If Terry could not be controlled, and he had no skeletons in his closet, the CIA's dirtiest secret could now become public knowledge.

For six stressful days, Terry attempted to entertain the Deskos to whom he had promised to show the hidden beauty of Mexico. As they drove through beautiful Mexican countryside, Terry's mind was elsewhere. He kept reassembling the major events in his life that had led him here and to this "Y" in the road where he now stood. Life was complex, yet simple, he realized.

You lose your way a little at a time. He felt he had made no one major decision in life that had put him here...It was just the opposite. It was those little decisions that were all adding up to a major problem. As he often did, he compared his situation to flying. It's like a pilot failing to make the minor adjustments in heading and attitude that keep a plane squarely on altitude and course. Instead, the unwary pilot looks up and wonders "How in the hell did this mountain get in front of me?" That's exactly how he felt.

It was good having Desko with him. As John sat in the right front seat and they relived their travail in Thailand and talked of the innocence they had then, the answer to his problem was becoming clearer. He had to go back and find and re-assemble the pieces of himself he had lost along the way. The pieces of his grandfather that he felt lived within him still. His hard-headed grandfather who saw things in black and white, would never have gotten this far off course. Had it been money? Was it power? Was it post-Vietnam stress syndrome? What had gotten him here?

He didn't have one singular answer, but he knew the solution to his problem was going to require inner strength and to do what he should have done a long time ago in Thailand. Stand up. *Just say no.*

When confronted with the gut-wrenching decision in Southeast Asia during his military service, that of participating in the destruction of American POWs, he had given in to their logic: "If *you* don't do it *someone else* will." This time it was going to be different. He felt like he was being given a second chance to do it the right way. This time they could do it *without him*, and he was prepared to suffer their wrath. He knew it would be the hard way.

He and John were the only two in the motor home who knew what had happened and talked privately of Terry's possible options. They both kept coming back to the same alternatives: Either turn your back and walk away or play ball. The second option was unacceptable. How many powerful men are out there, Reed and Desko wondered, who owe their fortune and their power to the CIA and its drug proceeds? Does anyone truly make it anymore on his own?

And what about the Israelis, he was thinking. It had been a while since he had seen Pat Weber. Were the Israelis in on drug trafficking with the CIA? Why was Weber hanging out with the likes of Rodriguez? He didn't have the answers to these complex questions.

But he was about to find out.

* * *

As soon as the Desko family departed for the states, Reed returned to Marr's house for another round of questions and answers. He didn't need to be coached by his dead, mule-trading great-grandfather in order to realize that his only trump card was the "evidence" he was "safeguarding".

Mitch was anxious to take possession of the missing evidence, but Reed wanted some answers to some nagging questions before any deal could be struck. He demanded from Marr an accounting of the remainder of the people he had been put into play with in "Screw Worm".

Marr swore on a stack of his favorite VHS tapes that Terry was in for no more shocking revelations. "Gomez is Rodriguez, Cathey is North, and I'm the authentic Mitchell Fuckin' Marr, that's it... no more surprises... I swear on top of my non-pirated copy of *Apocalypse Now*."

That sworn statement held water about as long as it took Terry to get to Mexico city to consummate the divorce proceedings of the joint venture with the Hungarians. They too were reading TIME magazine, *Newsweek*, *The New York Times*, and *Pravda* about the Iran-Contra scandal and were eager to get as far away from the Agency's *negocio mal* (bad business) as they could get.

Terry and Fenue sat in Cortec's office and talked into the night, sensing this would be their last contact permitted with each other. While trying their damndest to destroy their livers, his young Hungarian friend listened intently while Terry attempted to explain his motivations for dragging Technoimpex into this mess and doing the best he could to genuinely apologize.

The Washington scandal wasn't the only thing the KGB seemed to be well-informed on. Fenue said he had a full report on the cocaine activity and "his people" had concluded that Max Gomez and "friends" were behind it. But it was so intertwined, as he put it, into other Agency activities, both legitimate and otherwise, that it was impossible for them to know how high up the CIA chain of command approval for such activity went.

"It would be as difficult as determining if it were *only* the CIA and KGB who killed Kennedy," he said with a smirk and a gleam in his eye.

He went on to advise Terry not to get overly concerned, as he put it, about the Agency's trafficking problems, and said the KGB had been infected with this same problem for years except "Moscow's finest" preferred dealing in heroin instead of cocaine.

Fenue said he knew the true identity of the American agents Terry had been dealing with, and a lot more besides. After killing the last of the *Oso Negro* Mexican vodka, he added pensively, "You need to be careful comrade, you are traveling in a very high orbit. Higher than you realize perhaps, and I wouldn't want to see you shot down like Gary Powers....and your old friend, Barry Seal."

The effects of the alcohol dulled the wave of emotion that tried to sweep through Terry as he deciphered the Hungarian's coded transmission. He had no inkling, up to now, that Fenue even knew the name Barry Seal, and now he was finding his friendship with Seal was a matter of KGB record.

"George, where did you get the name Barry Seal, and what makes you think I was a friend of his?" Terry questioned in a low key manner, not wanting to cause a premature termination of the conversation.

The question forced Fenue to become even more cagey. "As Joe Bona [the KGB agent] always said, we aren't like the CIA. We don't have to wait until things happen in order to discover them."

While Fenue was still basking in the victory of this verbal touche, Reed decided to get serious with the drinking, thinking it might loosen his comrade's tongue. When he returned from the office refrigerator with some ice cold Corona, popped the tops on two, and took a long slow swallow, Fenue began, "Listen, Terry. I like you and Janis and your children. You don't have to get me drunk in order to get me in bed. You look in need of a friend. I'll quit playing games, what do you want to know? You get one question."

"Tell me all about Seal...for beginners," Reed responded letting Fenue know he would press for more than one question.

Fenue gulped down half a beer, belched and while staring at the ceiling, began,

"Adler Berriman Seal.

"He worked for the CIA since the early 70's.

"He was a CIA pilot....among other things.

"His handler was CIA Agent Leroy Tracta.

"Your government fucked him, arrested him, and put him on trial after his arrest on set-up explosives charges.

"He penetrated and worked directly inside the Medellin Cartel for both the CIA and your DEA...and others.

"He was the one who master minded the CIA/Sandinista sting operation.

"He worked on operations Jade Bridge and Centaur Rose with you in Arkansas.

"He took you to Panama for a meeting on 'Operation Screw Worm'...as you call it.

"He introduced you to the Israeli agent that is now involved in Screw Worm, Weber, Pat Weber is his code name.

"Bona approached and unsuccessfully tried to 'turn' him.

"He bribed and successfully 'turned' one of our agents here in Mexico.

"He bought from that agent a copy of a very *compromising* surveillance video showing your vice president Bush's children caught in a very *compromising* situation.

"He was killed not for the reasons alleged by your government.

"He took with him to his grave more secrets than I ever want to know.

"Have I left anything out? Let me see...oh yes, he was a Cancer like you, and strangely he shared your birthday. July 16th. He was born in 1939....you in 1948. You see, you aren't the only one with a photographic memory."

If Fenue could perform this well drunk, it was scary to think what he'd be capable of sober. Before Terry could absorb all that had been spit out, literally between gulps of Corona, Fenue added, "How's that for mind control, *Señor Estrella?*"

Shit, Reed thought, Fenue out-gunned any agent he'd ever met, professional or otherwise, military or civilian—Red, or Red, White & Blue. He even knew his code name. There was only one way he could know this much about the American intelligence operations....they had a mole....a double agent had to be in the American camp. He had reconstructed an entire dossier from a vision on a blank ceiling.

"Impressive...So who actually killed Kennedy?" Reed asked.

"You used up your one question," Fenue answered still staring intently at the ceiling.

"At least you have to tell me the real name of the Israeli you mentioned. Since you know it's a code name, you must know his true identity. Come on, impress me again," Reed baited.

"Sure, why not. Your side knows who he is. Our side knows who he is. His side knows who he is. You're the only one in the dark," he castigated Reed. "His true name is Amiram Nir, the Israeli Prime Minister's Advisor on Combating Terrorism. You should be honored to be orbiting with him, he's very connected.... He's also a nice guy, about our age."

With that Fenue inhaled one more beer and terminated the unsettling conversation. "There, I've crossed the line for you." He paused to belch then peered intensely into Reed's eyes. "Someday, comrade, I'll expect the favor to be repaid.....with interest, as you capitalists say."

CHAPTER 28

WHAT A BIRTHDAY PRESENT!

The sound of the airplane engine at red-line RPM and the propeller being cycled through its feather check was a welcome distraction to Terry Reed's task at hand, coming to grips with his decision to turn his back on the covert world.

He could not pay the price. He could not look the other way while the CIA trafficked in narcotics. His family, he was certain, was in danger, and it was up to him to extricate them from this mess. Once again, Terry was preparing a contingency plan.

This, for Terry, was worse than assimilating a scenario for nuclear war in which nations would be attacked. He had done that before while working for SAC (Strategic Air Command). For now, it was he and his family who were the targets that faced destruction.

As he sat and mulled this over, the decibel-shattering sound from the airplane engine being tested next door was rather like music to his ears, blocking out the considerable problems facing him that summer day at the Guadalajara airport.

An internal combustion engine straining and revving at full speed plied itself like an aphrodisiac to his psyche as he sat among the file cabinets and machine-tool manuals spread around the large room that served as corporate headquarters of Maquinaria Internacional, S.A.

Movement in the adjoining warehouse quickly brought him back to reality. Gazing through the large glass windows that separated his office from the warehouse, he saw a familiar face, a man gesturing with both hands and quietly motioning Terry to step out onto the airport tarmac.

Terry joined him outside and the man introduced to him earlier in Mexico City as Pat Weber was nervously scanning the area to see if anyone was watching them. Both men stepped into an area between the warehouse and Terry's plane parked outside.

The unexpected visitor spoke first. "I didn't want to talk inside," he said. "The place might be bugged." Terry got the uncomfortable feeling one gets when conversing with someone who has a floating eye, and he found himself looking at the glass eye rather than the good one.

He shifted his focus to the good one in order to concentrate on what the Israeli intelligence agent was saying. Pat Weber spoke first in native Hebrew and then quickly translated. "We have a saying in Israel...Jews survive by their cunning. And we need to be cunning right now. I tell you this because our people are very upset by the cowboy actions of your people. You are the only low key avenue to North that I know of, now that Seal is gone."

The date was July 16th, 1987, Terry's birthday, only days after Oliver North had finished his marathon testimony before the Iran-Contra committees in Washington and five days since John Desko and his wife had returned home.

Outside the office, before Weber got started with detailing his problems, Terry decided it was time to test the agent's behavior to his new-found knowledge pertaining to Weber's alleged true identity.

"I was told your true name is Amiram Nir and you are a highly placed agent working closely with the prime minister's office. Is that true? I need to know the truth...I need to know who I can trust."

Weber glared back intensely, asking "Who told you that...your people? I'll bet it was that drunk, Marr."

"Yes," Reed answered deciding to hang the security slip on Robert Duvall's clone.

"Well," the Israeli began, "I suppose it's best you know. We can go directly to the business at hand. I won't have to mince words, as you people say."

Nir then confided that he felt he could no longer travel safely and unobserved in the United States even under his alias. *He had been compromised.* His other contact, the one he had referred to was Adler Berriman Seal, who had been murdered 17 months earlier. So adrift in Mexico, and fearful of what he had pieced together through deduction, Nir said he had come to Terry desperately seeking a channel to North. His fear centered on Felix Rodriguez, the man Washington had put in charge of things in Mexico. The Enterprise was now in a free fall, reporting channels were severed and anyone of importance in Washington now had an attorney that had sealed his lips.

Referring to Rodriguez, Nir said in a tone bordering on fear and laced with disbelief, "That crazy Cuban madman is going to take us all down. I don't understand why your vice president (George Bush) can't control him. My God, he was the director of the CIA...doesn't he realize this incident had all the markings of an international double-agent setup? I'm effectively neutralized with the hearings in progress. I'm being watched. My phones are bugged. I can't travel. Shit, I'm even afraid for Pat Weber. Where can we talk that's for sure a safe place."

Terry could not believe the change in Nir's demeanor. The cool, calm man with the analytical mind he had seen in Panama, Mexico City and Zirahuen was now obviously gripped by paranoia and fear. What had happened to him? Why had Weber sought *him* out, Terry wondered.

(The Israeli's reference to Bush was no accident. Bush was definitely no stranger to this man. Just a year earlier in Jerusalem, Nir had briefed the then-vice president in detail about what had been called the Iran initiative involving the swap of American weapons for hostages being held in Beirut. The earlier meeting between Nir and Bush had been arranged by Oliver North. [1] But Nir's links to the upper echelon of the American government were now severed due to the shootdown of the C-123 over Nicaragua the previous October. That incident had not only led to the exposure of American involvement with the Contra supply effort, but also to the Israeli "cut-out" and their secret dealings with Iran on behalf of the U.S.)

Nir was sensing a double-cross and he believed Rodriguez was behind it. He needed to confide this to Terry, but was paranoid about being seen with him.

Terry had a solution to Nir's security fears. "Why not up in my airplane?" he suggested. "We can fly to Morelia and pretend to be inspecting the runway construction for 'Z.'* That will give us a couple of hours alone together. And surely, they can't eavesdrop on us at thirteen thousand feet."

But Nir hesitated. He had a thing about flying in small airplanes. "I don't trust those little airplanes, I'm sorry it's, how do you say, a phobia." In hindsight, this was an odd disclosure considering Nir's death in a small single-engine commuter aircraft 16 months later near Morelia where they were now heading. The accident came just a week after Bush's election to the presidency and it sealed forever the lips of the one man who could have revealed exactly how "in the loop" George Bush really was.

"My little plane is not so little," Terry reassured him. "Besides it's a twin [two engines] and I have over 3,000 hours pilot time. Come on, it's the only place I feel safe unless they shoot us down with triple A (anti-aircraft artillery). Just joking."

"The thought of triple-A fire reminds me of the Yom Kippur War," he answered.

"And Yom Kippur is how Cathey...I mean North and I believe a war should be fought," Terry stated while draining the fuel sumps on the left wing. He still hadn't gotten used to Cathey's real name.

To calm Nir's nerves, he had him assist in the pre-flight of the aircraft. "You Israelis are lucky, you don't have a fucked-up Congress. You have leadership with direction and you win decisively, Not like our Vietnam."

"This could turn out to be our Vietnam if it's not controlled properly," The Israeli noted somberly. "You must bypass Marr and Rodriguez and get to North...And about the way we fight. It's not that we have any better leadership than you. As I've told North, we just fight scared. Our backs are to the sea. It gives you motivation to win. The will to live is motive enough, don't you agree?"

"Yes, but I always thought you Jews had a couple of other hidden advantages."

"Oh, what are those?"

"You own the banks of the world and God is always on your side. Or is it the other way around?", Terry joked.

Nir laughed as he walked around the plane and assisted in the safety check, a strategy Terry often used to put passengers at ease. "By watching you safety check the plane, I feel more comfortable about flying in it. But I definitely would not go up in one with only one motor," Nir added.

As the Piper-Seneca II commenced its take-off roll, Terry brought the manifold pressure needles up to the red line...40 inches of mercury and the tachometer needles on both engines to 2,575 RPM. Exactly the correct reading for a high-density take off considering the 5,000-foot elevation of the Mexican runway.

The ground speed quickly built to 66 KIAS, Terry "rotated," cross-checked the attitude indicator, air speed, and confirmed on the vertical speed indicator a positive rate of climb. He then "sucked-up" the landing gear, and was once again absorbed in his love of flying. But somehow, he thought, flying had complicated his life. After all, it was his flying ability that impressed North, Barry Seal and Bill Cooper. Definitely, there's something to be said of a "pilot personality"—a calculated risk taker, he could hear Seal say.

---

*   This was the code name given the weapons plant being built at the Morelia Airport.

But what of Emile Camp, he thought, as he banked the airplane to a south-easterly heading. Camp had been flying a plane just like this one when he crashed in February, 1985, near Rich Mountain in Arkansas. That still haunted Terry considering the expertise he had seen exhibited by Camp. It just didn't add up, "buying the farm" that way.

He suddenly realized his mind was wandering, something deadly for a pilot. He forced himself back into the cockpit to relay his flight plan to the Mexican air traffic controller below.

"Roger, Guadalajara," he then reported. "Understand, November one-three Lima Mike is radar contact heading one-zero-zero degrees climbing through niner-point-five for one-three-thousand, cleared vector five, Morelia. Please inform Commandante Fierro that this is a 'Sierra Whiskey' sortie and to process the flight plan as usual."

The air traffic controller's voice changed markedly when he heard Fierro and the code name mentioned together. That meant that this was an intelligence flight that would require "special handling" by the ATC system in Mexico. In fact, once the craft arrived safely in Morelia, the ATC knew to erase all stored computerized data concerning this flight. He was to destroy all physical evidence of the flight plan. In other words, the ATC was to eliminate any and all data concerning "Sierra Whiskey" flights in and out of Guadalajara. Once the safety of the flight was insured, as far as the outside world would know, the flight never happened.

"Roger, Seneca one-three Lima Mike. Guadalajara copies. Sierra Whiskey in effect. Have a good trip, Capitan Reed."

The Israeli in the right front seat started to relax somewhat as the pilot leveled off at 13,000 feet and engaged the autopilot.

"OK, here we are alone. Lay it on me." He slid the pilot's seat rearward to get a better view of the Israeli. The plane was now flying itself at 200 MPH heading easterly toward Morelia.

And lay it on he did. Terry's worst nightmare scenario began to unfold. It was worse even than his discovery 11 days ago that the CIA and Rodriguez were trafficking in drugs.

Nir expressed to him the belief that Rodriguez was a double-agent—and directly responsible for the shootdown over Nicaragua the previous October of Bill Cooper's C-123 supply plane and the capture of Eugene Hasenfus.

How ironic this was, Nir pointed out, because he had warned Seal before his death that there was a "leak" in the Enterprise that could bring about a political thunderclap. And that's exactly what happened when the C-123 crashed and exposed to the world the deviousness of the Reagan administration.

There were too many disturbing coincidences to that crash. "Think about it for a minute," Nir demanded. "We're not so naive to believe that these happenings are circumstantial. Just try to explain away these events. Number one, you knew Bill Cooper much better than I. I've been told he was an excellent flyer. You don't live to be a 60-year-old pilot acting reckless! What was he doing flying many miles off his flight plan course, and directly over a Sandinista stronghold...a military training camp no less?

"Number two, why did the aircraft have unnecessary and *classified* documents aboard? Documents from prior missions reflecting the dates of the flights, the crew members' names, the tonnage and descriptions of the munitions and the coordinates of the drop zones.

"Number three. Why was the crew not sanitized as the orders always called for? My God, Bill Cooper even had his Southern Air Transport identification card with him. That we cannot accept as an accident. My God, a direct link to the CIA. Cooper knew better!

"Number four, this guy Hasenfus...the dumb ass survivor...what kind of a story is this? No one was to have a parachute. The intention is to always go down with the craft in case of an incident like this. You know from your training that is the procedure, no one is to live. No loose ends. Instead, this guy claims his brother bought him a parachute in Wisconsin? My God, if it wasn't so serious, it would be funny.

"Number five. How does he know the plane was hit by a surface to air missile? If he was blown out of the plane by the explosion as he claims, he wouldn't even have seen it coming, let alone recognize the type of weapon.

"No sir, it's all too convenient. Daniel Ortega 'accidently' captures an American flyer who immediately spills his guts and starts babbling 'CIA, the White House, guns, Southern Air Transport,' and then to top it off, he's put on trial as a war criminal, convicted for his crimes and released as a humanitarian gesture! Shot down in October and home by Christmas. I'll bet your Vietnam POW flyers would have liked such an opportunity. Just think of it all."

As Reed adjusted the heading "bug" on the auto pilot and fine-tuned the plane's engines, he was absorbing the Israeli's itemized list of fatal mistakes.

"But I've saved the best morsel for last, if that's not enough to convince you," his passenger tantalized. "We warned Seal back in early 1986. Just before his murder, we warned him your side had a leak."

Terry's mind flashed to his feelings about Fenue having too much in-depth knowledge of the Agency's operations. He had suspected a mole. Now Nir was confirming they too had suspicions. He decided to not interrupt and just listen.

"We knew something was going to happen to bring unwanted publicity to this operation. Again, what a waste of a good agent. That makes two friends of yours who are dead for no good reasons. Cooper and Seal."

"Three friends if you count Emile Camp," Terry added. "I still think his crash was sabotage. His plane was exactly like this one. He left Baton Rouge with three hours of fuel. He crashes two hours later. There's no post-crash fire. And no fuel in the engine lines. That's fuel starvation! Combine that with the fact he crashed in a heavily wooded area, miles off course, while executing an instrument approach to Mena in VFR conditions...No, he was definitely sabotaged. But by whom? Emile never got along with [Ramon] Medina."

Terry's comments about Medina stemmed from his observation of arguments on several occasions between "the camp Jefe" and Emile Camp. This had made him suspicious that Medina was involved in sabotaging Camp's plane.

"Oh, Medina, that's another example of your CIA stooping to use terrorists to do agents' jobs. What did Medina ever do besides blow up civilians in airliners. These damn Cuban rebels, they're just not professionals."*

---

* Medina, an alias for Cuban exile Luis Posada Carriles, is a friend of Felix Rodriguez and was charged with masterminding the bombing of a Cuban airliner that killed all 73 passengers. Shortly after Hasenfus was captured and interrogated by the Sandinistas, he identified both Rodriguez and Medina as CIA links he had been working with.

Reed almost wished to hear no further details, but Nir wasn't through.

"An agent of ours in El Salvador reports that Rodriguez boasted he was responsible for the killing of both Seal and Camp. You know Rodriguez, he must continually brag of his exploits. Who knows how many people he's either killed or caused to die? He's definitely..."

"...A loose cannon, as they say in the Navy," Terry said.

"Yes. A loose cannon. We don't see how this program can continue. It may not even be salvageable."

What came next was a surprise to Terry. The Israelis were keeping close tabs on Felix Rodriguez...he had a *shadow* and most certainly wasn't aware of it. This became evident when Nir revealed that he knew about drug shipments from San Miguel de Allende northward to Laredo, the same shipments that Terry had reported to Marr.

Nir was now confirming Terry and George Fenue's suspicions that Rodriguez was involved with the earlier shipments from San Miguel and Nir also said these drug shipments involved some of Rodriguez' unspecified relatives.

"That's simply profiteering for the sake of his relatives. It's ridiculous. Who's supposed to be in charge of this idiot?" Nir asked spitefully.

That was a good question. With North on the grill in Washington, Rodriguez was operating alone, and out of control.

"He's a runaway freight train with no engineer at the throttle," Nir said. He bolstered that comment by saying Israeli intelligence in Mexico had intercepted some very disturbing long distance telephone conversations. That Rodriguez, in violation of all intelligence rules, had called Washington directly from Central America on unsecure phone lines and discussed classified data.*

"My God, it's just so apparent to us, that he is a double-dipper (slang for double agent). He must be eliminated one way or the other."

Rodriguez might be the mole, the one who kept Fenue so informed and up to date on the Agency's plans, Terry thought to himself. After all, Rodriguez had been to Cortec's facilities several times and he knew Seal's dossier sufficiently well enough to pass it on to the KGB. Shit, I bet that's right, he thought. Rodriguez was probably the leak the Israelis had warned Seal about. It all made sense.

But talk of "eliminating" someone bothered Terry. "If you're talking elimination, do you have concrete proof, beyond the shadow-of-a-doubt proof? I mean he might just be an idiot, like you said before. A greedy idiot suffering from post-Bay of Pigs stress syndrome"

"Yes, we have the proof, and no idiot, as you suggest, could bring in an ex-Air America kicker and 'turn him' as quickly as Rodriguez did."

"So *your* people think he recruited and *compromised* Hasenfus?"

Nir was not specific as to how this information had been obtained. But he was certain about his facts, he claimed. "We know it for sure. And did anyone from your side tell you about Cooper and Sawyer, the co-pilot?"

"I've heard nothing new about the shootdown since the meeting with you and Rodriguez in Mexico City last December. What are you referring to?"

Terry was shocked, again, when Nir answered. "They were both dead *before*

---

* Oliver North reprimanded Rodriguez for violating secure communications procedures during a meeting in the Old Executive Office Building in Washington on June 25, 1986.²

their airplane took off on that supposed ill-fated flight."

By this time, Terry's head was reeling, but some things were starting to make sense. All the circumstances outlined by Nir earlier concerning the shootdown were coming into focus. Nir said the autopsy performed by the Nicaraguans, the results of which had been relayed to the CIA, indicated the crew had been dead several hours, maybe even 12, before the plane crashed. There was no evidence of the usual profuse bleeding associated with a crash when the victim is alive on impact. This had to mean they were dead before they went down, Nir concluded.

This probably explained why Cooper's body hadn't been returned for burial, Terry thought.

"My God do you think it's Hasenfus that killed them? Terry asked. "Marr told me Hasenfus knows how to fly a C-123 even though he doesn't have a pilot's license."

"We're not prepared to say that. But he had to know *the dead crew members* didn't pilot the airplane...if he was even on the plane at the time..."

"Why? Don't you believe that plane was even shot down?" Reed asked, now fearing the answer.

"No. The aircraft remains were put on display in Managua and our people there said it appears the plane exploded outward as if it had been rigged with explosives prior to its last flight and then deliberately destroyed."

Both men then wondered if this could have been accomplished with a re-mote detonating device after Hasenfus bailed out of the airplane.

Terry had yet another shock. Nir informed him that the other dead crew member was the man Terry had called "Ramon No.2," one of his trainees in Arkansas. Nir said "Ramon" did not die from the crash. His throat had been slit!"

"What a way to get rid of Ronald Reagan," Nir summarized. "The communists must be patting themselves on the back. They expose a covert operation that is in violation of Congressional law and get the President of the United States impeached—all at the same time."

This statement shocked Terry back into his role as a pilot. He scanned the instrument cluster, realizing he had become so engrossed in the conversation he'd nearly forgotten he was flying. His DME was showing only 25 miles out of Morelia. It was time to get busy.

"Morelia tower, this is Seneca november one-three lima mike, level one-three thousand, twenty-five DME west, inbound vector five, landing mike mike. Please advise altimeter and active runway."

Terry slid his seat forward in preparation of the landing task ahead. He banked the plane to the right in order to line up on runway 23 and dropped the landing gear. He then turned to his nervous Israeli companion and asked, "Are you afraid of Rodriguez? It sounds as if he's capable of anything."

While rolling wings level on final approach Terry could not help but be in awe of how fast things could happen, construction-wise that is, when a wel-come covert industrial complex was coming the way of an underdeveloped state such as Michoacan. It was reminiscent of how quickly things happened in Ar-kansas when the Agency began setting up operations there, in 1983. But here things happened even faster. He was getting, literally, a bird's eye view of the new Morelia airport named after Mexican General Francisco J. Mujica. He couldn't help but feel partially responsible for its new runway which now mea-sured exactly 7874 feet with 197 foot overruns on both ends. It was just as

Governor Cardenas had said, "I will provide you with 8000 feet." He was good on his word....when backed by CIA money.

As he "crossed the numbers" at the northeast end of Morelia's newly surfaced runway and did one final GUMP check to ensure the landing gear was down, it hit him how he and Seal had envisioned all this happening two and a half years earlier. A secret weapons manufacturing facility in a Third World country. Technology was definitely coming to Mexico and the governor and his people were there with open arms.

The tires of the Seneca's main landing gear chirped signifying contact and Nir exhaled as if to vent his pent-up tension. "Yes," he said.

It had been so long since Terry had asked the question, he had to pause in order to recall it. "Yes, what?

"Yes, I'm afraid of Rodriguez. He seems to have gained a lot of power during all this turmoil up in Washington. He's an opportunist and he's apparently seized the opportunity to promote himself while the chain of command has been broken due to your congressional investigation. Like I said earlier, with North neutralized, I don't know who's in charge. But Rodriguez is having secret meetings with your vice president and this bothers us."

To explain, Nir admitted matter of factly that Israeli intelligence was following Rodriguez and had placed him in several clandestine meetings with Bush. Nir indicated that this was disturbing to his country because the Israeli ambassador was being kept in the dark about these meetings.

"They are up to something, and we Israelis have a lot of exposure from this whole ordeal—unnecessary exposure I might add, especially considering what is going on here in Morelia."

"What do you suppose Rodriguez and Bush are secretly discussing?" Terry asked.

Before Nir could answer, they were both startled by a tapping on the wing by a Mexican soldier armed with an Uzi. They had been lost in their conversation and were unaware of the approaching squad of armed security personnel. Tight security was in effect at the airport's east side due to the construction.

"Why don't you talk to him," Terry suggested. "That way if he decides to shoot you first, at least you'll have died from a weapon made by your own country." Nir was not amused.

"I wish you wouldn't joke about death Sr. Estrella."

They then explained to the *Jefe* of the security squad that the purpose of their visit was to inspect the construction of the new building complex that would house the machinery scheduled to arrive soon. Terry had accepted the reality that this was a pipe dream, however, in light of the disintegration of the "joint venture". But he had decided to go along with it all and make no waves until he could eventually flee...somehow.

"We knew from your flight plan you filed in Guadalajara that you were coming to Morelia. It's just that Capitan Fierro did not know the reason for your visit or who your passenger was. Feel free to inspect the facility."

As soon as the armed goon squad walked away, Nir began to speak. "Shit!!!! I was hoping no one observed me at the airport. Based upon those comments Fierro knew you had a passenger when you left Guadalajara. You see, I *am* being observed and followed!"

"Calm down. Don 't let your paranoia run away with your logic. Maybe it's me they're observing and following and you just happened along."

"But why would they be watching you? They trust you don't they? You're not supposed to know enough to be dangerous. You're just their front, right?"

Nir apparently hadn't gotten the word that Terry had "crossed the line" from being a *silent asset* who turned a blind eye to the agency's true activities to a *complaining liability*.

By his question, it was obvious he was unaware of Terry's July 5th discovery in his warehouse. And Terry was learning a lot. Up to this point, he hadn't been sure if the Israeli knew about that discovery. Nir had little way of knowing that Terry was, by then, appearing to be the most dangerous thing someone can be in this situation—a whistleblower. Terry's demands for a thorough investigation of the Agency's cocaine trafficking obviously were not being passed along to the Israelis. Otherwise, Nir would have known why Terry was no longer trusted.

Terry suggested that they both walk over and pretend to be inspecting the massive pouring of concrete that was in process for the foundation of the arms manufacturing site known by its code name, Z.

"I'm glad you're confiding in me. I need a friend, too," Terry admitted. "This whole fucking operation is out of control...and yes, they have reason to be monitoring me."

"But why?" Nir shouted over the roar of the concrete trucks dumping their loads.

"I guess I know too much! And I'm sure they don't trust me any longer...at least after what happened July 5th."

After a brief discussion with the work crew about the density and thickness of the concrete, Reed and Nir returned to the plane in preparation for their trip back to Guadalajara. As Terry processed his flight plan over the plane's radio, his nervous companion disappeared behind the aircraft in order to relieve himself.

"Clear prop!" Terry shouted out the pilot's storm vent as he brought the Continental engine to life on the left side of the plane. The ensuing propeller blast caught Nir by surprise and he suddenly learned the aerodynamics associated with urinating behind an airplane.

He climbed into the right front seat appearing to be in need of clean trousers. Looking embarrassed from his ordeal he secured the cockpit door.

"Didn't your grandfather teach you to piss downwind?" Terry asked, chiding his passenger. "But I'm glad you went already, because what I have to tell you on the way back will probably scare the piss out of you!"

"I'll bet I can top what you're gonna tell me," Nir challenged as the plane taxied into takeoff position. Little did Terry know that this soon would be the case.

Terry advanced the throttles and departed Morelian airspace, setting a heading for the return leg to Gaudalajara. It was another strange alliance formed that July day in 1987.

He started to inform Nir of the Agency's drug smuggling activities, which he had now confirmed first-hand from the July 5th incident. But it seemed he was anxious for Reed to finish his lengthy story as if the Israeli had a more pressing matter to discuss.

Terry had just violated the cardinal rule. Not only had he told someone something that he didn't need to know, but worse than that he had confided it to a known agent of a foreign government. And Nir had done the same. It was a mutual Munich.

"OK, top that my friend." Terry had placed the plane on autopilot and was again looking in Nir's eye. "My own fucking government is in the drug business. There's supposed to be a war on drugs and I find out that it's our own CIA that just can't say no...It can't say no to the money, I guess. You know it looks like Lenin was right. Democracy just doesn't work!"

To say Nir had an interesting observation would be an understatement. "You don't know how close your comments are to the real problem. We don't think you have a democracy any longer!"

"What are you saying?"

"We think your country has had a very quiet, internal coup. Look at the evidence, it's all there." What followed then puzzled Terry. Was he once again he was being drawn involuntarily into yet another loop?

How did drugs and democracy dovetail into a briefing on geopolitics as seen through the eyes of the Mossad? Terry, like many Americans, had seen things in stark black and white. In Israeli intelligence, the world was seen differently, in shades of gray. Nir needed to make Reed see the world through a different prism, hoping to bend his mind to a different way of thinking.

"You have, or maybe I should say had, a very popular President. One who is hell bent on destroying communism. Now on the surface that may appear good. You know, a carry-over of your Cold War objectives. The U.S. wins, Russia loses. But if you'll look deeper, as we Israelis have, destroying or even crippling the USSR is not a very good idea.

"You see, as we know in the Middle East, you need a balance of power. Two rival countries, or even more than two, are much easier to manipulate and control than one. They are always turning to each other either overtly or covertly to assist in maintaining that balance, that harmony that nature intended. It's actually healthy for society, and people, too, to have goals and fears...it gives an order to things. That bond of unity, that bond of allegiance, that bond of ethnic identification.

"Nature always has two of everything...male and female... plus and minus. It is not intended for either the U.S. or the USSR to dominate completely."

This was becoming a little too esoteric for Terry. He was beginning to lose the meaning of this "briefing," which had turned very philosophical and sounded headed toward the merits of the puzzle of nature. Terry had always believed that "coups" occurred in other, less-developed countries and they were often engineered by the U.S. This he studied in intelligence school. He knew that when coups do occur, one of the most important factors of survival was to back the winner. Was this Nir's problem?

"So what are you saying? Your country has knowledge of a 'coup' in the U.S.? Something brought on by the USSR? Something you've assisted in order to maintain a balance of power?"

"You're partially right. But it's not something we've had a direct hand in....I don't believe. The facts support our analysis. The United States has been prospering...on credit, I might add...while Russia is declining. All brought about by Reagan's plan to destroy the USSR by bankrupting it. He calls it 'riding tall in the saddle as an American while the Russians call it 'going hungry while standing in the bread line.' You probably don't even know how bad things are. Why this thing in Nicaragua is probably the last foreign expedition they [the Russians] can afford, and the *last* thing they need to be doing with their limited resources. Between Central America and Afghanistan, it's sure to bring an end to communism as we know it."

"But why's that bad?" Terry asked. "That's what I've been trained to do. I'm a Cold Warrior. I would love to win. I would love to see the end of the USSR in my lifetime," Terry said emphatically.

"You sound just like North. You two have a lot in common. You're both very bright, but yet very stupid!"

"Well enlighten me then, Allah, because I just don't get it. You're saying the USSR is on the verge of economic collapse and that is bad? You mean if I help the U.S. in Nicaragua, that is bad? That's what I've been trained to do, WIN! You're beginning to sound like a football coach who wants his own team to lose the homecoming game."

"Think about China," Nir replied with a soft voice and after a long pause, "because we are. Who will replace the USSR as the power base of all of Asia if Russia collapses? China will. Don't you get it? The enemy of my enemy is my friend. We have much stronger ties, both the U.S. and Israel, I mean, with Russia than with China. China we fear...and so does your country, I might add. No, you need a healthy Russia to keep China in balance."

After a brief pause and scanning his eye across the beautiful Mexican countryside below, where he would later die, Nir added in a melancholy tone, "And it's not surprising you have difficulty understanding that, because your President Reagan doesn't understand it either."

"So you're saying Reagan is a threat to world peace, or so you perceive it?"

"Yes!" Nir snapped. "And it's not only us that perceive it that way. We have many supporters of this view, both friendly and enemy. So we Israelis would not normally care what happens within your government, unless we see ourselves being set up to be double-crossed and embarrassed. And worst of all, maybe not being aligned with the proper president of your government."

"What do you mean, proper President? Don't we have only one?"

"No," Nir answered. "You have two, Bush is now in charge and he's trying to overthrow Reagan. It's a coup, plain and simple." It was becoming painful to listen to.

"How do you convince me of that? Being from Missouri I've got to be shown, or haven't you heard?" Terry responded, still doubtful of the Israeli's wild statements and conclusions.

"Well, our agents have been co-mingling with your agents for years, just as you and I are today. And we have all been writing reports for years, advising our leaders on the merits of maintaining a balance of power between the U.S., Russia and China. But only in the past six years has your country had a leader....an actor, my God, who as president is hell-bent on winning this Cold War. And if he is successful, the world will be a much less stable place.

"It is our fear that the conditions of instability in which Israel finds itself in the Middle East will spread throughout the world if Russia declines. So we have been.. uh.. monitoring...that's a good word...*monitoring* a condition in your government in which you have a maniac at the helm, and a much more astute second in command in the shadows. George Bush, your ex-director of the CIA, understands these complex issues. He's a true player of chess and Ronald Reagan barely understand checkers, I think. Anyway, our people have been *monitoring* certain relationships within your government that lead us to believe that your CIA is closely aligned, and in agreement with, your vice president.

"We have all, unfortunately, been caught up in a foreign policy dispute in Central America. So along comes this Hollywood cowboy who's determined to kick the communists out of Nicaragua, even if he has to break the law and lie to your Congress and the American people in order to do it. You and I are even part of that lie, I might add. So your CIA and Mr. Bush recognize that they must somehow seize power and stop this madman."

Terry was now starting to see the big picture and, as they say, get his mind right. "So they do it by staging an international incident. Something that proves to the whole world that Reagan will violate the law to get his war in Nicaragua."

"Right!" Nir nearly applauded, seemingly relieved his student has finally drawn the right conclusion. "This whole shootdown is a staged event from the very onset. Something right out of the movies. Quite fitting for Reagan's demise, don't you think."

Terry was now feeling used, and sad. Cooper, he thought, had simply been one more pawn. "Except Bill Cooper died in order to keep the USSR alive," he pointed out sadly. "I wonder how he would have felt about that...given a choice, I mean."

Nir had a ready answer. "Soldiers are trained to die, you know that. Besides, he probably went the way he preferred." The "gray" thinker had a black and white answer when it was necessary.

Terry's confusion was now giving way to wonder. "Why are you telling me this? It seems like things are turning out just as you Israelis want it. The U.S. has another Watergate, Reagan gets impeached, or whatever, and Bush assumes power. He moderates our foreign policy. Russia doesn't collapse economically. And the world has a harmonious, three-way balance of power, the U.S. Russia and China, just the way God and Israel planned."

"Except something has gone wrong. It's been over nine months since the shootdown and we now feel that Reagan has somehow miraculously been able to survive. I was able to talk to North early on and apparently, right after the incident, your Attorney General and Secretary of State seized important documents and were able to contain the scandal by eliminating most of the damaging evidence. Like I say, it's been a miracle, but so far Reagan appears to have fought off the coup."

Now the Israeli's motivation was becoming clearer "So now you are frightened because your country had prior knowledge of the 'coup' and didn't alert Reagan, right? Maybe you didn't back the right guy, huh? Maybe you backed the loser of the coup."

"Yeah, that's about it." But the worst was yet to come. "And now it looks as if the people near Reagan are trying to drag us Israelis into the limelight. It's very embarrassing for us. We were never to have been exposed as the country dealing with Iran. Your George Shultz and Ed Meese are responsible for our embarrassment and exposure...we've been *compromised*. For Chrissakes, Meese even labeled it Iran-Contra. That alone put the media attention on the Middle East and Israel. North lured us into this plan and we need your help. Contact him if you can. We must know what your government is doing and thinking and, most of all, who's in charge."

But getting to North? That would be impossible for Terry. North was only accessible to him now by satellite television and newspaper articles. Terry hadn't even been able, so far, to get an "audience" with Rodriguez.

"But we're especially frightened by your government's behavior here in Mexico," Nir added. "They are proceeding with Phase 2 of Screw Worm as if nothing happened. And we're afraid we'll now be exposed as an accomplice in all of this. That wouldn't appear kosher to the world for Israel to be conspiring with elements of the CIA, KGB and DFS to arm the Third World."

"No, I suppose not," Terry said in agreement. "But has any direct action been taken against you, or are you just reacting out of paranoia?"

"We had a break-in at the embassy in Mexico City. It was very professional and they knew exactly what they were looking for. All the material stolen was very *compromising* data...data we had intercepted about the shootdown and evidence of our involvement in 'Screw Worm.'

"But even more disconcerting to me is that we must have a double agent in our own embassy. They knew exactly where to locate the pertinent files. Shit! Sometimes I hate this profession!"

"And you think Rodriguez and his group are behind the break-in?"

"Yes."

"So what can I do with this knowledge?" Terry asked. "It appears to me it's out of our control. I'm barely able to keep on speaking terms with Marr. I've demanded a meeting with Rodriguez, but I don't know if I'll ever get one."

With the twinkling in Nir's one good eye, Terry believed he was now, finally, going to find out what they really wanted. Camel jockeys, he thought. Always a hidden agenda.

"We know how to get a meeting," Nir continued. "That's where you come in. We could stage another international incident right here in Gaudalajara. All you have to do is alert me when another large shipment of cocaine comes through your facility. We could assist you in seizing and moving the entire shipment to another location, say by truck and that would give us all something to negotiate with. But most of all, that would neutralize Rodriguez. We could serve him up to Reagan as a gift. It is our fear that unless we do something drastic, he will blackmail us all, my government, me, you, your CIA. He will play us all against each other unless we get him first."

To prove their support to the winner, the Israelis now had to deliver big. And how to do that? If they could get the "goods" on the CIA and the ones behind the coup, they would have an ace to deal with. But they needed more than Terry's cooperation in order to do it the way Nir had just suggested. They needed his knowledge and information about "Screw Worm's" facilities and network in Guadalajara.

And what did he know? He knew the Agency was dealing in drugs. *That was valuable information.* That knowledge, in the right hands, is "neutralizing material". And now it was clear what the Israeli really wanted from Terry. He could help the Israelis neutralize Rodriguez.

Nir could probably see that Terry was wavering. He apparently felt compelled to play his last ace in order to portray Rodriguez as the evil man Terry believed him to be.

"We have agents who say they know for sure he was *compromised* years ago while in Southeast Asia by communist agents." Nir was playing the commie card.

"Did the *compromise* you refer to involve heroin out of Laos?" Terry asked.

"How did you know that?"

"I worked with Air America, remember? It was common knowledge at Air Force Intelligence level that communist elements were trying to lure Americans into the narcotics trade in order to *compromise* them and convert them into double agents."

"Yes we have confirmed that," the Israeli replied. "Rodriguez was *compromised*. But when the Agency found out, they felt it better to use him as a triple agent as is often the case than to embarrass itself through charges and an investigation. Shortly after his return from Vietnam, he was basically suspended during the investigation and then, allegedly, released by the Agency due to medical reasons. But we know the real reason. He and his supervisors in Vietnam were all dirty. They were trafficking out of the Golden Triangle."

"So your people know for sure that Rodriguez conspired with Ortega in order to stage the shootdown?" Terry asked, needing to be reassured once again.

"Yes, like I said we've been following him for years and we intercepted message traffic. I suppose you're right about one thing. Democracy just doesn't work."

Terry's head was now swimming from the avalanche of data relayed to him by the Israeli agent as Seneca N13LM was handed off to Guadalajara approach.

But most of all he was recalling the personal warning that Rodriguez had given him at the bunker meeting in Arkansas. "I am a professional agent," were his words. "You are an amateur. Don't play spook and don't cross us."

Terry was now thinking about doing both. Mainly, he knew that failing to report *any* meeting with a foreign agent would be considered collaborating with the enemy. He had already met secretly with Fenue and now here was Nir. But who could he trust to report it to? Who could he trust at all at this point? Was the Israeli his friend or was he just trying to use him to *compromise* Rodriguez?

Terry was feeling alone and there was no one in the intelligence community to turn to. He had been told to turn to U.S. Consul-General Daniel Darrach "in an emergency." But Terry had construed these instructions as applying in the event of him being *compromised* by *foreign* agents, not people from his own side.

And how deep did the conspiracy go? What if Darrach was in on the drug trafficking? That would be like walking into the lion's den and locking the door. He needed protection *from* the CIA, a safe haven similar to that afforded by the witness protection program. But where could that be found? Probably only in Moscow.

The worst thing he could do, he felt, was open another tier of problems by taking Darrach into his confidence. That would be a big risk...one he feared to calculate. No...he did not need to draw attention to himself and perhaps become a target of a DEA investigation while residing on foreign soil, if he wasn't already.

"Pick your time and pick your place," he again remembered his grandfather saying. He had to get out of Mexico, he felt, and deal with this problem on American soil and hopefully, surrounded by friends.

He had to turn to his inward strength—the strength that had always been there from his high school days in ROTC, to his military days in Southeast Asia.

Terry was certain of one thing. He decided that he would not tell Nir about the "drug samples" he had seized from the July 5th shipment. His priority was to get his family safely out of Mexico. His "evidence" was his only trump card in this deadly game. If an agent like Nir was afraid, Terry knew he was in over his head.

"Roger, one-three Lima-Mike is clear to land," the Mexican ATC said as Terry "hit the numbers" with his Seneca on that July 16th afternoon.

"Señor Fierro wishes you to report to his office, Capitan Reed," the ground controller said as the aircraft cleared the active runway. Fierro knew Terry had a passenger and probably knew who it was. The problem of reporting the Nir meeting solved itself.

Upon deplaning near Terry's office, Nir was unmistakenly anxious to make his getaway. "Okay, let's keep in touch and think about what we need from you. Come by the embassy whenever you're in Mexico City. But don't telephone me with any sensitive information. I have no confidence in the security of our communications, at least without a decoding device. But above all, if you don't trust us, try to get to North. Tell him we must meet. Rodriguez is out of control."

Nir then spotted the armed guard approaching the plane and shifted the discussion. "OK, the building progress appears on schedule. I'll file a report to that effect with my people. Keep up the good work. Let's make the project a success. And by the way, *feliz cumpleaños.*"

Yeah, happy birthday, Terry thought, as Nir walked way and the Mexican guard helped him push the plane into the hangar. Thirty-nine years old and involved in a foreign intelligence operation that was coming apart at the seams.

Someone had sabotaged the Mexican operation. Their motives weren't clear, but the results were. The prototype of cooperation that Terry had believed he was involved in was at an end. Snuffed out in its formative stage, the cooperation between the KGB, the Israelis, the CIA, and the DFS would not be truly tested. Or had it been? Until the likes of Felix Rodriguez and the other "professional" communist haters either die or are killed, experiments such as this are surely doomed.

No one was to be trusted and everyone was to be feared. Everyone except his wife and John Desko, he thought. A pretty small circle of friends after 39 years.

His goal of being a millionaire by the age of 40 was starting to slip from his grasp. His goal now was more modest: *Just to reach the age of 40!*

Maslow, the psychologist Air Force Intelligence used as its model of mind-control, was very much in his mind. He had hoped to attain the pinnacle of Maslow's pyramid of needs and be "self-actualizing" by the time he reached 40. Right now, however, his focus was on the bottom rung of the pyramid—survival!

* * *

That was the last time Terry ever saw the man he knew as Pat Weber. He would later hear about and view with great suspicion the circumstances surrounding Nir's untimely death. In November, 1988, Nir met his demise in the crash of a single-engine Cessna T-210 near Morelia. Why was he aboard a small private plane, a mode of transportation he so dreadfully feared, Terry wondered? The passport he was carrying listed the dead, one-eyed Israeli as "Pat Weber."

It also left the world wondering: What was Amiram Nir doing in this remote area of Mexico? Reed's account goes a long way toward answering that question. What the world knew of Nir's clandestine activities consisted only of whispered rumors.

It had been assumed that Iran-Contra had effectively put an end to Nir's political career as the Israeli Prime Minister's consultant on terrorism. In the Spring of 1988, he resigned from the Israeli prime minister's office and moved to London, with only a few knowing the nature of his work. He seemed to have dropped of the earth's edge. There were reports that Nir was preparing his cover for a new spy mission.[3] Death snuffed out the life of one of the few men who could possibly have known for sure the depth of George Bush's involvement in Iran-Contra and the "coup" he revealed to Terry.

1. *Report of the Tower Commission*, B-145, B-147; Deposition of Craig Fuller, Vice President George Bush's chief of staff, 3/30/87, PP 23-33.
2. *Report of the Congressional Committees Investigating the Iran-Contra Affair*, H. Rept. No. 100-433, Felix Rodriguez Becomes Disaffected, p. 72.
3. Raviv, Dan and Yossi Melman, *Every Spy A Prince*, Houghton Mifflin Company, Boston, 1990, p. 341-42.

CHAPTER 29

MAX OR FELIX?

The traffic on the outskirts of Mexico City was beyond congested as Terry Reed guided his orange Nissan pickup truck between the craters in the highway that August night in 1987.

To make matters even worse, it was pouring rain and his sole passenger, Patrick Juin, had not ceased talking for the nearly six hours since they had left Guadalajara. Their destination, the Hotel Century in Mexico City, situated on the edge of the *Zona Rosa* district, was still 40 kilometers away.

As he slowed the stiffly-sprung vehicle to a near stop to negotiate a series of *topes* (speed bumps), Terry turned to his chatting companion.

"Tell me, Patrick, with the Mexican highways as fucked up as they are from their natural state of disrepair, why does your government waste so much money constructing and maintaining these damn humps on the roads? Who the hell can speed anyway in all this traffic?"

Juin, who preferred to think of himself as a *Chilango* (the ruling class of Mexico whose ancestry could be traced to Europe), and an expert on all subjects, quipped: "This is something you Americans could learn from us. We call these *topes* 'sleeping policemen.' They serve the purpose of slowing the traffic without the need of so many patrolmen, as your country has. Speaking of which, why does the United States need so many policemen? When I travel there, it makes me paranoid!"

"Paranoid!" Terry shot back as he pulled the truck into a service station near the Toluca exit on the northwest edge of the world's largest city. "Patrick my friend, you have no idea of what paranoia is truly about."

Paranoia was the reason Terry was driving that day instead of flying his airplane, as would have been usual and much more practical. Paranoia, though Juin did not know it, was exactly why Terry had invited him along. Paranoia was the reason he had been losing countless hours of sleep lately as he planned a way to extricate himself and his family from the dangerous state of affairs that had developed since his discovery that the CIA was, in fact, in the drug business.

Terry had crossed the line. If he had been on an accountant's spread sheet, he would now be listed as a number in red, a *liability*; no longer a "black number," an *asset*. He knew too much. And that put him on Felix Rodriguez' shit list and maybe his *hit* list.

He kept rolling Nancy Reagan's slogan through his mind to keep his nerves calm in preparation for the next day's meeting.

"Just say no, just say no, just say no..." he kept thinking. "No matter what they offer, just say NO!"

Juin's constant boasting brought Terry from his trance as his Mexican friend and tour guide of the past 14 months offered yet another chapter in the life and times of Super Stud. "Have I ever told you the story of the time a virgin girl friend of mine called me and asked me to deflower her on the night before her wedding to another guy?"

As Terry aimed his truck toward the city's center, he actually welcomed the never-ending 'stories' his macho companion was conjuring up. They temporarily took his mind off his problems.

"No amigo, I don't believe you have, but I'll bet you're gonna tell me."

As Juin droned on, and on, about fulfilling his impassioned girl friend's desire to give her maiden head to the man she truly loved rather than her betrothed, Terry's mind drifted away to the problems and dangers at hand.

He flashed back to the July 5th discovery in his company's Guadalajara warehouse—to the aluminum conex containers filled with cocaine. That was the day his worst suspicions were confirmed.

CIA contract pilots and operatives were involved in a conspiracy to smuggle tons, literally tons, of cocaine through Reed's warehouse facilities, which were clearly being used as a transshipment and temporary storage area for narcotics.

This was not the way it was supposed to be. The business plan he had developed for the CIA was to conceal a weapons transshipment facility under the guise of a machine tool trading company. He would not have been part of any plan to use his proprietary to smuggle drugs into the U.S. The hypocrisy of his government's position on this infectious epidemic thoroughly disgusted him. One arm of the government which had taken on a life of its own, the DEA, was responsible for stemming the deadly flow of cocaine. The other arm, the CIA, was plainly fueling this so-called "War on Drugs."

From that day of discovery, Terry's world had changed forever. For the first time in his intelligence career, he had drawn the line. He had reached his moral bottom. And he feared not only for himself, but his family. He was demanding answers and getting concocted responses from his local "handler." Rodriguez, he knew, was the core of the problem. From what Amiram Nir and George Fenue had told him a month earlier, Rodriguez was not only dealing in drugs but was a double or triple agent as well.

All the key people who had drawn him into this mess were either not who they had claimed to be...or were dead. Thoughts of mortality were once again on the front burner. People had died! Agents had been "terminated", he was convinced! And that wasn't all that had been terminated.

Technoimpex was "terminating" their part in the operation. The Japanese were "terminating" Applied Technologies' existence by suing Terry in federal court. Business relationships that had taken him years to cultivate were disintegrating right before his eyes.

He had simply and unintentionally gotten in way over his head, and having noted Amiram Nir's behavior during their last visit, Terry wasn't the only one that was "reacting" instead of "acting". Even the Mossad appeared to be in over its head.

He was now convinced that the KGB was the only intelligence agency that knew what was really going on. He had felt like contacting Fenue again to see if Moscow knew who was actually running the United States at this point, or who was the real President. Fenue had given him more information on Barry Seal in 60 seconds than he had learned about him in three years.

He'd even dreamed of Barry. And he was laughing. From his grave, he was laughing. Not at Terry, particularly—just laughing. Laughing at the whole fucking mess. When Terry awoke, he walked outside and demanded Seal to return from his grave and give him counsel. That didn't work.

So, he had demanded a meeting with Rodriguez to negotiate his way out of this operation. His bargaining chip? The 20 kilos of cocaine he had taken from the shipment. On that day in the warehouse, Terry had the presence of mind to take two large bags of the drug and hide them. This would be the "evidence" that his handler, Mitch Marr, had demanded earlier as proof of his suspicions that someone inside the organization "was dirty." So far, he was sure that "evidence" was probably all that was keeping him alive.

Juin was just winding down with, literally, the climax of his story about deflowering his old girl friend when Terry pulled the truck up in front of the Hotel Century at Liverpool 152 in the *Zona Rosa* section of the city, the same "spook hotel" where he and Janis had stayed the previous Christmas. It was August 19th, 1987 and the major players of the Iran-Contra scandal by now could only be reached through their attorneys. Things were unraveling all over.

The preceding day, August 18th, a *SECRET* federal communiqué had been sent to the FBI in Arkansas and CIA headquarters alerting them that the national media had discovered Mena, Arkansas. The residue of the Agency's "dirty" operations there were in danger of becoming as visible as the dirty ring left in a bathtub after it drains. People were getting desperate, loose ends and ravelings had to be taken care of. (See end of chapter 18.)

Juin unloaded the truck in preparation for valet parking, something Terry hated. Valet parking, to him, was the Mexican equivalent of the demolition derby. Terry went to the front desk, announced his arrival and inquired as to the arrival of Señor Maximo Gomez.

The desk clerk summoned the manager, Victor Dorantes G., as his card read, who said Gomez would not be checking in but had been there earlier and had changed the time and the site of meeting to the following evening in San Miguel de Allende, a city 100 miles to the northwest. The manager informed Terry that Gomez had said to check in at the Hotel Posada de la Aldea when he got there and await further contact.

Just like in the movies, Terry thought to himself. To make sure your contact is not being followed, he is run from location to location so that he can be observed and approached in an environment of choice. Slick!

Terry and Juin would spend the night in Mexico City, which was good news to Juin because by now his story about the old girl friend had aroused in him an unyielding desire to find her, so he spent the evening pouring through the Mexico City telephone directory, without success.

"These fucking third world phone books!" he shouted in frustration. "At least America has a good phone system...too many policemen but a good phone system."

The next day the two left for San Miguel, arriving in the early afternoon of August 20th to check in at the appointed place. (See chapter end.) Terry's tension was beginning to show as they drove north and Juin's constant chatter was now wearing thin. Being cooped up with a overly talkative, know-it-all *Chilango* as he solved the world's ills, was, in itself, an ordeal.

Had it not been for the fact that Terry wanted a witness to the impending meeting, he would never have brought Juin along. But it was a poker game and Terry was building a bluff and Juin, hopefully, would be seen as a wild card. Juin, Terry was told by Marr, was rumored to be an intelligence operative of sorts, one of the network of underlings that kept tabs on foreigners and reported his findings to the DFS. Marr had cautioned him on this when he discovered the Reeds and Juins were befriending each other. He'd kept the information to himself thinking it might come in handy as a channel for disinformation. Terry had no way of confirming any of this rumor, passed along by a drunk, but now was the time to use any and all resources.

Terry knew that he might be exposing Patrick to danger, but he hoped Gomez would perceive Juin as someone he perhaps had confided in, thereby not being able to determine how widely disseminated the drug information might become...if something bad happened to Terry and his family. It was a risk...but a calculated one.

The city of San Miguel is one of Mexico's prime tourist attractions, with its rich history and old Spanish colonial architecture. For reasons not clear, it is also the retirement city of choice for many former American intelligence agents. What spiked Terry's curiosity was that two unauthorized shipments of "tools" and one confirmed shipment of drugs previously shipped through his company, had originated in San Miguel.

As the truck turned off the manicured, cobblestone Calle Ancha de S. Antonio and into the parking area bordering the lush gardens of the picturesque hotel, Juin volunteered, "I'll get the bags."

Once in the hotel the desk clerk informed Terry that no one had left any messages. The two checked into room 312, and being weary from the travel, the tension, and perpetual conversation, Terry decided to rest and to wait. He wanted a fully charged battery for the mission that lay ahead. Three hours later, at around 4 PM, the desk clerk phoned the room, awakening Terry from his nap.

"Mr. Gomez called and arranged a dinner meeting at 7 PM at *Restaurante El Faro,* it is one half block southeast of *La Plaza,*" the desk man said. The games go on, Terry thought to himself.

At 7 PM exactly Terry and Patrick walked into the restaurant, but not before Patrick had first scouted out the place himself to determine the ambiance. Terry had debated in his own mind whether to carry the Smith & Wesson 9MM pistol that was hidden in his truck. He decided it would be unnecessary to bring it to the meeting after Juin informed him the restaurant was high-class with a well-lit, open courtyard at the center of the main dining area, complete with a fountain. It seemed like an unlikely place for any kind of violence since Juin said the establishment was "jumping with action."

After an inquiry of the maitre d', they learned that no one named "Gomez" had yet arrived, so they decided to wait in the area containing an upscale bar.

Both ordered a drink and Juin, a musician himself, was drawn to the alluring flute and guitar music of the group playing across the room. Terry surveyed the room and saw no sign of the man he now feared, the man whose hands, he felt, held his family's safety and future.

About 30 minutes passed, when Terry's eyes rose to a small private balcony area overlooking the musicians, and suddenly spotted Gomez. He wasn't alone. He was sitting with a woman, a classic Latin beauty, at a table along the balcony's edge.

Upon making eye contact with Reed, Gomez excused himself from his female companion and disappeared through a doorway above. He reappeared in the entrance to the bar and Terry rose to meet him.

"Shall I call you Felix or shall I call you Max?" Terry asked, staring pointedly into Rodriguez' eyes. It was the first meeting since Terry had learned Rodriguez' true identity.

He was trying to block from his mind the information Marr had passed on after their confrontation. "Yeah, Gomez....I mean Rodriguez is one tough fuckin' hombre. He personally killed Ché Guevara, then cut off his fuckin' hands for Agency I.D. purposes. Only question is, was Ché dead or alive when Felix chopped 'em off?"

"I actually prefer Maximo, but Felix will do," Rodriguez replied coyly. Seeing Juin was having the desired effect. Rodriguez was visibly upset that Terry had a companion.

"Who's he?" Rodriguez asked glaring suspiciously toward Juin.

Terry mustered up a smile as he said, "Just a friend along for the ride. Who's the woman with you?

"Nobody you need to know about," Rodriguez shot back. Looking at Juin, Rodriguez informed Terry's highly attentive companion, "You'll have to excuse me and Mr. Reed. We need to have a private business discussion."

Things were going as Terry had planned, at least initially. He and Rodriguez were in a public place, and there was a witness. Terry felt safe, at least while they were inside the restaurant. The feeling of security would give him an emotional edge during the ensuing discussion.

Juin remained at the bar and the two men were shown to a table Terry had chosen earlier. It was strategically located so that Juin could observe them from a distance through the course of their conversation.

"So I thought you were a big boy, a trained spy," Rodriguez started immediately, in a taunting tone. "What's this cry-baby attitude all about? Misuse of our warehouse?"

Sitting there face-to-face with the man Nir had said was responsible for Bill Cooper's death had a nerve-wracking effect Terry knew he had to disguise.

Putting on his best poker face, Terry attacked back, "Transshipment of tons of narcotics through my business and me being concerned about the legal ramifications is not reflecting a cry-baby attitude! A narcotics investigation could bring down the whole operation. If you're going to continue with this attitude, I'll just walk out of here and go to the consul-general's office *and* the DEA and tell them *all* I know. Don't provoke me, Felix!"

Rodriguez' attitude changed immediately. He plainly had not anticipated a counter-attack, in a public place. "OK, so it's over for you. You want out and I want you out. The only thing standing between you and your family attaining safe passage out of Mexico is your vow of silence and the return of our stolen property."

Rodriguez was referring to the 20 kilos of cocaine Terry had taken from the shipment in Guadalajara. Marr originally had told Terry it was a "controlled delivery" by the CIA and Drug Enforcement Administration. A controlled delivery is, in essence, a sting operation undertaken in order to track the drugs' path and distribution and to ensnare traffickers and arrest them.

But if that had been true, Terry had reasoned, how did Rodriguez know exactly how much was in the total shipment and, therefore, how much was missing? And why would he care and be so concerned? But what really troubled Terry was the warning earlier by Nir about his suspicion that Rodriguez was actually a double-agent, that he was "dirty" and was a "loose cannon" about to expose everyone else's involvement in these clandestine affairs. No one could be sure of his motives. Was Rodriguez just *loco* or was there a more sinister motive?

What Terry did not know was, as this meeting was taking place, Mexican DFS (the Mexican CIA) agent Raul Fierro and his goons back in Guadalajara were ransacking Terry's office and warehouse frantically searching for the missing 20 kilos he had taken as evidence. Had they located it, this story probably would never have been told. Reed would have joined Seal and Camp and Cooper in that place where "ya don't need flight plans ta fly."

In the dining room, with Juin as an eyewitness, Terry put his cards on the table. It was time to cut a deal.

"I'm a businessman," he reasoned with Rodriguez. "That was your attraction to me in the first place. Let's negotiate an acceptable conclusion to these affairs. I've got something you want and you've got something I want."

Rodriguez had an offer at the ready. "In exchange for your silence, I'm prepared to pay a handsome severance package to help you relocate to Arkansas. In exchange, of course, I would expect that your 'evidence', as you call it, be given to Mitch prior to your departure.

"I would also expect you to do the proper thing and phase yourself out of the operation gradually over the next couple of months so that you don't bring unnecessary attention to yourself or *Maquinaria Internacional*. Let's stay friends. We're all in this together. Mitch tells me you know both I and Oliver North have appeared before Congress and that's not a fun place to be. They would like nothing better than to send us all to prison. They're all a bunch of communist cocksuckers. So you better keep your silence or you'll end up there, too. *Telling a very unbelievable story, I might add.*"

He paused to let Reed digest what he had said and then added in Godfather fashion, "You leave with my blessing. Just keep your end of the bargain."

In was all over in 20 minutes. Terry felt somewhat relieved. He had known that it would be dangerous to confront Rodriguez and now felt, foolishly as it turned out, that he had struck an honorable deal. But he didn't know what was happening in his office in Guadalajara.

Rodriguez exited the restaurant with his *mujer para la noche* (woman for the night) and Terry and Juin stayed to enjoy a leisurely dinner, the first relaxing one for Terry in the weeks since he found the cocaine. The perfect way to diet with immediate results, he now knew, was to be involved in a Mexican standoff with the CIA. He had finally lost the weight he had promised himself he would lose years earlier in Arkansas.

After finishing their dinner, Juin gave Terry a macho grin and suggested, "We're near the City of Leon. If we can drive through there tomorrow I'll try to locate an old girl friend of mine who plays the piano. She has a great sister, who's always had the hots for me. Maybe she's ready to be deflowered."

Terry chuckled, not realizing that the worst for him was yet to come.

Posada de la Aldea

LR 0001   Nº 424

Tels. 2-10-22 y 2-12-96   Canaco 104   R.N.T. 11209003701   R.F.C. ALD 8309303 AA

Nombre		Habitación No	Plan	Tarifa	Depósito
TERRY & KENT REED		312	E	28,100.00	PAGARE

Entrada	Salida	Tipo de Habitación	No. de Personas	Observaciones	
20-8-87	21-8-87	DOBLE	2	EL PRECIO INCLUYE EL IVA	

Fecha 20-8-87

28,100.00

POSADA DE LA ALDEA

CALLE ANCHA DE S ANTONIO
S. MIGUEL DE ALLENDE, GTO.
MEXICO

LA-2   Nº 4292

Reg. Fed. de Caus. ALD-830950-3A-A   Tels. 2-10-22 y 2-12-96
San Miguel de Allende, Gto.

TELEFONO LARGA DISTANCIA

Ciudad _Chula Jal_   No. Teléfono 5-22-49

Persona _Gic_

De parte de _Sr Reed_

Fecha 20-8-87

Autorizó _____ Gto. No. 312   Importe 767-

Nota _____ 566

Tlc 13   150

Total 4,483

29-1. Receipt from Hotel in San Miguel de Allende, where Terry Reed met the real "Max Gomez" i.e., Felix Rodriguez, and "crossed the Rubicon" from CIA asset to liability.

Lucas Service

Paul Villett
Gerente de Reconstrucción
de Componentes

Lucas Service Mexico S A de C V
RIO TIZAPAN No. 1525
COL. ATLAS
GUADALAJARA, JAL.
44870 MEXICO
TELS. 39-21-11 39-21-12 39-22-90

---

amisa s.a.

ORGANIZACION
MANTENIMIENTO DE
INMUEBLES

ARQ. ALFONSO GONZALEZ VELASCO

AV. GUADALUPE 1115
45000 GUADALAJARA, JAL.

TELS. 22-27-80
22-54-41

NISSAN
REPUESTOS ORIGINALES

VAMSA

LUZ DELIA ALVAREZ
VENTAS MOSTRADOR

VEHICULOS AUTOMOTRICES Y MARINOS, S.A DE C.V.

AV. NIÑOS HEROES 963
TELEX 684172
44100 GUADALAJARA JAL

TELS. 14-60-20
14-63-97
13-17-52

Colenta
Representantes de Equipos Foto Proceso

ELIAS PEREZGOMEZ M.
DIRECTOR GENERAL

16-43-45   15-72-01

COLENTA DE OCCIDENTE S. A.
Calle Paz 475 Col. Juan Manuel Vallarta Tels. 16-00-27 y 16-10-78 Guadalajara 44680 Mexico

---

felipe gonzalez lugo

**cromo
scanner**

cromoscanner s.a.
herrera y cairo no. 2771
fracc. circunvalacion Vallarta
tels. 91-36 17-17-59 17-41-95
guadalajara jal.
44680 mexico

durango no. 245-401
tels. 91-5-511-52-60 5-46-32-97
colonia roma
06700 mexico d.f.

29-2. As a result of Reed's "divorce" from the CIA's black operation in Mexico, he would be leaving behind many legitimate business activities he had developed while working undercover in Mexico.

CHAPTER 30

SEVERANCE PAY

Terry was aghast. He was looking into his normally-neat, well-kept office and realized he had been the victim of a black-bag job.

It had been a day and a half since leaving San Miguel and his meeting with Felix Rodriguez. He had returned to the Guadalajara airport, hoping to continue with business as usual and fulfill his agreement with Rodriguez. But he couldn't shake the fear that comes from knowing too much, and being a liability because of it.

He had crossed the line, and was surely now viewed as a whistle-blower. If there ever was an investigation, he would be the subject of it.

But after entering his office, which showed no signs of forcible entry, Reed found something very unsettling. Someone had ransacked his office records and had spent a great deal of time conducting a thorough search of the warehouse as well.

Plainly, someone had been looking for his "evidence," and probably any embarrassing documents that would provide police with information about other "unauthorized shipments" by the Agency.

What he didn't know, and had to find out, was *when* the illegal entry was made. If it had been done *after* his handshake with Rodriguez 36 hours earlier, Terry was being double-crossed. If the search had preceded the agreement in San Miguel de Allende, that would be understandable since Reed did, in fact, possess something that belonged to them. He had to confront Mitch Marr, and right away, to get the answer.

A short time later Terry was being let into the walled compound by the Marr's maid. He found Mitch in his usual condition, sitting in his papa-san chair next to his Rambo tapes with a bottle of bourbon within easy reach.

"So Mitch, have you been in contact with Felix since our meeting in San Miguel?"

Reed winced as Marr emptied the contents of the shot glass into his mouth and ran his tongue around the inside of the glass, a technique to extract the last drop. In answer to Reed's question he grumbled, "Yeah he contacted me. I'm glad you guys worked everythin' out. It takes pressure offa me and I don't need any more fuckin' pressure. I had enough pressure flying 123s for Air America."

Reed needed to divert Marr from the war stories that were always triggered by the booze and back to the matter at hand.

"So what was your understanding of our agreement?" Terry asked.

"It's simple. You give us our shit and we give you some fuckin' money," Marr replied.

"So, Felix didn't mention to you anything about a plan to undermine my negotiating position by 'locating' the evidence you've been trying to talk me out of?"

"Naw, naw... what the fuck do you mean?"

From the tone of Marr's voice, Terry was sure he was lying. But that didn't stop Marr from rambling on.

"Hey, this is the Agency you're dealin' with. These are honorable guys, patriots. They won't fuck ya. You been watchin' too many movies. Speakin' of movies, do you wanna see Stallone's latest. We can have a drink. My wife's gone ta the States. It's only me and the maid. Besides, I got some money here for ya. Here's two grand for your travel expenses."

"I don't have time for a drink, but since you brought up the subject of money, Felix discussed severance pay with me and said that you would inform me of how that would be worked out and how much we're talking about."

"I'm not sure about the amount, but they'll be generous. We'll pay you as you leave, provided we get your 'evidence' back."

"Since you don't think it was our people who rifled my office should I get the Mexican police over to the warehouse to officially complain about the illegal entry?"

"Christ, no. If nuthin' valuable is missin', just go on about your business. We don't want any fuckin' Mexican police pokin' around. You're a short-timer, you're goin' home. Besides, it was probably just some of Fierro's people lookin' for somethin' anyway."

Marr was unconvincing. Terry knew that he was lying by the forced expression on his face, but he knew that his priority now was to collect his "severance pay" and get his family out of Mexico. As he was leaving the house, Marr reached for the bottle and settled back into his chair dressed in his usual attire of an armless undershirt and Bermuda shorts to enjoy his latest pirated copy of Rambo. It was mid-afternoon and Marr was well on his way. He loved it when his wife was away since she could not nag him about hitting the bottle, or berate him for watching the violent movies she hated.

* * *

"It just won't work. We're in over our heads and these people could find us anywhere in the world," a worried Janis Reed argued as she feed the pigeons that day near the Benito Juarez statue in a Guadalajara park. "Besides, we would need a lot more money than we have now in order to take an indefinite 'vacation.'"

Both Terry and Janis had driven to the city for what he always called, from his Air Force days, a "standup briefing." It was the first time since his return from San Miguel de Allende that the couple had talked together in detail about their plight. They had decided against talking at home for fear that the Agency had placed bugging devices in their house in Ajijic. They were always concerned, too, about Geronimo, their over-nosey gardener who always seemed to be eavesdropping when they talked.

Terry knew his wife well and felt she could handle the truth. Theirs was a special relationship and she had never been a millstone around his neck, especially when they entered the dark world. Just the opposite, she had embraced it with enthusiasm.

"I'm gonna tell it to you straight if you promise not to revert to being a Baptist on me." The taunt was intentional because Terry knew Janis hated being categorized as a Baptist. "I was *raised* Baptist" she always corrected him.

While feeding the pigeons, Terry looked around to insure no one could hear his conversation.

"You remember the day I took John (Desko) with me to the warehouse? While I was alone that day I took the liberty of hiding two bags of white powdery substance that I intended to use as evidence to prove to Marr that his people were in the drug business. That evidence is now our ticket out of here if we play our cards right."

"Terry, what are you trying to tell me?" Janis screeched and then quickly lowered her voice to the level of a whisper. "Are you trying to tell me you've got cocaine hidden somewhere! And you're trying to blackmail our way out of here?"

Her mind worked quickly. "Terry, we're going to all end up dead out of this deal!"

A *cerveza* purchased from a vending cart did little to calm her as the gravity of the situation began to sink in. In a few moments, she regained her composure and began to think how best to grapple with their problems. She quickly realized they needed a plan.

"So the Air Force paid you to develop battle plans, you got any *good* ideas now?" Janis said forcing a smile. Terry lifted her chin and kissed her whispering, "You know I always do."

"I figured you were going to say that and...'*what's the worse that can happen?*'"

A plethora of alternatives were discussed and the most viable emerged: Plan A: They would leave immediately and head for the U.S. border and then split up just south of the Rio Grande. Janis would cross the border with the children and then Terry would take off to some as yet unknown destination, probably Thailand.

Or, they could opt for Plan B: Secretly, they would load the motor home, exchange the dope for the money, leave Ajijic abruptly during the night, zig-zag across Mexico to Cancun, put the motor home on a freighter, and disguised as tourists, head for some remote area like Australia.

And then there was Plan C, the one they both knew in their hearts they had to do: Go along with the Agency's divorce proceedings, return to the U.S. together, hopefully without being harmed in the process, and report their findings to the proper authorities, probably the Iran-Contra committees. Plan C, he knew, was doing the moral thing—doing it the hard way.

That day in Guadalajara, however, both were aware that to implement any of their plans required lots of money. Janis agreed for her husband to proceed with negotiations about the cocaine, but she made it clearly understood that she didn't want to know any of the details.

They returned to Chapala and immediately began preparations for a quick departure.

Janis, who had discovered early retirement in the *Land of Mañana* for a person of her age could bring on mental atrophy, was teaching in private school in Ajijic. She began quietly making plans for obtaining a replacement for her elementary class.

Terry began winding down his business operations in a manner designed not to draw attention to his departure. He told associates that the catastrophic devaluation of the Mexican pesetas was the basis for his reason to return home.

Janis, who acted as the family accountant, was concentrating on their financial needs and both she and her husband felt the urgency of finding out what Rodriguez' "severance package" would be. The amount would strongly influence their future plans.

Several days later, after several unsuccessful attempts to locate Marr, Reed found him at a local watering hole, The Posada, during Happy Hour.

Marr was sitting on an *equipali* chair in the corner drinking by himself. As Reed approached, Marr motioned him to sit down. "Since you're leavin', I guess it's OK that we be seen in public. What are you drinkin'?"

Terry ordered a Dos Equis dark and slid his chair closer to Marr, keeping his back to the wall. He was paranoid, extremely paranoid. Visions of Barry Seal being riddled with bullets kept flashing before him. It was totally out of character, but he was now carrying a concealed, 9MM semi-automatic wherever he went.

"We need to work out the conditions of exchange for everything," Terry began quietly. "And I need to know how much severance pay we're talking about."

Marr said Rodriguez was unhappy because he felt Terry was blackmailing his way out. So why, Marr asked, didn't Reed just turn over the drugs and he would be "rewarded handsomely later." Marr then said that if Reed did "the right thing" he would still be on the Agency's friendly side and could be eligible to "be tapped" for other assignments in the future.

Reed knew this was a ploy and he wanted no part of it. "Mitch, now you wouldn't do that. You didn't survive your years in Air America by being stupid. I don't consider myself stupid, so don't insult me with such offers. The only thing I'll find acceptable is a plan that gives me the security I need while I extricate my family and myself from this mess. Now, tell me a plan where we can all accomplish our objectives."

Marr emptied the tequila from his shot glass, bit the slice of lime and wiped his mouth on his bare arm. "Well, it was worth a try, but you're right, I wouldn't go for it either. OK, here's the deal. We'll pay ya a hundred grand in cash when ya hand me your evidence."

Reed countered immediately with the plan he had devised during many sleepless nights since his last meeting with Marr. "I'll give you half the evidence, you pay me the full amount and upon my safe arrival in the U.S., I'll telephone you and tell you where you can find the other half. I won't double cross them. They know where they can find me and my family in the event I did. And believe me the CIA is the last organization I would *ever* double cross. That, Mitch, is the only way I find acceptable. You can rest assured that I wouldn't try crossing the border with your evidence." Tongue-in-cheek he added, " 'Cause that, Mitch, would be construed as trafficking."

Marr had switched to Bohemia and was downing a mouthful when Terry finished. He brought up a hearty belch, and as he peeled the label from his bottle he said, "I see where you're coming from. I can't approve that, but I'll pass it along. It sounds fair ta me."

Terry got up to leave, tossed down some pesos to cover his bill, and started to turn from the table.

"You ought to be careful about carryin' a gun in Mexico, 'specially a concealed one. It's against the law ya know."

Terry spun around and challenged, "What makes you think I'm carrying a gun?"

Marr smiled. "Fuck, I would be."

Within several days, Marr came to Reed with the news that "they don't like doin' it this way, but I've convinced them that you won't fuck us when you get to the States. So when can I have half of the evidence?"

"Just as soon as I see 10,000 pictures of Benjamin Franklin smilin' at me," Reed said. "And you were right before when you brought up the subject of guns. I am carrying one. This is a dangerous country, you know. The State Department says so!"

Terry found the wait while preparing to leave stressful. So much so that he "grounded" himself and would not fly his airplane—convinced that it would be sabotaged and he would die in a plane crash, just as Emile Camp had more than two years earlier.

For this reason, he arranged for his plane to be flown back by a contract courier pilot so that way he could travel with his family on the return journey. Things appeared to be going as planned. The only thing that impeded their departure was finding a replacement for Janis at the school where she taught English.

The cover story was that Terry's silent partners in the states were re-evaluating their business options in light of the peso devaluation. They needed him there for a marathon meeting and Janis and the children would be traveling with him in order to visit relatives. Since their youngest child, Baxter, was only four months old, they would say that they decided to document their Mexican nanny and take her along as evidence to anyone watching that they intended to return. But Terry devised this as added security because if any violent action were taken against them, there would be one more person, a Mexican national, for the attackers to dispose of.

Outwardly everything appeared normal. But inwardly they were on "red alert," or DEFCON II, as it's called in SAC jargon. No one realized that Janis Reed was now carrying a .38-caliber Smith & Wesson, five-shot airweight pistol everywhere she went, even to school. Among other things, she feared a kidnapping attempt on the children. They allowed Duncan, their four year-old son, to continue his schooling, but only because he attended the same school where she taught and his classroom was two doors away from hers. Terry all but patrolled their home's walled compound and never allowed the other sons out of his sight when Janis wasn't home. "Each child must be continuously accounted for," was the inflexible rule.

All was quiet until Terry returned home from his warehouse on the afternoon of Sept. 18. Just before he walked in the door, Janis, as was her Friday ritual, had called their answering service in Little Rock to check for business messages.

There had been two unexplained calls that day from someone who identified himself as Gene Ogden. He gave no business name, but had left a Little Rock telephone number.

When Terry returned the call the following Monday, he was taken aback when a female voice answered: "Arkansas State Police."

Certain that he had dialed the wrong number, he gathered his composure and asked if a Gene Ogden worked there. He was further surprised when she gave no response and instead transferred him to an extension where a male voice answered "Ogden."

In the conversation that ensued, Ogden said he was with *Trooper Magazine*, a publication of the state police, and was soliciting advertisers. Since he had no business listing in the Little Rock phone book, Terry was curious as to how Ogden had come by the phone number.

When Ogden said he got Reed's number from the Yellow Pages, Reed knew something was not right, especially so when Ogden began to ask where Reed was calling from. "Gosh this sounds like long distance," Ogden said. "Where are you calling from?"

Reed said he was outside the United States on a business trip, but asked Ogden to forward his advertising rates along with a copy of the magazine to see if he would be interested in it for marketing purposes. Reed never received anything.

Though Reed was suspicious, he could not know then that a frame-up against him had started. He was becoming a disposable asset and the Arkansas State Police had been chosen as the instrument to manufacture a crime that would silence, discredit and financially drain him over the next two and a half years.

Being unaware of the "homecoming sting" being prepared for him, Reed had other things on his mind. He foolishly felt certain that he could handle whatever problems awaited him on the other side of the Rio Grande. His attention was diverted to protecting his family and taking care of the "escape" from Mexico. He had to "think like a pilot" and *prioritize* his worry about getting out of Margaritaville, safely. To be certain, they didn't needlessly expose their itinerary—neither Terry or Janis had informed their families, by phone or otherwise, that they were returning to the U.S.

On October 4th, Duncan's fifth birthday, the Reed's broke their communication silence and phoned both grandparents so they could wish the boy happy birthday. But even then, they made no mention of returning home.

But during their brief conversations with family, the Reeds were confronted with another puzzling development. Both grandmothers, who lived 175 miles apart, revealed they had received a telephone call from someone saying he was "an old flying buddy" of Terry's. The caller said he was in Arkansas and trying to find Reed. He left no name or number and said only that he would call back later.

Terry dismissed any concern about this at the time because he did have many old flying buddies, many of whom were former students who still resided in the Midwest.

Later, Arkansas State Police Capt. Raymond (Buddy) Young, then Gov. Bill Clinton's chief of security, would testify in federal court that he made these pretext calls in hope of learning the Reeds' whereabouts.

In Mexico, the packing of the motor home continued. Preparations were also under way for the "exchange" of the first half of the evidence that Terry had hidden in the rented garage, where he stored their BMW. A block from the Posada, on the lake shore in Ajijic, in a false bottom of a garage workbench lay the Agency's "evidence".

Little did the woman who rented the garage know that Terry had secreted there the 20 kilos of cocaine that was his proof the CIA was trafficking in narcotics.

One cool evening in mid-October, Marr rang the buzzer at the Reed home and disclosed that he had the money. "I got your Ben Franklin pictures ready. Come by the house anytime. Just be sure ta bring your half of the bargain."

Still wary of Marr, Reed asked if his wife had returned home, believing that if Marr planned anything unpleasant he would be less likely to do so in the presence of a nagging wife and a live-in maid.

"Yeah, the bitch is back. I'm goin' ta the Posada for a drink. Wanna go? For old time sake? For Screw Worm? Come on, I'll tell ya some more Air America stories." Reed declined. Marr then started to leave but paused and said, "You sure ya don't wanna sell me the gun before ya leave? They're worth a lotta money down here, ya know."

Reed put on his best stoic face. He was disturbed by the question, believing it a ploy to get him to admit he actually had a weapon. If he was actually going to be allowed to leave Mexico with $100,000, he wouldn't be concerned about turning a profit on a gun. He was leery the Agency was setting him up for an arrest by the police in Mexico where handguns are strictly prohibited, or simply to determine if he *really* had one.

"No. Hypothetically speaking, *if* I had one I may need it on the way out of here, you know, for banditos."

Marr chuckled. "You been watchin' too many movies. These are all honorable guys you're dealing with."

On October 16th, the exchange was made at Marr's house. At high noon, both men handed over what the other wanted. Terry got $100,000 in $100 bills and Marr got 10 kilos of "pure." The remaining drugs, they agreed, could be located after the Reed family safely crossed the border. A third person would contact Marr and arrange for a telephone conversation between the two men. Terry would then tell him where to find the other half.

"Sure is a lotta hocus-pocus among friends," Marr had said while shaking his head.

The last words he heard Marr speak that day in Mitch's den in Ajijic were, "Let's toast to the burial of Screw Worm and Bill Cooper. What a way ta go...ta die with your boots on in a 123. That lucky shit!"

It took less than a minute to end a 15-month chapter in Terry's life. A new chapter was about to begin.

That night, hopefully without the Agency or Marr knowing about it, Terry had a business appointment in Guadalajara. In anticipation of receiving consecutively-marked bills, which had been the standard form of payment in Mexico, Terry had devised a plan for eliminating the inevitable money trail, always a perfect way of tracking someone's movements. Again, the story of the trail of Hansel and Gretel came to mind. He certainly didn't want to leave "green" crumbs to be tracked by.

The man who had insured his airplane was a Mexican entrepreneur who had another business in addition to his thriving insurance agency—that of money changing. Terry had sought out his services because he had been told that he was "connected." After making sure he wasn't being followed, Terry rendezvoused at the insurance office to do a little after-hours banking. He had alerted the man earlier that he would be "coming into some money," which he would like to exchange this for different bills. He appeared to be accustomed to this kind of request as his money-changing service catered to the foreigners living in Guadalajara. He said he would have

the $100,000 ready for the exchange—for his usual fee...and a slight sur-
charge.

The previously-negotiated "fee" for this service was to be $2,000. But upon
seeing the Agency's consecutively-marked, uncirculated and newly-minted bills,
he reneged. After running the money through the machine that detects counterfeit bills, he demanded $3,000 more.

"It's not counterfeit, but due to its condition and appearance, I must ask for
a larger than normal fee," the money changer said. "I do not press my clients
as to the source of their problems...I mean money. But I'm afraid this *dinero* is
so hot I will have to exchange it for rubles just to unload it."

If the man was going to actually purchase Soviet currency in order to move
the cash out of the country, Terry laughed inwardly at the thought of leaving a
false money trail all over Siberia. That would keep a few agents busy.

Terry's negotiating skills reduced the total fee to $4,000. He departed the
office with used American bills of unknown origin, but only after he made the
Mexican run them through the counterfeiting machine.

On the drive back home, the thought of the money being tainted with cocaine residue kept rolling through his mind. He was going to have enough
problems explaining the source of the money to U.S. Customs. The last thing
he needed was a trained narcotics dog pissing on the side of their motor home
signaling the Reed's as traffickers.

So back home, their newly purchased Mexican washer and dryer did several
loads, the likes of which redefined the term "money laundering".

The next day the Reeds, the Mexican maid, the kids and the German Shepherd, Macho, all packed into the motor home and headed north. The motor
home was valued at $20,000, but on that day it was worth considerably
more...say, $100,000.

Reed had hidden the money in the waste tank, but that was only a temporary repository. Unknown to Janis, he had devised what he considered an in-
genuous plan to get it across the border undetected. It was not against the law
to have the money, it was only illegal not to report it to Customs when he
crossed. Terry didn't relish the thought of breaking the law, but this was an
emergency that could make the difference between life or death.

As Fawn Hall, Oliver North's secretary said to the Congressional Committee
investigating Iran-Contra, "Sometimes you have to go above the written law."

The Reeds spent the first night of their tense journey at the only three-star
hotel in Zacatecas where the maid slept in the motor home for the night as a
security precaution. To smuggle the money into the motel, Janis stuffed it in
the diaper bag along side her pistol.

Once inside, the Reeds began to implement their plan. Janis counted the
$100 bills for the first time and placed them neatly in waterproof plastic ziplock
bags. Her husband sat in the shower and carefully removed, with a surgical
scalpel, the so-called tamper-proof seals from two one-gallon plastic bottles of
Prestone anti-freeze.

He then packed the baggies into the bottle, refilled them with anti-freeze,
and, with super glue, replaced the tamper-proof seals. It was the most expensive anti-freeze on the face of the earth.

As she nervously waited for her husband to finish his tedious task, Janis
poured herself a glass of Mexican red wine. Her assignment finished, the
impact of what they were doing began to sink in. Terry, to keep his wife's

nerves steady, had promised her that this concealment was solely for security while in Mexico—to prevent it from being found and taken in the eventuality of an accident or robbery. When they reached the Texas border at McAllen, he told her, it would be declared, proper and legal.

He lied.

The next morning the tension heightened. They planned on making the border by nightfall, but that would be quite an accomplishment, he thought, after factoring in the unexpected delays he knew would result from traveling with the children, the maid and the dog. They hit the road at dawn to optimize the daylight hours.

Janis, he could sense, was on the verge of breaking from the stress and acute paranoia. To break her silence and to occupy her mind, Terry attempted to draw her into conversations of plans to rebuild his business, buying a house near Little Rock and blending back into the community. She knew what he was doing and feared not only for the trip to the border, but the future as well. She wouldn't share it with him then, but she felt deep inside their problems were only beginning.

Normally, they would have entered at Laredo. But the plan called for an abrupt change in border destination, crossing at an unexpected location on the Mexican side in the event someone might be there waiting for them.

Always do the unexpected, his intelligence training kept reminding him.

From their experience of living in Mexico, Reed knew that there was much more law and order in the interior than at the border. Border towns were something else. They reminded him of the bar scene in the movie *Star Wars*, a menagerie of misfits and cut-throats. From his observation, these towns were magnets for social mutants from both cultures. Unfortunately they were how most Americans pre-judged all of Mexico. But their rough and tumble atmosphere is what concerned him the most as they pulled into the outskirts of Reynosa after a rather uneventful trip. If someone was going to make a move on them, it would probably happen here.

It was Sunday evening, and by the time they arrived *en el centro de Reynosa*, Janis' nerves were shattered. To give her time to pull herself together, Terry decided it best to stay overnight there and cross early on the 19th. He also reasoned that spending an additional night in Mexico was, in fact, doing the unexpected just in case anyone had surprise plans for them.

"Always do the unexpected" again surfaced as he drove around getting the lay of the land and looking for the "right" place to spend the night.

He found a motel with a secure courtyard to park the motor home and, again, their maid slept in the RV. That night Terry tossed and turned while his wife slept soundly after "sedating" herself with a portion of a bottle of Mexican red wine.

From the motel window, Terry could see the American border and the city lights of McAllen. He was almost there, yet he felt the most dangerous leg of the journey, the crossing into the United States, lay ahead.

The impending crossing would be the test, he felt, of whether Rodriguez and his CIA cohorts were the "honorable, patriotic men" Marr had claimed them to be. He mulled over and over to himself: What will they be expecting me to do? Just do the opposite. His paranoia was running wild.

Even if they knew he was here, he rationalized to himself, they would not be expecting him to cross here. If he were, why would he be spending the night rather than crossing over earlier in the evening?

Do the unexpected, do the unexpected...

We are certainly visible enough, he thought as he protectively gazed at the three little boys lying on the floor in their sleeping bags. His gaze then drew to Janis who was lying next to him. What a woman he thought! Without her inner strength, her insistence on keeping the family intact, he would have probably opted for Plans A or B—flee or take the money and run. He finally dozed off, exhausted, with Smith and Wesson standing guard.

The next morning was Monday, October 19th, 1987.

As Janis loaded the last child into the motor home, she walked over to her husband and whispered, "Don't forget, you promised you would declare that money. You did drain the anti-freeze after I went to sleep last night, didn't you? "

He lied.

She knew what was in store when he didn't lift his sunglasses. He always lied when he didn't lift his sunglasses.

"Honey, this is one step at a time. How are we going to explain $100,000 in cash? I promise if they ask us about money, I'll declare it."

She gave him a look of disgust laced with disbelief, causing him to resort to a less tactful tone.

"Just get in the fuckin' motor home and let's leave."

With two pistols hidden in plastic bags in the sewage tank, and two $50,000 bottles of anti-freeze under their sink, they crossed the Rio Grande and pulled into the United States Customs inspection station. They were on American soil. They had purposely put their oldest son, Duncan, in an upper berth near a window and told him to wave at the Customs inspectors.

"Look wholesome," the nervous mother told him as the expressionless agent entered their Missouri license plate number, visible on the front of their vehicle, into the computer.

Had it not been for the *single* fact that the vehicle was registered in a company's name and not his own, their trip would probably have ended right there. Without knowing it, Reed and his wife were now the subject of an investigation.

They were motioned into the vehicle inspection area and three inspectors literally ransacked the inside of the motor home. Their immigration papers showed that they had been outside the U.S. for an extended period, and they were discovering how most Americans are welcomed home. Law abiding or otherwise.

There were questions about the maid, the vaccinations for the dog and Terry was about to give a sigh of relief when yet another inspector approached Janis and asked, "Are you carrying currency or negotiable instruments that are in excess of $10,000?"

It was a moment frozen in time.

If this had been a movie, it would now be shown in slow motion. Janis stood by motionless as Terry, carrying his 5-month-old child, had just answered "no" when asked that same question by another inspector looking under the sink at the anti-freeze bottles.

Oh fuck, he thought to himself as resourcefulness kicked in. He hadn't come this far to blow it all now with an arrest for a currency violation.

"Hey, I just lost my ass on peso devaluations in Mexico. Do we look like the kind of people who would have $10,000 left?", he reasoned with the expressionless agent.

The inspector looked benignly at Reed holding the infant and agreed, "Naw, I guess not. It's been really hard for American businessmen down there, hasn't it?" He walked away with the others following him.

"You lied to me!" Janis snapped after she got back in the motor home.

Terry didn't respond but simply slowly piloted the motor home over the last speed bump and crossed into McAllen. Both were on the verge of collapse from the weeks of tension they had been harboring inside. They were safe, they fatuously thought.

"I can't believe you did that," she kept saying.

"Honey, please shut up and turn on the radio, we're back in the U.S. now! Let's listen to some rock n' roll."

She was rotating the dial seeking a station, when the familiar voice of Paul Harvey came over the radio. "Don't jump. Don't jump, it's not worth it. It's only money. Let's not have a repeat of 1929."

Was this some kind of joke they thought as they pulled into a service station to fuel the motor home. Upon inquiring of the attendant what Harvey was talking about, he answered matter of factly.

"Oh haven't you heard, the stock market crashed." It was near noon on Black Monday. The Reeds had come home to a national financial disaster...among other things.

But after refueling, as they motored north toward San Antonio on I-35 and updated themselves on the Wall Street disaster, they took comfort in the knowledge that *their* assets were, truly, *liquid.*

Meanwhile, at the governor's mansion in Little Rock, the Arkansas State Police and the DEA were frantically putting together a computer profile of the Reeds and attempting to learn their whereabouts. They had miraculously slipped through the border net.

The "honorable men" Marr had talked about were anything but.

CHAPTER 31

DOUBLE CROSS

The phone rang in the North Kansas City motel room. It was November 3rd, 1987. When he answered the call, Terry Reed quickly recognized the voice. It belonged to the man he had known as John Cathey. By this time, the voice had become well known to the rest of America as well. The man on the other end of the line was Oliver North.

"Should I call you Oliver or should I call you John?" Terry asked the man he had known as his CIA controller as he regained consciousness from his interrupted sleep.

"It's unfortunate that deceit among friends is necessary," North replied stoically.

"I'm out of Mexico and I'm in deep shit," Terry exclaimed, getting right to the point.

North was in deep shit himself when he returned Terry's frantic call. In fact, everyone connected with the illegal Contra supply operation was in deep shit.

North had already testified about the Iran-Contra affair, and having watched some of the congressional hearings, Terry had been somewhat taken aback by the re-packaging of the Marine Lieutenant Colonel for media and public consumption. The North he knew had not behaved as a "rogue" operating on his own, as Attorney-General Edwin Meese had painted him to be. And from what Terry had gathered from the print media since returning to the states, North was now being drafted by the public as an American hero and someone bordering on idol worship. With his new found fame, Terry sure hoped North remembered his old acquaintances, especially those on the run from the CIA, FBI and Arkansas State Police.

Earlier, while waiting for North's call, Terry had paced the motel room, mentally developing a battle plan from his rapidly deteriorating alternatives. One particular acronym kept leaping from his memory bank of Air Force expressions. His present condition was most definitely FUBAR, or Fucked Up Beyond All Recognition.

It had been two short weeks since the Reed family had crossed the border, and now he was fighting minute by minute to control his paranoia. His overriding reason for wanting to leave Mexico had been his fear of becoming the patsy for the CIA's dirty operation...that he would be left to take the fall if it were exposed.

As events were unfolding, it was evident that someone, most likely Felix Rodriguez, was double-crossing him. *Now*, he wished that he had the "evidence" with him so he could prove his story when he went to Congress—his only logical alternative. As it was turning out, all he had was his word.

Terry and Janis had breathed a cautious sigh of relief after their motor home cleared the last known obstacle between the Rio Grande and their first planned stop-over in Carthage, Missouri. Janis' last panic attack occurred just prior to the "wet back" checkpoint north of McAllen, which they passed with no major fanfare on "Black Monday", October 19th. Once beyond, they actually began to relax somewhat, for the first time in many stress-filled weeks.

The "Reed Traveling Circus" arrived unannounced in Terry's home town on October 21st, having survived this 1,100-mile road trek in reasonable fashion. The plans called for a surprise visit to his mother's house, giving her the opportunity to behave as a typical grandmother and dote on her five-month old "Mexican" grandson, Baxter whom she had never seen.

Working from information obtained from his youngest brother Roland, they were informed his mother wasn't home, but in the country visiting relatives.

They decided it best to head for Kansas City hoping to get to Janis' parents by nightfall. On their way out of Carthage they spotted a concrete truck bearing the insignia "**REED CONCRETE CONSTRUCTION**". Terry stopped and had a brief 15-minute meeting with his oldest brother Gary, whose concrete company was working on a construction site nearby. Terry alerted him they would soon return for a proper and extended visit.

They had spent less than an hour in Carthage as they left and headed northward on Route 71, but they would later learn that they had been observed by *someone* who was an informant and alerted Arkansas Governor Bill Clinton's chief of security. It was an eerie thought that their every move was being shadowed.

The next 10 days were restless ones spent at Janis' parents home in Kansas City. Night-time conversation in the guest room was filled with discussions of what was "the right thing to do." One dimension of them wanted to shout out to the American public their knowledge of the unthinkable... there was no war on drugs! Worse yet, that factions of the Federal government were actually trafficking! But the other dimension, the more rational one that normally takes command in the daylight hours, kept saying, "Put your lives back together and quietly blend back into society."

They were torn emotionally and ethically. Terry had given his word to Rodriguez and had taken his money. He still owed Felix half the "evidence", and was beginning to wonder if Marr had not already *recovered* it on his own. Their repeated attempts to contact him were fruitless, being informed by the maid he simply wasn't at home. Terry found this bizarre and unsettling. Taking possession of the "evidence" should be *"numero uno"* on Marr's list of things to do, unless of course he was again a guest of a Betty Ford-style clinic in the States.

But many questions gnawed at Terry. How big of a liability was he? Would they leave him alone, considering the dangerous knowledge stored within his brain? How vulnerable was he legally? Could, or would, some "inventive" law enforcement agent or prosecutor construct a crime based on what he had done while involved in these black operations?

Already a special prosecutor in Washington was targeting Oliver North for an indictment. Would the same thing happen to him? He was hearing about a very old and sparingly administered law called the Neutrality Act being put to a very new use. People who had assisted the Contras were being indicted by its application. This prompted him and Janis to visit a law library in Kansas City to do a little research of their own.

They ascertained that the Neutrality Act was a law passed in 1909 that bars American citizens from engaging in any act of armed hostility against a country with which the U.S. is not at war. But Terry hadn't performed any "hostile acts", or had he? Doing further research under the laws defining "conspiracy", they regretfully concluded he probably had.

Depressed, they sought the daytime solitude of a place special to Janis' teenage years.

"Calm down honey," he consoled as she sobbed while sitting in the car at the waterworks overlook in North Kansas City. "Implicating me legally is the last thing they would do. Only an idiot would press charges. They won't launder their dirty underwear publicly, especially not in Federal Court."

He couldn't articulate it to her, but his true fears had nothing to do with conspiracy statutes. Legal exposure was one thing. In a trial, you can fight back, even sling dirt of your own. His paranoia was most extreme when he thought of Barry Seal and how he had been dealt with—by assassins' bullets from automatic weapons with silencers. He now knew the term "silencer" had more than one meaning. Their non-judicial technique had certainly silenced Seal.

He usually told Janis everything, but he couldn't share his fear of assassination with her. To do so would have resulted in total panic. He had to be strong. He had gotten them into this mess, he had to keep a level head and get them out.

While sitting in the park that November afternoon, reassuring one another while looking down at the Missouri River and the Kansas City skyline, old thoughts began to kindle within her. This was the very site where she had made her vow at the age of 17 to leave home and live life to its fullest. She shared with him those long-ago memories of being the rebellious teen—visions she had not revisited since their first date in Oklahoma City. Life certainly hadn't been boring, they both agreed, and most importantly they had found each other to share their lives with—for better or worse.

While relishing their closeness, the haunting lyrics of a once popular song resurfaced from Terry's subconscious. They took on a deeper and more sinister meaning, but it seemed as if the lyrics were written specifically for them:

> Paranoia strikes deep
> Into your mind it will creep;
> It starts when your heart is afraid,
> Step out of line
> The man comes and takes you away....
> There's a man with a gun over there,
> Tellin' me I got to beware.

They would come to adopt this Buffalo Springfield song as their "self-help sanity check" in order to ascertain if their actions were rational or driven by paranoia. It was cheap psychiatry, they decided, and available on cassette, LP or 45.

Two days before North's phone call, Terry had been to the Kansas City Public Library attempting to get the transcripts of the Iran-Contra hearings. In Mexico, other than the spotty news coverage, he had no way of knowing for certain what had become public knowledge. He was especially curious if Rodriguez had made any admission or inadvertent reference to "Screw Worm". The librarian indicated the transcripts were on back order due to the inability of the government printing office to meet the demand for orders, so he spent the afternoon reviewing newspaper and magazine articles. From what he read, there had been no mention of Jade Bridge, Centaur Rose or Screw Worm...yet.

Upon returning that evening, Janis rushed to him as he crossed her parent's front lawn. He could tell from her ashen face something horrible had happened. "Get in the motor home with me," she uttered in a demanding voice. "I've got something important to tell you, privately!"

Once inside, she closed the door to the vehicle and nearly screamed out with pent-up rage. "They're screwing' us! Your damn CIA friends are setting us up! The police are after us! What are we gonna do, Terry?" She broke down crying as she pounded the cabinets with her fists.

She began to reconstruct what had happened. Terry's mother had called saying that Terry had received urgent mail, sent in her care, from Carol Canino, the wife of the owner of the rented aircraft hangar in Little Rock. The message instructed them to immediately contact her. There was a problem in Arkansas.

Upon calling Mrs. Canino, Janis was told that the police had executed a search warrant on the hangar on October 14th, only five days prior to them crossing the border, and its contents—allegedly an expensive, single-engine airplane—was seized.

The Reeds were stunned and confused. At that point they were not sure what precisely had been seized since they had left behind only the Ultra-Light aircraft and file cabinets containing office records. Could it be that the Agency was trying to seize his old files and records, he wondered? Were they afraid he had "papers" in storage that could implicate them? Was this a duplication of or somehow linked to the ransacking that had occurred at his office in Mexico? He had no immediate answers, but Mrs. Canino had been frantic to inform them of what transpired so that her company wouldn't be held legally liable.

She had passed on to Janis a telephone number for a police officer named Raymond Young, who wanted to talk to them immediately. The name sounded remotely familiar to Terry, like a name he'd heard in passing, or a name he'd read somewhere.

"They've just made the decision for us," Terry said while comforting his wife inside the motor home. "I don't know what's going on, but let's get out of here. We're going to Washington. Start packing. We'll leave first thing in the morning."

As Terry sat watching the national weather report on television in preparation for their journey the next morning, a personal tragedy unfolded. Janis' 65-year-old father, Ken, exited the bathroom with his left arm hanging limply at his side, saying with a look of terror on his face, "I can't comb my hair."

Janis and her mother, Vera, immediately rushed him to the hospital. Terry couldn't believe the timing of yet another disaster. For a moment it dwarfed their CIA problems, but then self-preservation took hold as paranoia from the events in Arkansas surfaced.

Still stunned, and with the help of the maid, he continued loading the motor home and moved the children, maid and RV to a nearby motel. After checking them in, he joined his wife at the hospital where his father-in-law's diagnosis confirmed their suspicions. He had experienced a stroke.

"I've moved us out of the house," Terry informed her in the hallway adjoining the emergency room. "We've got to leave. We could be arrested anytime. We've got to get to Washington. I need to find North. Surely he can help."

Janis was frantic, torn in all directions. For all she knew her father could be dying. Thoughts of being apprehended at his bedside flashed through her mind. She couldn't bear to think her father's last visions might be of her arrest. These unthinkable events could aggravate his condition and even cause his death. For all she knew, she might never see him again, alive or dead.

But leaving posed a monumental problem. How could she monitor her father's condition? She would have to keep her parents in the dark about their whereabouts and their problems.

"You know we can't tell my mother what's going on or where we're going," Janis cried. "If anyone comes looking for us you know she'll be compelled to tell them the truth. She won't lie."

As if Terry didn't have enough problems, he now had to deal with the strict Baptist adherence to the Ten Commandments, and at the top of that list was— Thou Shalt Not Lie. The CIA was on his trail, he was sure he was being framed, now he was faced with Janis' father possibly dying and a mother-in-law who wouldn't mislead the police.

"Oh fuck," were all the words he could muster. "What else?"

If this meant he had relatives who wouldn't lie under any circumstances, then he and Janis would be forced to. Terry suggested Janis simply tell her mother they were going to Chicago due to a business "emergency" involving their Gomiya lawsuit and that the crisis demanded both of their presence since they each were corporate officers in Applied Technologies. With this problem rectified, there were others to deal with.

There was still the major nagging problem. They still had not been able to make contact with Mitch Marr to arrange the return of the remaining drugs to Rodriguez. Terry now knew he needed to contact Marr *and quickly*. He was part of a "cut-out" that was now being "cut-off". He would have gladly violated the intelligence rule of communicating "one up and one down," meaning having contact and exchanging data with only the person directly above or below you. In fact, by the rules of intelligence, it was even a security violation to *know* any others in the loop. But unfortunately, he knew of no one else to contact. Marr was above him but out of commission, and Terry was the bottom rung on the "Screw Worm" ladder. With the link to Marr now seemingly severed, Terry was floating through dark space alone and isolated.

"Go by your parents' home, don't be seen and try one more time to contact Marr from there," he instructed Janis. "I want you to leave a trail to their phone, just in case it's tapped. When you talk to Chapala Realty, spread some disinformation. Tell them everything is fine here and that we'll be staying with your parents for at least two more weeks, and then back to Little Rock. Maybe that'll buy us some time. Then make sure you're not followed and meet me at the motel. If your dad has stabilized, we'll leave KC tomorrow."

He assumed that by now his in-laws' phone was tapped and would thereby be an excellent pipeline to distribute disinformation. It could also underline to those listening that he was not double crossing anyone and was still trying to keep his part of the bargain.

"What are you going do?"

"I hardly slept at all last night. I'm going to try to get some rest in preparation for a marathon drive to Washington. In the morning, we'll call North and Lieutenant Young to try to find out what's going on."

After cautiously rejoining her family at the motel, Janis informed Terry that Diana, their contact in Ajijic, had not been able to locate Marr.

"It's like he vanished," she had told Janis in a very unsettling tone. She went on to say she had driven to his house and Marr's maid told her she thought he had gone to the States. That made the Reeds even more uneasy. Why would Mitch depart for the States without the evidence? This made no sense. Had Marr already found the drugs? And was planted cocaine what had been seized from the Little Rock hangar? That's probably how it would all end up, Terry thought. He'd be set up and labeled a drug runner, after all.

As he attempted to watch television with his children that evening, one thing was becoming crystal clear. There was no deal anymore, if there had ever been one, and it was now everyone for himself.

Marr's words brought a bitter taste to his mouth: "These are honorable men...."

After another sleepless night, they were thankful to hear that Janis' father was in stable condition. They were now faced with the need to gain intelligence of their own and to make the call to the police officer who had left his number with the owner of the hangar in Little Rock.

There was risk involved. If the phone was tapped, he knew that the 911 technology the FBI utilized could show the point of origin of their call. For this reason they drove to a pay phone on the south side of Kansas City to disguise their movements in a southerly direction, figuring if their actions were being predicted and monitored, it would appear they were proceeding back to Little Rock.

Thinking back to the odd "flying buddy" phone calls made to their parents, Terry guessed they had been pretext calls probably made to locate him...as early as late September. He decided to use the police technique and make a pretext call himself. He told his wife to call the number, pretend she was Terry's sister and find out what she could about what had happened at the hangar.

"Governor's mansion," the male voice said after Janis nervously dialed the Arkansas number. She was taken aback by this salutation and in a wary voice said, "I need to speak to Mr. Young."

"So you're his sister?" Young said to her in a condescending Southern drawl when he came on the phone. "You better tell him he's in deep trouble. We found the airplane he stole up in Joplin, Missouri, hidden in his hangar. He's wanted on multiple counts includin' interstate transportation of stolen property, insurance fraud and makin' false statements. He's in deep shit! Tell him he's a fugitive and he better call me right away."

Janis was barely able to contain her anxiety when Young asked her if she knew where Terry could be found. When she answered he was still in Mexico, Young responded with a startling revelation, "You're lyin'. We know he was in Carthage to see his mom just recently. I'll bet you're not his sister, either."

Janis slammed the phone down. She was barely able to speak as she attempted to relay to Terry Young's comments about being seen in Carthage. They were being *shadowed*, and it wasn't by any normally detectable undercover car...Terry would have noticed that. This was a *pro*.

When she calmed down she didn't need any further urging by her husband to get away from Kansas City, even with her father in the hospital.

"What'll happen if Dad dies," she said tearfully back at the motel.

Terry loaded both the 9 mm and the .38-caliber pistols and answered coldly without looking up, "They'll bury him, Janis."

He had gotten more intelligence from the pretext call than he had planned on getting. So far he was realizing the word "cocaine" hadn't surfaced, yet. But that was probably soon coming. For now, it sounded like what had been seized was his long lost Piper Turbo Arrow, the one that had disappeared from Joplin in March of 1983, over four and a half years earlier.

Terry began mulling over the dilemma. "This is out of control. I'm gonna try and call North," he said as he looked at a road map to compute his route and mileage to Washington.

He told Janis, "Get supplies for the trip, I'm sure it'll be fruitless but I'll call the FBI in Buffalo and ask for 'Carlucci', then I'm going to rest. I'm sure we'll be driving all night."

"Carlucci" was the code name for Cathey, which was the code name for North. It was beginning to sound like North's Project Donation could be responsible for this newly-discovered airplane "found" in Reed's hangar. Terry decided to call the FBI, but not for the purpose of giving himself up...not yet. He needed to reach North and it was through the FBI that he had always contacted his CIA controller in the past.

He called a number given him by North to use in case of an emergency—and was this ever an emergency. The number was for a phone located at an FBI office in Buffalo, New York.

When a voice came on the line, Terry asked for "Mr. Carlucci." In the past Reed would leave his name and telephone number and North would call him back. But now, things were different. With Iran-Contra unraveling, the voice at the other end at the FBI said she had never heard of "Carlucci." But Terry insisted.

His degree of isolation was beginning to affect him. Covert operations were inherently designed for deniability. This he learned in intel school. But what he was discovering now was the Agency's built-in ways to not only deny a person's involvement, but to take care of loose ends as well.

False criminal charges are one way, Barry Seal's fate was another. Since there was nothing to hold over Reed, it seemed that something had to be quickly manufactured. It was all coming to bear on Reed—it appeared as if he was going to be charged with a theft.

Terry realized that while he had been recruited as a deniable asset he had now become, probably as a result of crossing Rodriguez, a *disposable asset*. He felt like he was being flushed once again. That same feeling he had when he returned from Asia—discarded, used, abandoned. What he needed was a little help from his friends, if, in fact, he still had any. North surely wouldn't deny him assistance, he thought. He needed to hear from Oliver North, but he doubted it would happen.

His thoughts went back to nearly five years earlier, back in Oklahoma, when North had first told him about what he called "Project Donation." He recalled North telling him that participation in the program was voluntary. But now he was beginning to wonder if he had "involuntarily" donated to the cause. Could that have been the case? Had someone stolen his plane and made it available to the Contra cause? Or had it been "recovered" earlier by the FBI or others and was now being used as a way to dirty him up? * Had a false crime been created to destroy his credibility and keep him from testifying before Congress? That would really look good all right...testifying from behind bars.

He thought of Bill Cooper and the hangar. That day he and Cooper had recovered the Charlie Cuatro, July 31st, 1986, there certainly wasn't any Piper Arrow in his hangar. His thoughts then raced to the Arrow that Cooper had flown in. But that plane wasn't his stolen plane, even though it was the same make and model. It wasn't turbo-charged like his had been. Lots of questions and no answers. But he concluded the government was using the plane to play hard ball and it was only the first inning. Had they planned to set him up as far back as 1983?

What he didn't know that day as he rested in the motel was how hard they were playing. He would learn that someone had inserted information into government law enforcement computers saying that Terry was suspected of drug trafficking in Mexico and was "armed and dangerous"—a warning, in effect, to any law enforcement officer approaching him to shoot first and ask questions later.

He had to talk to "Carlucci," but doubted he would ever hear from him as he finally drifted off to sleep.

But two hours later North called back, awakening Terry from his sleep. As the conversation developed and Terry pulled his wits together, he became more and more angry. He vented his frustration about being set up, and North's platitudes didn't allay his fear or anger.

"Goddam it, this is no time for diplomacy," Terry told North. "I need to be extricated from this mess, and right fucking now!"

North listened, expressed compassion then concern when Terry outlined his plans to go to Washington and expose the lack of the "war on drugs".

North said adamantly, "I definitely wouldn't do that if I were you. Walsh is looking for blood. He's going after Secord and the whole cast, and so far Screw Worm hasn't been *compromised*. If you show up, that'll open up a whole new bucket of worms. Terry, take my advice and stay as far away from Washington as you can get. Your appearance here can only get you in further trouble...and indicted at best."

He asked Terry for a chance to intercede in his behalf prior to him doing anything "irrational". He said he would see what he could do. He had a friend highly placed in the FBI.

"I'll contact him as soon as we hang up. Things should work out all right."

---

* A case in point proving the FBI does create crimes around individuals: A civil complaint lodged in the United States District Court Western District of Arkansas, Index No.84-2368, and filed December, 21, 1984, alleged the FBI and other law enforcement persons used a stolen aircraft that had been earlier recovered and not returned to its owner as a means to entrap two individuals involved in the Mena operation. Had the FBI been successful in creating a crime and implicating these CIA assets, two men Reed had worked with at Mena, the results unquestionably would have resulted in multiple felony charges. The case was dismissed for lack of evidence. But in July, 1993, Reed and his attorney, Robert Meloni, through Federal Court discovery procedures, came into possession of a classified FBI internal memo and file outlining the details of the "sting" operation, thus proving the original complaint. [1]

When the talk turned to the narcotics trans-shipment through *Maquinaria Internacional's* warehouse, North replied, "Yeah, I heard about that from our Israeli friend," in a reference to Amiram Nir. "Terry, I would never condone such behavior. I truly want to apologize for getting you involved with such wild cards as Rodriguez. He's definitely not cut from the same cloth as we are."

The brief conversation terminated in a warning and an offer of help.

"Don't do anything fucking stupid and expose your position or there'll be 'incoming' on your ass right fucking now," North cautioned. "I'll do my best to arrange for a SAR mission and pluck you out of the wreckage."

If North could just intervene in his behalf with the FBI and Justice Department, that should neutralize the problem, all right. Surely this whole fiasco in Arkansas was just the renegade behavior of Rodriguez, he and North concluded. Why would the Agency needlessly bring attention to the residue of "Jade Bridge", "Centaur Rose" and "Screw Worm"?

Based on the conversation and advice from "Carlucci", the trip to Washington was out, for now at least. There was no sense in becoming an open threat to the Agency. He wanted to give North time to "fix things" as he had promised.

When Janis returned with the supplies, Terry was more upbeat, but hastily preparing for the family to change motels. Fearing that the FBI may have put a trace on his phone, he informed her that they were leaving immediately, probably for Kansas. At least, he told her, someone in the know had listened and given advice.

"I've got good news. You won't believe this, but North actually called. He said to lay low and he would try to take care of things, and for us to definitely not go to Washington."

"Where are we going to go? Off on another adventure, I suppose?" she said caustically.

"Remember the movie, *The In-Laws*?" he asked, drawing her memory to one of their favorite shows in which a spy is chased throughout a third-world banana republic. "Serpentine, serpentine, serpentine," he said, recalling a funny line from the movie and attempting to put his wife in a better mood. He knew the underlying application of the term meant to become a moving target. Moving targets were harder to sight in on, but his military survival training never factored in a wife, three children, a dog and a Mexican maid all packaged into a motor home.

In their early years of marriage, Janis had found her husband to be a metaphor for excitement. They had lived high and fast, in love and in money. Now it had all changed and they were about to become fugitives. It was more than she had bargained for as tears started to replace passion when she found herself forced to hold herself, and a family, together as they moved from state to state while her husband formulated a plan.

For the next five months, the couple traveled 30,000 miles, "serpentining," as they called it, back and forth across the country, traveling aimlessly and "laying low" as North had instructed. Their days were spent comforting their children, pretending all was normal, but their nights were spent comforting each other and crying in the darkness while their upper-middle class life-style fragmented and collapsed into one of survival and stark existence as they became fugitives.

Constantly wary of CIA shadows, the Reeds would rather have been pursued by 10 FBIs than the faceless assassins they were sure were at their heels. Buffalo Springfield's cassette was played so often even the children began to sing the lyrics as the Reed vehicle zig-zagged across America with a bumper sticker that read: "I'm not paranoid. I know I'm being followed."

1.   Little Rock, Arkansas FBI File # 87C-18534 and 12B-283 Volume #2, Serials 2-32.

CHAPTER 32

SERPENTINE

"Mommy, daddy, wake up," Duncan exclaimed that Thursday morning of January 14th, 1988. "The snow is all the way up to the windows."

Thinking her 5-year-old son was again demonstrating his father's gift of hyperbole, Janis Reed pulled the covers over her head and groaned, "Duncan, please go back to bed and let mommy sleep."

She had not slept well in a long time. In fact, neither she nor Terry had actually "slept in" since that fateful day in Kansas City back in November when they discovered they were being double-crossed by the CIA.

They were now on the run. Their journey had led them to the Sequoia National Park in California where they had checked into a rustic cabin in Grant's Grove late the previous evening. The snow had just begun to fall and the National Weather Service had predicted a "remote chance of small accumulations" over the weekend.

Duncan by now had awakened his younger brothers and was about to receive a stern scolding from his father, who, for the first time since they had taken to the road, had been able to shed his continual fear of imminent arrest.

Terry peered out the frost-free spot on the window which Duncan had earlier created and realized their son was not spinning a tale.

"Janis, you better get up and look at this! He's not exaggerating. The snow is higher than the window sills," he said, in disbelief. "I can barely see the road. I think we're buried in."

Sure enough the National Weather Service, which Terry as a pilot had grown to both love and hate, had been caught with its forecasts down again. Survival was on his mind, only this time it wasn't the fear of some assassin's bullet, it was laying in enough provisions to see them through Mother Nature's wrath.

Fortunately, parked outside was one of the few four-wheel drive vehicles belonging to the vacationers who had escaped Los Angeles and the Bay Area that weekend. It was the Reed family's newly-purchased 1986 Ford Bronco that they had already affectionately named "Bronco Billy." And it was standing by, hitched to what the children had named "Tommy," a small custom-built utility trailer sporting a matching paint scheme.

"Tommy Trailer" was bulging with the survival gear they had purchased in San Diego and along their route northward. Luckily, the Reeds had all the essentials and then some. The Reed's called their home on wheels the "escape module" after the small repair vehicle in the movie *2001: A Space Odyssey*. The term odyssey had become such a fitting one for their plight.

Not really believing the weather forecast, they had been lucky enough to stop in Visalia and take advantage of discounts on snow and ski suits. The area, which largely survived on the skiing and the tourism industry in the winter months, had been enduring a draught and had its slowest season in years. There had been no significant snow at all that year. At least not until the Reeds arrived.

By noon that day, as the snow continued to accumulate, the park rangers announced the park would be closing. Those wanting to leave were told to depart immediately by following the snow plow, a converted road grader, to the main entrance and the highway leading down to Visalia.

With their provisions now neatly stacked in their cabin, their shortwave radio tuned to the weather, the two gallons of "Prestone" stored under the bed, and their guns with sufficient ammunition to fend off the faceless enemy who might harm their children, the Reeds settled in for a long winter's night.

They and the other few who had elected to remain behind reminded Terry of the pioneer settlers marooned at the nearby Donner Pass until the spring thaw. From all outward appearances, no one would have guessed that the Reeds were fugitives, evading the net that had been drawn around them by the FBI, with assistance from the CIA.

Their heated log cabin was nestled in a group of rustic cabins that were a quarter-mile from the main lodge where only a skeleton crew of employees remained. Those guests stranded in the cabins would shovel a pathway there each night, and spend the evening socializing in front of the large fireplace. Luckily, the lodge was well-stocked with an ample supply of requisite essentials for the snowbound guests, namely bologna, beans and brandy.

Being snow-bound at high elevation and isolated from the chaotic world below them gave Terry a secure feeling, the first in so long, he had nearly forgotten the feeling. Now was the time to mentally heal and recoup. Analyzing his plan to date, he was rather pleased. So far so good. At least they were together as a family and hadn't yet been apprehended. His mind focused on the trail of disinformation they had strewn across the United States, Mexico and into Canada. Electronic communications had played a large role in throwing curve balls to any would-be pursuers.

He was hoping that Janis' parents' phone was in fact being monitored by the FBI. That would mean that Janis' deliberately placed phone calls to them laced with mis-information should have caused the search for them to be centered in Mexico, probably around the city of Puebla.

"I hope they drink the water," Terry thought as he pictured American agents dealing with Montezuma's revenge while scouring Mexico for "The Reed Bunch". This brought a smile to his now bearded face.

The forced isolation brought on by Mother Nature gave the Reeds a sense of security. For the first time in weeks they were able to let their guard down.

"Here I am in a one room cabin in the middle of nowhere with no phone, no TV, no maid service, no amenities," Janis mused. "No one ever could have told me that this is something I would aspire to, but at this point in my life, I couldn't ask for anything more. As far as I'm concerned, I hope it doesn't stop snowing until May."

Terry and Janis had been stretched nearly to the breaking point. The sleepless nights, the stress, the fear, the paranoia, and at times the terror they lived with daily, was emotionally exhausting. But it was becoming a way of life. They felt totally removed from the "system" they had been a part of since birth. It was a strange sensation of isolation...feeling you no longer belong to any country. They compared their feelings to that of refugees or nomads—or, as Janis likened, gypsies.

As Terry gazed at his family that night, he thought back to the leadership manuals he had studied in ROTC and the Air Force and realized that military tacticians had never taken into account the tact and patience required to "motivate" a family on the run. Wives are not military subordinates to be motivated by fear. There was enough fear in their lives already. Terry's leadership was being put to the test. He could not outwardly show fear. Just a small mental slip on his part could precipitate the crippling release of paranoia and terror that were constantly lurking in both of them.

Just as his old flight instructor had taught him, he had to disassociate himself from his fear, compartmentalize it, and contain it.

So, in order to keep Janis on an even keel, he felt he had to feign optimism that they would somehow survive this horrendous ordeal. He knew he desperately needed Janis' support right now, and he sensed her nerves were on the verge of shattering. He needed her, and the children needed her maternal nurturing. His job was to be a husband and a daddy; to establish an aura of make-believe by pretending that everything was well and under control.

"Look, Daddy, Elliott made a reindeer shadow," Duncan exclaimed as he interrupted Terry's thoughts.

The boys were having great fun making finger shadows with the light cast by a kerosene lantern. As the storm raged on over the California Sierras four more days, the family was able to bond as they ventured outside to play daytime games in the snow and told stories by the glow of the lantern at night.

"We're just really inconspicuous, aren't we?" Janis said sardonically to her husband as she watched Macho, who was being transformed into a sled dog, attempting to pull three giggling boys through the snow drifts. Even though the rambunctious German Shepherd might have drawn some unneeded attention, both parents felt an added sense of security with him around. Having been raised from a puppy in the presence of the children, he tolerated from *them* all sorts of "abuse" and was exceedingly gentle. On this recent trip, Janis had found the dog in the back of the motor home, patiently allowing Duncan and Elliott to wrap an entire roll of masking tape around his legs to "fix his boo-boo".

Macho was so passive with his little charges, but Janis and Terry knew that if anyone ever attempted to lay a hand on any of the boys that he could turn instantly ferocious. He would pace and growl at any stranger who violated the boy's territory, and his sheer presence would frighten the average intruder away.

Late at night, with Macho standing guard over the sleeping family, Terry couldn't suppress the thoughts of terror that would surface from nowhere and race through his idle mind. Were they out there somewhere? Were they on his trail, or had his plan to trick them worked? Terry's mind was in a swarm. The seriousness of it all was coming to bear. The adage *"what's the worst that can happen"* bore no humor at all! He knew what the worst could be. He would then fight to regain control, and as a mental diversion begin contemplating their next moves, over and over and over.

He couldn't allow them to find him. He had to become another person. He needed a new identity. He had developed a numerical point system of one to

10 to grade each action as to its degree of risk. Obtaining a new identification had to be a 10 pointer. But once accomplished, it would reduce the risk associated with other actions to the level it seemed worth it. That was it. He would somehow become a different human being...just as soon as the storm was over.

With the park now reopening and the roar of the snow plows outside their window, Terry knew they had to leave. They had been there too long. He had told the other vacationers he was combining a family vacation with a regional marketing survey. He now feared the park rangers would get suspicious if they stayed any longer. They had been there a week, and as the Bronco wound its way down the mountain and out of the Sierra Nevadas, Terry's mind drifted back to the start of their journey into anonymity. Back to the time they left Kansas City, to become "moving targets."

* * *

"What's wrong?" Janis asked nervously. She had been quitely observing her husband for the past 30 minutes as he drove westward across Kansas that dreary November night. She knew by his silence that something was eating away at him. He was behaving as if he was flying on instruments, in bad IFR weather, only this time there was no airplane involved. Perhaps, she rationalized, piloting this motor home with the children, a dog, and a Mexican maid aboard while evading shadowy pursuers might be as stressful.

She repeated, "What's wrong?" and this brought him out of his trance. It was well after midnight. The children and Macho were all asleep and Laura was in the rear reading a steamy Mexican paperback, oblivious to the Reeds' plight.

"I've got to change these plates," Terry informed, without breaking his concentration on the two lane road. "They might be looking for them by now."

He had neglected to tell her that he had "switched" license plates with another vehicle in the motel parking lot that morning while she was buying provisions. He rationalized away this act of chicanery as "trading", and not stealing, since he left the other Missouri motorist with his plates, which actually had a longer time before expiration. And hadn't he, after all, given them something of greater value?

"Terry, are you telling me you stole someone's license plates?"

"Janis, before this is over, I'm sure I'll have to do a lot of things that are not viewed highly by the law. This is an emergency and I'm gonna behave as such. Now if you're gonna sit there and bitch, I just won't tell you what I'm doing. It's your choice. You're the wife of a spook, and if the answers scare you, don't ask the questions."

It bothered her to hear her husband talking that way. But at the same time, she admired him that night for all those same reasons she had fallen in love with him. He was taking charge and doing whatever was necessary to insure the safety of the family. She, too, feared they would share the same fate as Barry Seal. She had to trust his judgment, so she decided to ask fewer questions. Maybe she didn't "have a need to know" everything her husband was doing. It was just that much more to worry about.

To Terry, this entire ordeal was turning into the equivalent of an on-board aircraft emergency. During his silence, he had been prioritizing his workload and weighing his alternatives. There were too many unanswered questions to define a true course of action right away. He had decided to confront the ordeal in the same method taught to a recovering alcoholic, one day at a time.

Right now, as he wrestled with his paranoia, his number one priority was "trading" plates again. This time he wanted to find a vehicle that would be heading eastward, back toward Kansas City, and preferably someone on vacation with an East Coast destination. That way, the switched vehicle would transport his current plates on an easterly course, opposite of their direction.

"If we head back up toward the Interstate, the map shows a rest area," he said to Janis as she poured him some coffee. "I figure if I can switch plates with an eastbound vehicle, we can rest easy until Denver."

A few minutes later, Janis held her breath as her husband bolted on their new Pennsylvania plates, which he had quietly "exchanged" from a parked RV as its occupants slept in the roadside park.

"OK, now we gotta get this bitch debugged," he told her. "If they knew we had been in Carthage, that means they *had* to know we'd been in Kansas City. And that means they had access to this vehicle when we weren't around it and sufficient opportunity to plant a transmitter on us. I won't rest easy until we have this thing swept."

"Now how are we going to do that?" Janis asked incredulously, almost afraid to hear the answer.

"Don't worry, this won't require anything illegal. In the morning, I'll call Jack and get some of his expert advice."

Jack was an old retired Air Force buddy of Reed's, who was an electronics genius and ham radio operator living on the East coast. The next morning near Denver, Terry was told by Jack that any good ham operator with the right equipment should be able to "sweep" his vehicle. By parking the motor home near the antenna, the operators' receiver, if run through the entire frequency spectrum, should detect a transmitter if one had been planted in or on the motor home, or so Jack said.

At Ft. Collins, Colorado, and after giving a $100 tip, Terry received the results of the electronic "sweep" of his RV.

"You're clean," they were told by the toothless, tobacco-chewing Army retiree, a "radio friend" of Jack's. "If I were you, I'd still wanna make sure I wasn't beein' optically ID'd."

The comment confused Terry. If his motorhome wasn't emitting a tell-tale electronic signal, how else, he asked the ham operator, could it be tracked?

"Visually from outer space," he answered as he spit brown tobacco juice on the white snow. "I was in satellite recon in the Army, and they got this special paint they put on things they wanna track from outer space. For war games we normally put it on the 'good guys' equipment...tanks, armored personnel carriers, artillery...stuff like that. Then a mobile command post sorta serves as a ground based traffic controller, givin' our guys vectors, via satellite, to find the enemy."

Reed had heard enough. Having worked in the early development stages of digital infra-red satellite reconnaissance in the Air Force, he knew that what the ham operator was telling him was within the realm of surveillance technology. He hadn't heard of this special paint though, so inquired further.

"It's clear in color and impossible ta see with the naked eye," continued the Army retiree. "It takes lacquer thinner or paint stripper and a whole lotta elbow grease ta get the shit off. If I were you, I'd do somethin' to the top of the RV, just ta be safe."

After "trading" plates again at a truck stop north of Denver, Reed put the RV through a truck wash, to clean the roof of the motor home in preparation for receiving paint. He reasoned that an even better way of insuring there was no trackable coating on their roof was to paint the the RV's roof with sealer. That way, if the tell-tale coating was there, it would be covered over.

At a recreational vehicle supply house parking lot, Janis, from within the comfort of the motor home, watched her husband scale the RV's ladder and climb onto it's roof. In the chilly November air, Terry applied two gallons of the thick, silicone-based roof sealer. Only afterwards, did he begin to rest a little easier, secure in the thought they weren't being tracked by satellite.

This technology, that most people think exists only in novels and movies, he knew was real. From his trip with Seal to Panama, he knew nearly anything was possible electronically. An ELT (emergency locater transmitter) carried in the tail of an airplane was a perfect example of a tracking device that was readily available to anyone, and this technology was easily accessible to the federal government, which owns and operates the FAA's tracking satellites.

"Damn! At times, I wish I was stupid," he would say to his wife. "I'd have a lot less to worry about. A dumb shit just wouldn't know about the technology that exists that could track us."

Through knowledge, however, one can reasonably separate true fear and concern from paranoia. Paranoia includes the fear of things that might not actually exist. His fears were real. They were being pursued by professionals, or at least he had to presume they were. Even if Oliver North had intervened on his behalf with the FBI, he still didn't trust Felix Rodriguez and company. Rodriguez was capable of anything, Terry now knew. Just ask Ché Guevara.

Meanwhile, Janis was desperate to learn of her father's condition. She had left Kansas City with him still in the hospital, having confided to no one in her family the true peril of their situation. No arrangements had been made to communicate securely, and she knew they could not risk a phone call from Denver.

One advantage to traveling with two gallons of "Prestone" was that money was not an issue. As the motor home sat parked in an overnight RV campground in Denver, Janis sat nervously aboard an American Airlines jet racing eastward to Chicago. The purpose of her journey was to place a phone call to her sister's place of business and to plant the devious seeds of disinformation. Janis' mission while there, besides checking on her father's condition, was to also make several strategically placed business calls that hopefully would be intercepted. Terry had instructed her to take a cab to the far north side of the city, near the Interstate, and to make her calls from there. If the Feds were tracking them by phone contacts, surely they would think the Reed's were making their way northward to Canada.

"He's getting better," said Janis' sister, Karen, by phone from her high rise office building. "But we've been worried about you. Your legal matters must have really been urgent for you guys to leave town that fast. Is everything OK?"

Standing at a pay phone, nearly shouting over the deafening roar of truck traffic adjacent to I-94 on Chicago's north rim, Janis mustered up every ounce of inner strength she had to keep from breaking down and telling her sister of her plight. Fighting back the tears, she said with mock enthusiasm, "Oh, everything's fine. It's just all this Gomiya legal junk has got me sorta down. While we're here, Terry's going to bid on a new project which might keep us on the road longer than we'd anticipated."

A short time later she was waiting in the bustling boarding area of the O'Hare terminal waiting for her flight back to Denver. Although she knew her husband wouldn't have approved, since she was instructed to not make calls from the airport, she made a quick "get well soon, I love you call" to her father as she was preparing to depart.

Watching the passengers deplane, she had never felt more depressed. Everyone seemed so happy, and her life was destroyed, maybe forever. While deep in thought, she was startled back into her frightening reality when she heard the assumed name under which she was traveling being announced over the loud speaker.

"Sheila Walton, please report to the ticket counter immediately."

It was the phone call to her parents house! How could they have tracked her that quickly, she thought! Terry had been right. The FBI was monitoring her family's phone lines. Trembling and barely able to breathe, her feet slowly and unsteadily carried her to the ticket counter.

"Miss Walton, can you do us a big favor? Would you mind trading boarding passes with this little boy so he can sit with the rest of his family?"

Frantically fumbling for her boarding pass, she watched her hands shake violently as she presented it to the ticket agent.

"Are you all right, Miss Walton?"

"Oh, uh, yes. Flying always just makes me a little nervous."

"He's getting better," the relieved Janis told Terry as she rejoined her family at Stapleton Airport. "And I've got more good news. I worked out a secure way to communicate. I talked to Karen's secretary and was able to get her travel itinerary for the next six months. That way I can call her in places no one will surely be monitoring and can keep tabs on Dad. I can rest a little easier now." She didn't inform him until much later about the call to her father and the breach of communications security.

Back on the road again with her family, Janis knew it was time to address the educational needs of her children. Duncan was becoming suspicious since no one was trying to force learning down his throat. Home schooling took on a whole new meaning as she set up her classroom in the motor home.

Later that week, she was back in her comfortable role of "school marm", demanding that Duncan continue improving his kindergarten skills. As the little boy practiced his handwriting by making "sticks and balls" on his Big Chief tablet, he was reassured that all was back to normal. As Terry surveyed the transformation of the interior of the motor home, he too was reassured that his wife was coping with their precarious circumstances.

He frequently referred to her as a "nester" and was amazed at how cozy she could make nearly any environment. Each of the boys had their favorite stuffed animal propped atop their beds. Colorful posters of shapes, ABC's and numbers were displayed, stapled to the overhead cabinetry. She had even purchased an exact duplicate of a poster the boys had in their room in Mexico and had attached it to the closet door at the little boys' eye level. It pictured a mother panda bear cradling her young and was captioned: HOME IS WHERE YOU GET CUDDLED. She was firmly convinced that if she abided by this motto, the children would have good memories of this chapter of their lives, rather than traumatic ones.

Earlier, in Mexico, Terry had built in an overhead cabinet housing a small television and VCR. This Janis now adapted as her primary "visual aid," and 2-year-old Elliott was content to watch Sesame Street educational tapes for hours on end. This would even entertain the baby as they traveled the seemingly endless stretches of highway.

"Mommy, you're the best cooker," Duncan commented one evening. "The motor home smells like Grandma's house."

Janis had just finished baking some "slice and bake" refrigerator cookies. The aroma of baking of cookies created that "warm and fuzzy" feeling.

"I've got an idea, Duncan. Tomorrow, let's get a cookie jar for the motor home. My new goal will be to keep it full of home-made cookies." That, and to evade our pursuers she thought to herself. What a paradox. She couldn't believe she was thinking of baking cookies and evading Federal agents all in the same thought process! One day at a time, she thought, I've got to take it one day at a time.

Terry had insisted their attitudes about the "system" did not spill over onto the children. Even though he was now deathly afraid of the U.S. Government and the unbridled power it could wield against them, he sought to ensure that Duncan did not become alienated by his parent's feelings of a government gone mad. He insisted that Janis place the standard classroom portrait of George Washington directly over the center cabinet door of the overhead storage. The one that was locked. The one that contained the guns and ammunition. He felt that America's true rebel, George, would have approved of his picture's location and what it was concealing.

Janis, while in Chicago, had done as instructed and tried, although unsuccessfully, to call Mitch Marr in Ajijic. The inability to find Terry's old handler and consummate the exchange bothered them both immensely. This should have been Marr's *number one* priority. What could be more important than sewing up this one last loose end?

Either it had by now become unimportant to communicate with the Reeds; perhaps they knew all along where the evidence had been stored; or was it something else? Maybe the Feds were one step ahead of him all the time. Maybe he was the mouse and the cat was only toying with him. He had to put this fear out of his mind and seek sanctuary.

Desko! I've got to get to Desko, Terry thought.

There would be extreme risk in communicating with him by phone. But less risk, Terry calculated, if he approached him in person without spending any time "loitering" in Albuquerque. Since the RV was now sporting California license plates, it occurred to him that Santa Fe would be the perfect place to go. They would fit right in with all the tourists and still be only a short drive from Desko's.

Two major priorities had made their way to the top of his mental checklist by now. First— *disinformation.*

They had left Chapala pretending to be only going north on an extended business trip/vacation. If they didn't return soon, people down there would become suspicious, especially since the Reed's had left many of their high value belongings there.

Somehow, they had to give the appearance of permanently leaving the

Chapala area and moving to a false location. Terry knew there had to be government informants living within the expatriate community. If he could create the proper illusion of moving somewhere else within Mexico, it might buy them more time and take care of the problem of vacating their leased home.

There was no way around it. He would have to go back to Mexico to create that illusion. If he were to return for just one day, vacate his residence and create the right cover story of moving the family to another Mexican city, the ruse might work. It might make the CIA think he was not a threat and was only seeking to reassemble his life and return to his old occupation of consulting for factory automation.

Yeah! That's it! The Volkswagen factory in Puebla was upgrading its capabilities to machine engine heads for the Beetle. He knew that was an on-going project. He would return and say he was moving the family to Puebla to work on the VW modernization project. That could create the proper illusion, if he handled it properly, especially if he was seen there in the Chapala area. But it would be risky. He could only stay one day. He would want to be in and out of Guadalajara during day light hours. Surely they wouldn't make an attempt on his life if he stayed in crowded public places. But who could he use as a bearer of this disinformation? Who would be sure to spread it all over the Chapala area?

Then, while driving south out of Alamosa, Colorado, it came to him. Laura, of course! Mexican maids and nannies blab everything about their foreign bosses to *everyone*. Their gossip network would be the perfect vehicle to spread the seeds of deceit. It would be better than taking out a full-page ad in the Chapala news bulletin, *Ojo del Lago*.

Perfect! This would be an ideal way to implement the plan and his predators might be fooled into thinking they were in Canada and Mexico at the same time. It could even create the illusion that the Reeds had split up, with Janis heading for Canada and Terry southward across the Rio Grande. The CIA would then be confronted with the same problem Hitler faced, a two-front war!

"God damn," he thought. "I'm gonna use what THEY taught me on them. After all, he had scored 95 in his class on disinformation."

After five days in New Mexico, and having discreetly contacted Desko, he felt rested but pressured to continue with his plan of appearing to be in two places at the same time.

Contributing to this pressure and growing sense of urgency was the fact that two days earlier he had discovered the telephone number at the FBI's office in Buffalo ,which he had earlier used to contact North, was now strangely "out of order".

To ensure his New Mexico location was not compromised from a telephone link intercept, Terry had hopped aboard Southwest Airlines and flown to Dallas in order to "reach out" for Carlucci one more time.

In Dallas, after listening to the telephone company's recording signifying the emergency phone number for Carlucci/Cathey/North was not in service, a montage of thoughts crept into his mind. Had the number been disconnected for security reasons and to prevent him from re-contacting North? Or was the Agency distancing itself even further from *Señor Estrella*? Terry rationalized he didn't dare call Buffalo information and contact the FBI through their published number for fear the call would be traced automatically through 911 technology. If his Southwest location was detected, it would destroy all the previous effort in creating the appearance of being in Chicago or Canada. He couldn't risk the call. It was best to continue on his existing "flight plan" and he decided to return at once to his nervous family awaiting in New Mexico.

His old friend let it be known the offer he made to him in Mexico was still good. "The desert can swallow you up," Desko had told him. It was a source of comfort to Terry, knowing that a fall-back plan was available as a last resort option. He again compared it to flying. Just as a good pilot always has an "alternate air field selected" he had an alternative if the going got too rough.

But there were still loose ends to tie up. He figured the excess baggage he was carrying, namely the highly-visible motor home and the nanny, could be used to his advantage. They would make perfect decoys to further throw off any pursuers. Just as in the movies, you leave a trail, but not one that leads to you.

If he was going to take up Desko on his offer, he wanted to return to New Mexico "clean" and more low-profile. Hopefully, the FBI now thought he was in Canada, or at least headed that way. The last place they would look for him was along the southern border, or so Terry calculated.

"Always do the unexpected," he could still hear his Denver intelligence instructor advising.

Yeah, he figured, with the concentration of law enforcement along the border, they would never believe he would head there, the place he had just fled and the place he feared the most. Go where your fear is! They won't look for you there. For this reason, he headed south out of Albuquerque on I-25 with an undecided destination, probably some large city along the border. A plan was beginning to take shape by the time they approached the outskirts of Truth or Consequences, New Mexico. This was an apropos place to get an idea, he concluded.

First, he would drive right into the heart of either L.A. or San Diego. Both were near enough to the Mexican border to implement his plan. The upside was, they were now within striking range of California. The down side was, they were in the worst place in America to be traveling with a Mexican: the Southwest. The border states were dotted not only with immigration checkpoints on every major highway, but also had roadblocks with agriculture inspectors' prying eyes seeking....fruit flies!!!! On all traffic arteries crossing into Arizona and California there were inspection stations looking for untaxed fresh fruit and vegetables, wetbacks and fugitives, and insects.

Number one priority—the nanny had to go back to Mexico before someone questioned her about her immigration status. He figured they could use her for a decoy, however, before terminating her employment.

Then, there was the second priority—*sanitized transportation.*

Even though Terry now felt sure the motor home was not carrying a tracking device, he knew that each "requisitioning" of new license plates was a high-risk maneuver. An estimated "six pointer" on the Reed Risk Scale. Sooner or later, he was sure to run into a roadblock or, worse, have an accident or get a ticket for a moving violation that could lead to police running his license number through their computer. And when this happened, the authorities were certain to find the vehicle didn't match the plates it was carrying. End of trip!

But how could he purchase a car and register it so that his or Janis' name didn't appear on the registration. The only secure way they could travel would be in a vehicle whose registration was in *no way* tied to them. The motor home they were traveling in was registered to his corporation. He found solace in that thought but was fearful there was an APB out for them. If this were the case, local police had probably been given a description of their vehicle since they had been surveiled in Terry's home town. And beyond that fear, he knew the level of sophistication of police vehicle registration computers gave them the ability to interrogate their computers for vehicles registered to an individual or corporation. This meant they could search for vehicles owned by any company which was tied to Reed, provided they knew the company's name.

The Agency certainly knew of his old company, Applied Technologies, Inc. He had no way of knowing if they were smart enough to research the motor vehicle records in order to tie the motor home to a company instead of him, thereby figuring out how the Reed's had been able to cross the border without being apprehended. All of these unanswered questions helped formulate contingencies that would neutralize his lack of information. He would have to form a corporation in which neither he nor Janis could be linked, and it in turn could own a vehicle that was unknown to the Feds. That's what he would do, just as soon as he executed the Mexican Disinformation Phase of the plan.

Terry had kept his electronic link to the outside world intact by keeping Applied Technologies' answering service in Little Rock. Janis called the service weekly to see of anyone was "reaching out" to them. It was strange, no one was calling and this added to their paranoia and confusion. Perhaps North had "fixed it all" and he had been forced to cut all ties to the FBI afterwards. Maybe that was why the FBI's phone number in Buffalo no longer worked. He just didn't know. It was like flying in solid instrument conditions after having experienced a total communications failure. Just follow the flight plan. That's all you can do.

"Janis, I've been thinking about this for the past 500 miles," he said as they drove west across Arizona toward California. "We've got to start a new corporation. If we put a 'clean' vehicle under a new company's name...a company we're in no way tied to personally...they would have no way of tracking us. That's what we have to do. Form a new company."

She made no comment, and continued with her classroom duties in the back of the RV. The pressure was beginning to mount again...he could tell by the tense look on her forehead. He had not shared with Janis his plans for his one-day, round-trip back to Mexico. He knew she would worry. But as they pulled into San Diego, he had no choice. It was time to let her in on it.

"Day after tomorrow," he said while grilling chicken at an RV campground between San Diego and the Mexican border, "I'll take Laura with me and fly back to Guadalajara on Mexicana Airlines from Tijuana. She and I can walk across the border into Mexico and won't have to show any type of identification.* We'll just pretend to be tourists. I'll escort her home and return the same day. Then, I'll just walk back across the border and rejoin you guys."

As he outlined the significance of the disinformation he would be spreading, Janis saw the beauty of the plan, but also saw a major weakness.

---

* For Americans traveling into the interior of Mexico, the only requirement is to prove U.S. citizenship. Acceptable for this purpose are a U.S. passport, a birth certificate or voter registration card. No ID is necessary to enter the trading zone along the border. Once on Mexican soil, a person may board an airliner for interior points with no identification.

"It's a great idea, honey, but it doesn't make sense for you to go. There's probably an APB out for you. And if Rodriguez' people were to apprehend you, they would probably kill you. We can't take that risk. I need to be the one that goes. Surely they wouldn't kill me. They don't see me as a threat like they do you," Janis said convincingly, knowing she was right. "I can spread the same rumors and I can tell Richard [Tingen] and Diana [Aguilar] about Puebla and say that you're already over there working for Volkswagen. And, if I accidentally bump into Mitch Marr I can tell him the same thing."

"Besides," she added after seeing he was digesting what she had said, "you need to be here guarding the boys. I wouldn't do that nearly as well as you can."

Terry had to give serious thought to her offer. He did not like the thought of his wife traveling to Mexico with the threat of danger looming over them, but on the other hand, there was merit to what she was saying. They may not even be looking for her. Rodriguez had been present that night in the bunker in Little Rock when Terry was told not to share operational knowledge with her, and they had no way of knowing exactly what she knew. She was his wife and not necessarily a liability to them, *alive*. But if she died under mysterious circumstances, an investigation and unwanted publicity would ensue. Gringos who die on Mexican soil were always given preferential treatment, not only by the State Department, but Mexican authorities as well.

The downside would be a kidnapping. But, he reasoned, if she were to arrive unexpectedly in Chapala during daylight hours, stay in a public place and depart the same day, the chances of that would be minimal. And again, a kidnapping would bring unwanted police and media scrutiny, too. He hated to admit it, but she was right. She should be the one to go. It took a lot of courage on her part to put herself willingly at risk. But was the disinformation plan worth putting her in danger? He would sleep on that.

"OK, you win," he reluctantly conceded the next morning, "I'll never forgive myself if this goes haywire. But if you're still up for it, I really think it's something we should risk. You stay here and get your things together. I've already told Laura she's going home and she's insisting she has to do some shopping before she returns."

"Oh, that's great," Janis responded testily, "why don't you take Laura to the mall while I stay here and do laundry and pack. Ever since she crossed the border she thinks she's been on vacation. I'm getting pretty fed up with this Mexican maid crap."

The next morning, as they sat outside the motor home drinking coffee and having breakfast, the "snow birds" in the lavish and well-groomed RV park surrounding them would never have guessed the stressful discussion the Reeds were having. Terry knew his wife was uptight but insisted on grilling her extensively on the details of their battle plan he had formulated and she had committed to memory.

To Terry it was the equivalent of a "pre-strike" briefing in Southeast Asia. To Janis, it was as if she were going to *solo* a 747 Jumbo Jet for the first time. The tension was high.

Janis was to leave on the 8 AM Mexicana flight from Tijuana the next morning. She would fly to Guadalajara, take an airport taxi directly to Chapala, return Laura to her home, execute the equivalent of a Mexican power-of-attorney to Richard Tingen so that he could handle their financial affairs, sow the

᛫ false seeds, be highly visible, telephone both her sister and parents to inform them the entire Reed family was back in Mexico but were moving to Puebla, and return back on the 5 PM flight to Tijuana. If all went as planned, Janis would be back to enjoy a barbecue dinner with the family at the RV park.

But Terry had worked out alternative contingencies as well. "I know, you should always have three plans," she said, tiring of his insistence to plan for every unexpected event. "That means I have to memorize two other plans, just in case. I don't know if my brain, or my intestines are up for all of this." Her husband's attention to detail tended to drive her crazy, but right now, she knew she had better pay close attention to his alternatives since their lives depended on them...literally.

The contingencies included all of the things they would rather not have thought about—the "what ifs". These had few pleasant consequences, but realistically they had to be dealt with. What if Janis was arrested? What if she was detained in Mexico and couldn't return as scheduled? What if Terry had to flee the campground? Where would they rendezvous? If Terry found it necessary to surrender, who would take care of the children?

They packed in three envelopes the necessary instructions and copies of the children's passports to cover all three contingencies. Inconspicuously labeled A, B and C, each contained cryptic essentials of all three plans and took into account elements such as secure communications, rendezvous procedures, bank account and phone numbers. These would serve as checklists since Terry knew from his military experience that in times of stress, people forget simple things and make stupid mistakes. Nothing was left to chance.

As they lay sleeplessly holding each other in bed that night, neither communicated to the other the true fear building inside them. It was best just to cling to each other, hoping for the best and conjuring images of someday recounting this ordeal to their children—and preferably not from prison.

Janis' and Laura buckled their seat belts on the Mexicana Airlines 737 the next morning, right on schedule. Janis was not in a good mood. She had kissed her sleeping boys good-bye that morning wondering if she would ever see them again. She and Laura had taken a cab to the border and walked across the bridge into Tijuana. Janis had dressed comfortably for the trip in slacks and loafers, but her maid, who had never flown before, took this opportunity to wear her new red, mini, "disco dress" and the three-inch black patent heels she had purchased the previous day. Her hair which was normally in a tight braid, was loose and flowing to her waist. She had allured enough attention at the border crossing that she had several *muchachos* falling all over themselves with offers to carry the bulky and unwieldy suitcase Janis had loaned her. Janis carried her own.

Using the same "Sheila Walton," the alias she had utilized before, she was attempting to get mentally prepared for what lay ahead as she sat tensely awaiting take-off.

"*Senora* Walton," a male voice boomed from the front of the plane. "*Senora* Sheila Walton, identify yourself, *por favor.*"

Janis watched in terror as two Mexican uniformed men accompanied by a female civilian marched down the aisle. Being one of the few *gringas* on the plane, she knew she was easily-identifiable. There was no way out.

Her ears were ringing and her eyesight began to blur. It's over, they found her. But how? She must have been followed since the alias hadn't thrown off the authorities. Janis realized she had *stupidly* used the same alias after it was probably *compromised* during the phone call to her father. Back at the campground, Terry was surely in custody. Her worst fears were being realized. She was under arrest! Slowly, she rose from her seat. Laura, who was sitting next to her, was too pre-occupied flirting with one of the male flight attendants to notice what was taking place.

"You will have to deplane," the woman told her firmly. "You need to report to Mexican Customs. Your luggage is waiting for you. I'm sorry, that is all I have been told."

As she and Laura exited the aircraft and walked down the portable boarding stairs, another uniformed official was waiting on the tarmac. The entourage of uniforms accompanied Janis and the nonplussed Laura across what seemed a never-ending runway as the jet taxied away for take-off.

A uniformed customs official, with the usual Third World arrogance, silently escorted them to a room that appeared to be an interrogation center.

"*Senora*, do you have a confession to make? I can make things much more pleasant for you if you do."

Trembling within, she looked at the burly Mexican who was displaying his medals on his uniformed chest, no doubt evidence of years of faithful devotion to duty. She *had* to maintain her composure and go on the offense, she thought.

With all the courage she could muster, she said indignantly and in her best Spanish, "*Que es la problema? Necisitamos ir a Guadalajara ahorita! Esta es muy ridiculoso!*"

In response to her outburst, the Custom's agent dramatically threw open the luggage Laura had packed and dumped its contents onto the table. In the midst of clothing, toiletries, and American candy bars, *three* brand new Sony Walkman's surfaced.

Janis' Spanish left her. Could it be? Had this whole experience resulted from "smuggling" Japanese radios into Mexico without paying the duty? She knew for a fact this was something Mexican Customs takes very seriously.

Janis looked at Laura.

"*Lo siento, Senora*," (I'm sorry), Laura whined.

Janis felt no change in her adrenalin level. She now wanted to strangle Laura. But her throat began to relax. She could finally speak normally.

"How much?" she asked with disgust and composure.

"One hundred U.S. dollars," the customs man replied without a millisecond's hesitation.

Now was no time to haggle, Janis thought. With the rapidity of her response as she handed him the $100 bill, the customs inspector probably wished he had asked for $200.

It was over. Janis arranged for the next available flight at noon.

Terry was pacing the campground. His wife had not returned the previous evening as scheduled. He had spent a sleepless night with the children, wondering what could have gone wrong. He had to call Chapala Realty and find out. After driving northward and locating the center of the Hispanic squalor near downtown Los Angeles, he found a pay phone situated in a barrio and took the risk of calling Mexico.

"Yeah, she's here," Diana Aguilar said in her usual "don't sweat anything" tone. "I saw her this morning. She and Richard were going to see an attorney to get some papers signed. She said to tell you she would be returning this afternoon and that everything is OK. By the way, congratulations on landing the project in Puebla. We will miss you all."

A tremendous feeling of relief swept over his body. Terry's anxiety shifted to the Chicanos who were eyeballing the hub caps on the motor home. He had purposely driven to a point in Los Angeles where he figured any pursuing FBI personnel that showed up would be mugged. Chicanos, he figured, also knew how to spot undercover *federales* by the tiny hub caps and antennas on their cars, and knew how to deal with them too.

When a taxi pulled up in front of the motor home that evening, the entire family rushed out to greet Janis.

"What in the hell happened?" Terry implored, shaking his head and hugging her at the same time. "You had me worried sick."

He felt like a parent whose errant child had just dashed across the street and missed getting hit by a passing car. His emotions were overwhelming him. His relief at seeing her safely back in the U.S. was mixed with the anguish he felt from her decision to change the plan without informing him.

"You didn't get my message I left at the campground office?" she asked incredulously. "I called for you from the airport told them it was urgent to let you know we were delayed in departing."

"No, I did not get any message. Do you know how worried I've been about you? Why didn't you call back?"

"Terry, I'm in no mood for a lecture. You have no idea what I went through. Now calm down and I'll tell you about my trip...over a drink," she admonished.

The objectives had been accomplished, she told him. She was certain she had not been followed while leaving Guadalajara. In fact, as planned, she had flown first to Mexico City and then to the border, taking flights with no advance reservations. And the good news was Marr had returned to Ajijic and she had given Aguilar the "envelope" with the diagram Terry had drawn which would lead Marr to the hidden "evidence." With any luck, the entire Chapala community, by this time, would think the Reeds were in Puebla...and the CIA as well if they were monitoring international telephone calls.

Janis recapped that she had spoken by long distance to both her parents and her sister, informed them of their new business opportunity in Mexico and that for now, they could continue sending mail to Chapala Realty which would eventually be forwarded to their soon-to-be determined new address in Puebla. To add to Janis' peace of mind, her father was much improved. He was now ambulatory and apologetic for lousing up their vacation in Kansas City.

"Let's not stay here," Terry said of the RV park. "I'm all packed and I want to get out of here. This RV is the only thing standing between us and anonymity. While you were gone, I've worked out a plan to get rid of it."

"That's what I was afraid of. Another plan," Janis sighed.

It was two days before Thanksgiving, and in a sense, they felt thankful. After moving the RV to a beachside campground north of San Diego, and while snuggling with her children later that night, she thought how happy she was to have her family back to just the five of them. She'd had it with hired help!

* * *

"Please take good care of my Bronco," the nurse in San Diego, California pleaded. "I bought it new in Arizona and my husband and I have really babied it. We've never even had it in four-wheel drive."

It was mid-December and Terry was taking delivery of the keys to the Ford Bronco he had just purchased. All that stood between him and vehicular anonymity was for the DMV computer terminal in San Diego to spit out the new title and registration showing his newly-formed California corporation as the vehicle's owner.

It had been a busy three weeks since Janis' return from Mexico. They were living in a condominium in the Old Town section of the city while processing the necessary incorporation papers, which was an essential part of his plan to escape the system. To be able to hide behind the corporation's name would give him the ability to not only register a car, but do banking and purchase insurance for the Bronco as well.

With the self-incorporation kit in hand and the aid of a portable, electric typewriter, Janis and Terry had on paper created a marketing analysis firm that would give them the cover to travel coast to coast on "company business." The company's address was a post office box, complete with a registered service agent approved by the state.

The motor home had been sold to a school teacher who fell absolutely in love with the vehicle after seeing the way Janis had decorated its interior and how meticulously Terry had maintained it mechanically. Under construction at a local welding shop was an angle-iron frame-work that would soon take the shape of a utility trailer Terry had personally designed and customized to fit the Bronco's dimensions and color schemes. The more professional and business-like you looked, they reasoned, the less chance of drawing attention and avoiding prying questions from nosey police.

To the outside world, they would appear to be a family on a working vacation—a wife and teacher simply traveling with her husband and family as he performed in-depth marketing analysis on some non-existent product for a mythical client. They were off to see this great land, they would say, and to teach their five-year-old about geography. Before the trip would end, Duncan would be the proud owner of 34 state patches and the Bronco Billy's odometer would indicate 35,000 additional miles.

They were traveling down the twisting mountain roads from the snow bound Sequoia National Park and onto the endless, flat irrigated farmlands south of Fresno, heading north with no set plan. In fact, the plan, at times, was to have no plan at all. Using the logic that a plan you don't possess can't be *compromised*, they simply prepared to wander aimlessly from one tourist point to another destroying any logic employed by a pursuer.

"The way I have this figured, Janis, if we don't know where the hell we're going, they can't be waiting for us when we get there," Terry assured.

Zigzagging their way through California, the Reeds could not shake the haunting fear they had about being stopped for a moving violation or being involved in an accident. Either scenario would force Terry to produce a driver's license, showing his real name.

For this reason, they had initially decided that Janis would do all the driving. Terry was the one the authorities were sure to be looking for. Janis' status was still unknown, and surely she wasn't on a "most wanted" list. But after about three days of pure torture for both of them, they rescinded this idea. Janis' driving made Terry a nervous wreck.

"Well, if you wouldn't be so critical of my driving, I wouldn't be so tense and I'd do a better job! All you do is tell me what I'm doing wrong. Quit acting like a damn flight instructor! I'm no student pilot! I don't care if the right front tire hits a damn curb. Since I'm so incompetent, you drive!" She pulled the vehicle to the side of the road, jerked to a stop, and jumped out. "In fact, I'll just walk!"

Terry got behind the wheel and eased on up the road. "All right, Janis. Get in. You made your point."

She reluctantly got back in. She knew she was being childish. The tension was getting to her.

"Why did you come after me if I'm such a horrible driver and worthless human being?" she snapped, still angry.

"Because I find you sexy when you're mad...and your ass looks great when you stomp away like that."

After they had traveled several miles, Terry broke the silence, "Janis, we've taken care of disinformation, we now have vehicle anonymity and a new corporation to boot, but I have to become another person".

They had just passed through a state police roadblock west of Reno, Nevada, set up to insure motorists had either chains or snow tires to safely negotiate the hazardous snow-packed winter road. The fear that could surface from nowhere at the sight of a police car's lights was unnerving. All it took to destroy the mood of each day was the sight of police cars parked innocently by the road. Their sole purpose could be traffic safety, but to Janis and Terry, visions of being apprehended would flash through their minds. Every peering set of eyes behind the wheel of a possible undercover car triggered terror. The wave of fear that would sweep over him from out of nowhere, and at the least-expected moment, was wearing him down.

"I've got to go back to Carthage," he said. "I know it's risky but I don't think they'll think I would ever go back there. And now that we have Bronco Billy, we can go to Missouri in a vehicle no one is looking for."

"Why do we have to go back there?" she asked.

"I have to assume the identity of a dead man."

* * *

Janis paced nervously in the motel in Joplin, Missouri. Her husband had been gone several hours and should have been back by now. Now *she* was learning what it felt like to have a plan go off-schedule and be in the dark about what was happening. Her fear was again surfacing and she *had* to control it. The children were watching Mr. Rogers on the motel's TV and she was hoping they couldn't feel her anxiety.

"It's a beautiful day in the neighborhood, a beautiful day in the neighborhood," Mr. Rogers droned that dreadful song her children adored, "Won't you be my neighbor."

Janis still had intense waves of denial and depression as she observed the rest of the world go on as if they had nothing to worry about. She felt she was on the outside looking in. How could people be so happy when her life was destroyed? Some days, she felt her only *raison d'etre* was her children and such trivialities as telling them time and again to brush their teeth.

Terry had been nagging her to read parts of his "Bible." She went for the Jeppesen-Sanderson Private Pilot Manual, turning to page 11-20 he had marked for her, the section headed "Anxiety and Stress." She began reading.

"Since a pilot in his aviation environment, is required to continually evaluate information, perform complex tasks, and make decisions, aviation psychology deals with a pilot's performance during various emotional states. Two of these states—stress and anxiety—may have adverse effects on pilot performance. The causes of emotional stress are many and varied. They can be divided into two categories. The first includes those situations not specifically related to flying such as family problems, financial or business considerations, or the demands of a pressing schedule.

"The second category involves situations directly related to flight: for instance, apprehension about adverse weather conditions, malfunctioning equipment, or the lack of confidence on the part of the pilot.

"Fear is a normal, protective emotion which can build some stress or anxiety. Fear progressing to panic, however, is certainly undesirable. Panic can be avoided or overcome by forcible maintaining or re-establishing self-control. A person who completely understands a situation can maintain control of his emotions, think more clearly and reason properly. Once reason and logic are applied to the facts, the proper decision can me made and the appropriate action taken."

Damn! She threw the book down. That's a bunch of crap! Maybe it works for pilots, but it's so clinical and calculated! Whoever wrote it couldn't have experienced real panic, she was convinced.

The phone rang, interrupting her outburst.

"Hi. It's me. I'm leaving Carthage and headed your way. I got what I needed. You're talking to the future Mr. _____ _____."

"I hate that name. I never did like it. I knew a real creepy guy in school named _____."

"Then, you can call me ____ if you like, that's his middle name."

While earlier driving across the desert Southwest and thinking about the problems associated with assuming a new identity, Terry focused on the pitfalls. What if you're questioned in detail about your past? What if someone really tries to get into your mind about your background, your hometown, your relatives and the rest. From what he'd read, this is where people normally assuming a new identity are tripped up. They make one little slip-up about a geographical location or some past significant event that they should have remembered.

For this reason, Terry had zeroed in on an ex-high school classmate. Not only had he gone to school with him, but they had worked together at the same grocery store while attending high school, both had attended ROTC together, and their birthdays were one day apart. Terry knew from friends that he had died very mysteriously after a very short illness in 1977. There was no better way, he thought, to be sure he didn't make those common errors about past events than to assume the identity of an individual you were raised with. In this way, he had the proper database to build his new identity.

In researching the "do's and don't's" in attaining someone else's identity, he had gone the extra mile by contacting the Office of Vital Statistics in Oklahoma to prepare himself for the questions that might be asked of him while getting a dead man's birth certificate. In that conversation, he had learned that most states were going through their death records and notifying the Social Security Administration to retire those individuals' numbers from the active files.

For fear this may be the case with his departed friend, Terry had decided all he really needed was a driver's license bearing another individuals name, but with Terry's photo on it. He had no intention of working and paying social security taxes under the dead man's name, for fear that the Social Security account had in fact been flagged as deceased.

On that morning in January, 1988, when he left his family in the Joplin motel room, all he knew for sure was that the dead man was probably buried in the largest cemetery in Carthage, Park Cemetery. After locating the gravesite, with the assistance of the caretaker, he then had the date of death from the tombstone. A quick trip to the local newspaper library gave him the published death notice, surviving relatives names and most importantly, the name of the funeral home that had handled the burial. He had been told it was a matter of normal business policy for undertakers to keep records on vital statistics of "clients."

Bingo...he had hit pay dirt. Not only did the funeral home have the record of the death in its files, but the record also contained the dead man's Social Security number as well.

Blind luck then struck! What caught his eye on the funeral home's ledger was the notation of the dead man's place of birth...the Panama Canal Zone. Now that he knew the exact place of birth, it would no longer be necessary to obtain a death certificate in order to extract that one piece of critical information. One phone call to the Pentagon gave him the phone number of the records section at the only Army hospital in the Canal Zone that could have delivered a dependent child in 1948. Terry now had in hand the Social Security number, a date and place of birth, the father's and mother's name and a money order for $25. From this he was able to obtain a certified copy of his friend's birth certificate.

With the certificate, he was allowed to take a driver's test in another state, and walk out a "new man."

It was now late January and the Reeds breathed a deeper sigh of relief as they motored eastward, secure in the knowledge that if stopped for a traffic violation, Terry had in his possession a foolproof new identity that could even get him a passport if needed.

But back in Kansas City, something strange was going on. Actually, nothing was going on, that was why it was strange. No one seemed to be looking for them. Janis had discreetly earlier obtained her sister's travel schedule and had been able to make contact with her while she was at an out-of-state seminar.

She asked Karen how their father was recuperating and if she was aware of anyone attempting to contact them through her parents, knowing that her sister would be fully informed since the family was close. She "pretexted" the question around a scenario of an old client of Terry's who was wanting to move to Mexico who perhaps had only her parents' address and phone number with which to contact them.

After being reassured that her father was recuperating nicely, Janis was relieved to be informed that there had been no callers or visitors asking questions. Most significant and yet curious to Terry was the fact no insurance investigator had been around asking questions. Wouldn't the insurance company, he reasoned, be the one most anxious to question him and demand their money back if in fact it was his stolen airplane N2982M that had been recovered from his hangar? And wouldn't it be logical that the company would have filed a lawsuit against Terry by now, seeking restitution. The only conclusion he could draw was that the insurance company, which had held the policy on his stolen plane, must have been an Agency proprietary involved in "Project Donation."

Maybe, he thought, North *had* intervened. It made no sense to Terry for the CIA to allow Felix Rodriguez and the others involved in the cocaine trafficking to bring attention to "Screw Worm" by setting him up and bringing prosecution under phony criminal charges.

But he felt it was too soon to ease off and let his guard down. He remembered North's instructions to lay low. Now that Terry was a new man, and driving a vehicle no one was looking for and having created the illusion of being in two foreign countries at the same time, they felt free to wander as they contemplated their dilemma. But the dread never left them, because, in the end, it was not the law they feared as much as the ruthless assassins like the ones who killed Barry Seal. Amiram Nir's admission of Rodriguez's boasting about having knowledge pertaining to Seal's and Emile Camp's deaths never left Terry's mind.

A favorite movie of Terry's, *The President's Analyst* with James Coburn, played over and over in his mind. It was the sterile attitude captured in the scene where the government agent, his .357 magnum in hand and displaying no emotion, had come to kill the hero solely because he had a signed death warrant authorizing the assassination. "Eliminate with extreme prejudice," is the clinical terminology the intelligence agencies use to mask the assassinations they later deny any knowledge of. "We don't do that," is always the response from the official spokesmen. "The United States does not condone such behavior."

Terry's fear was not based on a movie, however, it was based on first-hand experience. He had learned in Arkansas that he had inadvertently helped train an assassination team. He had unwittingly participated in the hypocrisy of his government. Their stated policies, he knew, were not the policies they practiced. After all, hadn't the world learned of the CIA assassination manual found in Nicaragua?

As they drove from motel to motel across the country, the terror never left them. The children were never allowed out of their well-armed parents' sight. It was never their intention to participate in a Bonnie and Clyde type shootout with the law since the Reeds had agreed early on to surrender themselves without resistance to law enforcement if the time ever came. They felt the weapons were necessary to protect their children from the spineless kidnappers who might be lurking in the shadows.

To the "Reedlets" as Terry and Janis affectionately called their little boys, it had all become a giant, on-going adventure, state to state, town to town, a sightseeing extravaganza. Nearly every night of their journey while east of the Mississippi, they checked into a different Red Roof Inn. Janis liked the concept that every room looked alike...every bedspread, every lamp, every end table...they were alike all across the country. Each night when they checked in, the boys were in familiar surroundings. It was home to them.

Although living with a perpetual sense of dread, each day took on a familiar monotony. They pushed themselves relentlessly, always up and on the road at day break, driving until dusk to a destination seldom predetermined.

Janis spent the mornings schooling her children. Two- year-old Elliott was infatuated with his *Once Upon a Potty* book and Janis was thrilled when he expressed a desire to imitate the main character, Joshua. Terry was less than thrilled with Janis' suggestion of a potty seat in the car.

"I can't believe I'm trying to potty train a two year old in a car! What am I supposed to do?"

"Hey, he can learn to go in a bottle. He'll be advanced for his age," Terry responded. "I'm not dragging around a damn latrine along with everything else."

One morning Janis found Duncan diligently writing in his Big Chief Tablet.

"What are you working on, Duncan?" she asked.

Very proudly he replied, "Look, Mommy, I can spell!"

He presented her with his tablet and said, "I can read too! Listen."

Methodically he pointed to each of the five words he had written: ice, men, women, gas, coke.

"Duncan, you're so smart! I didn't know you could spell so many words!"

"It's easy, Mommy," he confided. "All the gas stations have the same words outside."

She had to laugh. This wasn't a traditional education, but at least he was learning. She had taught him about wagon trains, pioneers, Lewis and Clark, the Grand Canyon and the Continental Divide as they wound their way across the country. As they drove through Texas and Oklahoma, Terry would explain to his ever-inquisitive son all about oil wells and pumping jacks and centrifugal force. But, one of his little co-pilot's favorite subjects was weather, and he impressed his father by pointing out all the cloud types.

"Cumulo nimbus is my favorite, Daddy. That means it might rain and they tear up airplanes, right?"

The Reedlets were amazingly good travelers. But every afternoon as if on cue Baxter, also known as the "Round Mound of Sound" by his brothers, delighted in hearing himself squeal for miles on end. The family could only stand so much of this torture and discovered quite by accident one day that a spin around a grocery store in a grocery cart was all he needed to calm down. This became an afternoon tradition for the family and a much anticipated break from the monotonous travel.

As the afternoon faded to evening, it was always a game to see who could spot the Red Roof Inn first. As Janis and Terry watched their children cheerfully clamor out of the Bronco each evening with their back packs, their dog, and their favorite toy, they knew their children were having a wonderful adventure, but the facade was so difficult for them to maintain. Janis found herself frequently on the verge of tears, tormented by her plight.

She worried constantly if they were being followed. She worried about her parents and her father's health. She worried about Duncan not being in school. She worried that they were spending too much money. She worried about having a car wreck. She worried about the safety of her children. She had a perpetual knot in her stomach and had to force herself to eat.

One day while Terry was paying for gas and she was studying a map, Duncan screamed , "Mommy, Elliott swallowed my tooth fairy money. My quarter's gone!"

"What?! How could that have happened?" she exclaimed as she inspected the empty mouth of the wide-eyed Elliott. "Are you sure he swallowed a quarter?"

"Not really."

Janis breathed a sigh of relief.

"Maybe it was a nickel."

Twenty minutes later, after a thorough search turned up the missing quarter in Baxter's diaper bag, Janis sighed, "I can't take this anymore."

Terry said nothing. He knew that one little slip-up in their routine could alter their future dramatically. He didn't know how much longer he could take this either.

By late March, their trip led them to the easternmost region of Maine, where an old friend of Janis' from Oklahoma City was living. After spending several days with her and her family on the rock-bound Atlantic coast, they were beginning to feel the wanderlust.

They couldn't keep doing this forever, or could they? Before their troubles beset them, they had dreamed of finding time and money to do nothing but travel. But like all good things in life, they must be taken in moderation. It was starting to get old. They sat on the beach listening to the seagulls and the pounding surf and discussed their plight. They felt as if they were in limbo. Some state of suspended animation. What, if anything, was the government up to. The question gnawed at them incessantly.

They didn't, for a minute, dare assume their problems had vanished and that they could look forward to a normal life. They did not allow themselves the luxury of letting their guard down.

"Let's go to New Mexico," Terry said one day while throwing bread to the seagulls. "I love the high-elevation desert and I feel comfortable with Desko nearby. Let's serpentine our way slowly west. And if no one has contacted your parents by Easter, let's just ease our way down to Albuquerque and figure out how we can blend into the surroundings there."

* * *

"Terry, I just got off the phone with my mother," a panic stricken Janis was saying by phone to the Reeds' home in Placitas, New Mexico, on July 29, 1988. " I've got real bad news. The FBI has been to my parents home. They say you've been indicted and that you're now considered a fugitive."

This time it was Terry's turn to develop tunnel vision and ringing ears. His old friend, fear, immediately consumed him. He could swallow, yet the yellow bile from his stomach was rising through his esophagus and attempting to erupt from his mouth. His stomach was pushing hard against his diaphragm, causing shortness of breath.

Shit! he thought. He rushed to the window preparing to see a SWAT team around his compound. But no one was there and Macho wasn't barking. Damn! I've got to get hold of myself, he thought. "I've got to think," he said out loud. Prioritize! Go through your check list, he shouted to himself as he paced like a caged animal trying to deal with this intangible catastrophe as if it were an aviation emergency. He roamed the house looking outside for signs of movement, any visual clue to forewarn of pending disaster. He finally tired, regained control and just sat, expecting to be arrested at any moment. All he could think of was, why? Why would the CIA bring attention to all of this? Hadn't he figured it all out? Wasn't his plan working, up to now? It made no sense. WHY NOW? He had proved he was no threat to them. He could be trusted. He hadn't gone to the press or Congress.

Here it was August...almost a year from the date he had met with Felix Rodriguez in San Miguel. Just as he was starting to get things sorted out and look at some business opportunities in automation in New Mexico...shit! How could this be happening now?

After all, he thought, Iran-Contra by now was a politically dead issue in the on-going Presidential race. The election was only three months away and the Democrats had not successfully fired one major Iran-Contra salvo at the Republicans, who were at the heart of the scandal. Terry rationalized both parties were probably *compromised* since each had aided and abetted the CIA in Arkansas while the White House and the Agency violated the Constitution. So it made no sense for the government to bring an unnecessary indictment and unwanted attention to the issue. Or was he a political pawn? Who could be using him, and for what purpose?

Or was this a way to guarantee his silence? He knew he HAD to be a liability to both parties and their candidates.

His serene world in the New Mexican desert began spinning around, topsy-turvy, end over end. He could almost hear voices uttering phrases he never thought would apply to him. Phrases like:

"Freeze! You're under arrest!"

"Book him..."

"You have the right to remain silent, if you give up that right, what you say, can and will, be used against you...."

After Janis returned home, they had to deal with the fact Terry was a wanted man. They had quietly joined the community of Placitas 20 miles north of Albuquerque and had been attempting to become productive members of the local community. Duncan was pre-enrolled in the first grade. Elliott, who had been diagnosed with a speech and hearing disorder, was seeing a much-needed specialist.

The Reeds were so convinced that North had "fixed" things and they were no longer being pursued, their household goods, which had been in storage in Arkansas since the summer of 1986, were now in New Mexico where they had set up housekeeping. They were living under their own names. A quiet, but productive lifestyle. They were even hoping to build an energy efficient solar adobe home on the beautiful and sandy foothills that led up to the Sandia Ridge overlooking Albuquerque.

Just as their life was appearing to get back to normal, they had been dealt what seemed a death blow.

Calls to the federal courthouse in Wichita, Kansas revealed a situation even worse than feared. The FBI agents who had been to Janis' parents house had lied! It was not only Terry who had been indicted, but Janis as well. The indictments had been handed up by a grand jury in Wichita and both were charged with four counts of mail fraud stemming from the theft of Terry's old plane back in Joplin in 1983.

He was learning that the grand jury had convened on June 1st, 1988 and his case was the first to be heard that day, for good reason. Only three days later, on June 4th, the statute of limitations would have run out on *any* activity involving the theft of that aircraft or the alleged defrauding of the insurance company.

Having never been involved in the Federal Criminal Justice System, the Reeds sought out and retained an attorney to counsel them on their rights and their legal status. Even the attorney was somewhat confused as to why they hadn't been already arrested. Terry was confused. Either he had been awfully successful in confusing them as to his whereabouts or they were still toying with him. He had been overtly living in New Mexico for almost five months.

But one thing was certain, he felt he was under direct frontal attack. And it wasn't he alone being attacked. While negotiating with an attorney in Kansas to represent them during the surrender process, he learned through his sister that his 72-year-old mother had been hospitalized.

"I don't know what's going on, Terry," his frantic sister told him over the phone. "But two FBI agents have been to mom's house twice and the sons of bitches have got her so shaken she's in the hospital. I think she's dying. She may have had a heart attack. Terry, I don't know what you did, but these guys want you *real bad*."

And they wanted him bad enough to have created a computer profile that would tempt even the most timid of law enforcement officers to come out of his police car with guns-a-blazin' hoping to receive credit for apprehending or felling such a seasoned desperado.

Arkansas Governor Bill Clinton's Chief of Security, Captain Raymond (Buddy) Young had a played a major role in creating that profile. He had supplied the FBI with the following: "BUDDY YOUNG ADVISED THAT HE HAS RECEIVED INFORMATION WHICH INDICATES TERRY REED MAY BE INVOLVED IN MEXICAN AND/OR SOUTH AMERICAN DRUG TRAFFICKING AND MAY NOW BE RESIDING IN GUADALAJARA MEXICO. YOUNG STATED THAT A SEARCH OF THE AIRCRAFT REVEALED SEVERAL MAPS OF SOUTHERN NORTH AMERICA."

Young had further served as judge and jury over Reed by concluding he was guilty of the crime eight and a half months before the Grand Jury handed up the indictment. Young's "verdict" was stored in a computer file at the DEA's El Paso Intelligence Center (EPIC).

EPIC is a federal intelligence center specializing in storing information about border trafficking and other surveillance activity by police and federal agencies. It is operated by the DEA but many federal agencies maintain offices there, including the CIA. Young's insertion into the computerized records maintained at EPIC read as follows:

"On October 16, 1987, it was reported to EPIC that the Arkansas State Police, Little Rock, Arkansas, reported aircraft N2982M was recovered on October 16, 1987, from a hangar in North Little Rock, Arkansas where the owner Kent T. Reed (aka Terry Reed) hid the aircraft to collect the $33,000 insurance claim."

Young's form of justice moved swiftly.

Even more disturbing was a "profile enhancement" to affect the way police officers behave when apprehending a suspect. It was listed on an FBI AIRTEL message dated 5-5-88 from the FBI in Kansas City sent to FBI field offices in Little Rock, Memphis, and Oklahoma City. Its purpose was to classify Reed as "instant matter now being carried as *armed and dangerous* due to information developed by the Little Rock division".

Reed's paranoia was not.

The Reeds were fugitives. The FBI and CIA just never go away...if you're an asset that becomes a liability.

CHAPTER 33

DEPARTMENT OF INJUSTICE

"Mr. Reed, you are not to leave the State of New Mexico without permission from this court. You are not to carry or be near a firearm. You are not to associate with any known felons and you are not to consume alcohol. These conditions plus a $50,000 bail are the conditions of your release pending trial on four felony counts of mail fraud."

As U.S. Magistrate John Wooley finished Terry Reed's bail hearing on August 24th, 1988, visions of the bullets ripping through Barry Seal's body raced through Terry's mind.

He couldn't erase the thought from his mind. Confined to a specified area and unarmed. This is just how they "eliminated" Barry!

Marilyn Trubey put down her pencil, removed her glasses and wiped her eyes as she surveyed the three yellow legal pads she had just filled with notes from Terry Reed's marathon narrative, detailing his life from 1980 to that day in 1988 when she had been assigned his case.

"Is that all?" she asked.

"Isn't that enough?" Terry responded.

She put the cap back on her pen, stacked the pads neatly one atop the other and looked at him intently.

"It looks like your friends did you in, Terry," she said, looking up from the stack of shorthand notes on her desk. It had taken him over six hours to outline the series of events to Trubey.

Strangely, for the first time since his indictment, Terry somehow felt secure. This prim, stoic lawyer sitting back in her swivel-chair in the Federal Public Defender's Office rekindled in him feelings akin to those of his childhood, when his parents put his frail health into the hands of the old family doctor who always eased his pain and fears. She reminded him of a young Barbara Stanwyck, cool and radiating self confidence.

He had learned a lot about her, he felt, just by reading a framed inscription hanging on the wall above her desk that read: "Capital punishment means them without the capital gets the punishment."

The federal charges against the Reeds were "capital related." Janis and Terry were each charged specifically with four counts of mail fraud, a crime that carries upon conviction a maximum five-year prison sentence on each count. The indictment charged that Reed stole his own airplane and then hid it in his hangar to fraudulently collect the $33,000 in insurance. Janis was charged with aiding and abetting him, though just how she did that was never spelled out. The mail fraud statute, a law federal prosecutors use as a catch-all when no other charge fits, or when they are desperate to make something stick, was invoked due to the insurance transaction being handled through the mail.

Terry was told by an Arkansas attorney he knew, "Be extremely careful with mail fraud charges, they are difficult to defend and can really 'bite ya in the ass' if not taken seriously. Mail fraud is sorta like steppin' on a rusty nail. If ya don't treat it right, ya can die from infection. Oh, yeah, one more thing...get ready ta spend a lotta money defendin' it."

It was October 11th and the leaves of the trees that day in Wichita, Kansas, had only begun their fall transformation. Terry had told his story over and over again and by now he was tired of re-telling it. It was, to almost everyone who had heard it, an unbelievable tale. To no avail, he had spent three days the previous month in Washington with an attorney for Senator John Kerry's Subcommittee on Terrorism, Narcotics and International Operations.

There seemed to have been plenty of interest in Washington in the Reeds' story. "It all fits," they were told by subcommittee investigator Jack Blum. "It confirms our suspicions about Felix Rodriguez and what we suspected was really going on. Go back and tell your attorney to draft a proffer (a formal statement). I'm sure that either [Independent Counsel Lawrence] Walsh or Senator Kerry will want to question you under oath. You'll be hearing from us soon." Trubey drafted the proffer, but there was never a call from Blum, Kerry, Walsh or anyone else.*

And prior to the Washington debriefing, there had been the man billed as the second best defense attorney in the State of Kansas—Steve Robison, a former federal prosecutor. Terry had quickly determined Robison belonged to the "grab-a-fee, cop-a-plea" school of expensive and fast-moving attorneys who liked to clean up cases in a hurry. Lawyers, for the most part, feel that time spent in court is time lost from the pursuit of profit and Robison had honed that philosophy to a razor's edge.

After spending four hours on the night of their first meeting, Terry covered the high points of his ordeal and Robison comforted him with his $250-an-hour advice by saying, "Hey, relax. So you got caught with your hand in the cookie jar. It happens all the time to good people. They charged you with four counts, but my advice is to plead guilty to one. You'll get two years, but you'll only serve six months. After all, it's only your first offense."

After rejecting Robison's plea advice, Terry and Janis would look with despair at their monthly statements. Robison was courteous enough to reduce his $250 an hour rate to his "discount rate" of $125 an hour for time spent reading select Iran-Contra books. Robison called it "research." His favorite book turned out to be Leslie Cockburn's, *Out of Control*. After finishing that one, he called Terry and asked, "Did Iran-Contra really happen? Or did the media just make up all this shit?"

After realizing that Robison wasn't the type of counsel he needed, Terry set about attorney shopping. He was beginning to feel like the victim of a car

---

* While in Magistrate Wooley's court room, Terry and Janis were forced to waive their rights under the "speedy trial act", a law which guarantees defendants be put on trial within 70 days of arraignment. The Reeds had nearly needed that much time just to find an attorney qualified to deal with the case's underlying issues, namely Oliver North and the CIA.

accident as he went from firm to firm trying to locate one that had the "correct talent, expertise and proper track record" to repair his legal problems. Just as one is wise to get three repair estimates on a wrecked car, Terry did likewise for his pending criminal ordeal.

While still under the by-the-hour care of Robison and prior to exhausting his legal expenses reserve, Terry took his case to a well-known Washington legal scholar who told him, "it sounds like your Wichita attorney needs an attorney." During that interview, Terry was told that it would take an "estimated" $450,000 to bring in the CIA and defend the case properly. It was also this man's off-the-record advice to, "declare yourself indigent and force the government to appoint you an attorney. That's all that will stop your financial blood-letting. You're dealing with the fucking U.S. Government, Terry. They've outspent better men than you. They've got the deficit on their side," he noted cynically.

He had obtained another estimate from an attorney in Kansas who said he would take the case for $250,000, if defense strategy was kept very simple and the CIA was not implicated.

Still another, who was seeking to make a name for himself offered, "I'll blow it out for $125,000 but you gotta pay me up front in cash and I get to keep the money regardless of what happens."

Does anyone honestly believe he risked this kind of legal exposure over a $33,000 insurance claim that netted him a "profit" of $2,500, after retiring the loan and covering his expenses, he asked? Unless you're a lawyer, he was finding, crime certainly does not pay.

Terry was emotionally numb. He was getting a crash course about the legal system and its prohibitive costs to a defendant facing a criminal charge. He was feeling outrage and despair. There oughta be a law, he said to himself.

And he was beginning to learn what anyone who observes the criminal justice system for any length of time learns: It only serves itself.

"This is a fucking industry," he told Janis after an "attorney shopping trip". "It has nothing to do with justice. All it has to do with is money, and the power and prestige money will buy you."

On their trip to Washington to "interview" for Senator Kerry's committee, Terry and Janis visited the Vietnam War Memorial for the first time. It was a very emotional experience for both of them. Looking at the wall, Terry began to think that the men whose names were etched into the marble were the lucky ones.

"They wouldn't want to see the way this country has turned into shit," Terry said to his wife, who quietly sobbed, overcome with emotion as she gazed at the memorial with the Capitol Dome looming in the background. "They probably died thinking they were still fighting for something." He was sure the country had lost its soul. He had fought for what he was told was "truth, justice and the American way." But he had found through working with the CIA, there was no truth and now he was learning the hard way there was also no justice.

"So, this must be the American way," he said to his wife.

Unlike aerial combat, which has some honor in it, there were no rules of engagement in this war game he was playing. The Bill of Rights, which supposedly defined the rules, was honored more in the breach than in reality and had become to the judges just a nuisance on the way to conviction.

This "Dial 1-800-RAT FINK" mentality that the government encourages by reporting everything to the police was undermining the value system Terry had built his life around. There was no "Duty, Honor, Country" in this war, fought in plushly carpeted, mahogany paneled offices and marble shrines built as monuments to power.

It was a faceless, heartless entity that was after the Reeds, seeking to destroy their family and their lives. It had no shape, no form, nothing a person could grab and wrestle with. Their attacker could only be defined by twenty-five letters neatly embossed from a typewriter, emblazoned atop the documents that now controlled their lives and had robbed them of their freedom of movement as surely as the paper shackles that had bound Barry Seal: THE UNITED STATES GOVERNMENT.

Back in New Mexico, from their Placitas homesite view of the desert mesa region south of Sante Fe, Terry and Janis would "dig in for the duration" and took little comfort in the fact their address and phone number were "allegedly" not available to the public through court records back in Wichita. Trubey had successfully argued to Judge Theis that the Reed's lives were possibly in danger, and Theis had ordered the Reed's whereabouts be sealed and their address held in abeyance by the court, only to be opened in the event of noncompliance with a mandatory court appearance. [Reed later learned that the CIA had his New Mexico address the entire time.]

Terry had little faith in a system that had access to documents in which the "enemy" controlled. The government was saying that the government couldn't have access.

Surrounded once again by fear and paranoia, pinned down and unable to evade their possible pursuers, they huddled with their children and just stared at their arrest warrants neatly typed on U.S. Government Form "AO-142 (Rev. 5/85)."

They couldn't believe their names were written under the heading "United States of America versus Terry and Janice(sic) Reed". It was so impersonal and overwhelming seeing the words "United States of America" (an entire nation!) against the two of them. Some GS clerk-typist who prepared this would be critiqued on his or her spacing, spelling and neatness. Had it been the same way in Germany when Jews' names were typed neatly on Nazi extermination orders by some faceless bureaucrat? Terry wondered, was there a form number for an execution order? He knew the answer was yes!

Then, they would read their FBI file and see the words "armed and dangerous" next to their names, along with the notation "Reed may be involved in Mexican and/or South American drug trafficking and may now be residing in Guadalajara, Mexico." Preposterous, Terry thought, this is what he had caught the CIA doing! In intelligence parlance, this is called "transference," a technique of making a "pre-emptive strike" on someone to neutralize damaging information he might possess. You simply accuse the other person of doing what you've done. It was killing him knowing what they were doing. And where were these faceless accusers? Hidden behind the FBI reports the government had based its case on that read "Source says...".

"What justice," he screamed! "Felix fucking Rodriguez or just who? They won't dare come out in the open and fight like men. Just remain cowards hidden behind redacted FBI form 302's."

The case was packed with neatly-collected fabrications and half-truths the government had constructed to discredit the Reeds. Things people had said, like Janis' former friend, Cherryl Hall.

"Cherryl Hall," the FBI report said," advised that the last house they [The Reeds] moved into in Maumelle was a $200,000 home...[she] felt this strange in that she did not think they could afford a $200,000 home. Cherryl Hall also advised that the Reeds seemed to act mysteriously when they moved into this last home in the middle of the night."

Janis was aghast. "What is this supposed to mean, 'we moved into the house in the middle of the night?' Why would we do that?" she shrieked. "Where are these lies coming from?"

Seth Ward, who had blackmailed his way into the arms loop in Arkansas, told an FBI agent interviewing him at the Capital Club, an exclusive men's club in the Worthen Bank Building in Little Rock, that Terry was "a swindler and an individual unworthy of trust."

Mark McAfee, who fled Arkansas after declaring bankruptcy and was the man who sicced the FBI on Aki Sawahata, "described Terry Reed as a devious individual, unworthy of trust. He further stated he knew Terry Kent Reed to carry a gun and felt that Reed was just unstable enough to use it." McAfee also told the FBI "that Terry Reed had asked him how hard he felt it would be to traffic illegal narcotics into the United States from Mexico."

Terry couldn't comprehend what was happening here. These were total lies and fabrications the FBI was accepting from people who were themselves guilty of violating federal laws. Did the FBI know that? Was this deliberate? Was this all being done at the CIA's behest?

Janis was stunned when she went to retrieve her FBI file that had been FedEx'd to New Mexico by her attorney. Naively expecting a business size envelope, her stomach turned over when she saw the large box that her file had arrived in.

"How could this be," she cried. "I haven't even DONE anything!" She later became physically ill after reviewing its contents. "It's all so twisted! It's all so false! But, Terry, who do we fight to straighten it out?!" she sobbed while rocking Baxter. "They're out to destroy us. And they're going to win."

When Terry noted the name of the FBI Special Agent who was leading the investigation against them, he had concrete proof, at least in his own mind, that he was being manipulated by the Agency. The man was none other than counter-intelligence Agent Mark A. Jessie. The man who had helped contain the investigation against the Agency front Overseas International and resident CIA agent Akihide Sawahata, back in 1985.

Special Agent Jessie had shown photos of Janis and Terry Reed to her former business associates when he interviewed them. Based upon what was said in Jessie's reports, the photos were grouped with the mug shots of convicts, line-up style, in order to sway the opinion of the interviewee and make the Reed's appear as if they were prior felons. It was clear from the FBI file that a profile was being created to make both Reeds look like unsavory people with connections to drug trafficking. Was he being drawn into the judicial system to be kept within their cross hairs until more charges could be filed? Or was he being set up to be killed?

True criminals, the Reeds were told, would be laughing at a mere mail fraud charge. But to the Reeds, who were the offspring of law abiding families with high religious and morals values, this "white collar crime" was equivalent to a death sentence.

Twenty years. Twenty years. This "crime" could get them both twenty years.

This gnawing knowledge remained unspoken between them. To articulate it made it real. They would not discuss it. They had three little boys to raise. Although unspoken, it was always there, every minute of every waking hour.

This indictment, Terry knew, had nothing to do with justice, or even with mail fraud. There was no victim. No one had been hurt. No insurance company had ever complained. This was the CIA, the government, trying to silence him and "dirty him up." His knowledge of how they operated made him full of rage. He knew what was really going on. He had been schooled in propaganda and disinformation. The justice system, devised to protect people's rights, had been turned into an illegal weapon. And he knew who had his finger on the trigger...Republican Presidential candidate George Bush, and the Republican Party.

Bush and the Republicans may have had their finger on the trigger, but the Democratic Party was probably passing the ammo, he figured. Terry could hear his great-grandfather laughing at him from his grave, "Got yourself in a fine fix, didn't ya boy? Both the Republicans and the Democrats want ya dead."

Terry knew that the last person who wanted him to leave Mexico in the Fall of 1988 and reveal the CIA secrets he had learned was Bush, who was running for President against Michael Dukakis. Terry's knowledge would have opened Iran-Contra all over again, exposing completely new levels of government duplicity. Bush, Terry was sure, wanted to make sure he had no real forum, and up until the trial Terry would be prohibited from saying anything, since by doing so could expose him to more charges.

And the last person who wanted Terry back in Arkansas was Bill Clinton. He, too, knew that Terry could destroy his chances of not only seeking the Presidency someday, but could probably keep him from being reelected as governor.

The Reeds, knowing they were isolated politically, took comfort from the serenity of the desert landscape that stretched for miles with its expansive views of Cabezon Mountain, the nightly sunsets, the winds, the sage brush and the dust devils.

Terry had selected the remote area in large part to be prepared to deal with the hired assassins who might try to dispose of him the way Barry Seal had been. To provide security for his family, he was ready to take whatever measures were necessary. For fear of wire taps, no telephone calls concerning court strategy were to be made from the house. He further isolated the home electronically by constructing a manual switching device that would sever all telephone lines to the house, as well as the one to the sheriff's department that controlled the burglar alarm. He knew any wire leading to the home could be used for surveillance purposes. He thought back and wished he still had the 500 pounds of C-4 plastic explosives that he had hidden for Cooper. The magistrate who had set his bail told him he couldn't have a gun, but he hadn't mentioned explosives or anti-personnel mines. So he went shopping. Lord help the unsuspecting coyote that happened to wander on the Reed property at night.

Out of fear, Terry took extreme measures to protect his family and as he contemplated their alternatives, Terry realized there was no ready refuge. In Mexico, he had been told, the local U. S. Consulate, in the event of an emergency would protect him from harm.

There is, they began to realize, no Witness Protection Program to protect people from a government that runs amuck and becomes the predator seeking to destroy those who have become liabilities.

Seated in their comfortable home in Placitas, Janis found herself withdrawing even more into their underground world. They were consumed with their quest for survival and talked of nothing else. She found her world revolving around Terry's daily trips to town and to the pay phone for discussions with Marilyn Trubey, and she would start to panic if he was gone too long.

Seven miles from their home on the banks of the northern Rio Grande was the small Hispanic community of Bernalillo, where Coronado had wintered as he traveled north from Mexico in search of gold.

On Main Street was the one and only Silva's Saloon, founded in 1933 and the site of many western movies. The second-generation owner, Felix Silva, ran a squeaky clean bar that doubled as a museum, which was filled with memorabilia of the Old West mixed with bare-breasted pin-ups. Prior to their indictment, it had become Janis and Terry's Hispanic "Cheers." Now Felix' pay phone was their communications center, and only telephone link, to the outside world. Felix had also become one of the Reeds' few confidants aware of their legal problems, and someone who offered solace when needed.

Early in their marriage Terry had told his wife that based on his intelligence involvement she should assume their phones were always tapped. But she never envisioned red stickers on her home phone that read "Don't be stupid. This phone is not secure." Even the utilities were not in their names so their address couldn't easily be discovered. And they never, never used a credit card, since they would reveal their location and could show a pattern of movement.

Terry lectured Janis continuously about computer trails that can be used to track an individual, and doctor's records, especially pharmaceutical prescription records, which are relayed via satellite and can be tapped into to determine a person's whereabouts.

In the winter of 1988 Baxter, the baby, had an ear infection and Janis took him to a local doctor. Having given the boy's vital statistics, the nurse informed her that she would have to provide her Social Security number and a photocopy of her driver's license.

"But I'm paying cash," Janis said as her breath quickened.

"It's our policy," the nurse said matter-of-factly.

The phone rang and as the nurse turned to answer it, Janis took the feverish baby and ran out the door as if running for her life. Her head was pounding violently.

Calm down, calm down, I've got to calm down, she told herself as she drove to a clinic in an Hispanic neighborhood where no questions were asked. But she couldn't calm down. She didn't know what forces were after her husband, but she knew they were forces who would be happy to see him dead and she had no idea how powerful and far-reaching this unseen enemy was.

"I am absolutely losing my mind," she thought while driving the baby home from the doctor's office. "How is this doctor's office going to be a link to the bad guys? Maybe I should have just let them copy my driver's license."

"You mean you even considered letting them Xerox your driver's license?" Terry said in astonishment after listening to his wife recount the day's events. "Haven't you heard that local pharmacy's commercial about getting your prescription filled anywhere, at anytime, in the country because they're linked via satellite? All you need is one slip up and your location will be accessible to anyone that wants it. Don't take any stupid chances," he reprimanded her.

A lecture was NOT what she needed to hear.

"Oh, sure. You tell the boys they can't get sick. They can't fall down. They can't ride a bike. Maybe they shouldn't run. Let's be sure they don't go down any slides. They might fall off and break an arm! We've got three little boys, Terry! What did you learn in spook school about hiding out a family of five! Yeah, a family of five with a German Shepherd the size of a horse! Was that in Advance Escape and Evasion? I bet you missed that chapter! You know, I think I'm coping amazingly well considering I'm pushing 40, living on the lam, have no contact with my family or friends, and can load most of my earthly possessions into a utility trailer while my ex-friends are dining at the country club and doing volunteer work for the Junior League! You're damn lucky you have me here taking care of our family, spending every waking hour of my life working on this case. Don't you think I've thought about running away from YOU?! But I won't and you know I won't because that's what they think I'm going to do. Now don't you lecture me about taking chances. You know I won't even let Duncan walk to the mail box by himself!"

Terry knew enough to say no more. Their nerves were shot. They talked to no one but each other and their attorneys, and the strain was taking its toll. They had been confused about being forced to have separate attorneys when they were first indicted. CONFLICT, they had been told. Two separate cases, two separate defenses. Now, it was starting to make sense. Conflict.

As Janis sat alone in her rocking chair in front of the fireplace that night, she was lower than she had ever been. Desperation and loneliness overwhelmed her. Would this never end? She had found herself doing strange things. She had developed a fetish about keeping her house immaculate. Was it because it was one small aspect of her life that she had control over?

Possibly. But she knew the real reason. She kept having a recurring dream that their home was invaded and agents were coming to take them away. But in her dream, she was always standing there in the doorway with her boys, and as the intruders searched the house she could overhear one of them saying, "We must have the wrong house. Look, this is a wholesome family that lives here. Let's go." As ridiculous as this dream was, she found herself meticulously arranging the toys in the children's room everyday, carefully placing the stuffed animals on their beds, displaying their Lego creations in a prominent location. "There is so much love in this family," she thought, "and they're trying to destroy us!"

As she sat there sobbing, she heard the patter of feet behind her. She turned to see three-year old Elliott scamper back out of the room, his padded pajama feet scooting across the floor. She became even more distressed that he had seen her crying since she and Terry both were so cautious about being even-tempered in front of the children.

But Elliott immediately returned. She watched as he toddled across the room with a fresh tissue in his little hand and to a flower arrangement sitting on a table. He plucked a flower from the vase and walked softly to his mother. He gently placed the flower in her lap and wiped her tears with the tissue. This beautiful expression of love melted her heart and was the turning point in her effort to fight her depression.

She took Elliott into her lap and rocked him until he fell asleep. He had given her a new strength she could feel growing within her as she rocked her small child. "I WILL NOT GIVE UP! We will survive this. We will overcome this! It could be so much worse. Look at the hostages in Beirut. What am I doing wimping around here?"

As she sat there with her sleeping child she began to re-evaluate her life. She knew she could not solely blame her husband for the mess they were in. She was always there, ready and eager to go along with his choices. She also knew she wouldn't be content with the shallow lifestyle of her old acquaintances. No, she had made a commitment to this marriage. For better or worse. Terry was certainly keeping his end of the bargain, living up to his vow: "It will never be boring."

"I could go for a small dose of boredom," she thought. She knew she was going to have to take charge of her life and she found herself thinking back to her religious upbringing she had so rebelled against. "I've just got to talk to someone," she realized.

She and Terry had made one attempt to talk to a counselor, but when their story was met with skepticism by the elderly counselor who refused to believe the government was tainted in any way, they left. Besides, they had no guarantees that their confidences would not be relayed to other sources.

But Janis realized for her own sanity that she must seek out a confidant and decided the church was the place to go. The next day she nervously approached the local minister, not knowing what to expect. "Can you please see me for just 15 minutes. I have to talk to someone," she pleaded.

Two hours later when she left she knew she was no longer alone. An enormous weight had been lifted. Instead of being condescending and judgmental as she had feared, she had found a caring and sympathetic minister who told her quite clearly that her family would find refuge within the church if need be.

He was highly knowledgeable about Iran-Contra and had been a political activist, someone she could relate to. No, he didn't think she was crazy. He admired her fortitude in fighting back.

"Few people could withstand the pressures you are experiencing, Janis," he told her. "I've seen your family here before. You obviously have done something right for you to have such happy, well-mannered little boys. If you ever fear for your family's safety, I want you to contact me immediately. This church is here to serve our community. You will be protected. No questions asked."

A burden had been lifted.

The church, she discovered, is a government, or at least a third party, a safe house willing to take you in without asking why you needed refuge. The pastor was more than willing to help them "disappear" in a modern version of the old Underground Railroad that would, if necessary, spirit them out of the country.

They both realized they had lived in the United States of America, had studied its Constitution and never fully understood the necessity for the separation of church and state until that fateful day.

They compared their plight to that of Christ—persecuted, not prosecuted, by an undefinable foe: The U.S. Government—whatever that is. Terry could put faces on his fears, faces like those of Felix Rodriguez and Ramon Medina. On paper it was a simple mail fraud charge, but to Terry it was a re-run of Barry Seal. Like Barry, he was pinned down where he could be found and told he could not have a gun. And now, he was forced to wait for the assassins he was sure would come.

The only two friends they could trust now were John Desko, Terry's old friend from Southeast Asia who still lived in Albuquerque, and Julie Dennison, a local realtor, who befriended Janis.

From having written war contingency plans, known as Emergency War Orders, during his Air Force days, Terry sat down to evaluate his options. Initially, he saw only three: He and his wife could flee together; they could flee separately or, last of all, something he did not want to think about, plead guilty.

"If Terry will plead guilty, I will drop the charges against Janis. That way, there will be one of them on the street to raise their children." That's what the prosecutor told both Steve Robison and Marilyn Trubey at one point. *"Must be George Bush's idea of family values,"* Terry responded when told of the offer.

And the worst thing the Reeds were both learning was that a criminal prosecution tests not only your love and your relationship to its limits, but it also exposes all weaknesses and character flaws, not only in yourself, but in your family and friends as well. You begin seeing things about other people that would never, ever surface without them having been exploited by the professionally trained federal manipulators, who cause internal conflict within people's value systems.

Janis' family, as the Reeds had feared, had a strength that the FBI was exploiting as a weakness, namely her parents' inability to tell a lie. By reading the FBI reports given them, the Reeds learned the FBI and Arkansas State Police had interviewed her parents and exploited their religious beliefs and convictions to the point they divulged the Reeds' fictitious location in Mexico.

The only thing that had prevented the Reeds' arrest and apprehension was the parents' lack of knowledge as to their true residence. Agents of the government had put two God-fearing senior citizens into a position of being forced to choose between family or religious conviction and authority, hedged in threats of criminal prosecution if the "government" is not supplied the proper information. How could a country that prides itself on its religious roots, family values and love of country lower itself to prey upon the very principles it pretends to promote and embrace?

This was destroying Janis. And the Reeds had no alternative. At a time when they needed family support, they had to cut themselves off from her parents. What else, the Reeds wondered, would they tell the FBI if exploited? Certainly, they were easily manipulated. Was the FBI exploiting "family values" at the instruction of George Bush's Justice Department?

Finally, they settled on another alternative, to take on and fight the legal system one a day at a time.

The first ray of hope Terry had found was in Marilyn Trubey, who had been assigned his case after he declared himself indigent. He had, without realizing it at first, turned the system on itself by fighting the government with a public defender paid by the government. And Trubey was no ordinary Public Defender.

Here was a dedicated, single woman in her late 30s who had learned the federal criminal justice system from the ground up, and inside out. Marilyn, the youngest of four children and a native of Kansas, had worked her way through law school after being employed by the Kansas State and Federal Public Defender's office. As an administrative assistant she had over thirteen years to observe the "do's and don't's" of defense and was appalled to see the errors made that literally cost people years of their lives.

But beyond the human mistakes made, she identified something more disturbing, something that would influence her decision to devote her life to attempting to rectify the injustices dealt out by the criminal justice system. Namely, it was all a game of money, she observed. She witnessed first hand how race and social status had a disproportionate share of leverage on the scales of the U.S. court system. In whatever way she could correct these inequities, she decided to commit herself and repair these injustices. Her years of devotion hadn't quite prepared her for Terry Reed, though. By the luck of the draw, a CIA spook with a big problem walked through her door and into her life, and would become a friend forever.

Now, more than a month after surrendering to face the charges, the Reeds were beginning to shake the "denial" phase of being framed and falsely accused and graduate to the "acceptance" phase of their plight. It was time to take charge of their defense.

Terry and Marilyn would become a good legal team, complementing each other's weaknesses.

He knew the intelligence world and how it worked. There were no rules on that side of the fence, he would teach her. She knew the legal world forward and backward, but still operated in a law school bubble, thinking there were rules for everything, and that they were strictly enforced. Trubey believed, then, that the judiciary could not be reached by the Executive branch or the Central Intelligence Agency.

After all, she, like most Americans, had studied about the triangular division of power within our government. Until this case, she had been convinced that the Executive, Legislative, and Judicial were separate branches that did not conspire to violate an individual's rights. She was in for a rude awakening.

The problem with lawyers, Terry was learning, is most suffer from terminal legal training and actually believe what they learn in law school—until it's too late.

Through Terry's experience and cynicism, he could moderate Trubey's structured, rigid view of the legal world. "Marilyn, don't you get it, we only have two branches of government now, the executive has absorbed the judicial," he would say. She would moderate his cynicism and outlandish thinking with legal precedents.

"It was like a marriage," she would say later of their two-and-a-half year legal ordeal. They often fought, and then made up. They each needed the other.

Another major player in this legal game was Joe Dunlap, a solidly-built investigator resembling a linebacker who worked for the Public Defender's office and whose relationship with the Reed case took him through the looking glass into a world he never knew existed. Joe was a college graduate who had 11 years service as a dedicated Wichita police officer. Like most jobs, police work has a routine, but it's not a routine one can settle into. Dunlap had settled in and made a near fatal mistake.

One night in 1978, he did not approach a suspect "by the book" and it nearly cost him his life. He took three shots at point-blank range from a .357 Magnum while approaching in his car to "interview" a pedestrian. Fortunately, he was able to coast his car into the street where he could be found, and miraculously was discovered in time, rushed to surgery, and lived. From then on, though, he was never the same man and was afraid that he was going to overreact and kill someone while on duty, if provoked.

Dunlap became a real find for the Public Defender's office because he, unlike other former cops, was able to turn himself around to a defense mode and apply his investigative skills to proving a client's innocence, rather than guilt.

"It's not that I didn't believe you when I first heard your story. It's just that I didn't want to believe our government did this kind of thing," Dunlap said to Terry later. He, like most people who hear stories of such grievous government misconduct, was, at first, in denial.

If it hadn't been for meeting Janis and the children, Dunlap said, he would never have believed Terry's story when he first heard it. "I just fell in love with Duncan and figured anybody that could raise a family this nice couldn't be what the FBI files say they are," he said.

Dunlap was a tenacious investigator whose style reminded Terry of the actor James Garner when he starred in The Rockford Files. He was street savvy and knew how to burrow into a case until he found the missing links and obtained the desired results. Terry's case would test him and his skills to the limits, and would open his eyes forever about our government's "secret government" and its felonious behavior.

* * *

While debriefing with Trubey and Dunlap, Terry went back in time to cover the events that occurred since that fateful day he learned of the indictment. Janis first learned of the indictment through a call to her parents, and Terry cautiously began preparing to surrender himself.

No big deal, the FBI Special Agents Gary Violanti and Sandra Bungo had said while sitting on the sofa in Janis' parents' living room in Kansas City, just "a small matter of white collar crime." But they neglected to tell them that Janis had been indicted as well.

Being drawn into the criminal justice system was a brand new experience for the Reeds. They weren't sure about their legal status as indictees and sought out an attorney to advise them. But they knew one thing for certain their lives were going to change. Once again, they considered the options: running away, disappearing or surrendering. In preparation for the third option, Terry got in touch with an attorney who told him the bad news. An indictment meant a warrant had been issued for the Reeds' arrest and if arrested outside of Kansas, they could count on a 10-day drive, with overnight stops at many jails in between, in the U.S. Marshal's bus to Wichita.

Terry began making arrangements to voluntarily surrender by contacting his Wichita attorney, Steve Robison. The lawyer had advised him it always looks better to the U.S. Magistrate, who hopefully would allow bail, if a fugitive surrenders and doesn't force apprehension. While dealing with the details of the possibility of being immediately incarcerated and being denied bail, Terry discovered the seriousness of the charges and the savagery of those trying to find him.

He became aware through his younger sister that his mother had been hospitalized as a result of FBI harassment and interrogation. She was 72 at the time and had suffered either a mental breakdown, a heart attack or both. It was thought she was dying.

Two FBI agents, Larry Nolan and another of the government's crime fighters, had made two trips to Terry's family home in Carthage, and refused to leave until his mother would inform them of her oldest son's whereabouts. They further stated, contrary to what Janis' parents had been told, that Terry was involved in serious "illegal activities" that would send him to prison "for many, many years." They further said the mother would be arrested, too, for "harboring a fugitive" if she refused to cooperate with them.

"I don't know what's going on, Terry..." his frantic sister had said. "They're gonna kill her if you don't do something. I ran them off after their second visit. These people are crazy and they don't care if they kill her...I don't know what you did, but these guys want you *real bad*."

That same day, the FBI in Kansas City was demanding that Karen, Janis' sister, come by their office for an interrogation session. They were threatening her, too, with charges of harboring fugitives. Her sister had the name one of the agents, Special Agent Violanti, from the Kansas City office. Terry called him, and that turned out to be a MAJOR mistake. He never actually spoke to the agent, instead he was told Violanti was too busy. A distraught Terry told the agent who picked up the phone, "I know you have a warrant for my arrest. I'm in the process of surrendering and if you guys kill my mother as a result of your searching for me, I'm gonna hold Violanti personally responsible."

"You just threatened a federal agent, buddy, so now you can add five more years to your sentence," the agent responded in an ominous tone. Terry hung up. He had never felt so helpless. Not only had he been stripped of his self-esteem, but now he was viewed as a hardened criminal. And this for trying to protect his mother, a human, natural instinct, he was being threatened with more charges.

He felt neutered. Incapable of defending himself or his loved ones. He had become the man the FBI created in their five-inch thick file. Although he had been convicted of nothing yet, he already had been reinvented as a man with a criminal past, a drug trafficker hiding in Mexico with countless aliases and someone described as "armed and dangerous." It was as if he had no name and no rights. He was just a fugitive, at best a defendant.

It was strange. FBI Agents in six states had been working countless man-hours, according to their own reports, on a mail fraud case involving an alleged $33,000 theft. In most federal districts, an overworked U.S. attorney would, at best, give a case like this his lowest priority, particularly since no insurance company had filed a lawsuit—or even claimed to have been injured.

Terry's efforts to live his life by his code and never taking the easy path just weren't paying off. He was finding that much of what he had done in life was being used in some manner to create the discrediting profile. A Vietnam veteran with a pilot's license who spoke Spanish, Trubey was telling him, was automatically part of a drug trafficker's profile.

* * *

"Ms. Trubey, I probably shouldn't say this, but those guys are lying," the U.S. Marshal said, referring to the government's star witness as he left the Wichita courtroom where the Marshal was assigned. The hearing was in its second day and the Marshal, who spends his working day listening to people testify, knew the government was faring badly.

Trubey was feeling elated. Victory, she felt, was in sight. She had utterly destroyed the earlier testimony given in Arkansas by the government's two witnesses against Janis and Terry.

The judge had ordered the recess so that phone calls could be made back to Little Rock to straighten out conflicting information about the file number originally assigned to the Reed investigation. She had them on the run. Assistant U.S. Attorney Robin Fowler, the chief Government Prosecutor, was not present and Jack Williams, another government attorney, was not prepared to counter the disclosures his own witnesses were making about their falsification of key documents.

If the result of the phone calls back to Little Rock confirmed what Terry and Trubey suspected, the government had been looking for him long before his stolen airplane was discovered in Terry's old "Contra training hangar" at the North Little Rock Airport.

As the courtroom was emptying for the recess that afternoon on June 21st, 1989, and after U.S. District Court Judge Frank Theis had returned to his chambers, the marshal who had heard all the testimony, made the unusual gesture of approaching the defense table and sharing his professional observations about the false testimony he had just heard.

"I'm glad you drew that conclusion. I hope the judge does also," she told the marshal. "I owe all my evidence to my investigator, Mr. Dunlap."

Nine months earlier, when Trubey and Dunlap had been assigned to the case, all they had to go on was testimony given by an Arkansas State Police official and a private detective who were seeking a state court warrant to search an aircraft hangar in North Little Rock and seize its contents.

And "its alleged contents" was none other than Terry's airplane stolen five years earlier from the Joplin, Missouri airport. And the plane was found in the hangar Terry had rented initially at CIA Agent Akihide Sawahata's behest and the same hangar that Robert Johnson had told Terry to keep rented while he was in Mexico.

Dunlap's first visit to Little Rock in October of 1988 made him a believer about Terry's story. Not only did he find flaws in the affidavit for the state search warrant, but he discovered something much more unsettling in Arkansas—the mind set of the police there. He was encouraged to check into a motel room that Dunlap later learned was permanently bugged electronically for prying out-of-state "agitators." The police, as if trying to hamper his freedom of movement, began shadowing him and even showing up at the bar of the motel Dunlap had chosen upon state police recommendation.

On that first trip, Dunlap couldn't quite shake his paranoia that was building from the knowledge that this case might involve some very important people in Arkansas, and this was not his turf. He was considered a meddler from the "Yankee Government" and his U.S. Government license plates were drawing a lot of attention. He had to interview some critical witnesses, two of whom were the people who had witnessed Terry's meeting with Arkansas Governor Bill Clinton at Juanita's Restaurant in Little Rock on April 19th, 1986.

These were people Terry wanted to call as defense witnesses not only to corroborate part of his story, but Trubey felt they would be needed to establish a motive for the government to set him up. If she could prove Terry possessed knowledge of Clinton's involvement in the illegal Contra operations, Clinton himself could have had motives to create a crime around Terry. And wasn't it interesting, she thought out loud, that one of the people helping to frame the

Reeds was the man in charge of Clinton's security staff who had an office in the governor's mansion?

The two people Dunlap wanted to interview were Wally and Cherryl Hall, both of whom now worked at the *Arkansas Democrat*. On his way to the newspaper that day, Dunlap noticed a car driven by a black man, following him. After unsuccessfully trying to shake him, Dunlap gave up and went to the newspaper only to discover the Halls were unavailable. When he left the newspaper office, the man following him remained parked there as Dunlap drove off. But he saw him again a short later in an unlikely and strange place...in the DEA's parking lot at an office complex that houses the DEA's undercover headquarters on the west side of Little Rock.

Earlier, when Dunlap had tried to interview Arkansas State Police Sergeant Don Sanders, he had been denied access to the DEA facilities. Upon returning to the parking lot, and while sitting in his car to fill out his reports, Dunlap observed the same car with the same black driver pulling in to park. The driver, without noticing Dunlap, entered the DEA's facility. Dunlap was sure he was being followed and probably that same person was keeping tabs on the subjects of his interviews.

When Dunlap finally did get to interview the Halls, they informed him that they had indeed dined with the Reeds, but couldn't recall that particular evening. How odd, the Reeds thought, considering Cherryl's penchant for gossip and earlier excitement about Terry leaving the restaurant with Clinton and his aide that night.

What bothered Dunlap *the most* was the man who showed up at his motel on that first investigative trip to Little Rock. It was Lieutenant Raymond (Buddy) Young, chief of Clinton's security unit at the governor's mansion and the man who had stood outside the van in 1986 when Terry met with Clinton, as he *inhaled* marijuana. That night, and earlier at the Camp Robinson bunker meeting, Terry had not been introduced to Young and he had never put a name with the security man's face. Until Young walked into the courtroom in Wichita in June of 1989, Terry did not know that the man in charge of the investigation against him, and the man who stood guard for Clinton at both meetings, were one and the same.

Young was simply one of the two names appearing on the Arkansas search warrant affidavit. The other was Tommy Baker, a former State Police Sergeant, who was now a private investigator in Little Rock.

The affidavit on the surface appeared simple. Baker, a pilot, was taxiing by a row of hangars at the North Little Rock airport and "a hangar door flew open."

"I looked in to make sure nothing was damaged," he stated. "I saw an airplane in there that appeared as if it had been abandoned." Baker said he looked at the plane's N-number and it "didn't look right." He then said he called Young, an old friend and, it was revealed much later, a business associate.

"I called Lt. Young and got the 'N' number ran on it," he stated. "And the plane with the 'N' number on it is supposed to be in Germany, according to the FAA records. So, I went back and found the serial number of the plane in question here on the aileron [wing area] of the airplane and was able to trace it down through Lt. Young and NCIC (the FBI's National Crime Information Center) as being stolen from Joplin, Mo."

Young said in the same affidavit, "I checked with the FBI in Joplin, Missouri. They also have a case report on it. I have done some follow-up work and determined that it was paid off by an insurance company and that the plane is still carried as stolen and has never been recovered."

However, FBI documents recently provided to Reed under court discovery in 1993 show that Young did not tell "the whole truth" as the witness oath requires. This was Young's first sworn testimony in the Reed case and he is still telling the same story, even though the FBI telex shows it to be untrue.

The FBI telex from its Kansas City office to its Little Rock and Oklahoma City offices and dated October 13, 1987, states: "On October 9, 1987, Ken Copeland, sergeant, Joplin Missouri, Police Department, advised Lieutenant Buddy Young, Arkansas State Police, Little Rock, Arkansas, advised aircraft recovered Little Rock area *in barn* on or about October 7, 1987. Drug Enforcement Administration and FBI Little Rock notified."

This clearly shows that Reed was set up and the aircraft had *not* been discovered in Reed's hangar as Baker and Young had testified to obtain the state search warrant. It further shows that Young had discovered and recovered the plane nearly a week *before* ever seeking the search warrant. This was suppressed and never turned over to the defense at Reed's trial by the government as the rules of evidence require.

From their appearance before a sitting judge and from his perjured testimony, Young was issued a search and seizure warrant from "Special Judge," [an attorney who fills in for a judge] Harlan Weber, on October 14th, 1987. Later, when questioned by Trubey about the frequency of "oral affidavits" being used in Arkansas to obtain search warrants, Young testified that in his experience it was unprecedented.

As a result of his first interviews, Dunlap discovered a third person was involved in the investigation, one whose name did not appear on the affidavit. He was Arkansas State Police Sergeant Don Sanders, who was assigned to a joint federal-state drug task force. Without the key information he supplied to Baker about the registration of the aircraft found in Terry's hangar, that it had been de-registered and sold in a foreign country, there would have been no search warrant affidavit in the first place.

They would only have what they called an "abandoned" airplane in a "rented" facility, a contradiction in terms. It would be impossible for an airplane owner to "abandon" his own aircraft in his own hanger. And certainly no crime would have been established.

Dunlap returned to Wichita to digest the new and confusing information. What he had found was a shadowy third person lurking in the background, a person with connections to the federal government *and* the Drug Enforcement Administration. What was bothering both Trubey, Dunlap and Terry as well, was the elusive report in Terry's FBI file that he was "trafficking in narcotics in Central and/or South America." Where did all this come from? The Teletype report was not signed and had no letterhead. But it said something very interesting. It said that Young had passed on information to the FBI that Terry was trafficking in narcotics "out of Central and South America."

This smelled of a tip. And it sounded like the FBI was passing along a DEA "profile." Could Sanders have been the conduit for a tip that emanated, Terry figured, from Rodriguez or maybe someone else in Mexico?

Secondly, Dunlap had ruled out the unlikely story about the wind blowing open the hangar door, as Baker had claimed. The hanger manufacturer provided detailed engineering data indicating the hangar and its doors were stressed to withstand over 120 knots of wind—hurricane speeds. The highest wind gusts the day Baker said the door flew open, he had found, were about 10 miles an hour.*

Dunlap also had interviewed the hangar owner and the locksmith who maintained the hangar and both said they had no knowledge, records or repair orders to reflect a problem with Terry's hangar or its door. But even if there had been a problem, the hangar owner faxed a receipt to the court showing adjustments and retrofits were made to all of the hangars' locks prior to October 7th. The locksmith's invoice to the hangar owner for this work was dated October 7th, 1987, the day Baker claimed the wind blew the door open.

The final blow to the wind scenario came from the hangar owner who later testified that the locksmith's work had to be performed before the 7th, since it was not his policy to invoice until the work was totally completed.

These facts proved Baker was lying about how he gained access to Reed's hangar. But why?

While driving back to Wichita, Dunlap realized that if this airplane had been discovered as the result of good detective work, as Baker had said, Dunlap would not have found these inconsistencies. Maybe, he thought, Terry *was* being set up. The thought that he was perhaps dealing with the CIA and the likes of Felix Rodriguez was unsettling.

On Dunlap's second trip to Little Rock on February 21, 1989, he would find no answers, only more questions. First, why had Baker visited a Piper dealership and FBO (fixed-base operator) at the North Little Rock Airport, shortly after the plane's seizure, and divulged he had discovered the plane as a the result of "a tip?"

Second, why had Young hidden critical evidence in the governor's mansion for more than 16 months and not turned it over to the FBI when the case was handed off to federal authorities? What Young had held back was potentially more incriminating to Terry than the airplane. It was Terry's old flight bag that had been in his airplane, N 2982M, when it was stolen in Joplin in 1983. It contained maps, charts, log books and personal effects of Terry's and *if* this was found in the aircraft in the hangar as Baker claimed that would be the key piece of evidence that would tie Terry to the plane and assure a conviction. Why, Dunlap wondered, wasn't this turned over to the Feds?

After a search warrant is executed, police must inventory everything seized and return the inventory to the court that issued the warrant. But the itemized inventory that Young had sent back to the court made no mention of the flight bag, leading Dunlap to believe it was not in the aircraft when it was seized.

The story Young and Baker were telling was beginning to shred. The key item missing in the FBI file, which by this time had been turned over to the defense, was Young's personal investigative file. Young's name was mentioned on only two items in the FBI file. What should have been there was Young's complete investigative file that all police maintain as they work. It lists their activities, the people they questioned and what had been said.

* National Weather Service report for October 7th and 8th, 1987, recorded by the weather reporting station located at the North Little Rock Airport, Little Rock, Arkansas.

When questioned about this by Dunlap, Young produced what appeared to be onion skin copies of unformatted reports whose dates had been "whited out." He would not give Dunlap copies of those, saying he could not do so without permission from the U.S. attorney's office in Wichita. Oddly, Young would not even allow Dunlap to inventory, or make copies of the bag's contents. Dunlap thought this whole thing was beginning to emit a peculiar odor.

Dunlap analyzed what he had found to date.

1. The single piece of evidence used to indict Terry, namely the plane, had seemingly disappeared.
2. The plane had been released by the police without a court order as if they were anxious to get rid of it and prevent its being inspected. And there was certainly skepticism whether the aircraft had even been in Reed's hangar since no photographs of it were taken while it sat there in it's alleged abandoned state.
3. Critical evidence that could have be used to convict Terry had been kept from the FBI and hidden from both the prosecution and defense.
4. Necessary police reports were being kept from the defense, if they had ever been written in the first place.
5. Entry to the hangar had not been gained as Baker had alleged in his testimony.
6. Baker had been led there as the result of a tip.
7. And most importantly, a federal agent had been involved in the initial investigation and his name had been purposely withheld from the judge issuing the search warrant.

All this subterfuge gave Marilyn Trubey the argument she needed to force a hearing to deal with these disturbing anomalies, a hearing to present evidence showing why the judge should suppress the plane as evidence. Since the plane in question was unavailable to the defense, she wanted to make it technically unavailable to the government. Without the aircraft being admitted into evidence in Terry's trial, the government would have no case and there would be no trial, or least that's what she thought.

The plane Young seized October 14, allegedly was removed from Terry's hangar. There were no photographs ever taken showing any plane in Terry's hangar. After seizure it supposedly was stored by the Arkansas State Police in a different hangar rented in the state's name. It allegedly bore the tail number N 30489, *which is the same number that was on the plane Cooper flew into Little Rock carrying the C-4.* Young said the plane was removed from Terry's hangar to safeguard the aircraft because he feared this key piece of evidence would "disappear."

"I put it under my lock and my key," he later testified.

The plane did, indeed, disappear later, but as a result of Young's doing. He released it prematurely to an independent insurance adjuster, and with no court order. This was the one and only piece of evidence that had been used to indict Terry and it would now suddenly vanish and not be available to for him to use in his defense.

Much could have been learned from examining the aircraft. For example, what fingerprints would have been found? What type of insects were in the engine cowlings. Were they indigenous to a tropical climate? What frequencies and headings were set in the plane's radios and instruments? What tell-tale maintenance stickers and stamps existed on the plane and its avionics which could leave a trail of mechanical work performed, etc. And the one looming problem that still needed clarification was whether or not the alleged plane was actually N2982M, Terry's stolen plane.

The circumstances surrounding the plane's release and the motivations for doing so are still shrouded in mystery. The bottom line is that no one—except for Young or Baker—can place that airplane, Piper Arrow N30489, a non-turbo charged craft, in Terry's hangar because no photographs of it were ever taken. This normally is routine police procedure and these photos should have been submitted as evidence against Terry.

On June 21st, 1989, the suppression hearing was convened before Judge Theis. Then 81 years old, Theis was the senior judge for the District of Kansas and had been appointed by Lyndon Baines Johnson, of whom a portrait measuring six feet by four feet hung behind Theis' desk in his luxurious chambers.

Federal judges are above political control, Terry thought cynically as he looked at Johnson's portrait. Upon being notified they had drawn Theis as their judge, Steve Robison informed, "You could've done worse and you could've done better. I was hoping we'd draw Judge Kelly since he's the most liberal judge we have in Kansas and loves to catch the government misbehaving. I'm glad we didn't draw Judge Crow though, he's a conservative Republican and in his mind the government does no wrong. The only problem with Judge Theis is he's normally not awake long enough to know what's goin' on."

Robison cautioned Terry about courtroom behavior. "When the judge falls asleep, it's real important not to make a big deal about it and embarrass him. His secretary, who he sleeps with, will notice it eventually and go over and wake him up. The judge has narcolepsy."

After meeting Theis in his courtroom for the first time, and looking at the giant, looming portrait of the judge hanging on an adjacent wall, it was clear to Terry that the judge had declined considerably since it was painted. He now had a drooping eye, probably the result of stroke and a rambling mind normally focused on the famous Karen Silkwood Case, which he tried earlier and talked about continually.

"Sure is a pretty day," the judge said one day when entering the courtroom. "The weather sort of reminds me of the weather we had during the Silkwood trial." Theis' résumé included not only the Silkwood case, involving plutonium theft from Kerr-McGee, but the tampon toxic shock syndrome case as well.

Terry threw up his hands. His life, as well as his family's, was in the hands of a droopy-eyed judge who couldn't stay awake. A man who had to be briefed by his secretary about what had occurred in the courtroom. The only positive thing he could think of was that his grandfather would have approved of Theis' political affiliation. He was a Democrat.

But contrary to the warning about narcolepsy, Theis was wide awake that first day. In fact, Robison noted, "I haven't seen the judge this perky in a long time. The name of Oliver North seems to have reignited some old fire in him." A Wichita newspaper had just printed an article saying North's name would surface in the case.

Then, there was Robin Fowler, the federal prosecutor. From the time Terry and his wife were indicted until their first appearance in Theis' courtroom, there had been no face or voice for "the government," this elusive monster set on devouring them.

On June 21st, 1989, the monster finally had one. It was Fowler's face, an Assistant United States Attorney schooled in the East and brought in to be the personal protégé of United States Attorney Benjamin L. Burgess Jr., whose supporters were distributing bumper stickers saying "Burgess for Governor." It was rumored that Fowler would be his running mate and candidate for lieutenant governor.

Fowler was 32 at the time and Terry was told his personal life was in a shambles. His wife was seeking a divorce and he was now "in the party mode" and spending most evenings cruising the Wichita singles bars.

The yuppified attorney was sporting the best in polyester suits and the latest in men's permed hairstyles, apparently not realizing that both looks were passé. Based on his protruding stomach, which shadowed a distasteful belt buckle sporting the letter "F," it was apparent from what Trubey had told Terry that Fowler wasn't spending much time at the gym, but instead probably occupied himself drinking beer and lounging around. Terry was certain from Fowler's demeanor that the government hatchet man believed every lie he had read in the Reed's FBI file.

It was apparent as he faced Terry that Fowler believed he was a trafficker who had eluded justice, and the government's only chance to nail him was on petty mail fraud charges.

"Robin thinks you are real bad people," Robison said to Terry and Janis on the courthouse steps the second day of the marathon hearing. He had worked with Fowler, knew him well, and used him as a private pipeline into the prosecutor's office.

On that first day, the judge, referring to Janis said, "What's she doing here?"

"I don't know, Judge, what she's doin' here. I guess it's because she's married to him," Robison answered, referring to Terry.

The government said it intended to prove she had been Terry's accomplice, an interesting point since nothing presented to the grand jury showed that. And yet Fowler, who presented the case to the grand jury, asked for and received indictments against both. As usual, the grand jury had done what the prosecutor instructed—administer one-sided justice by returning, on a national average, a 98 per cent indictment rate.

Maybe the judge didn't know why Janis had been indicted, but Terry knew why. It had nothing to do with her being an accomplice, it was to silence her, keep her from the media, and to use her as a bargaining chip to force Terry into a plea of guilty. She was simply a pawn.

On the first day of the hearing, the government's star witness was Baker, the private detective who "found" Terry's plane. As he ambled into the courtroom, he was the epitome of the state of Arkansas, Bubba in dungarees. He looked and spoke like the stereotypical southern sheriff, and with his enormous beer gut and his waddle, it was obvious he had given up worrying about his appearance a long time ago. The blue jeans he was wearing were tight enough at the waistband to force them to ride so low on his physique they barely covered his massive derriere. To match this insulting choice of attire for an appearance in federal court, his undersized perma-press shirt was straining to cover his bulky "spare tire".

After a day on the witness stand, it was apparent that Baker was lying, not only to the judge and the attorneys on both sides, but also to the marshal in the courtroom. Baker, as his testimony continued, kept shooting himself in the foot with a total disregard for his possible peril, namely perjury charges. Perhaps, he forgot he wasn't testifying in Arkansas, a place Terry affectionately had labeled "the People's Republic of Arkansas," since it appeared the hog state protected civil rights about as aggressively as did the People's Republic of China.

It was clear the defense was dealing with a professional witness who had a convenient memory and could remember only what was beneficial to the prosecution. Trubey was hoping to show Baker as an extension of, and under the control of the police. That would make his an illegal search and accomplish her objective of forcing Theis to suppress the evidence and, therefore, dismiss the case.

By Baker's own admission, he continued his investigation of the airplane using information solely supplied by the police. As a civilian, he knew he did not need probable cause to enter the hangar as a police officer normally would.

And from his demeanor on the stand, it was obvious he was used to behaving any way he wished, undoubtedly because he was a prosecution witness. He displayed open contempt for the defense by saying he had ignored the defense request to bring his investigative file with him.

The hearing on June 21st, 1989, began with Baker emphatically saying, "I can say without any hesitation it's October 8th, yes," when asked if he was sure about the date he found the airplane.[1]

Trubey found this interesting since she had in her possession a copy of an FBI-NCIC (National Crime Information Center) report showing the Arkansas State Police investigating the crime on October 7th. This seemed to confirm what Dunlap had discovered, that Baker was working on a tip when he "found" the plane. Under cross-examination, and after saying multiple times he was certain it was the 8th, Baker began waffling and said it "could have been the 7th" when he realized the defense was attacking the validity of the date and had in its possession the NCIC supplied data, showing police activity on the 7th.

The questioning also confirmed that Baker had, in fact, been in the hangar on multiple occasions before the search warrant was issued. Each time he returned, it was as a result of being supplied more "confidential police data" by Young and Sanders that allowed him to continue his investigation.

Baker's testimony was as follows: The first N-number he had was N30489, which was stenciled on the outside of the plane. When that number was initially run for him by Young, it came back negative. It had not been reported stolen. But armed with information provided him by Sanders, namely that the number N30489 was decommissioned as a result of it being sold to a buyer in Germany, Baker returned once again. This time, he copied down the serial number embossed on an ID tag riveted on the tail.

He also said he entered the aircraft and retrieved a flight bag. In that bag, he found not only Terry's name, but another N-number, N2982M. After having Young run this information through NCIC, he determined that this was a stolen plane. To be sure it was the correct aircraft, Young wanted him to return and confirm what he believed he had found.

This time, Baker testified, he took with him someone who was an aviation expert and who pointed out to Baker a component of the plane that should bear the true serial number. By reading that number, he was sure he was dealing with N 2982M stolen from Joplin, Mo. in March, 1983 and belonging to "a Terry Reed out of Oklahoma City."

Photographs of the recovered airplane obtained from the insurance company after the plane was removed from the hangar clearly showed the left aileron was removed from the plane, as well as the engine cowling while in the possession of the Arkansas State Police. When asked if he had removed the parts, Baker testified he had not.*

This was done, he said, to disable the plane and make it incapable of flight. But when was it done? And by whom? If it was done before the search warrant was issued, and by Baker or the police, it would be illegal entry, trespassing, tampering, and theft, all violations of law, and would show the police disabling an aircraft before they had a warrant. But adding to the puzzlement, if the plane could not be flown because it had been disabled, why move it to another hangar?

As ridiculous as it was, Baker stuck with his convoluted testimony that the wind had blown open the hangar door, just as he happened to be passing by.**

Toward the close of the first day of testimony, Judge Theis was alarmed enough at the inconsistencies and holes in Baker's story to summon Young and warn him and Baker not to discuss the day's testimony that night while staying over in Wichita. In spite of the warning, both left together in the same taxi and stayed at the same hotel. The day was over.

Terry and Janis felt euphoric. They were sure they had won the first skirmish, the prosecution's lead witness was leaving the courtroom with holes shot through his story large enough to fly a Piper Turbo Arrow through.

What they didn't know was, as a practical matter, only defense witnesses can commit perjury. They would learn later, to their disbelief, of federal immunity statutes that hold government witnesses harmless for civil penalties when lying under oath.

They returned to the motel where Janis' parents had arrived to care for and protect the children from potential harm. As if they didn't have enough to worry about and occupy their attention, the thought of a kidnapping attempt on their children never left their minds. The Reeds had refused to leave the children in New Mexico for fear of reprisals, mainly from Felix Rodriguez, and Terry reasoned it would probably happen while they both were making mandatory court appearances.

The next day would be Young's turn and that of Don Sanders, if they could force his appearance. Already the term "national security" had cropped up as a result of a subpoena delivered to the Arkansas State Police demanding Sanders' appearance in Wichita. Sanders, due to his assignment working with the DEA, was being granted federal status. This meant that he could not be questioned in open court without first forcing the defense to outline in advance what they intended to ask him.

---

* Baker did a complete turnabout four years later in an oral deposition given in Little Rock in 1993 for Case LRC-91-414, when he admitted that he did, in fact, remove the aileron, a violation of FAA regulations and federal law.

** There was a second turnabout by Baker. He has since recanted the "wind" myth and in an affidavit subsequent to the 1993 deposition, gave a totally different version of his original story, now saying he was invited into the hangar by a friend named Rick Edwards. Edwards, in a separate affidavit, claimed he was in Reed's hangar because the lock was damaged and incapable of securing the door. The real truth may never be known.

On June 22nd, it was Arkansas Governor Bill Clinton's Chief of Security who sauntered into the courtroom, took his oath, was seated, and began chatting with the judge about good fishin' holes down in Arkansas. Young was dressed more appropriately for a court appearance and a person of his position. By Young's relaxed and cocky attitude, it was apparent he was accustomed to the court room environment, getting his own way, and answering to no one, except Bill Clinton...and possibly Hillary and Chelsea.

As the day wore on, it became crystal clear Young had little regard for the facts of the case—in the legal vernacular, as Judge Theis would later write, Young demonstrated a "reckless disregard for the truth."

He ended up looking worse than Baker. He hand-delivered his elusive investigative file, the one he would not allow Joe Dunlap to copy while in the Governor's mansion in Little Rock, as well as the flight bag he had so "professionally" stored there in a closet rather than turning it over to the FBI.

When copies of Young's file were delivered in court to the defense, Terry began digesting them while Trubey questioned Young. Terry took note of the file's cover sheet and knew immediately that something was wrong. By utilizing his intelligence analyst's skills, he probably knew more about Young than Young knew about himself, by this time.

Written on the file's cover was the date, 10/08/87, the day Young said he had dictated this report. But in it, he had listed his rank as captain. Terry knew this was incorrect, recalling that on the search warrant application only six days later he listed his rank as "lieutenant."

"How long have you been a captain?" Robison asked Young.

"One year this month," he testified. That meant he had been promoted to captain in September, 1988, 10 months *after* he said dictated his report.

When challenged by Trubey about the authenticity of his report, as well as the date, Young had to admit his entire file had been created "sometime after" Dunlap interviewed him for the first time in October, 1988...more than a year after the events he described in the report. But he insisted the reports correctly reflected what had occurred.

What did this mean? To Terry and the defense attorneys, it meant that Young never expected to be testifying in a federal court about this case. Young had been pursuing a state case in which Terry would have been tried in an Arkansas court and by the conduct he and Baker were exhibiting, the results would have been a foregone conclusion. Trubey could not understand why a man with Young's rank, stature and experience was so ill-prepared to testify. The answer, she was convinced, was unspeakable.

"Terry, I don't think they thought they would ever see you in a courtroom," Trubey told him later. "They probably would have stashed you in a cell in Arkansas, or even worse, in a grave somewhere down there."

But again when questioned, Young said, "Well it was dictated sometime later...Everything in one of these reports *may not have occurred on the date the report indicates.*"

Robison hammered away.

Q. Before today, have you told (the government) that you back dated this report?
A. No, sir.
Q. Did you tell anyone in the FBI?
A. No, sir.

Q. So I presume the courtroom is the first time this came out that you back
   dated these reports?
A. Yes, sir.
Q. Well, the day it was typed says 10/10/87. You said that's wrong. We don't
   know when it was typed, do we?
A. No, we don't. [2]

What, Terry wondered, would the judge be doing if this was a defense witness!

Throughout all this, Theis snoozed off and on.

Another point of interest to the defense was the internal file number assigned to the case by the Arkansas police record system. Since dates of police
activity were becoming a critical issue, Robison examined Young closely about
the file number and how its coded system worked. On the bottom of the cover
sheet, the one with the manufactured date, was a manufactured file number.
It was 64-129-87.

Young said, in decoding this, that 64 had no meaning, 129 meant this was
the 129th case of the year and 87 was the year. Trubey, meanwhile, had dispatched Dunlap to call the Arkansas State Police records section to determine
what date 64-129-87 was opened. She was hoping to find a date of police involvement even before October 7th.

When Dunlap called from the federal building in Wichita armed with confidential Arkansas State Police (ASP) file numbers, the chief of the ASP records
section, Lieutenant James Jenkins probably confused Dunlap's official capacity with the court for someone involved in the prosecution of the case. He unwittingly passed along embarrassing and *compromising* information that would
later lead him to claim Dunlap had tricked him into revealing further evidence of ASP conspiratorial involvement in setting up the Reeds.

To this day, the Arkansas State Police claims that Dunlap got this information under false pretenses and bears nothing but animosity and contempt for
him. They even tried later to arrest him and have his private investigator's
license revoked in Kansas on the grounds he had posed as a federal marshal to
get the information.[3]

While Dunlap was away taping his conversation with Jenkins, Trubey homed
in on the flight bag she believed had been pilfered. Key evidence that Dunlap
had seen earlier in the governor's mansion was now missing. Dunlap had seen
a white Spanish-language document bearing the Mexican government seal. He
had asked Young about its significance and whether it had been translated
into English. Young said no, and had refused to allow Dunlap to copy it.

Now, with a key document missing, things were getting interesting. Young
took the following positions: "Possibly" the missing document might not have
been there at all; he couldn't recall ever seeing it; but if it was missing, Young
inferred, it was because Dunlap stole it.

One other interesting point was emerging. It was Young's professed desire to
get rid of the case. "I didn't want to get involved in this case," Young testified.
"I tried to hand it off to the FBI." This puzzled Trubey and Robison, who knew
that police officers' careers are built on cases like the seizure of an aircraft
linked to narcotics.

"...I waited for the FBI to come and take over," Young testified. "They didn't
come, and at that point I went for a search warrant."[4] The FBI waited until the

21st of October to enter the case, 12 days after Young's first contact with the bureau. Why, they wondered? A hot airplane is a major crime in Arkansas.

This led Terry to think that Oliver North actually had intervened on his behalf, but Bush, and his Justice Department, probably turned the case back on once they realized the level of liability that was stored in Terry's head. It had, after all, been eight months from the time he had called North until an indictment was returned. And North by that time was coming up on the short end of an indictment himself. This would explain why the FBI spent so much time questioning Terry's neighbors and friends in Arkansas and Oklahoma. These people would have no knowledge of any plane theft.

But the FBI, fronting for the CIA, would want to know if Terry had revealed to these people his intelligence connections to the Arkansas training operations or any classified data related to "Jade Bridge" or "Centaur Rose."

But the most disconcerting thing to Terry personally, and which sent tremors through him, was when Young was confronted with a two-page FBI report saying Young had volunteered information that Terry might be a drug trafficker.

After reading this report into the record, Trubey asked, "Capt. Young, where did you get that information?

"I got that information from EPIC," he answered.

"From who?"

"El Paso Intelligence Center."[5]

Terry's worst fears were coming true. Up until that moment, he had no concrete evidence that anyone was truly out to get him. Now, here it was, a two-page FBI report labeling him a drug trafficker, something he definitely was not! For that exact reason, he had turned his back on the Agency and left Mexico. They were pinning this insidious accusation on him when, in truth, they were the ones guilty of drug trafficking. The clinical intelligence term for this action is "transference," but it was now taking on a very human meaning for Terry. He was now labeled as Barry Seal had been—a notorious drug trafficker. He felt like screaming with rage so loud it would wake up Theis.

He now knew this profile of him existed before he ever crossed the border back into the United States. That same profile labeling him "armed and dangerous" meant that someone wanted him dead, in a big way. Visions of lumbering across the Rio Grande with his innocent little children flashed through his memory bank. How fortunate they were some trigger-happy customs agent hadn't found them out and then opened fire, responding to the computer profile someone had created.

While Young was still smarting from the cross-examination, Dunlap returned after placing his call to Arkansas to inform Trubey that Lieutenant Jenkins said the file number 64-129-87 had been opened *on September 30, 1987*, and was not assigned to a case involving a stolen airplane, but to a totally unrelated case.

Why did the Arkansas State Police Captain, and the man who was the governor's chief of security, sit on the stand all day and lie? Terry was recalling the old Arkansas joke about the man who was such a liar he had to hire someone just to call his dog. Could it be that Raymond Young inspired that story?

This disclosure had been enough to wake the judge from his slumber. "I think we got a pie in the sky on this case number thing," Theis said, as the confused attorneys looked at one another. Theis decided to forgo further examination of Young until Arkansas authorities could respond about the mix-up on the case file number. In addition, the defense had requested from NCIC in Washington a printout denoting all police computer activity surrounding tail numbers, N30489 and N2982M and Terry Reed.

Trubey felt it was necessary at this point in light of all the government's conflicting evidence and testimony to go straight to the source of records for both FBI-NCIC and DEA-EPIC. It would be a risk, but she asked the judge to demand from the government these critical intra-agency reports. The defense team held their breath for fear of what the reports might say about Terry. After all, he who controls the computer data base can insert literally anything.

Sanders finally arrived on June 22nd and reluctantly took the stand to testify. By now, he had had time to hear from Baker and Young about the credibility problem surrounding when Baker first discovered the plane.

Sanders covered for Baker and attempted to defuse the whole date issue concerning whether Baker's activity occurred before or after the initial police involvement. He testified Baker first called him for information on the 7th of October, but it was not until the following day that he could access the FAA and provide Baker with information he wanted.[6] This would further cloud the issue of when Baker actually found the plane.

It appeared Sanders had been effectively and professionally coached. His testimony had diluted the whole date issue and included action by Baker on both the 7th and the 8th. This seemingly confused the old judge, who was frantically doodling on his scratch pad.

"God, he's a great witness for the government," Robison whispered at the defense table. "He's neutralizing the date issue. And he's obviously been coached." As a former prosecutor, Robison knew how the government worked and still marveled at their dirty tricks, even when they were being used against him.

Sanders purposely lied when he said he used only the telephone to conduct his investigation. He obviously said this because he knew Trubey was going after computer records. He probably felt that if he testified he used only a state telephone, it would be difficult to trace his efforts on Baker's behalf and there would be no telltale computer trail. He was wrong.

As a result of subpoena effort in 1993 in his civil case against Young and Baker, Terry gained access to Arkansas State Police computer records showing that Sanders not only accessed computer files for Baker and Young, but was *the first person at the state level to do anything* pertaining to this case. One can only guess at Sanders' motive for lying and what else was done by other people still unidentified.

What did this show? It showed that Sanders was willing to perjure himself to cover Baker. But even more significant, it further substantiated federal government activity in setting up Reed *occurring before* either Young or Baker were involved.

Harry Barrett, the FBO (fixed base operator) and Piper airplane dealer at the North Little Rock Airport, was the only witness called by the defense in the first hearing. He testified that Baker approached him sometime after the airplane was seized from Terry's hangar and stored in the state's hangar. During this interview, Baker confided to Barrett that he had discovered the plane as the result of a "tip."[7] This testimony contradicted all the government's evidence and the original state affidavit for the search warrant.

The government was licking its wounds after the first two days, and appeared relieved when Theis adjourned the hearing.

* * *

"Don't talk to me, I'm trying to concentrate on my driving," Joe Dunlap said nervously. "I'm trying to stay as close to this truck as I can so oncoming traffic can't see us. Can you tell if anybody's following us?"

It was a tense afternoon on September 8th, 1989. Terry and Dunlap had received a large dose of "Southern Hospitality" and were trying to get safely across the Arkansas State line and into Oklahoma before being arrested. It was Friday afternoon and Dunlap knew that was the worst time for anyone to be arrested. There would be no bail hearing until Monday and the thought of what would happen to them in an Arkansas jail over the weekend was not a pleasant one. Terry, trying to bring a little levity into a tense situation, began joking about the scene in the movie *Deliverance* in which actor Ned Beatty is sodomized by some backwoods survivalists. It didn't help.

Dunlap, from his years as a police officer, knew all too well what could happen to a prisoner the police choose not to protect while in their custody. So Terry shut up and helped Dunlap survey the traffic.

Back in Wichita, Marilyn Trubey was frantically trying to contact Robin Fowler to get him to intervene and call off the Arkansas State Police pursuit of not only her client but her investigator as well. Things had gotten a little out of hand in Little Rock, and regardless of the new face Bill Clinton's administration was trying to put on Arkansas, Dunlap was learning the hard way that the Old South was still alive and well.

Two days earlier, Dunlap and Terry had quietly and inconspicuously arrived by car in Little Rock to continue their investigation in preparation for the upcoming trial, estimated to start sometime in early Spring 1990. Several key defense witnesses had been intimidated by the FBI and state investigators, who had told the witnesses that *they did not have to talk* to anyone from the defense.

Terry was appalled to learn that old friends were avoiding Dunlap. From their interviews given the FBI, they had already convicted Terry in their own minds.

Trubey, as a last resort, reluctantly agreed Terry should accompany Dunlap in hope that his presence would change the witnesses' attitudes. After all, the people they wanted subpoenaed had been old friends or business associates with whom Terry had parted on good terms.

The first day, September 7th, went well. Linda Crow openly discussed her old boss and lover, Mark McAfee, and what she called his "sick, devious mind" and pent-up, vendetta-driven jealousy concerning Terry. The defense was going to have to neutralize McAfee since Robin Fowler had by now identified him as a government witness. Just what McAfee could or would testify to was unclear. But sensing that McAfee was unstable enough to say or do anything, and that he would be testifying under government granted immunity from perjury, Trubey didn't want to take any chances. And Crow had supplied them with all the ammunition Dunlap felt the defense would need, and then some!

Shelby Aaron, the locksmith who had performed all of the lock maintenance to Terry's hangar, had provided a sworn affidavit that stated, in effect, that the lock on the door of the hangar Terry rented had never required any type of repairs and, in his professional opinion, it would have been impossible for the wind to have blown it open.

Then came the trip to the Arkansas State Police Intelligence Center. After Terry's first hearing in Wichita, Major Doug Stephens, head of the criminal division, had written the Wichita court a letter attempting to explain away the file number mix-up. The letter was ridiculous in that it reflected no internal investigation of any kind and merely hypothesized about what might have happened with this key piece of evidence. After all, if the date on the front of the file folder assigned to Terry's case was correct it would show Young being involved as far back as September 30th, 1987, at least seven days earlier than he had testified. Aside from showing that Young had lied, the earlier date was crucial since it would show police involvement with Reed's plane long before Baker "stumbled" upon the so-called open hangar door. This gives substance to the defense theory that Reed had been set up from the beginning.

Dunlap, who had developed a telephone relationship earlier with Lieutenant Jenkins, the head of the records section, was hoping to speak personally with Jenkins to get to the bottom of the alleged mix-up. Terry waited outside in the car in the hot summer sun while Dunlap attempted to interview Jenkins. He returned a short time later, having struck out, because low and behold, none other than Major Doug Stephens just happened to intervene in the middle of the interview.

Jenkins' friendly attitude toward Dunlap changed abruptly in Stephens' presence and the interview was prematurely terminated.

The next morning, first on the list and the highest priority was to interview Bill Canino, the owner of the North Little Rock hangar, who had said some very disconcerting things to the FBI back in 1987. Namely, that he had never met any Terry Reed, but had rented a hangar to a Terry Kerr, whom he had never seen either.

Additionally, Carol Canino, his wife, had produced copies of corporate cashiers checks that Janis, as secretary-treasurer of Applied Technologies, Inc., had used to pay the hangar rent. The defense determined from grand jury minutes that these checks and correspondence about the hangar rental supplied by the Caninos were the sole evidence used to indict Janis as an accomplice in "aiding and abetting" her husband.

It was hoped that Canino, in the presence of Terry, could explain why he had become so confused about meeting him back in 1983, when he first moved to Little Rock. Beyond the rental arrangement for the hangar, Terry had even approached Canino at one point about purchasing an Ultra-Light. It was very confusing to Terry and his defense team as to why Canino's memory was so selective. Could it have been that Canino had been pressured by the investigators? Was he guilty of something and "working off a case"? They had to know and only in Terry's presence, they felt, would Canino "'fess up."

The first part of the interview went well. Terry had a checklist of topics to discuss with Canino, who as soon as Dunlap and Terry arrived, recanted his statement about not knowing Terry. The name mix-up, he theorized, was due to the fact that his wife, Carol, handled most of the business dealings concerning the hangar with Janis. Janis' hyphenated last name, Kerr-Reed, had probably caused her husband the problem. Mrs. Canino, Bill guessed, had confused Kerr as being the correct last name and set up the rental file under "Kerr."

But as the subject turned to an even more sensitive area, i.e. money—cash money—the money Bill Cooper had given Terry to rent the hangar space initially, Canino's friendly attitude quickly changed. This was obviously an area Canino did not want to discuss and, without allowing any further questions, said: "I don't want to do this. And I won't if you guys will leave right now. But I'm supposed to call in order to have you guys arrested. They know you're in town and they say he (pointing to Dunlap) has been posing as a U.S. Marshal and there's a warrant out for his arrest. And maybe you, too, Terry."

Terry was out of New Mexico without court permission since Trubey did not want Fowler to know he was going to Arkansas. This way, Fowler couldn't tip off the ASP and cause the two men to be followed, revealing defense witnesses and strategy. Linda Crow, who was turning out to be a key witness for Terry, was unknown to the state police then. The defense wanted to keep it that way.

Technically, Terry was legally in Dunlap's custody. But if Dunlap were to be arrested, this could give Terry problems with the court. And Terry was sure that Young and Baker would certainly like to conduct a weekend's interrogation of them both.

As Dunlap and Terry sped out of Canino's driveway, Terry found it interesting to witness his old companions, paranoia and fear, invading the mind of someone else for a change. With Terry as navigator, and knowing the back roads of Arkansas, they planned an escape route they hoped would keep them out of the law's hands.

Their nemesis, they feared, would be Dunlap's government license plates, which would surely lead to their doom. Dunlap rejected Terry's suggestion that they "borrow" someone else's license plates, electing instead to call Trubey for help. Terry had never seen Joe carry his weapon before. Normally he kept it in the trunk of his car, but as they drafted along in a semi's wake west of Russellville, Arkansas on I-40, his weapon lay loaded on the car's console.

Dunlap was learning fast what serious business this was. There was a lot more involved here than just mail fraud and a stolen airplane.

Dunlap turned to Reed and asked: "Who are you, really? Why do all these people want your ass so bad." From his comments, Dunlap at long last was coming to terms with what he was dealing with.

Through it all, Terry managed to joke about *Deliverance*, the PRA (People's Republic of Arkansas), and appeared to be controlling his stress and fear.

"God damn pilots!" Dunlap would snap. "You're all crazy!"

A couple of tense hours later, and with a sigh of relief, they crossed the Oklahoma line and managed a quick pit stop, to phone Trubey and tell her they had "escaped." They then began their drive toward Tulsa where Terry would fly back to New Mexico. Too tired from the stress of the day to talk, Terry thought about the multitude of problems facing him and Janis as they prepared for the upcoming trial. He still couldn't accept the fact they were actually going to trial in light of all the perjured and tainted evidence from the hearings.

Their lives were literally in limbo. Looking back at the summer of 1989, which plodded on as Trubey and Dunlap's investigations continued, Terry thought of the slow, long slide into depression he and Janis had undergone. Janis, due to her indictment, was unable to gain employment in her old profession, real estate, since it was impossible to be professionally bonded, a New Mexico state requirement, while awaiting trial.

Terry, likewise, had to pass up several lucrative automation projects since bail bond requirements placed him under severe travel restrictions. This produced the added burden of not knowing how he was going to provide financially for his family. His business life was a disaster since he felt obligated to tell his potential business associates about the indictment and how it would possibly interfere with his work schedule. To them, he had the plague. His future was uncertain and they could not be assured he would even be around to fulfill contractual agreements. And like Janis he, too, required bonding unavailable to him for large projects.

As the Reeds depleted what was left of their dwindling resources, they watched their lifestyle slowly decline. The one thing that sustained them was the love they had for their children. The thought of anything sinister happening to them was unbearable and went unspoken. The only defense for an attack on them was a well-rehearsed plan, Terry felt.

The Reeds had contingencies for everything. They had rehearsed over and over again their "battle plans" to the point at which they were prepared for almost any catastrophe.

Duncan was driven to school every day. And to prevent a kidnap attempt, the principal was given a cover story. She was told that Terry had a former wife who was unstable, could not have children of her own, and might resort to kidnapping Duncan. For this reason, his first grade teacher was instructed to allow no one to take him from school even in an "emergency."

Webster defines paranoia as "a psychiatric mental disorder characterized by systematic delusions and projection of personal conflict, that are ascribed to be supposed hostility of others." The definition fit their status with the exception of one word, the word "supposed." Trubey, Dunlap and the Reeds had plenty of "true life" events happening to separate their paranoia from reality.

Through the course of unearthing their evidence, a series of frightening events took place that would have an impact on not only Terry and Janis, but Trubey and Dunlap as well. First, there was hard evidence that their phones were being tapped. Having been trained in the Air Force about communications security, Terry was particularly wary about using unsecure phone lines to discuss the case and especially to map out defense strategy.

Trubey and Dunlap initially complied with his wishes to keep telephone communications to a minimum and communicate primarily by mail, but this was difficult to do and, over time, communications security began to erode. It came to a head one day when Dunlap asked the Federal Public Defender's office in Columbus, Ohio, to interview Barbara Williams, to whom the aircraft registration number N30489 had been assigned originally by the FAA. This was the registration number supposedly painted on the plane Baker "found" in Terry's hangar.

Dunlap had relayed the instructions for this task by phone to a female investigator in the PD's office in Columbus, Ohio, where Williams resided. And while enroute to interview Mrs. Williams, the investigator noticed she was being followed. The car, carrying two passengers, gave the appearance of an undercover police car, but it had civilian registration.

Concerned, she stopped at a phone booth and called her office to give the license plate number of the car. Her office, in turn, had the police "run the number," which automatically triggered an FBI alert system designed to protect the identity of their agents. She was, indeed, being followed by men in an FBI car.

With that, the FBI office in Columbus placed a call to the Public Defender's Office to complain about the Police Department's running one of the Bureau's undercover plates. It was then that Dunlap and the Ohio office knew that communications security had been *compromised*. Their office phones in Wichita, they were now sure, were being monitored by the FBI!

It was now all becoming very real to Trubey and Dunlap. Terry's paranoia was not paranoia at all but a legitimate concern. They had their phones swept, but the technician who conducted the sweep stated that the degree of sophistication for tapping available to the FBI made detection virtually impossible.

But more disturbing was the firebombing of a Volkswagen Beetle, which had been parked in front of Dunlap's house in Wichita. The car that had been firebombed belonged to a friend of Dunlap's daughter, but was identical to one owned by his oldest daughter. The fire department later determined the fire was caused by some type of incendiary device, probably thrown into the car through an open window.

Dunlap saw this as a direct threat to his family, and that he was being given a warning. He was upsetting someone because of his investigation into the Reed case. He apparently was doing too good of a job.

Shortly after that incident, his wife's car was intentionally rammed at an intersection by a hit and run driver, who by the glare his wife saw on the man's face, knew his target. Another motorist who witnessed the accident told police that the driver appeared to purposely ram Dunlap's wife's car and then casually backed up and left the scene.

Dunlap's personal vehicle was not spared either. The windows of his pickup truck were smashed twice and on each occurrence, his was the only vehicle on the block to be vandalized. The Dunlap family was now on "Red Alert", just as the Reeds.

As a result of all these sinister events, Trubey had the Reeds make copies of all their important records and files needed for the trial and advised them to store the records away in a safe place away from the originals. Not even Trubey was to know the location, so that their whereabouts could not be *compromised*.

Terry had amassed enormous volumes of files and records. He even kept notebooks to record each day's events, even as far back as his time in the Air Force. To accommodate all this data, he rented a small, storage facility in a secure compound, under an alias in Bernalillo, New Mexico.

Easter weekend of 1990, the Reeds planned a three-day camping trip to Carlsbad Caverns, thinking it might be their last opportunity to vacation before the impending trial. While they were gone, their storage unit was burglarized, and their files pilfered. Police later told them it was the work of a professional burglar.

The unknown perpetrator had somehow penetrated the elaborate chain link fence security, eluded the German Shepherd guard dogs, and proceeded to cut the lock on the door of Reed's storage unit. From evidence taken at the crime scene, the intruder had spent hours methodically opening boxes in which records were kept, but only removing select files. It appeared he knew exactly what he was after. He had even taken time to eat as he worked. Remnants of a sandwich were found on the floor. This was most definitely not an occurrence of paranoia and manifested fear. Paranoia does not eat ham sandwiches.

Who does one complain to when being victimized by the "system"? *The Department of Injustice*, perhaps?

This was the revised title Terry gave the criminal justice system as a result of Judge Theis' official Opinion and Order rendered as a result of weighing and digesting the material presented in the nearly six month suppression proceedings.

The 22-page order, dated December 15th, 1989, had struck down all pending defense motions with the exception of one. The Reeds could have their grand jury minutes.

The avalanche of conflicting data that Trubey and Dunlap had developed and dumped on the court had been explained away simply by Judge Theis' and his two new law clerks as irrelevant. The defense had wanted, in addition to the grand jury minutes, the suppression of the airplane as evidence, and separate trials for Terry and Janis. Also denied was critical discovery involving Iran-Contra that could prove the theory of the defense, that Reed had been set-up as a result of him becoming a liability to some very important people.

Their list of requests from the government included:
1. A list of all of Oliver North's aliases;
2. All documentation relating to Oliver North's involvement with the Donor Program;
3. All documentation relating to the Donor Program, including, but not limited to, the date of conception, all persons involved in the program, agreements between the United States Government and insurance companies, a list of persons who contributed to the Donor Program and the items contributed, documentation relating to how the donated items were used, and any and all other documentation relating to the Donor Program;
4. A list of all other litigation, both civil and criminal, pertaining to the Donor Program;
5. All phone records, travel plans, notes, etc., relating to Oliver North's activities on Feb. 18, 1982; Feb. 24, 1982 to October, 1982; March 11, 1983 to March 22, 1983; November of 1984; and July 19, 1985;
6. Oliver North's notebooks and diaries from 1982 to 1987;
7. All documentation concerning the relationship between the CIA and Southern Air Transport, Richard Secord, and William Cooper.

In denying all this to the Reeds and his attorney, Theis fell back on the argument that all this information and material was outside the possession, custody or control of the U.S. Attorney's office. He further held that if, in fact, the material existed and was in possession of the special prosecutor's office or congressional investigators, the U.S. attorney had no right to these. Therefore, this information was "undiscoverable."

The motion seeking suppression was denied on the grounds the defense had fallen short of proving Baker acted on Young's instructions. To the dismay of the defense, Theis put no significance on the one major piece of evidence discovered between the first court session in June 1989, and the second in October.

After months of labor and research, Theis dismissed this key piece of evidence as "not particularly relevant."

The "smoking gun" that Trubey found that would shoot holes through all of the Baker and Young's perjured testimony was the computer printout from

NCIC (National Crime Information Center) in Washington. Baker's story was built around his "discovery" of an airplane stenciled N30489. He claimed to have taken that number to Young and had it run through NCIC to determine if it was stolen.

Young said the first NCIC check showed it was not stolen. Baker, being "one heck of a detective," as he called himself, returned at a later date (by his own testimony, the next day or later) found another number N2982M, and had that number run by Young.[8] If that scenario was true, the NCIC printout from Washington, which was a record of law enforcement accessing, should have shown 30489 being run *before* 2982M.

It did not.

Not only did it show just the opposite, it showed something even worse. *Both numbers were run within ONE minute of the each other.* The significance of this information was that Young was in possession of the stolen airplane number from the beginning. This backed up the "tip" theory. Terry had been set up, plain and simple. But why couldn't Theis see that? Or did he?

Young had not "found" his way to the "fruits of a crime" as he had testified. But instead, he knew he had a crime from the very beginning. This meant there was a preponderance of evidence that Young had instructed Baker from the very beginning to develop probable cause for entering the hangar. Trubey felt confident this single piece of information would cast a reasonable doubt on Young's testimony and make the judge dismiss the case.

As far as Young's investigative files being "manufactured" 18 months after the fact, Theis wrote: "Young did damage his credibility by his admission that he prepared his case reports between nine and 18 months after the events in October, 1987. Young's explanation for his failure to timely dictate a report is reasonable...The court in no way condones Young's behavior, but does not find it seriously damaging to his credibility."[9]

Another great statement surpassing the explanation of the term "ambiguity", the Reeds thought!

Theis also explained away the perjured testimony in the state affidavit for the search warrant and taught the Reeds a lot about the law all in one fell swoop. Namely, the government is allowed to extract lies from an affidavit and then analyze what's left and if sufficient material is left, then it's all right to proceed. Somehow, in Theis' reasoning and the Reed's shock, this does not reflect upon the credibility of the person making the perjured statement.

Theis, referring to this, wrote: "In the present case, the court will assume that statements made by Baker and Young in the oral affidavit were made with at least a reckless disregard for the truth."[10] In the language of Terry's mule-trading great-grandfather, this would have been reduced to more simple terms: "These sons of bitches are lying and can't be trusted, and should be strung up." Oh where are those innocent days, Terry wondered?

As for the motion to sever, or separate the Reeds' trials?

Denied, on the grounds that the trial jury would be able to separate "and compartmentalize" evidence and the defendants. This, in light of the fact that Janis' attorney, Steve Robison, alleged prejudice in the following areas:

1. An absence of evidence against her regarding the theft of the airplane, the submission of documents or statements regarding the insurance claim, and the receipt or presentation of the insurance draft;
2. The assertion of an alibi defense for the date the airplane was stolen;

3. the probable use of statements by Terry Reed containing hearsay against Janis Reed;
4. Terry Reed will testify on Janis Reeds behalf at a separate trial;
5. A disparity of evidence between Terry Reed and Janis Reed;
6. The probability of guilt by association due to the relationship between the defendants.

The Reeds did get access to their grand jury minutes, but these were useless except to show that only oral testimony was presented and given by one FBI agent who was *not* the case agent nor the one who was the main investigator in Arkansas. The agent, Lawrence Nolan, did, however, attempt to taint the minds of the grand jurors with cryptic remarks about the Reeds that hinted at drug trafficking.

He tried to make them appear as criminals. "These individuals thereafter, it appears, left Little Rock in approximately December, 1986, after pulling some type of scam with Gomex (sic) Industries...and they fled to Mexico, and as far as we know have been in Guadalajara ever since," Nolan said.[11]

Theis did give Trubey two additional crumbs of discovery, which she had asked for verbally. These were records maintained at the FAA Intelligence Center in Oklahoma City (AC700 unit) and records from the El Paso Intelligence Center to confirm this Agency was the source of information Young said he had received and was in fact on file there. This latter discovery request was one Terry and Trubey almost wished Theis had denied. They were nervous about what it might contain. Felix Rodriguez probably had friends there, they theorized, since the CIA officed in the same building.

After Theis' 22-page decree, things were plain and simple...the Reeds were going to trial. Theis now would have Oliver North in his courtroom, evidence notwithstanding. Forget Silkwood and the Dalkon Shield! He now had a case that was serving as an elixir for his "attention deficit disorder".

* * *

"Terry, we're not going to trial on June 3rd," Marilyn Trubey said from her office in Topeka, Kansas. "I just got off the phone with Robin Fowler and the government is going to invoke *national security procedures.* I think that's good news. What do you think?"

It was Trubey's feeling this was a grudging acknowledgement by the government of Terry's intelligence linkage. After all, she reasoned, they wouldn't be invoking national security unless what he had been saying was true.

Terry, however, was furious and Janis was in disbelief as he briefed her after hanging up the phone. It was June 1st, 1990, they were just two days from trial and their life was in a shambles. Preparation for the trial, which had been scheduled to begin in two days, had totally consumed them. Just as athletes totally immerse themselves in training, the couple had dialed out everything but the preparation of their defense. Their lives and future were hanging in the balance, in the scales held by the blindfolded woman.

But Terry was learning the truth about the criminal justice system, the blindfolded woman with the sword and scales was peeking. Theis' earlier ruling had made Terry very apprehensive about getting a fair trial. Theis was ignoring Trubey's evidence and continually aligning himself with the government. From what he had been learning he now realized this is the way it works, that judges are there to help the government convict you. Judges, he gleaned, don't like to make tough decisions, they want to leave that to juries or appeal courts. As far as the whole criminal "injustice" system was concerned, Terry figured, you're guilty just because you're there.

The Reeds couldn't combat these mind-sets, so they had fallen back on their life experiences and education and had taken the only course available to them.

Prepare, prepare, prepare for trial. Now, Terry realized, a jury was his only hope. He had been slow to catch on to how the game is really played, still operating from his "Perry Mason mentality." The judges on TV always seemed to play fair....and stay awake.

What was gnawing away at him and Janis was the element of time applied to this game called justice. Judges, to his surprise, don't rule in court, or quickly. It had taken months between each hearing for Theis to weigh the evidence. He would vacation each winter in Florida, and ultimately rule against the Reeds. It had been *two years* since they had been indicted. To them, they were winning the skirmishes, but losing the war.

In the Air Force, Terry trained continuously under real and simulated combat conditions. But there, things made sense. You fire a salvo of missiles at your enemy and the success of the strike, or lack of it, and the need for a second attack, were relayed immediately from the battlefield. Here, it was months between salvos. They would wait weeks to find out they scored a direct hit, but the judge would then rule, through a sterile court decree, the missiles were duds.

The one "war-game rule" that Theis could remember was "Brady." This was a U.S. Supreme Court ruling that held the government must turn over to the defense *everything* in its possession that tends to show innocence on the part of a defendant.

The judge, who liked to appear in court and on the record as a civil libertarian, cited Brady continuously, but then it seemed he had his law clerks find some precedent to negate it. This became legal double-speak and somehow always accrued to the benefit of the government, which after all, pays his inflated salary and guarantees him lifetime employment.

It had been an uphill battle all the way, causing the Reeds to spend countless hours organizing their files and developing cross-reference systems so they could feed Trubey the legal ammunition she would need while engaged in battle.

As the Reeds looked around the mass of file boxes on the basement floor of Janis' parents' home in Kansas City, Terry was emotionally numb. Janis was coming down from the emotional high of having her indictment dismissed "with prejudice" (meaning the government could not renew these charges) four days earlier on May 28th. It worried her to see her husband in this continuing state of suspended animation. It was as if they were toying with him. The government was a gigantic, carnivorous cat, and he was a crafty little mouse. But every time he prepared to launch an offensive and attempted to escape, the cat would simply stand on the mouse's tail. Janis was fearful that the cat may now be tiring of the game and preparing to devour its prey, her husband.

They had prepared for the worst. All of their household goods were in storage. They were now homeless.

They had left New Mexico two weeks earlier, towing Tommy Trailer loaded to the roof with court data, records and essential personal effects and clothing to get them through what was predicted to be a six-week trial. Janis was school-ing Duncan at home once again, having had to take him out of school for the trial. Terry had asked, and was denied, the only extension of time he had re-quested since being indicted. His only true opportunity to earn a badly-needed income had surfaced early in the year and would require his involvement in a project in South Carolina through the month of June. Theis denied the re-quest, citing "this is *the* oldest case on my docket." Justice can be swift when it's the defendant who suffers, the Reeds were learning.

Although they dared not articulate it to each other, the Reeds had put their financial affairs in order for what Terry felt in his heart was a certainty...he was going to prison.

Trubey had begun counseling Terry like a doctor before major surgery, tell-ing him to think positively, but prepare for the worst. She had warned Janis that, among other things, a conviction for Terry would destroy her credit rat-ing. This was alien to her. She had been a successful businesswoman with a perfect credit rating, ever since leaving college. But now she was being told that somehow her husband's character would be factored into her financial status, simply because she was his wife.

Another discovery Terry had made throughout all of this was that a whole new service industry had grown up, composed of convicted attorneys who "coun-seled" clients on prison life and how it affects the family. They performed this service at half their old hourly rate, since they could no longer practice law. This seemed to him the only type of service industry the Republicans were capable of creating in the 10 years of the Reagan-Bush "law and order" poli-cies.

The Reeds had already decided secretly, while both under indictment and without either attorney knowing, that Terry would plead guilty if they saw the trial going badly, hoping that they could bargain his plea for his wife's free-dom.

Then Fowler, suddenly and without warning even to Robison who socialized with the prosecutor, walked into the final hearing on May 28th—the eleventh hour—and moved to dismiss Janis' indictment. He had held her hostage as long as he could. He had no evidence against her and probably knew it all along.

Fowler didn't know that he had played his trump card before Terry could play his. The trump card was Janis, she was the mutual pawn. This was unbe-lievably wonderful news, but it cut two ways. Janis was free, but now Terry had no bargaining chip. He would have to fight as aggressively as Amiram Nir had once described, "with your back to the sea." With Nir's words in mind, Terry had set out with Trubey and Dunlap's help, to develop his final battle plan. The way he viewed what was about to happen was a new application of his military training, to build nuclear war contingencies.

All nuclear war damage projections are based upon the two 75 kiloton weap-ons dropped on Japan in World War II. Not being familiar with the game he was now playing, he had decided to go into his personal arsenal and summon enough "yield" to vaporize his enemy. He might go down, he thought, but only after inflicting major damage and casualties.

Trubey's first salvo in mid-May 1990 consisted of more than 50 subpoenas directed at such targets as the CIA, the FBI, DEA, EPIC, FAA Intelligence and the Arkansas State Police. The missiles had "left the hole" and were streaking

454	TERRY REED AND JOHN CUMMINGS

silently toward their targets when Robin Fowler's phone rang reporting the first "hit."

Fowler, from his command post in Wichita, was relaying to Trubey's battle station in Topeka the "bomb damage assessment" of the weapon that had impacted on the neon pig, the savings and loan logo, sitting atop FBI headquarters in Oklahoma City.

Trubey relayed to Terry, "Robin just got a call from FBI Agent Wayne Barlow in Oklahoma City. This is great news, Terry. Not only does Barlow say he knows you, but his contact with you involved classified information that he won't discuss over Robin's unsecure phone. He made Robin go over to the FBI office in Wichita in order to discuss it on a secure line. Terry, I think we got 'em on the run."

That subpoena, which had triggered the first "secondary explosion," had been loaded with high explosive ammunition. Barlow's subpoena ordered him to appear in Wichita on June 11 and bring: "Complete files on: Northwest Industries, Inc.; Technoimpex; Barcorp Corporation; Emery L. West, a/k/a Veda; Reed Kane and Associates; Janis Kerr Reed; Terry K. Reed; Joseph (Jozsef) Bona; 1978 Piper Arrow PA-28 N2982M."

Barlow, by admitting he knew Terry, and saying his contacts with him involved classified information, was the crack in the wall of silence that had been built around the intelligence community. The silence up to this point, had been interpreted by Fowler as a denial of Terry's involvement with the intelligence world, and an unspoken approval to take Terry down.

The remainder of that day, the day that Fowler's case began to unravel, centered on "damage reports" from various federal agencies offering "regrets" and saying, in effect, they couldn't appear in court. Classified material was involved, they all said.

That day, another legal title had appeared in Terry's growing anthology of new legal terms. It was called the Classified Information Procedures Act, which the government was now invoking, *two days* before Terry's scheduled trial.

The law was enacted in October, 1980, and from the application of it came the term "graymail." From what Terry learned, the law was normally used to prevent government agents who had been indicted from blackmailing the government into dropping the charges against them by threatening to disclose classified material during the trial.

It prohibits "unauthorized disclosure for reasons of national security and any restricted data." It defines national security as encompassing "national defense and foreign relations of the United States." Trubey and Terry found this definition interesting because his involvement in intelligence did, in fact, involve the USSR, Mexico, Israel, Hungary, Japan, China...and *Arkansas*.

What the law says is that a defendant must notify the government in advance of a trial about any classified information that they plan to use or which might surface during the trial. If the defense fails to do that, the court can bar its use during the trial.

Up to this point, Theis had denied almost all of Terry's discovery demands. He had no classified information in his possession, and the government agencies contacted by Dunlap had refused to cooperate or admit knowing of any involvement by Terry in any intelligence operation. For this reason, the defense was preparing to go to trial with only unclassified material. All it had was Terry's story, him as a witness, and 50 subpoenas.

But this eleventh-hour move by the government not only gave Terry the credibility he needed, but in essence proved that the government had not been cooperating with either the defense, or the prosecution—an old story in cases like this. The CIA and the intelligence community has lied to the government's own attorneys on numerous occasions.*

Fowler was quickly learning that the fast track to a career change was for a government attorney to blindly accept a case on face value. He had clearly ignored a U.S. attorney's first responsibility: To be the brake that stops an unjust prosecution.

One could conclude by the government's actions during that presidential election year of 1988 and, now, by invoking the Classified Information Procedures Act (CIPA) in 1990, the criminal justice system had been perverted to silence an asset with embarrassing political knowledge. The use of the judicial system to gag him had worked up until now. But since Terry at last had subpoena power and could pry behind the layers of deceit that shrouded the truth, it was time for the government to re-trench and hide behind "national security," leaving Fowler to take the heat and the judge's wrath alone.

While Fowler filled out his DD Form 398 detailing his life's history in an attempt to get his security clearance in order to be able to talk directly with the federal agencies involved, Terry felt he was being jerked around once more by the government.

Terry would later read the results of the telephonic hearing, which occurred June 1st, 1990, between Fowler, Trubey and Judge Theis as Fowler outlined areas of classified information that were certain to come out in the trial.

"There are a number of areas, your honor, that I'm concerned about, "Fowler said. "I'd like to just briefly go through those for the record. I'm concerned with the potential testimony of Wayne Barlow, an FBI agent out of Oklahoma City. He has, in fact, told me that some of his prior contacts with Mr. Terry involved classified information. There are a number of other areas I'd like to just very briefly mention.

"The second area of concern is information accepted from the F.A.A. Intelligence Division. A third area of concern involves information accepted from the D.E.A.'s EPIC organization. The fourth, information potentially that would be brought out on direct or cross, particularly that of Oliver North, Jack Bloom (sic) and Robert Johnson, particular there's concern for information that the director of the C.I.A. has been ordered to produce in regard to certain files and information from the National Security Archives and finally, there's the possible testimony of the defendant which may or may not implicate classified information. I think there are a number of areas which it's reasonably expected at that point the classified information might be—that might come out at trial and I'm concerned enough about that to raise the issue here."[12]

By June 6th, Terry had had a chance to absorb what was happening. His frustration turned to rage! The subpoenas they had fought so hard to have served, were officially "on hold." The time for legal protocol was over. It was time, he decided, to take matters into his own hands. After thoroughly reading the CIPA act, he perceived it as a ploy to make him play out in advance to the

---

*   In 1983, former Attorney-General Ramsey Clark and Federal Judge John Curtin, a former U.S. Attorney, testified in a New York federal trial that the Central Intelligence Agency lied to them repeatedly about a case they were investigating back in the 1970s.

court and prosecutor his entire defense strategy. The CIPA law was forcing Trubey to itemize all elements of evidence they planned to put into play, so they could be screened for possible classified material, which he did not knowingly have. This would give the Justice Department a chance to neutralize anything embarrassing to the government.

The letter he wrote and filed with the court, without Trubey's knowledge or approval, was entitled "Statement of Position of Defendant, Terry K. Reed." He had decided that the only way to bypass the entire judicial system and communicate directly was through the court file, which he was sure the Agency was monitoring. He had no way to penetrate the dark world and "reach out and touch someone," since he was now persona non grata to the intelligence community. He still felt his plight had been brought on by a few selfish agents involved in "Screw Worm," with the situation escalating to its present state because of the breakdown in communications. It was as if the war had knocked down the telephone lines, so he decided to send a "carrier pigeon" to deliver the message. He was under attack and if the provocations continued, he would be forced to protect himself any way he could. Even if that meant exposing classified material and agents. (See chapter end.)

He wanted them to know he wasn't picking the fight. He was being boxed in by the "In-Justice Department" and wanted the Agency to intervene. Surely, he thought, if they realized he wasn't a threat and would quietly go away, they would possibly put an end to this madness.

Why, Terry asked in the letter, was the burden on him rather than the government, to outline possible areas of sensitive or classified information? By doing so, he said, he might be needlessly exposing something that should be kept secret.

Terry didn't know what effect, if any, the letter had on the CIA. He was quick to find out, however, its effect on the court. Theis was unhappy. He informed Trubey that he didn't appreciate such behavior by a "defendant." If Trubey could not control him, Theis said he would have his bail revoked and Terry could spend the remainder of his trial preparation time in jail.

Legal protocol had been violated, after all. That was much more important, they were discovering, than attention being given to the travesty of justice that was being acted out in Theis' courtroom.

It was 1968 all over again, he thought. Terry had been a young airman in Okinawa and LBJ had the North Vietnamese on the run. As the Air Force's B-52s relentlessly pounded Hanoi to the brink of oblivion, Terry and his fellow intelligence analysts sat in shock when they heard the bombing had been halted. Yeah, this was how he felt as he sat in his in-laws' basement with no job, or home to return to in New Mexico. The subpoenas they had fought so hard to have served were on official hold, just like the bombs that were piled up by the runway in Okinawa, unable to go to their intended targets. They just wouldn't let him win...again!

The intended targets of the subpoenas read like the who's who of Iran-Contra. At the top of the list was Oliver North, who through his attorney Brendan Sullivan, was already saying North would take the Fifth Amendment if forced to testify.

And then, there was Felix Rodriguez, the macho commie-fighter, who had hidden in his house in Miami for two days trying to avoid Dunlap's effort to serve his subpoena. Trubey finally had to get a court order from Theis to get

Rodriguez' phone number so that he could be called. Rodriguez agreed to talk with Dunlap after communicating with him through Rodriguez' uncle, an attorney, who was his registered service agent.

And the uncle agreed only after being told that continued evasion would result in a U.S. Marshal arresting his nephew. When Dunlap finally gained access to Rodriguez' house, he said it looked to him like a "memorial" to Felix' world-wide campaign of chasing Communists. Grisly photographs adorned the walls and included some of a dead Ché Guevara and photos of his severed hands.

In the subsequent interview, Rodriguez denied ever knowing "a Terry Reed" and told Dunlap he had never been to Mexico, even though Dunlap would later note that Felix' book, "Shadow Warrior," reflects the contrary. In the book, Rodriguez refers to living in Mexico City with his parents after Fidel Castro's takeover. While in Mexico, he had written, he became active in Cuban exile groups operating there.[13]

The subpoena of Jack Blum, Special Counsel to the Senate Foreign Relations Committee, was being blocked by the counsel to the Senate on grounds that Blum had given his information about Terry to Independent Counsel Lawrence Walsh. The argument was that this put Blum outside the reach of a court subpoena. This was still being argued on the day CIPA was invoked by the government. Terry and Janis had met with and been interviewed by Blum for three days in 1988 in Washington. Trubey wanted to know, in Blum's own words, why Congress and Walsh weren't motivated to act on Terry's information.

And then there was Arif Durrani, a Pakistani-American businessman then serving time in a federal prison for illegally selling weapons to Iran during the arms embargo. He claimed to have been recruited for this activity by North and had knowledge of "Project Donation."

The defense also had some "secret weapons" they had "discovered" within government files and which Trubey was hoping to "drop" during the trial. El Paso Intelligence Center had responded to the court order to produce the files that Young had claimed identified Terry as a drug trafficker.

EPIC's attorney notified the court that no such records on Terry existed. Not only did this cause Trubey and Dunlap to breath a sigh of relief, but the rest of the report was interesting as well.

The report said the only record of inquiries into Terry or the stolen airplane found in Little Rock, N2982M, had occurred on October 16th, 1987. This inquiry was not to retrieve data, as Young had testified, but rather to insert data into the EPIC's computer system. The entry read: "On Oct. 16, 1987, it reported to EPIC that the Arkansas State Police, Little Rock, Arkansas, reported aircraft N2982M, was recovered on Oct. 16, 1987, from a hangar in Little Rock, Arkansas, where the owner Kent T. Reed (aka Terry Reed) hid the aircraft to collect the $33,000 insurance claim. EPIC records reflect no other inquiries in connection with Terry Kent Reed and aircraft N2982M."

Young had lied when he testified that EPIC files portrayed Terry as a drug trafficker. Trubey found it interesting that Young didn't need the justice system to "convict" Reed, only two days after he had executed the search warrant.

Young had lied.

Why would a man of Young's stature, a man so close to Bill Clinton, perjure himself so blatantly? They were hoping to find the answer during the trial, since Young and Baker had been subpoenaed as well.

As for FAA intelligence, they were screaming national security to Fowler when all they had been asked to produce were the official FAA records on N30489 and N2982M, the tail numbers connected to the plane "found" in the North Little Rock Hangar. In addition to this, Trubey had added to the subpoena a request to "state whether either plane appears on the list of aircraft used covertly in the Contra operation in Nicaragua."

Direct hit!

If this simple request was triggering cries of "national security," then Terry's suspicions had to be true. His old airplane, the one Bill Cooper had been flying, or the one from Ohio that was supposed to be in Germany, must have been "donated" to the Contra cause in Nicaragua. And in addition, an FAA Computer report showed the FBI in Oklahoma City targeting N2982M as being the subject of a narcotics investigation on May 19, 1988, one month after Young released the plane to the insurance company without a court order.

It was Trubey's feeling this proved either one of two things: The insurance company was an Agency front company involved in narcotics trafficking or perhaps there was more than one plane with the number, N2982M, flying around.

Throughout June, after returning to New Mexico to breaking out their household goods once again from storage to continue their life of limbo, Janis and Terry watched their savings evaporate. As they contemplated their dire financial condition, they were once again thrust back into deep depression. While Fowler and everyone else involved in the judicial system were getting their bi-weekly federal paychecks, embossed with the Statue of Liberty, such was not the case for the Reed household. To them, everyone they had met since getting indicted, with the exception of the Public Defender system, was simply devouring them, a bite at a time. It was consuming not only them personally, but their family and their lifestyle, as well.

They were locked in a seemingly endless struggle with this hydra-headed monster called the criminal justice system. They were learning it could only be kept at bay by feeding it money...lots of money...which it insatiably devoured. This monster didn't breathe fire, however, it wore three-piece suits, had college degrees, tie bars, wing-tipped shoes, carried expensive gold plated fountain pens, and even had its own sterile vocabulary.

Courtroom combat, they saw, was fought between social parasites "dressed for success" who worked in marble "palaces" with mahogany paneled walls. The "war games umpire", referred to as "Judge", sits perched on his throne and quibbles over the foundation of each argument or impresses the contestants with the word of the day. A word probably selected at random, just prior to court proceedings, that is chosen to dutifully impress the assembled humble subjects.

Terry, the defendant, if mentioned at all, was referred to in impersonal, third person pronouns as if no name or face or body was attached. And what were the stakes??? Simply winning! Who was keeping score, the Reeds wondered? If the prosecutor wins, a human being is taken from his loved ones and goes to a urine-infested cage for "rehabilitation".

Terry and Janis were consumed with thoughts of raising their children without a father, and how this justice system gone mad, led by Mr. Law and Order, Robin Fowler, didn't seem to care if the Reed family produced three juvenile delinquents as a result of Terry's incarceration.

* * *

"You put that away," Judge Theis snapped in his chambers as he pointed his finger at Robin Fowler. "It's your office's fault that we're here today. All you should be carin' about is comin' out of this smellin' good!"

"Yes sir," the contrite Fowler said as he put the letter back inside the coat pocket of his polyester suit.

The letter Fowler was carrying was a written position statement from his office that he wanted to read into the record of the upcoming proceeding.

Terry, who was sitting on the judge's maroon leather tuck-and button sofa felt embarrassed for Fowler as the judge finished admonishing the government's attorney. Theis then turned to Terry to outline the scenario for what was about to happen shortly in his courtroom.

"Mr. Reed, do you understand exactly what's happening here?" Theis asked from behind his elevated desk, which resembled a pulpit. The office was plush, Terry thought, with its thick salmon-colored carpet, its built-in bookcases and the large portrait of Lyndon B. Johnson.

"It's my understanding from Ms. Trubey that if I waive my right to a jury trial that you will acquit me...find me not guilty," Terry said crisply.

"Yep, that's about it," the judge said as he leaned back and surveyed the group assembled in his chambers, then asked, "What I want to know is, though, who alerted the press? I noticed there are some out there in the courtroom." The question was answered with silence.

With that, Terry signed his jury waiver and the entourage consisting of Terry, Trubey, Assistant U.S. Attorneys Fowler and Jack Williams, the judge's two law clerks and Chief Federal Public Defender Charles Anderson left the chambers and filed into the courtroom.

The proceedings lasted less than 15 minutes. Terry sat impassively, not believing that the culmination of this two-and-a-half year ordeal was coming to such an anti-climactic end.

Theis, true to his word, 10 minutes into the session said: "...It's my opinion that no reasonable jury could really have found beyond a reasonable doubt that the defendant was guilty...and I do find, on the basis of stipulation of facts, that the defendant would be entitled to a verdict of acquittal in the case, and I'm going to so rule...I do know that no reasonable jury would have found him guilty under those tenebrous facts that the government's (sic) had."

What Theis was really saying, in polite language, was that the government had perpetrated a travesty of justice against Terry and Janis. Fowler had gone to the judge and admitted that the "evidence" he had presented to the grand jury in 1988 was all he had, and which had failed to show any complicity by the Reeds in the alleged fraud. After two and a half years, Fowler was now admitting, he had no case...and never did.

And what about the grand jury, that supposed bulwark against injustice, that panel of 23 citizens that is supposed to stand between a venal prosecutor and the individual? Once again, it had done what most grand juries do—acted like sheep and rubber stamped what prosecutors present to them.

Theis had one final thought:.

"...I might say I entered this [decision] with some regret because I think it would have been an interesting trial for the court to sit on. Had some of the defense's evidence developed and had some the — if they were able to prove part of things they thought they were going to be able to prove, it would have gone far beyond the confines of just a simple insurance fraud case. But, in view of that, we'll just have to read the adventure books and wonder what would have happened."[14]

In 1992, in an interview with co-author John Cummings, Theis added a postscript. The government's case against the Reeds, the judge said, *"had a high odor to it."*

The impossible had been accomplished. The conviction rate for federal indictees was more than 98 per cent. The Public Defender's Office in Kansas had just beaten the CIA and the massive government machinery behind it. David had actually slain Goliath.

Marilyn Trubey, by dissecting the government's case with a well-planned strategy, was victorious. Joe Dunlap, from vapor, had found evidence that made a shambles of the government's witnesses.

Terry, who had become an equal partner with this defense team, was relieved but angered at the result. He felt he had been robbed, cheated of his chance to show a jury his evidence, to win his way, to completely vindicate himself and send those who had perjured themselves to prison; those same people who had kept him in the jaws of the legal monster.

During the two and a half years spent in preparation for this day, all that kept him going was the conjured image of triumphantly leaving a courtroom filled with spectators, to face the waiting television cameras and reporters, eager to know how he felt in victory. Against all odds, he would be celebrated by the little people, people like him who had fought back and won.

But this was denied him. An ebullient Trubey hugged him and whispered, "We did it, Terry." He felt empty, and by the expression on his face she knew the disappointment he was feeling.

They had won, all right, but only because the government was not going to allow Terry to light up dark corners and expose the total hypocrisy of government policies. Revealing the seamy story of an Intelligence Agency trafficking secretly in drugs, while dedicated lawyers like Trubey defend young adults whose lives are being destroyed by the criminal justice system that nearly devoured the Reeds—not by the drugs being sold on the street corner.

As Trubey drove Terry from Wichita to Topeka where they would celebrate this hollow victory, Terry's mind went back to the day when the tide turned in his favor. The day the government invoked CIPA.

After accepting once again a government implemented court delay, the Reeds had returned to Placitas to settle in, temporarily. But as the summer wore on it became clear the government had total disregard for filing deadlines, mandated by the law. Terry came once again to the realization that the government does not have to follow its own laws and that there would be no immediate end to this game of injustice.

Insomnia was wearing him out. He had acquired a fear of the darkness. His uneasiness about the night was upsetting his biological clock to the degree that he had reversed his days and nights. Only in daylight hours did he feel secure enough to sleep. The government was winning, and he and Janis knew it. Time was on his persecutor's side. The wait for the battle to start was wreaking havoc. His weight had dropped to 155 pounds. Nights were filled with pacing and dry heaves, trying to vomit some uneaten meal. Janis would wake in the night to find no one beside her. Outside she would find her husband patrolling, pacing, guarding against some faceless enemy.

Janis identified that the idleness was killing them, that the mask of normality they were wearing for the children's sake was becoming transparent, and they knew it. They had to do something. They desperately needed a change of scenery and lifestyle. By now, the beautiful New Mexican landscape only reminded them of the anguish and pain they had suffered since their indictment over two years ago.

As September neared, they were feeling economic pressure and Duncan's education was becoming a major concern. The boy already had been taken prematurely from the first grade as they traveled to prepare for their summer trial in Kansas. How, they wondered, did this nomadic, gypsy behavior affect a six-year-old? In desperation, they sought to put down roots. But where? They were tired of the endless moving and yanking their children from school.

Terry had developed business contacts in the El Paso area that serviced the expanding twin-plant manufacturing concept that was developing along the Mexican border. He felt there was opportunity there for him. Janis, with her case now dismissed, was able to reinstate her New Mexico real estate license and was successful in getting a job opportunity in the New Mexico real estate market bordering El Paso, allowing them to move to the border.

Trubey, fearful for Terry's life while living along the border, went to Theis and won his approval to have the Reeds' new location kept secret from the government and to allow his travel into the border area of Mexico. She successfully argued that he was not a "risk for flight," he had been in the court system for more than two years and had not vanished yet.

With the advent of Fall, Terry still felt in business limbo and was having difficulty applying himself fully in his newly found work in Juarez, Mexico. Knowing he would need at least eight weeks away from work for the trial was disrupting any hope of long-term manufacturing projects. Janis, meanwhile, was suffering through the usual adjustment period associated with starting afresh in a new real estate environment.

No matter how hard they tried, they just didn't fit in. At least, they thought, the children seemed happy. Duncan and Elliott were taking root quickly in the New Mexican elementary school near their home in Santa Teresa.

A short distance down the road from their community, situated near the New Mexico-Texas state line, was La Tuna federal prison. Since the children were being absorbed into the culture and welcomed into their new environment, Terry and Janis had quietly selected this prison, if the unspeakable need arose.

From the highway it looked like an old Spanish mission with its white adobe walls and arched entranceway. If given a choice, Terry preferred to be imprisoned within La Tuna's walls, if he was going to be forced to live in a four-by-eight foot cage. But Trubey had told him there would be no guarantee of that. And probably, she had said, the government out of vengeance would send Terry to some remote location as they had in other cases she had handled.

Sitting on the floor of their New Mexico home with the children tucked in and asleep, Terry and Janis stared at the computer print-out Trubey had sent them.

"Janis, don't cry. Be strong. This is something we need to do and be prepared for," Terry soothed, as they looked over the list of federal prisons as if selecting a college. Amenities like college courses were even listed for those wishing to continue their education or work in a trade shop to obtain a skill. He would wake in the night to his wife's sobbing and he too would go outside and cry.

There were times he couldn't bear to look at them, knowing that prison life would kill him and that someone else would raise his children.

So, on the afternoon of November 8th, the last thing Terry expected to hear was Marilyn Trubey's voice exclaiming, "Terry, I just got off the phone with Judge Theis. He wants you here by noon tomorrow. If you'll waive your right to a jury trial, and promise not to talk to the media for 30 days, he'll acquit you."

Terry sat in his office in silence and disbelief. It took only a few moments for the anger to well up inside him. He was already formulating questions Trubey didn't want to hear. To her, Terry's position, by refusing the judge's offer, was like looking a gift horse in the mouth.

"No, Marilyn, I think I'll pass on that one," Terry said emphatically. "I want my day in court with a jury of my peers."

"Terry, listen to me. There's no better status to end all this than an acquittal," she replied.

Terry saw it differently and, besides, by this time he didn't trust anything the government or the court had to say. He had seen Judge Theis fall asleep as his life swung in the balance and then read the written results concocted by ill-equipped law clerks. And the government that denied him was no different than having a pet rattlesnake. It could only be handled with thick, leather gloves and could never be trusted. Why should we trust them now, he thought? And as much as he respected and admired Marilyn Trubey, there were times she still acted very naively about the system she served.

Marilyn broke from her stoic Barbara Stanwyck manner, lost her composure and snapped, "If you don't take this acquittal, you'll have to find another attorney. It just won't get any better than this, Terry."

The next day, as his jet airliner streaked toward Wichita to meet the noon deadline the judge had mandated, his mind was racked with rage. How could this be happening? He had found that the justice system didn't expose the truth, it contained it. How much dirty laundry was hidden behind the guise of national security? He felt betrayed.

At a time he should be joyful, he was at one of the lowest points of his life. They were even robbing him of his chance to share his promised acquittal with Janis. They had been through this two-and-a-half year nightmare side by side, every step of the way, and because of Theis' unyielding demand to appear immediately, Terry went alone.

The time spent enroute was occupied with filling the pages of the yellow legal pad in front of him. They were overflowing with the explosions of thoughts and anger he wanted to express to the judge, this senile manipulated remnant of a judicial system that had been devoured by an imperial Presidency and the real power behind that...the CIA.

Was he the only one who could see it for what it was? Why wasn't there a public outcry? Were they ALL brain dead? Behind the marble walls of the federal building in Wichita the serpent was putting on its bib and preparing to swallow the truth. Visions of the monster Jaba in *Return of the Jedi* [the third part of the *Star Wars* trilogy], sitting in slime and swallowing small creatures, came to mind as Terry compared this mental image to the criminal injustice system. How many people like him does it take to keep the monster full? They were sending him to his mental gallows, to be silenced and gagged.

Trubey didn't know what was happening in his mind that day when the jet landed. But a burning ember deep inside was beginning to glow. They hadn't killed it yet, but they had certainly fucking tried.

"Terry, what's important is for you to go in there, agree to the judge's conditions and don't rub the government's nose in all this," Charles Anderson had told him in his office. It was 1 PM, November 9th, 1990, and the Public Defender's office was awaiting notice from Theis' office that the paperwork was complete for the Reed trial.

Terry didn't like what he was hearing. Anderson had told him not only to avoid the media that was on its way to the court house, but that Anderson's office didn't want Terry reading his statement into the court record either. The terms Anderson and Trubey had hammered out with Theis were beginning to sound to him like a plea bargain.

"Charlie, it was my understanding I was coming here for an acquittal. I can't talk to anyone about this for 30 days and now you're telling me I don't even get to speak at my trial. I'm about ready to get back on the plane and go home."

"If you do that, the judge will just dismiss your case and you'll be walkin' around with a cloud over ya' the rest of your life," Anderson replied. "At least this way, you're being found not guilty." Terry felt he was being appeased.

"Terry, I know you've been through a lot. But think of your family. You need to get on with your life. Just put this down and go home. My advise to ya' is don't be pokin' no sticks at no tigers."

Oliver North wouldn't be coming to Theis' courtroom after all.

* * *

"All you and your office should be carin' about is comin' out of this smellin' good!" Theis' scolding of Fowler had even occurred in front of the defendant.

As Marilyn Trubey and Terry Reed motored east on I-35 that victorious evening, the last element of the Benjamin Burgess political machine was biting the dust in Wichita, Kansas.

November 9th 1990 would become known in criminal defense circles in Wichita as *"Robin Fowler Flame-Out Day."* That was the day Theis not only acquitted Reed, but had lectured Robin Fowler in front of the chief public defender for the state of Kansas.

He had been disgraced. He had been cruelly toying with the lives of two innocent people. His actions of keeping the Reed's mercilessly locked in the criminal justice system for over two and a half years had tarnished not only his record, but the U. S. Attorney's office as well.

If the prosecutor was not venal, then his only excuse was stupidity. Fowler never seemed to question anything the government told him. The Classified Information Procedures Act, way back in June—that should have been the clue. That's when he should have known that the day had come to dump the Reed case.

That was the day FBI Special Agent Wayne Barlow had called him. Up until that day he was just doing his job, prosecuting a simple mail fraud case. Or so his superiors had told him. From that point on, this case had been running him instead of him running it. Fowler had even been forced to get a security clearance just to stay on the case and be able to talk to his own department.

How was he to know Reed was an intelligence asset if they didn't tell him? How was he to know Reed had worked for the FBI and CIA? How was he to know Reed had become a pawn in a political "dirty-up job"? Before he got this case, he wasn't even sure if Iran-Contra really happened. After all, Wichita is a long way from Washington. Fowler even naively called KTOK-AM investigative reporter Jerry Bohnen in Oklahoma City and asked him if Iran-Contra had really happened, and for a list of books to read on the subject.

And then the FBI had continued to investigate the Reeds for the entire time they had them under indictment. If they had sufficient evidence for a conviction, what did they need to investigate? The FBI must have been desperate to get them charged with something else. Why had the FBI in Oklahoma City gone to the trouble of interviewing Reed's old neighbors and the family that bought his home way back in 1983, talking about events that occurred long before the airplane was stolen? Were they checking on the government's exposure?

And those three Keystone cops out of Arkansas, Young, Baker and Don Sanders. They had lied so frequently on the stand that Fowler had been forced to "recreate" the order of their individual involvement. And Baker and Young did not get even one date straight on *anything* that happened.

And yet the prosecutor went along with it all. The U.S. attorney not only prosecutes the guilty, he is supposed to protect the innocent person from overzealous investigators. He should have stopped the whole proceeding right then and walked out, right after the first suppression hearing.

Yet, on two different occasions, in court motions, Fowler tried to rearrange the chain of events and tried to claim that it was Don Sanders who had first gotten involved with the plane.

Then there was Colonel Goodwin, the commander of the Arkansas State Police, the man who reported directly to Bill Clinton. He had refused to comply with Theis' order to produce the Mena files. Trubey asked Theis to hold Goodwin in contempt. Fowler today doesn't know what's in those sealed files, even though Trubey had said in court Reed was working for the CIA and training Contra pilots in Mena. Why hadn't he listened?

Joe Dunlap had certainly been through a lot on this case being chased out of Arkansas and almost arrested. And then occasionally, when Fowler and Dunlap met in the halls of the Federal building, Fowler just couldn't help but play mind games with Dunlap and try to convince him that Reed was just a sleazy drug trafficker.

Another clue that Fowler ignored was a tactic well known in all fields of endeavor as the "lateral pass."

The U.S. Attorney in Springfield, Missouri, when he passed the whole thing off to Fowler in April, 1988, called it "a good case." If so, why didn't he prosecute it?

And in the end, what happened? Fowler had to go to Judge Theis and admit that he couldn't get a conviction. After keeping Reed and his wife in the "system" for over two years and then forced to admit he couldn't "produce" what he had promised the Grand Jury—Reed's head—that hadn't gone down too well with Theis.

And the way he had told Janis Reed to cop-out on her husband in exchange for her freedom—what a terrible trauma to put her through.

But the worst part was that Fowler lied and suppressed critical discovery that Trubey had asked for, on repeated occasions. He denied her the FBI interview transcript with Baker that clearly showed it was October the 8th when Baker went into Reed's hanger after the wind allegedly blew the door open".[15] Plus Fowler and his associate, Jack Williams, wrongfully suppressed Baker's own investigative report that also said it was the 8th when he first went into the hangar[16]. If those documents had been admitted into court, as they should have been, the judge would have had to rule in Trubey's favor. It would have all been over right then and there. The judge would have thrown the case out, 18 months earlier in June of 1989.

What could Fowler do now? After all, he was 34 years old, divorced, horribly out of shape, and with his personal life in shambles. Ben Burgess, the man who had brought him to Kansas, was gone. Fowler was all alone in defeat.

With Desert Shield in full swing that November night, Robin Fowler decided on a new course of action, one that people would perceive as noble, and redeeming. He would resign his position with the government and volunteer to do something completely different. *He would join the United States Army!*

And it wasn't some cushy office job in the Judge Advocate-General's division he would seek. No, something more challenging than that. Something that would test him, something adventuresome and dangerous.

He would become a paratrooper.

By January, 1991, as Terry Reed wrestled with getting his life back in order, Robin Fowler would be wrestling with basic training as an enlisted grunt. Sweating out of his body those endless calories from too many happy hours in Wichita bars. Ultimately he would waddle his way through boot camp with young men 14 years his junior. And he would make it. He would be transformed from an attorney into a soldier—a paratrooper—and serve with the US Army airborne forces in Korea. At time of discharge in May, 1993, Fowler's official title was:

Army Specialist Robin D. Fowler 243023944
82nd Airborne
D 21504 PIR
Fort Bragg, NC 28307

Jack Williams told Terry Reed in 1992 that Fowler resigned from the prosecutor's office and joined the Army "because Robin's very patriotic, you know, and he wanted to serve his country during time of war." One of the authors interviewed Fowler in June of 1993 and discovered he had made a grand total of *five* airborne jumps in his 28 months of Army service. For someone who now claims to have enlisted because, "I just always wanted to be a paratrooper", Fowler sure spent a lot more time on the ground than he did yelling "Geronimo."

Funny, Reed thought. Fowler didn't go in until January, 1991, the same month Desert Shield turned into Desert Storm and, as the "100 Hour War" raged on, Fowler was still getting his head shaved and learning his right foot from his left.

Oh, well... such is the case of *closet patriots*. At least Fowler wasn't in Wichita sending innocent people to prison.

1. Court Transcript of Tommy Baker in the United States District Court for the District of Kansas, Case No. 88-10049-01, 6-21-89.
2. Court Transcript of Raymond Buddy Young in the United States District Court for the District of Kansas, Case No. 88-10049-01,TIME2-89.
3. Oral Deposition of James Jenkins, in the United States District Court Eastern District of Arkansas, Western Division, Case No. LRC-91-414, March 9, 1993.
4. Court Transcript of Raymond Buddy Young in the United States District Court for the District of Kansas, Case No. 88-10049-01, 6-22-89.
5. Ibid.
6. Court Transcript of Don Sanders in the United States District Court for the District of Kansas, Case No. 88-10049-01, 6-22-89.
7. Court Transcript of Harry Barrett in the United States District Court for the District of Kansas, Case No. 88-10049-01, 6-22-89.
8. Court Transcript of Tommy Baker in United States District Court for the District of Kansas, Case No. 88-10049-01, 6-21-89.
9. Opinion and Order filed 12-15-89 in the United States District Court for the District of Kansas Case No. 88-10049-01 and 02 by the Honorable Frank G. Theis, U.S. District Judge.
10. Ibid.
11. Transcript of Grand Jury Minutes dated 6-1-88 In the Matter of the Grand Jury of the United States of American Sitting in Wichita, Kansas.
12. Transcript of telephonic court proceedings, 6-1-90 in the United States District Court for the District of Kansas, Case No. 88-10049-01.
13. Rodriguez, Felix and John Wiseman, *Shadow Warrior*, Simon and Schuster, 1989, pp.32-34
14. Court proceedings (trial) in the United States District Court for the District of Kansas, Case No. 88-10049-01, 11-9-90.
15. Tommy Baker FD-302 taken 4-11-88 by SA Mark A. Jessie.
16. Tommy Baker Form 1, file no. 88-1246, Investigator's Notes dated 3-15-88.

FEDERAL BUREAU OF INVESTIGATION

PROSECUTIVE REPORT OF INVESTIGATION CONCERNING

```
TERRY KENT REED, aka
Terry K. Reed,
Terry Reed,
A. K. Reed,
Terry Kerr;
Mrs. TERRY KENT REED, aka
Janice Ann Reed, nee Kerr,
Janice Reed,
Janice Kerr,
Janis Kerr
INTERSTATE TRANSPORTATION OF A STOLEN AIRCRAFT;
MAIL FRAUD
```

Copy to: 1 - Criminal Division, USDJ
1 - U.S. Attorney, Topeka, KS

ARMED AND DANGEROUS

33-1. Cover sheet of three-inch-thick FBI report showing the Reeds as "ARMED AND DAN-
GEROUS". The list of aliases is totally preposterous.

1   Date of transcription_____4/20/88_____

        TOMMY L. BAKER, Private Investigator, 1523 Broadway,
Little Rock, Arkansas, telephone (501) 376-7770, was contacted
at his place of business where, after being advised as
to the identity of the interviewing Agent and the purpose
of the interview, he supplied the following information:

        On October 8, 1987, he had been flying with
a friend and had just landed at the North Little Rock
Municipal Airport in North Little Rock, Arkansas, and
was taxiing the aircraft in which he had been flying to
a private hangar when he noticed the door was open to
hangar number 28, the hangar immediately next door to
the hangar which was his destination. He noted there
was a strong north wind that day and the hangar faces
the north and the normal-sized door, which is the entrance
to hangar number 28, had blown open. Noting the recent
amount of aircraft burglaries in the Little Rock area,
he decided to check inside the hangar to make sure everything
was secure. When he entered the hangar, he noticed that
there were no lights nor electricity and that the plane
inside the hangar was profusely covered with dust and
had apparently been sitting in the hangar for an extended
amount of time. He became curious as to why the Piper
Turbo Arrow III, which was listed in NATIONAL PUBLICATIONS
as being worth as much as $40,000, had been allowed the
deteriorate. Suspecting that the airplane was either
involved in narcotics smuggling or was stolen, he decided
to investigate. All the tires were flat and there were
piles of rust under the brakes. The tail number on the
airplane was N30489. It appeared to BAKER that the tail
numbers had been hastily applied and did not fit the value
of the aircraft. He noted that the serial number plate
near the left tail section of the aircraft bore serial
number 28R7887229 and plate number 008510. The model
of the aircraft was PA28R201T. BAKER advised that the
serial number plate had been visibly altered and it appeared
to him as if the airplane had been retagged. He took

Investigation on _____4/11/88_____ at _____Little Rock, Arkansas_____ File # _____LR 26B-31681_____ -3,

by_____SA MARK A. JESSIE/clb_____   Date dictated____4/14/88____

This document contains neither recommendations nor conclusions of the FBI. It is the property of the FBI and is loaned to your agency;
it and its contents are not to be distributed outside your agency.
        Indexing Certified _____

33-2. FBI 302, a key document illegally suppressed and kept from Terry Reed during his
Wichita trial. This document, which was found in court discovery two and one half years
after Reed's acquittal, proves that the private investigator working with Bill Clinton's chief
of security did not "find" Reed's stolen plane until October 8, 1987, one day *after* the
police began investigating on October 7, 1987.

IN THE UNITED STATES DISTRICT COURT
EASTERN DISTRICT OF ARKANSAS
WESTERN DIVISION

TERRY K. REED, et. al.   PLAINTIFFS

VS.   NO. LR-C-91-414

RAYMOND YOUNG, et. al.   DEFENDANTS

STATEMENT OF UNDISPUTED FACTS

Come the defendants, by their attorneys, and for their statement of material facts, filed in conjunction with their motion for summary judgment and pursuant to Local Rule 29, state:

1. Terry Reed claims that he was an "asset" of the Federal Bureau of Investigation (FBI) and the Central Intelligence Agency (CIA) between 1982 and 1987 and has suggested in deposition testimony that he may still be acting in that capacity. (Complaint, paragraph 8; Exhibit E, pp. 40-42)

2. Between July, 1984, and August, 1985, Reed helped train Nicaraguan nationals as pilots, (Exhibit E, pp. 46, 53) flying out of the Waldron, Arkansas, airport, having planes repaired at Mena, and generally operating out of a clandestine encampment disguised as chicken houses near Nella, Arkansas. (Exhibit E, pp. 52-59, 64)

3. Reed believes that he incurred the displeasure of the CIA when he discovered that it was using a warehouse he operated at the Guadalajara, Mexico, airport for an operation

---

33-3. List of Arkansas State Attorney General's undisputed facts in Terry Reed's lawsuit brought against Bill Clinton's chief of security and the private detective. Note that the A.G.'s office does not contest the fact that Terry Reed trained Nicaraguan Nationals at Mena, Arkansas.

FORMS.TEXT HAS 1 DOCUMENT

INBOX.1 (#559)

TEXT:

VZCZCKCO004

RR OC LR

DE KC #0004 2862230

ZNR UUUUU

R 132200Z OCT 87

FM KANSAS CITY (26B-65775) (SQ 5) (P)

TO OKLAHOMA CITY (ROUTINE)

LITTLE ROCK (ROUTINE)

BT

UNCLAS

UNSUB; THEFT OF 1978 FIFER ARROW PA28, TAIL NUMBER N2982M,

JOPLIN, MISSOURI. MARCH 23, 1983; ITSA; OO;OC

    RE KC AIRTEL TO OC, APRIL 19, 1983.

    ON OCT. 9, 1987, KEN COPELAND, SERGEANT, JOPLIN MISSOURI

POLICE DEPT., ADVISED LIEUTENANT BUDDY YOUNG, ARKANSAS STATE

POLICE, LITTLE ROCK, ARKANSAS, ADVISED AIRCRAFT "RECOVERED" LITTLE

ROCK AREA IN BARN ON OR ABOUT OCT. 7, 1987. DRUG ENFORCEMENT

ADMINISTRATION AND F.B.I. LITTLE ROCK NOTIFIED.

    FOR INFO LITTLE ROCK, AIRCRAFT REPORTED STOLEN MARCH 26,

1983. BY TERRY REED. OWNER CAPTIONED AIRCRAFT, TO F.B.I.

OKLAHOMA CITY, OKLAHOMA.

33-4. Critical FBI telex which was found in 1993 during the discovery process related to Reed's civil action in Arkansas. This report clearly proves Reed was setup and that his stolen plane was actually found in a barn, not in Reed's hangar. The report is dated one day <u>prior</u> to police getting the search warrant.

TRANSMIT VIA:
☐ Teletype
☐ Facsimile
☐ _____

PRECEDENCE:
☐ Immediate
☐ Priority
☒ Routine

CLASSIFICATION:
☐ TOP SECRET
☐ SECRET
☐ CONFIDENTIAL
☐ UNCLAS E F T O
☒ UNCLAS

Date   10/28/87

1 FM LITTLE ROCK (26B-31681) (P)

2 TO OKLAHOMA CITY ROUTINE (26B-4780)

3 KANSAS CITY (26B-65775) (SQ 5) ROUTINE

4 BT

5 UNCLAS

6 UNSUB; THEFT OF 1978 PIPER ARROW PA28, TAIL NUMBER N29CZM,

7 JOPLIN, MISSOURI, MARCH 23, 1983; ITSA; OO: OKLAHOMA CITY

8   RE KANSAS CITY TELETYPE TO OKLAHOMA CITY AND LITTLE ROCK

9 DATED OCTOBER 13, 1987.

10   ON OCTOBER 14, 1987, A SEARCH WAS CONDUCTED AT NORTH LITTLE ROCK

11 MUNICIPAL AIRPORT, HANGAR NUMBER 28, 2000 REMOUNT RD.,

12 NORTH LITTLE ROCK, ARKANSAS, BASED UPON A STATE SEARCH WARRANT

13 BY BUDDY YOUNG, LIEUTENANT, ARKANSAS STATE POLICE (ASP). A

14 SEARCH REVEALED A 1978 PIPER TURBO ARROW III, SINGLE ENGINE

15 AIRPLANE, MODEL NUMBER PA28R-201T, SERIAL NUMBER 28R7803156,

16 WHITE IN COLOR WITH ORANGE STRIPES, WHICH NCIC COMPUTER CHECK

17 SHOWED TO HAVE BEEN STOLEN.

   BUDDY YOUNG ADVISED THAT HE HAS RECEIVED INFORMATION WHICH

   INDICATED THAT TERRY REED MAY BE INVOLVED IN MEXICAN AND/OR

   SOUTH AMERICAN DRUG TRAFFICKING AND MAY NOW BE RESIDING IN

   GUADALAJARA, MEXICO. YOUNG STATED THAT A SEARCH OF THE AIRCRAFT

   REVEALED SEVERAL MAPS OF SOUTHERN NORTH AMERICA. YOUNG ADVISED

   PLANE IS NOW LOCATED AT THE NORTH LITTLE ROCK AIRPORT, 2000 REMOUNT

   RD., NORTH LITTLE ROCK, ARKANSAS, HANGAR NUMBER 27, PENDING CLAIM

   BY INSURANCE COMPANY.

   YOUNG ADVISED THAT BILL CANINO SUPPLIED TWO CASHIER'S CHECKS

   WHICH REED USED FOR PAYMENT ON RENTED HANGAR. ONE CHECK, DATED

   MARCH 27, 1987, CHECK NO. 51352, DRAWN ON THE VALLEY NATIONAL

   BANK OF ARIZONA, 30TH AVENUE, PEORIA OFFICE, PHOENIX, ARIZONA,

Approved: _____ Transmitted _____ Per _____
                                          (Number)   (Time)

☆ U S GPO 1987 — 181-486

33-5. FBI file in which Young falsely states that Reed was a drug-trafficking suspect and that this information came from the DEA.

U.S. Department of Justice

Drug Enforcement Administration

FEDERAL PUBLIC DEFENDER
DISTRICT OF KANSAS   SEP 2 2 1989   Washington, D.C. 20537

DEA   SEP 22 1989

MEMORANDUM

TO: Robin Fowler, Esq.
          Assistant United States Attorney
          Wichita, Kansas

FROM: Dennis F. Hoffman
          Chief Counsel

SUBJECT: Court Order Directed to the El Paso Intelligence Center
          in United States v. Terry Kent Reed.
          Case No. 88-10049-01

     In response to the above-subject court order and in light of
discussions between you and Donald Clements, an attorney on my
staff, we are providing the following information which we
believe is responsive to the court order and can be released to
the defendant through discovery under Rule 16 of the Federal
Rules of Criminal Procedure.

     Records of the DEA El Paso Intelligence Center (EPIC)
reflect two reports made to EPIC involving aircraft N2982M.

     On May 24, 1983, EPIC was notified that the Joplin,
Missouri, Police Department reported to the National Crime
Information Center (NCIC) that aircraft N2982M was reported
stolen on May 23, 1983, from the Joplin, Missouri, airport.

     On October 16, 1987, it was reported to EPIC that the
Arkansas State Police, Little Rock, Arkansas, reported aircraft
N2982M was recovered on October 16, 1987, from a hangar in Little
Rock, Arkansas, where the owner Kent T. Reed (aka Terry Reed) hid
the aircraft to collect the $33,000 insurance claim.

     EPIC records reflect no other inquiries in connection with
Terry Kent Reed and aircraft N2982M.

     Pursuant to your conversations with Mr. Clements on
September 20 and 21, 1989, we are forwarding a copy of this
memorandum to the above-named defendant's attorney.

cc: Marilyn M. Trubey
     Assistant Federal Public Defender
     Topeka, Kansas

33-6. Letter from the DEA which gives the lie to the testimony of Arkansas State Police
Capt. Raymond Young, who said he received information from the DEA stating that Reed
was a suspected drug trafficker. Paragraph four has information Young himself inserted
into the file.

For the courtesy of the Court, this has been re-typed for ease of reading since originals provided by Captain Young are barely legible.

ACIC Terminal Input Log Record   Grid J 13
Entry reads as follows:

SP00   ,DATE=100787 ,TIME=1204170,** AM   ARASP0000   MPF OHOHP1300
STATE HIGHWAY PATROL COLUMBUS OH
704-W AR SP LITTLE ROCK   100787   DRIVERS LICENSE FILES ON A BARBARA A
CAN YOU PLEASE CHECK FOR DRIVERS LICENSE. WE ARE NEEDING A DOB ON
WILLIAMS   WF OF 583 DYLN ST YOUR CITY.   PLEASE REPLY ATTENTION SGT.
THIS SUBJECT, IF THIS IS POSSIBLE.
DON SANDERS THANKS

33-7. Arkansas State Police computer terminal readout showing activity at 12:04 PM on October 7, 1987 concerning the registered owner of the plane found in Reed's hangar. The date and time are significant because it proves law enforcement knowledge at least one day prior to Tommy Baker's alleged entry into Reed's hangar. This proves that all the court testimony about the discovery scenario was a lie.

FILED
U.S. DISTRICT COURT
DIST_____ KANSAS

JUN 5   1 17 PM '90

RALPH ____ CH.

BY _____ ____ UTY
AT ____ __

Not being prolific in legal language, I feel it necessary to officially inform the court of my personal position regarding case number 88-10049-01. I am somewhat dismayed and yet relieved to now discover that my activities involving support of our government's policy which indirectly led to my indictment are now coming to light. At this point, however, I am compelled to go on record to state that my Missouri country logic is truly being tested to the degree in which I foresee no winners if the present course of action continues. Further, now being personally exploited by the Court's Friday, June 1, 1990 telephonic ruling with Robin Fowler, the prosecutor, and Marilyn Trubey, my defense attorney, I feel I am forced to either officially divulge what is apparently classified information or not defend myself to the fullest.

Common sense from the innermost depths of my soul tells me that the Classified Information Procedures Act (Pub.L 96-456, Oct. 15, 1980, 9- Stat. 2025) was never intended to be applied in this manner. From my view point, being on the outside of government and the defendant, it would appear that this legal maneuver on behalf of the U.S. government is only an attempt to assess their potential embarrassment or liabilities by forcing me to disclose my total defense posture. Furthermore, compliance with this order could possibly expose me to additional charges associated with the dissemination of national security items as well as to undermind my Fifth Amendment rights.

Being a former U.S. Air Force intelligence officer, I could fully understand the application of this law to an individual who is an official agent or employee of the U.S. government, and who is knowingly using classified information or materials in the pursuit of his defense. But for the government to now contend that I possess knowledge of classified activities of the U.S. government is totally absurd. How can it be construed that my civilian association with that of bona fide government agents be an extension of a cloak of security surrounding these items that I intended to use as my defense? Also, another consideration is the government's previous denial, officially and unofficially, of the existence of the bulk of the areas subpoenaed.

The government has been fully aware of my line of defense ever since a record of my debriefing by Jack Blum of the Senate Foreign Relations Committee was submitted to Lawrence Walsh, the independent prosecutor investigating the Iran Contra affair. The majority of items the government initially denied the existence of are now suddenly available but classified. It is outrageous for the government to now come forward in the 11th hour of my trial countdown in order to smoke screen their true objective of forcing me into a breach of security situation; especially since Mr. Fowler has been the government's liason in all defense requests per the Court's interpretation of Brady. Why is it not the Court's position to compel the government to set forth in writing the areas of my defense that may be classified, so that an immediate decision may be made to determine if I, the defendant, can avoid those classified areas and still put on a reasonable defense?

From the very onset of this case, all that I was expecting or hoping for from my government was the admission or acknowledgement of an apparently embarrassing program, and for the intervention of the intelligence community in my behalf. Even though embarrassing, I can fully comprehend the necessity of its existence.

It was never my intention to purposefully compromise or expose national security information in this case. The subpoena efforts put forth by myself through my attorney were merely an effort to present a reasonable defense. Now, burdened with the responsibility of either apparently exposing national security affairs in the vigorous pursuit of my defense or to unselfishly dilute my defense so as to not delve into this sensitive subject matter, as a patriotic servant of my government, I will be forced to take the latter; especially considering my interests in this matter are not only my vindication and return to productive activities, but also the long term security of my wife and children long after the burial of this case in the archives of the Federal Court in Kansas.

I, therefore, respectfully protest my forced compliance with the Classified Information Procedures Act.

Respectfully,

Terry K. Reed

33-8. Letter Reed wrote and filed with the court to "reach out" to the CIA and secretly communicate with them. It was his hope that the Agency would see that he was no threat, but would defend himself if forced to.

AO 89 (Rev 5/85) Subpoena

United States District Court

————— DISTRICT OF —————

UNITED STATES OF AMERICA,

Plaintiff,

v.

TERRY KENT REED,

Defendant.

SUBPOENA

CASE NUMBER: 88-10049-01

TYPE OF CASE	SUBPOENA FOR
☐ CIVIL ☒ CRIMINAL	☒ PERSON ☐ DOCUMENT(S) or OBJECT(S)

TO:

OLIVER NORTH
c/o Brendan V. Sullivan
839 Seventeenth Street, N.W.
Washington, D.C.   20006

YOU ARE HEREBY COMMANDED to appear in the United States District Court at the place, date, and time specified below to testify in the above case.

TO:

FELIX RODRIGUEZ
215 N.E. 2nd Avenue
Miami, Florida
                    33161
(305)891-5659
 (305) 591-1875

YOU ARE HEREBY COMMANDED to appear in the United States District Court at the place, date, and time specified below to testify in the above case.

TO:

WAYNE BARLOW
c/o F.B.I.
50 Penn Place
Oklahoma City, OK 73118

YOU ARE HEREBY COMMANDED to appear in the United States District Court at the place, date, and time specified below to testify in the above case.

PLACE	COURTROOM
UNITED STATES COURTHOUSE 401 North Market - Room 410 Wichita, KS 67202	Judge Theis
	DATE AND TIME
	JUNE 11, 1990 at 9:00 A.M.***

YOU ARE ALSO COMMANDED to bring with you the following document(s) or object(s): *

Complete files on: Northwest Industries, Inc.; Techno Impex; Barcorp Corporation; Emery L. West, a/k/a Veda; Reed Kane and Associates, Kerr Reed; Terry K. Reed; Joseph (Jozsef) Bona; 1978 Piper Arrow PA-2; N2982M.

***or at such other time as directed by defense counsel.

☐ See additional information on reverse

This subpoena shall remain in effect until you are granted leave to depart by the court or by an officer acting on behalf of the court.

U.S. MAGISTRATE OR CLERK OF COURT	DATE
RALPH L. DeLOACH	May 22, 1990
(BY) DEPUTY CLERK	

This subpoena is issued upon application of the:

☐ Plaintiff ☒ Defendant ☐ U.S. Attorney

QUESTIONS MAY BE ADDRESSED TO:

Marilyn M. Trubey
Assistant Federal Public Defender
444 SE Quincy, Room 365
Topeka, KS 66683   (913) 295-2595
ATTORNEY'S NAME, ADDRESS AND PHONE NUMBER

* If not applicable, enter "none".

33-9. Subpoenas issued by Terry Reed's defense attorney, including those of Oliver North and Felix Rodriguez.

AO 245A (7/87) Judgment of Acquittal ●

United States District Court

DISTRICT OF __KANSAS__

FEDERAL PUBLIC DEFENDER
DISTRICT OF KANSAS

NOV 14 1990

TOPEKA

UNITED STATES OF AMERICA

V.

CASE NUMBER:

88-10049-01

TERRY KENT REED

ENTERED ON THE DOCKET
DATE: _11-13-90_

The Defendant was found not guilty. IT IS ORDERED that the Defendant is acquitted, discharg
and any bond exonerated.

/s/ FRANK G. THEIS
Signature of Judicial Officer

HON. FRANK G. THEIS, SENIOR JUDGE
Name and Title of Judicial Officer

November 9, 1990
Date

FILED
U.S. DISTRICT COURT
DISTRICT OF KANSAS

Nov 9   3 48 PM '90

RALPH L. DELOACH,
BY   DEPUTY
WICHITA, KS.

JUDGMENT OF ACQUITTAL

33-10. Reed's judgement of acquittal. What a defendant is awarded after winning a 30-
month criminal prosecution, which nearly bankrupted the Reeds.

CHAPTER 34

P.I.S.S.

As the Reed van moved north up Mexico Highway Route 45 toward El Paso, Terry was unusually silent and wasn't concentrating on the pot holes too well in the highway in front of him. His mind was in a swarm.

The van was laden with not only the Reed family, but opened gifts from the Christmas holiday they had shared with Patrick and Patty Juin. It was January the 5th, 1991.

It had been the first time in over two years they had been able to travel freely from state to state, country to country without first being forced to get permission from Judge Theis and then being treated as threats to society by having to maintain continual telephone contact with a court designee.

Janis had been leery of returning to Lake Chapala for fear of reprisal from the CIA or the Mexican DFS. But Terry's logic that they were now no longer perceived a threat to the Agency and that any harm that came to them would only bring unwanted attention to the residue of his work with them, must have been correct. The trip had been enjoyable and uneventful and Janis had hoped it would be a period of relaxation and healing for the Reed family. Almost two months had elapsed since Terry's acquittal on that fateful date in November, when he had been released from the jaws of the monster that had nearly devoured them.

But this had not been the case. Under the surface, he was still in turmoil. Even though they had unwound at the Manzanillo beach with the Juin family and celebrated New Year's Eve in Ajijic with old friends, Janis could tell that Terry was only paying lip service to the holiday. He was remote and disconcerted.

He had been drinking throughout the Christmas season—way too much. This wasn't like him and was the opposite reaction she was expecting his acquittal to trigger. Surely she prayed, the three-year nightmare hadn't extinguished the flame, that hidden somewhere deep inside him was the same overly confident pilot and headstrong business man she had once known and loved enough to marry. She was afraid to interrupt his silence and ask the question. She instinctively knew what was eating away in his mind.

He had to cling to the premise that he had been forced to go through this legal orgy for a purpose. Why had he been singled out to be destroyed? Or had he been chosen for a test? One to determine his limits? If so, had he passed or failed in the eyes of his unseen master? There had to be a reason, didn't there? Was his conversion from an asset to a liability an accident...or was it predestined? Was it intended for him to be prosecuted, persecuted, survive and then become the messenger to the

American People about the corruption and inequities in the judicial system? Was it meant for him to be thrust into orbit with people like Marilyn Trubey? Was he supposed to fight the legal system from without or within?

His mind went back to the Cabal, that evening in the Arkansas bunker...when he felt he was being "knighted." Even after all he'd been through he still felt there was a purpose for him being selected. Had he been exposed to all this in order to be the one who screams out? Had he been thrust into the mumbo-jumbo legal world in order to expand mentally and absorb yet another dimension of our failed attempt at democracy?

Terry's thoughts went in an ever decreasing spiral until he felt his head would burst. Being engineering minded at heart, he decided on taking a new approach to solving his problem. For every plus there is a minus...that had been a guiding principle of his since he learned it in 9th grade physics. He knew the minus...he had been singled out, in part, due to his value system, and his life had been ripped to shreds. Now to find the plus to the equation. There is a reason for all action, that same physics teacher had told him, and backed up his teachings with Sir Isaac Newton's law: "for every action there is an equal and opposite reaction." Perhaps that explained what he was supposed to do. They, the government, had acted and now he had to react or he would be violating a law of physics. That was it he decided! He was still a member of the Cabal...and he had been chosen to REACT! He would go to battle! But the unanswered question was would Janis be capable of another extended fight?

As she gazed at the flat Mexican landscape north of Chihuahua, she took a deep breath and dared to ask, "What's bothering you?"

"You know what it is, honey," he answered without removing his stare from the road. "You know me by now. I just can't go on as if nothing happened. I feel like we've been raped and now they expect us to just pretend nothing happened. Janis, I have to fight back. You know if I don't this thing will kill me."

There was no mistaking it. Janis knew her husband meant every word. Unlike her, she knew that he had to fight back or it would destroy him. His unyielding value system was one of his qualities that drew her to him.

Quietly and without replying, Janis moved from her front seat in the van to the rear and returned with a yellow legal pad and pen. As she'd done so many times before in their nearly 10 years of marriage, she prepared to write while he drove.

The letter he dictated was to an anonymous attorney seeking help to right the wrongs done to him and his family by the United States government. He outlined their 30- month criminal prosecution sprinkling in the proper buzz words he felt sure would summons forth the help he needed.

Half way into the letter, Janis took an interest. She began participating and he was glad to see that she too still had the rage and anger buried in her that they needed to harness to help them fight back. The fervency of his words tore off the scabs she had tried to grow over her unhealed and now infected wounds. As the poison from her mind drained they had to stop by the road to hold each other and cry.

The writing of the letter had triggered the release of the pent-up emotion. Without realizing it at first, it had become their own method of therapy, and Janis realized he was right. They had to fight back, *together*.

The tribulation had to be ended properly to heal their minds. They had not sought psychiatric help during this painful period of their lives, reasoning that a person only goes to a therapist when they don't know what ails them. How could a therapist call off the vengeance of the CIA?

When they reached their home in Santa Teresa, they had what they thought would be the necessary documents to bring countless attorneys running to their aid in order to defend the Constitution of the United States of America. Surely they thought, their case was unique. They were only asserting that the executive branch of government had devoured the judicial branch, had it secretly under its control, and by doing so was undermining the basic freedoms upon which this country was founded.

Terry didn't realize it then, but he was locked into a mental state he would later self-diagnose as "post-indictment stress syndrome" (P.I.S.S.).

PISS, that was the cynical acronym he chose to call it. He would jokingly tell Janis that the legal system had left "emotional skid marks on his brain." Other people with whom he would come into contact, people with experience in dealing with those recently released from the *criminal injustice system* would say his feelings and attitudes were not uncommon. The period of relief after an end to such a traumatizing ordeal is often, they said, replaced by anger and hostility.

But it would pass, they said. Just go on about your life and the rage would die and be replaced with feelings of apathy. Soon they said, within six months in all probability, the old Terry Reed would be back smiling as usual looking for a way to make up for lost time.

This was not going to be the case, he knew. That glowing ember deep inside, the one that re-kindled that day on the plane enroute to his trial as he captured his emotions on paper, was now turning into a raging fire. The feeling of burning up inside was giving him energy, forcing a re-awakening and he was happy with the feeling. He was obsessed with thoughts of what he considered the moral thing to do. A way to strike back and correct the system. After all, he thought, hadn't life actually prepared him for this task? All of his training had gotten him through this ordeal. Why not now apply that survivalist mentality, that analytical aggressive attitude to lead the attack against those who had wronged him? That Missouri stubbornness that he was sure came from his great grandfather...that stubbornness he knew Harry Truman had...was what he needed to muster up from deep within for the battle that lay ahead.

The battle field he had selected was federal court! He had been analyzing for several weeks just what had happened in the final months of his 'persecution' in Wichita, and one thing was now very clear. *The government did not want his story told*! They didn't want the embarrassing facts spilling out of the court record and into the newspapers. They had denied him his trial! He had not had his day in court!

Court...yes, that's where this story belonged. Go right where they *least* want it. There, combined with the credibility and scrutiny offered between those marbled columns and perhaps the protection afforded him and his family by a sympathetic federal judge—it was the perfect arena for all the seamy details of the CIA's operations that had turned him into a liability to be heard. Surely, he rationalized, court was the only forum from which to tell this story. The world and the American people must be told about their government gone mad...their own CIA trafficking in drugs! Surely the Federal Court System was the place to expose this.

But what disturbed him even more than drug trafficking was how the CIA was hand picking and sponsoring candidates to the office of Presidency! *That had to be told.*

There had been, in Terry's opinion, a coup d'état in this country. A quiet revolution with no shots fired...or had there been? Had a young president by the name of John Fitzgerald Kennedy penetrated the CIA's veil and discovered this earlier? Could the conspiracy theorists be right?

Only with subpoena power could he ever hope to get to the bottom of this "black" dilemma that hung over him....and the nation for that matter. This matter belonged only in court where the classified material that was sure to come out could be protected. He didn't want to harm other innocent agents and assets who had been able to quietly sever themselves from these black operations. That was the problem, protecting others. That's why it belonged in court and not in the media event!

After all he and his family had been through he almost hated to admit it, but he was still patriotic. Yeah...that was what that tight, warm glow deep inside was all about! He was still patriotic! He still loved this country! He loved his home! And after all, as his father had taught him...it WAS worth fighting for! He had to fight...once again! Not for the government that had misled and exploited him—for the country that he so loved.

Back in Santa Teresa, and with Janis now firmly by his side, they prepared endless packets of material to send to all the famous legal names and law firms recognized as the flag-bearers of civil freedoms. At one point they felt their efforts surely must be subsidizing Federal Express, but few responses were forthcoming. There was no white knight arriving on a white charger.

"There's no real money in constitutional rights litigation," they were arrogantly told again and again. Or, "Haven't you heard....since the Christic case ruling, no one in his right mind sues the government." *

To their frustration, the typical response included, "God, this looks like a great case. And I'd love to take it, but only if you're willing to pay as you go.....Our firm doesn't do contingencies."

"I guess defending the constitution is only a capitalistic endeavor in this country," he would cynically tell Trubey by phone, who was stunned to believe Terry could find no one to take the case.

By now Terry and Janis were clinging desperately to economic solvency, making every effort to avoid bankruptcy, considering that their last resort. With long-standing legal bills and unpaid family loans, their financial world was in shambles, and they had no money to contribute to the estimated $250,000 they were told was the minimum they needed to properly litigate against the government.

---

*   Civil case No. 86-11-46, CIV-KING, filed in the United States District Court, Southern District of Florida, in May 1986. The complaint was filed by the Christic Institute, a non-profit, public interest legal group headquartered in Washington, D.C., and headed by attorney Daniel Sheehan. The suit was officially listed as Tony Avirgan and Martha Honey vs John Hull, Rene Corbo, ET AL, in which it was alleged that a total of 29 defendants had perpetuated a long term conspiracy in violation of U.S. racketeering statutes. The suit alleged a "secret team" of former intelligence and military personnel engaged in crimes that included murder and drug trafficking to support the Contras. The lawsuit was dismissed in June, 1988, by U.S. District Court Judge Lawrence King in Miami, with a sanction of approximately $1.2 million levied against the Christic Institute for filing a "frivolous" lawsuit. An appeals court affirmed that decision in 1991 and added another $400,000 for filing a "frivolous" appeal.[1]

Frustrated, Terry turned to those who claimed they wanted to help. Those who said they had experience in bringing these matters to public attention. The only avenue he figured that would publicize their dilemma and assist in securing an attorney: The print media.

First he sought out an old acquaintance in New Mexico named Jonathan Beaty, a senior correspondent with TIME magazine. After all, it was Beaty who sought out the Reed's back in the Fall of 1988, shortly after their surrender to the Feds, wanting their story, or least what he thought their story was.

With their attorney's permission in 1988, Terry and Janis had driven to Truth or Consequences, New Mexico, and met with Beaty and a photographer for TIME named Steve Northop.

A magazine with an investigative reporting staff as large as TIME's could certainly help prove out parts of Reed's story, which were strewn throughout several foreign countries and many U.S. states. In exchange for their help, maybe he would give them first rights to their ordeal. Or at least that was the idea behind the meeting. A trade, pure and simple.

Beaty, Northop, Janis and Terry had sat in a local park while Beaty attempted to grasp the larger elements of Reed's story. Being a seasoned reporter and having covered elements of Iran-Contra for TIME, Beaty wanted to immediately pry back the rocks covering the involvement of John Cathey aka Oliver North. This line of questioning eventually led to Bill Cooper and Southern Air Transport.

Throughout the questioning, Beaty had remained somewhat distant and just observed the Reeds until he asked Terry who he worked with at SAT?

When Terry informed him it was a man by the name of Robert Johnson, who was purportedly in-house counsel for SAT, Beaty turned to Northop and announced, "this guy [Reed] is for real."

"I know Johnson and that's a name that hasn't appeared in the press," Beaty revealed. Terry had passed the scrutiny test, for the time being, and the remainder of the interrogation went well.

It was Beaty who put them in contact with the senate investigator Jack Blum in Washington, D.C. Shortly afterward, however, Beaty said that his boss at the magazine had made a decision to pull him off Iran-Contra related stories since TIME considered it an old issue and the American public seemed burnt out on the subject.

Beaty did go so far as to print an article in the Grapevine section of the March 13th, 1989, issue outlining what he thought the Reed case involved. He talked of Oliver North and Project Donation and how Reed had been indicted and was awaiting a trial in Wichita, Kansas. "All for Ollie", he entitled the piece.

Jonathan had even extended a hand of kindness after seeing the dilemma the Reeds faced. They departed with what the Reeds felt was a foundation on which to build a future friendship, if they ever got out of this mess. Of course, back in 1988, Beaty did seem somewhat frustrated but understanding with the Reeds, realizing they were muzzled by the advice of their attorneys and were not talking to the media, being guided by the legal warning required under Miranda, "What you say can and will be used against you".

But now that he could talk, he was learning Iran-Contra was a dead issue. After all, it was 1991, over 4 years since the Cooper shoot down and miraculously, the Reagan-Bush White House had been able to contain the scandal

that everyone had said was more significant than Watergate. It involved, people
said back then, subversion of the constitution by Oliver North, Bill Casey and
the CIA. But that seemed a long time ago, and Terry had been successfully
silenced throughout those four years. And now, Beaty was telling him from his
ranch, that the new hot topic was a money investigation he was working on
that involved the Bank of Credit and Commerce International and a guy named
Clark Clifford, a name Reed knew from previous administrations, and conversations.

One night, as the Reed family barbecued chicken in their backyard in Santa
Teresa, Janis, realizing Terry's mounting frustration, suggested, "What about
that guy in New York? You know, that writer that was working on the Barry
Seal story."

She was referring to an investigative reporter and author by the name of
John Cummings. Cummings was one of those guys Reed didn't know whether
to trust, but he had grown to admire his bulldog attitude...he simply wouldn't
go away. But from the insatiable appetite for information Cummings demonstrated, Terry was afraid handling him might be compared to hand-feeding a
cheeseburger to a lion. It might be difficult not to get swallowed up to the
elbow in the process. Cummings had contacted Trubey on several occasions
asking for an interview saying he only wanted to talk about Barry Seal and he
was curious if Reed knew of any connection Seal had to the CIA. Cummings
had even driven through New Mexico in a vain attempt to locate them once. At
least he was persistent, Terry thought. He admired that in a person, but was
that enough?

"I don't know if I should call him, honey. After all, he's from New York and
my great grandfather always said you can't trust Yankees," Terry joked.

But the next day the call was made, and Cummings not only offered his help
to find an attorney, but extended the offer to bring along an investigator who
might "donate some time" to the case.

"You can call me Pierre, all my friends do," the looming investigator accompanying Cummings said upon entering the Reed home. The 60's-plus man with
the six-foot, four-inch frame, gray beard, slightly stooped shoulders, and sporting a black beret certainly would have difficulty blending into a crowd if his
wish was ever to travel incognito, Terry thought as they shook hands.

"Your reputation precedes you Pierre. I've been told by people who know
you that you are the world's greatest investigator," Terry said, just to let Pierre
know that he had been asking questions about him prior to his arrival.

"Well, I don't know about that...but I'm at least the most expensive", he shot
back with a warm, broad grin and a gleam in his eye that alerted you he would
be a formidable opponent in a match of wits.

Cummings and Pierre sat in Reed's living room grilling him, no—interrogating him for more than three days. Probing his brain for every nitty gritty dark
detail they could find, and looking continuously for a flaw in his story. Pierre,
Terry discovered, was a 30-year veteran United States Army investigator who
spent his entire career in CID (Criminal Investigative Division). Pierre had a
mind like a bear trap, and after two days of sitting quietly, taking no notes,
and chain smoking unfiltered Camels, Reed realized that Pierre could recite
any name, date or place from his "debriefing", verbatim.

"Holy shit!" he thought, "who is this guy? I hope he's not here to hurt me."

Reed had no reason to trust anyone, let alone this guy with the photographic memory that couldn't quite articulate his motives for being there, free of charge.

Terry would only learn later that Pierre was working for Daniel Sheehan of the Christic Institute, a public interest legal group in Washington, in hopes of adding defendants to the Christic complaint. He was actually a target of Sheehan's that day. But after Pierre grew to know and like the Reed family and heard first hand their pain and suffering, he decided to not only quietly remove Terry from the Christic "hit list" but to help them as well, free of charge!

He volunteered to attend any critical attorney interviews with the Reed's, theorizing that his presence may lend credibility to Terry and his story. Terry would grow to really like and respect this man from south of the Mason Dixon Line, who held nothing but disdain and contempt for the "Yankee fuckin' government" for which he had served for thirty years. Pierre, like Terry, felt that America's military had been misused by one President after another trying to remedy failed foreign policies. It was their common belief that the country was now being run out of Langley, Virginia, the headquarters for the CIA. And Reed knew that from what he had heard and witnessed, they weren't far off track with their views. But Terry couldn't share all his knowledge with them, yet. He had to keep them on track, if possible, and simply get his civil case to court!

And then there was Cummings. Pierre affectionately referred to Cummings as "a scribbler," a term he had created for investigative reporter/writers. Pierre let Reed know immediately that he held the bulk of the "world of scribblers" in contempt, feeling they did more to hurt a good investigation than they helped.

"What they add to the world of investigating is like comparing what depth charges add to sport fishing," Pierre grinned, "With the possible exception of a few. And John Cummings here is one of those exceptions."

From what Reed had learned of Cummings, this 59-year- old man had spent over 30 years with New York's *Newsday* as an investigative reporter, had written several books, was an expert on the mobster John Gotti, organized crime and the underworld, and in addition had immense interest in Cuba, the Bay of Pigs, Barry Seal, and the world of intelligence. His appearance, stature, demeanor and aggressive New York attitude made Terry initially wonder if the Mob hadn't actually sent Cummings at the time of their first meeting. But as the day wore on he discovered Cummings only projected a hard facade, and that underneath, had an interesting, almost scholarly yet street-savvy that caught Reed's attention immediately. Over the course of their "sessions," Terry would discover that Cummings was a Marine Corps veteran of the Korean war and a seasoned world traveler having covered many of the 'hot spots' around the globe for *Newsday*. He seemed expert on geopolitics and was very cynical and opinionated, probably a result of his years of covering courts for the newspaper. His years of dogged pursuit of the truth had helped his newspaper win a Pulitzer Prize in 1970.

Terry didn't know it then, but meeting Cummings would change his life forever, and at times in the future, would be nearly the only man to stay by his side.

Cummings and Pierre, these at first unlikely partners, departed El Paso with not only the outline of Reed's story, but with something much more important to him—the beginnings of friendship. They were building a bond. A bond of trust. They believed him and he believed them in that they both promised to help and not hurt him and his family. But as they departed El Paso he couldn't help but feel vulnerable and apprehensive. Terry had enlarged his circle of trust.

The spring of 1991 centered around endless telephone interviews with attorneys who Cummings and Pierre were flushing out. Document exchanges too numerous to mention were keeping Janis more than occupied as she shared her time between family, career, and her new-found job of "public relations director" for the Reed family. They were getting extremely frustrated, having seen no results from their efforts when the call came.

"Terry, I got your information. It's a hell of a story of two honest folks being wronged and I believe I would like to take your case. I'd like to meet you and Janis first, of course, so when can you get to Jonesboro?" Steve Clark said by phone from his office in Arkansas.

Terry couldn't believe what he was hearing. After all these months of effort, here was the ex-Attorney General of the State of Arkansas offering to take the case on a contingency fee basis. Terry was ecstatic and it took no time for him, Janis and Pierre to rendezvous in Little Rock and drive to Jonesboro Saturday morning March 2nd, for a "legal audition," as Pierre called it.

The interview went well and Clark said he wanted the case. He felt the Reeds had suffered a travesty of justice and from what they had described, it would make a perfect constitutional rights violation case at the federal level. There was only one problem. Steve Clark couldn't practice law in federal court. He was limited at the time to practicing only in Arkansas state court, the result of sanctions imposed by his conviction on state fraud charges.

When the Reeds lived in Little Rock, the name Steve Clark was in the news nearly as often as the name Bill Clinton. Steve was the boy attorney general who had sought and successfully attained that office at the same time another young man from Hope, Arkansas sought and attained the office of governor. He and Bill Clinton had served their time together in state government, with the exception of the two years that Clinton was not governor, having been defeated for one term by Governor Frank White. Terry and Janis knew from their time in Little Rock that Steve Clark harbored ambitions far beyond the office of attorney general.

He had gone so far as to organize a fund-raising committee in order to build the campaign chest and network necessary to run for governor. Janis and Terry had in fact attended one of these fund raisers in early 1986 and heard Clark deliver his practice "elect me for governor" speech.

But what had gone wrong? Why was Clark an ex-attorney general as they were interviewing with him that day and why couldn't he practice law in federal court? They even heard that Clark did announce his plans to challenge Clinton in January 1990. What happened?

He'd been convicted on state charges of misuse of his state credit card while using it for entertaining. They would be told that Clark had done nothing previous attorneys-general and most others in state government weren't doing, namely, offsetting their horribly low state salaries by padding their expense vouchers with non-existent meals or writing off personal business as state business. In fact, Reed was later told that this was considered one of the perks that "came with the job." But Clark had, for some reason, been caught in the act and pursued ferociously by state police investigators under the control of Bill Clinton, just as he announced his Democratic bid for governor in January, 1990.

Clark's official candidacy had lasted only 19 days! It was far too convenient, people were saying, to see Steve Clark fall from office in disgrace just at a time Bill Clinton was preparing his candidacy for the Presidency. After all, Clark would have been a shoo-in as the next governor, if Clinton left the post. He had built a solid political foundation during his nearly 12 years of dedicated service, with fighting corruption as his main issue.

No...it was just too convenient, people were saying, for Clark to come under such attack at a time when Bill Clinton's flank would be exposed since he would be forced to spend nearly a year out of state campaigning for the Presidency. It was being said that Clark posed such a formidable threat to Clinton that if Clinton ran unsuccessfully for President, he would probably have no governorship to return to. Clark would simply move over to fill the political vacuum left by Clinton, who would be wounded from his Presidential primary defeat, challenge Clinton, and defeat his old friend.*

Clark told the Reeds that his case was on appeal and he felt sure his conviction would be overturned. For that reason, he was telling them, it would be necessary to have another attorney file the case, but he would stay in the background and help run it. After all, he boasted, who knew better the inner workings of state government than he? And what intrigued the Reed's the most was Clark saying he thought they had a very good case against not only the Arkansas State Police, but the state as well, and he felt confident if the case was run properly, it would expand on its own, maybe even to a federal level.

"This guy has to have not only dirty laundry on damn near everyone in the state," Reed thought to himself, "but he's vendetta driven and was attorney general during the time of the whole Mena affair. He has to have inside knowledge. I wonder if he knows about OSI and Aki Sawahata. That's probably why he wants this case. And I'll bet he's got the real dirt on Clinton."

Prior to leaving Arkansas and heading back home that weekend, the Reeds and Pierre wanted to take time to do a little investigative work by interviewing an Arkansas man who had been in the local news of late. A man by the name of Larry Nichols. Since the Reeds had driven all the way from El Paso, they wanted to make good use of what time they would have with Pierre, and Terry was anxious to observe the world's greatest...er, most expensive, investigator in action.

What Reed had learned of Nichols prior to the meeting, and found most interesting, was his prior work on behalf of the Contra support network and his direct connection to some pretty big names in Arkansas State government, namely Bill Clinton and Bob Nash. In fact, Nichols had quickly become a thorn in Clinton's side because of a lawsuit he had filed against the state, a lawsuit he had announced with great fanfare on the State Capitol steps in Little Rock.

---

* Full-page headlines in the *Arkansas Gazette* on February 8th, 1990 read: CLARK DROPS OUT OF RACE. Arkansas State Attorney General Steve Clark had announced only 19 days after entering the governors race, that he was withdrawing his bid as a result of the scandal developing from the Arkansas State Police investigation into his filing "several erroneous expense claims with the state." Clark, at a televised news conference the preceding day, read a 78-word statement that included: "I have reached the conclusion that mistakes in my expense records and subsequent news coverage about those mistakes have virtually destroyed my ability to run an efficient and effective campaign for governor."[2]

At Bowen's, a family style restaurant in Conway, Arkansas, the Reeds, Pierre and Nichols sat down to breakfast and for what turned out to be more than a morning repast.

It was interesting for Reed to observe someone else for a change that appeared to be consumed with fear and paranoia. Was this how he had come across after first being indicted? He certainly hoped not. Here was this otherwise fairly normal looking executive-type, in what appeared to be his early forties, tastefully-dressed, articulate, well-groomed and babbling about people in the Clinton administration "out to get me."

As it turned out, Nichols did in fact have a lot to fear! Here, sitting across from Reed and speaking in a whisper, was the one man, other than possibly Reed himself, who could probably single handedly keep Bill Clinton out of the White House. His political "dirt" was not only good, it was fresh and it involved many of the same players Reed had worked with in Arkansas. And most interesting, it involved Nichol's former employer, the Arkansas Development Finance Authority (ADFA), Bill Clinton's financial creation that was designed to take Arkansas out of the stone ages and into the 21st century!

Terry knew that some of ADFA's capitalization had literally "fallen from the skies" out of Barry Seal's planes and he was curious how much Nichols knew of this.

"So is ADFA responsible for a lot of Arkansas growth?" Reed began, "It was just getting up to speed about the time Janis and I moved from here."

"You mean Bill Clinton's bank, don't you?" Nichols quipped. "All it's for is to loan money to his friends. It's a farce. And the poor people of Arkansas are just subsidizing Clinton's mistakes. I'm glad I'm no longer a part of that con scheme. I was not really there to do ADFA's work anyway. I worked on other things."

Nichols had worked for Clinton's ADFA all right...right up until he was forced to resign in 1988 for "misuse of the telephone." Nichols explained he had been in the marketing division of the state agency, responsible for attracting business to Arkansas by "selling" the attributes the state could offer to new businesses.

It seems that a state audit of long-distance telephone charges made on state government telephones had turned up a juicy tid-bit of information that was seized upon by the local media. Namely that Nichols was making phone calls to the prime Contra leaders, Adolpho and Mario Calero, two of Ronald Reagan's model "freedom fighters," men that Reagan called "the moral equivalent of our founding fathers."

The numerous calls had been made on Nichol's state supplied phone and most on state time. This information had become public and in order for Clinton to distance himself from the ensuing media investigation demanding to know why it appeared the state was in effect secretly working with the Contras, Clinton had Nichols fired. Or at least that was what this jittery man was saying who kept looking over his shoulder throughout the course of the interview.

Nichols claimed to be involved in some sort of secret network of people operating at a very high level in Arkansas state government who were not only supporting the Freedom Fighter cause, but were doing so with full knowledge and backing of the man at the top—the governor. When this became public, Nichols claimed, Clinton threw him to the wolves and disavowed any knowledge of his activities. Nichols even went on to say that he had personally arranged for Retired Army General John Singlaub and the Calero brothers to have Arkansas Traveler certificates, special VIP state passes, issued them.

The three men had supposedly visited the state so frequently that they had attained sufficient air mile credits traveling to and from Arkansas that they were issued frequent flyer bonus points on American Airlines. All of this, Nichols said, was done quietly and privately in order for Clinton to show covert support for the Nicaraguan Conflict. Reed found this interesting since, he remembered at the height of the Nicaraguan debate, Clinton appeared to give lip-service that led the public to believe he was against the war. That's what he said publicly.

In conflict to that verbalized disapproval however, he did send the Arkansas National Guard on a joint military exercise, where they maneuvered dangerously close to the Nicaraguan border from Honduras.

Other governors saw this simply as an antagonistic show of force by the U.S. Government and were fearful it could lead to an armed engagement between American troops and the Sandinistas. Mario Cuomo, the governor and the commander-in-chief of the New York National Guard, boycotted the exercise calling it "a provocation" on behalf of the Reagan Administration. Clinton sent his troops.

In reference to an incident that occurred while Nichols was the Caleros' guest and invited to witness actual combat between Sandinista soldiers and Contra rebels, Nichols abruptly put his foot on the dining table and produced proof. "I got this wound while being an invited observer to a fire fight down there," Nichols bragged, while pulling up his pant leg in order to show the breakfasting group a scar on his leg. Janis lost her appetite at the sight of the old wound.

"Adolpho [Calero] invited me down to write a public relations report about field conditions his troops were suffering and I got caught in the cross fire." His repeated secret travels to Nicaragua were done with full knowledge and approval of his superiors at ADFA, Nichols added.

Terry found this story very interesting indeed. Being aware of all the CIA's operations that he knew had existed in Arkansas in the mid-eighties, it certainly all fit. From what Nichols was describing, it sounded like the Agency had tapped some of it's idle resources at ADFA in order to develop a "marketing plan" to sell the war to the American people.

"I guess it was pay back time for some of the secret money the Agency pumped into ADFA," Terry would later conclude with his wife. "You see, in effect it is a form of money laundering. The CIA puts dirty money into ADFA and then they tap guys like Nichols to help run their propaganda machine and the state of Arkansas picks up the tab. I guess it all went well until some state auditor blew the whistle. I wonder what swamp he's lying at the bottom of?" It was a grisly thought. And now that Terry was no longer an Agency insider, he was seeing how perverted it had all become. If Nichol's story was true, and he had no reason to doubt him, then democracy *had* actually failed! If the Agency had state governments "indebted" to them and if state agencies like ADFA had been *compromised* and owed their literal existence to the intelligence community, who was in charge of this country? It definitely wasn't the people...or even the people elected by the people. The thought saddened him.

"But my lawsuit is what has got Clinton scared," Nichols continued. "It's going to expose all the corruption that surrounds him, as well as his womanizing. I'm going to be known as the man who keeps Bill Clinton out of the White House."

Pierre and Reed had heard of Nichols' lawsuit. He had filed a pro-se complaint in state court claiming wrongful dismissal. Being a man accustomed to manipulating the media for the advantage of state government, the CIA and the Contras, Nichols had decided to put his advertising talent to work for himself and had held a press conference on the steps of the state capital building.

The speech he delivered to the gathered media and passers-by not only covered the reasons for which he said Clinton had him wrongfully fired, but went into great detail about "extra-curricular" activities he had performed for the governor. He claimed his activities at ADFA were only one reason Clinton considered him a liability and didn't want him around any longer. He said Clinton had taken him into his confidence about a stable of other women Clinton was sleeping with... unbeknownst to Hillary Rodham Clinton. He even read their names from a prepared list he had made. On that list was the name Gennifer Flowers.

"I was sort of like a secret personal assistant to the governor," Nichols said, smiling for the first since they had begun. "I could move around behind the scenes and do things for him that he couldn't otherwise do."

"Like go to Nicaragua?" Reed asked.

"Yes, like going to Nicaragua and being his eyes and ears. I'd always personally brief him at the governor's mansion when I returned. But that isn't all I did. And that's what's got him worried."

"What else did you do?" Pierre asked, sensing that Nichols was dying to tell them.

"I procured women. Classy women," Nichols grinned, and then surveyed his three listeners, apparently to see if they were shocked by his statement. That apparently hadn't generated the desired effect, so with a solemn look he continued. "And I dirtied people up for him. That's why he's afraid of me. His chief of security, Buddy Young, picked me up and took me to the mansion just the other night to discuss a settlement. They offered to buy me a house and fix me up for life if I would just drop the case and be quiet."

Pierre wanted to know more about the term "dirtied-up" and asked Nichols to expand on that, figuring that the Reed's may have been victimized by such activity.

"I worked on neutralizing political opponents, things like that. You know, digging up dirt," Nichols added. "I guess the biggest thing I ever did for him was to eliminate Steve Clark, the ex-attorney general."

Nichols had no way of knowing that he was eating with three people who had spent most of the previous day sitting in Clark's office. One condition Clark had placed on taking Reed's case was for them to keep the fact confidential for now. And here Reed was, talking to the man who had destroyed Steve Clark's political career. The man who was taking credit for "dirtying him up" and turning Clark into a convicted felon. The man who had successfully kept Clark out of the governor's mansion. What an opportunity!

Reed could barely hold back his enthusiasm! "Tell us more about that."

"I did him for Clinton. Clinton considered him a threat. He came to me and asked me to quietly dig up dirt on Clark. I zeroed in on his personal expense account and bingo, I hit pay dirt! I made copies of everything I could find that looked suspicious and gave the file to Young. They did the rest. Clark got blindsided just as he made his announcement to run for governor."[3]

What a game Reed thought. Lives and careers are destroyed simply because one individual becomes a threat to another. He wasn't justifying Clark's actions. Obviously, Clark had demonstrated a major lack of judgement by charging off personal entertainment expenses as business of the AG's office. Clark was wrong, but the price for his sins was the equivalent of a political execution.

And Nichols was telling the sordid story in a ruthless, cold, matter-of-fact attitude that reminded Reed of an assassin's report back to his handler. Had someone like Nichols, perhaps Young or Baker or Sanders, nonchalantly briefed Clinton like this after they set Terry up on the airplane charge. Had the beginning of his whole nightmare began with, "It's done. Reed won't be a threat to you any longer"? Terry wondered.

"So why don't you take them up on the offer of the house and the 'pension?" Reed asked "Just drop the case and be quiet."

"That's not enough!" Nichols snapped "I want my good name back. Clinton took that from me and now he's going to pay. I'm going to hurt him like he hurt me. I'm going to destroy his name and keep him out of the White House. I may even get him kicked out of the governorship. I haven't decided yet what I'm going to do. But I've got plenty of ammunition. I'm sure I'll do him just like I did Clark.

Clinton needs to feel the pain!"

This had turned out to be one hell of an impromptu education. Not only had the Reeds and Pierre discovered who helped neutralize Steve Clark, but they now knew that it sounded like Bill Clinton was in the habit of using aides...men like Nichols and Young to do his dirty work. Reed and Trubey had always theorized that Terry's problems all stemmed from Mexico and Felix Rodriguez. But he was now focusing his suspicions on Arkansas. The thought of being literally run out of the HOG State that day with Joe Dunlap was coming to mind. Had they been getting too close to uncovering something? Was he, like Nichols, a perceived threat to Bill Clinton? Had he been "dirtied up" by Buddy Young? It certainly sounded feasible.

Reed only knew one thing for sure. Whatever Larry Nichols was afraid of...he deserved.

"There goes a dead man or a rich man," Terry said to Janis as they watched Nichols walk to his car. "I sure wouldn't want to be living in Arkansas and making enemies like this guy is. Bad things can happen to you down here."

Two weeks later, back in El Paso, the Reed's got even better news. Clark had found the proper counsel to not only file the case, but this same attorney was wanting to run it. His name was John Wesley Hall Jr., a famous constitutional law expert residing in Little Rock. This was too good to believe, the Reed's said to each other.

And, as it turned out, it was too good to be true.

The bulldog investigative reporter named John Cummings, who simply wouldn't go away, returned to El Paso and pressed the Reeds for more information on the life and times of Barry Seal. Only this time, he had a "carrot." He professed in their back yard while barbecuing that he was sure their life was interesting enough to do a book. Odd, they thought, how could their lives be a book? And besides, this conflicted directly with their intentions of playing

out their story in the only arena Terry felt it belonged for security reasons—
federal court. They were honored, but rejected Cummings offer.

Then came April. By now the "spooky-groupy" world, as Janis preferred to
call Terry's telephone contacts to the intelligence community, was abuzz about
their up-coming lawsuit. Not a day went by without a telephone call coming in
to wish them good luck and cheer them on from the sidelines. For the most
part, these "cheerleaders" simply occupied valuable time that Terry needed to
be earning a living, but still it was nice to know there were people out there
who believed in them and their cause. It was interesting to talk to most of these
well wishers, composed mainly of the Walter Mitty types; the ones who were
real good at coaching Reed and encouraging him to charge full speed into the
cave where lived the dragon, but who lacked the courage to do the "killing"
themselves.

Their conversations reminded him a lot of the aircrew briefings he had given
to crew members during the war, where frightened airman sat learning of the
enemies defenses before the day's aerial assault on Hanoi, by some expressionless intelligence briefer who couldn't identify with the terror they suppressed.
Yeah, that's how he felt...scared...scared once again.

And then there were the calls of congratulations coming from the people
who KNEW he and Trubey and Dunlap had done the impossible, that they had
done what was rarely accomplished...had slain the lion bare handed in the
arena...but to the cheers of only a few.

But Terry was leery! Hidden somewhere within this ever expanding group of
telephone voices he calculated there had to be a pipeline back to the CIA. He
was most apprehensive of those who seemed to talk forever, paying no heed to
what had to be horrendous long distance charges. To those he fed
disinformation, and then would "reverse course" in his planned legal strategy
just to confuse them. He had to make it to court! He had to make it to court!
Surely, he figured, someone out there was planting land mines along his route.

It would be up to him to try and not step on one.

1. *Civil Complaint No. 86-11-46, CIV-KING, Tony Avirgan and Martha Honey vs. John
    Hull, Rene Corbo, ET AL.* Filed in United States District Court, Southern District
    of Florida, Miami, May. 1986.
2. *Arkansas Gazette*, February 8, 1990.
3. *Ibid.*

FILED

FILED
U.S. DISTRICT CO.
EASTERN DISTRICT OF ...
JUL - 5 1991

CARL R BRENTS CLERK

By _____

UNITED STATES DISTRICT COURT
EASTERN DISTRICT OF ARKANSAS
WESTERN DIVISION

TERRY K. REED and JANIS REED,	)	
Plaintiffs,	)	No. LR-C-91-*44*
	)	
v.	)	COMPLAINT
	)	
RAYMOND YOUNG and TOMMY L. BAKER,	)	42 U.S.C. § 1983
	)	28 U.S.C. § 1343(3,4)
Defendants.	)	28 U.S.C. § 1367
	)	FOURTH and FOURTEENTH
		AMENDMENTS

C O M P L A I N T

The plaintiffs allege against the defendants as follows:

I. INTRODUCTION

1. This is a civil rights action alleging a conspiracy between the defendants to violate the constitutional rights of the plaintiffs. . . . . . . Defendants manufactured, altered, tampered, removed, and planted evidence against the plaintiffs. They also knowingly testified falsely to material matters in Pulaski County Circuit Court (to obtain a search warrant for the airplane hanger), submitted a report to be read to a federal grand jury (to procure an indictment), and testified falsely before a federal judge (in pretrial hearings) in the United States District Court for the District of Kansas (<u>United States v. Terry Reed and Janis Reed</u>, D.Kan. No. 88-10049). All this was in violation of the plaintiffs' rights protected by the Fourth Amendment protection against unreasonable searches of premises and seizures of their person by a false arrest and by the Fourteenth Amendment's due process protection. . .

and done with reckless disregard for the rights of the plaintiffs. Accordingly, the plaintiffs are entitled to punitive damages.

PRAYER

WHEREFORE, the plaintiffs are entitled to the following relief:

(a) compensatory and punitive damages in an amount to be determined by a jury;

(b) reasonable attorneys fees and expenses and costs under 42 U.S.C. § 1988; and

(c) any other relief that the law requires.

Plaintiffs demand a jury trial.

Respectfully submitted,

John Wesley Hall Jr.

John Wesley Hall, Jr
Ark. Bar No. 73047
523 West Third Street
Little Rock, Arkansas 72201
(501) 371-9131

Attorney for Plaintiffs

34-1. Terry and Janis Reeds' lawsuit against Raymond Young and Tommy Baker.

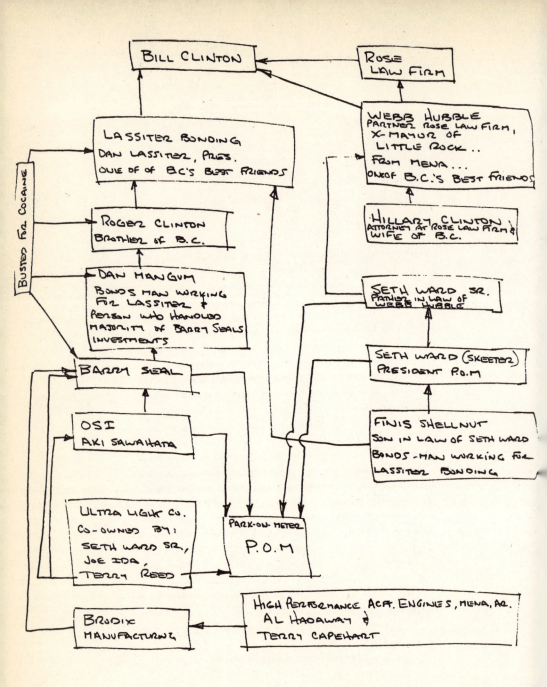

34-2. Document drawn by Terry Reed in January, 1991, and provided to co-author John Cummings. It shows Reed's inside knowledge of political relationships in Arkansas long before the media began publicizing them.

CHAPTER 35

SALVATION AT THE RACE TRACK

On March 10th, 1991, the Reeds decided to relax with their children and do something different for a change. After all, they had lived in El Paso over eight months and still hadn't taken the kids to see the horses race at Sunland Park Racetrack, as they had promised.

The track, which was in New Mexico and only a short drive from their home in Santa Teresa, was sponsoring a special event that Sunday, a car show, something sure to get Terry's attention, being a buff on sixties muscle car restorations.

Janis had to leave the festive event early that afternoon in order to perform "office duty" at the real estate company where she was working. She was disappointed at having to leave Terry and the children since they were truly enjoying themselves for the first time in a long while. Such is the unfortunate plight of the modern liberated woman.

Terry was too engrossed in the inspection of a vintage 1967 Corvette to notice the man who had taken a seat on the park bench by his children. They were busy consuming the hot dogs he had just purchased and Terry thought this would be a good opportunity to get a closer look at the workmanship done to the car's engine.

"I've got one just like it, except it's red and is a 427," the man's voice said to him as Terry pulled his head out of the car's engine compartment. Looking up, Terry saw a hulk of a man looming beside him. He had to be at least six- foot-six, 280 pound and didn't have an ounce of fat on him.

He had the look of a professional body builder whose biceps were barely contained by the day-glow, iridescent green Izod knit shirt he was wearing. Dressed in extremely tight fitting Wrangler blue jeans, cowboy boots and sporting a large western belt buckle that said "LET'S RODEO," Terry at first thought him to be just a car-admirer like himself. But the extremely tanned man, wearing a white cowboy hat came closer, extended his hand in a gesture of friendship and said in a raspy voice, "I'm a friend of a friend of yours."

By this time Terry was almost involuntarily shaking the hand that now enveloped his. "Oh, and who would that be?"

"He's right over there sitting by your children...and he wants to meet with you," the cowboy said with his face void of emotion.

Terry peered through the shrubbery that separated him from the park bench and his three boys, and could see the back of a man's head setting beside them. As he approached he could see, it was...Felix Rodriguez!!!!!!

Fear shot through his body, just like a bullet...like the bullet that he figured would be soon coming! Thoughts of JFK's head exploding like a watermelon streaked before him. His eyes swept the grandstands behind and beside them looking for the barrel of the weapon he was sure that was ready to fire! This would certainly be the perfect place to assassinate him! With all the noise from the crowd and the associated confusion no one would even notice if they used a silencer!

All of these thoughts occurred in a millisecond and reasoning finally took hold. No, he thought. If they had come to kill me, they wouldn't be talking to me. They'd just do it and I'd be dead already! Now his fear shifted to his children as he and his "escort" approached Rodriguez.

Felix rose, put his hand on Reed's shoulder and said in a relaxed, cordial tone, "Come my friend, we must talk. Don't worry about your children, they are safe. My friend will watch them while we chat over there by the cars you so admire."

He had no options, Reed figured. By this time the muscle man had taken a seat beside Baxter, who was playing contentedly with his toy cars. And Duncan and Elliott were so absorbed in the horse race they had disregarded their father's presence. There's probably more than two of them, Reed thought.

"Go on," the cowboy said. "You two have a lot to talk about...they'll be fine."

Over by the show cars, Felix got right down to business. His quiet, reserved demeanor reminded Reed of a Cuban version of Marlon Brando in The Godfather.

"A lot has happened since our last visit in San Miguel," Felix began. "You and you family have been through a lot of suffering. Needless suffering, I might add. Terry, you are just going about this all the wrong way."

"That's it! The same phrase!" Terry thought. That was the very same language Reed had been awakened to on the telephone on at least three separate occasions! The calls had all occurred at night after moving to El Paso and after he had began earnestly shopping for an attorney for his case. They had all aroused him from a deep sleep, and the anonymous caller always relayed the same message.

"You're just going about this all the wrong way," the male voice always said, and then hung up. But that wasn't Felix' voice, Terry recalled. It was an Anglo voice and it bore no discernible accent. He had not wanted to relay his fear to Janis, and had not told her of the caller's consistent message, only telling her that someone kept dialing the wrong number.

"What do you want?", Reed queried.

"I want you to forget about this foolish court idea," Rodriguez responded. "I now know that you did not leave Mexico with any intention of hurting the Agency. It was just that you were a perceived threat to some renegade agents who over-reacted, and then things got a little out of hand."

Rage was building within Terry! The fear had gone! His blood stream was now switching over to pure adrenalin! His ears were ringing! He was hearing what he had always suspicioned. He had been set-up! This nightmare he and his family had been through was all because "some renegade agents" had over-reacted!

Fuck! he thought. Rodriguez could reduce this entire four year ordeal to, "things got a little out of hand!"

If it hadn't have been for the welfare of his children he would have tried to strangle Rodriguez then and there! But slowly his grandfather began whispering from the grave, "choose your time and place." Terry fought back the animalistic rage! This was definitely Rodriguez' time and place. So he had better just listen. Reed remained silent, just staring at the man in white casual clothes and pilot's sunglasses.

"I have come to forgive you," were the next words to come from the Cuban's lips.

" Shit! Here we go again," Reed thought, just barely able to control himself.

"Put in the same circumstance, I may have reacted the same way," Felix continued in his godfather tone, "you were under a lot of stress and we were beginning to think you were going to spill your guts in court. But then I talked to North and he explained to me what had happened, you know... about those idiots of Clinton's setting you up. You realize they would not have done that without Clinton's instructions. You see, you are a major threat to that man and some other very important people in Arkansas. Centaur Rose and Jade Bridge may be history now, but their liability lingers.

"Most of your worst enemies come from your own side," Rodriguez went on in his instructional monotone. "This is something I learned early on in my work with the Agency...something that has kept me alive and out of jail. The man who trained me, my mentor, he always said, 'Keep one eye on your friends because chances are they are behind you and it is easier for them to stab you in the back.'"

"So," Terry asked, not believing that was the case, but fascinated by what he was hearing, "you are telling me that my problems all stem from my work in Arkansas and not from what happened in Mexico?" He was now glad he had not earlier strangled Rodriguez.

"That is mainly it, but it would also have made matters a lot easier if you had not acted the way you did in Mexico," Rodriguez added, now shifting to a more congenial tone. "But that is behind us now. That project was so poorly run by North and the others from the very beginning that it was destined to fail. It was never going to succeed with those Communists involved. But that is partially my fault. I should never have gone along with it. It's just that North and Johnson were in charge and they are such children when it comes to these matters. They are so naive! You may be somewhat naive also, but at least you are resourceful. Yes, for awhile people were acting in very unprofessional and dangerous ways.

"Then luckily you took matters into your own hands and wrote that letter to the court. From that point on we realized you were not out to hurt us...you were only being pressured. So then, we got involved and eliminated that junior fucking, yuppie prosecutor that had you by the ass like an alligator in the Everglades!"

"But I was acquitted!" Terry shot back. "You just told me that Clinton's men set me up! Felix, you knew I was innocent all along! You're not telling me that the Agency had anything to do with the outcome of my trial are you?"

Terry couldn't bear the thought that he and Trubey and Dunlap had not won on their own. What was Rodriguez trying to tell him? That the CIA had fixed the case?

Felix answered Reed's question with a question and a genuinely confused look. *"You do not know who Johnson really is?"* He asked. *"I figured you had already figured that out."*

"No Felix," Reed replied still confused, "I haven't figured anything out. Who is Johnson?" Felix just stared at Reed without answering.

Reed continued, "All I know is the earth has swallowed him up. My attorney and investigator in Kansas were never able to find him in Florida or at SAT. But the prosecutor must have found him since he was claiming Johnson's testimony would be classified."

"Your investigator from Kansas is lucky to be alive. My people and I had him in our sights more than once when he was in Miami to get me served for your trial," Felix retorted, returning to more like the person Reed had heard mix words with North in the bunker.

"He's just like all the rest of those government investigators I ever met...bar none," Felix said with a wink. "He couldn't find his ass in the dark with a flash light."

This conversation about Joe Dunlap's capabilities and his inability to locate Robert Johnson seemed to be upsetting Rodriguez. Reed decided to get the conversation back on track having assumed by now that Felix had not come to harm him, and wishing to return to his children who still hadn't missed their daddy. In fact, Baxter by now had "Frankenstein" playing with one of his cars.

"So why did you come Felix?" Terry asked. "Just to tell me that you guys got to the prosecutor? It's more than that isn't it?"

"Like I said before, you're just going about this all the wrong way," Rodriguez answered, visibly forcing himself to regain his composure. "We know about your attorney in Arkansas and your plans to sue. That's not wise. It could only lead to re-opening old wounds. I'm here to offer you a very lucrative position, if you'll come to your senses and drop all this court stuff."

Here it comes, Reed thought. The court case was the reason he was here. It would definitely open old wounds, all right. And Reed was hoping to inflict some new ones of his own. He decided to just listen and get more information.

"Go on", Terry said.

"I've picked out a very exciting and high paying job for you with one of our cut-outs up in Denver. If you're interested I'll pass your name along and they will get in touch with you. You will be compensated very well. You're already qualified for the position. It's flying.....you like that kind of work, don't you?", Felix asked expressing a *compromising* attitude. "Look, I know you need money. There will be lots of money in this."

"Flying for whom or, knowing you, Felix, flying what?" Reed said baiting him.

"I'll ignore that comment. I guess I had it coming," Felix snapped. "No, this is totally legitimate. It's an aerial photography company in Denver that has a contract with the Agency to do some 'special work' in Mexico and along the border."

Rodriguez went on to explain that an asset of theirs had put together an operation that was disguised as performing ecological services working primarily in the area of pollution control. The real purpose of the firm's activities, however, was to run surveillance on poppy fields in Mexico to pin point their locations and provide their coordinates to both the Mexican and American DEA. Through newly developed infra-red photography technology, they would also have the capability of identifying the radiation wave lengths emitted by other illegal plants, including marijuana.

The Agency's primary interest was not necessarily the eradication of the crops, Rodriguez said. Theirs was to find and surveil the international king-pins behind the production. Rodriguez went on to explain that the Bush Administration definitely felt that this whole drug epidemic was a communist-backed conspiracy to destroy the minds of our children. Most definitely, he said, the *jefes* behind the production had to be communists!

To Reed, after having gone through all he had; to know what he knew; to have seen all he saw; and then to hear Rodriguez attempt to distance himself from the entire drug epidemic by calling it in effect a communist conspiracy...well it almost too much to stand!

Here we go again, Reed thought. Felix can build a communism sandwich around any subject matter known to man. How many more of them like him are out there he thought? With hammers and sickles emblazoned on their brains. But that wasn't it, he knew.

Felix didn't believe his own line of shit, Reed guessed! It's just a ploy! It's just a cover! It's just a job! My God, he and others like him have turned this whole commie thing into a profession.

It saddened him and gladdened him all at the same time. He could now finally see through the smoke and mirrors that had formed his life. That made him happy. It was like finally whipping an addiction...yea, that's how he felt! Like when he ultimately whipped the demon nicotine back in 1973. When his body no longer screamed out for the 'fix' it had grown addicted to. That's how he felt.

All of this pain and suffering was perhaps what was necessary for him to finally rid his mind of the "communist demon" that his society had implanted there. It was like an exorcism, he figured, and he saw the image of the spirit leave his body that very instant. It was probably the closest Terry had ever come to a religious experience, but here he was, looking into his own reflection bouncing back from the sunglasses worn by the man who had undoubtedly killed Ché Guevera. And it was Sunday afternoon.

At that very moment he hated no man. He had no fear. He simply saw how ridiculous his motivations had been. His hot buttons had been disarmed. He was going to do the right thing! Even if it hurt...again!

"I'm through with all this communist hatred," Terry replied almost reverently. "I was wronged and no job offer in Mexico is going to correct my pain. I'm going to do whatever is necessary to right that wrong....in court. Felix, I wish you no harm. I'm going to take my sons and go home. *Vaya con Dios.*"

Under the glaring stare of Rodriguez and the cowboy, Terry gathered his cherished sons and walked away. They wouldn't dare shoot, he thought.

They're cowards, he suddenly realized.

They're outside the system, he concluded. Without the protection and immunity from arrest afforded by being in the "system", they wouldn't bring attention to themselves. In a strange way, this *was* his time and his place.

With his new found "religious freedom" giving him the drive to work long days and nights Terry wasted no time in setting a course he felt would lead him directly to court. His first duty was getting Steve Clark and John Hall up to speed on the case, as he saw it. He wasn't an attorney but after spending over three years surrounded by these "vultures in three-piece suits," he could now speak the language. He would spend countless hours on the phone exchanging information and strategy with Clark who was really growing to respect Terry's memory and grasp of the facts from the trial in Wichita. The document shipments to Arkansas were numerous as Clark built his files and organized the case.

The Reeds still hadn't met John Hall personally but were growing used to his monotone telephone voice. Hall had put them with his legal secretary Ruth, who Reed realized was the equivalent of Radar O'Reilly on the television series *Mash*. There was a tremendous amount of work to be done they all realized, and with Hall as chief legal strategist Terry and Janis set upon the tasks of rearranging their criminal case into a constitutional rights violation civil case.

By now, Terry and Janis had decided to leave El Paso as soon as school was out if opportunity elsewhere could be found. The talk of free trade combined with a recession in the automotive industry along the border was playing hell on Terry's business. And after Rodriguez' visit they were on a condition of red alert to such a degree that it was just wearing them down. They needed to get their case filed in Arkansas and then just "disappear" from the border area for security reasons. They really hated to think about leaving Santa Teresa, the children loved the school and the secure golfing community in which they lived. But Terry figured they had been a sitting target long enough, so it was once again out of the Land of Enchantment and off to the hog state.

Upon first meeting John Hall, the Reed's weren't sure if they were talking to a mad scientist or an attorney. His wild, unruly kinky hair combined with his 60's style wire- rimmed granny glasses gave him the appearance of a bespectacled Einstein. His professional, bedside demeanor consisted of an empty unfocused stare, not only betraying no emotion, but giving one the impression he wasn't even listening.

But they were confused. They had researched him in *Martindale and Hubbell*, the lawyer's directory, and his accomplishments were many. The sitting room leading to his office resembled a B. Dalton's bookstore due to the display racks for the law books Hall had written and which he sold there. Could this be the same man, they wondered? The famous constitutional rights expert who had successfully built case law before the U.S. Supreme Court.

Oh well, it wasn't time to be picky, and Clark was assuring them that Hall was a legal genius in disguise. When he won his appeal, Clark said, and had his conviction overturned, he would then surface as co-counsel and probably be the one who would present the case to the jury. This gave the Reed's comfort because if Clark was nothing else, he was a showman.

With this new-found legal team willing to work on a contingency basis, the Reeds immersed themselves into the "complaint development" phase of their lives. And on July 5, 1991.....did the impossible once again! They launched their counter attack directed toward the state officials and others who had previously wronged them. Hall's strategy as he outlined the complaint was to do what he referred to as a "reverse Christic" style case. The failure of the famous Christic Institute case was in large part due to the broadness of the scope of the complaint. They simply couldn't prove the bulk of their allegations.

Hall's remedy was to sue only the people the Reeds were certain of being able to win against and then hopefully they would "roll over" and implicate others. This would probably include the State of Arkansas and the federal government. That way the case would be self-expanding. This made sense to the Reeds, seeing as how they hoped to crack one layer at a time in order to gain access to the real discovery they knew they had to have—material in the possession of the NSC, NSA, FBI and CIA.

The complaint, filed as a 42 USC 1983 statute violation, involved the Reeds' civil rights being denied them under the Fourth and Fourteenth Amendments. The case was assigned the number of LR-C-91-414 and read in part as follows: They were accusing Captain Raymond Young of the Arkansas State Police, who was Bill Clinton's chief of security, and private investigator Tommy L. Baker of....

" [The] Defendants manufactured, altered, tampered, removed, and planted evidence against the plaintiffs. They also knowingly testified falsely to material matters in Pulaski County Circuit Court, submitted a report to be read to a federal grand jury, and testified falsely before a federal judge in the United States District Court for the district of Kansas. All of this was in violation of the plaintiffs' rights protected by the Fourth Amendment protection against unreasonable searches of premises and seizures of their person by a false arrest and by the Fourteenth Amendment's due process protection."

Hall went on to say "the conduct of the defendants constitutes the state tort of outrage as defined by Arkansas law in that the conduct was willfully and wantonly done and was so extreme and outrageous that it goes beyond all possible bounds of decency and should be regarded as atrocious and utterly intolerable in a civilized society."

The headlines of July 6th, 1991 in the Arkansas gazette read: "Suit alleges state link to Contra affair."

With the case now filed, Janis was anxious to depart Arkansas for friendlier territory. The state now held nothing but bad memories for her and symbolized how far this country has yet to go to guarantee personal freedom.

This was the supposed birthplace of the civil rights movement resulting in the forced integration of the schools by armed troops in 1957. But Blacks still couldn't get membership to the posh country clubs and most affluent whites simply sidestepped the whole integration issue by sending their children to expensive private schools. The Little Rock Police attitude to "shoot the black man first, and then ask questions" was what stuck in Janis' mind. Now that the Reeds had been a victim of unjust prosecution and had witnessed first hand how thin the veneer was that separated the police state from the people, Janis was always fearful of retaliation by the Arkansas State Police.

Terry would try to comfort her on their necessary trips to "The Natural State" by arguing logic. "Honey, nothing is going to happen to us there. I'm not afraid in Arkansas...if something did happen it would prompt a major investigation. It's when we're *not* there that worries me."

This did little to calm her fears, however, and now just the sight of the Arkansas State Line created tension and caused old, bad memories to resurface.

As they would near Texarkana, Texas, on their trips up I-30 heading toward Little Rock, Terry would normally kid her and announce, "Listen up! We're approaching enemy territory. We'll be behind enemy lines shortly. Those needing to relieve themselves prior to engaging the enemy had better do so in Texarkana." She found no humor in all this.

Arkansas State Police Captain Raymond Young and private investigator extraordinaire Tommy Baker likewise found no humor in Terry's actions. With their names now printed as "defendants" on federal court documents, they were being forced to seek counsel. Young, being an employee of the state, was eligible for cost free legal defense supplied by the office of Arkansas State Attorney General Winston Bryant.

Terry felt that by the AG's office representing Young, Bryant was clearly confronted with an acute case of conflict of interest. After all, Bryant had been elected to his post on a campaign pledge to get to the bottom of the controversy surrounding the unauthorized use of the Mena area by agencies of the federal government. And now Bryant was going to be defending Young, which in reality would force his office to suppress evidence of governmental wrong doing in order to defend Young and keep him distanced from the Agency's left-over trail from Centaur Rose and Jade Bridge, which Terry knew led right into the governor's mansion, where Young worked daily. He saw no way Bryant would be able to provide his voters with the promised thorough Mena investigation, which had been his campaign pledge. Clark, Hall and Reed saw this as an elevated personification of "conflict", and felt that eventually Bryant would have to declare it as such, thereby forcing Young to seek state paid-for, out of house counsel.

Tommy Baker, not being entitled to legitimately tap into the no-cost states' attorneys, for now at least, found it necessary to retain private counsel through an old lawyer friend of his by the name of Ray Baxter, of Benton, Arkansas. Steve Clark was elated to see Baker's choice of lawyers and likened Baxter to "an ambulance chaser type who has been know to practice law from his garage," a lawyer who had been sanctioned for ethics violations by the Arkansas Bar, and a person befitting Baker's representation.

Janis drew some minor comfort from the knowledge that Baker, at least, would be footing his share of legal expenses and not be "riding the gravy train" as Young was. Terry pointed out that now knowing Baxter's type of practice, Baker would probably just trade out investigative services for his legal bills. The Reeds bore no personal vendetta for Young and Baker, but were certainly hoping that the cost associated from being within the in-justice system could be tasted by the two of them, since it was they who had personally helped perpetuate the Reed's agony.

With the Reeds now holding a place in the line that administers justice and knowing who were the other team's players, Terry began earnestly looking for gainful employment hoping to catch up monetarily with where he had left off years earlier. The Reed family was upbeat for a change, convinced now that all the months of effort and the endless miles they had driven seeking counsel had been worth it.

Terry had not been a Don Quixote simply charging at windmills. They were happy to find a twinkle of light radiating from the black depression that had consumed them for over four years. The tide was turning they felt.

And maybe luck would be on their side for a change!

CHAPTER 36

DEEP THROAT IS SABOTAGED

"Janis, I just got off the phone with a guy who works for Yamazen Machine Tool in Arizona. He says they need a sales manager for their headquarters in L.A.," Terry shouted to Janis from the guest bedroom at his in-laws' home in Kansas City where the Reeds were visiting.

Thus began a new saga for the Reed family that hot summer month in late July of 1991.

As Bill Clinton huddled with trusted aids and advisors in mapping out his campaign strategy for the upcoming Presidential Primaries, the Reed family packed their belongings and headed to the west coast in order to do something entirely capitalistic for a change, hopefully make money.

By this time Terry and Janis' economic situation was desperate. For the entire seven months of 1991 they had been consumed with getting their case in court. Terry's work at the border had never developed as he had planned, due largely to the distraction of attorney-shopping. Janis was more than eager to pull up stakes and head for Los Angeles, just happy to see her husband's entrepreneurial spirit once again awakened.

The job Terry was taking was with one of the largest Japanese trading companies in the world, Yamazen Company, Ltd. The company's United States machine tool division, Yamazen USA, Inc., headquartered in Los Angeles, was in desperate need of some new marketing techniques. The West coast's economy was sliding from recession to depression and Yamazen's executive vice president, Joe Sakai, sensed a person with Reed's international machine tool experience was just what his ailing bottom line needed.

The job interview had gone extremely well with Sakai offering Reed a District Sales Manager's position and a promised shot at the coveted sales manager's job, if Terry could indeed assist in reversing the economic downslide his company was encountering.

For Terry it would be a totally new experience. He had been in the factory automation and machine tool world for over ten years and had sold a lot of Japanese manufactured computer numerically controlled equipment, but he had never worked directly for the Japanese.

After a whirlwind move to the Los Angeles area, Janis wrestled with the problems associated with starting up a household, getting three children enrolled in school, and pampering a husband suffering from California culture shock.

Terry enjoyed a brief honeymoon period with the new company, which included a week long product orientation seminar, and then came face to face with the reality of working in the bowels of an industry that was now nearly dominated by Japanese and Taiwanese transplant companies.

What he saw and heard, Terry did not like or approve of. At Yamazen, he discovered, there were two classes of people. The lower, working class....the peons....the expendables....comprised mostly of the American Anglos, and then there was the ruling class...the pure blooded Japanese. They were so racist and arrogant, they even discriminated among themselves according to how "diluted" their blood line had become since their ancestors had left ancient Japan. By observing the way the executives treated some of the employees, Terry believed that in the eyes of Yamazen's Japanese management the worst form of life seemed to be those who were the product of a "mixed marriage," with Korean ancestry being the most genetically inferior.

It was evident from the attitudes of his Japanese superiors and by the working environment within this multi-racial company, the American sales force was only considered a "necessary evil." Their job was to penetrate the American industrial base with the company's Japanese manufactured products. Through them, the American natives, a friendly face could be put on this "foreign invasion" into the American factory. At times Reed felt he was personally pulling the Trojan horse into the castle where lived the trusting civilians. The thought of helping to further undermine and contribute to the on-going destruction of America's machine tool industry, saddened him.

Oh well, he reconciled, this won't be for long. "I'll just have to hold my nose and tolerate it until our case gets to court," he told Janis in their suburban home northwest of L.A. "Maybe things will improve if they keep their promise and let me run the damn place. I certainly won't tolerate racism."

It was early winter and Janis could once again see the misery building within him. She knew he had taken the job with the family in mind, hoping to amass enough financial reserves to get them through the trial period in which neither of them would be able to work. But she knew her husband and saw his unhappiness in his eyes. He seldom complained, but she knew his heart just wasn't in it. She knew his problem....he needed his own company once again. Terry was not used to working for someone else. He was a leader, not a follower. She had seen him work eighteen hours a day in order to build their businesses in Oklahoma and Arkansas.

Their leased home in the bedroom community of Moorpark was small but elegant and belonged to a California State Policeman that lived two doors down the street. He flew helicopters for the state and was a survivalist-oriented kind of guy which gave the Reeds a secure feeling. Before anyone came looking for them, Terry calculated, they would first have to go through the landlord who was always legally armed, not to mention Macho, their German Shepherd, who lived in the fenced back yard. Terry viewed the relationship with the landlord as a free security service with a night time guard, only the trooper wasn't aware of the arrangement. He mistakenly thought the Reed's were just your average stressed out American couple with three well behaved children and a dog.

The Reed children had quickly taken root in the secure upper middle class neighborhood and school system. They rapidly made new friends and settled into the routine of household chores and homework. To the kids, it was another page in an adventure story, but to Janis and Terry it was a time of frugality and healing in order to prepare for another court battle.

This entire California experience was turning out to be one big sacrifice for the both of them. As they put in long hours with their work, Terry with his L.A. commute and job and Janis with her time sharing between family and her newly found real estate position, the only comfort they drew was that the clock was ticking in Arkansas and they weren't bankrupt.

"Janis!", Terry yelled outside to where she was playing with the children. "I just talked to John Cummings. The spooky-groupy network in Arkansas says that our judge has ruled. She feels there *is* sufficient evidence to conclude a possible *conspiracy* and that the statute of limitations has not expired."

The year 1992 was starting out in the Reeds' favor. It was January 5th and Cummings had just informed Terry that his judge in Arkansas, Federal Judge Elsijane T. Roy had ruled in his favor. For some strange reason the case had been laying motionless in court awaiting the judge's first action. Reed and Steve Clark were beginning to suspect the worst. Namely that Reed's case might be too politically sensitive to get to trial in an election year. Back in October, 1991, Bill Clinton had made it official. He was going to seek the Democratic nomination for President.

Already the local Little Rock media had seized on the Reed v. Young case and, for a while, not a week went by without headlines discussing the "avowed contra-trainer's" law suit against an Arkansas State Police officer sitting dangerously close to Bill Clinton. For the reporters there, it was a field day of wild speculation about the state's involvement in the whole Iran-Contra affair. John Hall had been deluged with questions about possible linkage between Reed's suit and the governor's office, and his lawyer's silence only fed the fires of speculation.

Terry was under instructions to lay low and save his ammunition for court. Only his immediate family, his attorneys and a few coveted friends even knew he was in California. And few of them had any way to contact him. The phone number was unlisted and the service as well as the utilities were under a corporation's name. For all practical purposes the Reeds had simply vanished out of Santa Teresa and were living anonymously. This was done primarily for security for the children since Rodriguez' visit was still fresh in their minds. And just as the teachers in New Mexico had been told, the teachers in California all thought Terry had an unstable ex-wife lurking about wanting to kidnap the kids.

The only way to readily attempt to locate Terry was through John Hall. Hall's office was under instructions to only relay messages, he wanted Terry making no statements to the press. The only official statements he had ever personally made about his involvement in the whole Mena ordeal had occurred in a deposition Steve Clark had arranged back in May 1991.[1]

Terry had been subpoenaed into a civil law suite between an ABC news affiliate and Southern Air Transport (SAT), both located in Miami. Terry had been deposed in Memphis by attorneys from both sides wanting to know if he had any knowledge of SAT aircraft transporting narcotics.

He testified truthfully, but incompletely, and even put SAT's ex-CIA attorney on notice that he did not consider an open-court deposition environment to be the place where classified material is discussed. Especially material that may jeopardize the lives of active agents and assets. He told them what he knew about the July 5th, 1987, incident in Guadalajara, and the SAT L-100 aircraft that had transported the narcotics that day. In the course of that deposition Clark, who was present, allowed Terry to answer questions about the Agency's operations in Mena. At the time he found that unsettling, but Clark had explained it away as being "necessary in order to establish your credibility." Anyone reading that sworn deposition can easily tell that Terry was reluctant to discuss the Mena operation, fearful that he may be exposing classified information.

But national security and concerns of classified material being *compromised* hadn't stopped the media from having a feeding frenzy with Reed's deposition, once they discovered its existence. For many of the reporters involved, it was the first real piece of credible evidence to surface that indicated a CIA operation had actually gone on under the noses of the Arkansas State Police. And more importantly, under the nose of a man who was by this time preparing for the New Hampshire Democratic Primary...Bill Clinton.

Judge Roy had strangely waited until the last day of the year to rule on a simple issue that had been pending before her since July. If she had not ruled that day the motion would have gone to her court of appeals. It certainly would have looked odd to force a higher court to rule on something as simple as whether the statute of limitations had expired. Their son, Duncan, would ask concerning the judge's lack of action, "What's the matter, can't she count to five?"

It was, after all, just a matter of the judge subtracting the date in which Young and Baker last appeared in Wichita...1989... the date of their last known overt act in the conspiracy, from the one in which the case was filed...1991. To Duncan it was easy, the answer was two. The answer to this complex problem in mathematics had to be greater than five for the Reeds to not have a case.

"It took her six months to subtract those numbers?" he asked, perplexed by this "adult" behavior. It had not only confused the Reed's but their attorneys as well. It looked as if for some strange reason the judge had delayed her action in order to push the case into the fall of 1992.

With Judge Roy's December 31st ruling on the Reed case now signed and put on public display in the court record in Little Rock, the media sharks began showing some life once again. There was definitely a faint scent of blood in the water, especially in the part of the judge's ruling that hinted a conspiracy might have existed to wrongfully prosecute the Reeds. By definition, a conspiracy can only exist if two or *more* people are involved in some devious scheme. The operative word for the Arkansas media being, *MORE*. They speculated wildly about who may have been the motivating forces *behind* Baker and Young.

The press knew they were on to something big and the headline in the *Arkansas Democrat-Gazette* that first day of January read: "JUDGE REFUSES TO DROP MENA CASE, SAYS CONSPIRACY POSSIBLE."

As Terry sat in daily gridlock in L.A.'s bumper to bumper traffic, and tolerated the Japanese management of Yamazen, he didn't know about the depth of the notoriety he was gaining back in Arkansas. He was slowly but surely becoming the unwilling "mascot" for conspiracy-oriented student groups and organizations he'd never heard of before.

Terry was, however, aware of a student group based at the University of Arkansas in Fayetteville and named the Arkansas Committee. From what he had heard it was just the type of left-wing do-gooder organization he needed to steer clear of. With it's unarticulated objectives, and what appeared to be a secret agenda, Terry felt that somewhere in it's enrollment lived the mind and soul of a disinformation machine.

It had all the earmarks of a group of well-intentioned people being manipulated by a few of its leaders. It was just the type of organization his old FBI counter-intelligence handler, Wayne Barlow, had been paid to penetrate back in the '60s. Barlow, back then, was undercover as a hippie style, love-and-peace college student trying to join The Students For A Democratic Society (SDS) and even worse, the bank-bombing Weathermen.

Barlow had shared with Terry what he thought these revolutionary groups had in common. Mainly charismatic leaders with hidden agendas who manipulate the masses for the advancement of their selfish and sometimes dangerous goals.

That seemed to fit the Arkansas Committee to a tee. A textbook definition he thought. At the top was a president by the name of Tom Brown. He reminded Terry of a leftover from the sixties student radical days and he was married to a journalist named Deborah Robinson, who worked with the local press. Between the two of them, she could regularly get into print whatever conspiracy theory Brown was articulating at any given moment.

But behind them, Terry felt, was the real leader. An articulate engineering student named Mark Swaney. Although not officially in charge, Swaney appeared to be the man who steered the group in the direction he wanted it to go. And this appeared to be after Bill Clinton, and bent on destroying his chances of having a shot at the Presidency.

Swaney, in Terry's eyes, was the equivalent of Jerry Rubin, the subversive student leader from the '60s. He was the mastermind, at least on a local level. What concerned Reed the most was wondering who, or what, was behind Swaney. Somebody's private agenda was being played out here, it appeared to Terry. Somebody with power and money and maybe even a vendetta.

In any case, Terry was sure he didn't need to be caught up in a political tug of war. Bad things can happen to innocent bystanders during a Presidential campaign and he had enough enemies as it were. The CIA, FBI and Felix Rodriguez were enough to keep him occupied. He certainly didn't need the Clinton campaign committee, and maybe even the Democratic Party, after him.

So when invited to address the group in June of 1991, Terry respectfully passed up the offer. He could see blood in the eyes of Swaney and others as they laid the foundation for their pursuit of Clinton's head. No, Terry didn't want any part of that fight—not in the media or picketing on the streets or in the assembly halls of the University of Arkansas. He and Janis had worked too hard to risk getting derailed now. Their destination was Federal Court, he told them politely.

There, they would be more than welcome to attend and listen to the unadulterated truth spill out. There, he might not only win his just legal victory, but perhaps be monetarily compensated as well.

The Arkansas Committee's agenda that summer had come down to pretty much one main topic—Mena, Arkansas and its professionally orchestrated cover up. They were demanding a new and independent investigation into all the dark activities that had occurred there. They claimed to have new evidence that government backed covert operations were still going on at the Mena airport, right under the noses of unsuspecting citizens.

Of course, the name Mena could not be uttered without including Barry

Seal and drugs in the same breath. There was still a connection they suspected between Seal and the Arkansas State government and the Federal Government, but they just couldn't put their hands on it. It would take an insider, they knew. Someone with real nuts and bolts, inside knowledge of the operation to blow the top off the scandal. They needed what the reporters from the *Washington Post* found during the Watergate scandal...another DEEP THROAT!

That's clearly what they saw in Terry Reed. They felt that he knew it all and it was driving them crazy he would not join their crusade. He, after all, was the *only* person to surface with a bona fide intelligence background and who was responsible for revealing parts of a story only because he had been forced to divulge them in court in order to protect himself. Reed's silence was only confirming his authenticity.

The decision was made. They would draft him if he wouldn't enlist. They would use him without his cooperation, and to hell with the consequences to him, his family and his personal agenda in federal court.

While the Arkansas Committee conspired to secretly induct Reed as their point man, Terry's attorney fired his first shots in court. John Wesley Hall, with the judge's ruling in hand, now had the green light to attack the state for discovery. He was making discovery demands of not only the defendants Buddy Young and Tommy Baker, but was also demanding that the Arkansas State Attorney General's office turn over their investigative files as well. Hall, with the aid of Steve Clark, had the new Attorney General Winston Bryant on the run. The headline read: "AVOWED CONTRA TRAINER IN COURT TO SEEK ACCESS TO FILES ON MENA AIRPORT."[2]

These headlines should have generated an atmosphere of celebration in John Hall's office as they finally got the Reed case moving. But such was not situation, as bad news had befallen the plaintiff's camp. Steve Clark's conviction had been upheld by the appeals court. He was now being forced to surrender his law license and pay his $10,000 fine. Terry wasn't informed if Hall would be finding a replacement for Steve, but for now at least, Clark continued to cheer from the side lines just like an injured athlete. It really saddened Janis and Terry to see Steve out of the "game", especially after being told that it was Larry Nichols, through a blind-sided tackle, while being coached by Bill Clinton, who had taken him out.

Hall and Clark had figured a quick way to obtain otherwise expensive discovery, was to get it from a government file. They knew there were extensive investigative files on the subject of Mena and Barry Seal, files that had taken years to develop, involving countless man-hours and no doubt hundreds of thousands of dollars. All those files that had been compiled by law enforcement agencies of nearly every variety, but from which no arrests had resulted.

How did they know those files existed? Besides Steve Clark knowing of their existence as a result of having been the state's Attorney General, the files had recently been the centerpiece of a front page newspaper article and photo in the *Arkansas Gazette* dated September 11, 1991. The photo showed Winston Bryant and U.S. Congressman William Alexander transporting those files to Washington, D.C. to turn them over to Iran-Contra prosecutor Lawrence Walsh.

With much media-hype and fanfare, this equivalent of a staged publicity stunt generated the illusion to the citizens of Arkansas that there was finally going to be a thorough investigation about, among other things, why the CIA and other federal agencies had gotten away with using Arkansas as their dumping ground for black operations.

Bill Clinton, Bob Nash, Oliver North, Terry Reed and a few other select individuals knew why the CIA had "gotten away with it." *The state had been "rented" by the Agency, just as Laos had been.*

By delivering the files to Walsh, Bryant was in essence admitting deceit and defeat. He was handing off the responsibility for the investigation he had known all along he could never undertake. Bryant had campaigned on and had been successfully elected from a platform that had as it's nucleus, one juicy issue. Namely, why had not his opponent, U.S. Attorney Asa Hutchison, aggressively sought indictments from a grand jury investigation in the Mena Affair?

It all smacked of a Washington led cover-up, Bryant had alleged. There was sufficient evidence, literally tons of it at this point, to prove that the late Adler Berriman Seal had been running a government-backed operation out of western Arkansas. Bryant had alluded to rigged grand jury proceedings, witness tampering and overall containment of one of Arkansas's worst scandals. All occurring while Hutchison was a U.S. Attorney and Clinton was governor.

The strategy worked. Bryant was elected. The brains behind the Bryant machine was a man by the name of Lawrence Graves. He was the campaign strategist who hired William Duncan, the 17-year veteran Internal Revenue Service Agent who investigated Mena and then walked away from his job and his government retirement after being told to perjure himself before Congress by denying the existence of some of his more "sensitive" information. With Duncan's inside knowledge on all of the wrong doing and lack of a thorough investigation into Mena, Hutchison had been blown out of the water.

But when Bryant had to make good on his campaign promise to aggressively investigate the whole Mena Affair, he then had a problem. He had no money and, more importantly, no power to do so. Besides having no funds for an investigation, the Attorney General's office in Arkansas has no constitutional power to initiate a grand jury investigation. That was something Bryant failed to mention during his appeal for votes.

With Bill Duncan now on Bryant's staff and assigned to the office's medicaid fraud division, all he really had to do was turn Duncan loose on the Mena case and bill out his time to some other investigation. After all, who was going to complain if the Mena story finally erupted, and all of the dark details came flowing out?

Bill Clinton, that's who!

By this time, in February of 1992, Bill and Hillary Clinton were having a little trouble getting their message across to the voters of New Hampshire. Their plans for the country, if elected, were being drowned out by demands to know more about Bill's indiscretions—"bimbo eruptions" as they were referred to.

Yes, Larry Nichols had made good on his promise to make Clinton feel the pain. He had blown the lid off the story about Clinton's womanizing. Gennifer Flowers' picture was now on the cover of *Star*, one of those supermarket tabloids, and she had greater name recognition nationally than some of the Democratic contenders for President.[3]

People magazine even ran an article on the boy friend Flowers had maintained while sleeping with the Governor, and he was none other than Finis T. Shellnut, Seth Ward's son-in-law and the man who retrieved Seal's "green parcels" from the Drop Zone near Little Rock.[4] He was also the bond-daddy who had worked for Dan Lasater's firm which had done the "preferred" state bonding business through the Rose Law Firm, the company where Hillary Clinton practiced law and where Shellnut's brother-in-law, Webster Hubbell, hung his law license. Lasater, who was now a convicted felon resulting from his guilty plea on cocaine charges, was also Bill's Clinton's investment banking friend who had employed his brother Roger Clinton as his chauffeur and had been "stung" by the younger Clinton, who was cooperating with the Arkansas State Police's undercover investigation back in 1985 after his bust by the ASP.

The Reeds were watching Clinton's world cave in around him, and the media had only dug deep enough to unearth the Flower's affair. What would happen when they discovered the incestuous maze that would lead them through the Ward family, the Rose Law Firm and into the questionable dealings within the bond business in Little Rock? Terry could almost hear Barry Seal laughing from his grave and saying, "He'll be lucky to get elected as a dog catcher..."

The last thing Bill Clinton needed was for the truth to come out about his state's involvement with the CIA. If that happened he might as well stay in New Hampshire... permanently! Steve Clark was privately enjoying the pain being inflicted on the Clinton family. Terry had relayed to Clark the revelations told him by Nichols. When informed, Clark said nothing for a moment and only stared intensely, as if rewinding his mental cassette tape, for an instant replay of key events that led to his "timely" downfall. Terry could tell by the twitching of Steve's facial muscles that it was all he could do to contain his anger that day.

"Thanks," he said, and walked away.

Back in California, Reed couldn't believe how dirty the primary was turning out. After the successful attack on Clinton's marital *faithlessness*, the remaining Democratic contestants were frantically seeking "new dirt" to dump on Clinton, hoping this next load would smother him for good. John Hall's phone was constantly ringing as a result of campaign managers and "political handlers" wanting to interview Terry to discover the mother-lode of dirt they were sure was stored within his head.

The political feeding frenzy at that time became so intense that a California campaign aide of Senator Tom Harkin of Iowa, one of the Democratic Presidential Primary aspirants, was trying desperately to tie Clinton to the Mena scandal by sending out mailings that included sensitive court documents from Reed's criminal case. The political backers of former California Governor Jerry Brown, another candidate, intercepted one of these mailings and called Reed's attorney in Little Rock. This led to Hall's suggesting to Terry that he meet with an aide of Brown's, who lived near the Reeds in Los Angeles. Hall felt the Brown backers could somehow be of benefit to the civil case. Hall instructed Terry to "sniff things out" and find out what the Brown aide wanted while, at the same time, not revealing anything to him. A few days later, in late winter of 1992, a female Brown campaign organizer visited the Reeds home in Moorpark for a quiet meeting where it suddenly occurred to Terry just how powerful his knowledge about Clinton and the Arkansas operations was. The woman confided that the faltering Brown campaign had hired a private investigator who was then in Arkansas trying to confirm Clinton's involvement with the CIA.

Terry would never have believed that he could have risen to the number-one position on Clinton's list of liabilities. It was not a warm and fuzzy feeling, as they say, but there was little he could do about it other than to sit quietly and hope, through his media silence, the Clinton camp would not perceive him as a direct threat. His strategy was not to single out Bill Clinton, per se, since he was sure that Clinton and the Democratic Party had the awesome power to sabotage Terry's efforts to go to trial.

But although he was doing nothing to hurt Clinton directly, his attorney and Judge Roy certainly were.

The judge had scheduled the Reed case for trial on September 11th, 1992. That would give John Hall just about eight weeks to completely destroy the Democratic Party's hopes of defeating the Republican contender if Bill Clinton was to end up being their man on the ticket.

And the Little Rock newspaper had headlines that kept the residents up to date on Hall's battles for the Mena files that Bryant had turned over to Walsh's office. "FBI TIES UP DOCUMENT ON MENA-CONTRA CONNECTION," headlined the newspaper.[5] The Attorney General's office was starting to look pretty bad. It was beginning to appear that perhaps Bryant's plan had been to "hide the files" in the abyss known as the Iran-Contra investigation, at least until the election was over.

By giving the files to Walsh's office, Bryant's attorneys were arguing that placed the material outside the scope of court discovery since the Justice department had no right to material under Walsh's control. The AG's counsel was even asking for a protective order from the court to prevent access to the Mena files and to make the AG and his staff immune to Reeds' subpoenas. It was like *déjà vu* for Terry and Janis.

The Independent Counsel Law was the argument the government had used in his criminal trial, which effectively kept North's notebooks out of Reed's mail-fraud case. Was Bryant running interference for Clinton? It certainly seemed so. After all, they were both Democrats and they were probably rallying around the party. John Hall was also a very active Democrat in Arkansas, and had announced his plans to run for Circuit Judge in a special election on the Democratic ticket in late 1992. This declaration made the Reeds uneasy. How could Hall aggressively pursue their case and let the dirt fall where it may, if he had to be careful not to soil Democrats? Democrats, were damned near all there were in Arkansas.

Hall assured the Reeds that his flirtation with seeking elected office would not interfere with their case since the trial would most likely be over before he would assume office, if he ran successfully. And even if the trial date slid into late 1992, he was confident he would still be allowed to try the case, he told them. The Reeds could only hope this posed no problem in the future, but Terry complained covertly to Janis about his doubts Hall would be able to keep his promise.

Duncan, the indefatigable former IRS investigator, was overtly complaining that there was no money for a new Mena investigation. That's what he had been promised by Bryant, his boss. There had even been a plan to assign him to the Arkansas State Police (ASP) and let him work directly under the control of the main man, Colonel Tommy Goodwin, in order to investigate Mena. That had been scrapped due to lack of funds, allegedly. Reed found it humorous that Goodwin was even giving the appearance of being interested. It was Goodwin who had *ignored* Judge Theis' order issued from the federal court in Wichita, the one that demanded he produce the ASP files on Mena. Goodwin, back then, acted as if he were willing to be held in contempt of court and appeared willing to stymie any attempt to re-open the state's Mena investigation. If he did allow Duncan to work under his control, Reed figured it would just be a way to further contain and control Duncan and the investigation. It never came to pass, however. A slot was never created for Duncan, again due to claims of "lack of funding."

Back in 1987, there had been an outcry for an investigation into Mena by Charles Black, the Polk County Deputy Prosecuting Attorney. Black said he had approached Clinton for state monetary help, saying that a thorough investigation would bankrupt the poor county in which Mena is located. Clinton pledged to help and there was talk that $25,000 of state funds had actually been made available to investigate the Mena scandal. When Black heard the dollar amount being allocated, he compared it to "trying to extinguish a forest fire by spitting on it."

He knew this amount wouldn't even cover the cost of helicopter fuel that would be needed to thoroughly explore the Ouchita mountains surrounding Nella for clues of Agency wrong-doing. But even more suspicious than the lack of sufficient funding, Duncan in 1992 was now being told there was no money available *at all* with which to investigate. This time the headline read: "$25,000 FOR MENA AIRPORT INQUIRY MISSING".[6]

Back in September, 1991, just before Bryant and Alexander delivered their "credible evidence" of federal wrongdoing to Walsh's office, Clinton was questioned once again about his state's role in the Mena investigation. Clinton responded by saying he had authorized the state police to tell local officials the state would help pay for a grand jury, which he expected would be costly because of the need to bring witnesses in from outside the state. But Black said he never saw any money. Bill Duncan was not finding any money. And yet Bill Clinton was saying the state did all it could in the Mena case.[7] Terry Reed would learn in March, 1993, through a sworn deposition of AG chief of staff Lawrence Graves that his office spent between $2,500 to $3,000 to investigate Mena.[8]

They were dealing with the most effectively orchestrated state and federal cover-up of a scandal, the magnitude of which makes Watergate appear insignificant. And the Arkansas Attorney General's office allocated approximately $3,000 to unearth it. Steve Clark, the ex-AG, could hide sums larger than that within his own expense account.

The blatant disregard by state and federal officials to respond to the public outcry for a new and thorough investigation into the government's activities at Mena, left the leaders of the cause with no recourse but to reach out to the private sector. This effort led them to Dallas, Texas, and into the offices of billionaire H. Ross Perot.

After being made aware of the results of the private probing into the Mena matter, Perot personally telephoned Little Rock and notes taken at the session read, "Perot says he has briefed Governor Clinton and 'everybody else' and nobody can stop [the] investigation now that it's out in [the] open." When the media seized on the "briefing," the headlines read: "PEROT CALLED CLINTON ABOUT MENA INQUIRY".[9]

Clinton later acknowledged the call and claimed he assured Perot there would be a complete and thorough state investigation.

Throughout February the Reeds kept their noses to the grind stone, followed the Democratic Primary in the news, began organizing documents for the September trial and longed to return to the simple life afforded them in rural New Mexico. The complexities of survival in this palm-tree lined, concrete jungle, far outweighed those of avoiding an occasional rattle snake in the desert.

On the good side though, Terry's job had improved considerably since his arrival. He was now in charge of a newly formed division entitled "the advanced systems group." Its purpose was to pursue larger, more complex automation projects available through Fortune 500-sized companies. The division was of his own creation and it was turning out to be a little like his own small company within this large Japanese dragon.

It was good to have his mind once again engaged with manufacturing problems. They are definable and solvable, unlike this world of courts and attorneys that had sucked his energy for so long. The ability to view the threat the Japanese pose to American industry, from within, gave him new drive to automate U.S. firms and hopefully make them once again globally competitive.

This "insider knowledge" about the Japanese invasion had led him on a search of clients who could readily identify with his preachings of "automate or die." Terry's "the sky is falling" caveat penetrated welcome ears in Phoenix, Arizona. There he met an extremely logical-minded, articulate and entreprenural-driven man named Clark Ronnow. Clark was heading up a start up manufacturing firm that held patents protecting a new bicycle product that would revolutionize the bicycle industry. Ronnow's plans were to automate the new factory to such a level that the bicycle manufacturing industry could once again return to American soil and compete heads-up with their Oriental competitors.

Terry's mind was on this exciting new project and not prepared for what happened that 13th day of March. He would again learn old enemies were constantly lurking, poised for retaliation.

"Come into my office and close the door," Ted Tokudome the new Yamazen vice-president told Terry. "It is time I got to know you better."

A lot had changed within company since Terry had arrived. There had actually been a shake-up of Japanese management, probably attributed directly to the huge losses the firm was suffering. Joe Sakai, the person who had hired Reed, had been forced into early retirement and the man who was demanding to speak with him that day, Tokudome, was Sakai's replacement and about Terry's age. So far Tokudome had seemed impressed with Reed and was giving him complete rein to do as he pleased in his newly formed division.

Tokudome was a new breed of Japanese manager, however. He was part of the new wave of white collar replacements from Japan that were being sent to retire the first group of managers. The original "front line commanders," the ones who had first penetrated the American markets, were for the most part aging. Many of them were due for retirement, ready to be put out to pasture, as Reed saw it.

But something else was going on here as well. Japanese firms were reducing their dependency on American management. The older men had come to America in the '60s and '70s. For the most part they spoke fractured English, didn't fully understand American attitudes and psyche and relied only on the superiority of their products to establish a beach head from which to launch their assault. These men needed Americans all around them as advisors, and front men, continuously relying upon their skills, advice and help to service the "foreign market" they were in.

But not guys like Tokudome. They had either been here since their early twenties and learned American ways and attitudes through observation and osmosis, or many of whom had gone to college here. These were the true clones, and they no longer had to make up for their short comings with *gaijin* advisors. From what he had heard, Tokudome fell into the first category having been with Yamazen in Houston and Chicago for many years before being promoted and sent to Los Angeles.

As Reed closed Tokudome's door and took a seat in his spartanly furnished office, he had assumed it was finally time for his "one-on-one", as the Japanese called it. It was Japanese custom for the "boss" to interview each employee privately. To learn the ills of the company and to get better acquainted. There lying spread on Tokudome's desk was the résumé Terry had given Joe Sakai the previous year.

"I have been reviewing your résumé," Tokudome said, masked with his expressionless piercing stare. "Can you explain to me why you played down your business relationship with Toshiba?"

Terry knew in an instant where this conversation was headed. Toshiba Machine Tool had been convicted in the court of world opinion in 1987 for making the world a much less safe place. They had stolen secret American nuclear submarine propeller technology and sold it and the necessary machine tools to manufacture the advanced technology parts to the USSR.[10] In lieu of a Congressional ban on all Toshiba products, of which there are many, the company self-imposed a five-year ban on selling machine tools to the U.S.

The aftershock of the scandal led to arrests and trials of Toshiba executives in Japan. The disgrace brought to the company by it all, caused the president of the machine tool division to "do the honorable thing." He killed himself, the old fashioned way...*seppuku.*

"Since you had your own company and you were dealer for Toshiba, you should put Toshiba at very top of résumé in big print," Tokudome chided. "Do you not agree?"

Earlier that week Reed had noticed Tokudome with a visitor in his office. He was a man Reed had seen someplace before, years ago, probably at some machine tool show. After the man left Tokudome's office, Reed had noticed some Toshiba literature left on Tokudome's desk. It was old literature dated back to the early '80s and depicted the same model of computer numerically controlled (CNC) gantry milling machine that had been illegally sold to the Russians in the early '80s. It was the same model John Cathey/Oliver North had Reed tracking for the CIA. This certainly was a lot of coincidence and why was this subject at the top of Tokudome's list of things to discuss?

"Ted, I purposely downplayed my relationship with Toshiba since I'm not very proud of having represented them. Besides trying to cheat me out of my commissions, Toshiba did some very dishonorable things," Terry answered.

"Toshiba did nothing that Cincinnati Milacron did not do!" Tokudome snapped back. "Cincinnati sold many machines to the Russians and they did not get into trouble!"

He was referring to the largest builder of American manufactured machine tools, or what was left of that company. Japanese competition for the world market of manufacturing machinery had driven most American builders into extinction. Cincinnati Milacron was retooling and trying to hold on to what market share they had left. But Reed found it interesting that Tokudome was overlooking the fact that Toshiba had been caught in the act of espionage, stealing and selling American defense secrets and selling computer controlled machine tools in violation of COCOM (the 15-nation Coordinating Committee for Export Control). Somehow in Tokudome's Japanese mindset, this compared to Cincinnati selling to the Russians internationally approved equipment, that did *not* possess the restricted technology.

"The machines Cincinnati sold to the Russians, Ted, did not contain computer programs stolen from the U.S. Navy," Reed shot back without thinking.

"You seem to know a lot about this affair," Tokudome snapped. "How do you know so much?"

"I read a lot and it was an issue that personally affected me," Reed bluffed, hoping that would satisfy him and they could maybe move on to something else. It didn't work. It only got worse.

"What do you think of a person who causes another to take his own life?"

"I don't think that is possible, Ted." Terry answered, knowing full well he was referring to the circumstances that led to the Toshiba executive's death. "Suicide is self-inflicted by definition. I don't see how someone can be accused of causing suicide. That would be a good one for the courts."

"I have also been told you are very experienced in court. And that is not on your résumé either! You should put that up at top also. Terry Kent Reed. Convict... and most of all...traitor! I knew president of Toshiba. He was honorable man, and you helped to kill him! You and your two-faced government!"

Here Terry sat looking at what surely would have made a model World War II Japanese officer. Tokudome's hostilities were spilling out of his tight thin lips. It was as if his slanted, expressionless eyes were trying to pierce into Reed's mind to see what he was thinking.

Without a doubt his cover had been blown. Someone had thrown him to the wolves. He was again expendable! Had this been World War II, Terry would now be treated like the spy that Tokudome knew he was. He would be tortured to death! He was now angry!

"Ted, whatever it is you think I did, I did not only for the safety of my country but that of Japan's as well," Terry responded, trying to control his anger.

Tokudome only sat there in rigid silence, nostrils flared and panting with pent up rage. There was no doubt about it, Terry had been *compromised*. Fuck it! He wasn't going to take this shit. The silence was killing him...might as well tell it like it is, he decided.

"Ted, Toshiba was wrong! Toshiba's president was wrong! And you are wrong! If this is the opinion of the Japanese community and Yamazen, then they are wrong! I did what was right and I'm not going to let any ancestor of any harbor-bombing son-of-a-bitch sit here and tell me otherwise."

Well, so much for the one-on-one.

It was Friday afternoon and Terry had plenty of time to digest the meeting while sitting in bumper-to-bumper traffic for the 62-mile drive back to his home west of the San Fernando Valley.

Tokudome had not actually fired him yet or maybe he had, he wasn't sure. The meeting had ended in a strange silence with both men simply staring each other down. Tokudome, with nostrils still flared had eventually just left the room.

Terry couldn't stand the word *traitor*, especially considering all he had been through for his country. But he had gotten the strange feeling that Tokudome now considered America his, and that by Reed doing anything against the Japanese was somehow an act of subversion. It was a weird circumstance indeed. Maybe the Japanese did own this country, he thought as he sat looking at the endless miles of "rice burners" creeping along I-405.

It had turned out to be a strange day. Being chastised for having done the right thing. For spying on behalf of the U.S. Government 10 years ago on a dirty company, a traitorous company, a company that through their own greed had brought the world a little closer to Nuclear Holocaust, he was sure he and his family would now ironically pay the price for his loyalty. How circumstances change. Once he was an insider and now he was an outsider. Once he was a hero and now he was a traitor. Once we Americans owned this great nation and now he worked for the Japanese, who own it. But that wouldn't be for long now. Someone else had seen to that.

"I wonder who *compromised* me?", he asked himself. "Probably someone with the Agency. When will it ever end?"

It was time to do what everybody in L.A. does when stuck in traffic. Get on the cellular phone and call home. He certainly wasn't looking forward to telling Janis, but she was strong and he knew she could take it. He would have to tell her that he was a free man once again...compliments of the intelligence community!

* * *

"Janis you've got to call John Hall immediately!" Terry nearly shouted from a pay phone near downtown Los Angeles. "I just got off the phone with Richard fucking Behar and he said if we don't turn over all our material to TIME, right now, that he is going to crucify me in the magazine. He said he's going to paint me as a con-man if I don't cooperate and give him our dirt. This is blackmail...I'm not gonna take this shit!"

Janis, from her real estate office, set about frantically trying to contact Hall in Little Rock to inform him of the pending disaster. After finally reaching him and informing him that Richard Behar of TIME magazine had turned on them and was literally blackmailing them to turn over all their evidence and court discovery, Hall's initial instructions were for Terry to cooperate with Behar.

"We certainly don't need any bad publicity at this point," were his comments to Janis.

Later that same day Hall called Janis back and reversed his earlier instructions and told her to tell Terry to have no further contact with Behar or anyone else at TIME until he could hopefully defuse this bomb that he had a hand in building.

The date was March 26th, 1992, and the Reeds' lives were crumbling before their eyes once again. They were under attack! This time by TIME magazine. Things had gone atrociously wrong!

To make matters worse, Terry had no job. On March 18th, just five days after their one-on-one, Reed had been summoned to Yamazen's office where Tokudome sat silently and watched Yamazen's Italian-American executioner, salesmanager Mike Ghiorso, chop off Reed's head.

It seemed there had been such an immediate downturn in business that Tokudome had been forced to eliminate the Advanced Systems Group that

Reed was in the process of forming. He wasn't fired...Tokudome was smarter than that. It was simply treated as a lay-off. Ghiorso the yes man, quietly approached Reed in the hall after the "ceremony" and with no Japanese present said, "I'm sorry about that. I was only following Ted's orders. I'll certainly recommend you highly if you need any references."

Nuremberg all over again he thought. Nobody is personally responsible and everyone was only following orders!

Oh well, he knew it was coming and knew why. The clown Ghiorso was probably in the dark about it all. Terry doubted seriously if the Japanese had referred to him as a traitor in Ghiorso's presence and shared their true motivation for canning him. It was best to leave quietly, but he couldn't help but think about the publicity damage he could inflict by calling the media and telling the truth behind his dismissal.

But he didn't have time for that. His world was in a swirl that day, things were truly in fast motion as he attempted to stomp out the small blazes that were erupting around him, hoping to smother them before they consumed him and his family. A job was only one of his worries as he once again fell back into the pilot mode and attempted to prioritize his emergencies. How had it all gotten out of control?

Bill Clinton had miraculously limped out of the New Hampshire Democratic primary. He was wounded, possibly gut shot, but was still alive even after all the scandal about his unfaithfulness to his wife. Larry Nichols had helped somewhat by "mysteriously" withdrawing his lawsuit against Clinton on the eve of Bill and Hillary Clintons' televised interview on CBS's *60 Minutes*. The main purpose of which was to convince the viewers that in spite of Bill's "infidelities," their marriage was solvent and that if elected they would be sleeping in the same bedroom.

Terry and Janis were wondering how large a house Nichols might have been promised and debating if he would get his hush money in monthly installments or one lump sum.

But as the Clinton Campaign Committee carried Bill out of the Northeast on a stretcher, the Democratic Party and Clinton's handlers were combing the trail up ahead for other hidden "booby traps." They didn't have to look very far. The other shoe was getting ready to drop.

Alexander Cockburn, a columnist for *The Nation* magazine, was writing a series of articles on Clinton, the State of Arkansas and most flammable of all topics at the time...Mena. He had somehow zeroed in on POM, the company in Russellville, Arkansas that had built weapons parts for the Contra resupply operation and was also showing a connection between it, ADFA and the Rose Law Firm where Hillary Clinton worked.

The scandal surrounding the lack of a thorough investigation into the governments activities in Western Arkansas had spilled out of the local Arkansas media into the pages of *The Nation*. A major firestorm was in the brewing and the winds of the media were fanning the flames of defeat for Presidential candidate Bill Clinton.

With Clinton now on the "critical but stable" list the media was now focusing on the survivors of the first major skirmish. The hotel rooms in Little Rock were now overflowing with "carpet-bagging" reporters from out of state, looking for the trail of blood from Clinton's wounds.

They too didn't have to look very far. The trail led them straight to Terry

Reed. Laying right there in the Federal Court House was a file marked **REED v. YOUNG**, case No. LRC-91-414. It didn't take much of a detective to be lead from there to the offices of John Wesley Hall, Jr. over on 3rd Street.

Hall, of course, was saying very little to the reporters, preferring to make his comments about the case in the form of motions to the court. And by now there were many! The Arkansas Attorney General's Office and its attorneys were really starting to "smell". They had a definite conflict of interest and were groping with the image problems this presented. Headlines from the Arkansas Gazette read: "BRYANT'S OFFICE REPRESENTING BOTH SIDES OF MENA AIRPORT CASE".[11]

Winston Bryant was beginning to appear as somewhat of a double dealer. The Indians call it "two speaker" or someone who speaks out of both sides of his mouth.

By the Attorney General's defending Captain Raymond Young they were being forced to suppress the Mena material Reed's lawyer was demanding. Hall hoped that somewhere in the "voluminous files" there existed information that could corroborate Reed's involvement with the CIA in Mena. By doing so, it was Hall's intent to establish motive as to why Young, Baker, the Arkansas State Police and others had conspired to attempt to illegally convict and incarcerate Janis and Terry. They hoped to show it had all been done to destroy Terry's credibility by converting him into a felon and thereby silencing him forever.

But Bryant's efforts in keeping Reed and his attorney from the files were creating the appearance of his reneging on his campaign promise to get to the bottom of the Mena controversy, once and for all.

With this internal conflict of having dual objectives and policies, Bryant was forced to erect what his office called an internal "Chinese wall". It was supposedly an attempt to isolate the two forces within the AG's office. One was trying to expose the crime associated with Mena and the other that was trying to contain it in order to protect Young.

Hall was having fun with the term "Chinese Wall," noting to Reed that the real wall in China built hundreds of years ago had been useless in keeping factions separated, and they had to assume this one was also. As they lobbed their mortar rounds over the wall, Lawrence Graves was forced to try to muzzle and isolate Bill Duncan. Duncan was ordered to do no further work on the Mena investigation, something laughable, since he had not been doing so because of no funding. He was also told to stop talking to the media concerning the Mena scandal. All part of the Chinese Wall, he was told.

To the Reeds, it was plain and simple. Bryant's office had joined the *Clinton For President Campaign* and would do anything in it's power to keep from him, the public and the media, the information he so desperately needed. Good ole boy politics was alive and well in the HOG STATE.

"Hey Bubba, have you seen the current issue of *The Nation* magazine?" Bill Duncan was asking Terry by telephone to California. "If not you better go find a copy. You're famous."

Duncan had called Hall's office earlier in the day, desperate to talk to Terry. The message was forwarded to Terry in California and he listened in disbelief after calling Duncan at the Arkansas State Attorney General's Office. Duncan was elated about an article appearing in the February 24th issue in the section entitled BEAT THE DEVIL.

The culmination of a three-part series by Alexander Cockburn aimed at exposing all the sin in Arkansas that could remotely be linked to the CIA was on page 222. The piece entitled "Chapters in Recent History of Arkansas" was featuring a story about a CIA asset who worked for Oliver North, aka John Cathey, and the infamous and now deceased, Barry Seal. Terry, after talking to Duncan, stood in a Book Star bookstore in the San Fernando Valley reading about himself in disbelief.

The one and a half page article pretty much said it all. It outlined his prior work with the CIA, synopsized his Wichita criminal case, and then got into the Reed v. Young case in Arkansas. He had been thrown into the fight. His story had been stolen from him and was being played out right where he did not want it...in the media!

Anyone reading the piece would draw the conclusion Terry had given an in-depth personal interview and was anxious to add misery to Clinton's misfortunes, but this simply had not been the case. Now, by being thrown into the limelight it could be perceived that Terry was even threatening Clinton, in much the same way Larry Nichols had.

Shit! Here he stood in L.A. feeling totally defenseless. He could see the political storm brewing on the horizon and he was beginning to feel like a lonely lightening rod. How could this have happened, he and Hall wondered? Hall took Terry at his word that he wasn't the source of the article. But it was apparent that Cockburn wanted to kill Clinton politically and was using Terry as the non-participating ammunition to assassinate him.

It didn't take Reed long to find the source of the material that had been fed to Cockburn. None other than the Jerry Rubin of the Arkansas Committee—Mark Swaney. Terry's earlier suspicions about Swaney were right. He was articulating someone else's agenda. The saboteur had even been paid by *The Nation* to research and piece together the various facets of Terry's story, all for $1,500, he was told. Terry and Janis had spent more than that in telephone charges while shopping for an attorney. The whole complexion of their case was now changing for $1,500. It was time to rethink their strategy, Terry concluded.

On February 23rd, a Sunday morning, Terry had gotten up early in order to watch one of his favorite shows, *Sunday Today*. He had special interest in watching this particular segment since Garrick Utley was hosting a 90 minute special on BCCI, the Bank of Credit and Commerce International.[12]

As the BCCI scandal unraveled over the years Terry had maintained a keen interest, always suspecting that the illegal money trail the investigators were following would eventually take them to Arkansas. Terry had not really been part of the "green flights" in Arkansas that Seal had been in charge of, but he figured sooner or later massive amounts of cash deposits would show up in the Arkansas bond or banking business.

Again, while working on a very limited discovery budget, he and Hall were hoping something major would happen to blow the whole Mena scandal wide open. If it was ever going to happen, they figured, it would have to happen now, with so many independent investigations still probing into not only Iran-Contra, but now BCCI money, which had trails into the Arkansas financial community as well.

With great interest and a note pad in hand, Terry watched the NBC special as Utley and guests described "the biggest fraud in the history of banking—

perhaps the biggest fraud in history, period. Billions of dollars—at least 8, perhaps 10 or 12, even more were taken, stolen, were gone."

How could that be, Terry thought? You simply don't hide 8 to 12 billion dollars. And the CIA was already being implicated in the scandal. He bet he knew where part of it was. Invested in Arkansas! With Seal's operation flying in the cash...the paper trail had been broken! There would be no record of wire transfers etc. to track...it all made sense!

That's what had been discussed in the bunker in Little Rock! The Agency was somehow involved in all these "lost funds" and Clinton's bunch at ADFA had probably been caught skimming from the profits. The money wasn't lost...it was right under everybody's noses. It had been re-invested in America through the issuance of industrial and municipal bonds. It was a great scheme the more he thought about it. Maybe it took all this transfusion of cash, which was being stolen from around the world, to keep our American lifestyle afloat. Maybe what Garrick Utley was describing as the biggest banking fraud in history was actually Reganomics at work!

Terry wondered?

The TV special then touched on names like Clark Clifford, Robert Altman, Bert Lance, Jimmy Carter and First American Bank. Terry thought he remembered from his time in Little Rock that there was some kind of connection between Jackson Stephens of Stephens & Company, the largest investment banker in Arkansas, and First American. This was turning out to be a really interesting show.

Utley then introduced a guest that was reporting live from Burbank, Jonathan Beaty of TIME magazine. Beaty had become an expert on the scandal and in fact was actually single handedly responsible for overturning some of the rocks that hid the largest scoundrels found to date. If he kept turning them over in the right direction he might find a couple of the missing billion right there in the "Natural State."

Beaty began by stating, "I think that this, in the end, will be seen as a bigger cover-up than Watergate ever was." He went on to say, "...intelligence agencies from both the Eastern and Western worlds needed this bank."

Peter Truell of the *Wall Street Journal* was saying things like, "There are several dealings related to the bank which—which come home to the Bush family." And at one point Truell said, "Everybody is trying to distance themselves from BCCI—from the tainted scandal."

Brian Ross, an NBC journalist, said, "It's frustrating because there are limits to what journalists can do. We can't subpoena records. We can't subpoena people to come. We can't compel them to testify. It's very frustrating."

Utley closed with a personal appeal, "If there is silence, indifference, BCCI will be forgotten, and many people will breathe easier and sleep better. But if the public demands a public accounting, government will react. In the end, the choice is to stay silent or speak up."

This was amazing, Terry thought. Here was the media appealing for help in order to continue an investigation that the Justice Department should be pursuing. That statement about the Bush family probably had something to do with why the Justice Department wasn't interested in BCCI. And Terry knew that if his suspicions were correct and that Seal's airborne deliveries were linked to the missing BCCI funds, then a thorough investigation would not only expose the CIA's involvement, but would lead right up the steps of the Arkansas State Capitol building as well. Probably right into Bob Nash's office.

And from there into ADFA.

And from there into the Arkansas investment banking and bond business.

And from there, into the pockets of some mighty important people.

Was this why Seal was killed? he wondered.

Terry sat there on his sofa and tried to absorb it all. He had definitely been involved in a lot more than training Contra pilots. The Agency and Clinton probably figure he knows all the details of everything that happened during "Centaur Rose," since he not only became friendly with Seal, but had been forced to assume Aki Sawahata's duties for a while as well.

No wonder Clinton had invited him out of Arkansas back in 1986. It was starting to fully impact him for the first time. He is truly a living liability to a lot of people. He knows too much!

That BCCI special had brought nearly everything into perspective. There was still, however, a missing piece to the puzzle. In order to contain a scandal of this magnitude, someone high up in the Justice Department would have to be running interference, for not only the Bush Administration, but for the Arkansas State Government as well.

Terry thought back to the Camp Robinson bunker meeting. From that night on he knew that the Republicans and the Democrats worked together on projects that were beneficial to the CIA's objectives. It was demonstratively clear that the CIA had compromised both parties. That's why there had been no real outcry about Iran-Contra by any of the Democratic candidates. It was appearing that Iran Contra wasn't even going to be an issue for the 1992 election. George Bush and Bill Clinton, if he were to become the Democratic candidate, would certainly not be able to sling mud at each other over Mena...that's for sure, he thought. It certainly was interesting to observe a presidential race in the making while possessing all the inside knowledge he had in his head. Watching them all maneuver, wishing they could annihilate each other, but not being able to because they're all compromised.

But what was really bothering him was wondering who in the Justice Department had been compromised in order for the CIA to be assured there would be no real BCCI investigation. He was thinking about Felix Rodriguez' comments about getting to the prosecutor. That would probably have taken someone in Justice to do that. And then what about the night in the bunker? In that meeting, there had been discussion of controlling the U.S. Attorneys in Arkansas in order to contain Mena and other things as well. He was rehashing Felix Rodriguez' comments about getting to the prosecutor when it **HIT HIM**!

"Shit! That's it! Johnson! *Who and where is Johnson?*" he said out loud, startling Janis who was now sipping coffee beside him. "That's it!" he again exclaimed.

He could now account for the true identity of everyone of importance in the bunker that night with the exception of Johnson. Cathey was North, Gomez was Rodriguez, Sawahata was...well he figured Sawahata wasn't his real name, but that wasn't important. Aki had never behaved like an attorney, and Johnson had.

Johnson had not only said he was an attorney and talked like one, but he had been in charge that night in the bunker. He said Casey had sent him and he was the one who shouted down Clinton that night. OK! That's solved! It's

Johnson, he decided. But how does he find Johnson? Marilyn Trubey and Joe Dunlap spent months trying to find him. Even the law firm in Miami that represented ABC in the case with SAT, they looked for Johnson. No one could find him.

But wait a minute! Robin Fowler, the "yuppie prosecutor" in Wichita, strongly implied that he had found him! He had even made mention of him during the CIPA hearing!

He ran to retrieve the CIPA transcript. There it was on page 5, lines 16-23 ...[Classified] "information potentially that would be brought out on direct or cross [examination] particularly that of Oliver North, Jack Bloom, (sic) and _Robert Johnson_, particularly there's concern for information that the Director of the C.I.A. has been ordered to produce..."[13]

"There it is in black and white," he yelled to Janis. "Fowler found Robert Johnson and he was concerned about his testimony being classified."

As Terry re-read the entire CIPA transcript he became more and more convinced that Robert Johnson was the door to the "black abyss." His name was separated from reference to the Director of the CIA by only 7 printed words.

While coming down from his near euphoric state, Terry realized there was still the problem of physically locating Johnson. Even though it appeared Fowler had interviewed Johnson, he probably would not be to helpful in locating him, Terry speculated. After all, it was Reed's case that had cost Fowler his career in criminal justice.

He was at a mental dead end when a possible solution came to him. Jonathan Beaty! It was Beaty who had sat in the park in Truth or Consequences, New Mexico, and talked of meeting Johnson down at SAT's offices in Miami. That's it, Beaty holds the key to the door.

And besides holding the key to locating Johnson and determining his true identity, Beaty held something else he needed. Investigative resources. John Hall was already complaining at how expensive this case could turn out to be. Terry had something Beaty and everyone else in the investigative world needed...information. First hand information. That had to have value. Maybe he could trade his information to Beaty for his help.

That afternoon Terry was able to locate his old acquaintance Beaty by phone who maintained a residence in the L.A. area. It had been a while since they last spoke but Beaty projected friendliness on the phone so Terry got right to the point.

"Jonathan, I just watched you on Utley's special. We need to get together soon," Terry suggested. "I think I know where a lot of the missing BCCI money ended up. Maybe we can help each other."

A couple of days later, and with Hall's permission, Terry met with Beaty in his oceanside home in Hermosa Beach. They then drove to a favorite bar of Beaty's to discuss how they could perhaps quietly help each other. Terry outlined where he thought some of the missing BCCI money had ended up and Beaty was quick to catch on to the genius of the Agency's plan. Their available time to spend together that day was short, but each departed on an upbeat note agreeing there were grounds to proceed with their newly-developed plan.

The plan, in essence, was for Terry to be debriefed in detail later by Beaty about the money aspects of his knowledge. Beaty, then armed with Reed's information, would direct a TIME magazine backed investigation into areas Reed led them. Beaty was fully aware where the trail might lead and by the expression on his face, the realization excited him.

TIME magazine would in essence bear the cost of the expedition since it had the resources and access to a grand jury. Terry would be the guide and point out which rocks to turn over and John Hall would be in charge of capturing what ever scurried out from under them. Beaty, in return, would get the story and the necessary ammunition to feed to a sitting grand jury in New York.

"Poor man's way to expensive discovery," is the way Terry described it.

John Hall had already made it clear to Terry that if he and Beaty were able to work something out that he wanted to be present for the interview. This way Hall would be assured the debriefing did not venture over into areas that might endanger the Little Rock civil case. So the first meeting was terminated with a plan to get together in Hall's presence. There was just one more pressing issue...Robert Johnson.

"Jonathan, on our first meeting in T or C you said you had talked to a man by the name of Robert Johnson who was my contact at SAT. Do you remember that?" Terry questioned.

Beaty came across very vague about the whole issue. This confused Reed since he had grown to appreciate Beaty's mind from the times they had spent together earlier. This was odd, Terry thought, but decided not to press the subject for now. He didn't want to share the significance he was placing on Johnson's role in all this with Beaty, not just yet anyway. It would be better to wait and bring up the subject again in John Hall's presence. But he left the oceanside meeting somewhat confused by Beaty's reaction to the Johnson issue.

Back in Little Rock John Hall was having to nearly take his telephone off the hook in order to get any work done. The encamped media was continuously calling, desperate to interview Reed as a result of his new found publicity, courtesy of *The Nation* and Mark Swaney.

Hall had come to the realization that Reed's story was going to be told with or without his input. Hall said he didn't like giving this advice, but since the story was already in the media perhaps Terry should be talking to a reputable network or show. In that way, Hall deduced, the publicity could be better controlled in their favor. Hall had been turning reporters away in numbers but when he received a call from ABC's *Prime Time Live*, he figured he'd better pass that one along to Terry in California.

Seated in a restaurant in the San Fernando Valley talking with Scott Shugar, a producer from *Prime Time Live*, Terry was getting good vibes about this guy. The clean cut, unpretentious man in his early thirties and wearing a khaki safari jacket was asking all the right questions and saying nothing stupid.

They had been there the better part of the afternoon in order to "sniff things out" and see if they could come to some sort of agreement about a *Prime Time Live* special Shugar was working on. It was tentatively titled "Covert Activity In Arkansas."

Terry had identified the reason he was getting along with Shugar was because he too had spent time in naval intelligence. He told Reed he had been in the U.S. Navy and his intelligence duties had put him into areas involving advanced weapons technology. Considering Terry's Air Force duty with Task Force Alpha this gave them common footing from which to build their relationship.

Shugar, he would find, was well known and respected in the world of journalism for his work on the Stealth Bomber project. He was the investigative journalist who had discovered and first reported that the Stealth bomber wasn't! Government test reports had been doctored to show the craft as being much more invisible to enemy radar than it actually was. His probing was detailed in an article it the *Washington Monthly* in 1991 entitled: "The Stealth bomber story you haven't heard; it doesn't work, and it'll probably crash."

Subsequently, in the summer of 1991, Shugar had been responsible for a *Prime Time Live* television special about the deceit surrounding the Stealth, and for his efforts he was nominated for an Emmy in 1992.

Prior to having the meeting, Hall had largely defined the conditions to which Shugar would have to agree in order to get Reed's cooperation. Shugar was planning to put together an hour-long special on intelligence activities centered in Arkansas. Hall had tentatively agreed to allow Terry to appear, provided he and his story were no more than 25 percent of the show. That way, Hall said, Shugar would be forced to thoroughly investigate the Mena Affair and would hopefully dig up information that would corroborate CIA involvement there, as well as other evidence beneficial to their case.

Shugar was way ahead on meeting Hall's requirement. As they sat and drank iced tea, Shugar was telling Reed some very exciting news. He said he had already located an Ex-Air Force Captain who had headed up a secret ground team whose job it was to help guide the black operation planes, which Reed knew were codenamed "Dodger", in and out of the U.S. to avoid radar detection. In fact, Shugar said, this was the person who originally directed his attention to Arkansas in the first place, and specifically to Mena! If this guy was authentic—and Shugar said his source already had passed a lie-detector test— it could prove that operation "Centaur Rose" was definitely government-backed and sponsored.

But then it got even better! Shugar said he had also found another man, living in Florida, who had performed "BLINDING SERVICES" for these black ops flights by turning off elements of the Defense Department Satellite Warning System orbiting in outer space. Visions of Barry Seal and him "flying on the darkside" flashed into his mind.

And Shugar had already found another pilot who claimed to have flown Agency flights that had penetrated America's electronic security fence without triggering an armed response. This man had even retained his CIA-supplied maps, charts, aircraft call signs, radio frequencies, etc., and had been authenticated to Shugar by then-United States Senator, Gary Hart (D-Colorado), as being "the real McCoy."

By Shugar going after the technical aspects of operation "Sea Spray" he would undoubtedly prove how all the "Screw Worm" flights were able to come and go without alerting our coastal defense system. All he needed now was for Reed to "come clean" and talk about the WHO'S involved in the operations. Shugar had already solved the HOW'S, it sounded like.

What a break, Reed thought! He'd make it to court yet. And by the time he and Hall get through putting on all the discovery evidence they had attained through *Prime Time Live* and TIME magazine, surely the world would acknowledge that the CIA operations at Mena were not only real...but were one of the best kept secrets of the century.

But he hadn't factored in Strobe Talbott and Richard Behar!

Strobe Talbott is an old schoolmate and personal friend of Bill Clinton. Not only are they both Rhodes Scholars and Oxford classmates, they lived together while being schooled in England. Since graduating from the world of academia, Talbott had worked his way up the editorial ladder at TIME magazine and, in the spring of 1992, held one of the coveted top slots, EDITOR AT LARGE. Talbott's forte, for TIME, was covering and writing about political events that shape the world's future.

Richard Behar, on the other hand, was not a Rhodes Scholar, nor a graduate of Oxford, and had not roomed with Clinton. He was simply an associate editor with Time. His claim to fame with the magazine, during the time of his first meeting with Reed, was the cover story he had written for the May 6, 1991, issue attacking the Church of Scientology. The church would later reward him and the magazine with a $416,000,000 libel suit for what the church said were Behar's savage and vindictive reporting techniques.

Beaty had been unable to get back immediately with Terry, citing a pressing writing schedule related to his soon-to-be published book on the BCCI scandal. In his stead, he had sent Behar to the meeting that was to take place in Hall's presence, a pre-established condition.

As Behar and Reed sat in the coffee shop of the Reno, Nevada, airport awaiting Hall's plane, which was weather delayed, the two men just chatted and sized each other up. Terry had earlier picked Behar out of the crowd of deplaning passengers arriving from New York, identifying him from his earlier self-description.

But as they sat and talked Terry kept wondering why Behar likened himself to the comic book character of Superman as portrayed by Christopher Reeves. Maybe, he thought, it came from the old "mild mannered reporter" verse written for the original TV series, because sitting there with his crooked front teeth, he bore very little resemblance. Terry would not have recognized him at all, had it not been for his long black coat, which he said he would be wearing, looking humorously out of place in Reno. The coat had another purpose, Terry would later discover. It concealed Behar's secret tape recording gear, which is illegal to use in Nevada.

Reed was expecting Beaty to send someone more seasoned. He had earlier described Behar as a "task force leader" but Terry was looking at a man who appeared to be in his early 30's and, after and hour's discussion, seemed to lack any in-depth knowledge of the world of intelligence. He was wishing Beaty had come. He didn't have time to baby-sit junior reporters and get them up to speed on the inter-workings of the CIA. When Reed challenged him on his seeming lack of experience and youthful attitude, he responded by saying, "I may be young, but I have an old soul."

So as they chatted and waited for Hall, Behar was reading from his hurriedly constructed notes he had made earlier as a result of Beaty's briefing. Reed listened intently, calling Behar's attention to mistakes he had made in his notes about Reed's criminal proceedings in Wichita.

"No, my case was not dismissed," Reed corrected him. "I was acquitted."

It was near midnight by the time Hall's flight arrived. Behar was just putting the final touches on his rendition of some of his earlier reporting of which he was most proud. He had described in great detail, and seeming enjoyment, the "hatchet job" he had done on the Jordache family of blue jean fame. He went on to say that a fellow journalist he had worked with, Christopher Byron, had also covered the story was now trying to get a book published on the Jordache affair.

Behar said he was going to muddy the water in the publishing world in order to prevent his old partner from getting it published. Quite a vindictive man, Reed thought. "I'm glad he's not after me," would flit through his mind.

Hall's flight was so late that the meeting was postponed until the next day. Per Hall's suggestion, the three men then rendezvoused at Hall's hotel in Lake Tahoe, California, where Hall had come to attend a legal seminar. In Hall's room, they got down to the business for which they'd come.

In their off-the-record conversation, Terry went through the money aspects of the Mena Connection, as he understood them. Behar sat in a chair by the window with Hall taking up a position on the bed, for the rather brief private discussion. Reed outlined the key players in the Arkansas black money loop and described in detail the mechanics of it all from the inside knowledge he had attained between the years 1984 through 1986.

Behar was quick to focus on the aspects of ADFA's possible involvement in money laundering and even could see the possible trail between the Arkansas investment banking industry, the bond business and BCCI. But of greater interest to him was the possible political fallout that could definitely have an adverse affect on Bill Clinton's bid for the Presidency. Hall and Reed made it perfectly clear to Behar that they had no axe to grind with Clinton and that Reed was only giving him the inside story on Arkansas finances so that TIME could throw their resources into the investigation.

At the meetings end, Hall felt it best for Behar to travel back to L.A. with Reed so that he could review key court document that Terry and Janis had meticulously maintained there. Some of these documents, Behar was told, were not part of the public record from Reed's trial in Wichita, since some had been sealed by the court after the Government invoked National Security. These, Behar agreed, would go a long way toward establishing Reed's credibility.

The two men then set out on a late afternoon flight from Reno to Burbank, California. From there Terry arranged lodging for Behar at a motel in Simi Valley which was overflowing with reporters who were staked out awaiting the verdict of the Rodney King beating trial that was in progress there. During check in, when Behar realized why the motel was so crowded, he said to the female desk clerk with a grin, "If I'd remembered about the King trial being here, I would have brought my golf clubs." She didn't laugh.

Saturday morning, Behar was to rendezvous at the Reed residence in order to inspect their documents. Terry had lowered his guard and even entrusted Behar with his home address and phone number in Moorpark. It was ridiculous to be paranoid and overly protective with a person who was out to help them, he thought.

Saturday afternoon, March 8th, about three hours late, Behar arrived. He apologized for his tardiness claiming an intestinal disorder had delayed him. In the Reed's living room Janis, Terry and Behar got down to business. They gleaned through the mammoth amount of files with Behar flagging the ones he wanted copies of...with John Hall's permission.

The two men talked into the afternoon about Behar's planned investigative trip to Arkansas, while Janis took files and documents to a copy center for duplication. She return with 338 duplicated pages and a bill for $29.92, which Behar gladly paid.

Terry felt it necessary to implement one precaution before giving the papers to Behar. He felt it best to send them to Hall's office in Little Rock via Federal Express later that day. In that way, he said, Hall could make the final determination on each document, before releasing them to Behar. It was agreed that Behar would go to Hall's office on Monday the 9th to review them with Hall. Behar then departed for Little Rock.

Reed's first telephone conversation with Behar after he arrived in Little Rock was to report he was staying at the Capitol Hotel. He gave Reed his room number and said he had the documents in his possession that Reed had sent to Hall. He was outlining his snooping itinerary with Reed for the next couple of days when Terry got the uneasy feeling that Behar was now modifying their game plan.

"You're not planning on just charging into ADFA and questioning Bob Nash about all this stuff, are you? "Terry questioned in disbelief. "I don't think that's the style of investigating Hall had in mind."

Behar informed Reed that he had already discussed the plan with Hall and that he had been given a green light to proceed. This didn't make much sense to Terry. That would be the equivalent of charging into the White House right after the Watergate burglary and demanding Richard Nixon to 'fess up.

"If Richard Behar had been Woodward or Bernstein, he would have published Deep Throat's true identity on the front page of the *Washington Post* and called him a liar," Terry sniped to Janis out of frustration over Behar's approach.

But Behar insisted that this was the only way to proceed. *He said he had to break the story first.* Since his arrival he had met with Bill Duncan who had secretly supplied him with portions of the Arkansas State Attorney General's documentation that had been sent to Independent Counsel Lawrence Walsh's office. The three-inch thick file Duncan slipped him contained some of the sensitive information that Reed was unsuccessfully trying to gain access to in federal court.

If that wasn't enough to corroborate portions of Reed's Mena story and light Behar's investigative afterburner, he had also secretly zeroed in on a self-appointed watchdog of the Arkansas bond business, a man named Roy Drew.

Drew was about Reed's age, a self-employed financial consultant and a man who was making enemies of some of the biggest and most powerful names in financial circles in Arkansas. When he met with Behar he had spent over 15 years in Little Rock's investment banking industry having worked for Merrill Lynch, Stephens Inc., and E.F. Hutton.

But after becoming self-employed, Drew had decided to take aim at the incestuous relationships between Arkansas Banks, the Arkansas bond industry, Arkansas bond lawyers, Arkansas Development Finance Authority and Governor Clinton. Drew had written several newspaper articles, which much to the chagrin of people like Jackson Stephens, detailed the immense profiteering taking place at taxpayer expense.* This was the result, Drew pointed out, of

---

*   In a guest column in the *Arkansas Democrat* dated June 7, 1988, Drew outlined what he referred to as "The Mushroom Theory" that exposed behind-the-scenes profiteering between Arkansas investment banking firms, lawyers and state agencies. He deftly noted that the fees added on for "services" rendered by subcontractors for the bond issue swelled the ultimate price by millions of dollars. This was his theory, "mush-

(see next page)

sweet heart deals and lack of true outsider oversight, considering the boards of the banks, the bond houses, the law firms and ADFA, shared the same men.

Behar had sought out Drew to serve as a financial consultant to TIME as he explored the money trails that Reed had described to him on the West coast. Drew had not only agreed to work with TIME, but had provided Behar with financial documentation that would help support Reed's private allegations about money laundering in Arkansas.

From all of this new-found information, combined with the media frenzy developing around the Mena story, Behar was telling Reed that the story was getting ready to break. And in light of the burgeoning media population that was present there, he probably was fearful it was going to break without him in the pilot's seat.

He wanted to be the first to attack the money end of the scandal, he said.

So much for the plan to quietly develop data and send it to the grand jury in New York.

Behar's behavior was reminding Reed of the story about the old bull and the young bull. In the story the inexperienced, overly energetic young bull was anxious to "run down the hill and service one" of the grazing heifers. The experienced, seasoned, calculating old bull said to the upstart; "Hold on son. Wait a minute. Let's walk down there and service them all."

Never, he thought, was the story more fitting. Behar was about to "run" into ADFA and blow the whole investigation. This surely would only send Bob Nash and the others underground and "scurrying to their shredders," now forewarned by such amateurish behavior.

Terry felt helpless, trapped in L.A. while a junior reporter was on the loose in Arkansas armed with his most sensitive information. Strangely enough, John Hall seemed to be going along with it all. It appeared as if he was "getting his jollies" by siccing his new found bulldog Behar onto the money establishment of Arkansas.

Reed could stand the isolation no longer and was scheduling his own flight to Arkansas in hopes of cutting Behar off at the pass when he heard the bad news.

Behar had already charged into ADFA and demanded that Bob Nash "come clean" on all the state's funny money business.

Armed with only his TIME magazine business card and wild accusations, he had put Nash and ADFA counsel Bill Wilson on notice that he knew the truth about what was going on there. Of course, he didn't know that Bill Wilson was among Bill Clinton's best friends and wasn't going to just cave in and spill his guts just because some Yankee reporter from TIME magazine was waving his business card at them.

So after Nash and Wilson did the honorable and logical thing to protect themselves and their political cohorts, by denying any wrongdoing, Behar retreated to his hotel room to plan his next assault.

> rooms are raised by being kept in the dark by the farmer and fed plenty of manure. From what I can see... this is the same system that certain legislators, the governor, a Little Rock investment banker and their lobbyists, and some bond lawyers have been using...and it has been quite successful. I'm a little confused about the governor [Clinton]. I have not been able to figure out whether he is administering the manure in order to find 'deep pockets' to finance his campaign or is he is just another mushroom who is being prepared for harvest."

A confrontation! *That* would get to the bottom of things, Behar suggested to Reed. First, he proposed a conference call to take place between Reed and Nash and he could "listen in." Nash initially agreed to the concept of a long distance confrontation, but then backed out.

Behar next proposed to have Terry flown into Arkansas to confront Nash in his presence. Nash would surely crack under such tremendous pressure and he could scoop the story since he would be sitting there listening to Nash's secretly taped confession, Behar argued.

John Hall demonstrated some constraint and nixed that idea, telling Reed by phone that such confrontational behavior could back-fire and only serve as a "rehearsal" for Nash's court appearance. But Behar wasn't through.

A polygraph! That would get to the bottom of things. He would challenge Nash to a polygraph test. He would wire up Reed and Nash in sort of an electronic duel. That would flush out the truth.

Terry, with John Hall's permission, agreed to take the test. TIME magazine agreed to have the test administered to Reed on the West Coast by a retired FBI polygraph examiner who did contract work for the magazine. Nash initially agreed to take the lie-detector test provided Reed took the test first. Terry again agreed to Nash's terms. But a short while later, Behar informed Reed that Nash had reneged on his agreement to take the test, doing so on advice of ADFA counsel Bill Wilson. The following morning, Nash abruptly left Arkansas on unexplained business and remained unavailable for the remainder of Behar's week in Little Rock.

"Well, Nash suddenly vanished." Behar informed Hall, while he covertly tape recorded the attorney.*

"Where to?", Hall asked.

"He's in Detroit...I left a message on Friday on his machine saying, I'm ready to move forward, I got Terry flying out here, come on."

"What, and he disappeared?", an astonished Hall shot back.

"And he left a message saying, I'll [Nash] be in Wednesday. He's in Detroit," an equally baffled Behar informed.

Reed was still waiting to hear where and when to report for the polygraph when John Hall called to report he had been contacted by Ron Brown, the Chairman of the Democratic National Committee.

It was March 12th, 1992, and it had been one hell of a week for the Reeds. But the next two would be even more exciting, only they didn't know it. Terry was listening to the details of John Hall's conversation with Ron Brown. Hall seemed somehow honored to have spoken with the man and his instructions were simple: Go home and decide how much money you would accept as a settlement.

Reed and Hall had never even discussed an amount of money that the Reeds would consider equitable to trade for the last four years of their life. He was telling Terry to put a pencil to the problem and to have a number ready for him the next day because he felt "a settlement offer was in the making." He said Brown had wanted to know how the Reed case might affect Clinton's chances at the Presidency.

---

*   Transcripts of portions of Richard Behar's tape recorded interviews were obtained
      through court discovery in Terry Reed's libel suit filed against Behar and TIME maga-
      zine.[14]

In that same conversation, Hall claimed that the Arkansas Legislature, for unknown reasons and through no request by Clinton, had mysteriously increased an emergency contingency fund that the governor could use on his own initiative. Hall said he suspected that perhaps this fund was being increased so it could be used to fund a settlement for Reed.

A settlement offer was something Terry and Janis had never planned for. All along they were just being driven by the desire to do the right thing. To fight back! To correct wrongs done them! Steve Clark and many other prospective attorneys had warned them from the onset that there "just wasn't much money in civil-rights litigation and defending the Constitution."

Even though the Reeds hadn't dwelled on the thought of a settlement offer, it had been on Clark's mind at least six months earlier. In a background conversation with John Cummings on September, 9, 1991, Clark expressed the opinion that any money for an out-of-court settlement paid by the State would be "reimbursed" by the federal government since it was after all Washington's dirty laundry that would be kept hidden. "Somehow, I would think, a way will be found to pass that money along without drawing attention to it," Clark said. "The government is always funnelling money to states for all kinds of things."

"We're not in this for the money!" Janis shouted that night when he told her about Hall's instructions. "How can money fix what has happened to us. They can't buy our silence! It's not for sale!"

Janis was not only angered at the whole damn system of justice in this country, but she was upset by Hall not informing her of why he had wanted to urgently contact Terry that day. She's the one who had relayed the instructions from Hall for Terry to contact him. Hall, she felt, should have informed her about the Ron Brown conversation.

She didn't appreciate being considered unworthy of consultation on such an important issue. After all she argued, this injustice had happened to her too, and she was co-plaintiff in the case.

They sat up late that night discussing their alternatives. Finally, the decision was made. Janis went to the type typewriter and wrote a letter to Hall dated March 13, 1992 that read in part as follows:

Dear John:
As a co-plaintiff in this case who is normally overlooked, I would like to go on the record officially with you regarding the possibility of a future settlement.
...I can't express sufficiently in words the emotion I feel when it comes to this case and the grief it has caused my family.
...But please don't think of me as a happy homemaker who wants to take the money and run so I can get on with my life and bake cookies for the PTA meetings. This has affected my life permanently and I realize I am just one person out there who has been unjustly treated. Are we supposed to accept the fact that cops lie and it's OK? ...if we don't take them to court, they will have gotten away with this and be free to continue their pursuit of corruption and deceit. I would like to continue approaching this case knowing we will see these guys in court. I am concerned that Rich [Behar] is alerting so many people to this that they will have time to contemplate their responses. I would much rather see the witnesses involved perjuring themselves under oath rather than just practicing their

lies with Rich or other reporters. I am not so naive as to expect them to tell the truth. As we know, most of these guys are pros. I feel like the easy way out would be a settlement. If we do this, my idealist senses say justice was not served. Someone has to take a stand. I am prepared to see this all the way through.

With this letter now written and sent to Hall, the Reeds probably became the largest threat to Bill Clinton's candidacy. It's real hard to deal with people that have values and can't be bought off. They require special treatment...

Coupled with all this talk about a settlement was Hall's disclosure to Terry that the United States Secret Service had contacted the attorney for background information on the Reed v. Young et al. case and on Terry Reed personally. Hall told Terry that he viewed this clandestine activity as the possible start of a secret line of communication between his law firm and Clinton, who, as a Presidential candidate, now had Secret Service protection.

So Terry was standing there on March 26th, 1992, listening into the pay phone in California as Richard Behar, safely separated by 3,000 miles, was calling Reed a con-man as he surreptitiously recorded the conversation. Terry had to come clean and turn over all his evidence, Behar was demanding, or Terry would be destroyed.

"Are you prepared to do that?" Behar challenged.

"I'm prepared to tell you, you better talk to John Hall. I'm prepared to tell you that you are probing into areas that I have purposely avoided so it'll come out in my civil litigation, if I ever get there [to court]. I have a September trial date," Reed responded.

"Terry, I am going to come out with some very, very, harsh conclusions about you."

"What, in TIME magazine?" Reed asked. Still in shock, he added, "Thanks a lot, Rich."

"Don't you think it's worthwhile to spend this time with me?"

"No, I don't. I don't feel I have to prove anything to you. If this is turning out to be a negative slam on me, you're going to set back my kind of litigation [civil-rights law suits] and what happened to me and Janis by a hundred years," Reed retorted, then dwelling for a second as the severity of Behar's threats impacted upon him.

Suddenly, realizing that Behar and TIME magazine had the ability to snuff out Janis and his hundreds of hours of effort to get their case to court, he added pensively, "I guess the power of the pen is mightier than the sword."

"There is evidence out there that you're a con man," Behar baited, probably referring to a "trash Reed file" provide him by private detective Tommy Baker, one of the defendants in Reed's civil-rights suit.

"That is not true!" Reed shot back.

"...Well. Fine. Why don't you -," Behar began to speak, but was then interrupted.

"Because this certainly wasn't how this started out," Reed reminded.

"Well, it wasn't how it started out, but it's certainly how it's going," Behar chided.

"So," Reed recapped. "You're going to write an article that will now be used against me in court."

"Well, I don't care," Behar answered. "I'm not interested in writing anything to be used for or against you."

This was certainly a reversal of the position Behar had originally taken when he came into Reed's life in Reno, Nevada. At that time he agreed to use TIME magazine's vast investigative resources to Reed's advantage, which was the only reason Reed had been willing to cooperate with Behar in the first place. Reed decided to remind Behar of the original intent of their collaboration.

"I thought you wanted to write an article about Jack Blum's coverup, about Lawrence Walsh's coverup," Reed said referring to an earlier conversation with Behar, in which Behar stated he felt there was strong evidence to prove Senator John Kerry's investigator, Jack Blum, had actually helped to stymie the Mena investigation.

Blum's job as Special Counsel to the Senate Committee on Foreign Relations was to not only provide investigative services to Kerry's Subcommittee on Terrorism, Narcotics and International Operations, he was to also funnel off pertinent leads he developed during the course of his investigation to Independent Counsel Lawrence Walsh's office, which was seeking indictments involving the Iran-Contra Affair. It was Blum who the Reeds had interviewed extensively with in Washington in 1988.

Behar had confided to Reed he felt Walsh, probably in concert with Blum, was indeed part of the Iran-Contra cover-up since Walsh's office had taken no action on Mena. Behar earlier cited the foundation for his suspicions stemmed from Walsh's lack of action on the preponderance of credible evidence provided directly to his office by federal, state and county law enforcement agencies, as well as the materials provided him by Arkansas Attorney General Winston Bryant and U.S. Congressman William Alexander concerning the activities at Mena.

Behar responded, completely reversing his earlier position on the Mena affair, "I'm not convinced there is a coverup."

* * *

Behar had made a complete turnabout, saying initially he believed there was a cover-up, and saying there wasn't. Why? In order to have come to the conclusion that he was still not convinced there had been a CIA operation at Mena and a subsequent coverup, one must put into perspective Behar's *own evidence* that he was willing to ignore and dismiss.

After his week in Arkansas (March 8th through 14th, 1992) and the subsequent telephone investigation he conducted after returning to New York, Behar was literally drowning in leads, conflicting accounts of critical events and experts willing to assist him in exposing the coverup. From court discovery obtained from Reed's federal libel suit against Behar and TIME, the following are excerpts from Behar's secretly-recorded interviews and telephone conversations during that time period.

As a result of Reed's off-the-record discussions concerning money laundering in Arkansas, Behar sought out the services of Roy Drew, a financial expert and former employee of Stephens, Inc., the largest investment banking firm in Little Rock. Behar was soliciting a professional opinion on the feasibility of the Clinton Administration's and other prominent Arkansans' involvement in these sordid money affairs.

DREW: Well I've been hired by the state. I've done due diligence on some bond issues. I've got a deal, an $85 million bond issue appealed back in 1989.

BEHAR: Who handled it, ADFA?

DREW: ADFA. But the Rose Law Firm (firm in which Hillary Clinton and Webb Hubbell practiced) and Stephens Incorporated and Beverly Enterprises and a whole bunch of folks were involved in. I worked for Stephens for a long time and I do know a lot about —

BEHAR: How big was that?

DREW: $85 million, $82 million.

BEHAR: Wow.

DREW: And they had done a deal exactly like it up in Iowa that last summer I appeared as an expert witness in. The exact similar case that got appealed here in Arkansas was done up in Iowa. That a judge ruled up there that it lacked any legitimate purpose and denied some tax exemptions for them and then called it a sham deal.

BEHAR: Who did it?

DREW: Well, it was, Stephens operated Beverly Enterprises nursing Homes, and were sold to a sham tax exempt operation controlled by a handpicked person of [the] Rose Law Firm and Stephens Incorporated...

BEHAR: ...When was it stopped in Arkansas?

DREW: It finally got killed in December of 1989 when the then-Attorney General of the state of Arkansas, Steve Clark [Reed's original attorney in the civil-rights lawsuit], accused the Stephens people of offering him a $100,000 bribe to remain neutral. All of this was going on while the Governor, Bill Clinton, [inaudible]—... (At this point in Behar's recording of the conversation, the tape conveniently becomes inaudible).

BEHAR: ...Are these [the Stephens group] bad guys?

DREW: Yes, they're real bad guys....Yeah, they're bad people. They're financial terrorists. They run the state. And Bill Clinton is the politician that makes it all go. That's the only reason he has been able to do that since 1980. He came in, he was a very ideological person in 1978, he lasted two years. And he got voted out of office because Stephens financed a guy named Frank White [former Governor] and he [Clinton] got religion.

BEHAR: You really think Stephens has that much power?

DREW: I don't think, I know. The conversation then shifted to a discussion of a $50 million bond issue involving Stephens and Clinton. Behar appeared to be getting confused from the details Drew was providing.

BEHAR: ...Well, let's try to keep it in —

DREW: There's no way to — hey, Bill Clinton is a very sophisticated person whose got very sophisticated advisors. This is a very sophisticated way that he has been able to gain money to run a campaign. He's been doing this since he was a teenager. It was very sophisticated because nobody like Boyd or Julie [state auditors] was supposed to be around to see through it. He [Clinton] has been milking, along with his conservators, for years, the retirement systems and the bonding systems and has gained a lot of friends from it. There is no simple way to approach it.

BEHAR: ...Okay, but what I need from you is just to spend about 20 minutes getting an overview.

DREW: I can't do it in 20 minutes. I can tell you, Bill Clinton has been mis-

managing the retirement systems and been putting money in people's pockets.

BEHAR: How is ADFA used?

DREW: Well, there's a number of ways that they can do it. I can show you one
that is in the process right now....I would suggest that you call me tomorrow.
I've been talking to reporters from the *Boston Globe*, from *The New York
Times*, and the *Wall Street Journal*, and the *Arkansas Gazette* today.

BEHAR: All today?

DREW: Yeah.

BEHAR: On this subject?

DREW: Yeah.

BEHAR: Wow.

DREW: Do you want to know Bill Clinton, and you want to know what's going
on? I mean it's sure not Gennifer Flowers.

BEHAR: I don't give a shit about her.

DREW: It's not that. But, I mean, this is the hard core...

DREW: ...You're going to run in - and I'm not lying. But I tell you what Richard, you're going to run in to some stone walls and some ruts without any
kind of back up...

BEHAR: ...Can I ask a couple of questions?

DREW: Certainly. I don't know that I'll answer them, but you can ask the
question.

BEHAR: Okay, are you familiar with Dan Lasater, (man who was handling the
deposits from Barry Seal's green flights, close associate of Bill Clinton and a
bond dealer who was convicted on cocaine charges as a result of Roger
Clinton's arrest).

DREW: Yes.

BEHAR: Do you have information about Dan and his operation?

DREW: Some.

BEHAR: In a nutshell, what is that.

DREW: I'm not going to tell you that.

BEHAR: Ever?

DREW: That's pretty sensitive...

BEHAR: ...I'm wondering if there has been some money laundering.

DREW: Through what?

BEHAR: Through ADFA.

DREW: *Hell, money's been laundered through the retirement system, it's all out
in the open, to Bill Clinton conservators.* It's not sexy enough for a guy [Lasater]
that's gone to prison on a dope deal. I know you guys got to sell newspapers
and I understand. I mean, he's [Clinton] laundered money through the retirement systems to a guy where he ain't gone to prison for a dope deal. I
know it looks better if you got a guy that the money was laundered through
from a dope deal...

BEHAR: ...Okay, and has it been laundered as well through ADFA?

DREW: Yeah.

BEHAR: And you can prove that? I don't know what we're going to be able to
get into...

DREW: Yes...I'm not interested in talking about Dan Lasater.

BEHAR: Okay, so we're not going to be able to get into Dan.

DREW: No, we're not going to talk about Dan Lasater.

BEHAR: Okay, let's leave that out. Are we going to talk about Mena?

DREW: *You're talking about the same thing...*

BEHAR: ...Now, most of what you have is laundering through the retirement system, or is it ADFA, or is it equal?

DREW: Both.

BEHAR: Both?

DREW: Both...

BEHAR: ...What about Bob Nash? (Clinton Administration's head of ADFA).

DREW: We can talk about him for awhile.

BEHAR: We can what?...

DREW: *...Hey look, Richard, this is some dangerous shit. I'm telling you.*

BEHAR: I know that. It's dangerous for me being here poking around.

DREW: Who have you interviewed?

BEHAR: I spent half a day with Bobby Nash.

DREW: Did he tell you anything?

BEHAR: Of course not.

DREW: He serves at the wheel of the government. I saw the guy threatened, I've got it on tape. He was threatened in a meeting by a white guy, to take him out in the alley and whip his ass.

BEHAR: This guy was going to take Nash out and whip his ass?

DREW: Right.

BEHAR: For what reason?

DREW: Because he wouldn't go along with a deal that he'd promised. And they invited him back. The Governor [Clinton] never said one word about it. You're talking about race relations, you think some pasty-face white guy comes up from Texas [Bruce Wallyer] and threatens to whip the ass of Bobby Nash on television in front of the reporters and the Governor doesn't say a word about it? Go figure.

And Bobby Nash doesn't come across the table and kill him? I mean, anybody - I mean, I thought Bobby Nash, you know, it was great restraint on his part...

BEHAR: ...Okay, can I ask you-

DREW: That's the kind of stuff that goes on and that's why Bobby Nash is not going to say anything.

BEHAR: Can I ask you one thing?

DREW: Yeah, sure.

BEHAR: The companies that received ADFA money, these small companies that get ADFA loans, are they all basically political favors?

DREW: *Yeah.*

That one conversation not only supported Reed's private allegations that Barry Seal's Mena black ops money was being run through Dan Lasater's firm and probably also the Stephens corporation as well, it also provided Behar with a totally independent and non-biased view from a financial expert, that money was allegedly being laundered through the state retirement system as well as ADFA. Something equally as important was Drew's assessment of Bob Nash as being a compromised individual who had been neutralized as a result of underhanded dealings. This too fit the profile Reed had provided Behar about Nash and ADFA, especially the information about making preferred loans to politically connected companies (POM and the other firms manufacturing the Agency's weapons parts).

Strangely, Behar never took Drew up on his offer to volunteer his expertise in proving fiscal wrongdoing in Arkansas. He chose instead to attack Reed's money allegations in the first paragraph of his slash-and-burn article and present them out of context and as an inconceivable myth.

Behar attempted to personally interview Wally Hall, the Little Rock sportswriter. It was Wally and his wife Cherryl who had dined with Terry and Janis the night Clinton forced the impromptu meeting outside of Juanita's Restaurant, where Clinton discussed Barry Seal's death with Reed.

During Behar's telephone questioning of Hall concerning his recollection of the events the night he dined with the Reeds, the following exchange was recorded:

BEHAR: I'm a writer for TIME. I've been here [Little Rock] for awhile and I'm covering a couple of things. I was hoping there might be a chance I might be able to get together with you, have a beer, and talk about something I'm certainly eager to talk about, even on a very deep off-the-record basis if we can do it.

HALL: What's it about?

BEHAR: Terry Reed.

HALL: ...But other than having dinner with them [the Reeds] 2 or 3 times, that was about the extent of our [relationship]...And I know very little about him other than he was a very intelligent person, very intelligent.

BEHAR: He's got a mind like a steel trap...Yeah, he's a pretty intense guy.

HALL: Yeah. I mean, I've kept up with this on-going story about his airplane and all that Oliver North stuff. But I would have no idea if that was true or not true.

BEHAR: You know what the one thing I need to know is...And again, it can be an off-the-record thing. He [Reed] talks about an incident happening in Juanitas where he was having dinner with you and Cherryl and Nash...

HALL: I really, Richard, I go to so many things ...that honestly, I mean, that could have happened...I can't say one way or the other...

BEHAR: ...Why don't we get together on Sunday...Let me buy you guys [the Halls] lunch here at the Capitol [Hotel], one o'clock Sunday...

HALL: ...You understand my concerns?

BEHAR: Absolutely. This is not exactly the lightest subject I'm bringing up.

HALL: We're not talking about basketball persons.

BEHAR: No.

HALL: *We're talking about government.*

BEHAR: I understand. This is rough stuff and it's very sensitive.

HALL: *And I do not want my family involved.*

Mysteriously, the Hall's cancelled the Little Rock luncheon scheduled with Behar to discuss the events of that night. Behar made no mention of this or the concerns expressed by Hall when he wrote in the TIME article that the Halls had never been to the restaurant with the Reeds. When Behar sought out Larry Nichols, a former employee of ADFA and the man fired from his job for making telephone calls to the Contras, at the expense of the state, Behar tapped into more dirt on Clinton than he had apparently bargained for. This probably explains why once again Behar's recordings have strategically placed gaps whenever Bill Clinton's name surfaces in extremely embarrassing and possibly incriminating ways. It is also interesting to note from the dialogue between the two men, it appears that Behar has recruited Nichols to lure and entrap some very prominent people into some very *compromising* conversations.

NICHOLS: Did you get the stuff I had delivered?

BEHAR: Yeah, just a couple of documents...Okay. You were supposed to come back here with tapes. (Nichol's tape- recorded conversations between himself, Clinton's Chief of Security Buddy Young, Clinton and others, concerning the on-going negotiations between Clinton and Nichols which were outlining the terms of getting Nichols to drop his lawsuit against Clinton for wrongful dismissal. Keep in mind, it was Larry Nichols who exposed the Gennifer Flowers scandal.)

NICHOLS: Right, that's what I was going to say. I'm meaning to come out there after she [Nichol's wife] gets back.

After the two men agree to meet later that night for a private meeting, the conversation leads into an area in which Nichols is alerting Behar of the intense media investigation into the Mena scandal, and the resulting articles being written.

BEHAR: ...Well, the one in *Nation* I think I'm aware of already....What was in the *[Boston] Globe*?

NICHOLS: Some story in the *Globe* was passing on information that the Arkansas traveler certificates that I had made up by Clinton to give Calero [Adolpho Calero, the head of the Contras] and Singlaub [Retired U.S. Army General and Contra fundraiser] were not on file, but yet everybody saw them get delivered. And he said it was quite, [sic] *Buddy [Young] says it connected him to Mena somehow.*

BEHAR: Who's him?

NICHOLS: Him, Buddy.

BEHAR: It connected Buddy?

NICHOLS: Buddy said - if I were Buddy, Buddy said, it connects me to Mena. What is this shit about?...I said, shit Buddy, I don't know.

BEHAR: What is it about?

NICHOLS: I mean, I don't know what is so sensitive to Buddy about that.

BEHAR: Well, nobody wants to be connected to Mena.

NICHOLS: Well, Buddy asked me if I had talked to anyone about his relationship with Mena. I said, yes, I did today at lunch.... I said to him [Buddy], you be sure and you call the Governor and you make sure he understands, with my little present that starting tomorrow, his world's turning to shit. And four weeks to the day from Sunday, he will be out of the governor's race, I mean the President's race.

BEHAR: Why four weeks?

(Tape fades out, conveniently)

BEHAR: You have this conversation on tape?

NICHOLS: Oh, no, no, no.

BEHAR: All right.

NICHOLS: Yours?

BEHAR: No, yours with Buddy.

NICHOLS: Oh, yeah, yeah. I thought you meant this conversation.

BEHAR: No, no, no, no. I'm talking about with Buddy,

NICHOLS: Oh, Yeah.

BEHAR: All right, Now, are you going to come over here with your other stuff?

NICHOLS: Yeah, you want me to come over after Kerry [wife] gets here, or is it too late? You want to do it in the morning?

BEHAR: No, let's do it tonight.

NICHOLS: What are your plans? Give me some clue. I know what my agenda is.

BEHAR: I have no plans until I see what you've got.

NICHOLS: Okay.

BEHAR: Remember I showed you at lunch, the distance on that *pen*. (A secret transmitter housed within a ball point pen, used for bugging a room.)

NICHOLS: Yeah.

BEHAR: You haven't moved it since I last saw you...I mean, you got your work cut out for you with me and, you know -

NICHOLS: What do you mean I got my work cut out for you in what way?

BEHAR: You've got to prove to me, you've got to show me what you've got that could concern him, first of all. And then you've got to bring me more of your taped conversations with Buddy and these people, if there are any others.

NICHOLS: Okay, number one, as I think I already told you, what I have that concerns them is, they are scared to death of me. I mean, they shouldn't be, but they are. They ought not be dealing with me. Something's got them - now, *I know, as you know, all the shit about it*. And I know which things are real because I heard them say it. I know who the women [women with whom Clinton had alleged extra-marital affairs] are that want to get the big money.

BEHAR: This is what I want to hear from you.

NICHOLS: ...You just need to calm down. Damn.

The following is from a follow-up, taped conversation which begins with a discussion of women Nichols alleges were involved with Clinton. By this time Behar was no doubt, feeling somewhat intimidated by the money laundering aspects of his investigation so apparently decided to focus on something he understood...infidelity.

BEHAR: Hello. Okay, Elizabeth Ward is a former Miss America. She's white, And the other woman is Lynn Cola Sullivan. She's black, former Miss America. They both live in Arkansas. No. [sic]

NICHOLS: One is in New York and one in California....

BEHAR: ...Now, you're not the only one with this information on Ward because -

NICHOLS: She's negotiating her own contract.

BEHAR: She's negotiating. Her lawyer in L.A., what's his name?

NICHOLS: Miles Levy.

BEHAR: And they're talking to newspapers. [sic]

NICHOLS: Talking to TV.

BEHAR: TV. What does she want?

NICHOLS: $250,000.

BEHAR: $250,000, that's right. She's been offered a hundred?

NICHOLS: She's been offered one and a quarter.

BEHAR: One and a quarter, by who?

NICHOLS: *Star*.

BEHAR: *The Star?*

NICHOLS: *Star Magazine* got it up to about 175. And then Gennifer Flowers went.

BEHAR: Flowers, okay.

NICHOLS: So then, *Star* didn't want to pay her that much money. So, then, when it looked like Clinton was losing in New Hampshire, they got in touch with me and said, could we get it back up to the 175 or 200 range again. I said, I don't know. I called Conafer [person not further identified]. Conafer said that they would be interested in talking to them, working towards a relationship. But then, Clinton lived through New Hampshire. And Miles Levy and all of them think that she's worth a lot more money if you consent to the—

BEHAR: ...Do you have any other information that you got from bugging? When you say you bugged the mansion, what did you actually do?...

NICHOLS: ...I had unique information sources that allowed me to hear and cover some strategies....

BEHAR: ...What else is there, drug use?

NICHOLS: There is a viable linkage to me, what I can get Adolpho Calero to say, and Clinton's relationship to them [the Contras]. I mean, I can make it too, I can present a case on the front that it would be inconceivable to believe the Governor didn't know about it.... Because if you don't have the element of Adolpho Calero, who's the absolute leader of the Contras, you see, you don't get the whole story.

BEHAR: Why would Calero come forward?

NICHOLS: Why would he not? I mean he's not being sued, he's not being tried, and he's a friend of mine. And all I need is just the proof. I just need the answers to the questions. I just need some help getting the questions that I need the answers to.

BEHAR: Has Calero already told you about Clinton's involvement with Mena?

NICHOLS: No. He has told me...that Mena was not a Contra feeder system.

BEHAR: Right.

NICHOLS: But he also said that there's no way that Clinton could not have been aware of the goings-on there since Calero, who didn't even live there, was aware of it. Now, Calero would, in Clinton's situation, going to become a hostile witness. Clinton will not be supported by Calero. The pieces of the puzzle at the Mena Airport fall apart because they sealed the files and got rid of all the players.

BEHAR: Right.

Behar's article in TIME made no mention of Adolpho Calero's comments, which were passed on by Nichols, nor is there any evidence that Behar took Nichols up on his later offer to arrange for Behar to conduct an interview with Calero in order to determine the depths of Arkansas' involvement in the CIA's Contra support operations.

The transcripts of Behar's taped interviews with: United States Congressman from Arkansas, William Alexander; Colonel Tommy Goodwin, Commander of the Arkansas State Police; Joe Hardegree, former Polk County Prosecutor (location of Mena); and Charles Black, former Deputy Prosecutor of Polk County—all seem to indicate Behar was convinced that there had not been sufficient funding to conduct a thorough investigation into the nefarious activities at Mena. He focused primarily on the elusive $25,000 of state funds that Clinton allegedly promised for state grand jury proceedings.

Probably the most credible evidence of a White House orchestrated cover-up of Mena came from Bill Alexander. And who should know better than a U.S. Congressman from Arkansas who was trying to gain access to intelligence information through the back door accounting channels offered him through the GAO (General Accounting Office).

BEHAR: ...Remember the GAO investigation in 1988?

ALEXANDER: Of what?

BEHAR: Mena.

ALEXANDER: Yeah. It wasn't just Mena, though, was it?

BEHAR: No, it wasn't just Mena...

ALEXANDER: ...But it included Mena as part of it and they stonewalled me.

BEHAR: That's right. Now, when that thing was stopped cold, is it accurate to say that the CIA and the State Department refused, on orders from the White House, to turn over Data? Is that accurate?

ALEXANDER: Let me think a minute about it. I've got a letter from GAO which I could share with you that says precisely what happened...[the letter says that the] National Security Counsel [N.S.C.] refused to participate, and ordered everybody else not to for security reasons. So, to the extent N.S.C. is part of the White House, that's correct.

BEHAR: Did they order—they are part of the White House.[sic]

ALEXANDER: Yeah, they are part of the White House. And you need to say N.S.C. because that says specifically what part of the White House ordered everyone to stop - they stonewalled me. They just said, none of your business.

BEHAR: Did they order it to the State Department, the CIA, how many different—

ALEXANDER: *Everybody across the board: Justice Department, CIA, Defense Department, everybody*. And I'll give you a copy of the letter if you want...I mean that's the kind of thing that really galls you when you're trying to find out what's going on.

BEHAR: And you get stonewalled.

ALEXANDER: And what they've done is thumb their nose at the Congress and the American people.

BEHAR: Right. Okay, second and last thing. Clinton, it's so cloudy, you know, his lack of interest. You know, he claims Arkansas did everything it can but it just doesn't seem that way. I remember you mentioned that you had asked for some support.

ALEXANDER: Well...I asked him [Clinton] to see the deputy prosecutor named Charles Black. And I said, Charlie Black is trying to see you about this Mena case, this Mena investigation that I have followed and I'm involved in. And I would encourage you [Clinton] to see him....

BEHAR: ...And you were trying to get federal money?

ALEXANDER: No. Charlie Black was trying to get state money for a grand jury investigation. And I asked him to help....you [Behar] ought to call him [Black].

BEHAR: Yeah, I spoke to him....He said that he hand delivered a letter to Clinton that didn't get an answer.

ALEXANDER: I see. Well, that was what I spoke to Clinton about.

BEHAR: But that's funny. In the newspapers in Arkansas in September, do you remember, Bill [Clinton] said that he'd made some attempt to get some money and then nothing ever happened with it. It was very odd...

ALEXANDER: ...Have you talked to Duncan? (Bill, former IRS investigator, then working for Arkansas Attorney General Winston Bryant).

BEHAR: Yeah....

ALEXANDER: ...What did he tell you?

BEHAR: You mean about his not being able to make phone calls?" (A reference to orders from Arkansas State Attorney General Winston Bryant that Duncan neither accepts nor places any phone calls related to Mena.)

ALEXANDER: Right.

BEHAR: Yeah. Something is going on over there [at the AG's office].

ALEXANDER: I just learned about this [about Duncan's gag order] this week....But did you talk to Duncan personally?

BEHAR: *Yes, of course....Yeah, I spent a lot of time with him.**

ALEXANDER: Because he [Duncan] couldn't talk to me over the phone....

BEHAR: ...Okay. Well, what Bill [Clinton] said to the press in September was, that he had authorized the state police to tell local officials that the state would help pay $25,000 for a grand jury but that nothing ever came of it.

ALEXANDER: I see.

BEHAR: But that's not true is it?

ALEXANDER: I don't know whether it is or is not. I know that there's been no grand jury investigation.

The reason Behar knew of Clinton's statement about the $25,000 still in question, was he had earlier interviewed the man who had approached Clinton for financial assistance to investigate Mena. His name is Charles Black.

BEHAR: ...I was interested in the Mena situation...And I just wanted to check something with you...the year that you hand delivered that letter [request for state assistance in investigating Mena] to Clinton asking for help was 1988?

BLACK: Yes, latter part of 1988...several of us had a meeting at the state police headquarters at Little Rock. Bill Alexander was there and Colonel Goodwin, the head of the state police and several others that had been involved in looking at this...And it was discussed whether I should go or would be willing to go ask him [Clinton] for any available state assistance...I did go and ask him [Clinton]. And he said that he'd check into it and get word back to me. I never heard from him again or never heard from anybody about it. But he's [Clinton] been quoted...as saying that he authorized Colonel Goodwin to communicate to us [county prosecutors office] the $25,000 was available. And I never got that word...

BEHAR: ...Right. Okay. But do you think in the end, he [Clinton] did as much as he could on the Mena situation or probably not? He's probably busy with other stuff.

BLACK: He [Clinton] probably could have. The only thing I could say is that he might have been a little more public about criticizing the way that that case [Mena investigation] was handled by the federal authorities.

BEHAR: Or trying to get a lot of state money together to do something.

BLACK: ...that's why I was going through him [Clinton].... I don't know if there was something else he could have done in that regard.

BEHAR: Well, if you were Governor you'd find a way.

---

*   Transcripts of conversations between Behar and Bill Duncan are being withheld from Reed in his Federal libel suit against Time and Behar on the grounds that Duncan is a "confidential source" of Behar's whose identity needs to be protected.

BLACK: ...It [Mena] was a situation tailor-made for handling by the federal-level authorities.

BEHAR: And tailor-made for covering up by them.

BLACK: Correct. Absolutely correct...I saw some well documented supported findings and requests that he [Bill Duncan] made in his investigation that certain people be indicted for CTR (money laundering) violations and perjury. And that information that he compiled, at substantial tax payers' expense, never was presented to the grand jury, federal grand jury, that were looking into it. Absolutely no reason or excuse. I don't think Duncan was ever subpoenaed to testify before the grand juries...I can't understand why Fitzhugh, that Assistant U.S. Attorney, didn't present that information to the grand jury...and it would have been very, very expensive.

BEHAR: ...Well, I'll tell you, this $25,000 that Alexander's gotten, that's about enough money to buy a big tarp that can cover up the coverup.

BLACK: ...that amount would have been tantamount to trying to extinguish a raging forest fire by spitting on it.

Behar then called Colonel Tommy Goodwin and questioned him about the elusive $25,000 that Black claimed to never have received.

BEHAR: ...Do you remember...Bill Clinton asked you to relay to local officials that there would be some money for a state grand jury probe?

GOODWIN: Of $25,000.

BEHAR: ...What ever happened? Did you ever relay that to the officials like Black?

GOODWIN: No, not Black...Hardegree, was the prosecuting attorney at that time. That is who I would have relayed it to...but [Hardegree] had denied anything about it...I know that Clinton told me that I could tell them [Polk County prosecutor's office] that he [Clinton] would furnish that amount of money for, to kind of defray the county cost of the grand jury.

BEHAR: But it never happened.

Behar at this point knew there had been a meeting in Little Rock in which Black had been dispatched to solicit aid from Clinton, but Black had received none. Yet, Colonel Goodwin, who was claiming to have been Clinton's messenger, was saying he personally communicated to Joe Hardegree, not Charles Black, that money was available.

It is difficult to believe that Hardegree and Black, two men who shared the same office and the same frustration that Polk County was undercapitalized and therefore unable to properly investigate Mena, did not communicate to each other that $25,000 of state money was available.

So Behar then telephoned Hardegree to get to the bottom of things. Colonel Tommy Goodwin, the Commander of the Arkansas State Police, had just told him that it was Hardegree to whom he had relayed the good news that funding was available forthwith.

BEHAR: ...Now, Clinton says that he made an offer to make some state money available for a grand jury probe to look into what the hell happened, and that he [Clinton] relayed that message to Goodwin. And Goodwin says that he called you and told you that the money is there if you want to do a state probe of this thing....

HARDEGREE: ...Oh, come on, Goodwin said that?

BEHAR: Yeah.

HARDEGREE: I'll tell you what...I cannot imagine him [Goodwin] saying something that is just false. But I have no recollection whatever of ever having had a telephone call from him regarding the subject in any way, and specifically no call about the $25,000 of funds for a grand jury investigation.

The taped conversation then later shifted to Hardegree's speculation as to what had actually gone on at Mena.

HARDEGREE:....It was simply that there was an indirect usage of the local facilities [Mena airport], maybe, in the political deal between the Reagan Administration and the Contras, and people working all over Central and South America and whatever else, I don't know....I never regarded it as remotely realistic to try to free up the federal grand jury. And, of course, I suspected all along that Reagan people were suppressing the local federal grand jury...and they certainly wouldn't help, wouldn't cooperate, and wouldn't do anything with the state grand jury investigation except block it, *subvert, suppress, obstruct, stonewall, and everything else.*

One can conclude, based upon Hardegree's firm response that he had never spoken to Goodwin about the funding, that Goodwin was lying to Behar. Yet, in his article, Behar made no mention of Goodwin giving the appearance of being willing to lie and white-wash the Mena scandal for his boss, Bill Clinton. And even more powerful were Hardegree's comments about grand jury tampering by the Reagan Administration, something else Behar deemed unworthy of mention.

And the person who most suffered the effects of this grand jury tampering was IRS investigator William C. Duncan, who had spent 10 years trying to unravel the Mena mystery.

Behar's investigation, on the other hand, involved spending one week in Little Rock, much of it in the Capitol Hotel, more than 130 miles from Mena. And yet Behar dismissed the results of Duncan's reams of reports and interviews documenting his years of probing behind the closely-guarded and protected money-laundering operation in Arkansas. At great personal and professional risk, because he had taken Behar into his complete confidence, Duncan went so far as to give Behar a portion of the key evidence provided by the Arkansas Attorney-General's office to Independent Counsel Lawrence Walsh in Washington.

Duncan, in a 1993 interview with the authors, said he had numerous discussions with Behar while he was in Little Rock, all of which Duncan thought was part of a serious journalistic investigation.

He now admits he learned the hard way that the media is not interested in anything "not served up on a silver platter."

"I feel personally betrayed by him [Behar]," Duncan said to the authors. Duncan likened to what happened in Mena as "complete breakdown of the judicial system." Yet, the only reference to Duncan, or the issue of the Justice Department's stonewalling its own investigation, in the entire TIME article was an allusion to "law enforcement officers [who] grumble that the case had been scuttled by higher-ups in Washington."

"I am disgusted and sickened by the entire media attitude," Duncan said, referring to the frenzy of media activity around the time of Behar's trip to

Little Rock and which only resulted in discrediting Duncan's 10 years of investigative work.

Duncan remains confused as to Behar's motives for nuking the Mena scandal and using TIME magazine's massive influence to sabotage the investigation. Especially so after Behar's telephone call to Duncan shortly after the article appeared. During the call, Duncan said, he "perceived Behar as sounding embarrassed...he sounded apologetic and used language to the effect he [Behar] had been under pressure to do a 'hatchet job' and had lost control of the article...and did not intend for the article to portray the issue the way it turned out."

Evidence of the quality with which Duncan had provided Behar required of a lot neutralizing. Back in New York, Behar set upon the search for tangible evidence to bolster his view that he was only dealing with a pack of liars. That pack included a U.S. representative, a 17-year veteran IRS criminal investigator, an Arkansas State criminal investigator, a county prosecutor and his deputy, a financial expert and a man who claimed to have "bugs" planted in the Arkansas governor's mansion. None of this mattered, obviously, as Behar zeroed in on his new found target, a man with 8 years of military intelligence experience and a veteran of three CIA black operations—Terry Reed.

Behar clearly set upon a course of rearranging the facts to fit his bias and then apparently wrote the article as he, or his bosses, saw fit. He then must have felt it necessary to perform some due diligence on the eve of his deadline for the article (March 27th, 1992) since he then contacted Oliver North for his comments on the developing Mena scandal. The powder-puff questioning of North by Behar signified that Behar was probably not wanting to disturb the "slant" his article had already taken.

The recorded telephone interview, which was placed through a conference call link-up with Nicole Seligman, one of North's attorneys from the firm of Williams and Connolly, listening on the line, sounds rehearsed. Behar had apparently provided questions to North prior to the interview and Behar's own words certainly set the stage for a get-to-the-bottom-of-things grilling.

BEHAR: I think this story is shaping into a story about a con man. That's what all the evidence indicates. But, basically, I thought it was useful to see if maybe there was a shred of truth, maybe he [North] had met him [Reed] or something or other, their paths crossed.

SELIGMAN: ...Let me see if I can even find him [North] and if he's inclined to say anything about anything...

BEHAR: At the very least, if I could use even a nonattributing quote, you know, an attorney close to him [North] or something.

SELIGMAN: No, we attorneys don't talk to the press. We haven't - no, I mean, even no, we just don't. We haven't from day one and we're not.

BEHAR: Sure, but if there was a way somehow to use that, then this would be a way to dismiss him...

SELIGMAN: ...Okay. Somebody will try to get back to you.

Later the same evening, with Oliver North on the line, this conversation took place.
SELIGMAN: Ollie, are you there?
NORTH: Richard?
BEHAR: Hello, Ollie.

NORTH: Hilarious hog wash. You can quote me.

SELIGMAN: No, but wait. Before you [North] say that, you're supposed to ask what it is that he's [Behar] asking about.

NORTH: All right, ask me. After the question I'll give you my comment.

BEHAR: I'm sure you probably get a lot of this.

NORTH: I do. I can't believe TIME magazine is going to waste good column mention on it. Go ahead...

BEHAR: ...*Okay. Yeah, well, there are reasons for us doing the story beyond how it may seem to you. You'll see when you see the story.*

NORTH: I'm sure I will. I'll just bend over.

BEHAR: But have you ever met Terry Reed?

NORTH: No. Go ahead, ask me the next question.

BEHAR: Never spoke to him?

NORTH: No, go on.

BEHAR: Well, then, I guess everything else kind of, everything else I shouldn't even bother asking then, because you obviously didn't introduce him -

NORTH: I thought it was funny, I thought it was great.

Later on in the "grueling" interrogation of the man convicted of lying to congress, Behar did get in a question about Mena, between barbs directed toward the press.

BEHAR: Well, it's difficult sometimes for the press to sort things out, especially when they don't give it a lot of time....But that's what they need to do. Was anything going on at Mena?

NORTH: At Who?

BEHAR: Mena Arkansas, having to do with the Contras?

NORTH: *I haven't been there.* I can't imagine that anything is going on at Mena with Contras since they're all out of business.

From the conversation it was clear Behar did not want any real answers, even if they had been offered. Behar never asked the key questions: Did North know Barry Seal? Did he know about Project Donation? Did he know FBI agent Wayne Barlow? Had he been to Oklahoma City? Why was he going to take the Fifth Amendment, as North's lawyers had said, when subpoenaed to Reed's criminal trial in Wichita?

Behar behaved as if he didn't know that he was interrogating the man who had expertly lied under oath about knowing Rob Owen, his very own Contra cut-out. Owen, North's bag man and battle field intelligence gatherer, later testified during the Iran-Contra hearings that he met with North on more than 100 occasions. Why then, did Behar allow North to disavow knowledge of Reed after only one question about him.

Instead, the conversation is allowed to drift into one based upon who could possibly have been using Mena to resupply the Contras. North suggests to Behar that conceivably a man named Tom Posey, a person who helped the "resistance, and organized an outfit called CMA," may have had something to do with Mena.

NORTH: ...But there were lots of organizations that were doing that. You know, conservative-focussed organizations and folks who felt very strongly that the policy of Congress was wrong and they wanted to help. And many of them were doing it totally independently, not everybody was Joe Coors...Don't bother putting Joe Coors in the article.

BEHAR: No, no, no I won't.

NORTH: This is just a little background...But this fellow Posey may have been from Arkansas. But Mena doesn't mean a thing to me.

BEHAR: You've never heard of it or been there?

NORTH: I may have, but there's obviously nothing in it that Larry Walsh [Independent Prosecutor Lawrence Walsh] ever asked me about...

Not only did North just contradict his earlier statement about having never been to Mena, the comments about Walsh never asking him about this whole affair are very disturbing. One would think that the materials provided Walsh by the Arkansas State Attorney General's office and those of Congressman Bill Alexander would have at least warranted Walsh's questioning of North in these areas. Behar was either ignorant of the importance of North's statement expressing lack of concern by Walsh's office, or Behar simply chose to overlook it since he questioned North no further about Mena.

The mystery surrounding Behar's lack of aggressiveness in questioning North about Mena is compounded by the fact that Behar had in his possession a report saying North had indeed been seen in Mena. Bill Duncan had earlier provided Behar with the results of an interview taken on December 21st, 1989, indicating that Ernal Cunningham, a Mena resident, had given strangers a ride from the Mena, Airport and dropped them off in town to dine. The event, which Cunningham said took place either in 1985 or 1986, involved transporting three white males unknown to him, but one of whom he would later identify from the televised Iran-Contra hearings as being Oliver North.

Ignoring or overlooking leads while investigating a coverup as complex as the one enshrouding Mena is one thing. But to be deliberately undermining other investigative efforts, and to jeopardize the life of your confidential source, is quite another.

Instead of quietly investigating and developing his own supporting evidence and sources to corroborate Reed's allegations about some very powerful people in Arkansas, Behar employed a technique that is sure to solicit a hostile and prevaricated response. He repeatedly went straight to the accused armed only with the off-the-record information supplied him by Reed. The accused person is customarily and logically the last person on a good investigative reporter's list of interviews.

Behar's reckless disregard for the safety of the Reed family and his total lack of journalistic professionalism is best captured in the transcripts of Behar's own taped interviews. The following is from a taped conversation with Seth Ward, the owner of POM and the man who leveraged his way into the CIA's gun parts business.

BEHAR: I'm going to try to get to the bottom of it [Reed's allegations].

WARD: We'll, you're at the bottom of it as far as I'm concerned, right now. You know everything that I know about Terry Reed. You know everything that my son [Skeeter] knows about Terry Reed. And after you talk to my son-in-law, Webb Hubbell, you'll know everything that Webb told you about Terry Reed...

BEHAR: Well, what can I say. He's [Reed] got your family linked to bringing illegal weapons down to the Contras in Nicaragua, manufacturing them for transport, working for Barry Seal.

WARD: ...That's the most farfetched, asinine thing I ever heard in my life....oh hell, I can give you a hundred brokers that's here in Little Rock, business-men who have known me for years....They'll say I've never been involved in anything disreputable.

BEHAR: All right. Well, I've taken enough of your time I think.

WARD: ...Yeah, but once you mentioned what Terry Reed was up to, I felt like I better tell you everything that I knew about it...

BEHAR: ...I'm sure it's very upsetting too. Does it upset you much? You don't seem particularly upset by it.

WARD: I'm a little bit numb....it would be difficult for it to upset me.

BEHAR: I see what you mean. But you'd certainly be upset if national publica-tions -

WARD: Yeah, I would. And I don't know what I could do about it. If there was any substance to Terry Reed, I'd sue the Shit out of him...

BEHAR: All right. Well I really appreciate all the time you've spent with me.

WARD: Let me ask you. What's the name of this newspaper you say you saw?

(Behar was confidentially shown an advance copy of *The Nation* by Bill Duncan. As a result of *Nation's* investigative efforts, a detailed article was com-ing out in the *Nation* on POM's involvement in the Contra support activities. By offering this information to the subject of the expose and alerting him of all their revelations, Behar was violating the oath of secrecy he promised Duncan, and was alerting the Ward family about the up-coming article.)

BEHAR: *Nation.*

WARD: That's a New York paper?

BEHAR: It's a liberal newspaper but it's sort of like, it looks like a little maga-zine but it's a newspaper. And it's based out of New York and it goes around the world, around the country.

WARD: I'll tell you one thing, if these allegations are in there....we'll sue the living hell out of them.

Subsequent conversation with Seth Ward.

BEHAR: Terry Reed has offered to take a polygraph examination.

WARD: I don't give a shit what he's offered to do.

BEHAR: Is that the kind of thing you'd be willing to take as well?

WARD: I ain't going to take a polygraph test. I'll show you records, I'll show you bottom line. I have nothing to conceal....you talk to Webb [Hubbell] on Monday.

Behar did talk to Webb Hubbell the following week, after he returned to New York. From portions of the transcript of the conversations with Hubbell it sounds as if Behar is doing his best to contain the Mena scandal; especially as it pertains to POM, the company for which Hubbell was corporate attorney prior to him moving to Washington to become Bill Clinton's Assistant United States Attorney General.

BEHAR: ....Do you remember Terry Reed?

HUBBELL: Yeah, not well. I mean I wasn't a close personal friend or anything, but I remember him.

BEHAR: ....Right. Are you aware of the nature of his allegations right now?

HUBBELL: I've read about them in the newspapers, you know...

BEHAR: Well, he [Reed] has drawn me a diagram showing all of the partici-pants in the resupplying of the Contras.

HUBBELL: Am I one?

BEHAR: He's got you right up here.

HUBBELL: ....Yeah. Well what did I do?

BEHAR: Well, you had knowledge....that you may not have been directly involved in the operation, but certainly Seth Ward, Jr.,[Skeeter] Finis [Shellnut], and Seth Ward, Sr. were involved in the operation to....Well, Finis was the one who Terry had to call when he was dropping parcels of cash from his airplane....

HUBBELL: Have you talked to Finis?...Okay. You better tell Finis why you're calling because he might think you're calling about something else. But—

BEHAR: Okay. And then POM, which you helped set up.

HUBBELL: Yeah.

BEHAR: ....Okay, well POM was apparently making, according to Terry, illegal autosears. It's an autosear, it's part of an M-16 rifle. Making these illegally in order to then transport these weapons down to the Contras.

HUBBELL: I think, I've been to the plant several times and I've only seen them making parking meters.

BEHAR: Do you think, has the company ever made anything for a weapon?

HUBBELL: It has made, I think a nose cone or something like that for LTV.

BEHAR: A rocket launcher? (The *Nation* article Behar had been shown by Duncan had made a connection between POM and other federal weapons contracts.)

HUBBELL: A rocket launcher or something like that. I do know they did that, yeah, made a part.

BEHAR: ...You think Terry was down there in Mena working for Seal?

HUBBELL: I have no idea...I didn't keep track of Terry's whereabouts...

BEHAR: Terry says that Bill Clinton was involved in overseeing this thing as well as Bobby Nash.

HUBBELL: That's ridiculous.

Subsequent conversation with Webster Hubbell.

BEHAR: Well, listen, can I make a recommendation to you off the record?

HUBBELL: Sure.

BEHAR: And this is, I don't particularly want these guys to know that I'm on this story, but it seems to me that *they're acting irresponsibly, The Nation* Newspaper.

HUBBELL: Uh-huh.

BEHAR: Apparently, I heard it through the grapevine they [*Nation*] had an interview with Skeeter [Hubbell's brother-in-law who runs POM].

HUBBELL: He shouldn't be talking to them.

BEHAR: And supposedly Skeeter told them that you guys have done exit cones on nuclear weapons at POM.

HUBBELL: He wouldn't have said that, he knows better.

BEHAR: Well, that's just the thing. I don't know why it would come back to me through the different channels about nuclear weapons unless the story is taking a life of its own. What you might want to do is give a ring to *The Nation* and speak to whoever is doing the story, and clear it up before they put it in their damned newspaper.

HUBBELL: Yeah.

BEHAR: But you didn't hear it from me.

HUBBELL: I appreciate it, I really do. Thank you.

Behar apparently wasn't content to get only the Ward family agitated and after Terry. As soon as he finished undermining *The Nation's* article, he called Toshiba Machine Tool in Chicago and got Takashi Osato, the Japanese former vice president of Toshiba on the line. Behar asked Osato, among other things, if he had known that Reed had been working for the FBI in an undercover capacity and spying on Toshiba. By doing so Behar compromised Reed's cover and ostracized him from the Asian machine tool industry, forever!

BEHAR: Well, let me tell you. Terry Reed has made a lot of different allegations.
OSATO: Oh really? I didn't know that.
BEHAR: Not about Toshiba, no. But it has to do with-
OSATO: Another company?
BEHAR: The CIA.
OSATO: Oh, really?
BEHAR: ...Can I ask you something?...Terry says that he did some intelligence work...For the FBI.
OSATO: For the FBI?
BEHAR: The FBI, while he was working with Toshiba.
OSATO: What?
BEHAR: Yeah.
OSATO: (inaudible)
BEHAR: He was working for the FBI. Do you know the FBI?
OSATO: Yeah, uh-huh.
BEHAR: Trying to find out how machinery is going from Japan to America, that he was working as an agent.
OSATO: Oh really?
BEHAR: For the FBI.
OSATO: I didn't know that. I haven't been told about it.
BEHAR: Does that sound crazy?
OSATO: Yes, sounds crazy but I really don't know. He [Reed] never told me such a thing.
BEHAR: ....Do you remember the scandal with Toshiba?...In 1986?...remember the president of the company committed suicide and that Toshiba apologized to America. Do you remember all this?...
OSATO: ...Uh-huh.
BEHAR: ...Terry says the work he did was part of this thing...that his work led to this thing. Is this crazy?
OSATO: Sounds crazy. Sounds crazy.
BEHAR: He was just a salesman, he was not working for the FBI.

For no logical reason Behar had just informed the very man Reed had "monitored" for John Cathey (Oliver North) and the CIA that it had been Reed who was the undercover agent spying on Toshiba's Houston warehouse. The same facilities Osato had managed when Reed was a Toshiba dealer in Oklahoma and when Toshiba committed their illegal and treasonist acts. Without a doubt, Reed was now a dead man—at least within the Japanese business community.

* * *

So even in light of over-powering evidence that there was a major, on-going cover-up—orchestrated initially by the Reagan White House, continued by the Bush Administration and now spilling over on Democratic Presidential hopeful Bill Clinton, Behar was choosing to put the burden of proof squarely in the lap of Terry Reed. Reed was overwhelmed by Behar's attack as he listened into the pay phone's receiver.

REED: I thought you wanted to write an article about Jack Blum's cover-up, about Lawrence Walsh's cover-up.
BEHAR: I'm not convinced there is a coverup...Prove it to me.
REED: Prove what to you?
BEHAR: Prove to me that you were involved in this resupply operation.
REED: Okay, let's fly down to Mexico at your expense.
BEHAR: No.
REED: Do you want to see Carlos [sic Raul] Fiero? [Mexico's DFS Chief in Guadalajara and liaison to CIA's Operation Screw Worm] Do you want to see where the weapons were stored?
BEHAR: You have not provided me with documentation.

Not only had the Reeds provided Behar with over 300 pages of evidence to prove their story, Behar had been covertly supplied with a portion of the materials sent to Lawrence Walsh by the Arkansas Attorney General's office (a 3 inch thick file). The source of these documents, combined with the inside knowledge available to him through Reed gave Behar the equivalent of two "Deep Throats" in order to expose what is probably the best contained U.S. government scandal of the twentieth century.

What did Behar elect to do? He sabotaged his Deep Throat (Terry Reed and family) so effectively that Thomas G. Whittle of *Freedom* magazine would write, "The magazine [TIME] must answer why, instead of helping to raise the lid off the Mena coverup, it evidently sought to drive more nails into it."[15]

* * *

Fearing for their children's safety, the Reed family literally fled Moorpark, California, in the middle of the day on April 1st, 1992. The fully loaded U-Haul truck pulled up in front of the Peach Hill Elementary School, precisely at noon, while Janis frantically collected her sons and they headed east, to a destination unknown.

Their old friend, fear, was once again trailing, just off their bumper. This time their pursuers might include the CIA, the FBI, the Democratic and/or the Republican Party, Felix Rodriguez, Ramon Medina and, now, Time magazine.

In a state of shock, and with no income, they pulled into Phoenix, Arizona, towing their belongings and keeping an eye on the rear view mirror. Terry took time while there to call on his prospective client, Clark Ronnow, and divulged to him that he was no longer with his Japanese employer, and would therefore be unable to continue working on Ronnow's bicycle project.

Ronnow asked no questions about Reed's departure from Los Angeles, and suggested he contract directly with his firm, so that Terry could complete the automation plan for the new product his company was scheduling to manufacture.

Terry and Janis were reluctant to take Ronnow into their confidence and share the details of their plight, for fear that he too would treat them as if they were carrying a contagions disease. More in error, they could not have been.

After deciding to take Ronnow up on his offer, and to return once again to a one day-at-a-time life style, they sought temporary, anonymous lodging, formulating plans to move on immediately if the situation warranted.

A few days after settling into a cautious work routine, the TIME article was published, just as Behar had promised and threatened. It was appropriately titled "ANATOMY OF A SMEAR" and appeared in TIME's April 20, 1992 issue.

It was worse than imagined. With the ink of his ball point pen, Richard Behar had most surely dealt the death blow to their uncountable hours of sacrifice and labor in preparation for their court case. NO ONE would believe them now. Not with a publication as credible as TIME calling Terry a charlatan, a thief and a liar...and claiming the operations in Mena never happened. Behar even vindictively printed the name of the small California town in which they had taken up residence. Why?

The Reeds only comfort was their children were safely with them, once again securely snuggled in sleeping bags on a motel floor, and that they had left Los Angeles on the eve of the riots resulting from the Rodney King trial.

After spending a sleepless and emotional night reading the piece over and over and over...wishing it to miraculously disappear, Terry left a still-weeping Janis and drove to the office to confront Ronnow with the article. He was fully expecting immediate abandonment by Clark and his firm.

Clark, a Mormon, sat quietly in his office savoring every grizzly, ugly, slanted, scandalous, untruthful and slander-riddled detail of the full-page, tabloid-style, slash and burn article. After appearing to read it at least twice, he lowered the magazine from his face and said, "Damn, I've been trying my whole life to get in this magazine, and you just made a full page!".

Reed just sat there in silent disbelief, so Clark added, "This article is your credibility, don't you see it? You must be a big threat to Bill Clinton or they wouldn't go to this much trouble to discredit you."

Terry could finally speak and then rapidly attempted to explain away every flesh-ripping word of the scathing article, causing Ronnow to interrupt with, "Slow down, I'm a believer. We can sit here and talk about this all day long if you like. Then I've got some stories for you, Terry."

As they talked that day of governments, hypocrisies, Intelligence Agencies, politics, life and the media, the conversation finally evolved to one of religion.

It was amazing and enlightening to Terry, how Ronnow compared the "persecution of the Reeds" to that of that of Joseph Smith, the founder of the Mormon Church. The Mormon Church, he was hearing for the first time, was built upon the premise of sheltering those being singled out and being punished for daring to be different.

How refreshing and uplifting the Summer of 1992 turned out to be for the Reed family as they were "harbored" by their new found friends, Clark Ronnow and The Mormon Church. The comfort and support provided them, not only help take the sting out of Richard Behar's words, it actually restored their faith in their fellow man. "Nice people actually still exist," Janis would say, in near disbelief.

Here they were, feeling protected by relative strangers, that seemed to respond to and be guided by an unspoken bond, a greater force. Their kindness will never be forgotten and will be carried as a debt until it can be repaid tenfold.

It was such a stark contrast to that of alleged friends, with the more typical words of consolation being, "Hey Reed, since the TIME piece, you're dead. You're history. Your stock just crashed!"

They learned a lot about people and friends that summer. And the Mormon religion as well.

* * *

Due to TIME's reckless attack on the Reeds, the fervor surrounding the Mena scandal would simply die off and go away. Scott Shugar would inform Terry that *Prime Time Live* was killing his special due to Reed's perceived lack of credibility.

Again quoting from *Freedom Magazine's* May 1993 article covering the TIME/Behar libel suit:

"In TIMEspeak, when one throws enough allegations, insinuations, and double-edged questions, the task has been accomplished: the victim, if not dead, has been bloodied and his reputation rendered a shadow of its former self."

A well-orchestrated and executed disinformation program had robbed Terry of the one thing he valued the most, his word. He was now considered a liar. It was as if he suddenly had a plague. He felt black-balled by the media. He was being treated as a leper.

Terry was discovering that the cynical writer in New York named John Cummings was right once again. "The major media all march in lockstep," he had said earlier. "What one does the other does. They're afraid to go take a piss without holding each other's hand."

And the Reeds' attorney John Hall? He was quick to abandon them. He would lie by saying that he was dropping the Reed case due to an argument Terry had with his secretary, Ruth. He would then tell reporters that he could not corroborate Reed's story, knowing all along he had not bothered to depose even one single witness.

But this was not the reason Hall publicly divorced himself from the Reeds. The transcripts of taped phone conversations between Behar and Hall effectively prove that Hall violated his fiduciary responsibility and attorney-client privilege and had inexplicably sided with Behar, becoming a willing participant in the effort to strip Reed of his credibility.

Once back in Little Rock from the Reed/Hall/Behar meeting in California, Hall apparently enlisted Behar as an investigator to investigate his own client, instead of keeping Behar focused on the money laundering aspects of his supposed probing. Unknown to, and without the permission of Reed, Hall was sharing with Behar confidential client/attorney correspondence, information, and strategy. Behar and Hall were talking privately about details of Reed's debriefing in Reno, Nevada and Lake Tahoe, California and the taped conversation was centering on the Clinton/Reed meeting at Juanita's restaurant in Little Rock.

HALL: The whole thing sounds a little squirrely to me, anyway.

BEHAR: Which whole thing?

HALL: Being in the van smoking a joint.

BEHAR: Yeah, I know.

HALL: In front of somebody you don't know. I could see him [Clinton] maybe doing it with somebody who had given him a blow job, but not in front of somebody he doesn't know.

BEHAR: Well —

HALL: I mean, cocaine possession is one thing. (This unexplained reference to cocaine must be from a private conversation Behar and Hall had concerning cocaine use by Clinton.)

BEHAR: It's the kind of thing that's almost so preposterous that it has to be true. Do you know what I mean?

HALL: It could possibly be true.

BEHAR: Well, have you found Terry to be, you know, credible in everything else? Or have you found discrepancies?

HALL: I haven't been able to corroborate him, that's the problem.

BEHAR: Yeah.

HALL: That's why I hope at least some of the stuff [federal court discovery] from the A.G.'s office will corroborate him.

BEHAR: Oh, you're hoping that I can. Yeah, I've been having some trouble.

HALL: That's part of the problem, that's the nature of the beasties. Out there on his [Reed's] own, expected to do all this stuff...That's the whole point.

BEHAR: Well listen, I just turned up something that I think I probably should not have gotten from you.

HALL: What?

BEHAR: Some letter from Janis [Reed] to you.

HALL: Okay. You got the original then?

BEHAR: Yeah. I got the original...But if she [Janis] asks you and you don't know, she might get upset.

HALL: Yeah, she would. She's kind of like that.

BEHAR: Have you asked Terry if he'd be willing to settle [the court case]?...Did you ask him if he had a bottom line financially?

HALL: Not this week. I might have made some comment about settling the case back when it was filed. It could be settled...

In a subsequent conversation, Behar and Hall seem very concerned in sheltering Reed from other media personnel, and again Behar begins probing into areas of confidential client/attorney privilege, and Hall allows him to do so.

HALL: ...And the *Washington Times* has seven reporters here now.

BEHAR: Are they interested in Terry?

HALL: Not yet. They have talked to me briefly about Terry but they haven't come back.

BEHAR: Anyone in the press really trying to get stuff on Terry or not yet?

HALL: Not yet.

BEHAR: ...You haven't talked to Terry about the Governor's increasing his fund? (The Governor's emergency fund that Hall had speculated to Reed was being increased in order to settle their case.)

HALL: No. That's common. The Governor's fund can be used for all kinds of things...it could, in fact, be used because there was talk of trying to get money out of that fund for the Mena case and they never did... I'm going to have to go on a sojourn to Iowa and Chicago pretty soon. I might take a side trip to New York so we can just sit down and put our heads together. Are you going to be in New York next week?

BEHAR: ...I'll let you know what my plans are.

HALL: Because I was, since the last time we've talked I've really been concerned about him [Reed]...But I've been having my own doubts. I shouldn't be telling you this because it probably violates attorney-client privilege so don't spread it around.

So here was John Hall, Terry and Janis Reeds' attorney, claiming to a TIME magazine reporter that he could not corroborate his client's story. Hall was conveniently not sharing with Behar the Reeds' concerns that no depositions were being taken and that their case appeared to be hanging from only the one fragile discovery demand Hall had made, that of the material requested from the AG's office.

During this period, Hall was sharing none of his concerns with his clients, the Reeds, nor was he informing them of the vast amounts of time he was spending collaborating with Behar against their interests. One can only speculate the agenda of Hall's planned trip to New York to confer with Behar, since Hall certainly didn't make the Reeds aware of the "sojourn."

Strangely, Hall himself, candidly admits his clandestine conversations with Behar were in violation of client-attorney privilege, the very fiber upon which all confidentiality is based. The Reeds knew nothing of Hall's doubts that he expressed to TIME magazine, and contrarily, in his conversations with the Reeds, reflected only optimism about the outcome of their pending civil rights trial—right up until May 1992 when he petitioned the court to be relieved as their counsel, leaving them without legal representation, only four months from their trial date.

And Independent Counsel Lawrence Walsh would do little but help contain the Mena scandal by inexplicably sitting on the evidence supplied him by Arkansas state Attorney General Winston Bryant and Democratic Congressman Bill Alexander. Walsh's office took no action on the reams of evidence supplied by the state, and instead waited until 1993 to cite that: Whatever statutes may have applied to criminal activities at Mena, have now expired. And even after this ambiguous position, Walsh's office ruled to not allow Reed access to the entirety of the materials supplied them on Mena, claiming *national security* grounds.

The Reeds were told their testimony, which they had volunteered to the Walsh committee, and which surely would have exposed the true depths of the Reagan/Bush Administration's complicity in the Iran-Contra conspiracy, was mysteriously "outside the scope of its investigation."

And Bill Clinton. Well, he limped along dodging one major disaster after another. He claimed to be incapable of inhaling a marijuana cigarette. How can this be possible, the Reeds said. Not only from what Terry had witnessed in the van outside the restaurant, but how could anyone even near their own age say anything so foolish, concocted and unbelievable. If this were any indication of how quickly Clinton could think on his feet when confronted with a difficult question. Well, he'll make one hell-of-a Commander in Chief, Terry concluded.

And, of course, then came Clinton's draft issue. That was a real problem. To counter that dilemma would once again require the aid of TIME magazine. His old friend and college mate Strobe Talbott, who is now number three man in the State Department and Ambassador at Large, would conveniently use his editorial powers at TIME to defend candidate Bill Clinton.[16] Talbott would be forced to switch from his covering of important world political events, i.e. the break-up of the Soviet Union, and write an article in defense of Clinton's draft record entitled "Clinton and the Draft: A Personal Testimony."

In the April 6th, 1992 article, Talbott would defend Clinton, by claiming that as a college student, his old friend may have enrolled in an ROTC program in order to avoid the draft, but that Clinton began to wrestle with his conscience and feel the guilt of *compromising* his values by taking on the obligation to later serve as an Army officer. Therefore, Talbott explained, Clinton withdrew from the ROTC program in order to become eligible for the draft, and cast his fate to the lottery system.

However the article failed to mention that Clinton experienced this new found moral conscienceness, only after finding his birth date afforded him a high lottery number, thereby making his chances of being drafted highly improbable.

Clinton would in fact selectively quote profusely from TIME magazine throughout the campaign, whenever it was to his advantage. After delivering a speech to the NAACP in Pittsburgh, Pennsylvania on April 21st, 1992, reporters approached Clinton about the Reeds' civil suit involving his state. They specifically inquired about the allegations that Mena had been used for Contra training operations and asked if Clinton's chief of security, Raymond Young, played any role in the cover-up of the Agency's activities there.

One reporter said that Clinton: "flew off the handle and shouted, *'That's bull. That fantasy was discredited by [TIME] magazine.'*"

As the Reeds hit their new emotional bottom after being abandoned by their legal counsel and saw the chances of having their day in court evaporate before them, the bull dog "scribbler" from New York came and sarcastically said in his usual condescending New Yorker tone, "You see, I told you they'd never let you get this subject into court. The offer still stands if you want to do a book."

* * *

While motoring through the "Land of Enchantment", two months after the publication of the TIME article, Terry would make a miraculous find. At long last, he would espy the *BIG PICTURE* of his Agency involvement by discovering that Robert Johnson was none other than...WILLIAM P. BARR, the Attorney General of the United States.

It was William P. Barr, who became President George Bush's Attorney General in 1991, an *apparatchik* who always has a way of emerging from the shadows when Bush needs his trail covered.

The 43-year-old lawyer and ex-CIA analyst, little known outside Beltway legal circles, had nonetheless an uncanny way of crisscrossing Bush's path at critical times. This confluence of careers within the world of intelligence became the precursor that empowered him to become the dark overseer of the cabal that subverted the U.S. Constitution he took an oath as Attorney General to uphold.

Barr was the man that William Safire, *The New York Times*' conservative columnist, called the Justice Department's "Cover-up General" in a 1992 column criticizing Barr's refusal to seek the appointment of a special prosecutor to investigate the Bush Administration's actions in continuing aid to Saddam Hussein after it was eminently clear that Iraq was about to invade Kuwait.[17]

Barr had joined the CIA in 1973 where his work brought him into contact with the future Vice-President while Bush was serving as the Agency's Director from 1976-77. By 1978 Barr had joined the Washington law firm of Shaw, Pittman, Potts and Trowbridge, a firm very much aligned with the CIA and with a history of providing criminal defense for intelligence agents.

From there Barr moved into a well-placed political position and became a member of the transition team of President-elect Ronald Reagan in 1980. Two years later he was deputy assistant director of Domestic Policy Council serving on the Reagan White House staff, where he again began orbiting in the same circles as George Bush and Bill Casey, then Director of the CIA.

In 1983, around the time Oliver North was forming "Project Donation" and was briefing Terry Reed on the CIA's efforts to bypass the Congressionally imposed Boland Amendment, Barr strangely left the White House and drifted into obscurity, allegedly back to the firm of Shaw, Pittman. This lower profile position—out of the media's eye and off the government's payroll—gave him freedom of movement and less chance of being discovered as he assisted the Agency and Southern Air Transport as they ramped-up for operation "Screw Worm" in Mexico and had need of "specialized" legal services.

Having survived the near catastrophe known as Iran-Contra, George Bush needed Barr's overt services in 1988 and returned Barr to the White House to aid in the selection of a running mate. He was forced to stay on however, through the campaign, and became a Dan Quayle handler when the vice-presidential nominee experienced trouble from his draft avoidance record during the Vietnam War.

By being a problem solver and helping his old CIA boss get elected President, he was given a position on Bush's transition team and, in April 1989, was appointed assistant attorney general for the office of Legal Counsel. By July, 1990, he was Bush's deputy attorney general, the number two man in the Justice Department shadowed only by Attorney General Richard Thornburgh, who he replaced in October 1991. He was 41 years old at the time, making him the third youngest attorney general.

Adding additional intrigue, it was Barr who drafted the legal opinion justifying the invasion of Panama and the arrest of Panamanian General Manuel Noreiga, a paid CIA asset.[18]

And it was Noriega who claimed it was the CIA, not he, that was trafficking in cocaine through his country. Could it be, Reed wondered, that the whole damn U.S. invasion had been designed to cover the Agency's trafficking trail and to silence Noriega about CIA involvement in Bill Clinton's state? After all, it was Noriega's people who Max Gomez had said were going to start "investing" in Arkansas, Terry recalled from the conversations in the bunker near Little Rock.

The Reagan Administration and the Agency most assuredly were the ones who engineered the assassination of Barry Seal, for the same reasons. Seal's name had rolled off the lips of Akihide Sawahata, Bob Nash, Felix Rodriguez, Oliver North, William Barr and Bill Clinton—in the same context that the CIA had grown to view Noriega—an asset becoming a liability.

Noriega must have been just *another* disposable asset, like Barry Seal and countless others like Terry Reed.

But Noriega will undoubtedly be replaced by someone less *compromising* now that the Agency has another of their men in the oval office.

* * *

P.S. Barry, I've gone as far as I dare in my attempt to correct the wrongs levied you...*at least for now*. I miss you, you calculated risk taker...and I can still hear you laughing.

SSSSSSSOOOOOOOOOOOOOOOOOOOOOOOOOOEEEEEEEEEEEEEEEEEEE!!!!

1. Transcript of sworn deposition of Terry Kent Reed, May 24, 1991, Southern Air Transport, Inc. vs. Post-Newsweek Stations, Florida, Inc., et al., in the Circuit Court for the Eleventh Judicial Circuit in and for Dade County, Florida, Case No. 87-23989
2. *Arkansas Democrat-Gazette*, February 25, 1992.
3. *STAR* magazine, January 28, 1992.
4. *People* magazine, April 1992.
5. *Arkansas Democrat-Gazette*, March 27, 1992.
6. *Arkansas Democrat-Gazette*, February 27, 1992.
7. *Arkansas Gazette*, September 11, 1991.
8. Transcript of sworn deposition of Lawrence S. Graves, March 9, 1993, Terry K. Reed and Janis Reed vs. Raymond Young and Tommy Baker, In The United States District Court, Eastern District of Arkansas, Western Division, Case No. LR-C-91-414 , Page 44.
9. *Arkansas Democrat-Gazette*, April 19, 1992.
10. *The Mexico City News*, May 2, 1987.
    Kansas City Times, July 20, 1987.
    Kansas City Star, November, 19, 1987.
11. *Arkansas Gazette*, October 3, 1991.
12. Transcript of National Broadcasting Company, Inc. (NBC), *Sunday Today*, 9:00-10:30 AM, 2-23-1992.
13. Transcript of Proceedings, United States of America, vs. Terry Kent Reed, In The United States District Court For The District of Kansas, 6-1-90, Case No. 88-10049-01
14. Transcripts of tape recorded conversations provided through Discovery, Terry K. Reed vs. Time Warner, Inc., Time Inc. Magazine company, and Richard Behar, in the U.S. District Court, Southern District of New York, April 16, 1993, Case No. 93CIV.2249.
15. *Freedom*, May, 1993, Pgs. 22,23.
16. *The Nation*, July 12, 1993, Pgs. 54-55
17. *New York Times*, August 31, 1992.
18. *Current Biography*, June, 1992, Pgs. 11-15

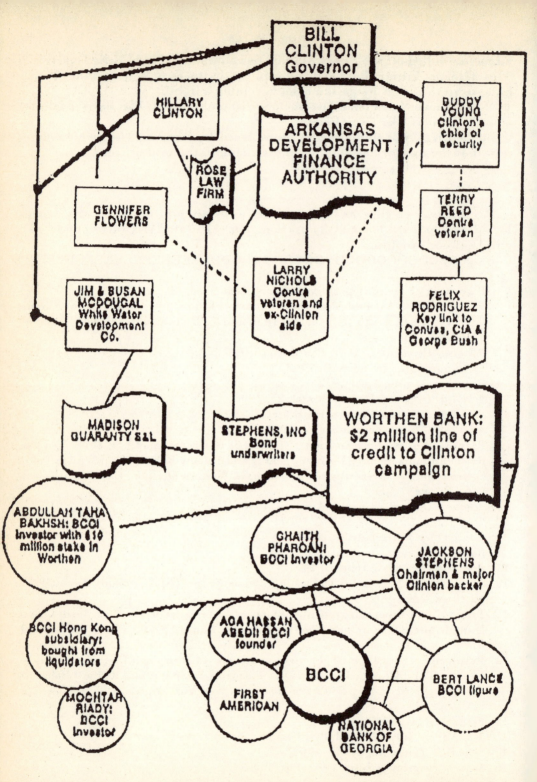

36-1. Document developed by the Harkin campaign committee during the 1992 Presidential Primaries. Reed contributed no information to the committee, but their chart is remarkably similar to the one Reed drew in 1991. (See end of chapter 34 for comparison.)

ANATOMY OF A SMEAR

Terry Reed loves to tell reporters scandalous tales about Bill Clinton and the contras. The trouble is the stories are false.

By RICHARD BEHAR LITTLE ROCK

To HEAR TERRY REED TELL IT, during the mid-1980s he was a key player in a covert "resupply network" that flew arms to the Nicaraguan *contras* and drugs back to the U.S., using a small airport in rural Arkansas as a base. On top of that, the enterprise was personally supervised by Governor Bill Clinton, whose state received 10% of the profits from the operation. And according to Reed, he even discussed the scheme with Clinton while the Governor smoked marijuana in a van parked outside a busy Mexican restaurant in Little Rock.

The only trouble with Reed's sensational tale is that not a word of it is true. That inconvenient fact has not stopped a busy rumor mill in Arkansas from cranking out ever more preposterous allegations, nor has it prevented some credulous journalists, including Andrew Cockburn, a columnist for the *Nation*, from using Reed as a source for absurdly speculative accounts. None of those who are taking Reed's wild stories seriously seem to have asked why Clinton, a vocal critic of U.S. aid to the *contras* who even then was considering running for President, would have done risky favors for the Reagan Administration. But then again, answering that question would spoil the fun.

As with most smears, Reed's allegations are built on a slim foundation of truth. Before being gunned down in Louisiana by a squad of Colombian hit men in 1986, a convicted drug smuggler and DEA informant named Barry Seal was involved in something fishy at the airport in Mena, a heavily wooded town 130 miles west of Little Rock. In 1984 Seal played a part in Oliver North's campaign to prove that the Sandinista government was in league with Colombia's Medellín cocaine cartel. In exchange for a reduced sentence on drug-smuggling charges, Seal flew his C-123 transport plane to Managua and picked up 750 kilos of cocaine from a high-ranking Sandinista official, recording the transaction with hidden cameras.

What does this have to do with Reed, a 43-year-old pilot and machine-tool sales-man who now lives in Moorpark, Calif.? He claims that in 1983 North recruited him to go to Mena to work with Seal and help train *contra* pilots. He also says North asked him to donate a Piper airplane to the *contras* and then report the plane as stolen so that insurance would cover his loss. Later that year, Reed and his wife Janis received a $33,000 insurance payment for the Piper. He says he quit the *contra* effort in August 1987 after he learned that it involved drug running. For that, he claims. the government sought revenge.

Two months later, a Little Rock private investigator named Thomas Baker stumbled on a rusted Piper in a local aircraft hangar. He asked his best friend, state police captain Raymond ("Buddy") Young, who has been Clinton's chief of security for a decade, to run the plane's identification numbers through the FBI's national crime data base. Lo and behold, it turned out to be Reed's missing plane. Reed and his wife were indicted for mail fraud in Wichita. The case was dismissed in 1990 after the government refused to turn over North's diaries. notes and phone records. which Reed claimed would back up his alibi.

Since then Reed has been waging a vendetta against Baker and Young. He began by filing a suit accusing them of fabricating a federal crime. More recently he has added Clinton to his list of targets. In an interview with TIME, he breathlessly proclaimed that "I just spoke to my lawyer and he says that a Clinton emergency fund was just increased considerably. and he seems to think that some kind of offer will be made to get this thing to go away." That was news to Reed's attorney, John Wesley Hall, a constitutional expert from Little Rock, who says he actually told Reed that no one would ever settle the suit. Adds Hall: "I haven't been able to corroborate [Reed's story]. that's the problem."

No wonder. There is absolutely no proof that Reed ever worked with either the CIA or Seal. Oliver North denies that he has ever met or spoken with him. A couple with whom Reed claims he was dining on the night of his alleged conversation with Clinton say they have never been to the restaurant with Reed.

Over the past decade, Reed has shuttled from one job to another. leaving behind a string of charges that he absconded with company funds. Among his victims: an Illinois-based Japanese machine-tool company named Gomiya, which currently has a $600,000 judgment outstanding against him. Last month U.S. marshals seized Reed's van for Gomiya. Reed blames the CIA.

Given Reed's track record, why does anyone take him seriously? In part because there are so many unanswered questions about what was going on at Mena. In 1988 a federal grand jury that

Terry Reed at a California airport

had investigated the affair for three years failed to return indictments, leading some state law-enforcement officers to grumble that the case had been scuttled by higher-ups in Washington. Clinton says the state has done everything it can to solve the mystery. But Charles Black. a deputy state prosecuting attorney, says when he asked the Governor to provide financial assistance so the state could conduct its own grand jury investigation in 1988. Clinton never got back to him. Last year Democratic Congressman Bill Alexander obtained $25.000 from the Federal Government to fund a probe by the state police. who will soon decide how to proceed with the investigation. That is a timely idea. if only to lay Reed's fabrication to rest. ∎

36-2. TIME magazine's article written about Reed and Mena.
Exhibit "A", United States District Court, Southern District of New York, case # 93 CIV. 2249.

April 22, 1992

Time Magazine Letters
Time and Life Building
Rockefeller Center
New York, NY 10020

To the Editor:

What an appropriate title for your article about my husband Terry Reed and me: "Anatomy of a Smear" (April 20, 1992)! But who is smearing whom, and why? I was distressed to see that TIME used its considerable reputation and authority to pass on to its millions of readers so many inaccuracies and omissions.

Example: In characterizing Terry Reed and his "sensational tale" regarding his knowledge of secret contra and associated drug operations, TIME described him as "a 43-year-old pilot and machine tool salesman". TIME does not mention that he served honorably for eight years in Air Force intelligence which included two tours of duty in the most highly classified operations of the war in Southeast Asia. Also, having been almost exclusively self-employed since 1982 by owning and operating his own high-technology marketing/consulting company, he has hardly established a pattern of "shuttling from one job to another".

TIME wrote that the Wichita fraud case relating to a missing plane brought against my husband "was dismissed". The truth is that he was brought to trial and found NOT GUILTY (acquitted). In a similar inaccuracy, TIME said that my husband, in subsequently bringing a lawsuit against Tommy (not Thomas) Baker and Buddy Young, chief of Bill Clinton's security force, "has been waging a vendetta". TIME never mentioned that the federal judge hearing the Wichita case wrote that the sworn testimony of these men (Baker and Young) was made with "a reckless disregard for the truth". Our federal suit filed in Arkansas names only two people and Bill Clinton is not one of them. Furthermore, no dollar amount has been placed on this suit. The actions that provide the foundation for this suit began in 1987, long before Bill Clinton announced his bid for president. Our intent has only been for a jury to conclude that there was a conspiracy to violate our constitutional rights.

Regarding TIME's reference to a judgment, we have made it no secret that Gomiya, a Japanese trading company, holds a DEFAULT judgment which surely will be overturned once their involvement in this affair is exposed. Gomiya's complicity in this matter was discussed in depth with congressional investigators in our 1988 debriefing in Washington.

When TIME wrote, " There is absolutely no proof that Reed ever worked with...the CIA...[and] Oliver North denies that he has ever met or spoken with him", it ignored two facts: 1) The Classified Information Procedures Act was invoked by the government in our Wichita case when the U.S. Attorney went on record saying that the FBI told him that it had "prior contacts with Mr. Reed [that] involved classified information", and 2) Oliver North has admitted his willingness to lie concerning national securtiy matters and was convicted of doing so.

TIME states that "Terry Reed loves to tell reporters scandalous tales about Bill Clinton and the contras" and gives as the main example an article in The Nation by Alexander Cockburn (whom TIME mistakenly identified as "Andrew" Cockburn). But neither of us have ever spoken to Mr. Cockburn or otherwise cooperated with the Nation's story which was drawn instead from court documents, depositions, and other public records. Which, of course, raises an important question: Why did TIME make all of the foregoing damaging mistakes when the truth is in publicly available materials? This is especially puzzling since my husband and I personally supplied most of these materials to the TIME reporter who interviewed us. We have tried to maintain a low profile regarding this case to protect our three small children from additional stress, and have not cooperated in general with the countless media persons, investigators, and political contenders who have pursued us for many months.

Nonetheless, if national attention is finally going to be focused on Mena, Arkansas and certain nefarious government activities, then THANK YOU TIME MAGAZINE for your article, even if it had to be at our expense!

Sincerely,

Janis Kerr Reed
c/o 523 W. Third St.
Little Rock, AR 72201...............(501) 371-9131

36-3. Letter Janis Reed wrote to TIME magazine, protesting Richard Behar's story.

AO 440 (Rev. 10/93) Summons in a Civil Action

JUDGE KNAPP **93 CIV. 2249**

United States District Court

SOUTHERN ———————— DISTRICT OF ———— NEW YORK

TERRY K. REED,

      Plaintiff

      v

TIME WARNER, INC., TIME INC.
MAGAZINE COMPANY and RICHARD BEHAR,

      Defendants.

SUMMONS IN A CIVIL ACTION

CASE NUMBER:

TO (Name and Address of Defendant)

TIME WARNER, INC.
75 Rockefeller Plaza
New York, New York 10019

TIME INC. MAGAZINE CO.
Time-Life Building
Rockefeller Plaza
New York, New York 10000

RICHARD BEHAR
c/o Time Inc. Magazine Co.
Time-Life Bldg.
Rockefeller Plaza
New York, NY

YOU ARE HEREBY SUMMONED and required to file with the Clerk of this Court and serve upon

PLAINTIFF'S ATTORNEY (name and address)

ROBERT S. MELONI, ESQ.
405 Park Avenue
Suite 1500
New York, NY 10000

an answer to the complaint which
this summons upon you exclusive
against you for the relief demanded

JAMES M. PARKISON

CLERK

DAVID ZAM

BY DEPUTY CLERK

---

such other amount as the jury may find necessary to deter and
punish the defendants for the malicious libel set forth in this
complaint.

    WHEREFORE, plaintiff prays for an award of damages against
all defendants as follows:

        1.   For general damages in an amount to be determined
at trial, but in no event less than the minimum jurisdictional
amount for this court;

        2.   For punitive damages in an amount not less than
$41,600,000;

        3.   For an award of plaintiff's costs and reasonable
attorney's fees;

        4.   For such other, further and different relief as to
this Court may seem just and proper.

Dated: New York, New York
          April 8, 1993

                   Respectfully submitted,

                   ROBERT S. MELONI, ESQ.
                   Attorney for Plaintiff Terry
                   K. Reed

     By:
                   ROBERT S. MELONI (RM-8087)
                   405 Park Avenue, Suite 1500
                   New York, New York 10022-4405
                   (212) 935-0900

36-4. Portions of the libel suit filed by Terry Reed against TIME and reporter Richard Behar.

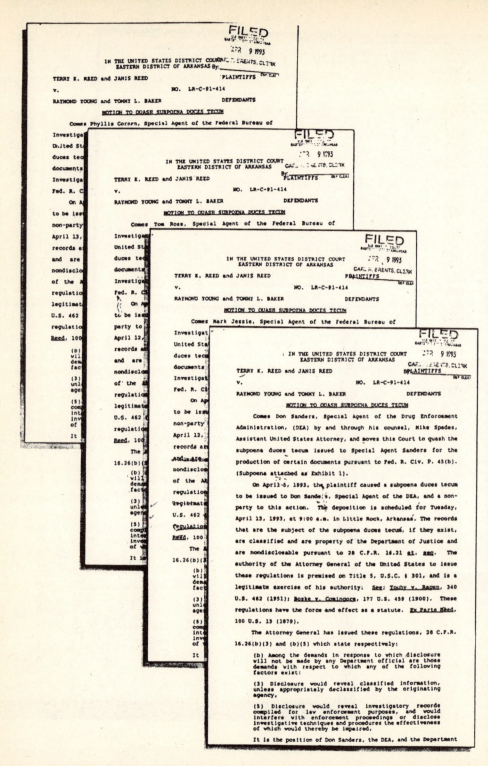

IN THE UNITED STATES DISTRICT COURT
EASTERN DISTRICT OF ARKANSAS

TERRY K. REED and JANIS REED   PLAINTIFFS

v.   NO. LR-C-91-414

RAYMOND YOUNG and TOMMY L. BAKER   DEFENDANTS

MOTION TO QUASH SUBPOENA DUCES TECUM

Comes Phyllis Cornrn, Special Agent of the Federal Bureau of

IN THE UNITED STATES DISTRICT COURT
EASTERN DISTRICT OF ARKANSAS

TERRY K. REED and JANIS REED   PLAINTIFFS

v.   NO. LR-C-91-414

RAYMOND YOUNG and TOMMY L. BAKER   DEFENDANTS

MOTION TO QUASH SUBPOENA DUCES TECUM

Comes Tom Ross, Special Agent of the Federal Bureau of

IN THE UNITED STATES DISTRICT COURT
EASTERN DISTRICT OF ARKANSAS

TERRY K. REED and JANIS REED   PLAINTIFFS

v.   NO. LR-C-91-414

RAYMOND YOUNG and TOMMY L. BAKER   DEFENDANTS

MOTION TO QUASH SUBPOENA DUCES TECUM

Comes Mark Jessie, Special Agent of the Federal Bureau of

IN THE UNITED STATES DISTRICT COURT
EASTERN DISTRICT OF ARKANSAS

TERRY K. REED and JANIS REED   PLAINTIFFS

v.   NO. LR-C-91-414

RAYMOND YOUNG and TOMMY L. BAKER   DEFENDANTS

MOTION TO QUASH SUBPOENA DUCES TECUM

Comes Don Sanders, Special Agent of the Drug Enforcement
Administration, (DEA) by and through his counsel, Mike Spades,
Assistant United States Attorney, and moves this Court to quash the
subpoena duces tecum issued to Special Agent Sanders for the
production of certain documents pursuant to Fed. R. Civ. P. 45(b).
(Subpoena attached as Exhibit 1).

On April 8, 1993, the plaintiff caused a subpoena duces tecum
to be issued to Don Sanders, Special Agent of the DEA, and a non-
party to this action. The deposition is scheduled for Tuesday,
April 13, 1993, at 9:00 a.m. in Little Rock, Arkansas. The records
that are the subject of the subpoena duces tecum, if they exist,
are classified and are property of the Department of Justice and
are nondisclosable pursuant to 28 C.F.R. 16.21 et. seq. The
authority of the Attorney General of the United States to issue
these regulations is premised on Title 5, U.S.C. § 301, and is a
legitimate exercise of his authority. See: Touhy v. Ragen, 340
U.S. 462 (1951); Boske v. Comingors, 177 U.S. 459 (1900). These
regulations have the force and effect as a statute. Ex Parte Reed,
100 U.S. 13 (1879).

The Attorney General has issued these regulations, 28 C.F.R.
16.26(b)(3) and (b)(5) which state respectively:

    (b) Among the demands in response to which disclosure
    will not be made by any Department official are those
    demands with respect to which any of the following
    factors exist:

    (3) Disclosure would reveal classified information,
    unless appropriately declassified by the originating
    agency;

    (5) Disclosure would reveal investigatory records
    compiled for law enforcement purposes, and would
    interfere with enforcement proceedings or disclose
    investigative techniques and procedures the effectiveness
    of which would thereby be impaired;

    It is the position of Don Sanders, the DEA, and the Department

---

36-5. Four government motions seeking to keep FBI agents from testifying in the Reeds'
civil case. "National Security" is cited as a reason.... all for a $33,000 mail-fraud case.

The Honorable Janet Reno   April 7, 1993
Attorney General of the United States
Department of Justice
10th and Constitution Avenue, N.W.
Room 4400
Washington, D.C. 20530

                    Re: Terry Reed

Honorable Madam Attorney General:

        I am the attorney for Terry Reed and his wife Janis
Reed in a pending Civil Rights action in the United States
District Court for the Eastern District of Arkansas, Western
Division entitled Terry K. Reed and Janis Reed v. Raymond Young
and Tommy L. Baker (No. LR-C-91-414 (J. Howard)). Terry Reed is
a former Air force intelligence operative who served in Task
Force Alpha during the Vietnam war and has served as an intelli-
gence asset for both the FBI and CIA during the last 15 years.
His duties included the training of contra pilots in the mid-
1980's in connection with the CIA's covert operations in the
State of Arkansas in support of the Nicaraguan contras.

        During the course of recent discovery proceedings in
the litigation, I had occasion to serve subpoenas duces tecum on
three special agents of the FBI, Mark A. Jesse (Hot Springs,
Arkansas), Thomas W. Ross (Hot Springs, Arkansas) and Roy Christopher (Little Rock, Arkansas). In addition, a subpoena duces
tecum was received by Don Sanders, an Arkansas State Trooper who
for the past several years has served on a joint task force with
the Drug Enforcement Administration in Little Rock, Arkansas.
Each of these agents responded to the subpoenas claiming that the
information sought was non-disclosable classified information
pursuant to 28 C.F.R. 16.21 et. seq. and since their disclosure
"would disclose investigative techniques and impair the effectiveness of law enforcement."

        Briefly, the information sought was narrowed to infor-
mation concerning Terry Reed and two Piper Arrow aircraft, registration numbers: N7062M and N3049G, as well as seven other
aircraft flown by Mr. Reed in the CIA's Mena operation' and a
stolen 1979 Cessna T210, Reg. No. 5468A, the last of which was
used in a 1984 FBI sting operation at the CIA facility at Rich
Mountain Aviation in Mena, Arkansas.
                        * * * * * * *
        It has become common knowledge that certain United
States intelligence agencies have, for many years, used stolen or
"laundered" airplanes in connection with their various operations. It is also become known that the CIA's Nicaraguan contra
operations in Arkansas also involved the use of so-called "laundered" airplanes. We believe that as many as nine of the airplanes Mr. Reed used to train the Nicaraguan contras in Arkansas
were also so-called "laundered" aircraft.

        I am writing to respectfully request your intervention
in what appears to be a specious and unjustified attempt to
prevent Mr. Reed from obtaining access to the files of various
intelligence agencies pertaining to these two aircraft, as well
as to Mr. Reed himself. If, in fact, the United States Government's intelligence agencies have used so-called laundered
aircraft in their operations, it can hardly be said that this
practice involves legitimate "investigative techniques" that will
impair the effectiveness of law enforcement. One need only ask
Congressman James Inhoff, who chairs the House Subcommittee on
Public Works and Transportation, which is investigating this
phenomena, since I understand that he himself had inadvertently
and unknowingly purchased one of these laundered aircraft for his
personal use. I also understand that Sen. David Boren is conducting his own investigation into this matter as well. Furthermore, the investigations of the Arkansas State Police, Arkansas
Attorney General Winston Bryant and former Congressman Bill
Alexander also revealed that laundered aircraft were used in the
CIA's covert contra operations in Mena, Arkansas.
                        * * * * * * *
        In light of the public disclosures of many facets of
the CIA's covert activities involving the Nicaraguan contras, and
the growing body of evidence concerning the use of stolen or
"laundered" aircraft by United States intelligence agencies, I
submit that any continued efforts by certain officials of the
United States government to conceal the information sought by my
client would be contrary to the public's right to know about
obviously improper and illegal conduct by these intelligence
agencies. Moreover, any claim that this information should not
be declassified is wholly without merit, insofar as the practice
of using laundered aircraft by these agencies is no longer a
secret. Full disclosure of this practice and an in depth investigation into such practices, rather than their continued concealment, would seem to be the only proper and just course to
take at this time.
                        * * * * * * *

                        Respectfully submitted,

                        Robert S. Meloni

36-6. Letter written to United States Attorney General Janet Reno by Robert S. Meloni,
Reed's attorney, listing the obstructions of justice by the government in Terry Reed's civil
trial. Reno never responded.

PART 4 IN A SERIES

'Anatomy of a Smear': The Arkansas Coverup

ANATOMY OF A SMEAR

Terry Reed loves to tell reporters scandalous tales about Bill Clinton and the contras. The trouble is the stories are false.

By RICHARD BEHAR LITTLE ROCK

TIME Magazine Sued for $41 Million Over 1992 "Slash and Burn" Article

"Will it never end for poor Richard Behar?... Now he's ticked off Terry Reed, a pilot and former CIA operative who was the subject of a Behar article.... Reed claims Behar went after his scalp because he refused to provide TIME with 'dirt' against Arkansas cops and Clinton."

— Newsday

In earlier articles in this series, FREEDOM exposed reports of drug smuggling, money laundering and other illegal activities centered around Mena, Arkansas — a quiet town in the western part of the state.

"The Drugging of America" has been prepared with the help of local, state and federal law enforcement officials, as well as members of the news media in Arkansas and elsewhere.

In the series, FREEDOM has pre-sented accounts of how, in the 1980s, Mena became a base for an international, multibillion-dollar cocaine transport operation.

As described in earlier articles, corrupt U.S. government officials were allegedly involved in covering up the illegalities, which included special aircraft modifications so drugs could be flown into the United States and weapons transported out.

One of the main cover stories about Mena has been that drug smuggling, arms running and related Central Intelligence Agency (CIA) covert operations died with Barry Seal, the smuggler, CIA asset and Drug Enforcement Administration snitch who perished in a fusillade of bullets early in 1986 outside a halfway house in Baton Rouge, Louisiana.

Few know this cover story better than

those personally involved in the smuggling operation or those courageous law enforcement officials who have battled — sometimes at risk to the lives and welfare of themselves and their families — to expose the illegal activities and bring those allegedly involved in drug smuggling, money laundering and related coverups to justice.

Terry Reed — One of the Players: According to knowledgeable sources interviewed by FREEDOM, Terry Reed was one of the players in CIA covert operations based at Mena.

Why, then, would TIME have devoted a full page in its April 20, 1992, edition to denigrating Reed and making strange assertions to the effect that he had no connection to the CIA or to drug smuggler Barry Séal?

That question may be answered by a lawsuit filed on April 8, 1993, by Reed against TIME Warner Inc., TIME Inc. Magazine Company and reporter Richard Behar, demanding more than $41 million in damages for allegations printed in TIME's April 1992 article.

Reed's 31-page complaint, filed in the U.S. District Court for the Southern District of New York, alleges: "The article contained a series of false and highly defamatory statements...in order to discredit Reed, a CIA asset who took part in significant CIA activity in the mid-1980s in the state of Arkansas involving that agency's covert operations supporting the Nicaraguan contras.

"...The article, ironically entitled 'Anatomy of a Smear,' did in fact, and upon information and belief was intended, to smear Reed's name and to completely destroy his credibility."

"Everything in [Reed's] Complaint Has Been Verified": In the TIME article, for example, Behar made an issue about a couple with whom Reed stated he was dining on the night of an alleged conversation with then Governor Bill Clinton. Behar claimed the couple said they had never been to the restaurant with Reed.

Reed's lawsuit discredits Behar's claim. It identifies the couple by name (the TIME article did not) as Cheryl and Wally Hall and states that they "never told Behar that they 'had never been to the restaurant with Reed.'" Furthermore, the suit states, "the couple refused to grant Behar an interview."

As another example, Behar quoted Reed's former attorney, John Wesley Hall, as stating, "I haven't been able to

Article published by *Freedom* magazine, highlighting Reed's lawsuit against TIME.

corroborate [Reed's story], that's the problem."

The lawsuit charges that was not at all what Hall said. What he actually said was, "I haven't been able to corroborate a few of the details of Reed's story, but that has not been a problem as everything in [Reed's] complaint has been verified."

Behar's article contained such sweeping statements as, "The only trouble with Reed's sensational tale is that not a word of it is true."

Reed's lawsuit countered this strongly and charged that "Reed was recruited by Lieutenant Colonel Oliver North for the purpose of training Nicaraguan contra pilots. This training took place in or around the Intermountain Regional Airport located in Mena, Arkansas.

"... This training was part of the covert resupply network supervised by Lieutenant Colonel Oliver North during the 1980s which provided covert arms and civilian training assistance to the contras in the Nicaraguan conflict."

Law enforcement officials have confirmed to FREEDOM that Reed was involved in the covert activities around Mena, and that information he provided was accurate.

Seeking "Dirt" and "Ammo": According to the suit, Behar took information obtained from Reed in confidence and used it to try to wrest additional "dirt" and "ammo" regarding certain Arkansas officials.

The suit alleges, "When Reed refused to provide Behar with such information and materials, Behar threatened Reed by stating that Behar would write a negative article about Reed, and would include in that article various off the record statements Reed had made to Behar earlier...."

It also charges, "Despite Behar's promise to Reed to keep confidential the location of Reed, his wife and three children, Behar maliciously disclosed in the article where the Reeds were living."

Reed claims Behar was selected by TIME for the article because of his "established proclivity for writing...slash and burn articles."

The Nation's Biggest Cocaine-Smuggling Operation: The lawsuit charges, "[A]t least 7 CIA aircraft that

Reed used to train contra pilots in the training program in rural Arkansas in the mid-1980s were both serviced, retrofitted and 'laundered' to conceal the identity of those airplanes at Rich Mountain Aviation, at the Intermountain Regional Airport located in Mena, Arkansas, under the management and control of Adler Berriman [Barry] Seal and the CIA."

Terry Reed's story — supported in many details by law enforcement officials at federal, state and local levels — raises troubling questions about what may have been the nation's biggest cocaine-smuggling operation. How could it have operated with impunity? Who in

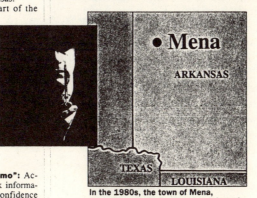

A CONTINUING COVERUP

• Mena

ARKANSAS

TEXAS

LOUISIANA

In the 1980s, the town of Mena, Arkansas, reportedly served as a base for a multibillion-dollar cocaine smuggling enterprise which operated without government intervention.

our own federal government was in league with the smugglers, and for what benefit?

It is not surprising that Terry Reed ran into problems after seeking to blow the whistle on accumulated corruption witnessed during his years as a trainer of pilots for the CIA. There are many people who want to keep Mena's skeletons buried.

National publications such as *The Nation* and FREEDOM, as well as certain local Arkansas newspapers, have published accurate accounts of covert activities at Mena. Legislators such as Congressman William Alexander have

endeavored to fully open up the matter. Law enforcement officials have pressed for effective investigations, but found their efforts blocked or scuttled.

Now it is TIME which is being called to account. The magazine must answer why, instead of helping to raise the lid off the Mena coverup, it evidently sought to drive more nails into it.

Analyzing Behar's coverage of the Mena saga, columnist Alexander Cockburn commented in *The Nation*, "Leaving aside for a moment the matter of Behar's motives, TIME's story was ludicrous, claiming that all reports of *contra* resupply and CIA activities in western Arkansas stem from allegations by Terry Reed, a former pilot, trainer of the *contras* and associate of George Bush's pal Felix Rodriguez."

Cockburn concluded, "Behar is certainly a terrible journalist....With TIME's story, it is as if the magazine, back in 1972, had used an interview with Nixon's Attorney General, John Mitchell, to denounce the Watergate revelations as 'a smear.' But then, moments before the final incriminating tape surfaced, in mid-summer 1974, prompting Nixon's resignation in August, TIME ran a cover story implying that maybe the press was going too far in pursuing Nixon."

"News Manipulation ... As a Matter of Office Routine": In the eyes of TIME founder Henry Luce, "News manipulation was sheer policy, TIME's way of life, performed as a matter of office routine."[1]

TIME was called for comment on the lawsuit, but no spokesman was available.

In TIMEspeak, when one throws enough allegations, insinuations, and double-edged questions, the task has been accomplished: the victim, if not dead, has been bloodied and his reputation rendered a shadow of its former self.

Terry Reed is one man who is fighting back.

— *Thomas G. Whittle*

1. W.A. Swanberg, *Luce And His Empire* (New York: Charles Scribner and Sons, 1972).

EPILOGUE

What you have read is only the prelude to the Terry Reed story. The official cover-up of these dirty secrets he has revealed goes on unabated.

To admit what really happened in Bill Clinton's Arkansas, to pull back the veil of U.S. government duplicity in drug trafficking would be disastrous for the political perpetrators, who as you read this, are hiding—and probably shredding—documents, protecting accomplices and suppressing evidence—all under the guise of "national security."

In five federal judicial districts, the Justice Department and the FBI are fighting Federal Court subpoenas to keep Terry Reed and his wife from obtaining the necessary documents that would reveal the truth about what was done to them. Imagine, "national security" is being invoked to mask the investigation of what the government said was nothing more than a $33,000 insurance fraud! For those who try to use the Freedom of Information Act to strip away the veil of secrecy, and after very great expense, this is an example of what the Government reluctantly turns over:

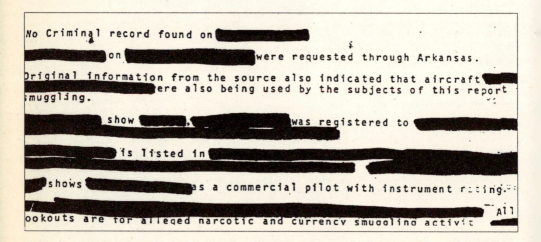

As the judge who acquitted Terry Reed said, this entire affair "had a high odor to it."

In addition, a massive disinformation machine has been put in play to destroy those who know the truth. And many of these people are now either dead, in prison and even in mental wards.

No government agency has investigated this, and none can be expected to—certainly not the U.S. Justice Department that was prostituted by George Bush and Ronald Reagan. This same perversion of justice continues under Bill

Clinton. In fact, one man who helped Clinton hide his Faustian political deal with the CIA now sits atop the Department of Justice.

Isn't it interesting that Bill Clinton never raised his voice at Bush's Christmas Eve pardons for the Iran-Contra criminals and, to this day, has fought against preserving key White House computer tapes from the Bush-Reagan years. Why?

This book provides at least part of the answer. It has shown how an intelligence agency co-opted and compromised both Bush and Clinton——and the presidency; how the black and covert operations, like a cancer, have metastasized the organs of government.

And Congress? This cover-up would not have been possible in the first place had it not been for Congress' political cowardice when it failed to expose this during the Iran-Contra hearings.

Terry Reed, as he said, is trying to bring this out through legal means, in a federal court with witnesses and documents. But he has been, and is being, stonewalled by the minions who served George Bush and those who now serve Bill Clinton. They know how expensive civil litigation is for the average citizen.

This has not been a pleasant story to tell, because of what it shows about you and me—we don't participate in the process of government and hold our politicians accountable. It shows that these dirty operations took place in secret and in an environment that existed in part because the American public, like a cancer patient in denial, would rather not know the depths of evil to which its government has descended while, at the same time, claiming to fight evil.

Like Terry, the nation surrendered its values and morality a little at a time in the years since the Bay of Pigs and now has awakened to wonder: How did we get here?

But Terry finally drew a line. And he, along with his New York attorney Robert S. Meloni, are fighting this monster virtually alone. So far not one person, not even the breast-beaters who claim to seek the truth and cry "cover-up," have been willing to help the Reeds.

Terry wrote a personal letter to Ross Perot, outlining what he knew, how he and his family had been victimized, and simply requested his help in locating an attorney for his civil lawsuit against the men who falsely testified against him. He told Perot, that champion of the "little man," that if the government can pervert justice to silence Terry Reed, the Constitution was meaningless. Then, no one is safe.

Perot did not even respond. And he was the one who called Bill Clinton "Chicken Man!"

Jerry Spence, one of the country's most noted criminal defense attorneys, put it best when he said "before the Government tries to convict someone, they first try to demonize him." I've been an eye-witness to this many times in my journalistic career. That's how Terry Reed suddenly became "armed and dangerous" and a drug trafficking suspect in 1987.

If that can be done to Terry Reed, do you think you are I are safe? What happens when it's your turn?

For me, Terry and Janis Reed have become both a Cold War Rosetta Stone and metaphor that translate into a bizarre and personal story about the more than 30 years of dirty and clandestine warfare this country had waged with its proxies, the Cuban exile mercenaries and assassins.

When I first met Terry Reed more than three years ago, I did not truly realize what I had found. Behind his deceptively insouciant demeanor hid a sensitive and dedicated man possessed with righting the wrongs done him.

At first, he was just another story. And my professional cynicism and disbelief about him were not easily overcome. He seemed at first like other intelligence assets I had met, some tarnished, some not; many of them men with a sense of both adventure and a need to somehow vindicate their Vietnam experience of coming home as perceived "losers" and "murderers."

But my experience with the Reeds and their children, all of whom I have come to think of as family, has made me realize what shallow people writers can be when they become prisoners of their own doubt.

"Scribblers" like me usually want only one thing, a story to tell. And we really don't care how we get it. And as we commit it to a narrative, it all becomes somehow mechanical and pro forma, like sidestroking through flotsam as though we are not affected by the things we write about.

In becoming the exorcist for this amazing tale of deception and hypocrisy by those who pretend to serve us, I have learned many things. Chief among them is the fact that there *are* things better left unsaid.

I began this quest to learn why Barry Seal was really murdered. Now, I know why, but I cannot reveal the true motive behind Barry Seal's murder. Suffice to say that his assassination took place because Seal's "ace in the hole" was also "neutralized." To go beyond that would expose some innocent people to extreme jeopardy. There are some things that even an investigative journalist must keep to himself.

Maybe, someday.

John Cummings
East Northport, N.Y.
November 25th, 1993

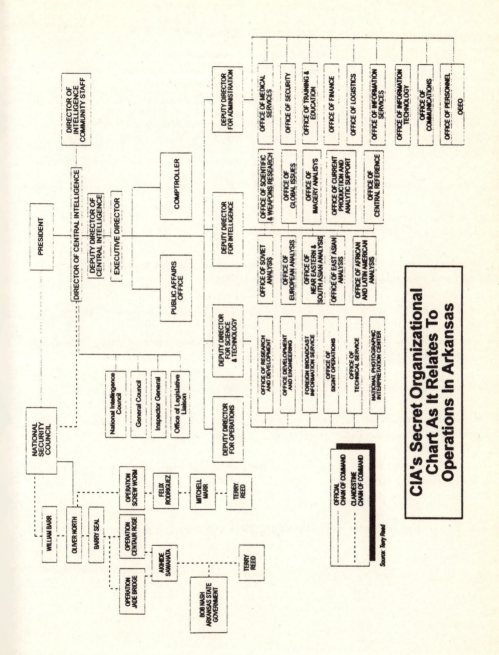

CIA's Secret Organizational Chart as it relates to operations in Arkansas and Mexico.

BIBLIOGRAPHY

Armstrong, Scott, Malcolm Byrne and Tom Blanton, *Secret Military Assistance to Iran and the Contras: A Chronology of Events and Individuals* (National Security Archive, 1987).

Bradlee, Ben, Jr., *Guts and Glory, the Rise and Fall of Oliver North*, (Donald I. Fine, 1988).

Draper, Theodore, *A Very Thin Line*, (Hill and Wang, 1991).

Raviv, Dan and Yossi Melman, *Every Spy a Prince, The Complete History of Israel's Intelligence Community*, (Houghton Mifflin, 1990).

Rodriguez, Felix and John Wiseman, *Shadow Warrior*, (Simon & Schuster, 1989).

Shultz, George P., *Turmoil and Triumph, My Years as Secretary of State*, (Charles Scribner's Sons, 1993).

Wise, David and Thomas B. Ross, *The Invisible Government* (Random House, 1964).

Report of the Congressional Committees Investigating the Iran-Contra Affair, 100th Congress, First Session, 1987. Report No. 100-433.

Drugs, Law Enforcement and Foreign Policy: Report of the Subcommittee on Terrorism, Narcotics and International Operations of the Committee on Foreign Relations, United States Senate.

Woodward, Bob, *Veil: The Secret Wars of the CIA, 1981-1987* (Simon and Schuster, 1987.)

ACKNOWLEDGEMENTS

Although this book bears the names of two authors, this work was not the result of their labor alone.

However, some of those, who supplied help and encouragement prefer to remain anonymous.

The authors would like to acknowledge publicly several people, chief among them Sue and Roger Lange, along with Louisa Potenza Muniz for editing, advice and help in making this book possible. Our thanks also go to John Bell, Julian Serer and Kent Carter of S.P.I. Books.

In their quest to continue turning over rocks until this <u>entire</u> sordid story is exposed, the authors have established a "spook hotline". For those wishing to keep abreast of the authors' efforts to bring forth another work dealing with the covert culture, call: 1-505-884-8822 and "reach out and touch someone."

If you wish to become a "participant" in leading the authors down the shadowy trails, just leave a message and your call will be returned by one of us.

We are especially interested in hearing from those assets or intelligence officers whose devotion to duty has been besmirched by renegade agents, or those who feel manipulated and exploited by failed policies.

Terry Kent Reed
John Cummings

TERRY REED LITIGATION FUND

Terry Reed's battle to redress the violations of his constitutional and other rights continues against Raymond "Buddy" Young and Tommy Baker, in Reed's civil rights lawsuit in Little Rock, and against media giant Time Warner, Inc., in Reed's libel lawsuit in New York City.

As Terry Reed and his attorney, Robert S. Meloni, are waging these battles, the straggering litigation costs continue to mount. Anyone who is willing to make a donation to help defray these costs may call the following number for information on making a donation. Your help would be greatly appreciated.

(212) 580-7477

Robert S. Meloni,
Attorney for Terry Reed

INDEX

COMPANIES/FIRMS

DRUGS/MONEY LAUNDERING

FINANCIAL INSTITUTIONS

GEOGRAPHICAL LOCATIONS

Fujikawa, Frank 194, 218, 282, 305, 309, 332, 339
Garrison, Karen 398, 399, 411, 430, 436
Gates, Robert 245
Ghiorso, Mike 502, 503
Gonzalez Certosimo, Raul 161, 316, 317, 334
Goodwin, Col.Tommy 238
Graves, Lawrence 495, 498, 504, 543
Gregg, Donald 72, 147, 184, 288, 290
Guevara, Che 187, 370, 398, 457
Hadaway, A.L. (Al) 146, 172
Hall, John Wesley Jr. 486, 487, 488, 491, 494, 496, 497, 502, 504, 505, 508-517, 522, 538, 539, 540
Hall, Homer (Red) 88, 122, 200
Hall, Wally 262, 432
Hampton, Fred 62, 67, 75, 109, 146
Hardegree, Joe 525, 528
Hart, Gary 510
Hasenfus, Eugene 289-293, 297, 299, 302, 303, 304, 353, 354, 355, 356
Hayes, Floyd 239
Helmer, Allie 296, 297, 298
Ho Chi Minh 16, 21, 113, 114, 286
Hubbell, Webster (Webb) 55, 67, 165, 167, 169, 171, 248, 486, 496, 519, 32, 533, 534
Hubbell Webster (Webb) 55, 56, 171, 447, 496, 534
Hutchison, Asa 495
Ida, Joe 3, 27, 49
Iturraldi, (Chief of documentation, Mexican Immigration) 314, 315
Jenkins, Lt. James 441, 442, 445, 466
Jessie, FBI Agent Mark 115, 151, 160, 422, 466
Joe Sakai, Joe 489, 499, 500
Juin, Patricia 280, 281, 282, 300
Juin, Patrick 281, 282, 291, 300, 301, 305, 331, 366, 369, 467
Kerr, Ken and Vera 386
Kerry, John 419, 518
Kissinger, Henry 11, 21, 25, 286, 339, 342
Laura, (the maid) 396, 401, 403, 404, 405, 406
Lloyd, Philip Lynn 54
Lopez Alcantara, Ricardo 330
Lopez Ramirez, Roberto 294, 328, 340
Marr, Mitch 256, 267-280, 282, 284-289, 291, 293, 299, 301, 304, 305, 308, 309, 314, 318, 319, 329, 331-334, 339, 340, 343, 344, 345, 347, 351, 352, 355, 356, 362, 368, 369, 370, 372-376, 378, 380, 382, 384, 387, 388, 400, 404, 407
McAfee, Mark 81, 82, 92, 93, 114, 115, 121, 150, 151, 153, 156, 160, 183, 194, 197, 273, 283, 422, 444
McCollum, Bill 241

McNamara, Robert 15, 16
McRainey, John 284, 285, 344
Medina, Ramon 94, 100, 101, 103, 104, 105, 106, 107, 110, 111, 113, 120, 124, 126, 127, 148, 149, 163, 183, 354, 426, 536
Meese, Edwin 230, 302, 307, 383
Meloni, Robert S. 390, 545
Mills, Wilbur 55
Mounetow, Andres 331
Nash, Bob 152, 153, 154, 155, 156, 158, 160, 161, 163, 166, 168, 169, 170, 171, 224, 225, 227, 228, 229, 231, 233, 236, 244, 246, 260, 263, 264, 265, 475, 495, 507, 513, 514, 515, 521, 522, 534, 543
Nichols, Larry 475, 476, 477, 478, 479, 494, 495, 496, 503, 505, 522, 523, 524, 525
Nir, Amiram 307, 310, 349, 351, 352, 353, 354, 355, 356, 357, 358, 359, 360, 361, 362, 363, 364, 365, 367, 370, 371, 391, 412, 453
Nir, Amiram (code name Pat Weber) 208, 310, 311, 312, 313, 323, 324, 325, 326, 327, 335, 347, 348, 350, 351, 364
Nixon, Richard 11, 18, 20, 21, 22, 25, 62, 120, 162, 286, 307, 513
Nolan, Larry 429, 451
Noriega, Manuel 249
Northop, Steve 471
Ogden, Gene 376, 377
Ortega, Daniel 95, 168, 269, 286, 291, 295, 301, 354
Osato, Takashi 39, 535
Owen, Rob 531
Perot, H. Ross 6, 75, 498
Pierre (pseudonym) 472, 473, 474, 475, 476, 478, 479
Poindexter, John 308
Palozola, Frank 220, 221
Ponce, Pablo 278
Posey, Tom 531
Proctor, George 235
Provance, Bob 296
Provance, Raquel 296, 297
Reagan, Ronald 1, 4, 41, 42, 53, 54, 63, 64, 72, 83, 98, 106, 122, 148, 151, 180, 223, 230, 235, 241, 242, 273, 289, 290, 291, 292, 307, 308, 317, 333, 353, 356, 359, 360, 361, 362, 366, 453, 471, 476, 477, 529, 536, 540, 542, 544, 545
Reed, Baxter Xavier Kerr 329, 376, 384, 413, 414, 422, 424, 482, 484
Reed, Duncan Charles Kerr 44, 46
Reed, Elliott Kent Kerr 98, 176,
Reed, Gary 22, 384
Reed, Harry 14
Reed, Martha 15, 522
Regan, Donald 308
Reno, Janet 36-6

Revell, Oliver (Buck) 25, 238, 306
Robinson, Deborah 493
Robison, Steve 419, 420, 427, 429, 436, 437,
    440, 441, 443, 450, 453
Ronnow, Clark 499, 536, 537
Ross, FBI Agent Tom 239, 240
Ross, Tom 239
Roy, Elsijane T. 491
Ruth 486, 538
Sanders, Sgt. Don 432, 433, 438, 439, 443,
    464, 466, 479
Sawahata, Akihide (Aki) 68, 69, 70, 75, 80,
    81, 82, 83, 84, 85, 87, 88, 92, 93, 95, 96,
    98, 99, 100, 101, 106, 107, 108, 109, 110,
    114, 115, 122, 123, 124, 126, 129, 130,
    131, 133, 134, 139, 140, 141, 142, 143,
    144, 145, 147, 148, 149, 150, 151, 152,
    153, 154, 155, 156, 160, 161, 164, 168,
    169, 170, 172, 176, 177, 180, 182, 183,
    184, 193, 197, 222, 227, 228, 232, 233,
    237, 238, 243, 244, 245, 246, 247, 249,
    250, 251, 422, 431, 507, 543
Sawyer, William (Buzz) 118
Seal, Adler Berriman (Barry) 49, 51, 52, 53,
    54, 55, 57, 58, 59, 60, 61, 62, 63, 64, 66,
    67, 68, 69
Secord, Richard 158, 218, 270, 285, 449
Seligman, Nicole 530
Shellnut, Finis 139, 167, 213, 232, 495, 496,
    534
Shugar, Scott 509, 538
Shultz, George 307, 310, 361
Silva, Felix 424
Singlaub, John 477
Stephens, Major Doug 445
Stephens, Jackson T. 232, 245, 247
Stodola, Mark 114, 129, 143, 259
Sullivan, Brendan 456
Sullivan, Lynn Cola 524
Sultan of Brunei 180
Swaney, Mark 493, 505, 509
Talbott, Strobe 510, 511, 541
Theis, Judge Frank 421, 431, 436, 438, 439,
    440, 441, 442, 444, 449, 450, 451, 452,
    453, 454, 455, 456, 459, 460, 461, 462,
    463, 464, 466, 467, 497
Tingen, Richard 191, 333, 334, 404
Tokudome, Ted 499, 500, 501, 502, 503
Tom Harkin 496
Tracta, Leroy 208, 209, 210, 211, 212, 323,
    325, 326, 348
Trubey, Marilyn 418, 419, 421, 424, 427,
    428, 429, 430, 431, 433, 435, 437, 438,
    440, 441, 442, 443, 444, 446, 447, 448,
    449, 450, 451, 452, 453, 454, 455, 456,
    457, 458, 459, 460, 461, 462, 463, 464,
    465, 468, 470, 472, 479, 480, 483, 508
Truman, Harry S. 4, 5, 12, 13

Turner, Stansfield 162
Urbiola Ledezma, Felipe 315, 316, 317, 332
Varnados, Ramon 103, 111, 127, 148, 177
Velazquez, Arturo 282
Vilines, Bobby 259
Violanti, Gary 429, 430
Wallyer, Bruce 521
Walsh, Lawrence 105, 457, 494, 513, 518,
    529, 532, 536, 540
Walsh, Lawrence 497, 498, 518, 532, 540
Walton, Sheila 399, 405
Ward, Elizabeth 524
Ward, Seth Jr. (Skeeter) 55, 56, 165, 170, 172,
    178, 179, 194, 213, 214, 215, 532, 534
Ward, Seth Sr. 49, 55, 65, 67, 81, 129, 138,
    164, 165, 170, 171, 232, 330, 422, 495,
    532, 533,
Weber, Harlan 433
Weinberger, Caspar 308
Welch, Russell 105, 146, 216, 238, 239, 240,
    250
West, Emery 27, 28, 30, 31, 38, 186, 454
Whitehead, John 308
Whitmore, Paul 238, 239
Whittle, Tom 536
Williams, Barbara 447
Williams, Jack 431, 459, 465
Williams, Jack 447, 530
Wilson, Bill 514, 515
Wooley, Magistrate John 418, 419
Young, Raymond (Buddy) 433, 478, 479, 494,
    523
Young, Captain Raymond (Buddy) 227 264,
    377, 386, 416, 432, 442, 466, 487, 504,
    541, 543

VIETNAM WAR
Arc Light, 17, 34
Disco 17
Ho Chi Minh 16, 21, 113, 114, 286
Human Shield 21
Igloo White, 15
Kissinger 11, 21, 25, 286, 339, 342
McNamara, Robert 15, 16
Nakhon Phanom
Nixon, Richard 11, 18, 20, 21, 22, 25, 62,
    120, 162, 286, 307, 513
POW: decision to bomb the POWs 22
Task Force Alpha (TFA) 16, 18
Teaball, 17
Vietnamization 62, 64, 71, 120, 286